FINANCE

Investments, Institutions, and Management

The Addison-Wesley Series in Finance

FINANCE

Investments, Institutions, and Management

SECOND EDITION

Stanley G. Eakins
East Carolina University

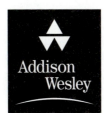

Addison
Wesley

Boston San Francisco New York
London Toronto Sydney Tokyo Singapore Madrid
Mexico City Munich Paris Cape Town Hong Kong Montreal

Editor in Chief: Denise Clinton
Acquisitions Editor: Donna Battista
Project Manager: Christine Houde
Development Manager: Rebecca Ferris
Managing Editor: Jim Rigney
Production Supervisor: Katherine Watson
Supplements Editor: Meredith Gertz
Media Producer: Jennifer Pelland
Project Coordinator: Electronic Publishing Services Inc., NYC
Manufacturing Manager: Hugh Crawford
Text Design: Electronic Publishing Services Inc., NYC
Illustrator: Electronic Publishing Services Inc., NYC
Electronic Page Makeup: Electronic Publishing Services Inc., NYC
Cover Design: Regina Hagen
Cover Photos: ©2002 PhotoDisc, Inc.

For permission to use copyrighted material, grateful acknowledgment is made to the copyright holders listed below copyrighted material throughout the book.

Library of Congress Cataloging-in-Publication Data
Eakins, Stanley G.
   Finance: investments, institutions, and management / Stanley G. Eakins.–2nd ed.
     p. cm.
Includes index.
   ISBN 0-201-72166-X
1.   Finance.   I. Title.

HG101 .E15 2002
332–dc21   2001022760

ISBN 0-201-72166-X

1 2 3 4 5 6 7 8 9 — DOC — 05 04 03 02 01

Dedicated to

MY FAMILY—LAURIE, CHAD, AND ALENA

Brief Contents

Detailed Contents

Chapter 11
Estimating Cash Flows and Refinements to Capital Budgeting 286

Chapter 12
The Cost of Capital 316

Chapter 13
The Theory of Capital Structure 341

Chapter 14
Financial Statement and Ratio Analysis 363

Preface

PURPOSE OF THIS TEXT

In the mid-1990s, the number of students in the school of business at East Carolina University dropped, as did the number of declared finance majors. The same was true in schools across the nation. This drop prompted the department to review the content of its Principles of Finance course. Surveys told us that students regarded it as one of the most difficult courses they would take during their college careers. Talking with students we learned that they were not getting what they expected or wanted out of the introductory finance course. They wanted to learn about all areas of finance, not just how large corporations practice finance. For example, they were very interested in investments and wanted to better understand popular business publications.

The revelations gleaned from our student survey inspired me to write this book. Most students in the introductory finance class will not take any other course in finance before they graduate. However, some find the subject so interesting that they will choose finance as their major field of study. Both of these groups can be better served by a course that introduces all the major areas of study in finance. Just as introductory biology does not focus exclusively on plants and introductory accounting does not simply cover taxes, introductory finance should not be limited to corporate applications.

TARGET AUDIENCE

This book can be used effectively by any university or college interested in providing a broad coverage of financial topics in the introductory course. The length of the text has been kept to a minimum so that most of it can be reasonably covered in a typical one-semester course. The text assumes that students have a basic understanding of accounting and a limited understanding of statistics, though statistical concepts are reviewed as needed. The lucid writing style will make the text particularly valuable to schools that expect their students to grasp the material with limited guidance from the instructor.

This text is appropriate for introductory courses that include both finance and nonfinance majors. Finance majors will find it provides an excellent foundation for their other finance classes. Nonfinance majors will appreciate its clear, comprehensive coverage of the full scope of finance. Both will come away from the course able to read and understand popular business publications and communicate effectively with finance professionals.

THE BENEFITS OF A BROADER APPROACH

This text includes coverage of the three main areas of finance: markets and institutions, investments, and managerial finance. The greatest emphasis continues to be given to corporate topics, since we are educating business majors and most will go on to be employed by corporations. However, by limiting some of the corporate finance detail and expanding areas that are of interest to a greater number of students, two benefits are achieved. First, the class becomes more interesting, relevant, and valuable to a wide range of students. A broader exposure to finance allows the nonfinance major to better comprehend financial information and make business and personal finance decisions.

A second benefit of a broader approach to finance is that some students may find one of the three areas of study particularly interesting and choose to become finance majors. This text makes it clear that not all finance majors have to work for large corporations. There are also jobs in financial planning, stock and security sales, and insurance, to name just a few. Students interested in these topics may be discouraged by courses that follow the traditional corporate finance approach. This point is emphasized with Careers in Finance boxes in each chapter.

CUSTOMIZING THE LEVEL OF DIFFICULTY

In writing this text I tried to address students' fear of this course. To this end, every topic is explained in clear terms to which students can easily relate. To further enhance the text's appeal, it has been classroom tested extensively, with bonus points given to students who identified any section that was the least bit difficult to understand or follow. These suggestions have helped make this a highly readable and student-friendly finance text.

Another unique feature of this text is the use of "Extension" sections within each chapter. These sections "extend" coverage of certain topics, allowing professors to customize the text's level of difficulty. During the manuscript review process, we learned that the survey approach to introductory finance differs widely from school to school: some instructors want more depth while others want less. Even within departments, we suspect there are different opinions on how far each topic should be taken. My approach satisfies both sides. For example, the modified internal rate of return is included in an Extension section: professors who want to skip this topic can advise students not to read Extension 1. Unlike end-of-chapter appendices, Extensions allow topics to be placed where they naturally fall in the development of the chapter. End-of-chapter problems that relate to Extension topics are clearly identified for those who choose to skip the material.

ORGANIZATION OF THE TEXT

There are many ways to organize a text to include the three main areas of finance. We chose the current organization because it best allows the topics to build naturally on each other, while presenting the most critical material within the first 13 chapters.

Part I provides an introduction to markets and institutions. By beginning here, students quickly become familiar with the terminology of finance, the major institutions that are involved, and the different financial securities available. Students learn how the actions of the intermediaries that participate in the different markets facilitate the flow of funds from those with a surplus to those with a need for the funds and how accurate prices are established along the way. Part I also introduces the role of interest rates and how they are established. It concludes with the role of the Federal Reserve in the creation of money and in establishing the level of interest rates.

Part II introduces the major topics in the study of investments. To capture their interest, students first learn the concept of the time value of money and its applications to personal finance issues. They then learn about the relationship between risk and return. Finally, they learn how various securities are priced. Chapter 9 also provides a discussion of whether the markets are efficient and whether the CAPM accurately measures the required return.

Part III covers traditional corporate finance topics. The topics have been divided into discrete chapters enabling instructors to cover only those topics that meet their needs. We begin with two chapters on capital budgeting, one that introduces the models and methods and another that shows how to evaluate cash flows and refine the capital budgeting models. Chapter 12 develops the cost of capital by reexamining the models used to value securities in Chapters 8 and 9. Chapter 13, which develops the theory of capital structure, is organized carefully around many extension sections so that professors can give this topic as much or as little attention as they deem appropriate. Financial statement and ratio analysis is placed immediately before the chapter on financial planning and forecasting. These two chapters naturally complement each other. We conclude our corporate coverage with a chapter on the management of net working capital.

Part IV concludes the text with a chapter introducing the major topics included in international finance and Chapter 18 is devoted to a case study that involves a small business owner making decisions that require the application of many of the finance topics discussed earlier in the text.

PEDAGOGICAL FEATURES

We have incorporated a variety of features to make this text as accessible as possible to students.

1. *Key terms* are highlighted and listed at the end of each chapter, reinforcing the most important concepts.

2. *Study tips* are included in each chapter to highlight or clarify issues that frequently cause students trouble. These tips reflect many years of teaching introductory finance to thousands of students.

3. Step-by-step *calculator solution*s are provided for many of the in-text examples, along with equation and factor solutions. This approach exposes students to all possible solution methods.

4. In addition to the many examples integrated throughout the chapter discussions, labeled *examples* often focus on real-life and familiar companies. These examples make the material more interesting and relevant to students.

5. *Problems* conclude each major text section so that students will pause and reflect on what they have learned so far, before moving forward. The answers are provided, upside down, at the bottom of the page.

6. *Finance in Practice* boxes discuss real-world applications of the chapter material that students will find both relevant and interesting. These boxes focus on global, ethical, and practical applications of the material.

7. New! *Careers in Finance* boxes place chapter concepts in an applied perspective and prompt students to consider finance-related occupations.

8. *Extension* features include advanced material so faculty can customize the course to suit the level of their students.

9. Each chapter concludes with a comprehensive section of *discussion questions* and a section of *problems*.

10. New! *Self-Test Problems* with answers conclude select chapters to give students even more sample problems to work through as they prepare for exams.

11. New! *Mini Cases* bring together major topics in each chapter, thereby enabling students to apply what they've learned to realistic situations.

12. New! *Web Exploration* assignments guide students to Internet sites with financial news and information.

13. New! *Spreadsheet problems* are included in many of the Web Exploration assignments and Mini Cases to familiarize students with Microsoft Excel. A spreadsheet tutorial is included on the text Web site.

SUPPLEMENTAL MATERIALS

The second edition of *Finance: Investments, Institutions, and Markets* includes a comprehensive program of supplementary materials. These include the following items:

FOR THE PROFESSOR:

1. *Instructor's Resource Manual*, prepared by the author, includes a sample course outline, chapter outlines, chapter overviews, key points for classroom discussion, chapter quizzes, and answers to the questions, problems, and Mini Cases in the text. In addition, it has Lecture Notes in transparency master format that comprehensively outline the major points covered in the text.

2. *Test Bank*, prepared by Oliver Schnunsenberg, St. Joseph's University, and David Zalewski, Providence College, contains 40 questions per chapter in multiple-choice and short-essay format.

3. *Instructor's Resource CD-ROM*, which contains the Microsoft Word files for the *Instructor's Resource Manual*, a PowerPoint lecture presentation, a separate PowerPoint with all the figures in the text, and computerized Test Bank files. The easy-to-

use testing software (Test-Gen EQ with QuizMaster-EQ for Windows) is a valuable test preparation tool that allows instructors to view, edit, and add questions. The CD-ROM is fully compatible with the Windows and Macintosh operating systems.

4. Companion Web site (located at www.aw.com/eakins) features links to financial data sources, spreadsheet and financial calculator tutorials, all Web Exploration questions and Mini Cases from the book, and a multiple-choice quiz for each chapter. The site also features a glossary of key terms and all Internet links from the book in up-to-date format.

In addition to the Companion Web site, the Web content is available in Course Compass and Blackboard versions. Course Compass™ is a nationally hosted, dynamic, interactive online course management system powered by Blackboard, leaders in the development of Internet-based learning tools. This easy-to-use and customizable program enables professors to tailor content and functionality to meet individual course needs. To see a demo, visit www.coursecompass.com. Please contact your local sales representative for more information on obtaining Web content in these various formats.

FOR THE STUDENT:

1. *Study Guide,* prepared by Scott Below of East Carolina University, includes chapter summaries, chapter outlines, study tips, and sample exams.

2. New! *Student Tutorial CD-ROM,* prepared by the author, is packaged with each new textbook. For each chapter, it includes an overview, summary and readings, sample problems with both written answers and audio explanations, and a complete sample test.

ACKNOWLEDGMENTS

Although this text is the result of many years of work and creative thinking, I also have received a great deal of generous assistance along the way. The following colleagues devoted a great deal of their own time and energy to this project, poring over many drafts and providing invaluable feedback. To these individuals, then, I would like to extend a heartfelt and most sincere word of thanks:

Tim Alzheimer, Montana State University at Bozeman

Vickie Bajtelsmit, Colorado State University, Fort Collins

Stewart Bonem, Cincinnati State Technical and Community College

Daniel Borgia, Florida Gulf Coast University

Jerry Boswell, Metropolitan State College of Denver

Michael Carter, University of Arkansas, Fayetteville

Kim Capriotti, University of North Florida

Choa Chen, California State University, Northridge

Ji Chen, University of Colorado at Denver

Dean Drenk, University of Montana

David Durst, University of Akron

Jeff Eicher, Clarion University of Pennsylvania

Marianne Hite, University of Colorado at Denver

Peppi Kenny, Western Illinois University

Edward Krohn, Miami-Dade Community College

Martin Laurence, William Paterson University

Thomas Liaw, St. John's University

Francis McGrath, Iona College

James Miles, Penn State University

Lalatendu Misra, University of Texas, San Antonio

Dianne Morrison, University of Wisconsin at LaCrosse

John Nofsinger, Marquette University

Thomas Patrick, Trenton State College

Robert Pavlik, Southwest Texas State University

Eric Powers, University of South Carolina

Laura Scroggins, California State University, Chico

Edward Stendardi, St. John Fisher College

Jerry Stevens, University of Richmond

James Stutzman, Southwest Texas State University

Amir Tavakkol, Kansas State University

James Tripp, Western Illinois University

Sorin Tuluca, Fairleigh Dickinson University

Joe Walker, University of Alabama at Birmingham

Jim Washam, Arkansas State University

Chester Waters, Durham Technical College

Howard Whitney, Franklin University

David Zalewski, Providence College

Many editors encouraged and helped shape my vision for this text. My thanks, then, to Donna Battista, who sponsored the second edition. I would also like to thank Christine Houde and Lake Lloyd for their valuable help and assistance. The efforts of Jennifer Pelland and Meredith Gertz on the print and media supplements are also appreciated.

Most important, I wish to thank my wife, Laurie. It is her support and affection that make all things worthwhile.

About the Author

Stanley G. Eakins has notable experience as a financial practitioner, serving as vice president and comptroller at the First National Bank of Fairbanks and as a commercial and real estate loan officer. A founder of Denali title and escrow agency, a title insurance company in Fairbanks, Alaska, he also ran the operations side of a bank and was the chief financial officer for a multi–million dollar construction and development company.

He received his Ph.D. from Arizona State University. Professor Eakins is Chair of the Department of Finance at East Carolina University. His research is focused primarily on the role of institutions in corporate control and how they influence investment practices. He has also studied the investment strategies of institutional investors.

A contributor to journals such as the *Quarterly Journal of Business and Economics,* the *Journal of Financial Research,* and the *International Review of Financial Analysis,* Professor Eakins is also contributing author to *Financial Markets and Institutions* by Frederic Mishkin (Boston, Mass.: Addison Wesley Longman ©2000).

An Overview of Finance

T his is a unique finance textbook. Introductory finance texts are usually titled *Financial Management* or *Introduction to Corporate Finance* and they focus exclusively on finance applied to business or *corporate* problem solving and decision making. However, finance is much broader in scope than these texts suggest. Finance also includes the study of investments and financial markets. The study of investments includes learning how to convert current dollars into a greater amount of future dollars. The study of financial markets includes learning how the interaction among the various players establishes security prices and facilitates security trading. Finance majors will take separate courses in each of these topic areas, but the course you are taking now provides a foundation in all of them. If this is the only course in finance you take, it will provide a sufficient background to enable you to read and understand popular financial literature. It will also provide a framework for how you should think about financial issues and prepare you for more advanced topics, should you choose to pursue the study of finance further.

This chapter briefly discusses the three major areas of study within the finance discipline. It then introduces the financial system and explains how we will approach the study of each element. Finally, the chapter discusses some fundamental assumptions that will be carried throughout the book.

This may be the most important course you will take during your college career. You will learn how to manage money on both the corporate

> ### Chapter Objectives
>
> By the end of this chapter you should be able to:
>
> 1. Define the major areas of study within the finance discipline
> 2. Identify the topics and some of the key concepts that will be studied in this course
> 3. Understand the scope of the financial system and the individual's role in it
> 4. Discuss the financial manager's role within a corporation
> 5. Describe the foundation assumptions that underlie the study of finance

and personal levels. You will learn to read business periodicals and understand investment advisors. You will learn the correct approach to solving business and personal investment problems. These lessons may have a tremendous impact on your career in business as well as on your personal wealth and security. For example, if you go to work for a firm after graduation, you will probably start your first day in the personnel office. There, you may be asked to choose how your retirement dollars are to be invested. You will learn in this course that one selection may leave you without enough funds to retire when you desire, but another, if history repeats itself, may let you retire early. In this course you will learn how to evaluate retirement options, select among auto and home loans, and analyze business opportunities. You will learn how to evaluate a firm's health and how to project its future.

WHAT IS FINANCE?

Broadly defined, **finance** is the study of managing money. At the most basic level this involves determining where to get money and what to do with it. Clearly, finance is central to a wide variety of jobs, disciplines, and activities. Bankers, accountants, financial planners, and many others make their living using financial concepts on a daily basis. Still others use the concepts less directly, but benefit from an understanding of the basics. It is difficult to think of any job that does not require at least some understanding of financial principles. Even an artist must price art fairly and deal with estimating cash flows. Additionally, everyone should take responsibility for his or her own retirement security and plan for it accordingly, which requires an understanding of finance.

It will become obvious as you read this book that many of the distinctions between the fields of study in finance are artificial. For example, the study of how interest rates are determined is normally considered part of markets and institutions. However, corporate managers and investors are keenly interested in interest rates and follow them closely. Similarly, both business managers and investors are concerned with how securities are priced. This text points out diverse applications as each topic is presented to help you achieve an integrated picture of the entire field of finance.

Markets and Institutions

A student majoring in finance will take at least one course in **financial markets.** The study of financial markets includes the determination of interest rates and how the market prices and distributes securities. To simplify the study of financial markets in Chapter 2, our discussion will be based on the maturity of the securities that trade there. **Money markets** are for securities that mature in less than 1 year. **Capital markets** are for securities that mature in more than 1 year. We will also investigate how financial markets facilitate trading and increase the accuracy of security pricing.

The study of **financial institutions** includes learning how banks, thrifts, the Federal Reserve, and finance companies increase the efficiency of financial transactions. Everyone interacts with financial institutions. Business managers deal with investment bankers who help take securities public. Individuals deal with banks for loans and with other investment institutions to invest for retirement. You will save money and time if you understand which institution specializes in each type of service you need. Additionally, by understanding the motives and constraints facing the various institutions, you are more likely to successfully obtain the services you seek. We begin our study of financial institutions in Chapter 3.

Another important topic covered in markets and institutions courses is the determination of interest rates. It is often important to both individuals and business managers to understand the factors that influence interest rates so that they can make educated predictions about future interest rates. For example, in 1992 long-term mortgage interest rates fell from about 10% to less than 8%. Many homeowners were faced with the question of whether they should refinance their home loans immediately or wait for rates to drop further. It turned out that long-term rates increased for two years before falling back to the level achieved in 1992. Homeowners who waited for rates to fall lost several years of lower payments. An understanding of interest rates can lead to better financial decision making. We will investigate how interest rates are determined and the factors that influence them in Chapter 4.

We extend our study of interest rates to the Federal Reserve, which is the central bank of the United States. Besides being the government's bank and the bank for banks, it also has tremendous control over the economy and interest rates. Because of the Federal Reserve's critical influence over both investors and businesses, we will study it separately from the other financial institutions in Chapter 5.

Investments

The second major concentration within finance is **investments.** The study of investments is the study of how dollars available today can be turned into more dollars in the future. At one time, most individuals had few investment choices. It was difficult to buy stocks with only moderate wealth, and corporate pension plans offered few options to employees. The investment landscape is very different today. As we will discuss later, investors build portfolios of securities. A **portfolio** is simply a group of different investments. Wise investors hold a variety of securities in their portfolios to reduce their risk, an investment strategy called **diversification.** Mutual funds enable investors with limited funds to buy a diversified portfolio of securities. Most corporations now give employees a number of investment alternatives. A thorough grounding in investments will help you to understand the implications of these alternatives and to select the best ones for yourself.

We begin our study of investments in Chapter 6 by learning how money grows when invested over time and how future dollars are worth less than dollars we have now. You will learn to solve many real-world problems in this chapter.

One of the most important topics in finance is the **risk–return tradeoff.** To get greater returns, you must be willing to incur greater risk. Although this concept seems straightforward, it gets more complex when we try to precisely define risk and to determine exactly how it affects returns. We will study the risk–return relationship in Chapter 7.

Anyone buying or investing in securities needs to know how the market arrives at a price. It is easy to find the value of bonds, but we will discover that it is much more difficult to accurately price stock. Like risk and return, asset valuation is important both to businesses selling securities and to investors buying them for their portfolios. We address asset valuation and explain how well our valuation theories work in practice as we discuss security pricing in Chapters 8 and 9. The discussion of market efficiency at the end of Chapter 9 ties our study of markets to our study of market pricing.

Corporate Finance

Corporate finance is finance applied in a business setting. This is the typical focus of introductory finance courses. We will cover most of the topics included in traditional corporate finance texts; however, we will include a personal investment slant whenever possible. Most of you will work for a corporation at some time in your future. You may even run your own firm. For this reason, even if you are never employed as a financial manager, you will benefit from the lessons taught here. Within the study of corporate finance, there are several subareas of study.

Evaluation of Long-Term Projects

The financial manager is responsible for evaluating whether a firm should pursue a particular investment opportunity. For example, Ford Motor Co. recently decided to make a multi–million dollar investment in engineering and production to produce right-hand drive vehicles for sale in Japan. The financial managers of Ford had to determine whether they could realistically expect to recoup this investment or whether Ford could use its resources better elsewhere. We will examine the most commonly used methods for project evaluation in Chapters 10 and 11.

Study of How to Acquire Funds

One of the most important yet difficult decisions facing the financial manager is how to fund the firm's investments. Consider the problems faced by many of the new dot com companies, such as Amazon.com. During its early years it focused on gaining market share as opposed to generating profits. Amazon's management decided that its long-run success depended more on building a customer base than on generating revenues. Many Web retailing firms believed this model. It is much like how the focus is on acquiring property at the beginning of a game of Monopoly. The winner will be the one with the most property, not the one with the most cash on hand.

The dot com companies had to find ways to support their growth until revenues increased sufficiently to generate profits. There are three options facing the firm: borrow a huge amount of money, sell stock to the public, or sell the entire firm to a larger corporation that has the resources to fund the expansion. The decision managers make will affect the very survival of the firm. We will look at how a decision such as this may be tackled in Chapters 12 and 13.

Analyzing Firm Performance

In Chapter 14 we analyze firms using ratios and common-size financial statements. Ratios help the financial manager to identify areas needing attention. Ratio analysis can help the financial manager identify the strengths and weaknesses of a firm. Chapter 15 extends the concepts learned in Chapter 14 by using ratios to forecast a company's future strengths and weaknesses.

We conclude our study of corporate finance by reviewing the management of short-term capital, which is how to correctly use current assets and current liabilities, in Chapter 16.

Chapters 17 and 18 conclude the text and integrate the various areas of finance by taking a look at how well the ideas and theories advanced earlier in the book can be used to solve real-life problems. In Chapter 17 we extend our discussion to international markets. In Chapter 18 we follow an entrepreneur through her life as she uses the financial lessons taught in this course to solve a variety of different business and personal finance problems.

To help link the various topic areas together into a cohesive unit we next introduce the financial system.

Self-Test Review Questions*

Answers to Self-Test Review Questions appear at the bottom of the page on which the question is located.

1. How is finance defined?
2. What are the three main areas of finance?

FINANCIAL SYSTEM

The earlier discussion might have led you to conclude, incorrectly, that the field of finance is segregated into distinct areas of study. In fact, all of the topics discussed in the last section fit together in the **financial system,** which is shown graphically in Figure 1.1. On the far left we see that three groups provide funds: individuals, businesses, and the government.

Individuals are the primary investors in the economy. Ultimately, they own every business asset. Individuals invest their savings in the financial system with the expectation of converting them into greater savings for the future. Figure 1.2 shows the typical life-cycle spending by individuals or households. During his or her early years, a person may spend more than is earned. For example, you may be borrowing money to pay for your education. Eventually, you hope to go to work and to earn enough to pay back these loans and begin building up a nest egg (a reserve sufficient to cover emergencies and retirement). You will use this nest egg when you retire and your income falls below your level of spending.

The financial system plays a critical role in the individual's financial life cycle. Initially, the markets and intermediaries provide a source of funds when you need to borrow. For instance, you will become acquainted with the mortgage market when you buy your first house. You may have already participated in the money markets if you have borrowed money to buy a car. Undoubtedly you have already dealt with banks, which are financial intermediaries.

Later in life, when your income rises, you will begin investing. This may be through an intermediary known as a pension fund, or it may be through banks and stock bro-

FIGURE 1.1
The Financial System

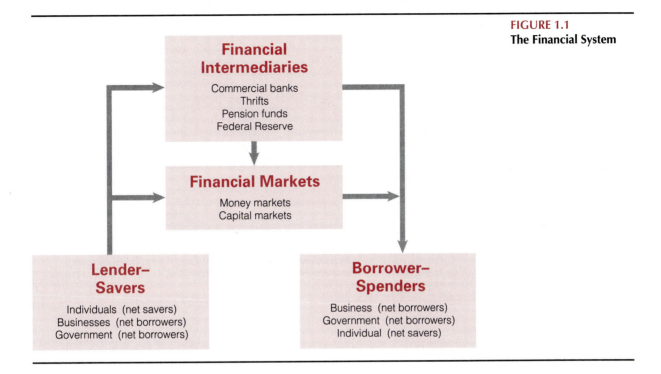

kerage houses. However you choose to invest, the markets, with the aid of intermediaries, will channel your savings to borrower–spenders. Borrower–spenders are listed on the right side of Figure 1.1. They include businesses, the government, and individuals. These borrower-spenders pay for the right to use your money for a period of time.

The financial system relies on all of its parts to function. Without you, the individual, there would be no money available for those who need to borrow it. Without the markets and the intermediaries, investors would have difficulty channeling funds to borrowers. Without the borrower–spender, investors would have nowhere to invest.

Note from Figure 1.1 that individuals, businesses, and the government are each sometimes lenders and sometimes borrowers. Businesses and the government often have temporary surplus funds to lend. Across the whole economy, however, businesses and the government borrow, which is why they are listed first in the Borrower–Spenders box. Similarly, individuals at times are borrowers. However, in aggregate, individuals are the source of investment funds and so are listed first in the Lender–Savers box.

Keep this diagram of the financial system in mind as we move through the text. In Part One we investigate the markets, intermediaries, and interest rates. In Part Two we look at investments, including how cash flows are adjusted for time, how risk and return are related, how assets are valued, and how we may evaluate a firm before making an investment. In Part Three we move our focus to the business. We study how businesses choose between using debt or equity to fund growth and how they choose between investment opportunities, plan for the future, and manage short-term assets.

Before we launch into our study of financial markets and institutions in Chapter 2, let us first establish what financial managers are attempting to accomplish.

FIGURE 1.2
Life-Cycle Spending by Individuals

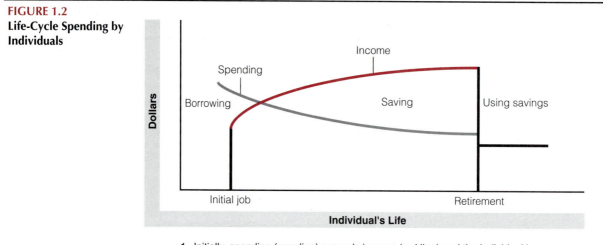

1. Initially, spending (gray line) exceeds income (red line) and the individual borrows.
2. To the right of the crossover point, income exceeds spending and the individual saves.
3. During retirement the individual uses savings.

ROLE OF THE FINANCIAL MANAGER

A firm's accountants report the recent history of the firm's earnings (the income statement) and provide a snapshot of the current fiscal condition of the firm (the balance sheet). As important as these functions are, no company succeeds by looking back. The financial manager is responsible for making decisions that affect the future of the firm. The financial manager evaluates future investments, projects, product introductions, and financing. On the basis of this analysis, the firm makes decisions that affect its very survival. It is helpful to have a single goal in mind when making financial decisions. This goal enables us to establish methods to make choices that will ensure profitability.

Maximizing Profit Is Not Enough

A rational goal to consider would be for managers to maximize the firm's profits. A manager who is maximizing profits makes decisions that result in the highest profits to the firm in every period. Is this really what we want our managers to do?

Consider the case of Fresh International, a privately held firm now run by the grandson of the founder. The California-based firm grows vegetables and sells them as salad. In the early 1980s the firm began developing a method to preserve salad in a bag. Initial efforts were a dismal failure (buyers found themselves with a bag of ugly brown mush). Clearly, the early efforts were a cost that the firm could have saved. They took money, time, and energy away from the firm's main business: growing and marketing lettuce. Finally, in 1989 Fresh International's scientists developed a special bag that lets out carbon dioxide without letting in oxygen. The result was bagged salad that would last on retailers' shelves. Total sales for Fresh International in 1995 were about $450 million, with about $350 million from the sale of bagged salads. Postponing current period profits for future sales seems to have paid off. This example suggests one problem with the profit maximization goal: ***Profit maximization can result in short-sighted management decisions.***

Another problem with the profit maximization goal is that it ignores risk. A manager whose goal is to maximize profits, if faced with two investment options, would choose the one with the highest expected profit, despite its having much higher risk than the alternative.

Finally, the timing of the cash flows is important. In general it is better to get cash flows to the company sooner rather than later. Suppose a manager was evaluating two projects. One gave large payments initially and the second gave large payments later. If the total profits of the second were larger, the manager with a profit maximization goal might choose it over the first. This may not be the best decision, as Chapter 6 will show.

Shareholder Wealth Maximization Should Be the Goal

Rather than profit maximization, we will assume that the manager's goal is to maximize shareholder wealth (which we will see later is equivalent to maximizing the value of the firm). Consider what this implies. Managers should make every decision with the goal of increasing the wealth of the shareholder. How is shareholder wealth increased? By increasing the stock price. So the goal of maximizing shareholder wealth is equivalent to the goal of maximizing stock price. Because investors buy stock for the sole purpose of making money, this goal will please them. Pleased shareholders will reelect directors, who will reward managers with higher salaries.

If the goal is to increase shareholder wealth, how can managers achieve this goal? Shareholder wealth is measured as the number of shares held multiplied by the price per share. For example, at the time of this writing William Gates, the CEO and largest shareholder of Microsoft, owns 741,749,300 shares of Microsoft stock. With Microsoft selling at $59.375 per share, Gates's wealth is $44.04 billion. To increase his wealth, Gates must increase the stock price.[1] Thus, the wealth maximization goal puts the emphasis on increasing the stock price rather than on profits or earnings per share (EPS). In Chapter 9 we will examine determinants of stock price in more detail, but we can briefly review them here. If a firm's risk falls, investors will pay a higher price for the stock. Similarly, if the projected cash flows increase, the stock price will rise, and it will rise more quickly if investors expect the cash flows sooner rather than later.

The wealth maximization goal leads to a very rational directive to managers: ***Increase the firm's cash flows, get those cash flows to the firm as soon as possible, and do this while minimizing risk.*** This goal allows us to develop strategies for evaluating projects that provide clear answers to investment questions.

---

[1]For more on Bill Gates's wealth, see the Bill Gates Net Worth page at http://web.quuxuum.org/~evan/bgnw1.html.

One type of agency cost is where managers use company funds to acquire perquisites that are primarily for the managers' pleasure.

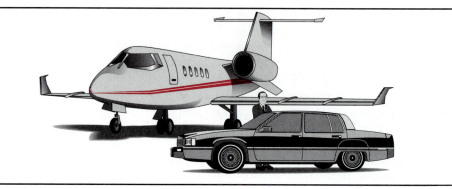

Straying from the Wealth Maximization Goal

In practice, managers do not always adhere to the goal of maximizing shareholder wealth. Consider that *Business Week*[2] reported that the cost of operating a private corporate jet averages nearly $10,000 per hour, including depreciation, pilot salaries, and insurance. Despite these high costs, many managers choose to buy a company plane rather than use commercial airlines. In these cases, managers may be looking out for their own welfare and comfort more aggressively than for the welfare of shareholders. This problem arises because managers, rather than owners, run many companies. *Managers, as agents of owners, recognize that they will not benefit as much from increasing shareholder wealth as they may by running the company to suit their own agendas.* For example, managers could have the company buy expensive luxury cars for their use. This does not increase the wealth of shareholders, but it may make the manager happy. An **agency cost** is any benefit a manager derives from a company that does not increase shareholder wealth and is not part of the manager's agreed-upon compensation. Agency costs include fancy offices, corporate jets, beachfront condos, and Friday afternoons off for golf. Less obvious costs of the agency relationship, but just as significant, are those associated with reducing agency costs. For example, hiring expensive accounting firms to monitor management decisions and provide accurate accounting and financial information is also an agency cost.

It is often difficult for shareholders to control agency costs. One reason is that the shares of stock in most large companies are so widely distributed that no one shareholder has the incentive or the power to discipline wayward managers. Many argue that the takeover market is one of the best sources of corporate discipline available. Managers who are looking out for their own interests over the interests of shareholders are likely to be replaced when the firm is taken over by another firm.

Boards of directors give many managers stock options and stock incentive plans to help align their interests with those of shareholders. One famous example of this was when Lee Iacocca became CEO of Chrysler. He received a salary of $1 per year plus stock options. At the time, Chrysler was near bankruptcy. By saving the company and increas-

---

[2]"An Updraft for Corporate Jets," *Business Week,* August 5, 1996.

Box 1.1 A Question of Ethics: Levi Strauss & Co. and Child Labor

In 1992 Levi Strauss was confronted with a difficult problem. Two of its subcontractors in Bangladesh were using child labor. Its first response was to consider ordering the subcontractor to fire the children and replace them with adult workers. On further investigation, Levi learned that if the children lost their jobs, they would probably be driven into prostitution to help support their families. Levi recognized that not only did the managers face an ethical dilemma, but there could be a public relations disaster if the press publicized the fact that they employed children. The dilemma: Lay off the children and force them into prostitution or keep them working at the factories, thereby contributing to child labor and opening the company up to bad publicity.

The solution Levi arrived at was both unusual and innovative. The children were taken out of the factories and Levi continued to pay their wages as long as they attended school full time. Levi guaranteed the children factory jobs upon reaching age 14, the local age of maturity. This solution benefited Levi in several ways. First, the risk of bad publicity was replaced with a conspicuous display of decency. Second, Levi began preparing a more qualified and better-educated workforce for the future. Finally, because the children had to attend school to get their wages, the families could be counted on to keep them in school—an important issue in a country where education is not strongly supported.

Innovative solutions to ethical problems such as these will be required in the future as the shareholder wealth maximization goal conflicts with social consciousness. Let us hope that managers will take the time and trouble to find appropriate solutions.

Source: Fortune, May 12, 1997, p. 104. © 1997 Time Inc. All rights reserved.

ing the stock price, Iacocca became a very wealthy man. This deal served shareholders very well.

At times, firm managers are caught in a position where their own personal ethics and social consciousness are at odds with the wealth maximization goal. For example, should a firm allow child labor in countries where it is legal and is the lowest-cost method of production? Box 1.1 describes how Levi Strauss & Co. dealt with this problem. Managers may need to be creative to find solutions to difficult problems such as this so that shareholders, managers, and the public are satisfied.

What About Bondholders?

Before we leave our discussion of the financial manager's goal, let us review what this goal means to the firm's bondholders. Bondholders lend money to the firm and are paid interest until the debt matures and they are paid back the principal. If managers are to maximize stockholder wealth, do they care about bondholders' wealth? Bondholders do not elect directors, set managers' salaries, or otherwise directly affect managers' welfare. To the extent that this is true, managers will not work very hard to make the bondholder happy. In fact, the wealth maximization goal suggests that the manager would be willing to take wealth away from the bondholder and give it to the stockholder.

Suppose it were possible for managers to set up a new company, sell bonds to the public, immediately distribute the proceeds to shareholders by declaring a dividend, and then file for bankruptcy. Certainly this transaction would please shareholders, but if this happened often, bonds would become impossible to sell. This explains why bondholders demand protection in the form of long, written agreements that constrain managers.

A typical provision prevents the firm from paying a dividend unless the firm meets certain cash flow requirements. Because managers already are looking out for them, shareholders do not need to be protected by these written agreements.

Self-Test Review Questions*

1. What is the goal of the financial manager?
2. Give three reasons why profit maximization is not a good goal.
3. Why would managers fail to maximize shareholder wealth?
4. Are managers likely to spend much energy looking out for bondholders?

FIVE KEY CONCEPTS OF FINANCE

This textbook covers many areas of finance. The lessons may be applied to nearly every aspect of our lives. This may suggest that it contains many unrelated topics, but this is not the case. A few basic concepts reappear throughout the text that help direct our study of the topic at hand. This section summarizes these concepts. We will initially assume that they are true and call them maxims, meaning an established principle or general truth. Later, we will see that there are shades of truth, and that even these fundamental concepts are subject to some controversy.

Greater Returns Require Taking Greater Risk

Study Tip

The distinction between required, expected, and actual returns can be confusing. The required return is what you *need* to be satisfied. The expected return is what you *think* you will get. The actual return is what you *actually* receive. If you expect a security to pay more than you require, you will buy it.

This assumption is at the heart of individual behavior. Before giving up consumption today, an investor will demand greater consumption in the future. Economists call the additional amount of consumption demanded the **real rate of interest.** It is independent of inflation. If I offer you the option of receiving a new pair of shoes today or next year, you are most likely to choose to receive them today. Wanting things *now* is part of human nature. I will have to offer you more in the future to induce you to delay consumption. For example, if I offer you the choice between a pair of shoes now or a pair of shoes plus a pair of socks next year and the socks are the minimum required to induce you to wait, then they represent your real rate of return. Real rates are expressed as percentages rather than as clothing accessories. This real rate is the minimum acceptable return, and it is based purely on human nature. We simply like to have things now rather than later.

However, if investors want something more than the real rate of return, they must incur more risk. Figure 1.3 shows the relationship between risk and return. The y-intercept is at the risk-free rate (the rate you can earn without incurring any chance of loss). As the level of risk increases, the required return increases. The required return is the

* 1. To maximize shareholder wealth.
  2. Profit maximization ignores long-term objectives, cash flow timing, and risk.
  3. Because they may look out for themselves before looking out for shareholders.
  4. No, bondholders have little influence over managers' welfare.

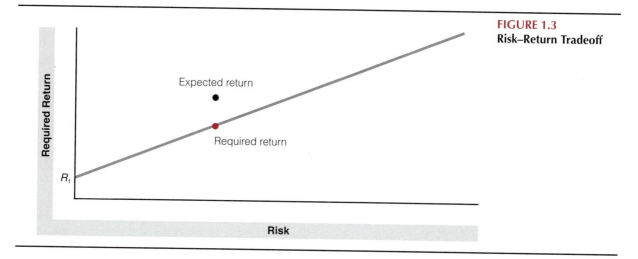

FIGURE 1.3
Risk–Return Tradeoff

minimum return needed to make the investor feel properly compensated for taking on additional risk.

Why does the risk–return line slope upward? Suppose an investor wants to save for the future. It is natural that this investor will choose the least risky investment available. However, there are securities for sale that have various amounts of risk. The only way that sellers of risky securities can entice an investor to buy these securities is to offer a higher interest rate. The seller will raise the return to the investor until the securities sell. Investors demand more return to compensate for the greater risk. If the return on assets did not fluctuate with risk, no one would be willing to buy riskier securities. As a result, not all of the securities in the market would sell.

Do higher-risk investments *always* provide higher returns? Absolutely not! If we knew what the return was going to be, the investment would not really be risky. When an investor buys a risky security, the *required return* is high. The *actual return* may indeed be equal to the expected return, or it may be even more. It also may be much less.

Investments are always made based on expected returns. The expected return is what investors think the future return will be. If they expect more than they require, they will buy the stock. Investment analysts make their living attempting to project future stock returns. We will pursue this topic further in Chapter 7.

The risk–return assumption can be summarized as follows:

Finance Maxim 1: Investors will not delay consumption unless they expect to get something extra in return, nor will they incur risk without being compensated for that risk.

Good Deals Disappear Fast

Suppose a new employee at Nordstrom's Department Store misunderstands the manager and, rather than putting last year's unsold merchandise out for sale, drastically reduces the price on a new shipment of Tommy Hilfiger shirts. Shoppers would quickly buy the shirts. Who would be able to take advantage of this good deal? Only shoppers who knew what the true price of the shirts should be and who happened to spot the bargain. Every shopper is looking for the same thing—good deals—but which shoppers are most likely to find them? The good deals go to those who know prices well enough to recognize a deal when it surfaces and to those who find it first.

The same situation exists in the securities markets. Every investor is looking for the same thing: a good deal. Good deals may occasionally surface. Who will be able to take advantage of them? The answer to this question leads to our next finance maxim.

Finance Maxim 2: Good deals go to the investor who is able to recognize them and reacts first.

For example, big investment fund companies employ a number of specialists who spend all of their time studying a few stocks or industries. When news about one of these stocks or industries is released, the mutual fund specialists can quickly buy or sell the affected security. Because the investment company controls large amounts of money, the price of the security will move quickly, and the opportunity for big returns disappears.

Consider this simplified example. In October 1995 China's leading car maker picked General Motors Corp. over Ford Motor Co. for a project valued at more than $1 billion to build sedans in China. General Motors stock was then selling at $44.50 per share and earnings per share (EPS) were $7.43. If GM distributed all of the earnings to the shareholders, the return would have been

$$\text{Expected return} = \frac{\text{EPS}}{\text{Investment}} = \frac{\$7.43}{\$44.50} = 16.70\%$$

If analysts projected that earnings per share would increase to $7.75 because of the deal with China, the projected return would increase to 17.42%:

$$\text{Expected return} = \frac{\$7.75}{\$44.50} = 17.42\%$$

If a return of 16.70%, as it was before the announcement, was adequate given the risk of this stock, then General Motors stock represented a good deal at $44.50, and analysts would have issued buy orders. The demand for millions of shares of the stock would cause its price to rise. Theoretically, investors would continue to buy shares until the price rose to the point where the return was again 16.70%. This happens when the stock price is $46.42:

$$\frac{\$7.75}{\$46.42} = 16.70\%$$

As new information becomes available to investors, security prices will adjust so that the return to investors is fair. Millions of investors are looking for mispriced securities every day. Many of these investors control large amounts of money that they can direct into good deals. As these securities are bought or sold, the prices move up or down until the good deal is gone. Exactly how quickly and accurately security prices reflect news is the subject of a tremendous amount of research and debate. We say that markets that do a good job of pricing securities are efficient. Few argue the logic behind **efficient markets,** but many disagree as to exactly how efficient the markets actually are.

What are the implications of efficient markets? If the markets were really able to assign the true intrinsic price to every security and investment offered for sale, every investment would be fair. It would not matter how the investor selected assets for a portfolio. A monkey throwing darts at the *Wall Street Journal* could pick stocks as well as the most learned professional. Obviously, the learned professional is not going to accept this idea easily. Chapter 9 discusses market efficiency in greater depth.

The concept of market efficiency can be summarized as follows: *If financial markets are efficient, the price of a security is an accurate estimate by the market of its true value.*

The Value of Money Depends on When It Is Received

Which would you rather have: $100 right now or $100 in 1 year? This is an easy choice. Even if you do not need the $100 now, you could invest it so that more would be available in a year. People pay more for things they prefer, so if investors prefer cash flows now rather than later, current cash flows are more valuable. The longer it will be before a cash flow arrives, the less valuable it becomes.

Much of the math we do in this course revolves around adjusting the value of cash flows to compensate for when they arrive. The value of assets depends on when the cash flows generated by the assets arrive. Investment opportunities depend on whether the values of future cash flows are greater than the initial investment. To make these calculations, we must recognize that the interest rate the initial investment could have earned is an **opportunity cost.** The higher the risk of the future cash flows, the greater the required return (remember the risk–return assumption) and the higher the interest rate.

Another way of looking at why we must adjust for when cash flows arrive is to consider what happens when we make an investment. Investors spend money today hoping that they will receive funds in the future. To decide whether the investment should be made, the investor compares what is being spent with what will be received. How can investors make this comparison if they receive the dollars at different points in time? Because the dollars have different values depending on when they are received, comparing dollars without adjusting for time is like comparing dollars with pesos without adjusting for the exchange rate.

We can summarize our third finance maxim, the time value of money concept, as follows:

Finance Maxim 3: A dollar received today is worth more than a dollar received in the future.

Cash Is King

In finance, cash flows are what matter, not accounting earnings or profits. This is because cash flows are what investors can invest and firms can use to pay dividends.

Accountants report earnings when they are earned, not when they are received. Because accounting profits cannot be invested or used to pay dividends, we must deal with cash. Another reason we deal with cash flows rather than accounting profits is that financial calculations always consider the exact timing of the cash flows and adjust for the time value of money. Accounting profits often have little to do with when funds will actually be received or spent.

The major difference between cash flows and accounting profits is how asset purchases are treated. Accountants depreciate an asset over its useful life. The financial analyst deducts the entire cost of an asset during the period when the firm buys it because that is when the cash expenditure takes place. Unfortunately, one problem with this adjustment is that firms pay taxes according to the accountant's way of recording asset purchase expenses. This requires that we compute taxes one way and report cash flows another. We will learn how this is done in Chapter 11.

Our fourth finance maxim, the concept that cash is king, can be stated as follows:

Finance Maxim 4: Cash flows determine value.

Not Everyone Knows the Same Things

In a business context, **asymmetric information** refers to the fact that not everyone knows everything. Investors may not know what the firm's insiders know. A bank may not know what a borrower plans to do with a loan. An insurance agent may not know how well an insured person will act to protect against loss. Each of these examples represents an opportunity for one party to gain at the expense of the other.

Consider Gina Day, owner of Rockies Brewing Co., a microbrewery located in Boulder, Colorado. During the first several years, she tried to convince investors that her firm was doing well and would provide excellent returns. Unfortunately, firm managers have no credibility with the public because they have an incentive to stretch the truth. Rockies Brewing Co. has survived and has grown by 1,000% since 1990. Too bad investors did not believe her!

The asymmetric information problem explains many events in finance. When a firm announces that it is going to borrow, the stock price usually rises. This is because investors believe that if management issues debt it is signaling the firm's ability to meet the required cash flows far into the future. Similarly, when it sells new stock, management is signaling that the stock is overpriced, so stock prices, on average, drop. Asymmetric information can explain many different financial events, such as why there are protective covenants and why firms may pay a dividend while simultaneously borrowing money. We will point out these issues as they arise later in the text.

In summary, our fifth finance maxim is as follows:

Finance Maxim 5: Asymmetric information is the difference in the information set held by different participants in the financial marketplace; these differences must be handled by business participants.

CHAPTER SUMMARY

Finance is the study of managing money. Because everyone must deal with money in one context or another, the study of finance is universally important. Finance can be distinguished from accounting by noting that the accounting function reports what has already happened, whereas finance involves making decisions that affect the future.

There are three main areas of study in finance. *Markets and institutions* deal with the financial intermediaries, who can be either suppliers or users of funds. The institutions that participate in the financial markets bring the suppliers and the users of funds together. The financial markets establish security prices so that all of the funds supplied are used and the markets clear. *Investments* is the study of how money is converted into more money over time. It includes how investment portfolios are created and how securities are selected. *Corporate finance* deals with financial problems and issues that face a firm. These include evaluating whether projects should be taken and how projects should be financed, and evaluating the financial health of the firm.

The goal of the financial manager is to maximize shareholder wealth. Maximizing profits fails to consider the timing and riskiness of the firm and may be short-sighted. Wealth maximization requires the financial manager to maximize the price of the firm's stock. This requires taking a long-term view of cash flows because the stock price is determined by the current value of all future cash flows.

The following five assumptions touch on much that will be discussed later in the text:

1. Greater returns require taking greater risk.
2. Good deals disappear fast.
3. The value of money depends on when it is received.
4. Cash is king.
5. Not everyone knows the same things.

Chapter 2 begins our study of the financial markets and institutions.

KEY WORDS

agency cost 10	diversification 4	financial markets 3	opportunity cost 15
asymmetric information 16	efficient markets 15	financial system 6	portfolio 4
capital markets 3	finance 3	investments 4	real rate of interest 12
corporate finance 5	financial institutions 3	money markets 3	risk–return tradeoff 4

DISCUSSION QUESTIONS

1. Why is profit maximization *not* an appropriate goal for firm managers?
2. Wealth maximization is the goal of financial managers. What, specifically, can the financial manager do to improve shareholder wealth? Discuss this issue in terms of the firm attributes that actually influence shareholder wealth.
3. Discuss the following in terms of agency costs.
   a. Why are financial managers not as concerned about bondholder wealth as they are about stockholder wealth?
   b. What do bondholders do to protect themselves?
   c. Why should financial managers be concerned with keeping bondholders satisfied?
4. Discuss the following in terms of the risk–return tradeoff.
   a. Distinguish between actual returns and expected returns.
   b. Distinguish between expected returns and required returns.
   c. Which must rise with increasing risk?
   d. If the expected return is less than the required return, will the investor buy the security?
   e. Will the actual return always be greater for higher-risk securities?
5. In an efficient market, if the required return is 10%, what is the expected return? Explain your answer.

6. Why are financial managers so concerned with computing cash flows when accounting earnings and income data are more readily available?

7. An investor was reviewing a company with the intent of purchasing shares of stock. In the annual report the president is quoted as saying that the firm's primary goal is to increase the value of shareholders' equity. However, after additional reading the investor learned of possibly contradictory actions by the firm. Discuss each of the following with respect to how the firm's stock price may react.

   a. The company contributed $5 million to the local hospital development fund. The firm is the major employer in a small town and the hospital is in danger of closing.

   b. The company is spending $500 million to open a new plant in Korea. The new plant will not be operational for 5 years, so the firm's net income will fall during this period.

   c. The firm is increasing its use of debt financing. The risk of the firm is not significantly increased by the additional debt.

   d. The firm is embarking on a plan to upgrade its production process using new, untried technology. If the new systems work, substantial savings could result. If the systems fail, orders will be delayed or unfilled and many customers can be expected to go elsewhere.

   e. The firm will decrease its dividend payout ratio. The firm proposes no new investment opportunities.

PROBLEMS

1. Expected earnings per share of a company's stock is $5.00. The current price of the stock is $50.

   a. What is the current expected return?

   b. If the stock price rises to $60 because of increased demand, what will the expected return be?

   c. If the stock price falls to $45 because a news release states that the firm is now more risky, what will the expected return be?

   d. Which maxim discussed in this chapter best explains the change in return computed in part c?

2. Expected earnings per share of a firm's stock are $1.50. This stock is selling for $35.

   a. What is the current expected return?

   b. If the stock price increases to $40, what will the expected return be?

   c. If the stock price falls to $30, what will the expected return be?

Financial Markets

Chapter Objectives

By the end of this chapter you should be able to:

1. Explain how the markets help establish security prices
2. Explain how the markets increase liquidity and reduce transaction costs
3. Discuss the structure of the financial markets
4. Discuss the money markets
5. Describe the capital markets

This chapter investigates the financial markets and the securities that trade in them. The financial markets include the money markets, where short-term securities trade, and the capital markets, where long-term securities trade. This chapter is important for three reasons. First, it establishes much of the terminology needed for understanding the chapters that follow. You will also need this terminology to read and comprehend publications such as the *Wall Street Journal* and *Business Week*. Second, this chapter explains how the markets help establish prices and increase liquidity. Finally, it introduces most of the securities available to investors. In later chapters you will learn how to compute the value of these securities.

One point you should keep in mind as you read this chapter is that not all countries have well-developed financial markets. Consider how important these markets are to the health of an economy. With poorly developed financial markets, it is difficult to raise funds, sell securities, and invest for retirement.

WHY FINANCIAL MARKETS ARE IMPORTANT

Within an economy there are those who have a surplus of funds and those who have a shortage of funds. In aggregate, households are net suppliers of

funds because they are saving money for later in life. Firms are net users of funds. A firm with many investment opportunities may need more funds than it can raise by simply retaining profits. In fact, corporations and governments do the most borrowing (consider that the entire $4 trillion national debt represents the amount the government has borrowed from the public). The financial markets help move funds from those who have a surplus to those who have a shortage.

One characteristic of a developed economy is well-developed financial markets. Consider the problems faced by entrepreneurs in Russia with its new market economy. The government controlled the economy until the recent breakup, so the financial markets were not developed. Without developed markets, an entrepreneur with a good idea will have trouble finding someone willing to invest money in the business. As a result, development is slow.

Financial markets provide several services. Among the most important are:

- To help establish equitable prices for securities
- To provide liquidity
- To reduce transaction costs

We will look at each of these services in the following sections.

Financial Markets Establish Prices

One of the most important roles of financial markets is establishing security prices. Setting accurate prices is a more difficult task than you might think. Consider the case in which something is bought secondhand. Both buyer and seller want the exchange price to be fair. The problem is how to set a fair price when neither the buyer nor the seller knows the price other people have set for the item. Suppose you want to buy a 1999 Ford Taurus from your neighbor. You would probably begin establishing the value of the car by consulting the *Blue Book* or NADA value guide. These guides collect prices by attending large auctions where dealers buy and sell cars. They set average prices for each year and make. You and your neighbor then adjust the actual price up or down depending on the condition of the car.

Now suppose that rather than buying the car from your neighbor, you want to buy his custom-made mahogany writing desk. The market for the desk is much thinner, meaning that not many of them are bought or sold. Therefore, you will have a more difficult time establishing its true value. There is no central market where similar desks are frequently traded and no value guide to consult. The result is that neither you nor your neighbor is sure what the true value of the desk should be. If you think that it is worth less than what your neighbor thinks, no transaction will occur.

What are the differences between the markets for late model used cars and custom furniture? First, the market for cars is a much **deeper market.** This means that many cars are bought and sold daily, which allows for price comparison. Second, there are many similar cars being bought and sold. In other words, there is standardization of the commodity. This allows traders to compare the price of one unit with another. Finally, there are dealers who participate regularly in the auto market. If they see a car that they can buy cheaply and resell at a profit, they enter the market. None of these factors are present to help price custom furniture. Of course, our current concern is how financial securities are priced. In the next section we will discover how well-developed markets facilitate their pricing.

High Volume of Trades

One feature of financial markets is that many similar securities trade in one forum. Some stocks trade on an organized stock exchange such as the New York Stock Exchange (NYSE) or the American Stock Exchange (Amex). Other stocks trade on the NASDAQ (originally named for the National Association of Securities Dealers Automated Quotation system, NASDAQ is discussed more fully in a later section). Similarly, there are also separate markets for other types of securities. *The result of organized markets is that because many similar securities trade at one location, traders know the true market price of the security at any moment*.

Standardized Securities

Another important feature of financial markets is that many securities are standardized. This means that one format is used for every security that trades on the exchange. For example, a futures option is a security that lets the holder buy something at a specified price, date, and time. If each one of these contracts had to be individually negotiated and attorneys had to be hired to write each contract, few contracts could be completed in a day and each contract would be different. This would greatly increase the difficulty of establishing a fair price. Instead, futures traders have agreed on one standardized contract to use in every trade. Because one contract is similar to another, traders can compare prices and an exact price can be established.

Concentration of Traders

A third feature of the financial markets that facilitates setting security prices is that there are many traders who actively participate. If traders observe a security for sale at a price below what it should be, they will buy the security. This demand for the security causes its price to rise. Traders continue buying until the price rises to what they believe is the fair market price. Alternatively, if a security's price is above what traders believe is fair, they will sell the security, causing its price to fall. *It is the activities of many traders, all buying and selling what they consider to be mispriced securities, that keep the markets efficient (meaning that security prices are correct)*. Chapter 9 will discuss market efficiency in greater detail.

Compare the market for securities to the one for custom-made furniture. The securities markets have high volume; there is low volume in custom furniture. The securities markets contain many similar securities; each item of custom furniture is unique. Securities traders gather together daily to trade; custom furniture auctions are rare. Because of these differences, the securities markets are much better at establishing accurate prices than are many other markets.

To summarize, *the market efficiently prices securities because of high volume, standardization, and a concentration of traders*.

Study Tip

Many students confuse high volume of trades with concentration of traders. High volume refers to the fact that many separate securities trade. Concentration of traders means that many separate traders trade these securities.

Financial Markets Provide Liquidity

Suppose that your roommate offers you the opportunity to invest in his new company that sells bicycle accessories to students through ads placed in university newspapers. Even if you have excess funds and believe the company will do well, you still might not invest because it could be very difficult to sell your interest in the company later when you need cash. **Liquidity** is the ease with which assets can be converted into cash; liquid assets are those that easily convert into cash. Many investors are reluctant to commit funds if they believe that it will be difficult and costly to liquidate the investment. Developed financial markets increase liquidity.

Dealers Increase Liquidity

One way financial markets increase liquidity is through dealers, who increase the liquidity of the market by being willing to step in and buy or sell securities if necessary. **Dealers** take ownership of securities, if necessary, and resell them later, much like car dealers. **Brokers,** on the other hand, do not take ownership of securities. They simply match buyers with sellers, much like real estate brokers.

To understand the role of dealers, consider D&E Communications, a stock that trades on the NASDAQ. Six hundred shares of D&E were traded on November 15, 2000. Suppose you own 1,000 shares of D&E and want to sell them. It is unlikely that at the exact moment that you call your broker someone else will be calling to buy the same number of shares. Several days could easily pass before another investor places a buy order for a security as thinly traded as D&E. Smaller regional companies have even lower transaction volumes.

Does this mean that these securities are not liquid? No: If another buyer is not available when the dealer receives your order to sell, the dealer buys the stock. You neither know nor care whether the sale was to another investor or to a dealer. All that matters is that you are able to sell the security at a fair price at the moment you wanted to sell. The dealer keeps the security in inventory until a buyer surfaces. When a buyer wants to purchase securities, it is again unlikely that another investor will be offering that security for sale at that exact moment. Instead, the dealer pulls securities from inventory to fill the buyer's order.

If you buy or sell securities, you will probably contact a broker, who will then contact a dealer to finalize the trade. *Remember that the broker does not hold an inventory of securities*.

Large Transactions Do Not Depress Market Prices

Another aspect of liquidity is the ability of the market to absorb large transactions while maintaining fair prices. Consider what would happen if you tried to sell 10,000 watermelons on your campus this afternoon. If you could sell them at all, it would be only after discounting the price far below what the melons would sell for in a deeper market. The security markets are big enough and deep enough that they can absorb large transactions while maintaining fair prices. When large pension funds or mutual funds sell hundreds of thousands of shares at a time, it is important that they not depress the market price of the securities. The sheer size of the financial markets usually ensures that this does not happen. Academic studies have looked at how long the market takes to absorb very large block trades (trades exceeding 10,000 shares). In less than 20 minutes the market price of a security rebounds from the effect of a large number of shares being sold at one time.

Financial Markets Minimize Transaction Costs

The most important functions of financial markets are to establish fair prices and provide liquidity. The markets can perform these functions only by keeping the cost of trading as low as possible. The lower the cost of trading, the more accurately priced and liquid are the securities.

High-Volume Markets

One way that securities markets reduce transaction costs is through economies of scale realized with high volume. Traders execute thousands of transactions per day, which drive down the cost per transaction. Securities generally trade in round lots, which consist of 100 shares. If you try to sell an odd lot (anything that is not divisible by 100), you will be charged a substantial odd-lot transaction fee. By encouraging trades to at least meet this 100-share minimum, the system keeps costs lower. When the newspapers report daily trading volume, they report only the number of round lots traded.

Rules

Another way in which costs are kept low is through the rules that protect the safety of market participants. For example, because access is limited to those who have the financial strength to back up their promises, losses due to bankruptcies are greatly reduced.

Standardization

Earlier we noted that standardized contracts are important to fair asset pricing. Standardized contracts also reduce costs. Not only is it less costly to prepare the contract, but potential buyers do not have to read and review each term of the contract before trading. The time and attorneys' fees saved are important to a smoothly functioning market.

Search Costs

Finally, the markets reduce search costs. Buyers and sellers of securities know where to go to find each other. Instead of advertising or relying on friends and acquaintances to bring traders together, the markets provide a central forum where everyone knows the rules and the products offered for sale.

Self-Test Review Questions*

1. List three features of the securities markets that help them set securities prices accurately.
2. Why are dealers so important to investors?
3. How do the markets minimize transaction costs?

---

* 1. High volume, standardized securities, and concentration of traders.
2. They provide liquidity so that investors are always assured that they can sell a security.
3. By capturing the economies of scale that come from high volume and standardization. Rules reduce risk and a central trading location reduces search cost.

STRUCTURE OF FINANCIAL MARKETS

We can discuss financial markets in a number of ways. Markets can be primary or secondary and organized or over-the-counter. The purpose of separating the markets into these different types is to highlight certain features. This section discusses each of the types of markets. Remember that any one market may combine these features. For example, the NYSE is an organized, secondary market.

Primary and Secondary Markets

Primary markets are for securities being offered for sale for the first time. A primary market transaction is one in which there is an initial sale of stock by a firm and the firm receives the funds raised by the sale. **Secondary markets** are where securities are traded after their initial sale. For example, in November of 2000, CoSine Communications went public with a stock offering of 11,500,000 shares at $23 per share. This was a primary market transaction because CoSine received the proceeds of the sale. A secondary market transaction occurs if those same shares are resold today, because CoSine would not receive any of the funds from this sale.

Organized and Over-the-Counter Markets

Organized markets have fixed trading rules and an established physical location, and trading is usually conducted by auction. Organized **auction markets** usually are called exchanges, such as the New York Stock Exchange (NYSE), the American Stock Exchange (Amex), and the Chicago Board of Options Exchange (CBOE). Box 2.1 discusses the growth of exchanges in developing nations.

Box 2.1 Developing Nations Want Their Own Exchanges

Everyone, it seems, wants to open a stock exchange. From Lebanon and Kazakhstan to Ecuador and Indonesia, businessmen and government officials in developing nations have been rushing to open or expand exchanges so they can be players in the global financial markets. The trend is a clear sign that globalization of the world's markets is entering a new stage, with easier access to capital for entrepreneurs, rising domestic savings, and more ways to invest globally. The opening of exchanges "globalizes the competition," as noted by Junius Peake, an expert in exchanges from the University of Northern Colorado.

Seven different groups from China alone are making plans for new financial exchanges. In addition, São Paulo (Brazil), Jakarta (Indonesia), Moscow, and Turkey are building new trading complexes. In eastern Europe, Romania, Latvia, and Estonia opened new exchanges in 1995.

The current frenzy of exchange building is a necessary but often clumsy step for nations shifting from centrally controlled command economies to free markets. There are widely varying degrees of liquidity, organization, and risk in the growing roster of new exchanges, according to industry experts. The problem is that in some of the new exchanges there is no way of discerning the value of the securities traded because there is no regulatory environment. For example, at one point in the early 1990s there were well over 400 stock exchanges in Russia and no system of regulation, research, or custodianship. These problems continue to plague the country today.

Adding to the woes are local officials who don't understand how a market works, says Peake, who has advised many nations on how to set up and run financial exchanges. For example, during a trip he made to China, one government official said, "They wanted a market where the stocks only went up." That would be nice!

Source: Wall Street Journal, November 14, 1995, p. 14.

In **over-the-counter (OTC) markets** trading takes place in a variety of places and a variety of ways. Trading usually occurs over the telephone or by computer. The **NASDAQ** (National Association of Securities Dealers Automated Quotation) computer system is an example of a computerized over-the-counter trading system. The over-the-counter market for stock is generally for stocks with less volume than those that trade on the major exchanges. There are many exceptions to this rule, however. Microsoft is listed on NASDAQ, yet over 100 million shares were traded on November 15, 2000.

About 15,000 securities trade OTC, of which about 5,100 are listed on NASDAQ. The balance of the stocks are from smaller firms of regional, rather than national, interest. By contrast, about 3,025 stocks were listed on the NYSE at the beginning of 2000 and 1,800 on Amex. Not every firm may list on the New York Stock Exchange, as discussed in Box 2.2.[1]

How Trading in a Security Establishes Its Price

Often, buy and sell orders do not arrive at the dealer at the same time. For example, it is unlikely that one customer will call the dealer wanting to buy a security just as another customer is selling it. To ensure an active market and hence earn commissions, dealers trade from their inventory. The dealer adds and subtracts stock from this inventory as demand warrants. Dealers want to begin and end each day with approximately the same inventory level.

If you call a dealer to sell a stock, you will be quoted a **bid price.** The bid price is the price dealers will pay for the stock. If you accept this price, the dealer will buy the stock. Similarly, if you want to buy a security, the dealer will quote the **ask price.** The ask price is the price at which the dealer sells the stock. To keep this more clear in your mind, remember: "Dealers buy at the bid."

> **Study Tip**
>
> One way to keep the bid and ask terminology straight is to remember the mnemonic "Dealers *buy* at the *bid.*" Alternatively, you can remember "The *bid* is *below* the ask."

---

[1]For more information on the exchanges, see www.nyse.com, www.amex.com, and www.nasdaq.com.

Box 2.2   Listing Requirements of the NYSE

To be listed on the NYSE a firm is expected to meet certain qualifications that affirm that it is a going concern, is of national interest, is stable, and is likely to remain important within its industry. The NYSE decides each case on its own merits but provides the following requirements as minimum.

1. Earning power of either $2.5 million before taxes for the most recent year and $2 million for each of the preceding 2 years, or an aggregate for the last 3 years of $6.5 million, together with a minimum in the most recent year of $4.5 million.

2. Net tangible assets of $40 million, but with greater emphasis placed on the aggregate market value of the common stock.

3. Market value of publicly held shares (subject to adjustment depending on market conditions) with a minimum value of $9 million.

4. A total of 1,100,000 common shares publicly held.

5. Either 2,000 total stockholders of 100 shares or more, or 2,200 total stockholders together with average monthly trading volume of 100,000 shares, or 500 total shareholders together with average monthly trading volume of 1 million shares.

The listing requirements are designed to ensure that only securities with high volume and frequent trading are listed on this exchange. This maintains the prestige of being listed on the NYSE.

Source: NYSE Fact Book for the Year 1999. (Available at www.nyse.com)

Suppose the dealer finds that the inventory level is rising. The dealer will respond by lowering bid and ask prices, thus making investors less willing to sell and more willing to buy the security. This reduces inventory. Similarly, if the dealer's inventory level falls below the desired level, the dealer can raise the bid and ask prices, which encourages more investors to sell and fewer to buy. This process is how market demand affects the price of a security. Many factors may drive investors to increase or lower their demand for a security. This change in demand is reflected in the stock's price as dealers adjust pricing so that their inventories remain approximately constant.

Dealers who operate in the organized markets are also called **specialists** because they specialize in a limited number of stocks. A specialist is a stock dealer who is responsible for maintaining an orderly market in a particular stock. Most specialists handle several securities. Like the dealers in the OTC, specialists maintain an inventory of securities so that orders can be filled immediately. If the inventory grows, the specialist lowers the price. If the inventory falls, the specialist raises the price. Again, demand and supply by investors in the market cause the price to adjust.

An interesting fact about the way security prices are set is that the dealer does not need to know a great deal about the stock to set the price accurately. An illustration may clarify this point. Suppose that you just graduated and your first job is to sell an odd-shaped retainer spring. You have no idea what it is used for or why anyone would want it. You are given an allotment of 1,000 per day to sell and told that that is all you can get. You are allowed to sell the retainer springs for any price you choose. The first day you set a price at $.10 each and sell out in an hour. You know that you set the price too low. The next day you set the price at $.20 and do not sell out until 2:00 p.m. You continue adjusting the price until you are able to just sell all of the retainer springs by the end of the day. In this way you have found the price where demand exactly equals supply and the available supply is sold. You never had to learn anything about the retainer. In the same way, the dealer does not have to know why investors are buying or selling a security. The dealer's only concern is finding a price at which demand equals supply so that the inventory remains constant. ***The point is that the investor's knowledge about the security drives the price, not the dealer's***.

So far in this chapter we have discussed in general what financial markets do, how they do it, and how they are organized. Next we will study the markets in greater detail by examining separately the money markets and the capital markets. We will first look at the structure of each market, then discuss its purpose; finally, we will define the major securities that trade there.

Study Tip

You may be confused about the distinction between dealers, specialists, and brokers. Dealers take ownership of a security and make a market by being willing to buy or sell a security if no one else will. Brokers do not take ownership; they bring buyers and sellers together. Specialists are dealers who represent a limited number of securities on one of the organized exchanges.

Self-Test Review Questions*

1. Distinguish between primary and secondary markets.
2. Distinguish between organized markets and OTC markets.
3. Summarize how prices are established by the markets.

* 1. Primary markets are for securities sold for the first time; secondary markets are for subsequent trades.
2. Organized exchanges have a centralized location with rules. In OTC markets, trading takes place in a variety of places and ways, usually over the telephone or by computer.
3. Dealers adjust the bid and ask prices so that their inventory of securities remains constant.

MONEY MARKETS

The term *money market* is a misnomer. Money is not traded in the money markets. However, the securities that do trade there are short term and highly liquid, and so are close to being money. The securities are usually large denomination and have low chance of defaulting, called default risk. Money market securities mature in 1 year or less from their original issue date. This means that a 90-day Treasury bill is correctly called a money market instrument. On the other hand, we do not usually call a 10-year Treasury bond issued 9 years and 6 months ago a money market instrument, although it may occasionally trade in the money market.

Money market transactions do not take place in any one particular location or building. Instead, traders usually arrange purchases and sales between participants over the phone and complete them electronically. This brings up another defining characteristic of the money markets. Money market securities usually have an active secondary market. This means that after the security has been sold initially, it is easy to find buyers who will buy it in the future. This makes the securities very flexible instruments to use to fill short-term financial needs.

Another characteristic of the money markets is that they are wholesale markets, where most transactions are very large, usually over $1 million. The size of these transactions prevents most individual investors from participating. Instead, dealers and brokers, operating in the trading rooms of large banks and brokerage houses, bring customers together. These traders buy or sell $50 or $100 million in mere seconds. This is certainly not a job for the faint of heart!

To summarize, there are four features that together distinguish the money markets:

1. Original maturity less than 1 year
2. Traded via phones and electronic markets
3. Active secondary market
4. Trade in large denominations

Purpose of the Money Markets

As discussed above, there is a well-developed secondary market for money market instruments. This makes the money market an ideal place for a firm or financial institution to warehouse funds until needed. The money markets also provide a low-cost source of funds to business firms, the government, and banks that need a short-term cash infusion.

Investors in the money market usually are not trying to earn unusually high returns on their money market funds. Rather, they use the money market as an interim investment that provides a higher return than simply holding cash. They may feel that market conditions are not right to purchase additional stock or that interest rates are low, so they do not want to purchase bonds. Investment fund managers often hold some funds in the money market so that they can take advantage of any investment opportunities they identify. Additionally, most investment funds and financial intermediaries (such as banks and savings and loans) hold money market securities to meet investment or deposit outflows.

Individuals participate in the money market with certain checking accounts offered by investment firms, who pool these funds and invest in the money markets.

The sellers of money market securities find that the money market provides a low-cost source of temporary funds. For example, the interest rates available on a variety of money market instruments are reported daily in the *Wall Street Journal*. See the box, "Money Market Rates." Banks may buy funds in the money market to meet short-term reserve requirement shortages. The government funds a large portion of the U.S. debt with Treasury bills (T-bills). Money markets permit finance companies such as GMAC (General Motors Acceptance Company, the financing division of General Motors) to raise the funds that it uses to make car loans.

Why are the money markets needed? The primary reason is that cash inflows and outflows rarely occur in unison. For example, the bulk of government tax revenue usually comes at certain times of the year, but expenses are incurred all year long. The government borrows short-term funds that it pays back when it receives tax revenues. Businesses also face problems caused by revenues and expenses occurring at different times. The money markets provide an efficient, low-cost method of solving these problems.

It is important to keep in mind that holding idle surplus cash is expensive. This is because cash balances earn no income for the owner. Idle cash represents an opportu-

Money Market Rates

The *Wall Street Journal* publishes daily a list of interest rates on many different financial instruments in its "Money Rates" column. (See "Today's Contents" on page 1 of the *Journal* for the location.)

The four interest rates in the "Money Rates" column that are discussed most often in the media are:

Prime rate: The base interest rate on corporate bank loans, an indicator of the cost of business borrowing from banks.

Federal funds rate: The interest rate charged on overnight loans in the federal funds market, a sensitive indicator of the cost to banks of borrowing funds from other banks and the stance of monetary policy.

Treasury bill rate: The interest rate on U.S. Treasury bills, an indicator of general interest-rate movements.

Federal Home Loan Mortgage Corporation rates: Interest rates on "Freddie Mac" guaranteed mortgages, an indicator of the cost of financing residential housing purchases.

MONEY RATES

Thursday, November 9, 2000

The key U. S. and foreign annual interest rates below are a guide to general levels but don't always represent actual transactions.

PRIME RATE: 9.50% (effective 05/17/00). The base rate on corporate loans posted by at least 75% of the nation's 30 largest banks.

DISCOUNT RATE: 6.00% (effective 05/16/00). The charge on loans to depository institutions by the Federal Reserve Banks.

FEDERAL FUNDS: 6 9/16% high, 6 3/8 % low, 6 7/16% near closing bid, 6 1/2 % offered. Reserves traded among commercial banks for overnight use in amounts of $1 million or more. Source:Prebon Yamane(U.S.A)Inc. FOMC fed funds target rate 6.50% effective 5/16/00.

CALL MONEY: 8.25% (effective 05/17/00). The charge on loans to brokers on stock exchange collateral. Source: Reuters.

COMMERCIAL PAPER: placed directly by General Electric Capital Corp.: 6.47% 30 to 31 days; 6.44% 32 to 59 days; 6.53% 60 to 75 days; 6.49% 76 to 95 days; 6.44% 96 to 130 days; 6.41% 131 to 153 days; 6.36% 154 to 184 days; 6.30% 185 to 239 days; 6.26% 240 to 270 days.

EURO COMMERCIAL PAPER: placed directly by General Electric Capital Corp.: 4.91% 30 days; 5.07% two months; 5.09% three months; 5.11% four months; 5.12% five months; 5.14% six months.

DEALER COMMERCIAL PAPER: High-grade unsecured notes sold through dealers by major corporations: 6.48% 30 days; 6.53% 60 days; 6.50% 90 days.

CERTIFICATES OF DEPOSIT: Typical rates in the secondary market: 6.55% one month; 6.65% three months; 6.64% six months.

BANKERS ACCEPTANCES: 6.50% 30 days; 6.57% 60 days; 6.84% 90 days; 6.47% 120 days; 6.45% 150 days; 6.41% 180 days. Offered rates of negotiable, bank-backed business credit instruments typically financing an import order.

LONDON LATE EURODOLLARS: 6.63% - 6.50% one month; 6.75% - 6.63% two months; 6.75% - 6.63% three months; 6.75% - 6.63% four months; 6.75% - 6.63% five months; 6.75% - 6.63% six months.

LONDON INTERBANK OFFERED RATES (LIBOR): 6.6200% one month; 6.7600% three months; 6.73313% six months; 6.73375% one year. British Banker's Association average of interbank offered rates for dollar deposits in the London market based on quotations at 16 major banks. Effective rate for contracts entered into two days from date appearing at top of this column.

EURO LIBOR: 4.93750% one month; 5.12000% three months; 5.17188% six months; 5.25000% one year. British Banker's Association average of interbank offered rates for euro deposits in the London market based on quotations at 16 major banks. Effective rate for contracts entered into two days from date appearing at top of this column.

EURO INTERBANK OFFERED RATES (EURIBOR): 4.937% one month; 5.123% three months; 5.174% six months; 5.253% one year. European Banking Federation-sponsored rate among 57 Euro zone banks.

FOREIGN PRIME RATES: Canada 7.50%; Germany 4.75%; Japan 1.50%; Switzerland 5.125%; Britain 6.00%. These rate indications aren't directly comparable; lending practices vary widely by location.

TREASURY BILLS: Results of the Monday, November 6, 2000, auction of short-term U.S. government bills, sold at a discount from face value in units of $1,000 to $1 million: 6.220% 13 weeks; 6.105% 26 weeks.

OVERNIGHT REPURCHASE RATE: 6.48%. Dealer financing rate for overnight sale and repurchase of Treasury securities. Source: Reuters.

FREDDIE MAC: Posted yields on 30-year mortgage commitments. Delivery within 30 days 7.78%, 60 days 7.81%, standard conventional fixed-rate mortgages: 6.125%, 2% rate capped one-year adjustable rate mortgages. Source: Reuters.

FANNIE MAE: Posted yields on 30 year mortgage commitments (priced at par) for delivery within 30 days 7.91%, 60 days 7.96%, standard conventional fixed-rate mortgages: 7.40%, 6/2 rate capped one-year adjustable rate mortgages. Source: Reuters.

MERRILL LYNCH READY ASSETS TRUST: 6.07%. Annualized average rate of return after expenses for the past 30 days; not a forecast of future returns.

CONSUMER PRICE INDEX: September, 173.7, up 3.5% from a year ago. Bureau of Labor Statistics.

Source: Wall Street Journal, November 10, 2000, p. C15

nity cost in terms of lost interest income. The money markets provide a way to invest idle funds and thereby reduce this opportunity cost.

Who Participates in the Money Markets?

An obvious way to discuss the players in the money market is to list those who borrow and those who lend. The problem with this approach is that most money market participants operate on both sides of the market. For example, any large bank borrows aggressively in the money market by selling large commercial negotiable certificates of deposit (NCDs). At the same time, it lends short-term funds to businesses through its commercial lending departments. Nevertheless, we can identify the main money market players and discuss their roles. They include the U.S. Treasury, the U.S. Federal Reserve System, commercial banks, money market mutual funds, and other financial institutions.

U.S. Treasury

The U.S. Treasury is the largest of all money market borrowers worldwide. It issues T-bills and other securities that are very popular with other money market participants. Short-term issues enable the government to raise funds until tax revenues are received. The Treasury also issues T-bills to replace maturing issues.

Federal Reserve

The Federal Reserve is the Treasury's agent for the distribution of all government securities. The Federal Reserve holds vast quantities of Treasury securities that it sells if it believes that the money supply should be reduced. Similarly, the Federal Reserve purchases Treasury securities if it believes that the money supply should be expanded. The Federal Reserve's responsibility for the money supply makes it the single most influential participant in the U.S. money market. We discuss the Federal Reserve and its control over the money supply and interest rates in Chapter 5.

Commercial Banks

Commercial banks hold a larger percentage of U.S. government securities than any other group of financial institutions (approximately 12%). This is partly because of regulations that limit the investment opportunities available to banks. Banks are also the major issuer of negotiable certificates of deposit (NCDs), bankers' acceptances, federal funds, and repurchase agreements (we will describe these securities in a later section). In addition to providing for their own liquidity, many banks trade on behalf of their customers.

Not all commercial banks deal in the secondary money market for customers. The ones that do are among the largest in the country and are often called money center banks. The biggest money center banks include Citibank, Bank of America, Chemical Bank, Morgan Guaranty, and Chase Manhattan.

Money Market Mutual Funds

Because many money market instruments are too large for the average investor to afford, money market mutual funds (MMMFs) are available that combine many investors' funds

FIGURE 2.1
Average Money Market
Fund Investment
Portfolio

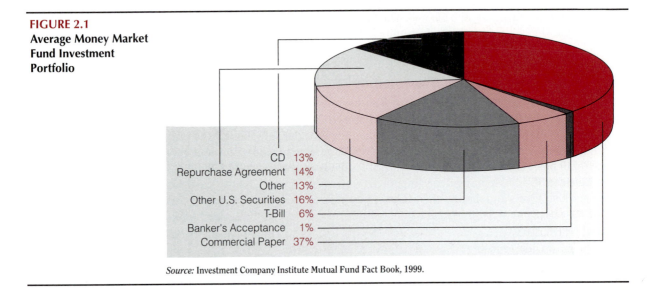

CD	13%
Repurchase Agreement	14%
Other	13%
Other U.S. Securities	16%
T-Bill	6%
Banker's Acceptance	1%
Commercial Paper	37%

Source: Investment Company Institute Mutual Fund Fact Book, 1999.

and buy money market securities. These funds became very popular in the late 1970s, when interest rates rose to record levels and federal law limited the interest rates banks could pay on deposits. Figure 2.1 shows the average money market fund investment portfolio. The securities included in this portfolio are defined in the next section.

Other Financial Institutions

Large diversified brokerage firms called **investment companies** are active in the money markets as well. The largest of these include Bear Sterns, Merrill Lynch, and Morgan Stanley. The primary function of these dealers is to make a market for money market securities by maintaining an inventory from which to buy or sell. These firms are very important to the liquidity of the market because they ensure that both buyers and sellers can readily market their securities.

Finance companies raise funds in the money markets, then lend the funds to consumers for the purchase of durables such as cars, boats, or home improvements. They lend funds to people that normally will not qualify for conventional financing, and they charge a higher interest rate to compensate for risk.

Property and casualty insurance companies must maintain liquidity because of their unpredictable need for funds. For example, when Hurricane Floyd hit North Carolina in 1999, insurance companies paid out billions of dollars in benefits to policyholders. To meet this demand for funds, the insurance companies had to sell a portion of their money market holdings.

Pension funds maintain a portion of their funds in the money market so that they will be liquid enough to take advantage of investment opportunities they identify in the stock or bond markets. Additionally, pension funds must have sufficient liquidity to meet their obligations to beneficiaries. However, because their obligations are reasonably predictable, large money market security holdings are unnecessary.

EXTENSION 2.1

Money Market Instruments

One aspect of entering a new field of study is learning the vocabulary. The press often discusses changing interest rates and market conditions based on the performance of commonly traded securities. Part of your understanding of market conditions depends on recognizing these securities. In this section we briefly introduce many of the securities that regularly trade in the money markets. You may find that you will invest in some of these securities, either individually or through your employer's retirement program.

Treasury Bills

To finance the national debt, the U.S. Treasury Department issues a variety of debt securities. The most widely held liquid investment is the **Treasury bill,** or T-bill. T-bills have either 91-day, 182-day, or 12-month maturities. The government issues T-bills in denominations of $10,000, $15,000, $50,000, $100,000, $500,000, and $1 million. The usual minimum purchase is a round lot of $5 million. Investors wanting to buy amounts smaller than this contact one of the major dealers, who buy T-bills from the government and resell them to the investor. See Box 2.3, which discusses how the Treasury auction works and how it once went haywire.

Federal Funds

Federal funds can be formally defined as immediately available short-term funds transferred (lent or borrowed) between financial institutions, usually for a period of 1 day. The term *federal funds* (usually just *fed funds*) is misleading. Fed funds really have nothing to do with the federal government. The term comes from the fact that banks with excess funds lend them to other banks at a rate close to that available from the Federal Reserve.

The main purpose of fed funds is to provide banks with an immediate infusion of funds. Banks can borrow directly from the Federal Reserve, but many prefer to borrow from other banks so that they do not alert the Fed to any liquidity problems. The reason banks like to lend in the fed funds market is that money held at the Federal Reserve does not earn any interest. So even though the interest rate on fed funds is low, it beats the alternative. One indication of the popularity of fed funds is that on a typical day, over $250 billion in fed funds are purchased.

You are unlikely to ever buy or sell fed funds; however, their interest rates are the most closely watched and reported of all money market instruments because fed funds rapidly reflect adjustments to the money supply by the Federal Reserve. The Federal Reserve cannot directly control fed fund rates, although it can and does indirectly influence them by buying and selling government securities. The Federal Reserve often announces its intention to raise or lower the fed fund rates. Although these rates directly affect few businesses or consumers, analysts consider them an important indication of the direction the Federal Reserve is taking the economy.

Study Tip

The term *fed funds* often confuses students into thinking that these funds are somehow related to the Federal Reserve. They are not. Fed funds represent money lent between banks.

Box 2.3   T-Bill Auctions Go Haywire

Every Thursday the Treasury announces how many 91-day and 182-day T-bills it will offer for sale. Buyers must submit bids by the following Monday, and awards are made the following morning. Twelve-month T-bills are offered similarly once per month. The Treasury accepts the bids offering the highest price.

The Treasury auction of securities is supposed to be highly competitive and fair. To ensure proper levels of competition, no one dealer is allowed to purchase more than 35% of any one issue. About 40 primary dealers regularly participate in the auction.

In 1991 the disclosure that Salomon Brothers had broken the rules to corner the market cast the fairness of the auction in doubt. Salomon Brothers purchased 35% of the Treasury securities in its own name by submitting a high bid. It then bought additional securities in the names of its customers, often without their knowledge or consent. Salomon then bought the securities from the customers. As a result of these transactions, Salomon cornered the market and was able to charge a monopoly-like premium. The investigation of Salomon revealed that during one auction in May 1991, Salomon managed to gain control of 94% of an $11 billion issue. During the scandal that followed this disclosure, John Gutfreund, the firm's chairman, and several other top executives with Salomon retired. The Treasury has instituted new rules since then to ensure that the market remains competitive.

T-bills have virtually no default risk because even if the government ran out of currency, it could simply print more. Inflation risk is low because of the short term to maturity. The market for T-bills is extremely deep and liquid.

T-bills do not pay interest; instead, they are sold at a discount, which means that the buyer pays less for the security than it will be worth at maturity. The investor's return is based on the difference between what the T-bill initially cost and what ultimately will be received when it matures.

T-bills are very close to being risk-free. As expected for a risk-free security, the yield earned on T-bill securities is among the lowest in the economy. Investors in T-bills have found that in some years their earnings even fail to compensate for changes in purchasing power due to inflation. Figure 2.2 shows the yield on T-bills and the inflation rate over the last 20 years. For example, in 1973–1980, the inflation rate matched or exceeded the earnings on T-bills. Clearly, the T-bill is not an investment to be used for anything but temporary storage of excess funds.

Repurchase Agreements

Repurchase agreements work much the same as fed funds except that nonbanks can participate. A firm can sell securities in a repurchase agreement (also called a *repo*) in which the firm agrees to buy back the securities at a specified future date. Most repos are very short term, with the most common being for 3 to 14 days. However, there is a market for 1- to 3-month repos.

Government securities dealers often engage in repos. The dealer may sell the securities to a bank with the promise to buy the securities back the next day. This makes the repo essentially a short-term collateralized loan. Securities dealers use the repo to manage their liquidity and to take advantage of anticipated changes in interest rates.

Because repos are often collateralized with Treasury securities, they are usually low risk; therefore, they have interest rates similar to those of other money market instruments. Losses have occurred in these markets, however. In 1985 ESM Government Securities and Bevill, Bresler, and Schulman declared bankruptcy. These firms had used the same securities as collateral for more than one loan. The resulting losses to municipalities that had purchased the repos were over $500 million. In addition, these bankruptcies caused the failure of the state-insured thrift insurance system in Ohio.

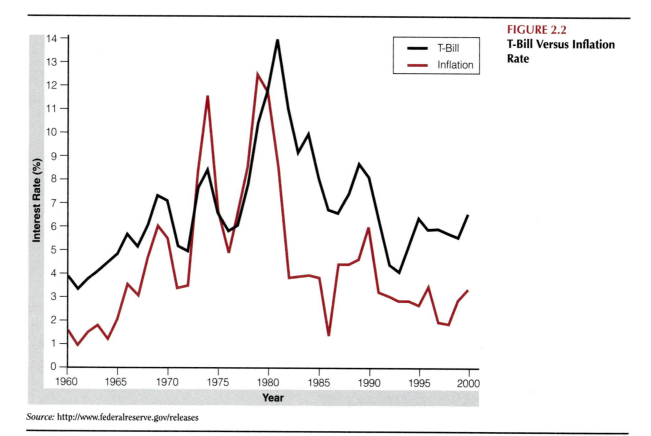

FIGURE 2.2
T-Bill Versus Inflation Rate

Source: http://www.federalreserve.gov/releases

Negotiable Certificates of Deposit

A **negotiable certificate of deposit** (NCD) is a security issued by a bank that documents a deposit and specifies the interest rate and maturity date. Because a maturity date is specified, an NCD is a term security as opposed to a demand security, which can be redeemed at any time without penalty. For example, your checking account is a demand security because you can take the money out whenever you want. An NCD is also a bearer instrument, which means that whoever holds the instrument at maturity receives the principal and interest. The NCD can be easily bought and sold until maturity.

The denominations of NCDs range from $100,000 to $10 million. Few NCDs are denominated less than $1 million. The reason these instruments are so large is that dealers have established the round lot size to be $1 million. As noted already, a round lot is the minimum quantity that can be traded without incurring extra costs.

NCDs typically have a maturity of 1 to 4 months. Some have 6-month maturities, but there is little market for ones with longer maturities.

Figure 2.3 plots the yield on NCDs and T-bills. The rates paid on NCDs are negotiated between the bank and the customer. They are similar to the rates paid on other money market instruments because the level of risk is low. Large money center banks can offer rates a little lower than other banks because the market recognizes that the

FIGURE 2.3
NCDs Versus T-Bills

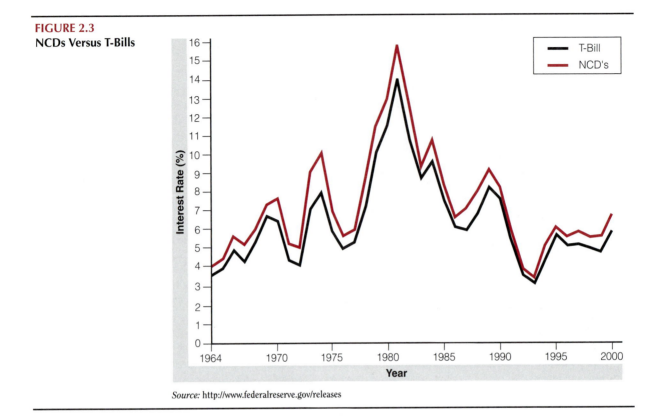

Source: http://www.federalreserve.gov/releases

government's "too big to fail" policy makes these banks' obligations less risky. NCD rates tend to be slightly above the T-bill rate because of the slightly greater chance of default.

Commercial Paper

Commercial paper securities are unsecured promissory notes issued by corporations. Because these securities are unsecured, only the largest and most creditworthy corporations issue commercial paper.

Commercial paper always has an original maturity less than 270 days, so as to avoid the need to register the security issue with the Securities and Exchange Commission (SEC). To be exempt from SEC registration, the issue must have an original maturity less than 270 days and be intended for current transactions. Most commercial paper actually matures in 20 to 45 days. Like T-bills, most commercial paper is issued on a discounted basis (meaning no interest is paid, and the increase in price provides the return).

Corporations use commercial paper extensively to finance the loans that they extend to their customers. For example, General Motors Acceptance Corporation (GMAC) borrows money by issuing commercial paper and uses the money to make loans to consumers buying General Motors cars, with repayment to come from customers making their monthly payments. Similarly, Household Finance and Chrysler Credit use commercial paper to fund loans made to consumers.

Bankers' Acceptances

A **bankers' acceptance** is an order to pay a specified amount of money to the bearer on a given date. Bankers' acceptances have been in use for hundreds of years. They are used to finance goods that have not yet been transferred from the seller to the buyer. For example, Built Well Construction Company wants to buy a bulldozer from Komatsu in Japan. Komatsu does not want to ship the bulldozer without being paid because it may not know Built Well and realizes that it would be difficult to collect if payment was not made. Similarly, Built Well is reluctant to send money to Japan before receiving the equipment. A bank can intervene in this standoff by issuing a bankers' acceptance. In essence, the bankers' acceptance is a promise to pay the shipper in the event there is a problem with the buyer. The bank charges Built Well a fee for their intervention.

Interest Rate Comparisons

Figure 2.4 compares the interest rates on each of the money market instruments discussed above. The most notable feature of this graph is that all of the money market instruments appear to move together over time. This is because all are very low risk and have short-term maturities. They all have deep markets that are priced competitively, and because these instruments have so many of the same risk and term characteristics, they are close substitutes for each other. Because they are substitutable, should one rate temporarily depart from the others, market supply and demand forces soon cause a correction. Figure 2.4 also demonstrates how volatile money market rates have been over time, ranging from over 8% in 1990 to about 3% just 3 years later. Table.2.1 summarizes the various money market securities.

FIGURE 2.4 Interest Rates on Money Market Securities

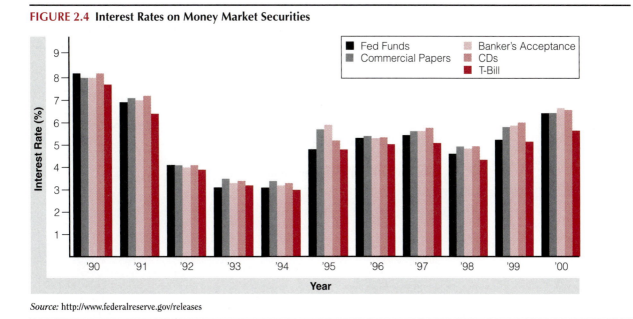

Source: http://www.federalreserve.gov/releases

TABLE 2.1 Summary of Money Market Securities

Money Market Security	Description
Treasury bills	Sold by the U.S. government. Lowest possibility of default. Available in 91-day, 182-day, or 12-month maturities.
Federal funds	Short-term (often overnight) funds exchanged among banks.
Repurchase agreements	Funds sold with a promise to repurchase on a specified date. Usually secured by Treasury securities.
Negotiable certificates of deposit	Term deposits issued by commercial banks. Usually denominated from $100,000 to $10 million. They are payable to the bearer.
Commercial paper	Unsecured securities issued by large, well-known companies. They are often used to finance loans to customers.
Banker's acceptances	Used in international trade to substitute the creditworthiness of the bank for the buyer. It is a promise by the bank to pay when goods are delivered.

Self-Test Review Questions*

1. What is the purpose of the money markets?
2. Why is the interest earned on money market securities so low?
3. What are money market mutual funds?
4. What does it mean for a security to sell at a discount?

CAPITAL MARKETS

In the previous section we learned that securities with less than 1 year to maturity trade in the money markets. This section discusses securities that have an original maturity *greater* than 1 year. These securities trade in the capital markets.

Capital Markets Defined

As just noted, the capital markets are where securities with original maturities greater than 1 year trade. The primary capital market securities are:

- Long-term government notes and bonds
- Municipal bonds
- Corporate bonds

* 1. Because the interest rates on money market securities are so low, they are used only for temporary storage of funds.
2. Money market securities are short term and the issuers are considered to be very stable and safe.
3. MMMFs combine funds contributed by many investors to purchase various money market securities.
4. The security is sold at a price below its value at maturity. The increase in price provides the return to the investor.

- Corporate stock
- Mortgages

Notes and bonds are securities that represent a debt owed by the issuer to the investor. Stock represents an ownership interest held by the investor. Mortgages are long-term loans secured with real estate.

Purpose of the Capital Markets

Capital market participants have very different motives from those of money market participants. The money markets are primarily for warehousing funds until a more important need arises. *The capital markets, on the other hand, are for long-term investments where the purpose is to significantly increase the investor's wealth.* See Box 2.4 for a discussion of initial public offerings.

Capital investments are expected to last over 1 year and produce a stream of future returns. The capital markets are used to finance capital investments. We study how to select these investments in Chapters 10 and 11.

The federal government issues long-term notes and bonds to fund the national debt. The government never issues stock because it cannot sell ownership claims. State and municipal governments also issue long-term notes and bonds to finance capital projects, such as schools and swimming pools.

Corporations issue both bonds and stock. One of the more difficult decisions faced by a firm may be whether it should finance its growth with debt or equity. We address the issues involved in this decision in Chapter 13. Corporations may enter the capital markets because they do not have sufficient capital to fund their investment opportunities. Alternatively, firms may choose to preserve their capital to protect against unexpected needs. In either case, the availability of efficiently functioning capital markets is critical to the continued health of the business sector.

Study Tip

Be sure to note a point that has been made several times in this chapter: Households are net *suppliers* of money and businesses are net *users* of money. Households invest in businesses and businesses invest in productive assets.

Box 2.4   Initial Public Offerings

One of the most widely publicized capital market transactions is the **Initial Public Offering (IPO)**. An IPO occurs when securities are offered by a firm that has never previously issued any securities to the public. The reason these transactions receive so much attention is that they sometimes result in large gains for the buyers of these securities. For example, Ixia went public (meaning it issued stock to the public for the first time) on October 18, 2000. By November 14, 2000, its price had risen 112%. Similarly, Synplicity gained 88% and Transmeta gained 117% within 2 months of their IPOs. There is no guarantee, though, that the price will rise after issue. TNPC lost 42% between October 5 and November 14 of

2000 and Advanced Switching Comm lost 18% within a month of its IPO.

Despite the hype surrounding IPOs, on average, an investment in an IPO underperforms investments in similar firms by 17%. This well-documented fact is exacerbated when the issuing firm is smaller. Another factor regarding IPOs is that your ability to buy shares in one depends on whether your broker chooses to sell shares to you. The better the prospects for the IPO, the less likely it is that a small investor will be able to buy any shares. Instead these shares go to the broker's largest investors.

For more discussion of IPOs, see www.e-analytics.com/ipo/.

The largest purchasers of capital market claims are households. Individuals, often through their employee-sponsored programs, invest in stocks and bonds as a means of preparing for retirement. Financial institutions are also large purchasers of capital market securities, because individuals and households often deposit funds in financial institutions that use the funds to purchase capital market instruments such as loans.

A firm must file a registration statement with the Securities and Exchange Commission (SEC) before it can offer securities for sale to the public. The SEC was established following the Depression in the 1930s to oversee the securities markets. The SEC does not audit the information for accuracy or monitor the firm to determine whether future filings and reports are accurate. Incorrect or inaccurate filings open the firm's managers to civil and criminal prosecution. The rewards for manipulating the security prices by releasing inflated income figures have caused investors substantial losses. See Box 2.5 for a discussion of the ethical issues involved.

Capital Market Securities

As noted above, capital market securities have original maturities greater than 1 year. In this section we introduce and define various types of bonds and then discuss common and preferred stock.

Bonds

Bonds are debt securities that usually require the issuer to make a series of equal semiannual interest payments followed by a final maturity payment. The holder of a bond

---

Box 2.5 Financial Managers Face Ethical Pressure

In February 1997 Mercury Finance Co. failed to repay over $100 million of maturing commercial paper. In the scandal that followed, Mercury Finance, a used-car lender, disclosed accounting irregularities that had overstated profits for the previous 4 years. The firm blamed its senior vice president and controller, James Doyle, for bookkeeping irregularities. However, Doyle responded that he had been pressured "to participate in the charade taking place at Mercury." The reasons for the questionable accounting that resulted in overstating income by 100% are obvious. Both Doyle and Mercury's president, John Brincat, were compensated according to the performance of the firm's stock. The misstated financial statements caused the stock price to soar, netting the president a bonus of over $1.6 million and Doyle $725,000.

The temptation to engage in questionable accounting and reporting is not rare. Phar-Mor, Inc. and Chambers Development Co. both experienced $1 billion stock market plunges in 1997 that occurred after questionable accounting practices became known. In one of the largest losses ever sustained on Wall Street by managers attempting to manipulate stock prices, Bre-X planted gold in ore samples sent in for assay. The results convinced shareholders that Bre-X held the world's largest gold mine and the stock value increased spectacularly. When the ore was later reassayed, only trace amounts of gold were found and the shareholders lost nearly $4.5 billion.

Students of finance and accounting may well find themselves in positions of sufficient authority to exercise control over information that will affect stock prices and their own compensation. Recognizing in advance that such opportunities are likely to arise and deciding beforehand how such situations will be handled can prevent the manager from succumbing to temptation.

Source: Wall Street Journal, February 3, 1997, p. C1, and May 7, 1997, p. A3.

has a claim on the assets of the issuer should the terms of the bond not be met. The amount that the issuer must pay at maturity is called the par, face, or maturity value of the bond. The coupon rate is the rate of interest used to compute the semiannual interest payments. This rate is usually fixed for the duration of the bond and does not fluctuate with market interest rates. Figure 2.5 shows a bond issued by Sohio/British Petroleum to help fund construction of the Alaska pipeline. Note that on the face of the bond the par value is listed as $1,000 and the coupon rate is stated as 8⅝%.

Treasury Notes and Bonds   The U.S. Treasury issues notes and bonds to finance the national debt. A **Treasury note** has an original maturity of 1 to 10 years and a **Treasury bond** has an original maturity of 10 to 30 years. Note and bond prices are quoted as a percentage of the $1,000 face value, as are T-bill prices. Oddly, the fractional part of the quotation is in 32nds. So a quotation of 120:17 means 120 17/32, which in turn is $120.531 per $100. *To convert the quoted price to the actual bond price, first convert the fractional portion of the quoted price to a percentage, and then multiply the quoted price by 10*. For example, if a $1,000 bond is quoted at 120:17, you would first convert 17/32 to .531 (17/32 = .531). Next, you would multiply 120.531 by 10 to get the price of the bond as $1,205.31 (120.531 × 10 = 1,205.31).

Treasury bonds have very low interest rates, reflecting their absence of default risk. Investors in Treasury bonds have found themselves earning less than the rate of

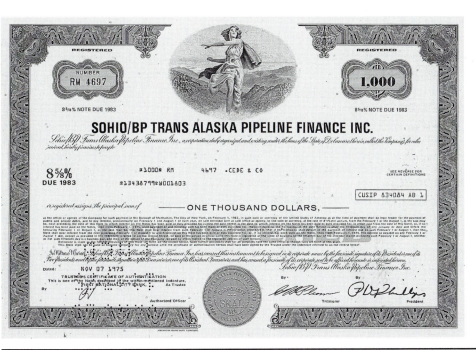

FIGURE 2.5
Sohio/BP Corporate Bond

inflation in some years. Most of the time, however, interest rates on Treasury notes and bonds are above those found on money market securities. We investigate why long-term interest rates are usually above short-term rates in Chapter 4.

Agency Bonds   The U.S. Congress has authorized a number of U.S. agencies to issue bonds; hence, these securities are called **agency bonds.** Although the government does not explicitly guarantee these bonds, most investors feel that the government would not allow them to default. Issuers of agency bonds include

- The Government National Mortgage Association
- The Farmers Home Administration
- The Federal Housing Administration
- The Veterans Administration
- The Resolution Trust Corporation
- The Federal National Mortgage Association
- Federal Land Banks
- The Federal Home Loan Mortgage Corporation
- The Student Loan Marketing Association

These agencies issue bonds to raise funds that are used for purposes that the Congress has deemed to be in the national interest. For example, the Government National Mortgage Association (Ginnie Mae) issues bonds to raise funds that are used to finance home loans. Similarly, the Student Loan Marketing Association (Sallie Mae) issues bonds to fund student loans.

The risk of these bonds is actually very low. They usually are secured by loans that are made with the funds raised by selling the bonds. Additionally, should they have trouble meeting their obligations, the federal agencies have lines of credit with the Treasury Department. Finally, it is unlikely that the federal government would permit a default. Despite this low level of risk, these securities offer interest rates that are significantly higher than those available on Treasury securities. For example, on November 9, 2000, Federal National Mortgage Association 30-year bonds yielded 7.35% while 30-year Treasury bonds yielded 6.07%. Many investors feel that agency bonds are an attractive alternative to low-rate Treasuries.

Municipal Bonds   **Municipal bonds,** sometimes called *munis,* are securities issued by local, county, and state governments. The proceeds from these bonds are used to finance public interest projects such as schools, utilities, and transportation systems. Municipal bonds that are issued to pay for essential public projects are exempt from federal taxation. This allows the municipality to borrow at a lower cost because investors will be satisfied with lower interest rates on tax exempt bonds. There are two types of municipal bonds: general obligation bonds and revenue bonds.

General obligation bonds are backed only by the creditworthiness of the issuer. Most general obligation bond issues must be approved by the taxpayers because the taxing authority of the government is pledged for the repayment.

Revenue bonds are backed by the cash flow of a particular revenue-generating project. For example, revenue bonds may be issued to build a toll bridge, with the tolls being pledged as repayment. If the revenues are not sufficient to repay the bonds, they may go into default and investors may suffer losses. This occurred on a large scale in 1983 when the Washington Public Power Supply System (since called "WHOOPS") used revenue bonds to finance the construction of two nuclear power plants. Falling energy costs and tremendous cost overruns resulted in the plants never becoming operational. Investors in these bonds lost their investments.

It is important to note that municipal bonds are not free of default risk. For example, defaults on municipal bonds amounted to $1.4 billion in 1990. This high rate of default was attributed primarily to the weaker economy in 1990. However, it shows that governments are not exempt from financial distress. Unlike the federal government, local governments cannot print money, and there are real limits as to how high they can raise taxes without driving the population away.

Corporate Bonds   When large corporations need to borrow funds for long periods of time they may issue **corporate bonds.** Most corporate bonds have a face value of $1,000 and pay interest semiannually. The degree of risk varies widely among issues. Bonds are a popular source of funds for businesses. Figure 2.6 shows the volume of bonds issued since 1983. Firms tend to issue more bonds when interest rates are lower.

A variety of different types of corporate bonds are available:

- *Debentures* are long-term bonds backed only by the general creditworthiness of the issuer. There is no specific collateral pledged to repay the debt. In the event of default, the bondholders must go to court to seize assets. Collateral pledged to other debtors is not available to the holders of debentures. Debentures are the most widely used form of corporate bond.

- *Mortgage bonds* are used to finance a specific project. For example, a building may be the collateral for bonds issued for its construction. Because these bonds have specific property pledged as collateral, they are less risky than comparable unsecured bonds.

- *Variable-rate bonds* are a financial innovation spurred by increased interest rate variability in the 1980s and 1990s. The coupon interest rate on these securities is tied to a market rate, such as the rate on Treasury bonds, and is adjusted periodically.

Corporate bonds have been changing in recent years as issuers introduce innovative securities in an effort to attract investors at lower prices. The following represent some of the more common provisions.

- *Sinking fund.* A sinking fund is a requirement that the firm retire (pay off) a portion of the bond issue each year. This provision is attractive to bondholders because it reduces the probability of default when the issue matures. By making the issue more attractive, a sinking fund provision reduces the bond's interest rate.

- *Protective covenants.* Financial managers are hired, fired, and compensated at the discretion of the board of directors, who represent stockholders. This implies that the

Study Tip

It is easy to estimate the effect on a security's interest rate of a special feature. Features that investors like lower the interest rate and make it cheaper for the firm to borrow. Features that investors do not like raise interest rates and make it more costly for the firm to borrow.

FIGURE 2.6
Total Bonds Issued per Year

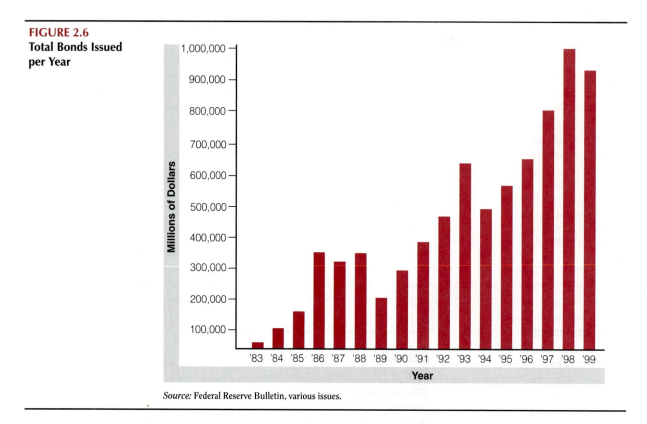

Source: Federal Reserve Bulletin, various issues.

managers are going to be more interested in protecting stockholders than they are in protecting bondholders. Because bondholders cannot look to managers for protection when the firm gets into financial difficulty, they must include rules and restrictions on managers designed to protect the bondholder's interest. These rules and restrictions are called protective covenants. They usually limit the amount of dividends the firm can pay and the ability of the firm to issue additional debt. The covenants may restrict other financial policies as well.

- *Call provisions.* Most corporate bonds are callable. This means that the issuer has the right to force the holder to sell the bond back. The call provision usually requires a waiting period between the time the bond is issued and the time when it can be called. This is so that investors will not buy a bond and be faced with the firm immediately calling it in and forcing the holder to incur the cost of buying another bond. The price bondholders are paid for the bond is typically set at the issue price plus 1 year's interest payment.

  One reason for call provisions is to allow the firm to take advantage of falling interest rates. If interest rates fall, the price of fixed-rate bonds will rise. If rates fall enough, the price will rise above the call price and the firm will call the bond. We examine why bond prices move in the opposite direction of interest rate movements in Chapter 8.

Careers in Finance

Investment Banker

One of the best paying jobs in the business field is that of investment banker. Investment bankers are responsible for helping firms sell securities to the public. They facilitate both IPOs and seasoned (already existing) issues. When a company wants to sell stock to the public, it will contact one of the major investment banking houses, such as Merrill Lynch, Salomon Smith Barney, or Morgan Stanley Dean Witter. Investment professionals at these institutions will help prepare the SEC registration documents, set a price for the securities, and market the securities to the public. This is a high-pressure job since errors in pricing the securities can cost millions of dollars. As compensation for the risk, successful investment bankers earn substantial salaries ranging from $75,000 to $300,000 after a number of years in the business.

A second reason that issuers of bonds include call provisions is to make it possible to buy bonds according to the terms of the sinking fund. A third reason is that firms may have to retire a bond issue if the covenants of the issue restrict the firm from some activity that it deems in the best interest of shareholders. For example, bond covenants often restrict the firm from issuing additional debt. If managers feel new debt is required, it may need to call in existing debt and issue new.

Call provisions put a limit on the possible price appreciation bondholders can hope to earn from a bond. For this reason investors do not like call provisions, so callable bonds have a higher yield than comparable noncallable ones. Still, firms typically issue callable bonds because of the importance of the feature.

- *Conversion.* Some bonds are convertible into common stock. This permits bondholders to share in the firm's good fortunes if the stock price rises. Most convertible bonds state that the bond can be converted into a certain number of common shares at the discretion of the bondholder. The conversion ratio is such that the price of the stock must rise substantially before conversion is likely to occur.

Bondholders like the conversion feature. It is very similar to buying just a bond, but receiving both a bond and a stock option (a right to buy stock in the future). The price of the convertible bond reflects the value of this option and is higher than the price of comparable nonconvertible bonds. The higher price received for the bond by the firm implies a lower interest cost. This feature gives the bondholder upside potential with downside protection.

Corporate Bond Interest Rates   The interest rate on corporate bonds varies with the level of risk. Several rating agencies evaluate the creditworthiness of bonds and assign ratings. A highly rated bond with little chance of default is rated AAA. Bonds that are investment grade but not as safe as the above may be rated AA, A, or BBB. If a bond has a rating below BBB, it is considered too risky to be called investment grade and is called speculative or junk quality.

FIGURE 2.7
End of Year
Interest Rates on
Corporate Bonds

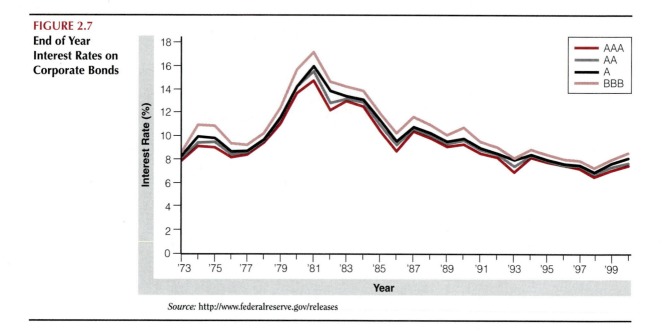

Source: http://www.federalreserve.gov/releases

Figure 2.7 shows the interest rates since 1973 on bonds rated between AAA and BBB. As expected, the interest rate is lowest for the higher-rated bonds and highest for the BBB bonds. The different bonds track together over time.

Self-Test Review Questions*

1. What is the purpose of the capital markets?
2. How much would you pay for a bond quoted in the newspaper as selling for 98:20?
3. What are debentures?

Stock

Stock, another type of capital market security, represents ownership in a corporation. A stockholder owns a percentage interest in a firm consistent with the percentage of out-standing stock held. This gives the stockholder the following rights:

- *Residual claimant.* The stockholders have a claim on all assets and income left over after all other creditors have been satisfied. If nothing is left over, they get nothing. However, it is possible to get rich as a stockholder when the firm does well. This is unlikely to happen to bondholders.

3. Bonds secured by the general credit of the issuing firm. No specific collateral is pledged.
2. $986.25 (20/32) = .625, .625 + 98 = 98.625, 98.625 × 10 = 986.25).
* 1. For long-term investments expected to increase the investor's wealth.

- *Right to vote.* Most stockholders have the right to vote for directors and on certain issues, such as amendments to the corporate charter and whether new shares should be issued.

There are two types of stock: common and preferred. Common stockholders vote, receive dividends, and hope that the price of their stock will rise. There may be various classes of common stock, usually denoted as type A, type B, etc. Unfortunately, the type does not have any standard meaning. The differences among the types usually involve either the distribution of dividends or voting rights. It is important that an investor in stocks knows exactly what rights the stock being contemplated provides. Figure 2.8 shows a certificate for 15 shares of Wien Consolidated Airlines common stock.[2]

Preferred stock is as much like bonds as it is like common stock. The preferred stockholder usually receives a fixed dividend that never changes. Because the dividend does not change, the price of preferred stock is stable. Preferred stockholders usually do not vote unless the firm has failed to pay the promised dividend. Preferred stockholders hold a claim on assets that is senior to common shareholders but junior to bondholders (meaning that bondholders have a claim on assets before preferred stockholders and preferred stockholders have a claim before common stockholders).

---

[2]This stock certificate was issued to your text's author when he was 15 years old and made his first stock purchase. The reason he still has the certificate is that the firm subsequently went bankrupt and the shares became worthless.

FIGURE 2.8
Wien Consolidated Airlines Stock

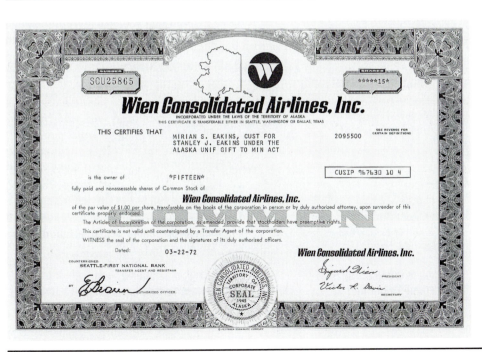

FIGURE 2.9
Volume of Newly Issued Common Stock

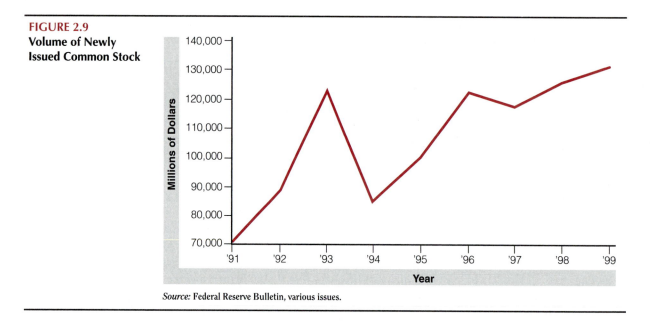

Source: Federal Reserve Bulletin, various issues.

Figure 2.9 shows the amount of common stock issued per year since 1991. Note that the total volume of stock issued is much less than the volume of bonds issued. Over $940 billion in new bonds was offered to the public in 1999 (see Figure 2.6). Firms offered just over $131 billion in stock in that year. One reason is since the interest payments on debt are tax deductible, the cost of borrowing is lower than the cost of equity. Also, stockholders do not have to share earnings with bondholders.

TABLE 2.2 The Thirty Companies That Make Up the Dow Jones Industrial Average

1.	Alcoa	16.	IBM Co.
2.	American Express Co.	17.	Intel
3.	AT&T	18.	International Paper Co.
4.	Boeing Co.	19.	J.P. Morgan & Co.
5.	Caterpillar Inc.	20.	Johnson and Johnson
6.	Citigroup	21.	McDonald's Corp.
7.	Coca-Cola Co.	22.	Merck & Co.
8.	DuPont Co.	23.	Microsoft
9.	Eastman Kodak Co.	24.	Minnesota Mining & Manufacturing Co.
10.	Exxon Corp.	25.	Philip Morris Co.
11.	General Electric Co.	26.	Procter & Gamble Co.
12.	General Motors Corp.	27.	SBC Communications Inc.
13.	Home Depot Inc.	28.	United Technologies Corp.
14.	Honeywell International	29.	Wal-Mart
15.	Hewlett-Packard	30.	Walt Disney Co.

Source: http://averages.dowjones.com/djia_cos.html.

Box 2.6 How to Read Stock Quotes in *The Wall Street Journal*

The figure below shows the *Wall Street Journal*'s listing of the NYSE. Review the entry for AFLAC. The first two columns report the 52-week high and low for this stock. AFLAC stock sold for as much as $74.94 and for as low as $33.56 at some time during the preceding year. The third column is the firm's short name. If the firm has a ticker symbol, it appears in the fourth column. The annual dividend is reported in the fifth column. Note that most stocks pay dividends every quarter. To find what the quarterly payment would be, divide this annual amount by 4. The next column lists the dividend yield of .5%. The dividend yield is the annual dividend divided by the price per share. The price/earnings ratio is in the next column, followed by the total number of shares traded that day. The Hi and Lo reported in the next two columns are the high and low price for the stock on that trading day. So on November 8, 2000, AFLAC stock went up to $70.68 and down to $69.63. The close is the price of the security when the exchange closed on that trading day. The last column reports the net change in price from close on the last trading day to close on the current day.

Stocks have traditionally been reported and traded in eighths. This system was established in the 1700 when the world's most stable currency was the Spanish milled dollar, known as pieces of eight. That coin was divided with a hammer and chisel into halves, quarters, and eighths, and the eighth became the standard increment for stock prices for centuries. The United States switched to the decimal pricing system during the summer of 2000. Beginning August 22, 2000, the *Wall Street Journal* began reporting NYSE quotes in dollars and cents instead of fractions.

Various symbols appear in the left-hand margin. These symbols indicate when stock splits, dividends, and other significant events occur. The symbols can be interpreted using a legend that is printed at the bottom of the first page of stock prices. For a discussion of bond quotes, see www.ny.frb.org/pihome/fedpoint/fed07.html.

Stock prices are quoted daily in most local newspapers and in *The Wall Street Journal*. Box 2.6 discusses how these quotes are read.

Stock Market Indexes

Various stock market indexes are reported to give investors an indication of the performance of the stock market. The most commonly quoted index is the Dow Jones Industrial Average. This index is based on the performance of 30 large companies, which are changed periodically due to their circumstances. The companies included in the Dow in November 2000 are listed in Table 2.2. Box 2.7 offers a detailed look at the Dow Jones Index. There are other useful indexes to use to follow the performance of different groups of stock. For example, Figure 2.10 shows the S&P 500, the NASDAQ composite, and the NYSE composite. The *Wall Street Journal* reports 23 different indexes in the Stock Market Daily Data Bank.

FIGURE 2.10 Stock Market Indexes

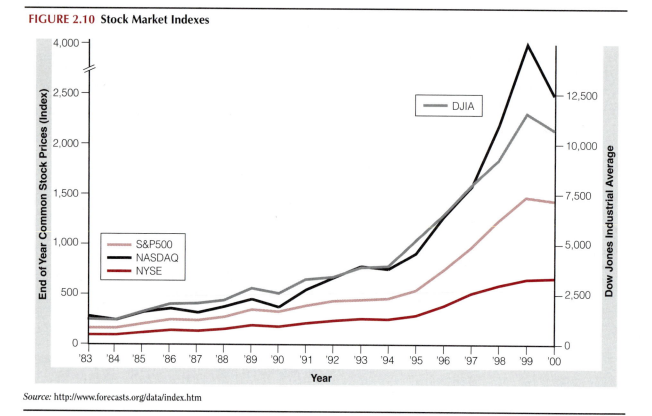

Source: http://www.forecasts.org/data/index.htm

Box 2.7 Dow Jones Stock Index

The Dow Jones Industrial Average (DJIA) is an index composed of 30 "blue chip" firms. On May 26, 1896, Charles H. Dow added up the prices of 12 of the best known stocks and created an average by dividing by the number of stocks. In 1916, 8 more stocks were added to the average and in 1928 the 30-stock average made its debut.

Today, the editors of the *Wall Street Journal* select the firms that make up the DJIA. They take a broad view of the type of firm that is considered industrial; in essence, it is almost any company that is not in the transportation or utility business (because there are also Dow Jones Averages for those kinds of stocks). In choosing a new company for the DJIA, they look at substantial industrial companies with a history of successful growth and wide interest among investors. The components of the DJIA do not change often, but they were altered in November 1999, when Home Depot, Intel, Microsoft, and SBC replaced Sears, Chevron, Union Carbide, and Goodyear. General Electric is the only one of the original 12 still included in the DJIA.

Most market watchers agree that the DJIA is not the best indicator of the market's overall day-to-day performance. Indeed, it varies substantially from broader-based stock indexes in the short run. It continues to be followed closely primarily because it is the oldest index and was the first to be quoted by other publications. It does track the performance of the market reasonably well in the long run.

CHAPTER SUMMARY

Financial markets are important because they help establish the fair value of securities and provide liquidity to investors. The markets establish the value of securities by having a large number of similar securities trade at known locations where many informed traders can interact. These same traders also provide liquidity for investors by buying or selling securities when there is a temporary trade imbalance. By helping set prices and improve liquidity, the markets provide a service that is critical for a vibrant growing economy. These activities increase the availability of funds to businesses, make it safer and easier to save for the future, and increase the confidence of all market participants.

There are both primary and secondary financial markets. A primary market is one in which securities are offered for sale for the first time and the initial issuer receives the proceeds of the sale. The secondary market is for the resale of securities. The NYSE is the largest secondary market in terms of total dollar volume. Organized markets can be distinguished from over-the-counter markets. An organized market has a specific place of business, rules that govern trading, and trade by auction. The over-the-counter market usually conducts trading over the phone or by computer. There is no central location for trading, and prices are quoted by dealers.

One way in which security markets establish prices is through dealers, who strive to maintain constant inventory levels. As the inventory held by a dealer increases, the dealer lowers the bid and ask prices. If the inventory falls, the bid and ask prices increase. In this way the security's price reacts to changing demand conditions in the market.

The money markets are where securities that have an original maturity of less than 1 year are traded. These securities include T-bills, commercial paper, federal funds, repurchase agreements, negotiable certificates of deposit, and bankers' acceptances. Money market securities provide a safe, low-interest way to warehouse funds for short periods of time. Similarly, the money markets provide a cheap source of short-term funds.

The capital markets are where securities that have an original maturity greater than 1 year are traded. These securities include stocks and bonds. Investors use the capital markets to earn higher returns. Firms obtain funds in the capital markets to finance long-term growth.

KEY WORDS

agency bonds 40
ask price 25
auction markets 24
bankers' acceptance 35
bid price 25
bonds 38
brokers 22
commercial paper 34
corporate bonds 41
dealers 22

deeper market 20
federal funds 31
finance companies 30
general obligation
    bonds 40
Initial Public Offering
    (IPO) 37
investment companies 30
liquidity 22
municipal bonds 40

NASDAQ 25
negotiable certificate of
    deposit (NCD) 33
organized markets 24
over-the-counter (OTC)
    markets 25
pension funds 30
primary markets 24
property and casualty
    insurance companies 30

repurchase agreements 32
revenue bonds 41
secondary markets 24
specialists 26
stock 44
Treasury bill 31
Treasury bond 39
Treasury note 39

DISCUSSION QUESTIONS

1. List and describe the two most important services the financial markets provide.
2. Explain the difference between the organized markets and the over-the-counter markets. Name an example of each.
3. Define the following terms:
    a. Primary market and secondary market
    b. Common stock and preferred stock
4. How do dealers facilitate price setting by the securities markets? That is, describe how prices change when new information is released.
5. What are the reasons why an investor would use a money market fund?

6. List the primary players in the money market and discuss their roles.
7. Explain what it means to say that T-bills are sold at a discount.
8. What is the primary difference between federal funds and repurchase agreements? (Extension 2.1)
9. Discuss the difference between the purpose of the money markets and the capital markets.
10. Discuss what municipal bonds are and list two examples.
11. Why do bondholders prefer noncallable bonds over callable bonds?

PROBLEMS

1. How much would you pay for a bond listed at 110:10?
2. If a note was listed as selling for 94:8, how much would you pay to buy this note?
3. If a bond was selling at a price of $1,301.56, how would it be listed in the paper (as a percentage)?
4. If a bond was selling at a price of $951.87, how would it be listed in the paper?

WEB EXPLORATION

1. Investigate the data available from the Federal Reserve at www.federalreserve.gov/releases. Answer the following questions.
    a. What is the difference in the interest rates on commercial paper for financial firms as compared with nonfinancial firms?
    b. What was the interest rate on the 1-month eurodollar at the end of 1971?
    c. What is the most recent interest rate report for the 30-year Treasury note?
2. Visit www.forecasts.org/data/index.htm. Click on Stock Index at the very top of the page. Now choose U.S. Stock Indices—Monthly. Review the indexes for the DJIA, the S&P 500, and the NASDAQ composite. Which index appears most volatile? In which index would you have rather invested in 1985 if the investment could compound until now?

MINI CASE

You have been hired by Risky Ventures as a consultant to predict market and interest rate trends. They believe that history is likely to repeat itself in the financial markets. After discussing the project with them, you decide to do as they ask even though you doubt the validity of their methods. The biggest task you must immediately face is collecting market and interest rate data. You know the best source of this information is the Web.

a. You decide that your best indicator of long-term interest rates is the 30-year U.S. Treasury note. Your first task is to gather historical data. Go to www.federalreserve.gov/releases and scroll down to weekly releases. Now select H.15 Selected Interest Rates| Historical Data|. Scroll down to U.S. Government Securities| Treasury Constant Maturities| 30 Year. Scroll over to the right and click on Annual.

b. You have located an accurate source of historical interest rate data, but getting it into a spreadsheet will be very tedious. Then you remember that Excel will let you convert text data into columns. Begin by highlighting both columns of data. Right click on the mouse and choose Copy. Now open Excel and put the cursor in a cell. Click Paste. Now choose Data from the tool bar and click on Text to Columns. Click on Fixed Width, then on Finish. The list of interest rates should now have the year in one column and the interest rate in the next column. Label your columns.

c. You now want to analyze the interest rates by graphing them and plotting a trendline. Again highlight the two columns of data you just created in Excel. Click on the Charts icon on the tool bar. Select Scatter Diagram and choose a type of scatter diagram that connects the dots. Let the Excel wizard take you through the steps of completing the graph. Once the graph has been completed, click on one of the lines on the graph. The dots should turn yellow. Now right click on the mouse and choose Add Trendline. Choose the linear regression option. Next, click on the Option tab at the top of the dialog box. Enter that you want to forecast ahead 1 period and that you want the equation written on the chart along with the R squared. Does the R squared indicate that this is a very good method for predicting interest rates?

d. You want to impress Risky Ventures by flooding them with well-presented data. Repeat the steps outlined in parts b and c for the bank prime rate and Aaa and Baa bonds.

e. Now go to www.forecasts.org/data/index.htm, click on Stock Indexes at the top of the page, and again repeat the steps outlined in parts b and c.

C H A P T E R 3

Intermediaries

Chapter Objectives

By the end of this chapter you should be able to:

1. Identify the distinguishing features of commercial banks
2. Identify the distinguishing features of thrifts
3. Understand why the savings and loan crisis occurred
4. Identify the distinguishing features of other depository institutions
5. Understand the role played by nondepository institutions

Certain institutions facilitate the transfer of financial assets and obligations between various market participants. These institutions intermediate between the suppliers of funds and the users of funds. Banks, for example, receive deposits from those with excess funds and lend to those with a shortage of funds. Intermediaries have advantages in information gathering, transaction costs, economies of scale, and diversification of risk.

There are many financial intermediaries that facilitate the transfer of funds between savers and users of funds. One way to classify these institutions is by whether they accept deposits that customers can redeem on demand. Naturally, these types of institutions are called depository institutions. Nondepository institutions may accept investment funds but do not offer investors the ability to write checks or otherwise easily access their funds.

This chapter introduces these various institutions. An understanding of the role and purpose of the various intermediaries will help you deal with them more effectively throughout your business career.

DEPOSITORY INSTITUTIONS

Depository institutions accept deposits that customers can redeem on demand. They include commercial banks, savings and loans (S&Ls), mutual savings associations, and credit unions. Although some brokerage houses now accept checkable deposits, they are not usually classified as depository institutions. Clearly the distinction between the different types of intermediaries is blurring as each institution attempts to capture business by expanding into new areas. This trend is likely to continue, and we will point out the major changes in this chapter.

Commercial Banks

We begin our study of institutions with commercial banks because of their pervasiveness in the economy. Individuals and businesses deal extensively with commercial banks on a regular basis. Additionally, banks are a major employer of finance graduates. We begin with a review of the history of banking in the United States because that is the only way to understand why we have our current and somewhat unusual banking system.

Brief History of Banking

In the 1600s the United States had a largely agricultural colonial economy unsuited to the rapid development of banking. Farmers purchased goods offered by local merchants on credit, and merchants in turn relied on credit offered by their British suppliers. This system worked well enough for limited agricultural development, but was unable to meet the needs of land-rich but cash-poor landowners who wanted to finance the development of their properties. To meet the needs of these landowners, land banks were established in some of the colonies. These land banks issued **bank notes** to make loans against property. Bank notes are promises to pay that are backed by the value of the property held by the land bank. Land banks tended to issue notes larger than the value of the land, and many failed.

During the Revolutionary War, British credit was eliminated. Several states chartered banks to help raise money to pay for the war effort. The first state-chartered bank was the Bank of North America, founded in Philadelphia in 1781. For the next 80 years, most growth in the banking industry occurred with state-chartered banks. These institutions accepted deposits and in turn issued bank notes that were payable on demand to the bearer. Bank notes became the money of early America. The problem with using bank notes as legal tender was that they were backed only by the assets of the issuing bank. If the bank ran into trouble, holders of bank notes stood to suffer losses. When these notes traveled outside the issuing bank's region, merchants were reluctant to accept them in payment for goods because they had no way of knowing whether the issuing bank was still in business.

Difficulties in financing the Civil War and the desire to provide a uniform currency prompted passage of the National Bank Acts of 1863 and 1864, which gave the federal government power to charter banks. Congress then gave nationally chartered banks the exclusive right to issue bank notes. The initial effect of the loss of the right to issue bank notes was a decline in state banking. Later, state banks began accepting deposits and offering checking accounts as their principal form of liability.

The role of private banks grew during the Industrial Revolution between 1890 and the 1920s. These private banks extended their business by acquiring commercial banks and merging underwriting activities (issuing stocks and bonds) with traditional commercial banking activities. Meanwhile, commercial banks began moving into the securities business to capture some of the profits being earned there.

Glass–Steagall Act   The Industrial Revolution came to an abrupt close with the Great Depression in 1929. Only about 15,000 of the original 30,000 banks were still solvent by 1933. Responding to the failure of so many banks, Congress passed the Glass–Steagall Act of 1933 to prevent further losses to the public. The two most significant features of the Glass–Steagall Act were the introduction of Federal Deposit Insurance Corporation (FDIC) insurance and the separation of commercial banking from investment banking.

One of the principal causes of bank failures during the Depression was a series of bank runs. During a bank run, depositors withdraw their funds because they fear that they may lose their deposits if the bank fails. Bank customers often started runs on mere rumors of bank insolvency, which is the bank having more liabilities than assets. Banks became insolvent in the 1930s because the value of their assets (loans) became much lower. Consider the customer who hears that his bank may have taken a big loss from a real estate deal. The customer can carefully investigate the accuracy of the rumor, or just withdraw funds. The simplest and most expedient approach is to withdraw funds. As word circulates that a bank is losing deposits, other customers try to withdraw their funds while they still can. Banks cannot pay depositors all their money because most of it has been lent to borrowers. The result is that a rumor of a bank problem could actually cause the bank to collapse. This problem is unique to banks.

The Glass–Steagall Act introduced Federal Deposit Insurance. **The Federal Deposit Insurance Corporation (FDIC)** insures depositors against losses that may result from a bank's failure. After FDIC was in place, customers no longer felt the need to withdraw funds if a rumor suggested that a bank was in trouble, because they knew the government would make good on any losses they sustained up to the limit of FDIC coverage. *The FDIC is responsible for stopping bank runs in the 1930s and saving the industry from collapse.*

Banks pay an insurance premium based on the risk of their investments, their equity, and their size. The FDIC uses these premiums to reimburse depositors when a bank fails. Currently the FDIC insures all accounts up to $100,000.

Figure 3.1 shows the number of banks in existence since 1920. In 1925 there were about 30,000 banks operating in the United States. This number dropped to under 15,000 by 1940. The number stayed fairly constant until 1985, when failures and consolidation led to a further decline. During the late 1990s, there were only one or two bank failures per year, yet the trend toward consolidation continues.

Investment banking is the sale of securities to the public. For example, if a firm wanted to sell stock to the public to raise funds for new projects, it could contact an investment banker. Investment banks buy securities issued by corporations for the very first time, called underwriting, and resell them to the public. Before the Glass–Steagall Act, commercial banks could engage in investment banking services. Many economists felt that some failures during the Depression were caused by banks investing in securities that failed to sell to the public. To preserve the safety of the banking industry, Congress mandated that commercial banks could not engage in investment banking. More

FIGURE 3.1
Number of Banks Each Year 1920–2000

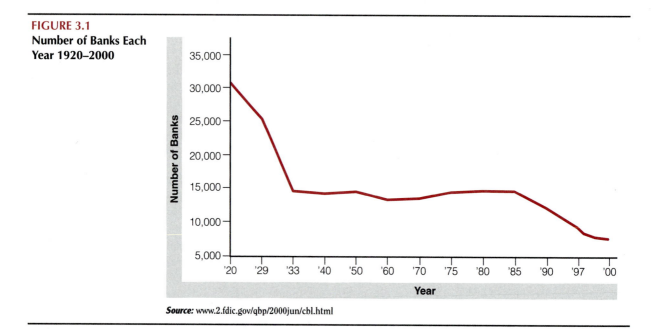

Source: www.2.fdic.gov/qbp/2000jun/cbl.html

recently, economists have expressed doubts that investment banking caused many bank failures. Primarily small regional banks failed during the Depression, but most investment banking was done by the larger money center banks.

To limit excess competition among commercial banks, Regulation Q, a section of the Glass–Steagall Act, imposed limits on the amount of interest banks could pay on savings accounts and banned the payment of interest on checking accounts. These restrictions did not limit the growth of banking during the early part of the century, because interest rates were lower than the maximum limits imposed by Regulation Q and there were no other institutions offering checkable deposit accounts. The purpose of Regulation Q was to reduce the likelihood of a bank failing by limiting the cost of funds to banks. Because banks could not pay interest on checking accounts, these funds were essentially free.

Problems in the Industry   Between 1940 and 1970, banks enjoyed an extended period of stability and profitability. Consider the advantages banks had during this period.

- The government granted charters only when applicants could show that their entry into the market would not harm existing banks. This restricted the competition for customers.
- Regulation Q guaranteed that banks would have a large source of low-cost funds (demand deposits) that banks could lend at market interest rates.
- Regulation Q required that banks pay a low rate of interest on savings accounts.

In effect, these regulations provided banks a protected customer base that gave them free money to invest. It took truly incompetent bank management to fail under these circumstances, which was exactly the intent of Congress.

This situation changed in the 1970s. Market interest rates rose well above the statutory limit and security firms began offering money market mutual funds that paid interest on checking accounts. The result of these changes was *disintermediation:* deposits flowing out of traditional intermediaries, such as banks and S&Ls, and into nontraditional intermediaries, such as brokerage firms.

Disintermediation caused serious problems for depository institutions. The loss of low-cost deposits meant that institutions had to replace the funds with higher-cost certificates of deposit (fixed-maturity securities that pay a much higher interest rate than regular deposits). The extra cost of these securities in turn led to losses and ultimately to the failure of many banks and thrifts. The term **thrifts** refers to S&Ls, mutual savings banks, and credit unions. Additionally, because the Federal Reserve did not control securities companies and these companies did not have to maintain reserves, a percentage of each deposit held at the Federal Reserve Bank to guard against liquidity concerns, the Fed was concerned about losing control of the money supply. (We will discuss the Fed's control over the money supply in Chapter 5.) This concern by the Fed led to new legislation.

Deregulation   The Depository Institutions Deregulation and Monetary Control Act of 1980 (DIDMCA) was the most significant banking legislation to be passed since the 1930s. A number of factors motivated Congress to pass the DIDMCA.

- Thrift institutions were experiencing devastating problems (we will discuss these problems later in this chapter).
- Limits on interest rates caused by Regulation Q were causing disintermediation (that is, the movement of funds out of banks).
- The Fed was losing membership because states tended to impose lower reserve requirements than the Fed imposed on nationally chartered banks. Because reserves do not earn interest income for the bank, large reserve requirements are costly.)
- Nondepository institutions were invading markets traditionally held by depository institutions and reducing bank profitability.

The combined effect of these problems was a seriously weakened financial system. The DIDMCA attempted to confront these issues with new legislation that provided what bankers called a level playing field on which to compete. The principal provisions of the DIDMCA include:

- *Uniform reserve requirements* for both state and nationally chartered banks. This effectively eliminated any advantage to being state chartered and stopped the switching of national charters to state charters.
- *Regulation Q reform.* The DIDMCA called for a gradual removal of interest rate ceilings. This transition was to take place over a 6-year period. Actually, virtually all limits were removed in less than 3 years.

- *Negotiable order of withdrawal (NOW)* accounts were authorized. These accounts provided limited checking and permitted the payment of interest. They were designed to compete with the money market mutual funds offered by security houses. A NOW account is a cross between a savings account and a checking account because it pays interest and also permits a few checks to be written each month.

- *S&Ls received broadened lending powers* that included the authority to make consumer loans. This provision of the act was intended to shorten the average maturity of S&L portfolios. Prior to this, S&Ls were only allowed to make long-term mortgage loans.

The Garn–St. Germain Act of 1982 followed the DIDMCA 2 years later. This act effectively removed interest rate caps from banks and thrifts and allowed S&Ls to make all types of loans. Although these acts did slow the tide of disintermediation, they did not limit the increase in the cost of funds to banks and thrifts. Savings and loans, especially, continued to fail in the mid-1980s, although many of their problems ran deeper than an increase in the cost of funds. We discuss problems of the S&L industry later in this chapter.

Structure of Banking

To those outside the banking industry, the structure and ownership of banks may seem complex and inexplicable. Actually, it is the result of how the industry grew up and how bankers maneuvered around various regulations.

Dual Banking System   The result of the various acts discussed so far is that all banks must operate with a charter. The United States is unique in that banks may obtain charters from either a state or the federal government. This is called a **dual banking system.** Nationally chartered banks must designate their affiliation by putting *National* or *N.A.* in their names. State banks cannot use these terms. In the past only national banks had access to Federal Reserve services. With the DIDMCA, Federal Reserve services became available to all banks, although they all now pay transaction fees. The principal remaining difference between state and national banks is who examines them.

Figure 3.2 shows that despite the consolidation in the banking industry that has reduced the number of separate banks, the number of branches has actually increased. In the last 10 years, more than 10,000 new bank branches have been opened.

Bank Holding Companies   **Holding companies** are shell companies that own other firms. Holding companies are popular in banking because they:

- Increase the flexibility of banks. For example, banks may sometimes use the holding company to circumvent interstate and intrastate bank branching restrictions.
- Increase access to capital.
- Reduce risk by allowing banks to diversify in ways that may not be possible otherwise.

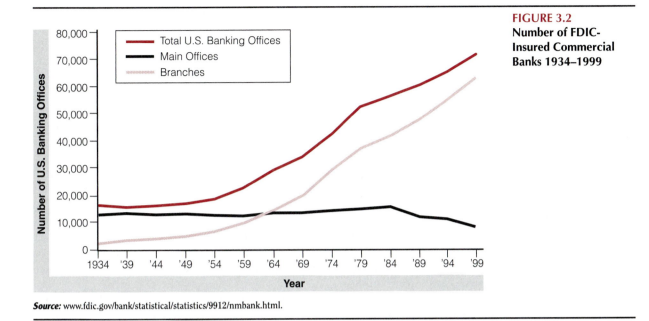

FIGURE 3.2
**Number of FDIC-
Insured Commercial
Banks 1934–1999**

Source: www.fdic.gov/bank/statistical/statistics/9912/nmbank.html.

Holding companies currently own over 70% of all banks, and over 90% of all deposits are in banks owned by holding companies.

The Bank Holding Company Act of 1956 restricted bank holding companies that owned two or more banks from engaging in activities that were prohibited by the banks themselves. This regulation did not restrict the activities of one-bank holding companies.

One-bank holding companies (OBHC) grew rapidly during the 1960s. These firms operated businesses ranging from banking to agriculture and mining. In 1970 Congress amended the Bank Holding Company Act to include all holding companies. OBHCs had to divest themselves of any prohibited businesses. Today the holding company is still an important organizational form, particularly for expansion purposes.

Bank Branching   Each state has the authority to restrict the number of branches banks can operate. By 1900 many states were very restrictive about branching. Their intent was to keep banks from becoming too large and powerful. They feared that large banks would take deposits out of some communities and not extend loans back. The most restrictive states were called unit states and they allowed only one full-service branch per bank. Others limited expansion to within one county or to some other geographic distance. Some states had no branching restrictions at all.

Most unit branching states were in the Midwest, whereas eastern states permitted limited branching and western states tended to permit statewide branching. In recent years most states have removed branching restrictions. The last unit bank state, Colorado, began permitting limited branching in 1991. One result of bank branching restrictions was that they kept banks from growing and capturing market share. For example, Table 3.1 lists the top 15 banks by size. Note that none of them are based in Texas—which had restrictive branching laws—despite its healthy economy and rapid growth. Three are based in North Carolina, which, despite not having as robust an economy as Texas, never restricted statewide branching. It is interesting to note that before consolidation in the banking industry there were many foreign banks that dwarfed the largest U.S. bank. For example, as recently as 1996 the Bank of Tokyo was over twice as large as the largest U.S. bank, Chase Manhattan. Now, the Bank of Tokyo is still the largest, but its lead has almost disappeared.

The McFadden and Douglas Amendment to the Bank Holding Co. Act effectively prohibited expansion across state lines (called **interstate banking)** except where expressly permitted by state law. These laws were in response to a fear by the American public of concentrating too much economic power in the hands of people not elected by the public. Congress assumed that if banks were restricted to a limited geographic area, this would in turn limit their size. The fact that the United States currently has about 8,400 banks, whereas most other industrialized nations have fewer than 300, attests to the accuracy of this assumption. In fact, Japan, England, and Canada each have fewer than 100 banks.

In 1975 Maine and New York became the first states to allow **reciprocal interstate banking,** meaning that banks from one state can branch into another if the second agrees to allow banks from the first to enter. In 1982 Alaska became the first state to allow free entry by any out-of-state bank as long as it was by acquiring an existing Alaskan bank. Currently, every state has some form of interstate banking regulation. Most require either reciprocal banking or entrance by acquisition.

TABLE 3.1 Fifteen Largest Banks in U.S.

Rank	Name	Main office	Size(000)
1	Bank of America, National Association	Charlotte, NC	604,683,000
2	Citibank, N. A.	New York	356,826,000
3	Chase Manhattan Bank, The	New York	320,476,000
4	First Union National Bank	Charlotte, NC	236,103,000
5	Morgan Guaranty Trust Company of New York	New York	173,606,056
6	Fleet National Bank	Providence, RI	147,334,000
7	Wells Fargo Bank, National Association	San Francisco	101,188,000
8	Suntrust Bank	Atlanta	96,986,322
9	Bank One, National Association	Chicago	95,794,841
10	HSBC Bank USA	Buffalo, NY	81,815,903
11	U.S. Bank National Association	Minneapolis	80,796,662
12	Keybank National Association	Cleveland	75,907,839
13	Bank of New York, The	New York	74,186,121
14	PNC Bank, National Association	Pittsburgh, PA	68,109,551
15	Wachovia Bank, National Association	Winston-Salem, NC	66,610,160

Source: http://www.ffiec.gov/cgi-bin/pbisa60.dll/nic_prod/uo_extract_top_bhcs/getinfo?ai_top_bhcs=1.

The growth of interstate banking has resulted in extensive changes in the banking landscape. The number of banks chartered in the United States dropped from 14,870 in 1980 to about 8,400 today. This consolidation is expected to continue.

In September 1994 the U.S. Congress approved the Riegle–Neal Interstate Banking and Branching Efficiency Act, which allows banks to operate interstate branch networks. Beginning in 1997, the bill gave banks the ability to operate branches outside their home states, but only if the affected states allow it. Before passage of this bill, banks that wanted to extend services regionally or nationally had to incorporate separate banking subsidiaries. The bill permits bank holding companies to acquire banks outside their home states regardless of state laws. This bill is one reason we continue to see rapid consolidation within the banking industry.

Uses and Sources of Funds   The assets of a bank are its cash balances, loans, investments, and deposits held at other banks and at the Federal Reserve. The liabilities of a bank are the deposits it accepts from customers, funds purchased (such as repurchase agreements or fed funds), and other borrowings. We often think of checking accounts as assets because we keep our transaction balances in them. But to a bank, your deposit is its liability because it owes the money to you.

Similarly, we think of loans as liabilities. Loans are the primary earning assets of a bank. It is correct to think of the lending function provided by commercial banks as their principal function. Over 65% of the average bank's assets are in its loan portfolio.

Changes in Bank Activities

The Federal Reserve Board regulates the activities of banks and bank holding companies. In 1933 the Glass–Steagall Act was passed to restrict banks from underwriting and selling corporate stocks and bonds. The Bank Holding Company Act of 1956 said that the Federal Reserve Board is to limit bank holding companies to activities that are closely related to banking. Several factors motivated these early restrictions.

- Congress believed that certain commercial bank activities reinforced the stock market crash of 1929.
- The stock market crash led to the breakdown of the banking system.
- Transactions between commercial banks and their securities affiliates were believed to lead to abuses. For example, banks were lending money to customers for the purpose of purchasing securities that the banks had underwritten.

Table 3.2 lists some of the activities that the Federal Reserve board has approved and denied. Activities that the Federal Reserve board has approved generally include the usual banking services traditionally reserved for banks. Thus, loans and loan servicing, trust services, gold handling, and some investment advising are allowed. Also approved are some securities brokerage activities.

The Federal Reserve board denies banks the right to sell insurance; broker, own, or manage real estate investments; run armored car services or travel agencies; and underwrite most securities.

Study Tip

Make sure you understand the difference between brokers and underwriters. A broker facilitates the transfer of securities between the seller and the buyer, without taking ownership of the security, just as a real estate broker brings sellers and buyers together. Underwriting securities means that the underwriter takes ownership of the stock offering in order to transfer it to a buyer. Underwriting takes place when securities are first offered for sale. The underwriter prices the security, then markets it.

TABLE 3.2 Activities Approved and Denied by the Fed

Approved Activities	Denied Activities
Credit extensions	Insurance premium funding
Loan servicing	Real estate brokerage
Trust company operation	Land development
Investment advising	Property management
Data processing services	Underwriting private mortgage insurance
Performance of appraisals	Operation of a travel agency
Buying and selling of gold	Armored car services
Securities brokerage	Real estate advising

Restrictions on Investment Banking Activities   The Glass–Steagall Act bars commercial banks from certain investment banking activities. Banks can neither underwrite securities nor act as dealers in the secondary market for securities. There are two exceptions to these restrictions.

- Banks are permitted to underwrite and deal in U.S. government obligations.
- Banks are permitted to underwrite and deal in municipal general obligation bonds.

More recently developed securities, such as interest rate and currency swaps, are not specifically forbidden to commercial banks.

These restrictions have frustrated bankers' attempts to expand the scope of banking for many years. Commercial bankers complain that securities companies can offer traditional banking services while legislation restricts commercial banks from entering the securities business. The increased competition has lowered banks' profit margins.

Breaking Down Investment Banking Restrictions   As the distinctions between the types of institutions and their products blurred, the financial services industry began pressing Congress to change Federal law. After years of debate and compromise, the Gramm–Leach–Bliley Act was signed into law on November 12, 1999. This Act represents the most significant change in the U.S. financial services industry in 66 years. The Act permits banks, insurance companies, securities firms, and other financial institutions to affiliate under common ownership and offer their customers a complete range of financial services. Financial holding companies may now offer financial services previously outlawed. The events leading to this act are listed below.[1]

1933: Glass–Steagall Act separated commercial and investment banking.

1956: Bank Holding Company Act limited activities of companies with two or more bank subsidiaries to managing and controlling banks or activities closely related thereto.

1970s: Securities firms began offering deposit-like mutual fund accounts paying market interest rates with access to funds through drafts.

---

[1]For a more complete discussion of this act, see www.clev.frb.org/bsr/GLBA/glba_brochure.pdf.

1980: Monetary Control Act began the process of deregulating interest rates on deposit accounts, allowed NOW accounts, and expanded thrift powers.

1982: Garn–St. Germain Act authorized money market deposit accounts and prohibited bank holding companies from providing insurance activities, except in specifically enumerated instances.

Office of the Comptroller of the Currency (OCC) approved formation of an operating subsidiary to engage in discount securities brokerage for the general public.

1983: Board of Governors of the Federal Reserve System (hereafter simply "Board of Governors") approved a bank holding company's acquisition of a discount securities broker.

1987: Supreme Court approved OCC action allowing national banks to own discount brokerage subsidiaries.

Board of Governors approved bank holding company applications to underwrite and deal in certain ineligible securities at a 5–10% level.

1989: Board of Governors approved bank holding company applications to expand securities underwriting and dealing to all corporate debt and equity.

1990: Courts upheld OCC action allowing a national bank to form an operating subsidiary to sell insurance throughout the United States from a town with a population of 5,000 or less.

1995: Supreme Court decided national banks could sell annuities because they are investment products, not insurance.

1996: Board of Governors increased gross revenue limit on ineligible securities underwriting and dealing to 25% and eliminated cross-marketing restrictions.

Supreme Court ruled that state law could not significantly interfere with a national bank's exercise of its authority to sell insurance from a small town.

1998: Board of Governors approved Travelers' application to acquire Citicorp.

1999: President Clinton signed the Gramm–Leach–Bliley Act.

As a result of these events, many banks have been aggressively expanding their brokerage service activities.

Self-Test Review Questions*

1. What is a unit banking state?
2. Why has the number of banks in the United States dropped in recent years?
3. What is a bank holding company?
4. What is a dual banking system?

---

* 1. A state in which banks can have only one branch. There are currently no unit banking states.
2. Changes in regulations have allowed banks to expand across state lines. This has led to many acquisitions.
3. A company that owns banks.
4. The presence of both state and national charters for banks.

Thrifts

In the last section we discussed commercial banks, which are the largest depository institutions. However, S&Ls, mutual savings, and credit unions—collectively called thrift institutions or thrifts—are important, though smaller, institutions. S&Ls were in the news in the early 1990s because of the huge losses occurring in the industry. This section investigates the causes of these losses.

Brief History

Mutual savings banks were the first thrifts in the country. The first one was chartered in 1816 in Boston. **Mutual ownership** means that there is no stock ownership. Technically, the depositors are the owners. There are currently about 500 mutual savings banks concentrated on the eastern seaboard. Most thrifts are state chartered because federal chartering of savings banks did not begin until 1978. Because they are state chartered, they are state regulated and state supervised as well.

Mutual savings banks and S&L associations are similar in many ways, but they do differ.

- Mutual savings banks are concentrated around the northeastern United States and S&Ls are spread throughout the country.
- Mutual savings banks may insure their deposits with the state or with the FDIC.
- Mutual savings banks are not as heavily concentrated in mortgages and have had more flexibility in their investing practices than S&Ls.

Because mutual savings banks and S&Ls are generally very similar and because few mutual savings banks remain, the balance of this section focuses on S&Ls.

Savings and Loan Associations   The original mandate to the S&L industry was to provide funds for families wanting to buy a home. In the early part of the nineteenth century, commercial banks focused on short-term loans to businesses. Congress decided that part of the American dream was home ownership and to make this possible it passed regulations creating S&Ls and mutual savings institutions. These institutions were to aggregate depositors' funds and use the money to make long-term mortgage loans.

There were about 12,000 S&Ls in operation by the 1920s, but they were not an integrated industry. Each state regulated its own S&Ls and regulations differed substantially from state to state. Congress created the Federal Reserve System for commercial banks in 1913. No such system existed for S&Ls. Before any significant legislation could be passed, the Depression caused the failure of over 1,700 thrift institutions. In response to the problems facing the industry and to the loss of $200 million in savings, the Federal Home Loan Bank Act of 1932 was passed. This act created the Federal Home Loan Bank Board (FHLBB) and a network of regional home loan banks. The act gave thrifts the choice of being state or federally chartered.

In 1934 Congress established the **Federal Savings and Loan Insurance Corporation (FSLIC,** called Fizz-Lick by industry insiders) to insure deposits in much the same way as the FDIC. The institutions were not to take in checking accounts; instead, they were authorized to offer savings accounts that paid slightly higher interest than was available from commercial banks.

S&Ls were successful low-risk businesses for many years. Their main source of funds was individual savings accounts that tended to be stable and inexpensive. Their primary assets were mortgage loans. Because real estate secured virtually all of these loans and its value increased steadily through the mid-1970s, loan losses were very small. Thrifts provided the fuel for the home building that for almost half a century was the centerpiece of America's domestic economy.

S&Ls in Trouble

Congress initially imposed a cap on the interest rate that S&Ls could pay on savings accounts. The theory was that if S&Ls obtained low-cost funds, they could make low-cost loans to home borrowers. The interest rate caps became a serious problem for S&Ls in the 1970s, when inflation rose. By 1979 inflation was 13.3%, which caused short-term interest rates to rise to over 15%, but S&Ls were restricted to paying a maximum of 5.5% on deposits.

At the same time, securities firms began offering a new product that circumvented interest rate caps. These new accounts were money market accounts that paid market rates on short-term funds. Though not insured, the bulk of the funds invested in money market funds were in turn invested in Treasury securities or commercial paper. Investors left the S&Ls for the high returns these accounts offered.

Most of the assets of S&Ls were long-term, fixed-rate mortgage loans. When the low-cost savings accounts fled, the S&L had to replace the funds with higher-cost CDs and borrowed money. This meant that the return on assets (loans) was fixed at low rates that could not be increased and the liabilities (savings accounts) were costly short-term securities.

S&L Crisis   By the late 1970s most S&Ls were losing money rapidly. Many had no equity left. The problem this industry suffered is called the S&L crisis. Several factors contributed to the S&L crisis.

- The industry was essentially deregulated with the passage of the DIDMCA in 1980 and the Garn–St. Germain Act in 1982.

- The number of regulators was reduced as part of the Reagan administration's effort to make government less intrusive to businesses.

- Many states (especially California and Texas) reduced the criteria needed to own and manage an S&L.

- Fraud by S&L owners resulted in losses.

- Brokered deposits replaced small time deposits that left for the higher returns they received from money market mutual funds. This resulted in the rapid growth of many S&Ls.

- Deposits continued to be insured by the government, so depositors did not monitor the riskiness of S&L activities.

Study Tip

The S&L crisis refers to the problems the industry faced with rising interest rates, fixed-return loans, and mounting losses, which drove many S&Ls insolvent.

Once Congress deregulated interest rates, S&Ls grew rapidly in the early 1980s because they could attract large sums of money by offering high interest rates. Deposit brokers searched the country each day for the S&Ls paying the highest rate and deposited funds in $100,000 blocks on behalf of their clients. By not depositing more than $100,000, the brokers made sure that the funds were covered by insurance. S&Ls were able to attract large amounts of money at low, risk-free interest rates because depositors knew that the deposits were guaranteed by the government. Depositors did not care what the S&L did with the funds, nor did they care about the risk taken by the S&L. Compare this situation to the market for corporate bonds. When a firm becomes more risky, investors demand a higher rate of return as compensation for that risk. **_With deposit insurance, the deposits were not risky, so depositors did not monitor the riskiness of the S&L_**. The government had too few regulators to adequately monitor the loans being made by S&Ls, so they were able to make high-risk loans unimpeded. Their motivation for making these high-risk loans was that they could charge customers higher interest rates and fees on higher-risk loans. Because many S&Ls had lost virtually all of their equity before being deregulated, they had little to lose if the loans did not pay. On the other hand, if the loans were repaid, there was the chance of returning the S&L to solvency. Unfortunately, the real estate market began weakening after 1985 and many of these loans defaulted.

The public became aware of the problems in the S&L industry in 1987 and 1988. To stop the losses, the Financial Institutions Reform, Recovery and Enforcement Act (FIRREA) was passed in 1989. This act:

- Eliminated the FSLIC.
- Formed a new insurance agency called the Savings Association Insurance Fund (SAIF). The FDIC administers this new agency.
- Required S&Ls to have a 3% capital ratio by January 1995.
- Eliminated the Federal Home Loan Bank Board that had historically regulated S&Ls.
- Established the Resolution Trust Corporation to deal with insolvent S&Ls.
- Increased the penalties for officers of financial institutions convicted of fraud.
- Required that in the future S&Ls use 70% of their assets for housing loans.
- Banned S&Ls from some risky investments, such as junk bonds.

As a result of the failure of S&Ls and the FIRREA, the total assets of S&Ls have fallen since 1988.

Cost of the S&L Crisis   The final cost of the S&L crisis has changed repeatedly over time. This is because many of the bad loans were secured by real estate that has changed in value over time. Additionally, regulators often are not aware of all of the bad loans and losses a given S&L will suffer until some time after the institution has been closed.

Initial estimates of the cost of the bailout were about $7 billion. In July 1988 the FHLBB increased its estimate to $15.2 billion. By October 1988 the estimate was up to $50 billion. Then, 3 months later, the estimate changed to nearly $100 billion. By August 1989, the General Accounting Office stated that the cost of the bailout was $166 billion.

In September 1994 the Resolution Trust Company estimated that the cost of the bailout was going to be around $112 billion. This reduction in the estimate was due to increased prices being paid for real estate acquired in the closing of defunct S&Ls and to falling interest rates that have increased the profitability of surviving S&Ls. The increased health of the surviving S&L industry is confirmed by the fact that only one S&L failed during the first 9 months of 1994. Final estimates put the cost at $145 billion. To put this loss into perspective, every person in the country will have to pay about $580 in additional taxes, not counting interest, just to pay for the losses the government suffered.

Since the S&L crisis in now well behind us, it may seem like an unnecessary review of ancient history to have discussed it in such detail. However, the lessons taught by this experience are far too important to forget. When the rules that govern the free market system are broken, in this case that higher returns should require greater risk, the system can fail. In retrospect, the collapse of the industry was very predictable as soon as legislation was passed that allowed an S&L to make high-risk loans with low-risk insured deposits. Because of FSLIC insurance, depositors did not restrict or monitor S&L risk taking, thus passing the responsibility on to the government, which would be held accountable for paying on losses. When the number of regulators was simultaneously reduced, disaster was guaranteed.

S&L Industry Today

The S&L industry has witnessed a substantial reduction in the number of institutions. Many have failed or been taken over by the Resolution Trust Corporation. Others merged with stronger institutions to avoid failure. The number of S&Ls declined about 54% between the end of 1987, when there were 3,600 S&Ls, and the end of 1999, when there were 1,640. Only one S&L failed during 1999. This suggests that both the industry and the economy are now stronger.[2]

One issue that has received considerable attention in recent years is whether the S&L industry is still needed. Observers who favor eliminating S&L charters altogether point out that there are now a large number of alternative mortgage loan outlets available for home buyers. A reasonable question to ask is whether there is a need for an industry dedicated exclusively to providing a service efficiently provided elsewhere in the financial system. Many S&Ls have been acquired by commercial banks. If this trend continues, the number of S&Ls is likely to fall even further.

Credit Unions

In this chapter, we have discussed mutual savings banks and savings and loans. A third type of thrift institution is the credit union, a financial institution that focuses on serving the banking and lending needs of its members. These institutions are also designed to serve the needs of consumers, not businesses, and are distinguished by their ownership structure and their common bond membership requirement. Most credit unions are small.

---

[2]The Office of Thrift Supervision publishes a fact book about thrifts on the Web. It contains thousands of statistics about thrifts. See www.ots.treas.gov/docs/48080.pdf.

In the early 1900s commercial banks focused most of their attention on business borrowers. This left small consumers without a ready source of funds. Because Congress was concerned that commercial banks were not meeting the needs of consumers, it established S&L associations to help consumers obtain mortgage loans. In the early 1900s the credit union was established to help consumers with other types of loans. A secondary purpose was to provide a place for small investors to place their savings.

One reason for the growth of credit unions is the support they have received from employers. They realized that employee morale could be raised and time saved if banking facilities were readily available. In many cases, employers donate space on business property for the credit union to operate. The convenience of this institution soon attracted a large number of customers.

Credit unions are organized as mutuals; that is, they are owned by their depositors. A customer receives shares when a deposit is made. Rather than earning interest on deposited funds, the customer earns dividends. The amount of the dividend is not guaranteed, like the interest rate earned on accounts at banks. Instead, the amount of the dividend is estimated in advance and is paid if earnings make it possible.

The single most important feature of credit unions that distinguishes them from other depository institutions is the **common bond** member rule. The idea behind common bond membership is that only members of a particular association, occupation, or geographic region are permitted to join the credit union. A credit union's common bonds define its field of membership.

The most common type of common bond applies to employees of a single occupation or employer. For example, most state employees are eligible to join their state credit union. Similarly, the Navy Credit Union is open to all U.S. Navy personnel. Other credit unions accept members from the same religious or professional background.

Credit union membership has increased steadily from 1933 to the present. The steady increase is expected to continue because credit unions enjoy several advantages over other depository institutions. These advantages have contributed toward their growth and popularity.

- *Employer support.* As mentioned earlier, many employers recognize that it is in their best interests to help employees manage their funds. This motivates firms to support their credit unions.
- *Tax advantages.* Because credit unions are exempt from paying taxes by federal regulation, this savings can be passed on to the members in the form of higher dividends or lower service costs.
- *Strong trade associations.* Credit unions have formed many trade associations, which lower their costs and provide the means to offer services the institutions could not otherwise offer.

The main disadvantage of credit unions is that the common bond requirement keeps many of them very small. The cost disadvantage can prevent them from offering the range of services available from larger institutions. This disadvantage is not entirely equalized by the use of trade associations.

Self-Test Review Questions*

1. What is a mutual association?
2. What was the original intent of Congress in establishing S&L charters?
3. Name one major factor that contributed to the thrift crisis.
4. What is a common bond membership requirement?

NONDEPOSITORY INSTITUTIONS

Nondepository institutions are intermediaries that accept funds for investment, but do not generally provide check-writing privileges. In recent years the distinction has blurred between nondepository and depository institutions because in some cases both offer nearly the same services. Still, this method of classifying the different types of institutions remains useful. In this section we discuss four types of nondepository institutions: insurance companies, brokerage firms, investment companies, and pension funds.

Insurance Companies

Types of Insurance

Insurance is classified by the type of undesirable event that is insured. The most common types of insurance are life insurance and property and casualty insurance. In its simplest form, **life insurance** provides cash to the heirs of the deceased. Many insurance companies offer policies that provide retirement benefits as well as life insurance. In this case the premium combines the costs of the life insurance with a savings program. The cost of life insurance depends on:

- The age of the insured
- Average life expectancies
- The health and lifestyle of the insured (e.g., whether the insured smokes)
- Operating costs of the insurance company

Life insurance policies tend to be long-term contracts.

Property and casualty insurance insures against losses due to accidents, fire, disasters, and other causes of loss of property. For example, marine insurance, which insures against the loss of boats and related goods, is the oldest form of insurance, predating even life insurance. Property and casualty policies tend to be short-term contracts subject to

Careers in Finance

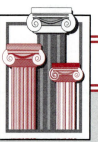

Commercial Banking

Commercial banks are in the business of providing banking services to individuals, small businesses, and large organizations. While the banking sector has been consolidating, it is worth noting that far more people are employed in the commercial banking sector than in any other part of the financial services industry. Jobs in banking can be exciting and offer excellent opportunities to learn about business, interact with people, and build up a clientele.

Today's commercial banks are involved in more different types of business than ever before. You will find a tremendous range of opportunities in commercial banking. These range from branch-level services, where you might start out as a teller, to a wide variety of other services such as leasing, credit card banking, international finance, and trade credit. Bank loan officers usually specialize in commercial, real estate, or consumer lending.

If you are well prepared and enthusiastic about entering the field, you are likely to find a wide variety of opportunities open to you. Trainee salaries in banking start around $27,000. A junior loan officer earns about $38,000 and a senior loan officer should earn $65,000 or more. Larger banks tend to offer higher salaries than banks with under $100 million in assets.

_____

Source: www.careers-in-finance.com/cbsal.htm.

---

frequent renewal. Another significant distinction between life insurance policies and property and casualty policies is that the latter do not have a savings component. Property and casualty premiums are based on the probability of sustaining the loss.

Fundamentals of Insurance

All insurance is subject to a few basic principles:

- There must be a relationship between the insured and the beneficiary. Additionally, the beneficiary must be in a position to suffer potential loss.
- The insured must provide full and accurate information to the insurance company.
- The insured is not to profit as a result of insurance coverage. The goal of insurance is to make people whole again, not to provide them profits.
- If a third party compensates the insured for the loss, the insurance company's obligation is reduced by the amount of the compensation.

The purpose of these principles is to maintain the integrity of the insurance process. Without them, investors may be tempted to use insurance to gamble or speculate on future events. Taken to an extreme, this could undermine the ability of insurance companies to protect policyholders.

Why People Buy Insurance

The purpose of insurance is for individuals and businesses to transfer risk to others. Individuals and businesses have the option of **self-insuring.** When self-insured, any unexpected losses must be paid for without outside help. The alternative is to pay an outsider to share in the risk. The outsider is in the business of evaluating risk and predicting the likelihood of incurring a loss. This lets the outsider properly price the risk it is agreeing to incur.

The price the insurer must charge is equal to the expected value of the loss plus a profit margin. The expected value of the loss is equal to the probability of a loss multiplied by the expected size of the loss. For example, if there is one chance in 1,000 that a house will burn down during a given year, and the house is valued at $100,000, then the insurance premium should be $100 per year (0.001 × $100,000) plus profit. Because insurance will cost more than the expected value of the loss by the amount of profit the insurance company charges, why are people so willing to pay an outsider to share in the risk? It is because most people are **risk averse.** This means that people prefer to pay a **certainty equivalent** (the insurance premium) than to accept the gamble. In other words, because people are risk averse, they prefer to buy insurance and know what their wealth will be with certainty than run the risk that their wealth may fall substantially.

Growth and Organization of Insurance Companies

Table 3.3 shows that insurance companies can be organized as either stock or mutual firms. A stock company is owned by stockholders and has the objective of making a profit. Most new insurance companies organize as stock corporations. As Table 3.3 shows, only 117 of 2,065 insurance companies are organized as mutuals.

Assets and Liabilities of Life Insurance Companies

Life insurance companies derive funds from two sources. First, they receive premiums that result in future obligations that must be met when the insured dies. Second, they receive premiums paid into pension funds managed by the life insurance company. These funds are long term in nature.

A life insurance company can predict with a high degree of accuracy when death benefits must be paid by using actuarial tables that predict life expectancies. For example, Table 3.4 lists the expected life of people at various ages. A 25-year-old woman can expect to live another 55.2 years. Because insurance companies have many beneficiaries, the law of averages tends to make their predictions quite accurate.[3]

TABLE 3.3 Age of Insurance Companies

Years in Business	Stock	Mutual	Total
100 years or more	9	23	32
50–100 years	133	38	171
25–50 years	589	43	632
Less than 25 years	1,217	13	1,230
Total	1,948	117	2,065

---

[3]An interesting exercise is provided at www.northwesternmutual.com/games/longevity. At this site after you answer a series of health and lifestyle questions, you are told your exact life expectancy. You can then see how changes to your lifestyle affect your life expectancy.

TABLE 3.4 **Expectation of Life at Various Ages in the United States**

Age	Male	Female	Average
0	72.5	79.1	75.7
15	58.2	65.0	61.6
25	49.0	55.2	52.2
35	39.8	45.6	42.8
45	31.0	36.2	33.7
55	22.5	27.2	25.0
65	15.4	19.2	17.5
75	9.5	12.2	11.1
85	5.3	6.7	6.2

Insurance companies also have invested heavily in mortgages and real estate over the years. In 1992, about 17.9% of life insurance assets were invested in either mortgage loans or directly in real estate. This percentage is down substantially from historic levels. The decline in mortgage investment has been offset by increased investment in corporate bonds and government securities.

The shift to stocks and bonds may be the result of losses suffered by some insurance companies in the late 1980s. As insurance companies competed against mutual funds and money market funds for retirement dollars, they found that they needed higher-return investments. This led some insurance companies to invest in real estate and junk bonds. Deteriorating real estate values brought on by overbuilding during the 1980s caused some firms to suffer large losses. The combination of large real estate losses and junk bond investment contributed to the failure of several large firms in 1991. The best known examples were the failures of Executive Life and Mutual Benefit Life, with assets of $15 billion and $14 billion, respectively.

Insurance Regulation

Insurance companies are subject to less federal regulation than many other financial institutions. The primary federal regulator is the Internal Revenue Service, which administers special taxation rules. Most insurance regulation occurs at the state level. The purpose of this regulation is to protect policyholders from losses due to the insolvency of the company. To accomplish this, insurance companies have restrictions on their asset composition and minimum capital ratio.

Brokerage Firms

Brokerage firms facilitate the buying and selling of securities. If you want to buy 100 shares of Microsoft, you can call the local office of Merrill Lynch and request that the broker buy the shares on your behalf. Brokerage houses can be classified as either full service or discount. Full-service brokerage firms provide investment advice and planning as well as transaction services. Discount brokerage firms usually offer limited advice

Box 3.1   The Most Expensive Seat in Town

On August 23, 1999, a seat on the NYSE sold for $2.65 million, the highest price ever paid. The last three seats sold during 2000 went for $2 million each. Owning one of the 1,366 NYSE seats is the admission ticket to trading on the world's largest stock exchange. Membership gives the hold-ers the right to trade stocks and vote at exchange meetings. As expensive as a seat on the exchange is, consider this: It doesn't even include a chair. If you want to sit down, you have to bring in your own stool.

Source: www.nyse.com.

and are engaged principally in the buying and selling of securities on behalf of their clients. The fees charged by full-service brokerage firms are naturally higher than those charged by discount brokerage firms. If you know which securities you want to purchase, you may save by using a discount broker.

Regardless of which type brokerage firm you choose, both will hold seats on the major exchanges and have NASDAQ computer links. Suppose that you place an order for 100 shares of IBM with your local Merrill Lynch office. Your broker sends an electronic message to the Merrill Lynch traders who work on the floor of the NYSE to buy 100 shares of IBM in your name. Merrill Lynch has purchased a number of "seats" on the exchange for its traders, as discussed in Box 3.1. On the floor of the NYSE are circular work areas for specialists in each security traded on the exchange. Each specialist is responsible for several different stocks. The Merrill Lynch floor trader knows where the IBM specialist is and approaches him or her to fill your buy order. Confirmation of the purchase is then communicated back to your local broker, who informs you that the trade has been completed.

The two most common types of orders are the market order and the limit order. In the example above you placed a **market order,** which instructs your broker to buy or sell the security at the current market price. When you place a market order, there is a risk that the price of the security has changed significantly from what it was when you made your investment decision. If you are buying a stock and the price falls, no harm is done, but if the price goes up, you may regret your purchase.

An alternative to the market order is the **limit order.** Here, buy orders specify a maximum acceptable price and sell orders specify a minimum acceptable price. For example, you could place a limit order to sell your 100 shares of IBM at $120. If the current market price of IBM is less than $120, the order will not be filled. Unfilled limit orders are reported to the stock specialist who keeps track of them. When the stock price moves in such a way that limit orders are activated, the stock specialist initiates the trade. If at all possible, the specialist fills new orders that come in from limit orders that are waiting. If no limit orders are activated, then the specialist trades from inventory. Knowing the status of unfilled limit orders helps the specialist judge the market and to move the bid and ask prices appropriately. An example of working a limit-order book is provided in Box 3.2.

Investment Companies

Investment companies manage pooled funds, commonly called mutual funds, and invest in a variety of securities. Investment companies offer small investors the opportunity to own securities that would be unavailable otherwise. For example, commercial paper is seldom sold in denominations of less than $500,000. Few individual investors are able to put this much into a single investment. By pooling funds, investment companies can purchase these high-priced securities.

A second important advantage investment companies offer to the individual investor is the ability to diversify even when only small sums of money are available for investment. Suppose an investor has $1,000 to invest. It would be impossible to buy enough different stocks to properly diversify. By pooling small sums from many investors, diversification is possible.

Closed- Versus Open-End Funds

Investment companies are organized as either closed-end funds or open-end funds. **Closed-end funds** operate much like other corporations. The company sells shares to the public. The funds raised are used to purchase various securities. The shares give the

---

Box 3.2 Using the Limit-Order Book

Suppose a trader on the NYSE is a specialist responsible for Circuit City stock. The limit-order book might look like the following:

Unfilled Circuit City Limit Orders

Buy Orders		Sell Orders	
37	100		
37⅛	300		
37¼	100		
		37⅜	200
		37½	500
		37⅝	100

Listed under Buy Orders are the highest prices investors are willing to pay to buy the stock. Listed under Sell Orders are the lowest prices investors holding Circuit City are willing to accept to sell. Currently, no transactions occur because there is no crossover or common prices. In other words, there is currently no one willing to sell Circuit City at a price anyone is willing to pay.

Now suppose the specialist receives a new 200-share market order to buy, an order to be filled at the best market price currently available. The specialist consults the Sell Orders column and fills the order at $37.37.

Next, the specialist receives a 300-share limit order to sell at $37.12. Again, the specialist consults the book, but this time looks under the Buy Orders column. The limit order is filled with 100 shares at $37.25 and 200 shares at $37.12.

Next suppose that a limit order to buy 500 shares at $37.87 is received. Because there is no sell order for this amount, the order is added to the book, which now looks like this:

Unfilled Circuit City Limit Orders

Buy Orders		Sell Orders	
36⅞	500		
37	100		
37⅛	100		
		37½	500
		37⅝	100

Your broker can help you buy or sell securities that trade on other exchanges or over-the-counter as well. These important intermediaries offer a broad spectrum of investments such as bonds, annuities, limited partnerships, and shares in real estate investment trusts. Full-service brokers help their clients find the investments that best suit their risk and return requirements.

holder an ownership right in the assets of the company. If the value of the securities held by the company rises, the value of the shares also should rise.

Theoretically, the aggregate value of the outstanding mutual fund shares should exactly equal the value of the securities purchased by the investment company. Often, however, the value of the shares drifts above or below this theoretical value based on the market's perception of how the management of the funds is expected to perform in the future. At times, if the market value of the shares falls far below the theoretical value of the investment company, the company liquidates the closed-end fund by selling all of the assets held by the funds and distributing the proceeds to the investors.

An alternative to the closed-end fund is an **open-end fund.** Open-end funds are also called mutual funds. Open-end funds offer shares at the current **net asset value (NAV)** of their portfolios and redeem outstanding shares at this same price. Unlike closed-end funds, open-end funds can accept new money at any time. The number of shares in open-end funds is not fixed, but is increased to accommodate increased demand by investors. This new money simply is invested in new securities on behalf of the shareholders. Open-end funds tend to be more popular than closed-end funds and account for much of the rapid growth of investment companies. When you invest in an open-end fund you buy shares at the NAV (adjusted for any fees), which fluctuates as the values of the underlying assets change. Box 3.3 discusses how the NAV is computed.

Box 3.3   Calculation of Mutual Fund NAV

If you invest in a mutual fund, you will receive periodic statements summarizing the activity in your account. The statement shows funds that were added to your investment balance, funds that were withdrawn, and any earnings that have accrued. One term on the statement that is critical to understanding the investment's performance is the *net asset value (NAV)*. The NAV is the total value of the mutual fund's stocks, bonds, cash, and other assets minus any liabilities such as accrued fees, divided by the number of shares outstanding. An example will make this clear.

Suppose a mutual fund has the following assets and liabilities:

Stock (at current market value)	$20,000,000
Bonds (at current market value)	10,000,000
Cash	500,000
Total value of assets	$30,500,000
Liabilities	$ 300,000
Net worth	$30,200,000

The net asset value is computed by dividing the net worth by the number of shares outstanding. If 10 million shares are outstanding, the net asset value is $3.02 ($30,200,000/10,000,000 = $3.02).

The net asset value rises and falls as the values of the underlying assets change. For example, suppose the value of the stock portfolio held by the mutual fund rises by 10% and the value of the bond portfolio falls by 2% over the course of a year. If the cash and liabilities are unchanged, the new net asset value is calculated as follows:

Stock (at current market value)	$22,000,000
Bonds (at current market value)	9,800,000
Cash	500,000
Total value of assets	$32,300,000
Liabilities	$ 300,000
Net worth	32,000,000

$$\text{NAV} = \$32,000,000/10,000,000 = \$3.20$$

The yield on your investment in the mutual fund is then

$$\text{Yield} = \frac{\$3.20 - \$3.02}{\$3.02} = \frac{\$.18}{\$3.02} = 5.96\%$$

When you buy and sell shares in the mutual fund, you do so at the current NAV.

Load Versus No-Load Funds

Many mutual funds are sold by salespeople, who earn a commission for marketing the fund. These salespeople may work for brokerage houses, insurance companies, or banks, or as private investment counselors. Because these commissions are paid when the mutual fund is sold, a fee must be charged the buyer. This one-time fee is called a load. A fund that charges a load is a **load fund.** Loads vary between 0.5% and 8% of the amount invested.

Funds that are sold directly to the public without a fee are called **no-load funds.** However, even no-load funds are subject to service charges. The managers of both load and no-load funds deduct a percentage of the fund's assets each year to cover their costs. One of the secrets to choosing a good mutual fund is to review the fees charged and to pick one that has provided high returns with low costs.

Most mutual funds specialize in a particular type of security. One fund may invest in stock whereas another invests only in bonds. Even among funds that invest only in a particular type of security, there is additional specialization. Some stock mutual funds invest only in small firms; others invest only in growth stock. With over 6,700 different mutual funds available, investors can find one that closely suits their needs and preferences.

Figure 3.3 shows how rapidly mutual funds have grown since the early 1980s.

Money Market Mutual Funds

One particular type of mutual fund deserves special notice. The money market mutual fund can be credited with initiating major changes in the structure of the financial

FIGURE 3.3
Number of Equity, Hybrid, and Bond Mutual Funds

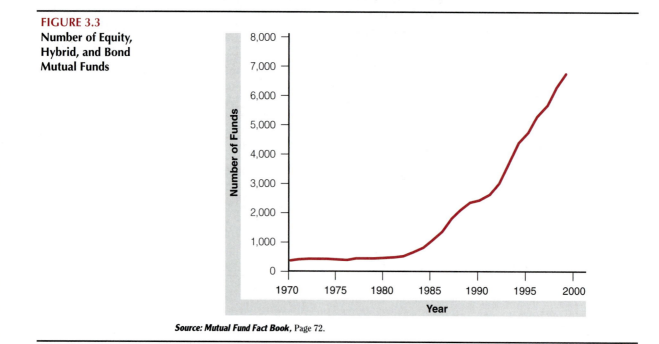

Source: Mutual Fund Fact Book, Page 72.

system. **Money market mutual funds** are open-end funds that invest in short-term, low-risk securities. These funds were first introduced in the early 1970s by brokerage houses as a way to simplify investment. Customers of the brokerage house could deposit money into the mutual fund. When the investor wanted to buy or sell a security, the broker would either withdraw funds or deposit funds into this account. The mutual fund account saved the expense and inconvenience of writing and mailing checks.

As discussed earlier, interest rates rose dramatically in 1978. Regulation Q limited banks and S&Ls to paying low rates on deposits. Depositors could earn market rates by putting their money into mutual funds. Massive amounts of money were moved out of banks and S&Ls during 1978–1980. Earlier in this chapter we discussed how this disintermediation led to the failure of many S&Ls, large government losses, and a greatly restructured regulatory environment.

Money market mutual funds pay investors the return earned on short-term investments such as Treasury bills. Money market mutual funds continue to be a popular alternative to bank savings accounts. However, the current low rates have stifled any rapid growth.

The distinction between brokerage houses and investment companies can be confusing because you can buy shares in mutual funds by contacting both directly. Brokerage firms offer access to many different mutual funds offered by many different investment companies, including some sponsored by the brokerage company itself. Some investment companies offer mutual funds that are sold only by brokerage firms. The mutual funds sold by brokers typically have higher fees so that brokers can be compensated for their time selling the fund. Other investment companies accept funds directly from the public and, because these funds do not pay commissions, the fees can be much lower. For example, the annual fee on a typical index fund offered by one brokerage house is about 1.5% of the amount invested. A similar fund that investors can contact directly has an annual fee of about 0.2%.

Pension Funds

A **pension fund** is an asset pool that accumulates over the working years of an individual and is paid out during the nonworking years.

Types of Pension Plans

There are both public and private pension plans, although in many cases there is very little difference between the two. When a government body sponsors a plan, it is a public plan. Plans sponsored by employers, groups, and individuals are private plans.

Public Plans   The largest public plan is the Federal Old Age and Disability Insurance Program (often simply called **Social Security).** This pension plan was established in 1935 and is a **pay-as-you-go system.** This means the money that workers contribute today pays benefits to current retirees. Future generations will be called on to pay benefits to those now contributing. Many people fear that the fund will be unable to meet its obligations by the time they retire. This fear is based on problems the fund encountered in the 1970s.

FIGURE 3.4
Net Assets in the Social Security Trust Fund

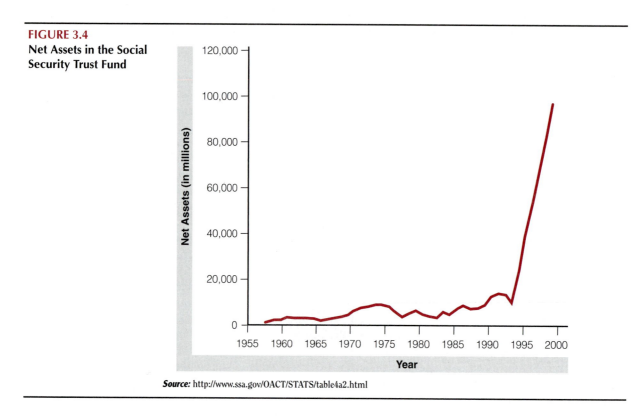

Source: http://www.ssa.gov/OACT/STATS/table4a2.html

Figure 3.4 shows that in the mid-1970s the net assets held by the Social Security Trust Fund fell. The total assets in the fund decreased at the same time as the number of insured people was increasing. During the mid-1980s and into the 1990s, adjustments were made to strengthen the fund. These adjustments included raising the program's contributions and reducing the program's benefits. The fund has also been bolstered by the strength of the economy during the 1990s and by the unexpected surge in new immigrant workers who contribute to it. Currently, the fund has sufficient assets and cash flows to pay retirees. However, most analysts are concerned that as the average age of the U.S. population increases, fewer people will be paying into the system and more will be receiving benefits. Despite the rapid increase in trust fund assets, projections still show that by the year 2037 the fund balance will fall to zero. The question of whether the Social Security system will be there when current workers retire is a critical element of retirement planning. It is likely that the system will require some adjustment, such as benefits starting a year or two later than they do currently. The benefit payments also are adjusted for inflation. Economists argue that the inflation adjustment has been larger than the true rate of inflation, so a task force has been appointed to determine whether there is a more accurate way of computing inflation. In the future, beneficiaries of Social Security will probably see smaller increases in their year-to-year payments. Economists and politicians note that small adjustments to the system, such as those discussed here, can keep it solvent.

Over the next several years, Social Security is likely to get a great deal of attention. It was a major issue of debate in the 2000 presidential election. One issue to watch is President Bush's proposal to invest a portion of Social Security in stocks and bonds.

The next largest group of public plans is state and local employee plans. Currently, these plans cover over 17 million government workers. The Federal Civilian Employees plan covers over 5.5 million federal employees. The Railroad Retirement plan covers 1.1 million workers.

Private Plans   Private plans may be administered by private corporations or by insurance companies. Over 30% of the total number of people covered by a pension plan are covered by a private plan. There has been a dramatic increase in the popularity of private pension plans. Nearly 50 million people have enrolled in private plans administered by insurance companies. There are several reasons for this growth. First, people expect to live longer and to retire earlier than in the past. This leads to better retirement planning. Second, many investors are more sophisticated than those of past generations. This leads them to capture the tax advantages of being enrolled in approved pension plans. Money contributed to an approved retirement plan is not subject to taxes until it is withdrawn during retirement. Finally, as noted above, many people are not confident that Social Security will be there when they retire. This motivates them to provide for retirement themselves.

Private Pension Fund Assets   In the past, private pension funds invested mostly in government securities and corporate bonds. These are still important pension fund assets, but corporate stocks, mortgages, and time deposits have a significant role. Private pension funds are now the largest institutional investor in the stock market. This makes pension fund managers a potentially powerful force if they choose to exercise control over firm management.

Employee Retirement Income Security Act

The most important and comprehensive legislation affecting pension funds is the Employee Retirement Income Security Act (ERISA), passed in 1974. This act set certain standards that must be followed by all pension funds. Failure to follow the provisions of the act may cause the plan to lose its advantageous tax status. The motivation for the act was that many workers who had contributed to plans for many years were losing their benefits when plans failed. The principal features of the act are that it:

- Established minimum guidelines for funds to be qualified
- Provided that employees switching jobs may transfer their credits from one employer plan to the next
- Required that plans provide minimum vesting requirements
- Established the Pension Benefit Guarantee Corporation, which guarantees workers against the failure of private plans
- Increased the disclosure requirements for pension plans

Despite ERISA, many plans still remain dangerously underfunded.

Self-Test Review Questions*

1. Why do people buy insurance even though it costs more than the average expected loss?
2. What is the difference in the investment portfolios between life insurance companies and property and casualty insurance companies?
3. What is a load fund?
4. Why does the Social Security system run the risk of running out of money?

CHAPTER SUMMARY

This chapter introduced the major institutions that make up the financial system. Depository institutions take in funds and make them immediately available to the depositor. Alternatively, nondepository institutions hold investor funds for longer periods of time.

The major depository institutions are commercial banks and S&Ls. The Federal Deposit Insurance Corporation insures commercial bank deposits against loss. This insurance is critical to instilling confidence in depositors. Without this confidence, banks are subject to failure.

In the late 1970s banks began to feel the effects of competition from nonbank institutions such as brokerage houses. To help banks compete, Congress passed new regulations that permitted them to engage in more activities and to pay more competitive interest rates. Additionally, recent regulatory changes have permitted banks to expand across state lines. This has led to a period of rapid consolidation within the industry.

The S&L industry is responsible for major losses to the government and represents a case study in how not to deregulate an industry. S&Ls were suffering losses when interest rates rose in the late 1970s. Congress attempted to help by deregulating the industry. Unfortunately, Congress did not see the need to increase supervision over the industry. Deposit insurance removed any motivation depositors might have felt to monitor risk taking by S&L managers, so the managers could use cheap, risk-free deposits to invest in high-risk loans. The results were many S&L failures, for which the government was required to pay depositors. The industry was reregulated in 1989.

Credit unions were established by Congress to provide a way for consumers to borrow money for nonmortgage loans. They are usually small because of the common bond membership rule. They enjoy tax advantages, employer support, and an extensive array of trade associations that allow them to offer lower interest rates on loans and lower account service fees than other depository institutions. Credit union growth is expected to continue in the future.

Nondepository institutions include insurance companies, investment companies, and pension funds. Insurance companies are important in that they provide long-term funds that are used by corporations. Insurance companies take on risk for a fee.

Investment companies offer investment advice and administer investment funds. There are closed-end funds and open-end funds, with the former limiting the amount of new investment whereas the latter can accept new deposits at any time. These funds may be no-load or load funds depending on whether a fee is charged for making deposits or withdrawals.

KEY WORDS

bank notes 52
certainty equivalent 69
closed-end fund 72
common bond 66
depository institutions 51
dual banking system 56
Federal Deposit
   Insurance Corporation
   (FDIC) 53

Federal Savings and Loan
   Insurance Corporation
   (FSLIC) 62
holding company 56
interstate banking 58
investment banking 53
investment companies 72
life insurance 67
limit order 71

load fund 74
market order 71
money market
   mutual fund 75
mutual ownership 62
net asset value (NAV) 73
no-load fund 74
open-end fund 73
pay-as-you-go system 75

pension fund 75
property and
   casualty insurance 67
reciprocal interstate
   banking 58
risk averse 69
self-insuring 68
Social Security 75
thrifts 55

DISCUSSION QUESTIONS

1. Define the term *depository institution.*
2. What are reserve requirements? Who sets the reserve requirement?
3. What events led to the Glass–Steagall Act? What are the responsibilities of the Federal Deposit Insurance Corporation?
4. List and explain the principal provisions of the DIDMCA.
5. Why did many states limit bank branching?
6. What has prompted the rapid increase in mergers and acquisitions among banks?
7. What is one important difference between S&Ls and commercial banks?
8. What caused trouble for the S&Ls in the 1970s?
9. Why was the Financial Institutions Reform, Recovery and Enforcement Act passed in 1989?
10. Why might it be reasonable to eliminate S&L charters?
11. What lessons can we learn from the S&L crisis?
12. List and define three types of nondepository institutions.
13. Define the following terms:
   a. Closed- and open-end funds
   b. Load and no-load funds
   c. Limit order and market order
   d. Money market mutual funds
14. Describe how an order to buy stock is filled by a broker.
15. What is a pay-as-you-go pension plan? Why do experts fear that the Social Security system will have problems meeting its obligations in the next 30 to 40 years?

PROBLEMS

1. What is the expected value of a loss if the probability of an auto accident is 5% and the amount of a loss, if it occurs, is $10,000? If an insurance company wanted to earn a 15% profit, how much would it charge in insurance premiums?
2. Suppose that your house is valued at $250,000. What would be the insurance premium if each year there is a one in 1,000 chance that the house will burn down?
3. You are considering buying mutual funds and have decided to buy from a private investment counselor who sells load funds. The load is 1.5% and you are investing $150,000. What would be the counselor's commission?

WEB EXPLORATION

1. Morningstar is a well-known company that specializes in analysis and review of mutual funds. There are a number of Web sites that report Morningstar's results. Go to www.quicken.com/investments/mutualfunds/finder/. Perform the EasyStep Search according to your own preferences for investment. Can you find funds that provide the return you want with the expense ratio you are willing to pay?

2. The Internet has many calculators available to help consumers estimate their needs for various financial services. However, when using these tools you should keep in mind that they are usually sponsored by financial intermediaries that also hope to sell you products. Visit one such site at www.finaid.org/calculators/lifeinsuranceneeds.phtml and calculate how much life insurance you need. Are you the beneficiary of any life insurance policies? Use the calculator to see if that policy is large enough.

MINI CASE

Jenny Cabycar, a mutual fund manager for a number of years, has recently been moved into the financial institutions research division. In her first meeting with her boss, Ernie, she learns that the company plans to aggressively purchase the stock of small banks that may be the target of takeover attempts by larger banks. Ernie is aware that takeover targets often experience large increases in price as a result of the acquiring firm buying shares. This particular investment strategy is inspired by the rapid consolidation that has been taking place in the banking industry. Ernie asked Jenny to prepare a one-page report outlining the viability of this plan and making a few tentative suggestions for how to proceed in the selection of banks for the new portfolio.

1. Discuss whether the trend toward consolidation will continue. Will the number of banks decrease due to failure or due to acquisition by another bank?

2. Discuss what features may make a bank a good target for a larger bank to attempt to buy it.

3. Identify sources of information about banks on the Web. You may choose to look at the following for help: www.fdic.gov/, www.bog.frb.fed.us/, www2.fdic.gov/qbp/cool.cfm?report=%2F, and www.fdic.gov/bank/statistical/statistics/index.html. Is there sufficient data available to prepare reports about individual banks and their competitors?

4. Conclude your report by identifying a strategy that uses the available data to select target banks and state an opinion as to whether the plan is viable.

The Structure of Interest Rates

Chapter Objectives

By the end of this chapter you should be able to:

1. Establish the importance of interest rates
2. Identify the factors that affect the level of interest rates
3. Explain the yield curve
4. Know why corporations are so concerned with interest rate levels

An understanding of the determinants and behavior of interest rates is critical to both investors and businesses. For example, in 1984 Sadco Development, a development/construction company in Fairbanks, Alaska, was financing a new eight-story office building. The building was fully leased, mostly with national tenants such as IBM, so lenders were eager to provide long-term loans. After sorting through the loan options, the two best were essentially identical except for one important feature. The first option offered a fixed rate of interest over the term of the loan, with a prepayment penalty. The second option offered a variable rate of interest. Because interest rates had been very high since 1978, the interest rate on the fixed-rate loan appeared low, and because it was transferable if the building was sold, Sadco's management decided this loan would actually increase the marketability of the building. After projecting that interest rates were not going to fall any lower in the near future, the firm accepted the fixed-rate loan.

Unfortunately, the management of Sadco did not accurately project future rates. Interest rates did level off for a few months, but then fell. When Sadco attempted to sell the building, it found that buyers did not want the fixed-rate loan (now well above current rates) and that the penalty for paying off the loan early amounted to hundreds of thousands of dollars. Lost profits from this major project, coupled with other weaknesses in the local economy, ultimately caused the firm to file for bankruptcy. Sadco could have been saved if management had better understood the nature of interest rates. By choosing a floating-rate loan with no prepayment penalty, Sadco could have sold the building regardless of which direction interest rates moved.

An understanding of interest rates is important in other finance applications as well. Later in this course you will learn how to compute the value of stocks and bonds by finding the current value of the future cash flows. The interest rate used in these calculations has a very significant effect on the value of the security. In Chapter 10 we study how firms make capital investment decisions. Again, the level of interest rates plays a pivotal role in the decision process. In this chapter we begin our study of interest rates by introducing the factors that affect the level of interest rates. In Chapter 5 we extend our understanding of interest rates by learning how the Federal Reserve can influence them by changing the amount of money in the economy.

RENTING MONEY

If you want to rent a car, a tool, a VCR, or an airline seat, you will be quoted a rental price in dollars. But what is the rental price of money? As you can surmise from the title of this chapter, *the rental price of money is the interest rate*. When you rent a car you will be told how much it will cost for a given period of time. Restrictions on how the car can be used and provisions for extending the rental period may be included in the rental contract. When you rent money, the rental rate is usually quoted as the cost of using the money for 1 year. Additionally, there is usually a contract that specifies the conditions under which the money will be lent.

The rental price of money has varied substantially over time. Figure 4.1 shows the yield on 3-month Treasury securities since 1960. In the early 1960s the interest rate on Treasury bills was about 2%. The rate rose to over 14% by 1981 and fell below 6% by 1985. Since then the yield on Treasury bills has varied between 7.5% and 3%.

FIGURE 4.1
3-Month T-Bill Returns over Time

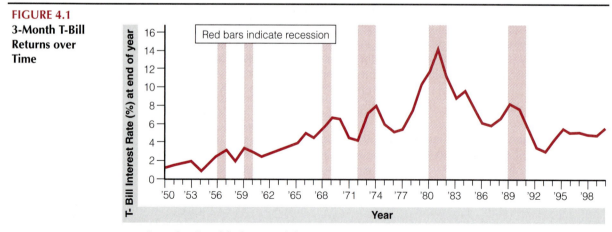

Source: http://www.federalreserve.gov/releases

Self-Test Review Questions*

1. What is the rental price of money?
2. What are the highest and lowest interest rates on Treasury bills since 1960?

FACTORS THAT DETERMINE THE LEVEL OF INTEREST RATES

As with any commodity, the price of money is a function of many factors. When a late freeze reduces the size of the Florida orange crop, the price of orange juice rises. Similarly, when the money supply is restricted, the price of money rises. Other factors, such as the expected rate of inflation, the riskiness of the borrower, the liquidity of the borrowing instrument, and the time to maturity, also affect the interest rate. In this chapter we investigate these factors.

Opportunities for Investment Affect Interest Rates

Interest rates are established by the financial markets so that the demand for money just equals the supply. For example, if businesses want to borrow more money than is supplied by households at the current interest rate level, interest rates must rise to discourage business demand and to increase supply by encouraging more savings by households. The result of the supply–demand relationship is that as business opportunities increase, so too will interest rates, all other things held constant. Let us explore how this may occur.

Suppose that a new technology has been perfected and is in great demand by consumers, such as automobiles that run on water. To meet this demand, businesses must invest in new plants, distribution warehouses, inventory, and advertising. Because many industries are affected by the production of automobiles, there is likely to be increased demand for funds across the whole economy. However, if interest rates are constant, there is no reason to think that more funds will be supplied to meet this demand. We now have a situation in which there is too little money available to supply those who need it. The question becomes, which businesses will obtain the funds they need?

Consider this question for a moment, as it is critical to the efficient functioning of a free market system. If a factor of production is in short supply, such as a chemical reagent or a type of fuel, who gets the limited factor? The answer is that the business willing to pay the most for the factor will get it. This works well because the result is that factors of production are allocated to those with the most valuable use. This is why they are willing to pay the most. This concept is also at work in the market for money.

If money is in short supply, who will get it? The money will go to the business willing to pay the most.[1] The price of money is its interest rate. Businesses bid against each

* 1. The interest rate.
   2. The lowest was 1% in 1954 and the highest was 14.2% in 1980.

---

[1]This discussion assumes equal default risk among the firms competing for funds. This simplification does not affect the conclusions.

other by increasing the amount of interest they will pay until an equilibrium interest rate is established. At this new higher interest rate, many businesses will choose not to borrow. Additionally, more households will supply funds. The important point, however, is that *limited funds are allocated to the business with the most profitable opportunities for investment*.

Business demand ebbs and flows even without the invention of cars that run on water. These changes in business activity are called **business cycles.** Although business cycles do not occur at any predetermined interval, historically, recessions have occurred every 5 to 10 years. Once again review Figure 4.1, which shows the level of interest rates over time along with the business cycles identified as colored bands. We see that during periods of recession, when demand by businesses for investment is low, interest rates often fall dramatically. Conversely, during periods of growth, when demand by businesses for investment is high, interest rates rise. Note the exception to this rule during the 1983 to 1987 time period. The inflation rate was falling over this interval and that influence on interest rates overwhelmed the effect of increased demand. We will discuss this situation in greater detail later in this chapter.

As interest rates rise due to increased demand by business, investment spending begins to slow. As investment spending slows, general economic activity falls and the economy may enter a recession. Can this recession be prevented? That is the goal of the Federal Reserve. Whereas many economists accept business cycles as a necessary and inevitable evil, the Fed tries to maneuver the economy to avoid or at least lessen the severity of business slowdowns. By increasing the money supply, the Fed can lower interest rates and encourage continued business expansion. Unfortunately, other factors of production, such as labor or raw materials, usually begin increasing in price so that inflation increases. When inflation increases, the Fed stops increasing the money supply and allows the economy to cool off. We explore the Federal Reserve and how it functions in Chapter 5.

Self-Test Review Questions*

1. Which firms will obtain investment money when money is in short supply?
2. What can the Fed do to prevent a recession or business downturn?
3. What is the usual frequency of business cycles?

Other Factors That Affect the Level of Interest Rates

In the last section we investigated how changes in the supply and demand for money result in changes in interest rates. This analysis is useful for predicting future interest rates and for interpreting how economic events may affect interest rate levels. However, it falls short of explaining why interest rates are at a particular level for a particular firm at a specific time. In the following section we look at the factors that determine why, for example, the borrowing rate for Sears is 7% and for J.C. Penney it is 8%.

3. Five to 10 years.
2. Increase the money supply.
* 1. Those with the most profitable opportunities.

This section introduces a number of different **interest rate premiums,** which are increases in the interest rate that compensate the investor for additional risk. How are they combined to establish the level of interest rates for a particular company? The good news is that they are simply added together. If N is the nominal or quoted interest rate for a bond, the equation for how it was derived is as follows:

$$N = r + INF + LP + DRP + MRP \qquad (4.1)$$

where

N = the nominal or published rate of interest
r = the real rate of interest
INF = the expected rate of inflation
LP = the liquidity premium
DRP = the default risk premium
MRP = the maturity risk premium

Each of these risk premiums is defined in the following sections.

Inflation: The Real Versus Nominal Rate of Interest

To understand interest rates we must begin by distinguishing between the real rate of interest and the nominal rate. Although everyone talks about wanting more money, what they really want is the ability to buy more things or services. We would not want more money if it were not for its purchasing capacity. When we save, we do so with the expectation of buying *more* in the future than we can today. The amount of extra purchasing capacity we get in exchange for delaying consumption is the **real interest rate,** or real rate of return. The **nominal interest rate** is the real rate of interest adjusted for inflation plus any appropriate risk adjustments.

It is important to think of the real rate of return in terms of purchasing power. For example, suppose you have enough money to buy a large pizza, but your roommate has asked for a loan of that amount. After negotiating, your roommate promises to buy you a large and a medium pizza next week. If this is the minimum amount of repayment you would accept, then a medium pizza per week is your real rate of interest. The point is that *real* interest rates relate to purchasing power, not to dollars. The distinction between purchasing power and dollars is the effect of inflation. If inflation has reduced the purchasing power of a dollar, then more dollars are required to buy the same goods in the future. As inflation increases, the real rate remains unchanged, but the nominal rate must increase, so the dollars earned over time give the same purchasing power as when there was no inflation.

We can now define the real rate of return as *the compensation you require to delay consumption*. The nominal rate of interest is the real rate of interest plus an adjustment for expected inflation. In equation form, if r is the real rate of interest, N is the nominal rate for treasury securities, and INF is the expected rate of inflation, then

$$r = N - INF \qquad (4.2)$$

You can see from Equation 4.2 that the nominal rate must increase to compensate for an increase in inflationary expectations. As inflationary expectations rise and fall, the

Study Tip

It is important to understand the distinction between the real interest rate and the nominal interest rate. The real interest rate is never seen directly and will never be printed in a newspaper as the rate for a security. It is the increase in consumption required by the investor. The nominal interest rate is the real rate plus risk premiums. One of the risk premiums is inflation. We will discuss additional risk premiums in later sections.

nominal rate must also rise and fall. As long as the nominal rate compensates for changes in inflation, the real rate remains unchanged.

More commonly, Equation 4.2 is written to express the nominal rate for Treasury securities in terms of the real rate and inflation:

$$N = r + \text{INF} \tag{4.3}$$

This relationship is commonly called the Fisher equation (named after the economist who developed it).[2]

E X A M P L E 4.1   Calculation of Nominal Interest Rate

Assume that the real interest rate was 4% and expected inflation was 3%. What is the nominal rate of interest?

Solution
Applying Equation 4.3 results in

$$N = 4\% + 3\% = 7\%$$

The nominal rate would be 7%.

Notice that INF is defined as the *expected* rate of inflation. Lenders set interest rates before lending funds and they set the rates to compensate them for giving up the use of the money during the loan period. Of course, the actual inflation rate for the *next* year is not known when they establish the interest rate. The lender must guess. When inflation rates are stable, as they have been since 1991, this is much easier to do. However, when they are volatile, as they were between 1970 and 1985, this is much more difficult. Inflation rates can be estimated using the Consumer Price Index.

Because we do not know what the market expects inflation to be (how do you accurately measure expectations?), we cannot directly compute the real rate. Using the best estimation techniques available, economists think that on average it varies between 2% and 4%. This does not mean that *your* real rate is 4%. Consider a man dying of thirst in the desert. His real rate for delaying consumption of a glass of water would be far higher than someone who just finished a third glass. The nominal rates set by the market tend to reflect the lowest real rate available from large investors, who can absorb large amounts of funds.

The nominal rate of interest reflects adjustments to the real rate of interest due to risk premiums. The largest risk premium and the cause of the greatest changes in the nominal rate over time has been inflation. Figure 4.2 shows how the return on Treasury bills has adjusted to the annual rate of inflation.

Let us summarize our discussion of the effect of inflation on interest rates.

- Historically, inflation has had the largest effect on interest rate levels of any factor.
- Real rates of interest must be adjusted to reflect the erosion of purchasing power due to inflation.

---

[2]The Fisher equation is more accurately expressed as $N = r + \text{INF} + r(\text{INF})$. The last term is usually dropped because it is very small (for example: $0.05 \times 0.03 = 0.0015$) compared with the built-in error that results from estimating the real rate and expected inflation.

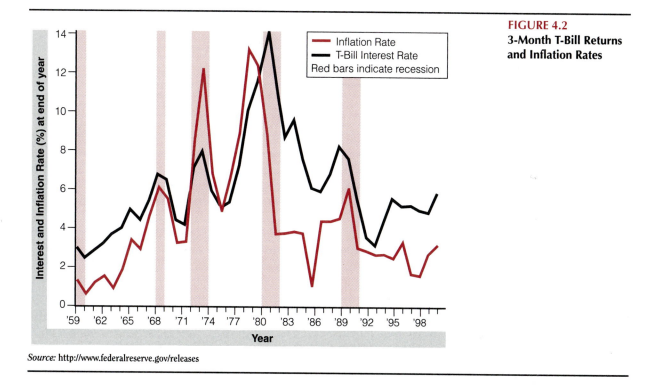

FIGURE 4.2
3-Month T-Bill Returns and Inflation Rates

Source: http://www.federalreserve.gov/releases

- The nominal rate is the real rate of interest plus the *expected* level of inflation and any other risk premiums.
- Even for otherwise risk-free securities, errors in estimating future inflation introduce inflation risk.

Adjusting Interest Rates for Liquidity Risk

Some investments are highly liquid, meaning that they can be easily sold at predictable prices and thus converted into known amounts of cash. Treasury securities are highly liquid because there is a deep and well-established market for these investments. Similarly, stocks traded on the major exchanges have well-developed markets that lower the cost of conversion into cash. However, it may be both costly and time-consuming to convert other assets into cash. Real estate may take months or years to sell and large sales commissions may be required. Other examples of nonliquid investments include diamonds, collectibles (stamps, trading cards, etc.), art, and the securities of small, closely held firms.

Buyers demand a liquidity premium to compensate them for the cost, time, and inconvenience associated with nonliquid investments. The size of this premium depends on the buyer's perceived cost of liquidating the asset in the future.

Self-Test Review Questions*

1. What does the real rate of return measure?
2. What does the nominal rate of return measure?
3. What factor has historically had the greatest effect on interest rates?

Adjusting Interest Rates for Default Risk

So far our discussion of interest rates has centered exclusively on compensating a saver for giving up current consumption and for recouping purchasing power lost to inflation. Clearly, however, some borrowers have a greater chance of defaulting, or failing to pay as agreed, than do other borrowers. For example, few analysts see any signs that Intel or Microsoft will fail in the next few years. On the other hand, the futures of Amazon.com and Apple are less certain.

Technically, default can occur in a number of ways, such as failure of a borrower to make interest or principal payments or to follow the terms of the contract that establishes the conditions of the loan. For example, when a loan is obtained, either from a financial institution or by selling bonds, the borrower agrees to a wide variety of conditions. These conditions are spelled out in detail in the loan agreement. If bonds are sold, the terms of the loan are in a document called an **indenture.** The loan terms may establish such things as the minimum working capital level, dividend policy, reporting requirements, insurance coverage of the collateral, maintenance of the collateral, and any other conditions the lender feels will increase the probability of timely repayment. If the borrower fails to keep *any* term of the contract, the lender has the right to declare the borrower in default and to demand immediate repayment.

A borrower's probability of defaulting depends on two factors: the firm's degree of business risk and the firm's degree of financial risk. The degree of **business risk** refers to how cash flows from operations fluctuate over time. A firm in an industry that regularly experiences booms and busts has greater business risk than a firm in a stable industry. One factor that influences the degree of business risk is how much of the firm's operating costs are composed of fixed costs. If sales fall, a firm operating with all variable costs can simply shrink until sales rebound. On the other hand, a firm with a large amount of fixed cost may be unable to shrink sufficiently and may not be able to pay its bills. For example, Delta Airlines has a large percentage of fixed cost. It makes little difference in cost whether it flies full or empty planes. Its variable costs are composed mainly of meals and the difference in fuel usage between full airplanes and empty ones.

Compare the business risk of Delta to Arthur Andersen Accounting. The principal cost to the accounting firm is personnel. If business falls, employees can be laid off quickly. Typically, service firms have lower business risk than manufacturing firms because service firms have lower fixed costs. Note that a firm can choose to reduce its fixed cost by subcontracting some of its business to other firms, by establishing short-term leases on equipment, or by hiring part-time or temporary employees. The problem is that this flexibility usually comes at a cost. These increased costs may reduce the firm's competitiveness.

Study Tip

Some students are confused by the distinction between business risk and financial risk. Note that business risk cannot be changed by the level of debt. Business risk is the variation in cash flows due to the type of business the firm engages in.

TABLE 4.1 Business and Financial Risk

Type of Risk	Description	Source of Risk
Business risk	Changes in cash flows from operations	Amount of fixed assets
Financial risk	Changes in cash flows due to financing	Amount of debt used to finance assets

The degree of **financial risk** increases as the amount of debt held by a firm increases. A firm with zero debt can hardly default. It can go out of business, but if no money is owed, there is no loan on which to default. As the amount of debt increases, so does the chance that a downturn in revenues will make the firm unable to meet its debt obligations. When interest or principal payments are missed, lenders may declare the firm in default. The difference between business risk and financial risk is summarized in Table 4.1.

If a firm has high business risk because the type of industry it is in requires a great deal of fixed assets, such as a steel mill, it may decide to keep its debt low in order to control its total risk. Similarly, firms with low business risk can afford greater financial risk and hence greater debt without pushing total risk too high.

Various companies, such as Standard & Poor's and Moody's, rate the debt offered by firms. These ratings help guide investors to match their risk preferences with various bonds. Table 4.2 lists the ratings given to different debt. The interest rates typically rise as the rating falls, as shown by the average interest rates listed for the top four ratings.

Self-Test Review Questions*

1. How could a firm reduce its business risk?
2. How could a firm increase its financial risk?
3. Is a firm in default if it fails to insure an asset as required by its loan agreement?

Adjusting Interest Rates for Maturity

Long-term bonds have higher interest rates than do short-term bonds. This is to compensate lenders for the risk associated with long-term investments. There are several reasons why long-term investments have more risk than short-term investments. One reason is that it is more difficult to predict the health of a firm 30 years into the future. Second, the value of long-term bonds is influenced by changes in interest rates more than is the price of short-term bonds. The fact that bond values change with changing interest rates is called **interest rate risk.** Interest rate risk is one type of risk that even the most conservative investor cannot escape.

Suppose you buy a bond for $1,000 that yields 10%. After a couple of years, if new bonds are being issued for $1,000 that yield 12%, no one will be willing to pay $1,000

* 1. Reduce its use of fixed assets, say by leasing equipment.
  2. By borrowing instead of issuing more stock.
  3. Yes.

TABLE 4.2 Debt Ratings

Standard & Poor's	Moody's	Interest Rate (8/25/00)	Definition
AAA	Aaa	7.54%	Best quality and highest rating. Capacity to pay interest and repay principal is extremely strong. Smallest degree of investment risk.
AA	Aa	7.69	High quality. Very strong capacity to pay interest and repay principal and differs from AAA/Aaa in a small degree.
A	A	8.02	Strong capacity to pay interest and repay principal. Possess many favorable investment attributes and are considered upper medium-grade obligations. Somewhat more susceptible to the adverse effects of changes in circumstances and economic conditions.
BBB	Baa	8.25	Medium-grade obligations. Neither highly protected nor poorly secured. Adequate capacity to pay interest and repay principal. May lack long-term reliability and protective elements to secure interest and principal payments.
BB	Ba		Moderate ability to pay interest and repay principal. Have speculative elements and future cannot be considered well assured. Adverse business, economic, and financial conditions could lead to inability to meet financial obligations.
B	B		Lack characteristics of desirable investment. Assurance of interest and principal payments over long period of time may be small. Adverse conditions likely to impair ability to meet financial obligations.
CCC	Caa		Poor standing. Identifiable vulnerability to default and dependent on favorable business, economic, and financial conditions to meet timely payment of interest and repayment of principal.
CC	Ca		Represent obligations that are speculative to a high degree. Issues often default and have other marked shortcomings.
C	C		Lowest-rated class of bonds. Have extremely poor prospects of attaining any real investment standard. May be used to cover a situation where bankruptcy petition has been filed, but debt service payments are continued.
CI			Reserved for income bonds on which no interest is being paid.
D			Payment default.
NR			No public rating has been requested.
(+) or (−)			Ratings from AA to CCC may be modified by the addition of a plus or minus sign to show relative standing within the major rating categories.

Source: Federal Reserve Bulletin. Average interest rates are reported in the bulletin only for the top four risk categories.

for your old 10% security. If you want to sell your bond you will have to reduce the price so that investors will earn 12%. The amount of the adjustment required increases with the number of years remaining to the maturity of the bond. In Chapter 8 you will learn exactly how to compute what an interest rate change will do to the price of a bond. For now it is only important that you understand the following relationship:

As market interest rates ↓ ⇒ price of bond ↑.
As market interest rates ↑ ⇒ price of bond ↓.

The relationship between maturity and return is so important and pervasive that it has been given a special name: the **term structure of interest rates.**

Term Structure of Interest Rates

Figure 4.3 shows Treasury yield curves from the *Wall Street Journal* from January 1, 1980, and January 1, 2000. A yield curve is a graph that has the time to maturity on the horizontal axis and the yield on the vertical axis. First, look at the January 1, 2000, yield curve. On this date, investors could choose among Treasury securities with various maturities and yields ranging from about 6% on a 1-year Treasury bill to 6½% on a 30-year Treasury bond. The Treasury yield curve appears in the *Wall Street Journal* every day. Yield curves could be prepared for corporate securities and the graphs would fall above the Treasury yield curve because of default risk premiums, but the shape would be about the same.

The January 1, 1980, yield curve demonstrates that the shape of the yield curve is not constant over time. In the early 1980s, short-term rates were very high. However, investors expected them to fall in the future, so long-term rates were lower. Downward-sloping yield curves are unusual. For this reason an upward-sloping yield curve is called normal and a downward-sloping yield curve is called **an inverted** (or abnormal) **yield curve.**

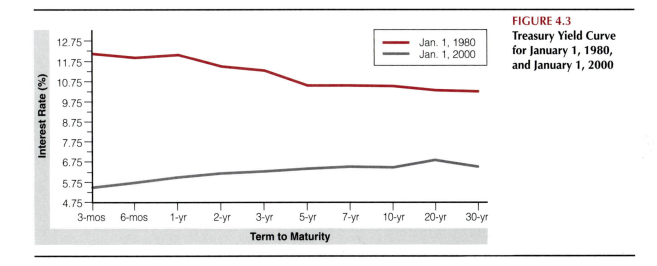

FIGURE 4.3
Treasury Yield Curve for January 1, 1980, and January 1, 2000

If the normal yield curve slopes upward, this means that long-term interest rates are usually higher than short-term interest rates. We discussed one reason for this in the last section: Investors demand higher rates to compensate them for interest rate risk. Other theories attempt to explain the shape of yield curves. One is the pure expectations theory.

Pure Expectations Theory

The **pure expectations theory** holds that the rate charged on long-term loans is an average of the interest rates *expected* during each period that the loan spans. For example, if the interest rate expected over the next 12 months is 10% and the rate expected during the subsequent 12 months is 12%, then the 2-year rate would be 11% [(0.10 + 0.12)/2 = 0.11 = 11%]. This relationship is shown graphically here:

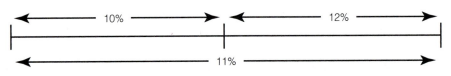

Similarly, the rate on a 3-year loan would be the average of the three 1-year rates expected to be in effect. To illustrate, suppose you are applying for a car loan. If inflation is expected to increase continually over the next few years, the bank may estimate the 1-year rates that will be in effect in the future as in Table 4.3. The last column of Table 4.3 shows the multiyear interest rate you may be charged as a result.

We can put this relationship into a generalized equation form. We use the following definitions:

i_t = today's interest rate on a 1-year bond (time t)
i^e_{t+1} = interest rate on a 1-year bond expected for next period (time $t + 1$)
i_{2t} = today's (time t) interest rate on the 2-year bond

Then for a 2-year bond,

$$i_{2t} = \frac{i_t + i^e_{t+1}}{2} \tag{4.2}$$

and for an n-year bond,

$$i_{nt} = \frac{i_t + i^e_{t+1} + i^e_{t+2} + \cdots + i^e_{t+(n-1)}}{n} \tag{4.3}$$

TABLE 4.3 Estimated Long-Term Rates Using Expectations Theory

Year	Expected Annual Interest Rate	Calculation	Expected Average Interest Rate from 2001 to Indicated Year
2001	10%		10%
2002	12	(10 + 12)/2	11
2003	14	(10 + 12 + 14)/3	12
2004	15	(10 + 12 + 14 + 15)/4	12.75

The interest rate on a multiyear bond is the average of the rates that are expected during each year over the whole interval.[3]

If interest rates are expected to increase due to inflationary pressures, the yield curve will be normal and upward sloping. However, if inflation is currently high, but expected to fall, the yield curve will be inverted. This was the case in 1980. Inflation was over 10%, but most investors felt that the Fed would soon get control over the money supply and that inflation would fall. In fact, that is what happened when the Fed reduced the money supply. This shortage of money raised short-term interest rates to record levels, which reduced investment spending by companies. Unemployment reached double digits and a recession occurred. This reduced the inflation rate. Soon interest rates fell below 8% on long-term home mortgages.

EXAMPLE 4.2   Calculation of Interest Rate Using Pure Expectations Theory

Assume that the 1-year rate is 16%. The 1-year rate expected to be in effect 1 year from now is 12%. The next 1-year rate is projected to be 8%. What are the 2- and 3-year rates?

Solution

First look at the problem graphically:

The 2-year rate is found by taking the average of the first two 1-year rates:

$$2\text{-year rate} = \frac{16\% + 12\%}{2} = 14\%$$

---

[3]We can prove the accuracy of Equation 4.2 as follows: Suppose we invest $1 in the 2-year bond and hold it for the 2 years. After the second year, the $1 investment is worth $(1 + i_{2t})(1 + i_{2t})$. Subtracting the $1 initial investment from this amount and dividing by the initial $1 investment gives the rate of return:

$$\text{Rate of return} = (1 + i_{2t})(1 + i_{2t}) - 1 = 1 + 2i_{2t} + (i_{2t})^2 - 1 = 2i_{2t} + (i_{2t})^2$$

Because $(i_{2t})2$ is extremely small—for example, if $i_{2t} = 7\% = .07$, then $(i_{2t})2 = .0049$—we can simplify the expected return for holding the 2-year bond for the 2 years to $2i_{2t}$. An investor could instead buy a series of two 1-year bonds. After the first year, the $1 investment becomes $1 + i_t$; and this is reinvested in the 1-year bond for the next year, yielding an amount $(1 + i_t)(1 + i^e_{t+1})$. Subtracting the $1 initial investment from this amount and dividing by the initial investment of $1 gives the expected return for the strategy of holding a series of two 1-year bonds:

$$\text{Rate of return} = (1 + i_t)(1 + i^e_{t+1}) - 1 = 1 + i_t + i^e_{t+1} + i_t(i^e_{t+1}) - 1 = i_t + i^e_{t+1} + i_t(i^e_{t+1})$$

Because $i_t (i^e_{t+1})$ is extremely small, we can simplify this to $i_t + i^e_{t+1}$. For there to be equilibrium, the return on the 2-year bond must equal the return on the consecutive 1-year bonds. So

$$2i_{2t} = i_t + i^e_{t+1}$$

Solving for i_{2t} in terms of the 1-year rates, we have

$$i_{2t} = \frac{i_t + i^e_{t+1}}{2}$$

This tells us that the 2-year rate must equal the average of the two 1-year rates.

The 3-year rate is found by taking the average of the three 1-year rates:

$$3\text{-year rate} = \frac{16\% + 12\% + 8\%}{3} = 12\%$$

The 2-year rate would be 14% and the 3-year rate would be 12%.

The results of Example 4.2 show how the pure expectations model can help explain the inverted yield curve in 1980. Interest rates on current 1-year bonds were high because inflation was high. Investors expected inflation to fall, so the 1-year rates projected for 1981 and 1982 were lower than for 1980. As a result the 2- and 3-year rates were less than the 1-year rate, as seen in the example.

A useful application of Equation 4.2 is the calculation of implied interest rates. If we know the current rate on 2-year securities and the current rate on 1-year securities, we can compute what the market expects the rate to be on 1-year securities that will be available next year.

E X A M P L E 4.3   Calculation of Expected Interest Rates Using Pure Expectations Theory

If the current period 1-year security has an interest rate of 10% and the current 2-year security has an interest rate of 12%, what rate is the market expecting on 1-year securities that will be available 1 year from now?

Solution:
The current period 1-year security has interest rate $i_t = 10\%$, and the current 2-year security has interest rate $i_{2t} = 12\%$. Using these values in Equation 4.2, we get

$$12\% = \frac{10\% + i^e_{t+1}}{2}$$

Solving this equation for the expected 1-year rate in 1 year, we find

$$24\% - 10\% = i^e_{t+1} = 14\%$$

The market expects that in 1 year a 1-year security will have a 14% interest rate.

The pure expectations theory effectively explains inverted yield curves, but it falls short of explaining why the yield curve would normally be upward sloping. After all, there is no reason to think that future interest rates will always be increasing. The liquidity preference theory may help out.

Liquidity Preference Theory
The **liquidity preference theory** holds that lenders prefer to make short-term loans whereas borrowers prefer to borrow long term. Borrowers must pay a premium to induce lenders into making long-term loans.

Borrowers are assumed to be **risk averse.** This means that they prefer to avoid risk whenever possible. But if they must assume risk, they want to be compensated for it. Because they are risk averse, borrowers prefer to finance purchases with long-term loans rather than with a series of short-term loans. Consider the homebuyer faced with the option of financing with a 30-year mortgage or with a 1-year adjustable-rate mortgage. If interest rates increase, the 30-year loan will be the best. If interest rates fall, the adjustable-rate loan will be the best. Because of risk aversion, however, most homebuyers opt for the long-term fixed-rate loan. They know that they may miss an opportunity to benefit from falling interest rates, but this is preferable to running the risk of interest rates increasing to the point where their mortgage payment becomes too burdensome.

Corporate borrowers behave the same way. They prefer long-term fixed-rate loans. They would rather miss benefiting from an interest rate decline than going bankrupt because interest rates increase so that they can no longer pay their debt. Put another way, *to risk averse borrowers, the downside risk of an interest rate increase overwhelms the possible benefit of an interest rate decline.*

Even though borrowers prefer to finance with long-term fixed-rate loans, *lenders* prefer to make short-term adjustable-rate loans, hence the name *liquidity preference theory*. The savings and loan (S&L) crisis clearly shows why. S&Ls made long-term fixed-rate loans. When interest rates increased because of high inflation in the late 1970s and early 1980s, they were no longer able to obtain funds at a cost below what they were receiving on these loans. With the cost of money greater than the revenues generated by the loans, many S&Ls became insolvent. If the S&Ls had made short-term or adjustable-rate loans, they could have increased the revenues on their loan portfolio to keep pace with their cost of funds. Profitability could have been maintained.

A second reason lenders prefer short-term loans is that it is difficult to predict a borrower's financial health many years into the future. A company that is doing well today may be struggling for survival 10 years later. Short-term loans give lenders the option of not renewing the credit if lenders feel that the firm may not be able to repay as agreed.

Clearly there is a problem. ***Borrowers want long-term loans, but lenders want to make short-term loans. According to the liquidity preference theory, the solution is that borrowers must pay a premium to lenders to compensate them for making the long-term loans.*** The longer the loan, the greater must be the interest rate premium. Table 4.4 shows the interest rate offered on home mortgage loans for 30-year, 15-year, and 1-year adjustable-rate loans.[4] The spread between the 1-year and the 15-year loan is greatest, reflecting the fact that most mortgage loans are repaid in less than 10 years when the home is sold. The difference between the 15-year and the 30-year loan is usually 0.25 to 0.75%.

TABLE 4.4 **Mortgage Interest Rates, August 2000**	
30-year fixed rate	7.625%
15-year fixed rate	7.375
1-year adjustable rate	6.875

Source: www.fastcash.com.

---

[4]Adjustable-rate mortgages (ARMs) usually have caps that limit the amount of interest rate increase that can be imposed in any one year and the maximum amount that it can increase over the life of the loan. Similarly, there is usually a floor, which guarantees the lender a minimum return.

Market Segmentation Theory

The **market segmentation theory** suggests that the market for funds is segmented between those who supply and demand funds at each different maturity. For example, there is a supply and demand for 1-year funds. The interest rate for 1-year funds will adjust until the supply just equals the demand and the market clears. A separate supply and demand equilibrium is established for each different maturity. Figure 4.4 shows equilibrium conditions with market segmentation.

The key assumption in the market segmentation theory is that securities with different maturities are not substitutes for each other. Thus, the equilibrium return established by supply and demand for securities with one maturity do not affect the equilibrium return for securities with a different maturity.

If, as seems likely, investors prefer short-term maturity securities because they have lower interest rate risk, then longer-term securities will have higher rates. (Remember, investors will accept lower rates on securities with features they like.) This helps explain the usual upward sloping shape of the yield curve.

Reconciling the Theories

Let us review the theories that have been offered to explain the shape of the yield curve.

- *Interest rate risk* (the change in the value of bonds due to interest rate changes) increases with long-term loans, so an interest rate premium is paid by long-term borrowers to compensate for the increased risk.

- The *pure expectations theory* suggests that long-term rates are an average of the expected short-term rates between now and when the loan matures. The short-term rates are influenced primarily by the expected inflation rate.

- The *liquidity preference theory* says that borrowers must offer an interest rate premium to induce lenders to abandon their preferred short-term adjustable-rate loans to make the long-term fixed-rate loans that borrowers prefer.

- The *market segmentation theory* says that there is an equilibrium between the supply and the demand for funds at each maturity.

FIGURE 4.4
Equilibrium with Market Segmentation

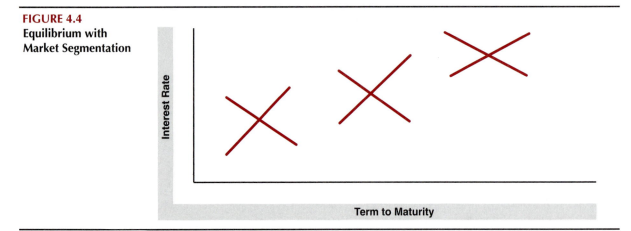

Which of these theories is correct? They probably all are. The level of interest rates is based on future expectations about the money supply and inflation. The yield curve is normally upward sloped because premiums are added to the average expected interest rate. These premiums result from interest rate risk and the preference by lenders to stay liquid. At times, expectations of falling inflation overwhelm these risk premiums and the yield curve becomes inverted. The demand and supply of funds at each maturity also influence rates.

One reason that the yield curve is so closely watched is that many analysts think it may hint at the future of the economy. This is further discussed in Box 4.1.

E X A M P L E 4.4   Computing Nominal Interest Rates

What is the nominal rate of interest for a 10-year corporate bond if the real rate is 4%, expected inflation is 3% per year, the liquidity premium is 0.5%, the default risk premium is 2%, and the maturity risk premium is 0.3% per year?

Solution

To find the nominal rate we must first compute the total maturity risk premium:

$$\text{Maturity risk premium} = 0.3\% \times 10 = 3\%$$

Plug the given figures into Equation 4.1:

$$N = r + INF + LP + DRP + MRP$$
$$N = 4\% + 3\% + 0.5\% + 2\% + 3\% = 12.5\%$$

Note that the above equation does not tell the whole story. We also discussed how the level of interest rates changes when the money supply is increased or decreased. Equation 4.1 does not capture this effect. In fact, changes in the money supply by the

Box 4.1 Reading the Yield Curve

The shape of the yield curve is often looked upon as an indicator of the future of the economy. For example, when it is steeply upward sloped, i.e. when short-rates are low compared to long-term rates, economists may forecast a growing economy, because low short-term rates may be due to the Federal Reserve stimulating business. When the yield curve flattens due to short-term rates approaching those on long-term securities, the economy may be slowing. This is because the Federal Reserve increases short-term rates to slow economic activity.

Other factors may complicate the story, however. Richard Fritz, Vice President and Chief Economist of the Federal Home Loan Bank of Atlanta, writes that the inverted yield curve observed at the end of 2000 was caused by two factors. First, the Fed was raising short-term rates to slow the economy. Second, because of budget surpluses the U.S. Treasury found that it needed to retire maturing bonds. Some bond investors, especially those dealing in long-term maturities, are facing a new challenge. Long-term investors who prefer long-term bonds are driving the prices of these bonds up, which cause the yields to fall. By retiring a respectable portion of the national debt at the same time the Federal Reserve was tightening short-term interest rates, supply and demand conditions were being artificially altered. Therefore, the inverted yield curve was not the result of the same conditions experienced previously over the past four decades.

By mid 2001, the yield curve had returned to its usual upwardly sloping shape. The fed had lowered short-term rates in an aggressive effort to revive a lagging economy. Once the economy recovers and short-term rates rebound, we can expect to still see an upward sloping yield curve, but one that is not as steep as before long-term rates fell due to budget surpluses.

Federal Reserve can actually complicate the determination of interest rates. For example, the supply of money can have a large effect on inflationary expectations. If the Fed decreases the money supply, we may initially conclude that interest rates will increase. However, if the decrease in the money supply reduces inflationary expectations, interest rates may decline. It is no wonder why the Fed, as well as bankers, investors, and government forecasters, have so much difficulty accurately predicting future interest rates.

Self-Test Review Questions*

1. What kind of risk increases when the market for an investment disappears?
2. What is interest rate risk?
3. What is the major point made by the pure expectations theory?
4. What is the major point made by the liquidity preference theory?
5. What is the major point made by the market segmentation theory?
6. Which theory is true?

Effect of Interest Rates on Stock Prices

The level of interest rates affects stock prices in two ways. First, when interest rates are high, corporate profits tend to decline. Second, when interest rates are high, other investments may appear more attractive.

How Interest Rates Affect Corporate Profits

When interest rates rise, corporate profits suffer. One reason is because many firms are constantly renewing old debt and issuing new debt. When interest rates increase, the cost of this debt rises. We can review the effect increasing interest rates have on debt payments by looking at what happens to the payments on a typical house loan. Table 4.5 shows the monthly payments on a 30-year $125,000 loan at a variety of interest rates. As the interest rate increases, the payments rise substantially. Increasing interest rates are clearly important to home buyers, but they also affect corporate profits.

Another reason why high interest rates affect profits is because they tend to depress economic activity. High interest rates reduce the level of investment spending by companies on new plants and equipment. When investment spending falls, the firms that supply the equipment and do the construction have reduced revenues. This leads to reduced employment and a generally less robust economy. When the entire economy is depressed, spending by consumers falls and corporate profits fall. Falling corporate profits lead to reduced stock prices. Consumer spending is also affected by interest rates because many consumers use credit to finance their purchases. For example, when interest rates rise, home sales fall, as do the sales of new cars.

* 1. Liquidity.
2. The risk that changes in interest rates will cause the price of bonds to go up or down.
3. That the interest rate offered for a period of time reflects the average of the interest rates expected over that period.
4. That lenders prefer to lend short-term and borrowers prefer to borrow long-term, so equilibrium occurs when borrowers pay a higher interest rate to induce the lender to lend long.
5. That there is a supply and demand equilibrium at each maturity.
6. They probably all are.

TABLE 4.5 **Monthly Payments on $125,000 30-Year Loan**

Interest Rate	Principal and Interest Payment
5%	$671.03
6	749.44
7	831.63
8	917.21
9	1,005.78
10	1,096.96
11	1,190.40
12	1,285.77
13	1,382.75
14	1,481.09

Thus, there is a two-pronged stab at corporate earnings. First, earnings suffer because of increased financing costs. Second, they suffer because of reduced sales. It is no wonder that corporate America is so intensely concerned with the level of interest rates.

Self-Test Review Questions*

1. How do interest rate premiums affect the nominal interest rate?
2. What is the nominal rate if the real rate is 3%, the DRP is 4%, and MRP is 2% per year, assuming that inflation is zero and there is no LP?

How Interest Rates Affect the Competition for Funds

When interest rates are low, investors tend to buy stocks because the earnings available on bonds and certificates of deposit from banks are low. When interest rates rise, some investors sell stocks and buy bonds. The fixed and higher-priority returns available on bonds can appear very favorable compared with uncertain corporate returns. When investors sell stock to buy bonds, the price of the stock falls and the price of bonds rises. This process reverses itself when rates fall again. We often observe bond and stock prices moving in opposite directions as each investment competes for funds.

The combined effect of reduced corporate profits and the competition for investment funds results in corporations viewing high interest rates very negatively. This underscores why it is so important that the Federal Reserve be kept independent of politics. Corporations will clearly attempt to influence Congress to reduce interest rates if profits are suffering. Congress would find it difficult to resist the pressure because campaign dollars would be at stake. Because the Fed is independent, Congress can publicly criticize the Fed to appear supportive of its corporate constituents and still let the Fed do the hard work of keeping the economy healthy in the long run. We take a closer look at the Fed and its role in the economy in the next chapter.

* 1. They are added to the real rate and expected inflation to calculate the nominal rate.
  2. 9% (simply add them up).

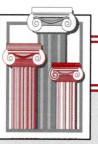

Careers in Finance

Mortgage Loan Officer

Lenders usually specialize in one of several broad types of loans. These include consumer lending, commercial lending, construction lending, and mortgage lending. Mortgage lenders have a unique job in that virtually all of the loans they make are intended for resale. Once the loan has been extended the bank sells the loan to one of several long-term financing agencies, such as the Federal National Mortgage Association. This means that the loans must satisfy the rules of the financing agency or the bank will be stuck holding the loan until it pays off. Mortgage lenders must understand all the intricate details of how to qualify borrowers and how to amass the documentation so the sales of the loans to the secondary lenders go smoothly.

Many mortgage bankers work for mortgage companies rather than for banks. They also work for savings and loan associations. Salaries range from the mid $30,000s to the upper $70,000s for mortgage company branch managers.

CHAPTER SUMMARY

Interest rates are the price of renting money. As the amount of money available falls, the price increases. Conversely, as the amount of money available increases, the price falls, just like the price of any other commodity.

Interest rates are a function of many factors in addition to the supply and demand for funds. The real rate of interest is the return required by an investor to compensate for delayed consumption in terms of actual purchasing power. The nominal rate adjusts this real rate of interest to take into account the effect of inflation.

The nominal rate is also affected by the probability that the debt will not be repaid as promised. This is called default risk. Default risk is affected by the firm's business risk and the amount of financial risk. Business risk increases as the level of fixed assets increases. Financial risk increases as the firm uses more debt to finance its assets. Bond rating agencies publish reports on the default risk of most publicly traded firms.

Other factors that affect the nominal interest rate include the liquidity risk and the maturity risk. Liquidity risk premiums are added to the return required on investments that may be slow or costly to convert into cash in the future.

The maturity risk results in increased interest rates on longer-term securities. The relationship between interest rates and the time to maturity is called the term structure of interest rates. The pure expectations theory of the term structure holds that long-term rates are simply the average of the short-term rates expected over that period. The liquidity preference theory says that a premium is offered to lenders to induce them to make long-term loans because they would rather make short-term loans. Borrowers are willing to offer this premium because they want to avoid the risk of being caught unable to pay their interest should interest rates increase. The market segmentation theory says that there is a supply and demand for funds at each different maturity. The interest rate is established when the supply of funds equals the demand. A separate interest rate is required to clear the markets at each maturity. In fact, all of these theories have some truth and help explain the shape of the yield curve at different times.

Interest rates affect the price of stock in two ways. First, increasing interest rates reduce corporate profits because financing costs are increased and sales are likely to fall. Second, with higher interest rates, many investors sell risky stock to capture the attractive rates being offered on fixed-rate bonds. Stock prices are depressed by the selling activity. For these reasons, corporations dislike high interest rates.

In the first four chapters of this text you have been introduced to the markets and to the securities that trade there, to the institutions that facilitate trading, and to theories regarding the determination of interest rates. In Chapter 5 we extend our understanding of interest rates by studying the Federal Reserve System and its control over the money supply. We will learn how money is created by the banking system and learn a simple way to estimate the effect on interest rates of major economic events.

KEY WORDS

business cycle 84
business risk 88
financial risk 89
indenture 88
interest rate premium 85

interest rate risk 89
inverted yield
    curve 91
liquidity preference
    theory 94

market segmentation
    theory 96
nominal interest rate 85
pure expectations
    theory 92

real interest rate 85
risk averse 94
term structure of
    interest rates 91

DISCUSSION QUESTIONS

1. Explain what the real rate of return is and why the real rate of return is different for each individual.
2. List reasons why long-term investments have more risk than short-term investments.
3. The pure expectations theory, the liquidity preference theory, and the market segmentation theory attempt to explain the shape of the yield curve. Explain these three theories. Which theory probably explains how long-term rates are established?
4. What is a yield curve? How would a yield curve facing a company such as IBM or Wal-Mart compare with a yield curve for U.S. Treasury securities? Draw a graph to illustrate your answer.

5. Why do long-term borrowers pay an interest rate premium?
6. How do interest rates affect corporate profits?
7. What is a business cycle? How often do they usually occur?
8. What factors affect the level of interest rates? Which factor usually has the greatest effect?
9. What is interest rate risk? How does it affect long-term interest rates?
10. What is the usual relationship between interest rates and stock prices? Explain why this relationship exists.

PROBLEMS

1. If the nominal rate is 13% and the real rate of interest is 10%, what is the expected rate of inflation?
2. What is the default risk premium of a corporate bond if the real rate is 4%, the expected inflation is 2%, the liquidity premium is 1%, the maturity risk premium is 4%, and the nominal rate is 14%?
3. The 1-year interest rate is 6%. The 1-year interest rate expected in 1 year is 8%. The 1-year interest rate expected in 2 years is 10%. What are the 2-year and 3-year interest rates predicted by the pure expectations theory?
4. Assume that the real rate of interest is 4%, the default risk premium is 3%, the liquidity premium is 1%, and the maturity risk premium is 0.2% per year. Additionally,

expected inflation is 5% next year, 4% the year after, and 3% from then on. What are the nominal interest rates for a 1-year, a 5-year, a 10-year, and a 20-year bond? Graph your results.
5. Given the following, what are the nominal interest rates on a 1-, 5-, 10-, and 20-year bond? Graph your results on a yield curve.
    Real rate 3%
    Default risk premium 4%
    Liquidity premium 1%
    Maturity risk premium 0.1% per year
    Inflation 3% next year
        2.5% in 2 years
        2% in 3 years and from then on

WEB EXPLORATION

1. The amount of additional interest investors receive due to the various premiums changes over time. Sometimes the risk premiums are much larger than at other times. For example, the default risk premium was very small in the late 1990s when the economy was so healthy that

business failures were rare. This risk premium increases during recessions.
    Go to www.federalreserve.gov/releases/ and find the interest rate listings for AAA and Baa rated bonds at three points in time: the most recent, June 1, 1995, and June

1, 1992. Prepare a yield curve on one graph that shows these three time periods (See Figure 4.3 for an example.)

2. As discussed in this chapter, the largest single influence on the level of interest rates is inflation. There are a number of sites that report inflation over time. Go to ftp://ftp.bls.gov/pub/special.requests/cpi/cpiai.txt and review the data available. Note that the last columns report various averages. Move this data into a spreadsheet using the method discussed in the Mini Case at the end of Chapter 2. What have the average rates of inflation been since 1950, 1960, 1970, 1980, and 1990? What year had the lowest level of inflation? What year had the highest level of inflation?

MINI CASE

As a junior financial analyst at MainStar Enterprises, a regional development company, your work is assigned by the Chief Financial Officer, Mr. Otym. Mr. Otym has called you into his office to explain that the company wants to refinance one of its shopping malls and is evaluating various competing loan alternatives. The main difference between the alternatives is that some are adjustable-rate loans and others are long-term fixed-rate loans. He wants your help preparing for a meeting with the company president. Mr. Otym complains to you that the yield curve in the *Wall Street Journal* every day only lists interest rates on Treasury securities. MainStar is very leveraged and its securities are often rated as Baa. He wants you to investigate the shape of the yield curve for these lower-rated securities.

1. What is an adjustable-rate mortgage? Is it more like a long-term loan or a short-term loan in terms of the interest rate it will offer?

2. How do you think the yield curves on Treasury securities, AAA rated, and Baa rated securities will compare? Sketch a rough graph showing all three together.

3. Go to www.federal reserve.gov/releases/ and find the listings for interest rates on Treasury bonds and bonds with both high and low ratings.

4. How much default risk premium is there between Treasury securities, high-rated bonds, and low-rated bonds? (Compare the rate on 30-year Treasury bonds with the rates reported for AAA and Baa rated bonds.)

5. Prepare a yield curve for AAA and Baa rated bonds by adding the interest rate differential to the interest rates on Treasury bonds with different maturities.

6. Discuss any sources of error the method outlined above may introduce. Is there a large interest savings for taking the risk of borrowing short term instead of long term?

The Federal Reserve and the Money Supply

Chapter Objectives

By the end of this chapter you should be able to:

1. Describe the structure of the Federal Reserve System

2. Know the primary responsibilities of the Federal Reserve

3. Appreciate why and how the Federal Reserve is independent of political pressure

4. Explain what money is

5. Describe how money is created and how banks participate in money expansion

6. Use the loanable funds theory to analyze how interest rates affect the money supply

Although the typical business or individual may never deal directly with the Federal Reserve or enter the lobby of one of its branches, it is the single most important and influential financial institution in the nation. The Federal Reserve is responsible for the stability of our economy, the security of our banks, and the creditworthiness of our government. In this chapter we will focus on the Federal Reserve's role in the determination of the money supply and its control over the state of the economy. Investors, businesses, and the government all carefully follow the actions of the Federal Reserve because it has such a significant impact on all aspects of the economic environment. For example, in December 1996 and again in February 1997, the Federal Reserve chairman touched off a major selling frenzy in the stock market with a casual comment in a speech about "irrational exuberance" by investors.

The Federal Reserve suffered several setbacks before becoming the powerful institution it now is. A precursor to the Federal Reserve was the First Bank, established in 1791. Unfortunately, because of fraud and favoritism, Congress did not renew its charter when it expired in 1811. The Second Bank was chartered in 1816, but its charter was also not renewed when it expired after 20 years. Congress did not make another attempt at establishing a central bank until 1913, when it chartered the current Federal Reserve Bank (the Fed).

RESPONSIBILITIES OF THE FEDERAL RESERVE

A **central bank** is very important to the stability of the economy and health of the financial system. The **Federal Reserve Bank** of the United States (usually called just **the Fed)** has four primary responsibilities.

- *Supervising and regulating commercial banks:* The Fed shares regulatory responsibility over commercial banks with various other agencies. It also regulates bank holding companies and supervises state-chartered banks.

- *Serving the banking industry:* The Fed is the **banker's bank.** It facilitates the transfer of checks between commercial banks, provides wire services, replaces worn bills, and even provides loans to nationally chartered banks. The Fed holds and maintains accounts for national banks. These services are critical to the smooth operation of the industry.

- *Holding the U.S. Treasury checking account:* The U.S. government uses the Fed as its bank. The government writes checks, makes deposits, and otherwise does its banking using the New York branch of the Federal Reserve.

- *Implement monetary policy:* **Monetary policy** involves adjusting the level of the money supply in a way that stimulates or slows the economy. Monetary policy influences the economy through changes in interest rates.

The Fed's control over monetary policy is its most important function. When the Fed increases the amount of money in the economy, interest rates fall. This makes sense if you think of money as any other commodity, where the interest rate is the price of money. As with any commodity, when the supply increases, the price falls. So when the supply of money increases, interest rates fall.

Falling interest rates tend to stimulate the economy. Low rates make it cheaper for firms to borrow money, which increases investment in new plants, equipment, and other factors of production. This expansion by business increases the number of jobs, lowers unemployment, and otherwise increases economic activity. We can summarize this sequence of events symbolically as follows:

$$\uparrow \text{Money supply} \Rightarrow \downarrow \text{Interest rates} \Rightarrow \uparrow \text{Investment} \Rightarrow \uparrow \text{Employment} \Rightarrow \uparrow \text{Economic activity}$$

Similarly, if the Fed believes that the economy is overheated and that inflation is likely, it can slow the economy by reducing the money supply. A reduced money supply increases interest rates, which makes borrowing more expensive and slows corporate investing. This sequence of events can be summarized as follows:

$$\downarrow \text{Money supply} \Rightarrow \uparrow \text{Interest rates} \Rightarrow \downarrow \text{Investment} \Rightarrow \downarrow \text{Employment}$$
$$\Rightarrow \downarrow \text{Economic activity}$$

The Fed has several mechanisms for controlling the money supply. These include:

- Open market operations
- Adjusting the discount rate
- Adjusting the reserve requirement

The most important of these mechanisms are **open market operations,** *which are the buying and selling of government securities*. The Fed can increase the money supply by buying government securities. When the Fed buys securities, it makes a deposit in a bank's account at the Fed in exchange for the securities. This deposit is now available to the bank for lending to its customers. The Fed can reduce the money supply by selling securities. When securities are sold, the Fed takes funds out of the bank's account at the Fed. This reduces the amount of funds banks have available to lend. By buying and selling government securities, the Fed respectively raises or lowers the amount that banks have available for lending. As we will learn later in this chapter, changes in the amount banks have available for lending ultimately results in changes in the money supply. These changes in the money supply, in turn, result in changes in interest rates.

The difficulty in controlling the economy with monetary policy is that there is a substantial delay between when a change in the money supply is made and when the economy reacts. This means that the Fed must project what changes the economy needs well in advance. This is a little like trying to drive a car when there is a 60-second delay between movement of the steering wheel and any change in the car's direction. It is generally agreed that it takes between 6 months and a year for changes in the money supply to affect the economy. Predicting what the economy needs up to a year in advance is tricky work. When the Fed makes a mistake it can be serious, because the economy can enter a recession or become overstimulated and have high inflation.

In addition to open market operations, the Fed has two methods for controlling the supply of money. One is to adjust the **discount rate,** the interest rate charged by the Fed when banks borrow money. In theory, if it costs more for banks to borrow money, they will charge higher rates on loans. This will slow investment spending by businesses and cool the economy. In truth, commercial banks seldom go to the Fed to borrow money. The money markets are sufficiently deep to provide all the funds banks require. The main purpose of the Fed changing the discount rate is to signal investors its intentions for future short-term interest rates.

The final tool available to the Fed is its authority to change **reserve requirements.** Every bank and S&L is required to set aside a portion of each deposit in its vault or in an account at the Fed. This reserve ensures that banks have sufficient liquidity to meet unexpected demand for cash from their depositors. As we will see later in this chapter, the reserve is also needed to control the growth of the money supply. We will return to our discussion of using changes in the reserve requirement to control the money supply after we learn how money is created. Table 5.1 shows the reserve requirement as it stood in November 2000.

TABLE 5.1 Reserve Requirements of Depository Institutions

Type of Deposit	Reserve Requirement	Effective Date
$0 million–$44.3 million	3%	12/30/99
More than $44.3 million	10	12/30/99
Nonpersonal time deposits	0	12/27/90
Eurocurrency liabilities	0	12/27/90

Source: Federal Reserve Bulletin, November 2000, table 1.15. See also http://www.ny.frb.org/pihome/fedpoint/fed45.html for more information on reserves.

The Fed has focused on various targets over the years while trying to control the economy. For example, between 1951 and 1965 the Fed set interest rate targets. When this failed to work well, it began targeting total reserves (1966–1970). Later, it focused on the monetary base (1971–1982) and more recently on various measures of the money supply. The Fed balances the benefits of low unemployment with the harm caused by high inflation. As investors gain confidence in the Fed's ability to avoid inflation, long-term interest rates continue to fall.

ORGANIZATION OF THE FED

Figure 5.1 shows the structure of the Federal Reserve System. Nationally chartered banks are required to be members of the Federal Reserve System. Each **member bank** subscribes to stock in the Fed and receives a fixed 6% dividend on the investment. The governing body of the Federal Reserve System is the Board of Governors. The Board of Governors and the chairman are appointed by the president of the United States and confirmed by the Senate. Each of the 12 district Federal Reserve Banks is supervised by its own board of directors consisting of nine members. Six are elected by the member banks of the district, and three are appointed by the Board of Governors. The 12 district banks are spread across the country, where they can facilitate check clearing and supply commercial banks with

FIGURE 5.1 Federal Reserve System

currency. There are a total of 24 branch banks that help serve commercial banks. Figure 5.2 shows the location of the 12 Federal Reserve Districts and the District Banks.

The seven members of the Board of Governors and five representatives from the Federal Reserve Banks form the **Federal Open Market Committee (FOMC),** which decides what action the Fed needs to take to keep the economy healthy. The president of the N.Y. Fed is always one of the five Fed members. This committee meets about every 6 weeks. Immediately following the meeting, the FOMC issues a press release that discusses in a brief and obscure way what the committee decided. Box 5.1 contains a copy of a typical press release. The full minutes of each meeting are released just following the next scheduled meeting, hence about 6 weeks after the meeting.

Before we investigate further how the Fed controls the economy, let us first review how it is able to take politically unpopular positions.

Self-Test Review Questions*

1. What is the function of the Open Market Committee?
2. Who appoints the chairman of the Board of Governors?
3. What are member banks?

---

* 1. To establish monetary policy, which is how the economy is to be controlled by changing the money supply.
  2. The president of the United States.
  3. All nationally chartered banks and other commercial banks that choose to join the Federal Reserve System.

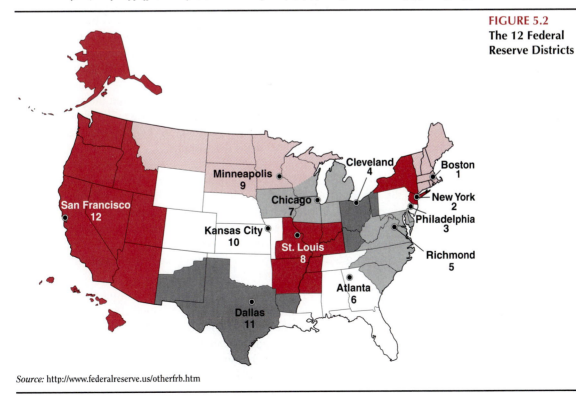

FIGURE 5.2
The 12 Federal Reserve Districts

Source: http://www.federalreserve.us/otherfrb.htm

Box 5.1 Federal Reserve Press Release, November 15, 2000

For Immediate Release

The Federal Open Market Committee at its meeting today decided to maintain the existing stance of monetary policy, keeping its target for the federal funds rate at 6½ percent.

The utilization of the pool of available workers remains at an unusually high level, and the increase in energy prices, though having limited effect on core measures of prices to date, still harbors the possibility of raising inflation expectations. The Committee, accordingly, continues to see a risk of heightened inflation pressures. However, softening in business and household demand and tightening conditions in financial markets over recent months suggest that the economy could expand for a time at a pace below the productivity-enhanced rate of growth of its potential to produce.

Nonetheless, to date the easing of demand pressures has not been sufficient to warrant a change in the Committee's judgment that against the background of its long-run goals of price stability and sustainable economic growth and of the information currently available, the risks continue to be weighted mainly toward conditions that may generate heightened inflation pressures in the foreseeable future.

Source: www.federalreserve.gov/BoardDocs/Press/General/2000/20001115/DEFAULT.HTM.

FED'S POLITICAL INDEPENDENCE

Consider the control the Fed has over the economy. It can reduce unemployment, increase inflation, and otherwise dramatically influence the state of the economy. Clearly, politicians are very concerned with the activities of the Fed. For example, many political historians say that George Bush lost his 1992 presidential reelection attempt primarily because the economy faltered during his reelection year. Similarly, Bill Clinton won reelection in 1996, despite several brewing scandals, largely because the economy was extremely healthy. Given the political importance of the Fed's activities, how independent is it from political pressure?

The original founders of the Federal Reserve System appreciated the political pressure that may be put on the Fed to manage the economy according to the whims of politicians rather than what may be best for the country. Congress therefore organized the Fed to minimize the effects of political pressure. For example:

- _**Members of the Board of Governors are appointed for 14-year nonrenewable terms**_. Additionally, the terms are staggered so that no one president will appoint a majority of the board during one term. Long terms with no reappointment remove much of the pressure that could be placed on board members. Unlike elected officials, they do not have to answer to any constituency. Note that the concept is similar to that used for appointing Supreme Court justices, who have lifetime appointments and do not answer to any political power.

- _**The Fed has its own sources of income**_. The Fed holds large numbers of U.S. Treasury securities. The interest from the securities goes to the Fed to pay for its operations, with the surplus being returned to the Treasury. The Fed also receives revenues from member banks for services rendered and from bank membership fees. By having its own source of funding, the Fed cannot be threatened by a Congress attempting to force its own agenda by reducing funding.

The independence of the Fed allows it to pursue hard, politically unpopular monetary policies. For example, in the early 1980s, in an effort to reduce inflation, the Fed increased short-term interest rates to nearly 15%. This caused double-digit unemployment and a great deal of human suffering. On the other hand, it effectively reduced inflation to a level that has been maintained ever since. Most economists agree that the long-term benefits to the economy far outweigh the short-term hardship the Fed caused. It is unlikely that the Fed could have raised interest rates as high and for as long as was needed if it was not politically independent.

Congress often raises the issue of whether it is appropriate that officials who have never been elected by the public should have as much power as is entrusted to the governors of the Fed. Congress gave the Fed the independence to make the hard decisions needed to keep the economy healthy. As long as it does an effective job, this is unlikely to change. However, if Congress feels that the Fed is abusing its freedom, changes can be made. The influence that the Fed and, specifically, the Federal Reserve chairman hold over the markets is highlighted in Box 5.2.

The primary reason we are interested in the Federal Reserve in this course is that it has control over the money supply and through this control it influences the level of interest rates. Figure 5.3 shows the money growth rate and interest rates on the same graph. Although the money growth rate appears more volatile, interest rates and money clearly tend to move together. When the money growth rate rose between 1950 and 1980, the interest rate on long-term bonds rose as well. In the late 1980s and into the 1990s, the growth rate in the money supply fell, as did the interest rate on long-term bonds. The Federal Reserve controls the amount of money in the economy. Before we investigate how it does this, let us first explore exactly what we mean by the term *money*.

Box 5.2   Fed Chairman's Voice Heard Around the World

On December 5, 1996, in a scholarly after-dinner lecture to the American Enterprise Institute, Federal Reserve Chairman Alan Greenspan proved once again why he may be the second most powerful man in the country. With a single question, Greenspan sent the financial markets reeling around the world.

"How do we know when irrational exuberance has unduly inflated asset values, which then become subject to unexpected and prolonged contractions, as they have in Japan over the past decade?" Greenspan asked his audience.

Although Greenspan did not answer his own question, as soon as reports of his comments flashed across the screens of traders, stock prices tumbled as they absorbed the fact that the chairman of the most powerful central bank in the world was wondering out loud about "irrational exuberance" in stock and bond markets. The Tokyo exchange, which was open at the time of the speech, suffered its biggest 1-day loss of the year and stock markets from Sydney to London began falling as well. The next day the Dow Jones Industrial Average fell 140 points during the first hour of trading (although it recovered all but 55 points by the time the exchange closed for the day).

The Fed chairman can cause the market to rise as well. In March 1997, the Dow Jones Industrial Average rose 93.13 points, or 1.36%, its largest increase in over a year, when Greenspan told members of a House subcommittee that monetary policy should not be used as a means of stemming the recent rise in stock prices.

Source: Wall Street Journal, December 7, 1996, p. A4, and March 6, 1997, p. C2.

FIGURE 5.3
Money Growth Rates and Interest Rates for Each Year 1950–2000

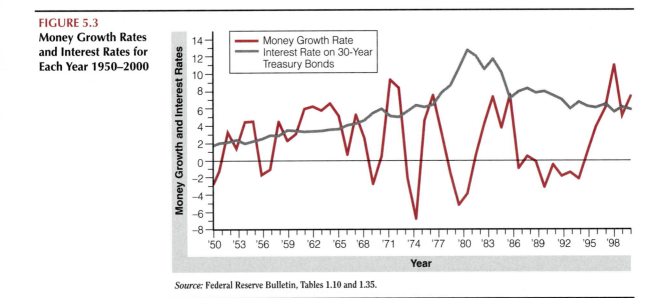

Source: Federal Reserve Bulletin, Tables 1.10 and 1.35.

Self-Test Review Questions*

1. Why is it important that the Fed be politically independent?
2. What features make the Fed independent?

WHAT IS MONEY?

Historically, many items have been used as money. Specific types of shells served the purpose on South Pacific islands. Stones and metal also have been used as money at different times in history. Even in the United States, paper and various types of metal have been used as money. At one point gold coins were the predominant form of money, but today they are seldom used in trade.

You probably have some idea about what money is and is not. For example, we all agree that cash and coins are acceptable for paying debts and for buying goods, but consider other methods regularly used to pay for goods and services. Most of us have checking accounts and have found that checks are usually accepted by merchants. This suggests that the balances you hold in your checking account should also be considered money. Money held in savings accounts can be readily accessed and also used to pay for goods. Money, then, is anything that is generally acceptable in payment of goods and ser-

*1. So that it can make politically unpopular decisions about fixing problems with the economy.
2. Long-term nonrenewable terms for governors and independent funding.

vices and for paying debts. For an item to be generally acceptable, the majority of the population must agree that the item has value and be willing to accept it in trade. Additionally, merchants must believe that the money represents a safe way to store wealth. Why will a jeweler agree to give you a diamond ring in exchange for a few small pieces of paper? It is because the population has agreed that these pieces of paper have value beyond their production cost. Why does a population agree that worthless paper currency has real value?

Back in history, people used to carry gold or other valuable goods around with them to meet their transaction needs. Somewhere along the line, a bright banker suggested that his customers leave the gold with the bank for safe keeping. The bank issued transferable receipts for the gold. In other words, the bank would give the gold to anyone who presented the receipt to the bank. Because the bank's customers found it much more convenient to use the receipts than to use gold, which was heavy and required weighing whenever used in trade, gold receipts became very popular. Everyone was willing to accept them because they knew they could be exchanged for gold at any time. Eventually, the government took over the business of printing the receipts and kept the gold that backed the receipts in Fort Knox. Each paper bill stated on the front that it could be exchanged for gold at a Federal Reserve Bank. Much later, the government dropped the gold standard, and gold receipts were replaced with Federal Reserve notes. The population continued to accept the notes as money because they trusted the government not to print too much. Currently, there is not nearly enough gold in Fort Knox to redeem all of the Federal Reserve notes in circulation. Paper currency continues to have value simply because the population has agreed that it does.

Money serves a number of purposes. It is a medium of exchange, a store of wealth, and a unit of account. Without money, the primary means of transacting business would be by barter, where one good is exchanged for another. Barter economies continue to exist in countries where the currency is not generally accepted as having value, as when a government has printed too much money.

It is clear that one of the important factors that affects the value of money is how much money is in circulation in the economy. Before we discuss the amount of money in the economy, we must define more precisely how the money supply is measured. M-1, the most basic definition of money, is coins and currency in circulation plus balances held in checking accounts at banks (called **demand deposits).** This also includes accounts held in negotiable order of withdrawal (NOW) accounts and in traveler's checks. Recall from Chapter 2 that NOW accounts are interest-bearing checking accounts held at banks. M-1 has been deemphasized in favor of M-2. M-2 is a broader definition of money that includes M-1 plus savings accounts and small-denomination time deposits. M-3 includes M-2 plus large time deposits, repurchase agreements, shares in money market mutual funds held by large corporations and financial institutions, and Eurodollars held by U.S. residents. Table 5.2 summarizes the components of the money supply. Each method of measuring the money supply provides different yet valuable information to those attempting to control it.

TABLE 5.2 Measures of the Monetary Aggregates

	Value as of August 2000 ($ billion)
M1 = Currency	523.1
+ Traveler's checks	9.2
+ Demand deposits	328.5
+ Other checkable deposits	241.2
Total M1	1,102.0
M2 = M1	
+ Savings deposits including MMDAs	1,813.1
+ Small time deposits	1,022.8
+ Money market mutual funds (retail)	890.3
Total M2	4,828.2
M3 = M2	
+ Large time deposits	777.6
+ Money market mutual funds (institutional)	704.9
+ Repurchase agreements	363.3
+ Eurodollars	174.1
Total M3	6,848.1

Source: Federal Reserve Bulletin, September 2000, Table 1.21.

HOW MONEY IS CREATED

Now that we know what money is and how it is measured, let us investigate how it is created. It may surprise you to learn that the amount of money in our economy is actually much more than has been issued by the government. This is because our banking system creates money in the process of making loans. Let us explore how this happens by looking at a very simplified example.

Suppose that First National Bank has the following balance sheet. It has $1,100 in capital, $900 in deposits from customers held in checking accounts (called demand accounts), $1,000 in cash, and $1,000 in government securities.

Initial Balance Sheet of First National Bank

Assets		Liabilities	
Cash	$1,000	Deposits	$900
Gov. securities	1,000	Capital	1,100
Total	$2,000	Total	$2,000

Suppose the Federal Reserve has set the reserve requirement at 10% of deposits. A loan by First National Bank of $910 to Joe Smith leaves $90 in reserves, which is 10% of the $900 deposit on hand. It must keep 10% of the deposits as reserves. Reserves can be in the form of cash held in the bank's vault or as deposits held in the bank's account at the Federal Reserve Bank.

Balance Sheet After Loan to Joe

Assets		Liabilities	
Cash	$90	Deposits	$900
Gov. securities	1,000	Capital	1,100
Loan to Joe Smith	910		
Total	$2,000	Total	$2,000

Suppose that Joe now deposits this loan back into First National. The following balance sheet results. (It does not matter whether Joe makes the deposit back into the same bank or another one. For simplicity we assume a one-bank system.)

Balance Sheet After Joe Deposits Loan Proceeds

Assets		Liabilities	
Cash	$1,000	Demand deposit	$900
Loan to Joe S.	910	Demand deposit to Joe S.	910
Gov. securities	1,000	Capital	1,100
Total	$2,910	Total	$2,910

As a result of the loan to Joe Smith, total deposits have increased by $910. These extra deposits provide the funds to make additional loans. A total of $1,810 is on deposit (the original $900 plus the $910 deposited by Joe Smith). Reserves on this total deposit amount are 10% of $1,810 = $1,810 × 0.10 = $181. With $1,000 in cash in the vault, the bank can still lend an additional $819 ($1,000 − $181 = $819). Now suppose that Mary Cate wants a loan for $819. This is the most that the bank can lend and still maintain a reserve of 10%. If this loan is also redeposited at First National, the following balance sheet results.

Balance Sheet After Second Loan is Made and Deposited

Assets		Liabilities	
Cash	$1,000	Original demand deposits	$900
Loan to Joe S.	910	Demand deposit for Joe S.	910
Loan to Mary Cate	819	Demand deposit for Mary C.	819
Gov. securities	1,000	Capital	1,100
Total	$3,729	Total	$3,729

Notice a few things about what is happening. First, because banks are required to maintain reserve requirements, the amount that can be lent to each subsequent borrower declines. Second, the total amount of demand deposits is increasing. Originally, there was $900 in checking accounts; then, after the loan to Joe Smith, there was $1,810. Now there is a total of $2,629 ($900 + $910 + $819 = $2,629) in checking accounts at First National. Remember how we measured money? The narrowest measure was M-1, which included cash and *demand deposits*. It does not matter whether there is only one bank in the economy, as in this example, or many different banks. When loans are made, the proceeds are typically deposited into transaction accounts. Aggregate demand accounts across the banking system increase.

Look at the First National balance sheet one more time. There is $2,629 in total demand deposits. The amount of reserves required on the $2,629 in deposits is $262.90 ($2,629 × 0.10 = $262.90). With reserves equal to $1,000, the bank can continue to lend. If we were to extend this example until no excess reserves were available, we would find that the bank can create $10,000 in new money with its initial $1,000 cash. Later we will show an easy way to compute how much the money supply can expand.

What if there were no reserve requirements? ***If banks could lend 100% of deposited funds, then the money supply could increase infinitely. Recall our earlier discussion that money has value only because the population agrees that it does. If the money supply were to increase without restriction, it would stop having value.***

Fed's Role in the Money Supply Process

In the last section we saw how the money supply increases as banks lend and relend funds. Now suppose that the Federal Reserve buys government securities from the First National Bank. In this transaction, First National gives securities to the Fed and the Fed pays for the securities by making a deposit into the bank's account at the Federal Reserve Bank. This deposit can be used to satisfy the bank's reserve requirements, so it is often called a reserve. Reserves are included with the bank's cash balances when computing how much is available for lending. The money expansion process begins again. The process will also occur if the Federal Reserve buys securities from individuals or from businesses. Ultimately, the proceeds from the security sale are put into a bank, where they are lent, and the money supply increases. The following balance sheet for First National shows the effect of the Fed buying the bank's securities and putting the proceeds in the bank's account with the Fed (before any new money has been created as in the examples in the last section). Note that the government securities are gone and reserves have increased.

Balance Sheet Sale of Securities to Fed and Completion of Money Expansion			
Assets		**Liabilities**	
Reserves and cash	$2,000	Original demand deposit	$900
Total loans	10,000	Total new deposits	10,000
		Capital	1,100
Total cash in vault	$12,000	Total liabilities and equity	$12,000

There are now excess reserves available for increased lending. If the Fed were to *sell* securities, total reserves in the banking system would *decrease*. When the Fed sells securities, money is taken out of the bank's account at the Fed and the bank receives securities in exchange. This reduces the amount that bank can lend. The effect of the Fed buying and selling securities on the money supply and interest rates is summarized in Table 5.3.

TABLE 5.3 Summary of the Effect of the Fed Buying and Selling Securities

Federal Reserve Action	Effect on Money Supply	Effect on Interest Rates
Fed **buys** securities	Money supply increases	Interest rates fall
Fed **sells** securities	Money supply decreases	Interest rates rise

Exactly how much will the money supply increase given an increase in cash at a bank? We can calculate the increase using the money multiplier.

Money Multiplier

The relationship between the change in the money supply and the change in reserves initiated by the Fed is expressed by the following equation, called the **money multiplier:**

$$\Delta D = \frac{\Delta R}{RR} \tag{5.1}$$

where

ΔD = the maximum possible change in demand deposits that can result from a change in reserves

ΔR = the dollar amount of the change in reserves

RR = the reserve requirement

The money multiplier can be used to compute the theoretical change in the money supply and a change in the reserves.

E X A M P L E 5.1   Change in the Money Supply

Suppose the Fed buys $100 million in bonds from banks and that the reserve requirement is 3%. What is the maximum amount that the money supply could increase from this transaction?

Solution

Plugging the numbers into Equation 5.1 yields

$$\Delta D = \$100,000,000/0.1 = \$1,000,000,000$$

A $100-million increase in reserves could increase the money supply by $3.3 billion. It is important to note that ΔD is the *potential* change in the money supply. ***The actual increase in the money supply will be much less than this amount***. First, not all of the money lent by banks will be redeposited. Some of it will be used as transactional balances held by the individuals receiving the loans. This means that banks will not have the full amount of each loan available to relend. Second, not all of the banks will lend the maximum amount permitted by law. Often, there are not sufficient loan requests for a bank to lend all of its loanable money. Additionally, bank management may be conservative and want to maintain excess cash reserves.

One final point: The expansion of the money supply takes time. Many loans must be made before the full effect of an increase in reserves will be felt. Because it is not certain exactly how much the money supply will increase, and because it takes many months for a change in reserves to ripple through the economy in the form of new loans, controlling the money supply is clearly a very difficult process.

In this section, we have discussed only one tool the Fed might use to change the money supply: buying and selling securities. In fact, this is the most common method used. Earlier we noted that an alternative method available to the Fed is adjusting the reserve requirement. The problem with this method is that a small change in the reserve requirement has a *tremendous* effect on the money supply because *all loans are affected*, not just new loans. Changing the reserve requirement to adjust the money supply is overkill and is rarely done.

Self-Test Review Questions*

1. What is the most important tool for controlling the money supply?
2. When is the Fed likely to decrease the money supply?
3. If the Fed wants to increase the money supply, will it buy or sell securities?
4. What is the greatest possible change in the money supply that would result from the Fed buying $100 million of government securities if the reserve requirement were 3%?

E X A M P L E 5.2   Federal Reserve and Changes to the Money Supply

Suppose the Fed has determined that the country is about to enter a recession and wants to avert a serious slowdown in the economy. The Fed determines that an increase of $50 billion in the money supply will be about right. How would the Fed go about increasing the money supply by this amount? Assume a 3% reserve requirement.

Solution

The first task is to decide whether the Fed needs to sell or buy securities. Because it wants to increase the money supply, it wants to increase reserves. This is done by buying securities. The second task is to estimate how much in securities the Fed needs to buy. We can solve for this figure by using the money multiplier:

$$\Delta D = \frac{\Delta R}{RR}$$

$$\$50 \text{ billion} = \frac{\Delta R}{0.03}$$

$$\$50 \text{ billion} \times 0.03 = \Delta R$$

$$\Delta R = \$1.5 \text{ billion}$$

If the Fed sells $1.5 billion in securities the money supply could increase by $50 billion. In fact, the Fed would have to sell more than this because not all reserves are used to increase the money supply.

* 1. Open market operations.
  2. If inflation is increasing.
  3. Buy.
  4. $3,333.33 million ($100/0.03 = $3,333.33).

Now that we understand how the Fed controls the money supply, we can examine how changes in the money supply relate to changes in interest rates. One of the simpler yet most useful models for understanding how changes in the money supply influence interest rates is the loanable funds theory of interest rates.

EXTENSION 5.1

Loanable Funds Theory of Interest Rates

The **loanable funds theory** of interest rate determination focuses on the supply and demand for loanable funds. This simple theory ignores many issues that may be addressed in an economics class. However, this simplicity is what makes the theory useful. Once you understand it, you will be able to predict how interest rates will behave without complex models or computer-based estimation techniques. When you read an article in the paper, you will be able to mentally evaluate the topic's effect on interest rates. Whether you are investing on your own behalf or making investment decisions for your business, a basic understanding of how macroeconomic factors affect interest rates is critical. As we proceed in this book you will soon see that many individual and business decisions depend on the interest rate.

The concept behind the loanable funds theory is that the *supply* of funds available for lending must equal the *demand* for funds by those who want to borrow. Interest rates adjust to ensure that this equilibrium exists. Equilibrium occurs when the markets clear. "Clearing markets" is economic talk for supply equaling demand.

We will develop the theory by discussing first the determinants of the supply of loanable funds, then the determinants of the demand for loanable funds. Finally, we will put the supply and demand curves together to see how changes in either supply or demand affect interest rates.

What Determines the Supply of Loanable Funds

The supply of loanable funds is determined by two basic factors. One is the supply of savings by households, businesses, and government. The other is the amount of new money created by the Fed and the banking system.

Savings by households rise when interest rates are high. The reward for delaying consumption is greater with higher interest rates, so households save more. This positive relationship between savings and the level of interest rates is not as strong as one might think, however. Many savers have a wealth goal that motivates the amount they save. With higher interest rates, less must be saved to reach this goal.

The relationship between savings and interest rates is weaker for businesses and government than for households. The amount of savings here is usually determined more by earnings than by interest levels. *To summarize, an increase in interest rates results in greater savings, although the relationship is somewhat weak.*

Savings is the principal source of loanable funds. However, new money introduced into the economy by the banking system can significantly increase the supply of loanable funds. As discussed in the last section, the amount of new money created is determined jointly by the Federal Reserve and the banking system. The Fed's introduction of

Careers in Finance

Academia

One career path often overlooked by undergraduate students is academics. Both the Federal Reserve and universities hire people with Ph.D.s to perform research and to teach. The academic lifestyle can be very appealing.

Most universities require a Ph.D. in the field in which the applicant plans to teach. There are about 100 universities in the country that offer Ph.D.s in finance. Faculty are typically in the classroom from 6 to 12 hours per week, depending on the research expectations of the school. The balance of the time faculty pursue their research interest.

The demand for finance faculty is very high, which is reflected in the starting salaries currently being offered. According to AACSB (American Assembly of Collegiate

Schools of Business, International Association of Management Education), the accrediting body for schools of business, the average starting salary for new Ph.D.s in finance in 1999 was $90,000 for a 9-month contract. Most faculty started at over $100,000 when summer compensation was included.

To earn a Ph.D. you will spend about 4 years attending school after receiving you master's degree. During this time you will take classes, teach undergraduates, help sponsoring faculty with research, and write a dissertation. Most schools provide stipends that students can live on while working on their degrees.

If academics sounds appealing, talk to several of your professors about their careers and their experiences in graduate school.

new money is based on its expectations regarding the state of the economy. The expansion of the money supply based on this new money is determined by the commercial bank's ability and willingness to lend.

There is little evidence that either the Fed or commercial banks are influenced by interest rates in the money supply process. The principal factor that determines the amount of new money is the Fed's monetary policy. The Fed's goals are to minimize inflation, maximize employment, and maintain constant economic growth. The level of interest rates helps achieve these goals, but is not a part of them. *In summary, then, there is little relationship between the level of interest rates and the amount of new money created*. New money in the economy can affect the level of interest rates, but not the other way around.

The supply of loanable funds is the sum of the savings and the new money created. This is graphed by adding the two curves together. The effect of adding the new money curve to the savings curve is to simply shift the supply curve to the right, as in Figure 5.4.

What Determines the Demand for Loanable Funds?

Loanable funds are demanded by individuals, businesses, and governments. The relationship between each of these and the level of interest rates differs.

Research shows that a large change in interest rates is required to change individual borrowing demand. Certain types of consumer demand are more sensitive to interest rates than other types. For example, mortgage borrowing is more sensitive to interest rates than is short-term consumer debt. As interest rates increase, the demand for loanable funds falls.

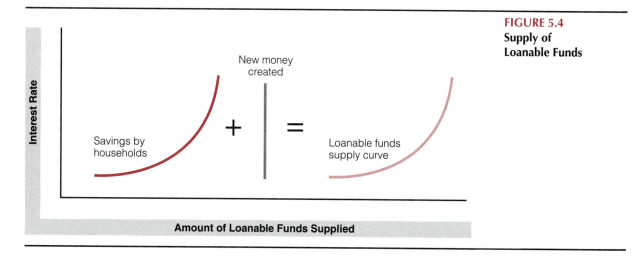

FIGURE 5.4
Supply of Loanable Funds

Business demand for loanable funds is influenced by a number of factors. The primary factors are spending for inventory, plant, and equipment. Borrowing for inventory is primarily a function of demand for the goods offered by the firm. When interest rates rise, firms become more aggressive about controlling inventory levels and reducing borrowing needs.

The demand for loanable funds to finance plant and equipment purchases is influenced primarily by long-term rates of interest, and small fluctuations have little impact on the demand for funds. Similarly, fluctuations in short-term rates have little effect on business demand.

There is little evidence that government demand for funds is influenced by interest rate levels. The difference between tax revenues and the demands by growing populations have more to do with the amount of government borrowing than do interest rates. In some isolated situations, governments take advantage of low rates to finance construction projects that might otherwise have been skipped or delayed.

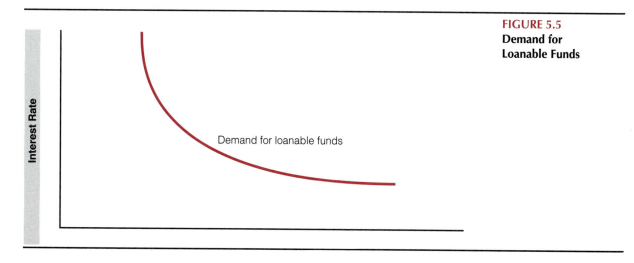

FIGURE 5.5
Demand for Loanable Funds

> *To summarize, the demand for loanable funds is a function of the demand for funds by individuals, businesses, and the government*. In each case, the link is negative, but weak. This means that as interest rates fall, demand increases, but not by a large amount. The relationship between the demand for loanable funds and interest rates is graphed in Figure 5.5 (page 119).

Combining the Supply and Demand for Loanable Funds

When the demand and supply curves are combined on one graph, their intersection tells us the level of interest rates and the quantity of loanable funds that will clear the market. In Figure 5.6, the interest rate in the market is i and the quantity of loanable funds supplied and demanded is Q. If the interest rate in the market was above i, say at i', more funds would be supplied than would be demanded. Equilibrium exists when the interest rate has fallen to i.

The determinants of the supply and demand curves for loanable funds are summarized in Table 5.4.

The real value of the loanable funds theory of interest rates is that it makes it possible to interpret changes in one of the variables. For example, what happens to interest

Study Tip

When drawing supply and demand curves, always remember that the *demand* curve slopes *down*.

FIGURE 5.6
Demand and Supply of Loanable Funds

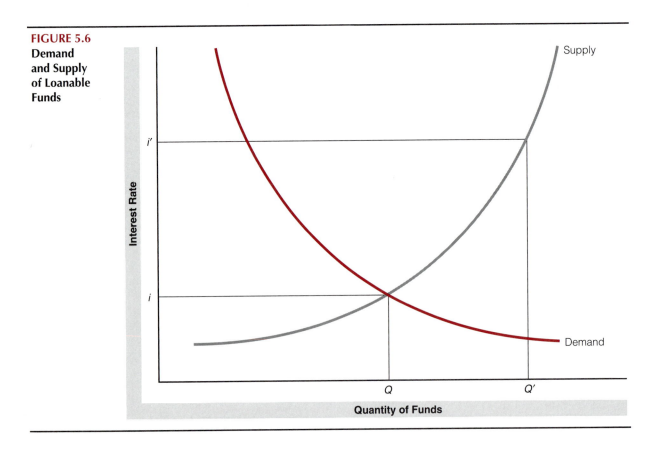

TABLE 5.4 Factors That Affect the Supply and Demand for Loanable Funds

Factors That Affect Supply of Loanable Funds	Factors That Affect Demand for Loanable Funds
Savings by individuals, business, and government New money created by the Fed	Demand by business, individuals, and government

rates if the Fed increases the money supply? From our earlier discussion we know that this will cause the supply curve to shift to the right. Figure 5.7 shows the effect of a shift in the supply curve. Interest rates fall from i to i' and the quantity of funds supplied and demanded increases from Q to Q'. We could easily find the effect of the Fed decreasing the money supply as well. The supply curve would shift left, interest rates would increase, and the quantity of funds demanded and supplied would fall.

Self-Test Review Questions*

1. What will happen to interest rates if consumers believe a recession is imminent and cut back on spending and borrowing?
2. What will happen to interest rates if the Fed buys bonds?

---

* 1. Demand will fall, so the demand curve will shift left. Interest rates and quantity demanded will fall.
2. If the Fed buys bonds, it is replacing bonds with cash in the economy. This increase in reserves shifts the supply curve right, lowers interest rates, and increases the amount of loanable funds.

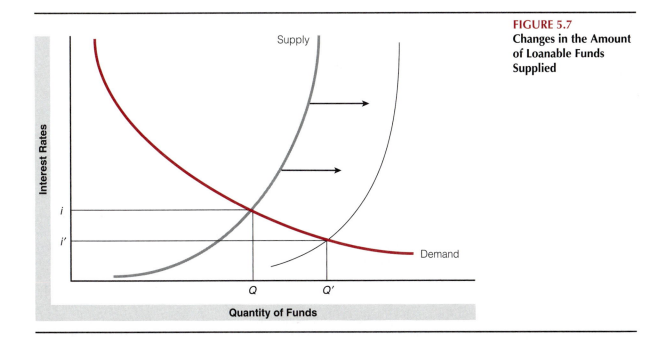

FIGURE 5.7
Changes in the Amount of Loanable Funds Supplied

Study Tip

Many students are confused by the difference between moving *along* a supply or demand curve and moving the *whole* curve. In this application, the determinants of supply and demand move the whole curve. We find the effect on interest rates and the money supply by finding the new intersection point.

The loanable funds framework can be used to anticipate the future of interest rate changes due to other macroeconomic factors as well. For example, suppose that you needed to predict next year's interest rates and after a thorough analysis of the economy decided that businesses were going to be expanding over the next 12 months. Business expansion would increase the demand for loanable funds. This would cause a shift in the demand curve to the right. Figure 5.8 shows that as the demand for loanable funds by businesses increases, interest rates increase from i to i' and the amount of loanable funds supplied increases from Q to Q'. Many economic issues can be analyzed using this simple framework. It also points out the important role interest rates have in the economy.

FIGURE 5.8
Changes in the Demand for Loanable Funds

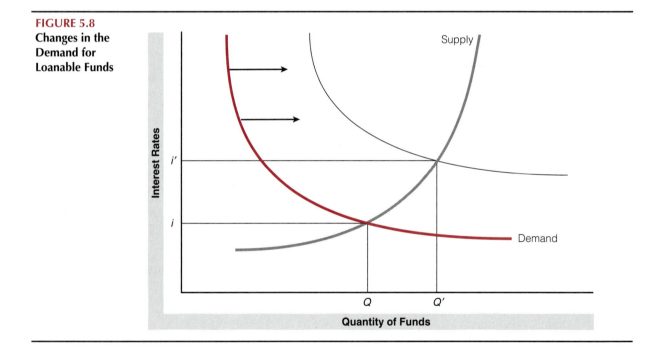

CHAPTER SUMMARY

The Federal Reserve Bank of the United States is the single most influential financial institution in the economy. It has many important responsibilities, but the most significant is the control it exercises over the economy. By changing the supply of money the Fed can affect interest rates, which in turn affects economic activity.

The Fed is organized with a Board of Governors, which sets overall policy, and district banks, which carry out the duties of the Fed. The seven members of the board plus five of the district bank representatives, including the president of the New York Fed, meet frequently to set monetary policy. Monetary policy controls the economy by altering the supply of funds.

The Fed is charged with the task of maintaining a healthy economy while keeping inflation under control and allowing for future growth. At times, this means setting policy that is politically unpopular. The Fed is organized to minimize the effects of political pressure. By having long, nonrenewable terms and an independent source of funds, the Fed is able to follow the course of action it believes best for the country, despite what the president and Congress may suggest.

The Fed, along with the banking system, creates money. When the Fed deposits new money in a bank, a portion of the deposit is held as a reserve and the balance is lent out. The loan is subsequently deposited in a bank, where a reserve is held and the balance is again lent out. This process continues until no more can be lent. With the actual reserve requirement at about 3%, this means that $1 of new money could eventually create about $33. The actual increase for $1 of new money will be less than this because not every loan will be entirely redeposited and not every bank will make the maximum allowable loans.

When the Fed increases or decreases the amount of money it puts into the economy, it has no way of knowing exactly what the resulting effect on the money supply will be. This, as well as the difficulty in predicting the state of the economy months ahead of time, makes the job imposed on the Fed very difficult.

The loanable funds theory of interest rates is a useful tool to illustrate how Fed actions affect interest rates and to help you interpret how economic events might affect interest rates. The theory notes that interest rates fluctuate to make the demand for loanable funds equal to the supply of loanable funds. The supply of loanable funds increases when interest rates rise. The demand for loanable funds increases when interest rates fall. By adjusting the supply and demand curves, we can see how interest rates are affected by different events.

In the first five chapters of this text you have learned about many of the institutions, securities, and markets in the economy. Additionally, you have achieved an understanding of how interest rates are established by the markets and changed by the interaction of the Fed with the banking community. You now have an excellent background for continuing your study of finance. In Part Two we study investments.

KEY WORDS

banker's bank 104	Federal Open Market	loanable funds theory 117	open market
central bank 104	Committee	member bank 106	operations 105
demand deposits 111	(FOMC) 107	monetary policy 104	reserve requirements 105
discount rate 105	Federal Reserve Bank	money multiplier 115	
	(the Fed) 104		

DISCUSSION QUESTIONS

1. What factors increase the independence of the Federal Reserve?
2. Why is it important that the Federal Reserve be independent of political pressure?
3. What are the primary responsibilities of the Federal Reserve? What is its most important responsibility?
4. Describe how an increase in the money supply can affect economic activity.
5. What are open market operations?
6. What are reserve requirements and what purpose do they serve?
7. Why is a population willing to accept paper currency as money?
8. Describe how the banking community can increase the money supply.
9. How is the supply of loanable funds determined? (Extension 5.1)
10. What factors affect the demand for loanable funds? (Extension 5.1)
11. Using the loanable funds theory, determine graphically what will happen to interest rates if consumers become convinced that the economy is failing and thus increase their savings. (Extension 5.1)
12. Using the loanable funds theory, determine graphically what will happen to interest rates if businesses project rapid future growth and begin to borrow to build new plants. (Extension 5.1)
13. Suppose that the Federal Reserve has reviewed masses of economic data and has reached the conclusion that the annual inflation rate will exceed 4% in about 6 months. The Board of Governors deems this too high to be tolerated and feels that immediate action is required. Discuss what the Fed is likely to do. Demonstrate how the Fed's actions will affect interest rates using the loanable funds framework. (Extension 5.1)

PROBLEMS

1. Consider the following scenario. Customers have made deposits of $2,000, and the bank also has $3,000 in capital, $2,500 in government securities, and $2,500 in cash. If the Federal Reserve has set the reserve requirement at 10%, what is the most money the bank can lend out? (Assume the funds are *not* redeposited into the bank.)

2. If the Fed buys $1,000,000 in bonds from banks and the reserve requirement is 10%, how much could this increase in reserves increase the money supply?

3. The actual increase in the money supply in Problem 2 will probably be less than the answer you found. Explain why.

4. If the Fed sells $250 million in securities and the reserve requirement is 3%, what will be the change in the money supply? (Be sure to note whether it will increase or decrease.)

WEB EXPLORATION

1. The Federal Open Market Committee (FOMC) meets about every 6 weeks to discuss the state of the economy and to decide what actions the central bank should take. The minutes of these meetings are released after the next scheduled meeting; however, a brief press release is made available immediately. Find the schedule of minutes and press releases at www.federalreserve.gov/fomc/.
    a. When was the last scheduled meeting of the FOMC?
    b. Review the press release from that meeting. What did the committee decide to do about short-term interest rates?
    c. Review the most recently published meeting minutes. What areas of the economy seemed to be of most concern to the committee members?

2. The Beige Book is published for public review. Go to the site listed above and find the Beige Book. What does it contain?

3. The Federal Reserve offers jobs and internships to business graduates. Go to www.federalreserve.gov/default.htm/ and click on the career opportunities link. Find the job that most appeals to you and report the following:
    a. Job title
    b. Job description
    c. Salary range

MINI CASE

You have been assigned as a research assistant to the most recently appointed member of the Board of Governors of the Federal Reserve System, Dr. Bello. Dr. Bello is a highly regarded economist from the University of Columbia who has a firm grasp of monetary policy and its implementation. Your work to date has been more focused on financial analysis of troubled banks and you feel unprepared for the meeting scheduled with him for tomorrow to discuss the upcoming FOMC meeting. While you do not expect to become an economist overnight, you do wish to familiarize yourself with some of the topics he is likely to bring up.

a. Your first step is to learn what took place at the most recent FOMC meeting. Find and summarize in one short paragraph the contents of the press release (available at www.federalreserve.gov//fomc/).

b. You decide that the press release is too brief to give you a good idea of what the board was discussing. To get more information, review the most recently published

FOMC minutes and summarize the major issues of concern to the Fed.

c. You remember from your finance class that the Fed seemed to be very concerned about the level of inflation. Find the most recent inflation figures and determine whether you feel inflation is currently a serious problem. Consumer price data can be found at ftp://ftp.bls.gov/pub/special.requests/cpi/cpiai.txt. (See the Mini Case from Chapter 2 for a discussion on how to move this data into a spreadsheet.)

d. Identify factors that you think may lead to increased inflation. For each of these factors, discuss whether the situation is improving or deteriorating.

e. Based on your analysis, what action do you think the FOMC should take at its next meeting?

f. What actions do you think the FOMC may need to take sometime over the next year?

PART II

Investments

The Time Value of Money

Chapter Objectives

By the end of this chapter you should be able to:

1. Compute how much a sum deposited today will grow to in the future
2. Compute the value today of a sum you will not receive until some future date
3. Compute how much a series of equal payments will grow to over time
4. Compute the value today of a series of equal payments
5. Apply the time value of money methods to answer a variety of questions

When plumbers or carpenters tackle a job, they begin by opening their toolboxes, which hold a variety of specialized tools to help them perform their jobs. The financial manager also needs a toolbox in order to perform the job. In this chapter we begin to fill the toolbox with the skills required to solve many of the financial problems faced by businesses and investors. The particular tools learned here will be applied extensively throughout the text.

The title of this chapter, "The Time Value of Money," implies that money has different values at different times. This point can be demonstrated by asking yourself whether you would rather have $100 now or a year from now. You probably answered that you would rather have it now. But suppose you know that you really do not need it until next year. You would still rather have it now because you could invest the $100 and have more than $100 in 1 year. The point is that your preference depends on when the $100 is received. You probably do not care too much whether the money is paid today or tomorrow, but you probably have a strong preference for receiving it now rather than in 10 years. This means that there will be a small difference in value if the delay in payment is short, but a large difference if the delay is long.

The time value of money (TVM) depends on the investment opportunities that could be taken if the money were currently available. However, another factor also influences the TVM. Chapter 1 noted that not all cash flows are known with certainty. Future cash flows are subject to fluctuations that can only be estimated in advance. Consider your preference for receiving funds now rather than later. In addition to the fact that you could invest them, it is also possible that the future cash flow may not actually materialize. The fluctuations inherent in business enterprises mean that the money may not be available as promised. With this in mind, it makes sense that the riskier the cash flows, the greater your preference for receiving them now.

Recall that one of the assumptions introduced in Chapter 1 is that the value of money depends on when it is received. In this chapter you will learn to compute precisely how the value of money changes over time. You will use these methods repeatedly throughout the balance of the text. In fact, *of all the tools you will acquire in this course, an understanding of the TVM is the most important.* There are many self-test questions in this chapter. It is important that you have your calculator out to work these problems as you read through each topic. If you are unable to work the self-test problems, go back and review the topic again before proceeding to new material.

BASICS OF THE TIME VALUE OF MONEY

Graphing Time

Sometimes the English language is less precise, or at least not as efficient, as we might like. For example, what does it mean to say that you received $100 per year for 5 years? Did the money arrive at the beginning, the end, or in the middle of each year? A simple tool to solve this problem is the **time line,** a graphic representation of cash flows. Review the following diagram:

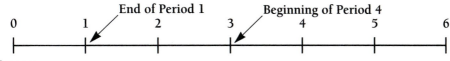

Time 0 is the present. It is also the beginning of the first period. Time 3 is the end of the third and the beginning of the fourth period.

The interval between ticks on the time line can be years, months, weeks, or even days. The cash flow that occurs at each interval is written directly on the time line.

Suppose you will receive $100 at the beginning of period 1 and at the end of period 4. These cash flows are placed on the following time line:

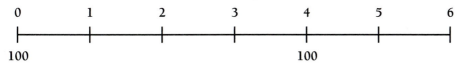

Study Tip

Be particularly careful when putting the cash flows given in a word problem onto a time line. If the problem says the cash flow occurs at the end of the time period, do not put it at the beginning of that time period.

Study Tip

Pay attention to the difference between points in time and periods of time. The numbers on our time line represent points in time, but growth in the value of money occurs during the intervals between the points.

Study Tip

Many students are reluctant to use time lines when solving TVM problems. Although they do take a few extra moments to draw, you will find this time is well spent. Skipping this step often results in having to redo problems because you did the computations using the wrong number of time periods.

If an interest rate is specified, it is placed between the tick marks as in the following diagram:

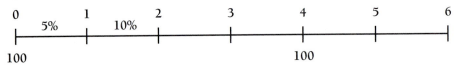

In this example, the interest rate is 5% during period 1 and 10% during periods 2 through 4. By convention, you do not need to repeat the interest rate between each interval.

The sign of the cash flow is used to indicate whether the cash flow is a cash inflow or a cash outflow. Inflows, cash you receive, have a positive sign (typically the + sign is dropped), as implied in the above examples. A cash outflow, cash you spend, has a negative sign, as shown in the following time line:

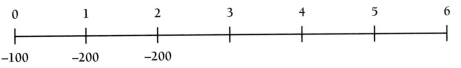

In this example, a $100 investment is made at the beginning of the first period and $200 investments are made at the beginning of the second and third periods.

Time lines are useful as an aid to solving TVM problems. They can help keep you organized, especially when the cash flows become complex. Even experienced finance professors rely on them to help visualize problems. To practice using them, we will show how to use time lines as we solve several of the examples in this chapter.

Compound Interest

Simple returns do not earn interest on reinvested interest. A balance is deposited and at the end of the investment period, interest is computed and paid. In the following example, we compute the simple interest earned on a deposit.

E X A M P L E 6.1   Simple Interest

Compute the simple interest earned on a 1-year $100 deposit that earns 5% per year.

Solution

The interest is computed as the principal amount multiplied by the interest rate:

$$\text{Interest} = \$100 \times 0.05 = \$5$$

Simple interest is easy to compute and understand, but most of the time, we want our interest payments to be reinvested. For example, if you put money into a savings account, the bank automatically deposits the monthly or quarterly interest payments back into the account so that during subsequent periods interest is earned on a higher balance. This is an example of **compound interest,** which is interest earned on interest. Virtually all of the calculations performed in finance require compound interest calculations. We will begin our study of compound interest by finding future balances.

FUTURE VALUE OF A SUM

Annual Compounding

If you make a $100 deposit into a bank that pays 5% interest once per year, you will have $105 at the end of one year. We call the amount we have today the **present value** and the future balance the **future value.** In this case, we found the future value by multiplying the $100 by one plus the interest rate $(1 + i)$. Where did the "1" come from? The "1" adds the original balance back to the interest that has been earned to give the total balance in the account. The formula for computing the balance after one period is

$$FV_1 = PV_0(1 + i)$$
$$\$105 = \$100(1 + 0.05)$$

The process of computing a future balance is called **compounding** because the investor is earning compound interest. Notice the use of the subscripts in the above formula. The subscript denotes the point on the time line when the cash flow occurs.

Now suppose that you leave the above deposit in the bank to compound for another year without withdrawing any money. Using the above formula, the balance grows to $110.25:

$$FV_2 = FV_1(1 + i)$$
$$\$110.25 = \$105(1 + 0.05)$$

During the first year the account earned $5, but during the second year it earned $5.25. The extra $0.25 was from the interest earned on the first period's interest. We can simplify these calculations by noting that FV_1 is equal to $PV_0(1 + i)$. By substituting $PV_0(1 + i)$ for FV_1 into the above equation, we get

$$FV_2 = PV_0(1 + i)(1 + i)$$
$$FV_2 = PV_0(1 + i)^2$$
$$\$110.25 = \$100(1 + 0.05)^2$$

If the funds are left untouched for a third year, the balance continues to grow:

$$FV_3 = FV_2(1 + i)$$
$$\$115.76 = \$110.25(1.05)$$

Again, by substituting $PV_0(1 + i)^2$ for FV_2, we get

$$FV_3 = PV_0(1 + i)(1 + i)^2$$
$$FV_3 = PV_0(1 + i)^3$$
$$\$115.76 = \$100(1.05)^3$$

Similarly, each subsequent period of compounding increases the exponent by one. The generalized equation for finding the future value of a deposit is given as

$$FV_n = PV_0(1 + i)^n \qquad (6.1)$$

Study Tip

Note the subscripts on the FV and PV variables. These subscripts refer to the time periods. PV_0 means the PV at time 0. FV_1 refers to the FV at time 1.

where

> FV_n = the future value of a deposit at the end of the *n*th period
> PV_0 = the initial deposit made at time 0
> i = the interest rate earned during each period
> n = the number of periods the deposit is allowed to compound

Let us illustrate with an example.

E X A M P L E 6.2   Future Value, Beginning-of-Period Deposit

What will the balance be in an account if $1,500 is deposited and allowed to compound for 20 years at 8% with interest being paid annually? How much interest will be earned on the original deposit?

Solution
Substituting these figures into Equation 6.1,

$$FV_n = PV_0(1 + i)^n$$
$$FV_{20} = \$1,500(1.08)^{20}$$
$$FV_{20} = \$1,500(4.66) = \$6,991.44$$

The balance at the end of 20 years will be $6,991.44.
To find the interest earned, we subtract the principal (the original amount) from the ending balance:[1]

$$\text{Interest earned} = FV - PV$$
$$\text{Interest earned} = \$6,991.44 - \$1,500 = \$5,491.44$$

If simple interest, rather than compound interest, had been earned in Example 6.2, $120 per year would have been earned ($1,500 × 0.08 = $120). Twenty times $120 is only $2,400. So $3,091.44 was earned because of compounding ($5,491.44 − $2,400 = $3,091.44). Put another way, $3,091.44 in interest was earned on interest. In this example, more interest was earned on the interest than was earned on the original principal balance! *This is the power of compounding.*

Not all deposits are made at the present time. We sometimes need to compute future balances on deposits that will be made in the future. The method does not change. Simply count the intervals between when the deposit is made and the ending point on the time line to determine the number of periods.

---

[1]It is easy to compute the value of a sum raised to any exponent by using the **Yˣ** key on your financial calculator. In the example given, first enter 1.08 and then press the **Yˣ** key. Next enter the number of periods for which compounding will occur, in this case 20. Now press the **=** key. You should get 4.6610. If your calculator only shows two digits to the right of the decimal, you may want to format it. On the TI BA-II Plus you do this by pressing the **2nd** button and then **Format**. Now enter the number of decimal places you want to see and press **Enter**.

EXAMPLE 6.3   Future Value, End-of-Period Deposit

If a deposit of $100 is made at the end of the current period, what will be the balance in the account at the end of the fifth period if interest is paid annually at 5%?

Solution

To solve this problem, begin by drawing a time line. Note that the initial $100 investment is given a negative sign because it is a cash outflow (money is going from your pocket into an investment):

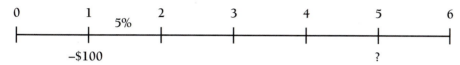

To find the number of compounding periods (*n*), count the intervals during which the deposit can grow. There is one interval between 1 and 2, another between 2 and 3, a third between 3 and 4, and a fourth between periods 4 and 5. Because there are four intervals, *n* = 4. Using Equation 6.1 we find

$$FV_n = PV_1(1 + i)^n$$

$$FV_4 = \$100(1.05)^4$$

$$FV_4 = \$100(1.21) = \$121.55$$

Study Tip

Pay attention to the terminology used in Example 6.3. The initial deposit was made at the end of the first period, yet we still called it the *present value*. The cash flow farthest to the left on the time line is always the PV. The cash flow to the right is always the FV.

Self-Test Review Questions*

1. You are about to graduate from college at the age of 22. You just learned that your grandfather invested $10,000 in your name when you were born and it is available for you to withdraw today. If the stock market earned an average 12% over the last 22 years, how much should be in the account today?
2. Suppose that instead of investing the $10,000 in the stock market, your grandfather invested it in Treasury bonds, which averaged 5.5%. How much would the investment be worth today?

Nonannual Compounding Periods

In the above examples, interest was paid once per year. This is called **annual compounding.** Often, interest is paid more often than once per year. Most bank accounts, for example, pay interest every month. We must adjust our formula to allow for any interest payment schedule that may arise.

Semiannual compounding occurs when interest is paid every 6 months. To compute the future value under semiannual compounding, recognize that the exponent in the formula for future value is the number of *periods,* not the number of years. Similarly, the interest rate is the interest paid during the *period,* not the annual interest rate. In the last

Study Tip

If you skipped the Self-Test Review Questions, *stop* and go back! It is critical that you read this chapter with calculator in hand and work each example and self-test question as they occur.

section, when we were discussing annual compounding, each period was 1 year so n equaled the number of years and i was the annual interest rate. If we want to compute the future value when each period is 6 months long, we must adjust n and i to reflect the number of 6-month periods and the interest paid during each 6-month period. This is demonstrated by the following time lines:

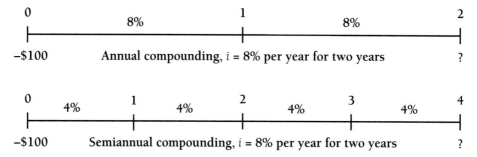

Suppose that you deposit $100 for 2 years, and the bank pays interest semiannually at an annual rate of 8%. There are four 6-month periods in 2 years, so n must be multiplied by 2. If the interest rate is 8% for 1 year, then 4% is being paid every 6 months. Substituting these figures into Equation 6.1, we have

$$FV_n = PV_0(1 + i)^n$$
$$FV_2 = \$100(1.04)^4 = \$116.99$$

Notice that the balance at the end of two years is $0.35 higher under semiannual compounding than it would be with annual compounding [$100(1.08)^2 = \$116.64]$.

To adjust to semiannual compounding, we multiplied the number of years (n) by the number of periods per year (m) and we divided the annual interest rate by the number of periods per year. Equation 6.2 shows how to adjust for any number of compounding periods per year:

$$FV_n = PV\left(1 + \frac{i}{m}\right)^{mn} \tag{6.2}$$

where

FV_n = the future value of a deposit at the end of the nth year
PV = the initial deposit
i = the annual interest rate
n = the number of years the deposit is allowed to compound
m = the number of times compounding occurs during the year

E X A M P L E 6.4   Multiple Compounding Periods

What is the future value of a $1,500 deposit after 20 years, with an annual interest rate of 8%, compounded quarterly?

Solution
Substituting these numbers into Equation 6.2,

$$FV_n = PV\left(1 + \frac{i}{m}\right)^{mn}$$

$$FV_{20} = \$1,500\left(1 + \frac{0.08}{4}\right)^{4\times20} = \$1,500(1+0.02)^{80} = \$7,313.16$$

In Example 6.2 we found that \$1,500 deposited for 20 years at 8% compounded annually grew to \$6,991.44. It turns out that the more frequently interest is paid, the greater is the future value. Now review Figure 6.1. This figure shows the future value of \$100 at 12% compounded at different frequencies. The increase in future value from additional compounding periods increases at a decreasing rate because the length of the compound periods is getting smaller.

The last column shows the future value, assuming continuous compounding. In this case we assume that the number of compounding periods increases into infinity.[2]

Effective Interest Rates

If the bank increases the number of compounding periods, the amount earned on a deposit increases. This implies that a higher **effective interest rate** (EIR) is being earned. The effective interest rate is the amount you would need to earn with annual compounding to be as well off as you are with multiple compounding periods per year. To determine the exact effective interest rate, given multiple compounding periods per year, we find the FV of \$1 after 1 year and then subtract the initial dollar. What is left is the earnings for the year, which equals the effective interest rate. The FV of \$1 is found by applying Equation 6.2 with PV = 1 and n = 1. The effective rate is computed by subtracting 1. Equation 6.3 computes the effective interest rate:

$$\text{Effective rate} = \left(1 + \frac{i}{m}\right)^m - 1 \tag{6.3}$$

---

[2]The formula for computing the future value, assuming continuous compounding, is $FV_n = PV \times e^{in}$, where e = 2.71828, i = annual interest rate, and n = number of years.

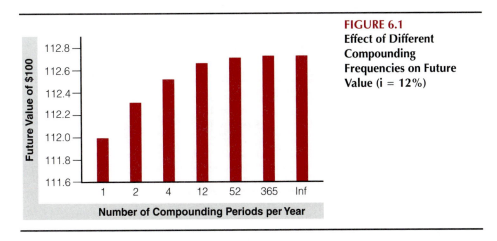

FIGURE 6.1
Effect of Different Compounding Frequencies on Future Value (i = 12%)

Future Value of $100

Number of Compounding Periods per Year

EXAMPLE 6.5   Effective Interest Rate Calculation

What is the effective rate of interest if 12% is compounded monthly?

Solution
Applying Equation 6.3 and substituting the numbers, we get

$$\text{Effective rate} = \left(1 + \frac{0.12}{12}\right)^{12} - 1 = 0.1268 = 12.68\%$$

Study Tip

Be sure to use the decimal equivalent when computing effective rates. For example, enter .08 into your calculator—for an 8% interest rate.

This result is interpreted to mean that an annually compounded interest rate of 12.68% is equivalent to earning a 12% annual rate that is compounded 12 times per year. Table 6.1 shows the effective rate at different compounding intervals when the annual rate is 12%. As in Figure 6.1, we see that the effective rate increases at a decreasing rate.

Investors are more interested in the effective rate of interest than they are in the annual rate. Suppose that you were attempting to choose between two bank savings accounts. The first pays 5% compounded annually and the second pays 4.9% compounded monthly. Which would you prefer? To answer this, you must compute the effective rate of each alternative and pick the largest one. The effective rate of the first is unchanged, 5%. The effective rate of the second is 5.01%, so you would choose the bank offering 4.9% compounded monthly.

Self-Test Review Questions*

1. What is the future value of $2,000 invested for 20 years with quarterly compounding at 8%?
2. What is the effective rate of 8% compounded quarterly?

Using Financial Tables

In working the examples above, we needed to compute exponents. Many calculators have this function available. An alternative way to solve TVM problems is to use tables

TABLE 6.1 Effective Interest Rates with 12% Annual Rate

Compounding Interval	Equation 6.3	Effective Rate
Annual	$FV = (1.12)^1 - 1$	12.00%
Semiannual	$FV = (1.06)^2 - 1$	12.36
Quarterly	$FV = (1.03)^4 - 1$	12.55
Monthly	$FVC = (1.01)^{12} - 1$	12.68
Weekly	$FV = (1.0023)^{52} - 1$	12.73
Daily	$FV = (1.0003288)^{365} - 1$	12.7475
Continuously	$FV = e^{0.12} - 1$	12.7496

*1. $FV = \$2,000(1.02)^{80} = \$9,750.88$.
2. Effective rate $= (1 + 0.02)^4 - 1 = 8.24\%$.

TABLE 6.2 Future Value Interest Factors (FVIF)

n	4%	5%	6%	7%	8%	9%	10%
3	1.125	1.158	1.191	1.225	1.260	1.295	**1.331**
4	1.170	1.216	1.162	1.311	1.260	1.412	1.464
5	1.217	1.276	1.338	1.403	1.469	1.539	1.611

that have worked a portion of the problem for you. Review Equation 6.1, $FV_n = PV_0(1 + i)^n$. This equation is sometimes written as

$$FV_n = PV_0(FVIF_{n,i}) \qquad (6.4)$$

$FVIF_{n,i}$ is the *future value interest factor,* and it is reported in tables at the end of the text and on the inside of the front cover. $FVIF_{n,i}$ is *equal to* $(1 + i)^n$. The tables contain factors for commonly used values of i and n. A portion of Table A.1, found in the Appendix, is reproduced in Table 6.2. To find the FVIF for $n = 3$ and $i = 10\%$, look down the left column until you find 3. Then look across the top row until you find 10%. The row and column intersect at **1.331.**

E X A M P L E 6.6   Future Value Using FVIF Table

Use the FVIF table to find the future value of $100 deposited at 10% for five periods with annual compounding.

Solution

The $FVIF_{5,10\%} = 1.611$. Substituting this into Equation 6.4, we get

$$FV_5 = \$100(FVIF_{5,10\%})$$
$$FV_5 = \$100(1.611) = \$161.10$$

This result can be verified by using Equation 6.1:

$$FV_5 = \$100(1.10)^5 = \$161.05$$

The results of using the table and the formula are close, but not exactly the same. The table rounds to the nearest three decimal places, whereas your calculator will probably use at least eight decimal places when the formula is applied.

Using a Financial Calculator

Financial calculators are available today at very reasonable prices and can ease solving many types of time value problems. It is best to begin by learning to solve the problems using the equations, then to progress to using the calculator. By using the formulas, you learn to adjust for nonannual compounding and other issues that will surface later in the chapter. These issues do not disappear when you begin using a calculator.

A financial calculator is distinguished by a row of buttons that correspond to the inputs to TVM problems. The five most common buttons are

Study Tip

Many students experience frustration trying to use financial calculators. Additionally, they often make errors when using them on exams. The only way to get past this problem is to work many problems using both financial calculators and the equations. If your answers do not match, it is almost always due to the issues discussed in this section.

where

$$N = \text{the number of periods}$$
$$I = \text{the interest rate per period}$$
$$PV = \text{the present value or the initial deposit}$$
$$PMT = \text{the payment (this button is used only when there is more than one equal}$$
$$\text{payment)}$$
$$FV = \text{the future value}$$

These buttons appear either on the face of the calculator or on the calculator's screen.

There are a few common errors students make when using financial calculators. First, be sure that the number of compounding periods is set correctly. The default is usually 12 periods per year. If the number of periods is set to 12 periods per year, the calculator divides the interest rate by 12 before performing calculations. Most new calculators are preprogrammed to divide the interest rate by 12. Additionally, whenever the batteries are replaced the calculator will revert to dividing by 12. (Check your calculator now and set it to one period per year. Refer to your owner's manual.)[3]

A second common error pertains to the assumption the calculator makes regarding the timing of cash flows. A cash flow can arrive at the beginning or at the end of a period. Most calculators have a way of setting the mode to match the timing. Be sure this mode is set correctly.

There is no consensus regarding whether it is best for students of finance to use calculators, equations, or tables to learn to solve TVM problems. With this in mind, this chapter will show some examples solved all three ways.

Accumulating a Future Balance

Another application of future value is computing the initial deposit required to accumulate a future balance. Suppose you want to have $5,000 in your bank account at the end of 10 years. If you can earn 5% annually, how much must you deposit today? To solve a problem like this, begin by writing down the formula for future value, then plug in the values that you know. For example,

$$FV_n = PV_0(1 + i)^n$$

The future value amount must be $5,000, so

$$\$5,000 = PV(1 + 0.05)^{10}$$

Now solve for PV:

$$\$5,000/(1.05)^{10} = PV$$
$$\$3,069.57 = PV$$

If you deposit $3,069.57 today in an account that pays 5% annually, you will have a balance of $5,000 at the end of 10 years. (Of course, if you invested in the stock market and earned 12% rather than 5%, your future balance would be $9,533.62 [$3,069.57(1.12)^{10} = \$9,533.62$] instead of $5,000.)[4]

---

[3]To check the number of periods on the TI BA-II plus press the **2nd** key and then the **I/Y** button. Your calculator should display P/Y = 1.00. If not, enter 1 on the keypad and press **Enter**.

[4]The stock market has earned an average of 12% per year over the last 65 years. In some years it suffered losses and in others it earned substantially more than 12%.

A similar application of future value is computing the change in purchasing power due to inflation.

E X A M P L E 6.7   Inflation Adjustment

How much will you need in 20 years to have the same purchasing power that $100 has today, if inflation averages 3% per year?

Solution

This example is a little different from the others in this section because there is no deposit and no future balance to calculate. On the other hand, the concept of future value applies. The $100 will be compounded at 3% for 20 years. To find the equivalent future amount, you can use any of the following methods.
Equation solution:

$$FV_n = PV_1(1 + i)^n$$
$$FV_{20} = \$100(1.03)^{20}$$
$$FV_{20} = \$180.61$$

Table solution:

$$FV_n = PV_1(FVIF_{i,n})$$
$$FV_{20} = \$100(1.806) = \$180.60$$

Calculator solution:

= $180.60

If an item costs $100 today and inflation averages 3%, the item will cost approximately $180.60 in 20 years.

Self-Test Review Question*

Suppose that you are trying to decide when you will be able to retire. You decide that if you have the equivalent annual spending power given by $50,000 today, you will be happy. You realize that with inflation you will actually need more than $50,000 every year during your retirement. If you plan to retire in 35 years and if you estimate that inflation will average 4% per year, how much will you need during your first year of retirement?

Solving for Number of Periods and Interest Rates

In all of the examples shown so far we have used the basic future value equation to solve for how much a deposit today can grow to in the future. There are occasions, however, when we already know both the future and present values and want to solve for one of the other variables in the equation. For example, we may want to know how long it will take to accumulate a future balance given a known interest rate and initial deposit. We may want to solve for what average compounded rate of interest has been earned if we know how long a deposit has been invested and its current balance.

Solving for these different variables is not difficult. Simply identify the future and present value amounts and at least one other variable and plug them into Equation 6.1 or 6.4. Use algebra to solve the equation for the unknown variable. In the next example we solve for the interest rate.

E X A M P L E 6.8   Future Value, Solving for i

Just as you were about to enter college you learned that a great aunt had established a college trust fund for you when you were born 20 years ago. She deposited $5,000 initially. If the balance is now $19,348.42, what average compounded rate of return has been earned?

Solution
This problem can be solved most easily using either financial factor tables or a financial table.

Table solution:

$$FV_n = PV_0(FVIF_{i,n})$$
$$FV_{20} = PV_0(FVIF_{i,20})$$
$$\$19{,}348.42 = \$5{,}000(FVIF_{i,20})$$
$$3.8697 = (FVIF_{i,20})$$

Now go to the FVIF table and look for the FVIF equal to 3.8697 on the row corresponding to 20 periods. When you find the factor, look at the top of the column to determine the interest rate. In this example the interest rate is 7%. The trouble with solving these types of problems using the factor tables is that if the investment rate is not a round number, you will not be able to determine the exact answer.

Calculator solution:

|20| | −$5000 | 0 | $19,348.42 |
| N | I | PV | PMT | FV |

$$= 7\%$$

Notice that the sign on the $5,000 initial deposit is negative and the sign on the future value is positive. Some calculators require that the signs be different. Other calculators require that the signs be the same. You will have to experiment with yours to see which method works.

Equation solution:

$$FV = PV(1 + i)^n$$
$$\$19{,}348.42 = \$5{,}000(1 + i)^{20}$$
$$3.86968 = (1 + i)^{20}$$
$$\sqrt[20]{3.86968} = (1 + i)$$
$$i = \sqrt[20]{3.86968} - 1$$
$$i = 1.0700 - 1$$
$$i = 7\%$$

You will have an opportunity to solve TVM problems for the unknown interest rate in Example 6.22.

Intuition Behind Compounding

It is important that the student of finance develop an understanding of how the compounding process works beyond simply applying the equations. Two things should be noted. First, as the *number of compounding periods increases,* the future balance increases. Second, as the *interest rate increases,* the future balance increases. Figure 6.2 shows how the future balance changes given different interest rates and number of compounding periods.

One of the more important features of TVM calculations is that the methods can be applied to anything that grows. In Example 6.7 we showed how the effects of inflation were computed. We can also use the same equations to find future sales, if sales grow at a constant rate. We can estimate future stock dividends as well, if dividends are assumed to grow at a constant rate. The method can be applied to any constant growth situation, whether it be money, sales, profits, populations, or trees.

Self-Test Review Questions*

1. If sales are currently $1,000 per year and are expected to grow at 5%, what are the projected sales 5 years in the future?
2. If the U.S. population is 273 million today and is projected to grow at 3% per year, what will the population be in 35 years?[5]

---

*1. $1,000(1.05)^5 = \$1,276.28.$
2. $273,000,000(1.03)^{35} = 768,184,450.$

---

[5]We can compute the average compounded growth rate between 1990 and 1999 as well. www.ameristat.org/estproj/basics.htm shows the 1990 U.S. population as 249 million. This data gives us a 1.03% annual growth rate.

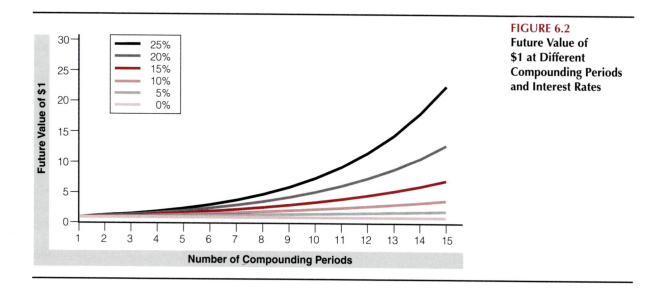

FIGURE 6.2
Future Value of $1 at Different Compounding Periods and Interest Rates

FUTURE VALUE OF AN ANNUITY

In the last section, we computed the future balance of a single deposit or sum. Often, many equal deposits or payments are made. For example, you may make equal monthly deposits into a retirement account. You could find the future value of these deposits by computing the future value of each one separately and then adding them together, but this becomes tedious if there are many deposits. An easier way involves using annuities.

What Is an Annuity?

An **annuity** is a series of equal payments made at equal intervals. Despite being called annuities, annuity payments do not have to be made annually. They can be made monthly, weekly, or even daily. The critical factors are that the payments equal each other and that the interval between each one is the same.

An annuity in which payments are made at the *end* of each period is an **ordinary annuity.** For example, deposits to a retirement account typically are made at the end of each month when you get paid. An annuity in which payments are made at the *beginning* of each period is an **annuity due.** Apartment rental payments usually are due at the beginning of the month, so the annuity is called an annuity due. ***Ordinary annuities are more common than annuities due (as the term implies), so in this book, the annuity may be assumed to be ordinary unless otherwise specified.***

Computing the Future Value of an Ordinary Annuity

Suppose that you want to know the future balance in your account after 3 years if you make three equal annual deposits that each earn 10%. To solve this problem using Equation 6.1 you would find the future value of each deposit, then add them together:

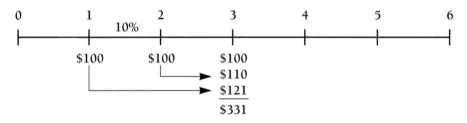

Notice that this is an ordinary annuity because the cash flows are received at the end of the period. Also note that the last payment does not earn any interest. In other words, the last payment is deposited and the balance in the account is immediately checked.

If the total future value is the sum of the future values of the individual payments, the following equation applies:

$$FV_{\text{ordinary annuity}} = PMT_1 + PMT_2(1 + i) + PMT_3(1 + i)^2$$
$$+ \cdots + PMT_n(1 + i)^{n-1}$$
$$FV_{\text{annuity}} = PMT \sum_{t=1}^{n} (1 + i)^{n-t} \qquad (6.5)$$

Unfortunately, Equation 6.5 is not much help in solving annuity problems. Students of algebra will recognize that Equation 6.5 is a geometric progression for which standardized solutions have been found. Annuity problems are best solved using either the tables or a financial calculator because the formulas are fairly complex.[6] (The solutions are listed in Appendix A, Table A.2.)

Financial tables compute the value of

$$\sum_{t=1}^{n} (1 + i)^{n-t}$$

These values are called the future value interest factor of an annuity (FVIFA).

If the financial tables are to be used to solve annuities, the formula becomes

$$FV_{\text{annuity}} = PMT(FVIFA_{i,n}) \qquad (6.6)$$

where

PMT = the equal payment made at regular intervals
$FVIFA_{i,n}$ = the future value interest factor of an annuity from Table A.2

E X A M P L E 6.9   FV of Ordinary Annuity, Accumulating a Nest Egg

Suppose that you win the lottery. The winnings consist of 20 equal annual payments of $50,000. You decide to save all of this money for your retirement, and deposit it into an account that earns 8% per year. What is the amount of your retirement nest egg?

Solution
Using the financial tables and applying Equation 6.6, we get

$$FV_{\text{annuity}} = PMT(FVIFA_{i,n})$$
$$FV_{20} = \$50,000(FVIFA_{8\%,20})$$
$$FV_{20} = \$50,000(45.762) = \$2,288,100$$

Calculator solution:

20	8	0	−$50,000	
N	I	PV	PMT	FV

= $2,288,098.21

---

[6]The factors in Table A.2 are the sum of the geometric progression. The formula is

$$FVIFA_{i,n} = \frac{(1 + i)^n - 1}{i}$$

Fortunately, just as compounding makes the effects of inflation seem severe, compounding makes it easier to reach a future goal. Let us look at an example that shows how small regular deposits can accumulate large ending balances.

Study Tip

Without exception, the number of periods in an annuity is equal to the number of payments received. This is true even if payments do not start for several periods. The factors in the tables and the algorithms in the calculators assume that n payments are actually made.

E X A M P L E 6.10   FV of Ordinary Annuity, Computing Future Balances

Because we cannot depend on winning the lottery, we must prepare for our retirement with our own funds. What will be in your retirement account after 35 years if you make $2,000 annual deposits that earn (a) 10%, (b) 5%, and (c) 12%?

Solution

Again, we can use the financial tables and apply Equation 6.6, with (a) $i = 10\%$, (b) $i = 5\%$, and (c) $i = 12\%$.

(a) If $i = 10\%$,

$$FV_{annuity} = PMT(FVIFA_{i,n})$$
$$FV_{35} = \$2,000(FVIFA_{10\%,35})$$
$$FV_{35} = \$2,000(271.024) = \$542,048$$

Calculator solution:

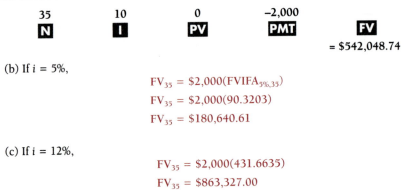

(b) If $i = 5\%$,

$$FV_{35} = \$2,000(FVIFA_{5\%,35})$$
$$FV_{35} = \$2,000(90.3203)$$
$$FV_{35} = \$180,640.61$$

(c) If $i = 12\%$,

$$FV_{35} = \$2,000(431.6635)$$
$$FV_{35} = \$863,327.00$$

To solve with $i = 5\%$ and 12% using the calculator, input the variables as you did for 10%, then input $i = 5\%$ and compute FV. Then input $i = 12\%$ and compute FV.

Not all annuities begin with the current period. We sometimes have a delay before the annuity begins paying. For example, if you start a business, it may not begin making a profit for several years. The next example demonstrates how to compute the future value of a **deferred annuity**.

E X A M P L E 6.11   Deferred Annuity

In 2 years you will begin receiving an annual payment of $500 that will be made for 3 years. If the annual interest rate is 10%, what will be the balance in your account at the end of the fourth year?

Solution

Begin by drawing a time line:

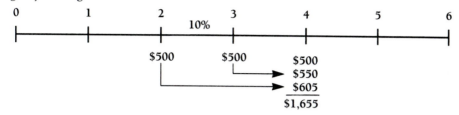

The first $500 deposit compounds for two periods. The second deposit compounds for one period, and the final deposit does not earn any interest. To solve this problem using tables, find the $FVIFA_{10\%,3}$:

$$FV_5 = \$500(FVIFA_{10\%,3}) = \$1,655.00$$

Notice that even though we are computing the balance at the end of the fourth period, we looked up the *three-period* annuity. This is because *three payments* were made.

Computing the Future Value of an Annuity Due

As we noted earlier, sometimes cash flows occur at the *beginning* of a time period rather than at the end. When an annuity's payments occur at the beginning of each period, we call the cash flows an annuity due. The following time line shows a three-period annuity due:

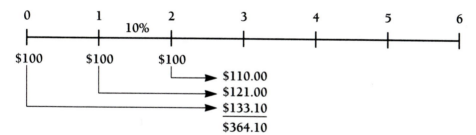

Compare this time line with the one shown for a three-period ordinary annuity. Each cash flow earns interest one period longer in this example. For instance, the final cash flow is compounded one period whereas the ordinary annuity's final cash flow is not compounded at all. Similarly, the first and second cash flows are compounded for one more period.

The tables at the end of the book for computing future values and the default settings on your calculators all assume ordinary annuities with end-of-period cash flows. Most of the time you will want to use either tables or a calculator to solve annuity problems, even if it is an annuity due. ***To compute the future value of an annuity due, multiply the future value of an ordinary annuity by (1+i). This compounds the cash flows for one more period.***

> **Study Tip**
>
> An ordinary annuity is just an annuity due that has been deferred for one period.

EXAMPLE 6.12   Annuity Due

Compute the future value of the annuity due shown on the above time line, assuming i = 10%.

Solution
The future value of a three-period ordinary annuity of $100 is found by multiplying $100 times the FVIFA$_{10\%,3}$:

$$FV_{ordinary\ annuity} = \$100 \times (3.31) = \$331$$

Now, multiply the result by 1.10:

$$FV_{annuity\ due} = FV_{ordinary\ annuity} \times (1 + i)$$
$$FV_{annuity\ due} = \$331 \times (1.10) = \$364.10$$

Study Tip

If you choose to change the mode of your calculator to compute annuities due, remember to change it back or all future annuity problems will be computed in that mode.

To solve this problem using a financial calculator, compute the future value as if the cash flows were for an ordinary annuity, then multiply by 1.10. An alternative calculator solution is to change your financial calculator from *end* to *begin* mode. The default mode on most calculators is *end*, which means that the calculator will treat the cash flows as if they occur at the end of each period. When the mode is switched to *begin*, the calculator treats the cash flows as if they occur at the beginning of each period. (Refer to your owner's manual for directions on how to change the mode of your particular calculator.)

Let us look at a slightly more complex example.

Study Tip

The tables and your calculator will compute the value of an annuity at the point in time when the *final payment of the annuity occurs*. In Example 6.13, this is at the end of period 5. Ordinary annuities always provide a value at this point. The annuity due adjustment simply computes the FV one period later.

EXAMPLE 6.13   Annuity Due

Cash flows of $1,500 occur at the beginning of periods 1, 2, 3, 4, 5, and 6. What is the future value of this cash flow at the end of period 6, assuming i = 10%?

Solution
First draw a time line as follows:

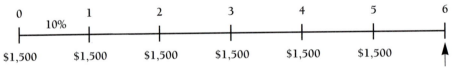

We want to compute the future value of the cash flows where the arrow points. We can do this by computing the future value of an ordinary annuity, which will give us the value at the end of period 5, and then multiplying by 1.10:

$$FV_{annuity\ due} = \$1,500(FVIFA_{10\%,6\ yr})(1.10)$$
$$FV_{annuity\ due} = \$1,500(7.716)(1.10) = \$12,731.40$$

PRESENT VALUE OF A SUM

Often we need to determine what the value is today of sums that will be received in the future. For example, if a firm is evaluating an investment that will generate future income, it must compare today's expenditures with expected future revenues. To compare sums across time, future values must be adjusted to what they are worth today.

There are many applications of present value methods. Assets are valued as the present value of the cash flows they generate. For example, stock is valued as the present value of the future cash flows the investor expects to receive, and bonds are valued as the present value of the interest payments plus the maturity payment. Capital investments are evaluated by subtracting the present value of cash expenditures from the present value of cash revenues generated by the investment. Loan payments are found by applying present value techniques. These applications make this section particularly important to grasp.

Luckily, if the concepts discussed under future value make sense, it will not be difficult to understand present value.

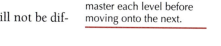

Study Tip

Go back and review future value concepts in this chapter if you have doubts about your understanding so far. TVM concepts build on one another. You must master each level before moving onto the next.

Present Value Equation

We already derived Equation 6.1, which establishes the future value of a deposit. Take another look at this equation:

$$FV_n = PV_0(1 + i)^n$$

Future value has been defined in terms of present value. To find the equation for computing present value, we only need to rearrange the terms in the above equation. If both sides are divided by $(1 + i)^n$, we get the equation for present value:

$$PV_0 = \frac{FV_n}{(1 + i)^n} \quad \text{or} \quad PV_0 = FV_n\left[\frac{1}{(1 + i)^n}\right] \tag{6.7}$$

The process of computing the present value of a future sum is called **discounting**. Remember that a future sum is not worth as much as a sum you have today. To convert future amounts to their present values, the future amount must be reduced, or *discounted*.

Study Tip

It is important to keep the terminology straight with regard to TVM. *Compounding* refers to the process of computing *future* values. *Discounting* refers to the process of computing *present* values. Further, the **discount rate** is the interest rate used when discounting.

E X A M P L E   6.14   Present Value

In 1 year John expects to receive $100 in repayment of a loan. He really needs the money now, however. How much would you give him today if he were to transfer the future payment to you? Assume that you have investment opportunities available at 10% that have similar risk.

Solution

You will pay John the present value of the future amount. Applying Equation 6.7,

$$PV_0 = \frac{FV_1}{(1 + i)^1}$$

$$PV_0 = \frac{\$100}{1.10} = \$90.91$$

You would pay $90.91 for the right to receive $100 in 1 year. You would pay this much because if you invested the $90.91 it would be worth $100 in one year:

$$\$90.91(1.10) = \$100$$

We are devoting a great deal of time to learning present value techniques. One reason for this emphasis is that many investment decisions are made by converting all relevant cash flows into present value terms. In the next example an investment opportunity is evaluated.

E X A M P L E 6.15   Present Value

Your great-grandmother has left you $100,000 in a trust fund that you cannot have for another 5 years. You have decided that you really need this money now to pay for your college expenses. You discuss your problem with your attorney, who offers you $75,000 for an assignment of the proceeds of the trust. If you can get a student loan at 8%, should you accept your attorney's offer?

Solution

This problem can be solved two ways. You can find the future value of $75,000 and see whether it is more or less than $100,000, or you can find the present value of the $100,000 and see whether it is more or less than the $75,000. Using the present value method,

$$PV_0 = \frac{FV_5}{(1 + i)^5}$$

$$PV_0 = \frac{\$100,000}{(1.08)^5} = \frac{\$100,000}{1.4693} = \$68,059.62$$

Because the $100,000 trust payment is worth only $68,059.62 to you today, you would be happy to receive $75,000 for it.

You can think of discounting as moving dollars to the left on the time line. Whenever dollars are moved to the left, their value gets smaller. The further to the left it moves and the higher the interest rate, the less the dollars are worth. Figure 6.3 shows the relationship between the interest rate, the number of periods, and the present value of $1.

Figure 6.3 shows that as you discount money by moving it backward in time (to the left on the time line) the value of $1 decreases. As always, if you compound money by investing it, the value of $1 increases.

FIGURE 6.3
Present Value of $1 at Different Discount Rates and Compounding Periods

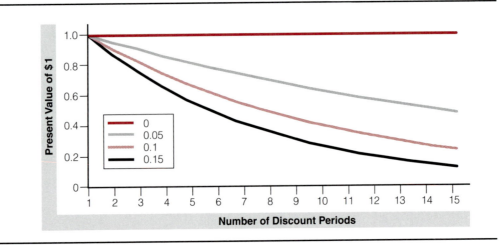

You do not always want to move cash flows all the way to time period 0. Present value calculations include moving future sums to any earlier period.

E X A M P L E 6.16   Present Value, Deferred Cash Flows

Compute the value of $100 at the end of the second period. Assume that it will be received at the end of the fourth period and there is a 10% interest rate.

Solution
Begin by drawing a time line:

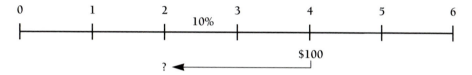

There are two periods for the $100 to discount. PV_2 is the value at the end of the second period, which is computed using Equation 6.7:

$$PV_2 = \frac{\$100}{(1.10)^2} = \$82.64$$

Using PVIF Tables

Financial tables have been computed to make present value calculations easier. Review the present value equation. The right-hand side can be separated into two terms:

$$PV = \frac{FV_n}{(1 + i)^n}$$

$$PV = FV_n \times \left[\frac{1}{(1 + i)^n} \right]$$

Table A.3 in the Appendix contains the expression in parentheses for various commonly used interest rates and periods. When the PV interest factors from the tables are used, the present value equation becomes

$$PV = FV_n(PVIF_{i,n}) \tag{6.8}$$

Study Tip

Students often use the wrong table when under the stress and time pressure of a test. There are two things you can do to combat this problem. When doing homework and studying examples, get used to the normal values of the factors. For example, PVIFs are always less than 1 and FVIFs are always greater than 1. Second, take a highlighter and label each table in broad 4-inch letters.

E X A M P L E 6.17   Present Value, Using Factors

What is the present value of a $500 sum that will be received in 6 years if the interest rate is 8%?

Solution
Using Equation 6.8 and Table A.3, we get

$$PV = \$500(PVIF_{8\%,6})$$

$$PV = \$500(0.630) = \$315.00$$

Intuition Behind Present Values

We will use the present value concept often throughout the balance of this course. It is important for your future success in finance that you understand the intuition behind the concept.

What does it mean that the present value of $100 to be received in 1 year at 10% is $90.91? *It means that you are indifferent which you get: the $90.91 today or the $100 in 1 year*. What if you do not really need the money today but expect to need it in 1 year? Then you can invest the $90.91 today and it will grow to be exactly $100 by the time you need it. The interest rate used to discount the $100 back to the present is selected so that you will be properly compensated for the risk that you may not be paid and for the delay in receiving the cash flow.

Still another way of defining present value is that if you have the present value of a future sum, *you can exactly match that future sum by investing what you have today at the discount rate*.

Present Value of Mixed Streams

Thus far, we have focused on computing the present value of a single, lump sum future cash flow. However, there are many occasions when you must find the present value of a series of *unequal cash flows*. For example, if you are evaluating an investment in a business, it is unlikely that each year's cash flows will be the same. To find the present value of mixed streams, simply find the present value of each cash flow individually, then add them together.[7]

Study Tip

If you solve this problem by calculator, your answer may display as −$754.80. Your calculator will always give the opposite sign on the PV as you have on the FV. Simply ignore the negative sign in this case.

EXAMPLE 6.18   Present Value of Mixed Streams

You are contemplating introducing a new product line that is expected to generate cash flows of $100 at the end of the first year, $200 at the end of the second year, $300 at the end of the third year, and $400 at the end of the fourth year. What is the present value of the cash flows if the appropriate interest rate is 10%?

Solution

Begin by drawing a time line:

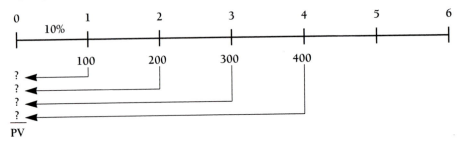

---

[7]If you have an advanced financial calculator such as the TI BA-II plus or the HP-10, you can enter the cash flows and the interest rate to compute the present value. Refer to your calculator's owners manual under NPV calculations.

$$PV = \$100(PVIF_{10\%,1}) + \$200(PVIF_{10\%,2}) + \$300(PVIF_{10\%,3}) + \$400(PVIF_{10\%,4})$$

$$PV = \$100(0.909) + \$200(0.826) + \$300(0.751) + \$400(0.683)$$

$$PV = \$754.60$$

The calculator solution is $754.80.

Self-Test Review Question*

Suppose that you have estimated the cost of your room, board, and tuition for the next 4 years of your education (you have decided to get your MBA) to be as follows: $5,000 due at the end of the first year, $5,500 at the end of the next year, $6,000 at the end of the third year, and $6,500 at the end of the fourth year. Assume a discount rate of 7%. How much must you invest today to pay for your future education?

Increasing the Compounding Periods

Computing present values with multiple compounding periods per year is very similar to computing future values with multiple compounding periods per year. The annual interest rate is divided by the number of periods per year to find the interest rate per period. The number of years is multiplied by the number of periods per year to get the number of periods the future value will be discounted. Present value with multiple compounding periods is computed as

$$PV = \frac{FV_n}{\left(1 + \dfrac{i}{m}\right)^{mn}} \qquad (6.9)$$

where

m = number of compounding periods per year
n = number of years
i = annual interest rate

On occasion you may need to find the present value of a sum that will be received in a few days or months. The concept remains the same. Convert the interest rate to the interest rate in effect for that period and raise the denominator by the number of periods.

E X A M P L E 6.19   Present Value with Monthly Compounding

H&R Block offers taxpayers instant tax return refunds for a fee. Suppose you had $1,000 coming from the IRS and you were offered an instant refund for a $35 fee. Would you take the

*Find the present value of each cash flow separately and add them together:
($5,000/1.07) + ($5,500/1.07²) + ($6,000/1.07³) + ($6,500/1.07⁴) = $19,333.42. If you have $19,333.42 now and invest at 7%, you will be able to pay for the balance of your education.

instant refund if you could borrow $1,000 at 12% and if you expected the IRS to pay you in 2 months?

Solution

The first step is to convert the annual interest rate into a monthly interest rate. This is done by dividing 12% by 12. The monthly interest rate is 1%. Next plug the monthly interest rate and the number of periods into Equation 6.9:

$$PV = \frac{\$1,000}{\left(1 + \dfrac{0.12}{12}\right)^{12 \times \frac{2}{12}}} = \frac{\$1,000}{(1.01)^2} = \$980.30$$

This problem can also be solved using the factors where the interest rate is the interest rate per month and the number of periods is the number of months:

$$PV = \$1,000(PVIF_{1\%,2})$$
$$PV = \$1,000(0.98) = \$980.00$$

Your $1,000 future tax refund is worth $980 today. If you take the instant refund, you are essentially selling the refund today for $965 ($1,000 − $35 = $965). Because you are a rational investor, you would not sell something worth $980 for $965, so you would reject H&R Block's offer.

PRESENT VALUE OF AN ANNUITY

Just as we sometimes need to find the future value of a stream of equal cash flows, we also may need to find the *present value* of a stream of equal cash flows. If the cash flows are different from each other, there is no shortcut other than using a financial calculator. If the cash flows are equal to each other and occur at regular intervals, we can find the present value using the present value of annuity tables.

Review the following time line:

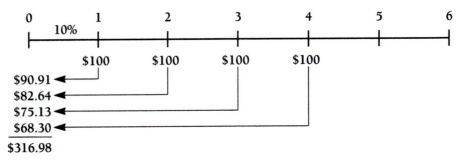

One way to find the present value of the annuity shown on the time line is to find the present value of each cash flow separately and then add them together, as shown. Obviously, if there are many cash flows, this can become tedious and time consuming. The solution to the above problem could be written as

$$PV = \$100(PVIF_{10\%,1}) + \$100(PVIF_{10\%,2}) + \$100(PVIF_{10\%,3}) + \$100(PVIF_{10\%,4})$$

The $100 can be factored out of each term in the equation. The solution is then rewritten as

$$PV = \$100 \times (PVIF_{10\%,1} + PVIF_{10\%,2} + PVIF_{10\%,3} + PVIF_{10\%,4})$$

This is another example of a geometric progression that has a standardized solution. The solution to the equation for various interest rates and number of periods has been computed and appears in Appendix A, Table A.4, at the end of the book.[8] Using these factors, the equation for the present value of an annuity can be written as

$$PV_{annuity} = PMT(PVIFA_{i,n}) \qquad (6.10)$$

where PMT = the amount of the equal annual payments.

E X A M P L E 6.20   Present Value of Annuities

Find the present value of the cash flow stream on the above time line using Equation 6.10.

Solution

The payment is $100, n is 4, and i is 10%. Plugging these figures into Equation 6.10 gives us

$$PVIFA = \$100(PVIFA_{10\%,4})$$
$$PVIFA = \$100(3.170) = \$317.00$$

Financial calculators are most valuable when used to solve annuity problems. The problem with using tables is that, although they are easy to use, they limit you to whole interest rates and certain numbers of periods. By using the financial calculator, you can solve problems with present values of fractional interest rates, as well as any number of periods. To solve the above problem with a financial calculator, input the data as follows:

= $316.99

In the last section we noted that the present value of a future sum can be used to exactly match the future sum by investing what you have today at the discount rate. We can reemphasize this important point using the present value of an annuity.

We have already computed that the present value of a four-period stream of equal $100 cash flows is $316.99. This means that if we have $316.99 to invest today we can exactly reproduce the future stream of cash flows. You would invest the $316.99 at 10% and have $348.69 1 year later. The first $100 cash flow is then subtracted from the balance, which is reinvested. One year later the balance is $273.56 and an additional $100

[8]The PVIFAs (present value interest factors for annuities) in Table A.4 are the solutions for the following equation:

$$PVIFA = \frac{1 - \left[1 / (1 + i)^n \right]}{i}$$

is subtracted. This process continues as shown below until the final $100 is subtracted and the remaining balance is zero:

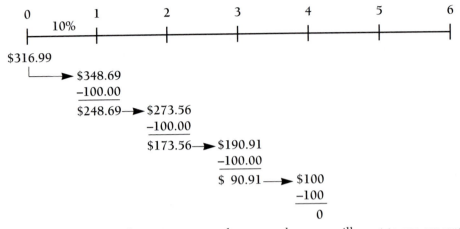

This example provides an important clue as to when you will want to use present value equations. Anytime you want to know how much you need today to create a future cash flow stream, find the present value of the cash flow. For example, in Box 6.1, present value and future value methods are used to compute how much must be saved to achieve a particular retirement goal.

Box 6.1 Will You Retire a Millionaire?

Have you ever asked yourself whether it is likely that you will end up a millionaire by the time you retire? If you are pursuing a degree that offers career opportunities with modest salaries and if you are not planning to go into business for yourself, you may feel that the chances are slim. Let us review this question in a little more detail.

Suppose you determine that you will need the spending power provided today by $50,000 every year during your retirement. However, we expect inflation to erode the spending power of the sum, so we must adjust for inflation. If inflation averages 3% over the next 35 years, you will need $140,693 during the first year after you retire ($50,000 × 1.03^{35} = $140,693). If inflation continues during your retirement years, you will need $286,000 during your 25th year of retirement to have the same spending power provided by $50,000 today.

To determine how much you will need in your retirement nest egg to finance a series of annual withdrawals, we need to find the present value of the series of cash flows. Remember that the present value of a cash flow stream is sufficient to exactly reproduce that income stream if the present value amount is invested at the discount rate. In this case, using an Excel spreadsheet that first computes the annual inflation-adjusted cash flow each year and then computes the present value of that amount, we find we need a nest egg of $1,621,493, assuming we can invest at 10%.

Small changes in our assumptions make a big difference in how much money we will need to retire. Suppose that inflation averages 4% instead of 3% and that we invest the nest egg at 7% instead of 10%, because most retirees are conservative. Under this set of assumptions we will need $2,386,258 in our nest egg.

Clearly, you will need to be a millionaire by the time you retire. In fact, to be safe you will probably want to be a multimillionaire. Because of the effects of compounding, it turns out that this is not as farfetched as it may seem. If you invest $371.06 per month at an average rate of return of 12%, you will have $2,386,258 in your nest egg 35 years later. Because most companies match their employees' contributions to their retirement plans, you would only need to invest half of $371.01, or $185.53 per month to meet your goal.

Self-Test Review Question*

You have just won the lottery and will receive equal payments of $50,000 at the end of each year for the next 20 years. Your attorney offers to pay you $500,000 today if you will agree to give him the stream of payments. If you think that you can invest at 10%, should you accept this offer?

PERPETUITIES

Annuities are equal payments that go on for a fixed number of periods. If the annuity continues forever, it is a **perpetuity.** The term *perpetuity* comes from the word *perpetual,* which means continuous or indefinitely. The cash flows received from preferred stock are an example of a perpetuity. Preferred dividends are fixed at a known level at the time the stock is issued. The dividends do not rise or fall with the fortunes of the firm. Because stock never matures, the cash flows are perpetual.[9]

The cash flows from a perpetuity are illustrated by the following time line:

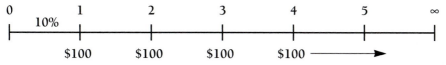

To find the present value of this perpetuity algebraically, we would begin with the expression

$$PV_0 = \frac{\$100}{(1.10)^1} + \frac{\$100}{(1.10)^2} + \frac{\$100}{(1.10)^3} + \frac{\$100}{(1.10)^4} + \cdots$$

Because the $100 appears in every term, it can be factored out:

$$PV_0 = \$100 \left[\frac{1}{(1.10)^1} + \frac{1}{(1.10)^2} + \frac{1}{(1.10)^3} + \frac{1}{(1.10)^4} + \cdots \right]$$

The term in parentheses is a geometric series. The solution to the sum of this endless geometric series is

$$PV_0 = \frac{\$100}{0.10} = \$1,000$$

---

[9]Most preferred stock has fixed dividends and does not mature, but firms are being more creative with the terms of securities they issue. It is now possible to buy floating rate preferred stock that matures.

*To evaluate this question, compute the present value of the lottery payments and compare this amount to $500,000: $PV_{lottery} = \$50,000(PVIFA_{10\%,20}) = \$50,000(8.5136) = \$425,680$. Because $PV_{lottery} < \$500,000$, you should accept the offer.

Study Tip

The idea behind the perpetuity equation is really very simple. For the cash flow to continue indefinitely, only the earned interest can be withdrawn. The amount of interest earned each year is the principal times the interest rate (PV × *i*) = PMT. By rearranging this equation we get Equation 6.11.

In general terms, the formula for a perpetuity is

$$PV_0 = \frac{PMT}{i} \qquad (6.11)$$

Let us illustrate Equation 6.11 using an example. Suppose we wanted to determine the present value of a share of preferred stock. We know that it promises to pay a $2 dividend forever and we assume an 8% interest rate.

The dividend of $2 is the constant payment. The interest rate is 8%. Plugging these figures into Equation 6.11 yields

$$PV_0 = \frac{\$2}{0.08} = \$25.00$$

As an investor, we would be willing to pay $25.00 for a share of this stock.

Self-Test Review Question*

An endowed faculty chair is created when a benefactor makes a donation of sufficient size that the earnings from the donation pay the salary and benefits of a professor. How much would need to be donated to endow a chair in your name if the salary and benefits were $80,000 and the after-inflation interest rate was 7%?

Study Tip

The PVIFA equation (Equation 6.10) finds the present value *one period before* the first payment is received. Go back and review the time line just before Example 6.19 to see this.

UNEVEN STREAMS

It is not unusual that cash flows have some payments that differ as well as some that are the same. When an annuity is mixed with other irregular payments we have an *imbedded* annuity. One reason we will see this cash flow pattern in this course is that we can often estimate the next couple of cash flows with some degree of confidence. However, as we make predictions about cash flows that are far in the future, it is often a rational simplification to assume that they will remain constant.

To solve for the present value of mixed cash flow streams, we find the present value of the annuity, then add the present value of any other cash flows. The simplest mixed cash flow is one in which there are several periods before the annuity begins. Thus, the stream consists of several periods of zero cash flows plus an annuity.

Consider the following example. Suppose an annuity does not begin at the end of the first period, as in the earlier examples. Instead, it begins one period later. As we noted in our earlier discussion of future value (see "Computing the Future Value of an Ordinary Annuity"), an annuity that begins *any time after* the end of the first period is called a *deferred annuity*.

*Because the chair position is expected to go on forever, the cash flow is a perpetuity. The given figures should be substituted as follows:

$$PV = \frac{\$80,000}{0.07} = \$1,142,857.14$$

A sum of $1,142,857.14 would need to be donated to create a chair in your name.

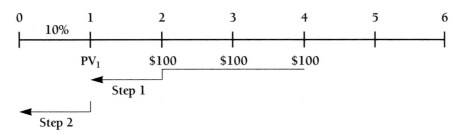

Study Tip

Pay close attention to when the PVIFA and the PVIF factors are used.

To solve this type of problem, we first apply the present value method to the annuity. When we do this using the Equation 6.10, we find the value of the annuity one period *before* the first payment (we label this point as PV_1 on the time line):

Step 1 $PV_1 = \$100(PVIFA_{3,10\%}) = \$248.70$

We are not finished yet because we need the value at time zero, not at time 1 (the end of the first period). To move the value of the annuity back in time one more period, we treat the solution to Step 1 as a new problem, and find its present value:

Step 2 $PV_0 = \$248.70(PVIF_{1,10\%}) = (\$248.70)(0.909) = \$226.07$

Steps 1 and 2 can be combined as follows to save time:

$PV_0 = \$100(PVIFA_{3,10\%})(PVIF_{1,10\%}) = (\$100)(2.487)(0.909) = \$226.07$

Let us review carefully what we have done. $\$100(PVIFA_{3,10\%})$ discounts the value of the three-period annuity back one period to the end of period 1. Multiplying by $PVIF_{1,10\%}$ discounts the annuity back to time 0. Our goal was to obtain the present value at time 0.

What happens if the annuity is deferred more than one period? For example, suppose that an annuity does not begin until three periods later. We find that the method is unchanged:

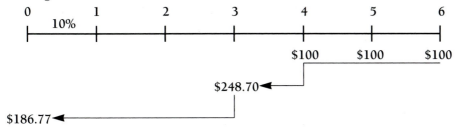

$PV = \$100(PVIFA_{3,10\%})(PVIF_{3,10\%}) = (\$100)(2.487)(0.751) = \$186.77$

Study Tip

The number of periods in the annuity is *always* equal to the number of payments, even when the annuity is deferred. One way to view annuities is to recognize that the annuity begins one period before the first payment is made and ends when the last payment is made.

You use the three-period PVIFA because three payments of $100 are received. This discounts the annuity back to the end of period 3. Next, discount back three more periods to compute the PV at time zero.

A slightly more complex example has two annuities. In the following example, find the present value of each annuity separately, and then add them together.

Study Tip

Be sure you thoroughly understand and can do each of these examples. These models will appear over and over in different sections of the text.

E X A M P L E **6.21**   **Present Value of an Annuity**

Suppose that you have two annuities, one beginning one period later and another beginning four periods later. What are the present values of each of the annuities and what is their combined PV?

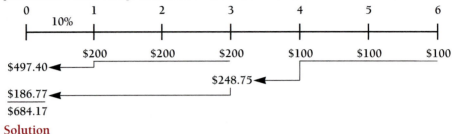

Solution

$$PV = \$100(PVIFA_{3,10\%})(PVIF_{3,10\%}) + 200(PVIFA_{3,10\%})$$

$$PV = \$100(2.487)(0.751) + \$200(2.487) = \$684.17$$

The present values of the separate annuities are \$186.77 and \$497.40. Their combined present value is \$684.17.

Note that you find the PV of each annuity separately, then add them together. Instead of multiplying by $PVIF_{n,i}$, you could multiply by $1/(1 + i)^n$. Pay close attention to when PVIFA and PVIF are used.

Self-Test Review Question*

You are considering buying a business. You have determined that it will generate \$1,000 per year for 5 years, then \$2,000 per year for an additional 5 years. How much would you be willing to pay for this business if you felt the discount rate should be 15%? (Hint: The value of a business asset is simply the present value of the cash flows.)

EXTENSION 6.1

Loans

Loan Amortization

Another useful application of TVM methods is the calculation of loan payments and loan amortization schedules. Loan payment calculations are performed using the present value of an annuity formula. This is because the bank making a loan must be indifferent between the money it is lending at the present time and the future cash flows it will receive in return. In other words, the loan amount must be the present value of the loan payments.

Loan Payments

In the section above, we learned how to compute the present value of an annuity. Suppose that we already know the present value, but we want to know what annuity payment equals that present value. To find this, we need to know the length of the annuity and the interest rate. Given these figures, we can compute the payment amount.

*$PV = \$1,000(PVIFA_{15\%,5}) + \$2,000(PVIFA_{15\%,5})(PVIF_{15\%,5}) = \$1,000(3.3522) + \$2,000(3.3522)(0.4972)$
$= \$6,685.63$. You would be willing to pay \$6,685.63.

Let's illustrate using an example. Suppose you have decided to buy a new car as a reward for acing your finance exam. You will need a loan of $15,000 and would like to make payments for 2 years. The dealership has offered a 12% interest rate on the loan. What will your monthly payment be?

You begin by writing down the formula for the present value of an annuity:

$$PV = PMT(PVIFA_{i,n})$$

Note that there are 24 monthly periods and that the interest rate is 1% per period. Because you will receive the loan proceeds today, the loan amount is the present value. Substituting these figures into the above equation yields

$$\$15,000 = PMT\left(PVIFA_{1\%,24}\right)$$

$$\$15,000 = PMT\left(21.2434\right)$$

$$\frac{\$15,000}{21.2434} = PMT = \$706.10$$

Monthly payments of $706.10 will be required to pay off this loan. To solve this equation using a financial calculator, you would enter the numbers as follows:

$$= -\$706.08$$

As the length of the loan increases, the amount of the monthly payment falls, but the amount of interest you pay over the course of the loan increases. Box 6.2 demonstrates the importance of selecting the shortest possible repayment period for a mortgage loan.

Loan Amortization   In the above example, monthly loan payments of $706.10 are required. These payments pay the interest that has accrued from the last payment as well as a portion of the principal owed. Each period, the interest due falls because the principal balance is declining. As a result, the portion of the payment that goes to reducing the principal increases. An amortization schedule details the distribution of funds between principal and interest. To prepare an amortization schedule, compute the amount of interest that has accrued and subtract this from the payment to find the principal reduction.

The sample amortization schedule that follows is for a 3-year loan of $10,000 at 10% with three annual payments:

A Beginning Balance	B Payment	C Accrued Interest (A × 0.10)	D Principal Payment (B − C)	E Ending Balance (A − D)
$10,000	$4,021.15	$1,000	$3,021.15	$6,978.85
6,978.85	4,021.15	697.988	3,323.27	3,655.58
3,655.58	4,021.15	365.56	3,655.58	0

Box 6.2 How to Save $150,000 Dollars

Suppose that you have graduated, gotten married, secured that good job, and now want to buy a house. After a diligent search, you and your spouse decide to buy a $170,000 house on a quiet cul-de-sac in a nice neighborhood to raise kids. You go into your local bank to apply for financing and are asked whether you would prefer a 30-year loan or a 15-year loan. Knowing that the 30-year loan will have lower payments, you select that. What is the long-term implication of this decision? To find out, let us compute the payment and total interest paid in each scenario.

Assume that the interest rate on the 30-year loan is 8% and on the 15-year loan it is 7.5% (remember that the usual shape of the yield curve causes short-term rates to be less than long-term rates). You pay a 5% down payment, so you will borrow $161,500. Using a financial calculator, the payments are as follows:

30-year loan: 360 payments of $1,185.03

15-year loan: 180 payments of $1,497.12

The total interest paid in each case is found by multiplying the number of payments by the monthly payment amount and subtracting the loan amount.

30-year loan interest paid

$$= 360 \times \$1,185.03 - \$161,500 = \$265,110.80$$

15-year loan interest paid

$$= 180 \times \$1,497.12 - \$161,500 = \underline{\$107,982.49}$$

$$\$157,128.31$$

By choosing the 30-year mortgage, you will pay an additional $157,128.31 in interest over the life of the loan. Most loans allow you to pay more than is required each month. You could take the 30-year loan, but make payments as if it were a 15-year loan. However, you will have to pay a higher interest rate on the 30-year loan than if you had just obtained a 15-year loan to start with. Some people prefer having the option of being able to reduce their payments should they get into a financial pinch, and this option is worth the extra interest cost to them. Others feel they need the discipline a 15-year loan will impose on them. Otherwise, they may not make the larger payments.

Notice that as the beginning balance falls the accrued interest also falls. This leaves a greater portion of each payment to go to reducing the principal.

Self-Test Review Question*

You plan to finance a $100,000 plant expansion over 5 years at a 12% annual interest rate. What will the monthly payment be?

EXTENSION 6.2

Compounded Growth

Growth Rates

The following table shows that K-Mart sales increased over the period 1990–1994:

*$PV = PMT(PVIFA)$, $\$100,000 = PMT(PVIFA_{1\%,60})$, $\$100,000/44.955 = \$2,224.45$.

K-Mart Sales 1990–1994 (thousands)				
1990	1991	1992	1993	1994
$27,670	$28,133	$29,419	$31,416	$34,557

You can use the TVM equations to compute the average compounded growth in sales. You might be tempted to find the average growth rate by computing the percentage increase in sales for each year and then taking an average. This might seem logical at first glance, but on second thought, it does not work. The problem is that taking an average of each year's increase ignores the effects of compounding. The proper method is to recognize that a growth rate is the same thing as the interest rate used with compound interest problems. You can use either the future or present value formula to solve for the interest rate.

E X A M P L E 6.22   Compound Growth Rate

What is the average compound growth rate in sales for K-Mart between 1990 and 1994?

Solution
Let us use Equation 6.1:

$$FV_n = PV_0(1 + i)^n$$

The PV is the earlier occurring sales figure (this is the figure farthest to the left if the data were plotted on a time line, in this case $27,670). The future value is the most recent sales amount, or $34,557.

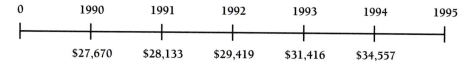

We can determine the number of periods by counting the intervals during which growth can occur. In this example, there are four periods of growth. Substituting these numbers into the equation yields

$$\$34,557 = \$27,670(1 + g)^4$$

A little algebra results in the following:

$$g = \sqrt[4]{\frac{\$34,557}{\$27,670}} - 1$$

$$g = \sqrt[4]{1.2489} - 1$$

$$g = 0.0571 = 5.71\%$$

The average compound growth rate for K-Mart's sales between 1990 and 1994 was therefore 5.71%.

Note that you can find fractional roots on most calculators by entering the exponent as a fraction.[10] This problem could also be worked by solving for the FVIF and looking

Study Tip

Note that on most calculators the sign of the PV and FV terms must be different or an error message results.

---

[10]You can find any root if your calculator has a ▉ button (or otherwise lets you compute exponents).

up the interest rate that corresponds to four periods. The problem is that only whole interest rates are reported in the tables, so only an approximation can be found.

Growth rates are easily computed using financial calculators. Input the PV, FV, and number of periods and solve for i:

$= 5.71\%$

![open book icon]

IS IT PRESENT VALUE OR FUTURE VALUE?

Study Tip

In setting up problems, it may help to draw or visualize a time line. Amounts on the left of the time line are present values. Amounts on the right are future values. Begin each problem by putting everything on the time line that is in the text of the problem. Solve for what is missing.

Mastering the TVM techniques presented in this chapter is a significant step toward solving TVM problems. However, an added layer of complexity is the need to determine whether a particular problem is a present value or a future value problem. Consider the following example. You want to determine the amount that must be accumulated to pay a fixed $25,000 per year during your expected 20-year retirement, assuming a 10% interest rate. Is this a present value, future value, present value of an annuity, or future value of an annuity problem?

For most students, the hard part of learning TVM concepts is not mastering the equations, but rather determining which equation to use to solve a particular word problem. Table 6.3 offers some guidelines to help. Remember, there were only four different equations presented in this chapter:

- Future value of a lump sum: $FV = PV(1 + i)^n$
- Future value of an annuity: $FV = PMT(FVIFA_{i,n})$
- Present value of a lump sum: $PV = FV/(1 + i)^n$
- Present value of an annuity: $PV = PMT(PVIFA_{i,n})$

To determine how to solve new, unfamiliar types of TVM problems and to pick which of the above equations to use, follow these steps:

1. Review the cash flows in the question to determine whether they are annuities. Once you have made this determination, only two equations remain. In the above example, because regular equal payments will be made, it is an annuity problem.

2. Review the information given in the problem and jot down what is known. If you are confused, draw a time line. PVs are to the left and FVs are to the right. For

---

TABLE 6.3 Guidelines for TVM Problems

- Use *future value* to find the balance resulting from an interest-earning deposit.
- Use *future value of an annuity* to find the payment needed to achieve a known future balance.
- Use either *present* or *future value* (without an annuity) to compute growth rates.
- Use *present value* on all loan calculations.
- Use *present value* to value assets.
- Use *present value* to evaluate investments.

instance, in the above example, we know that the regular payment amount is $25,000, so write down PMT = $25,000. We also know $n = 20$ and $i = 10\%$. We do *not* know PV or FV.

3. Determine what you want to solve for. In the above example, we want to know how much is needed now to generate a series of payments (PV = ?). This lets us choose an equation. We will use the PV of an annuity equation because it is the only one that includes all of the variables that are given plus the variable for which we need to solve.

Here is one last suggestion. If you are attempting to solve a problem and find that you cannot determine what to plug into the equation for each of the variables, it may be because you are using the wrong equation. Try another.

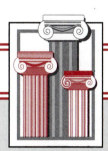

Careers in Finance   Financial Planners

Financial planners help individuals plan their financial futures: How are you going to cover your retirement needs? What do you have to do today to put your children through college?

This work can be personally and financially rewarding and requires excellent interpersonal skills. A good financial planner understands investments, taxes, and estate planning issues, and he or she knows how to listen. This work can be done within a company such as IDS Financial Services or by yourself, as a sole proprietorship.

Most planners go solo or work within smaller practices. It is essential that you have a certain amount of entrepreneurship, given that you will be running your own business. The work pays well and is rewarding if you like to help people. Many financial planners obtain the Certified Financial Planner (CFP) designation. This certification adds a great deal of credibility to the planner, and many customers look for it. The CFP designation requires work experience and the passage of a multipart exam.

CHAPTER SUMMARY

In this chapter we learned that dollars received in the future are not worth as much as dollars received today. As a result, we must adjust for differences in the time value of money. Four basic equations are used either independently or in combination to move money around in time.

We can compute the value of money invested over time using the future value equation. A lump sum invested today will grow to a larger amount over time. The longer the investment period and the greater the interest rate, the more will be the future balance.

At times, we may want to compute how much a series of equal payments will accumulate. For example, if you make regular contributions to a retirement fund, what will be available for retirement? Problems of this nature are solved using the future value of an annuity equation. If we know what the future value should be, we can also use the future value of an annuity equation and solve for the payment required to reach this balance.

More often in the remainder of this text, we are going to need to compute the present value of a future sum to be received. We use present value often because it is best to evaluate investments by evaluating all cash flows in the present so that cash inflows can be compared with cash outflows. There are two equations for determining present value. We can find the present value of a lump sum or the present value of an annuity.

TVM techniques are useful in many applications. For instance, we find the present value of the cash flows from an investment to determine how much that asset is worth. We can compute loan payments and amortization schedules using present value of an annuity methods. In later chapters we will use these methods to evaluate projects and acquisitions.

KEY WORDS

DISCUSSION QUESTIONS

1. Why are you indifferent between having the present value of a cash flow and the cash flow itself?
2. Define the term *annuity*. What is an embedded annuity? What is a deferred annuity?
3. Would you rather make a deposit into an account that pays 6% compounded annually, quarterly, monthly, or daily? Does it make any difference which account you choose?
4. What is the relationship between factors found on the FVIF table and those on the PVIF table? (Hint: How could you mathematically convert one into the other?)
5. What is meant by the term *discounting* and what is meant by the term *compounding*?

6. Demonstrate how you can derive the equation for the present value of a future amount from the equation for the future value of an investment.
7. What is the distinction between an annuity and a perpetuity?
8. What is meant by the statement, "You can exactly reproduce a future cash flow if you have the present value of that cash flow"?
9. What is a loan amortization schedule and why might you want to construct one?
10. Describe how you would determine the compound growth rate in sales over a period of time.

PROBLEMS

1. The financial manager at Zimmer Industries is considering an investment that requires an initial outlay of $30,000 and is expected to result in cash inflows of $5,000 at the end of year 1, $8,000 at the end of years 2 and 3, $15,000 at the end of year 4, $12,000 at the end of year 5, and $10,000 at the end of year 6. Without doing any calculations,
   a. Draw and label a time line depicting the cash flows associated with Zimmer Industries' proposed investment.
   b. Use arrows on the time line to demonstrate how compounding to find future values can be used to measure all cash flows at the end of year 6.
   c. Use arrows on the time line to demonstrate how discounting to find present value can be used to measure all cash flows at time zero.
2. Use the basic formula for future value along with the given interest rate, i, and number of periods, n, to calculate the future value interest factor (FVIF) in each of the following cases.

Case	Interest Rate, i	Number of Periods, n
A	10%	2
B	8	4
C	6	3
D	4	2

3. For each of the following cases, calculate the future value of the single cash flow deposited today that will be available at the end of the deposit period if the interest is compounded annually at the rate specified over the given period.

Case	Single Cash Flow	Interest Rate	Deposit Period (yr)
A	$ 100	6%	30
B	5,000	10	25
C	12,500	12	7
D	23,200	14	10

4. Calculate the balance you would have in an account after 4 years assuming $6,000 was deposited today at 16% compounded annually, semiannually, and quarterly.

5. For each of the following cases, find the future value at the end of the deposit period, assuming that interest is compounded semiannually at the given nominal interest rate.

Case	Initial Deposit	Nominal Interest Rate	Deposit Period (yr)
A	$500	8%	2
B	300	6	5
C	300	10	7

6. Calculate the future value of the annuity, assuming that each case is an
   a. Ordinary annuity
   b. Annuity due

Case	Annuity	Interest Rate	Deposit Period (yr)
A	$4,000	10%	7
B	2,500	8	30

7. For the following mixed stream of cash flows, determine the future value at the end of the final year if deposits are made at the beginning of each year into an account paying annual interest of 10%, assuming that no withdrawals are made during the period.

Year	Cash Flow Stream
1	$1,000
2	500
3	2,000

8. Using the basic formula for present value along with the given discount rate, i, and number of periods, n, calculate the present value interest factor (PVIF) in each of the following cases.

Case	Discount Rate, i	Number of Periods, n
A	5%	5
B	10	3
C	12	2

9. Ted Roberts has been offered a $1,000 future payment 3 years from today. If his opportunity cost is 7% compounded annually, what value would he place on this opportunity?

10. Find the present value of the following mixed stream of cash flows using a 10% discount rate. (Assume deposits are made at the end of each year.)

Year	Cash Flow Stream
1	$20,000
2	15,000
3	10,000

11. For each of the following cases, calculate the present value of the annuity, assuming that the annuity cash flows occur at the end of each year.

Case	Annuity	Interest Rate	Periods (yr)
A	$10,000	10%	5
B	20,000	12	10

12. In the following case the mixed end-of-period cash flow stream has an annuity embedded within it. Calculate the present value of the cash flow stream, assuming a 10% discount rate.

Year	Cash Flow
1	$10,000
2	8,000
3	5,000
4	5,000
5	5,000
6	5,000
7	3,000

13. Determine the present value of each of the following perpetuities.

Perpetuities	Annual Amount	Discount Rate
A	$10,000	10%
B	20,000	5
C	50,000	8

14. A retirement home at Westbrook Manor Estates now costs $80,000. Inflation is expected to cause this price to increase at 5% per year over the next 30 years before Chris O'Neal retires. How large an equal annual end-of-the-year deposit must be made each year into an account paying an annual interest rate of 10% for Chris to have the cash to purchase a home at retirement?

15. Determine the equal annual end-of-year payment required for each year over the life of the following loans to repay them fully during the stated term.

Loan	Principal	Interest Rate	Term of Loan (yr)
A	$10,000	14%	10
B	15,000	10	5

16. Calculate the average annual compound growth rate associated with each cash flow stream.

	Cash Flows		
Year	A	B	C
1	$ 500	$200	$2,000
2	600	300	2,500
3	800	400	2,600
4	1,000	500	2,800
5	1,200	600	3,000
6		700	3,250
7		800	
8		900	

17. You are saving money for your retirement. How much will you have on deposit in 40 years if you invest at 12% as follows:
    a. At the end of each of the next 8 years you deposit $2,000. After 8 years you do not make any more deposits, but the balance continues to compound at 12% for the next 32 years.
    b. Your first $2,000 deposit is made at the end of the eighth year and at the end of each subsequent year for the next 32 years.
    c. How much was invested in total in part a? In part b? Which investment plan appears to be superior?

18. Suppose your credit card balance is $1,125. The minimum payment amount is $22 and the annual percentage rate is 18%.
    a. If you make a constant monthly payment of $22, how long will it take you to pay off the credit card balance? (Note: You will need a financial calculator to solve this problem because monthly compounding requires that the 18% annual rate be divided by 12.)
    b. How much interest will you pay if you elect to make the minimum payment?

19. You bought a house 2 years ago with a $100,000 mortgage. This loan requires only annual payments for 15 years. You are now preparing your taxes and want to know how much interest you paid during the second year of the loan. If the loan interest rate is 8%, prepare an amortization schedule that shows second-year total interest paid and the end-of-year loan balance.

20. You have just taken out an installment loan for $100,000. Assume that the loan will be repaid in 12 equal monthly installments of $9,456 and that the first payment will be due 1 month from today. How much of your third monthly payment will go toward the repayment of principal?

21. You have graduated from college and landed a good job. You want to replace the junk car you are driving but do not want to take out a car loan. Instead, you decide to invest $350 per month. You will put the money in the stock market and hope to earn 12%. If the market performs as you are hoping (a very optimistic assumption), how long will it take to accumulate $20,000?

SELF-TEST PROBLEMS

1. What is the value today of $1,250 to be received 3 years from now, assuming a 12% discount rate?
2. What is the future value of a 5-year ordinary annuity with annual payments of $200, evaluated at a 15% interest rate?
3. What would be the present value today of $1,250 to be received 3 years from now, assuming a 12% discount rate and quarterly compounding?
4. What is the present value of a 5-year ordinary annuity with annual payments of $200, evaluated at a 15% interest rate?
5. What is the present value of a series of $200 payments to begin at the end of the current year and to continue for 20 years, assuming a 12% discount rate?
6. What is the present value of a series of $100 payments made monthly for 5 years, assuming a 12% discount rate?
7. What is the present value of a series of payments in which $100 is received at the end of the current year, $200 is received at the end of the following year, and $300 is received at the end of the next year, assuming a 10% discount rate?

8. If a 5-year ordinary annuity has a present value of $1,000 and if the interest rate is 10%, what is the amount of each annuity payment?

9. You have the opportunity to buy a perpetuity that pays $1,000 annually. Your required return on this investment is 15%. You should be essentially indifferent to buying or not buying the investment if it were offered at what price?

10. How much will be in an account earning 10% at the end of 5 years if $100 is deposited today?

11. How much will be in an account earning 8% at the end of 5 years if $100 is deposited today, assuming quarterly compounding?

12. What is the annual payment due on a $1,000 loan payable in equal annual payments over 3 years at 10%?

13. What is the present value of a $100 payment that will continue to be paid annually forever, assuming a 10% interest rate?

14. How much will be in a retirement account if $2,000 is deposited at the end of each year for 20 years and the account earns 12%?

15. Assume that you will receive $2,000 a year in years 1 through 5, $3,000 a year in years 6 through 8, and $4,000 in year 9, with all cash flows to be received at the end of the year. If you require a 14% rate of return, what is the present value of these cash flows?

16. Suppose the present value of a 2-year ordinary annuity is $100. If the discount rate is 10%, what must be the annual cash flow?

17. If $100 is placed in an account that earns a nominal 4%, compounded quarterly, what will it be worth in 5 years?

18. You are financing a new car with a loan of $10,000 to be repaid in five annual end-of-year installments of $2,504.56. What annual interest rate are you paying?

19. You are given the following cash flow information. The appropriate discount rate is 12% for years 1–5 and 10% for years 6–10. Payments are received at the end of the year. What should you be willing to pay right now to receive the following income stream? (Hint: First discount years 6–10 at 10% back to the end of year 5. Then discount this amount back to year 0 at 12%. Finally discount years 1–5 back to year 0 at 12%.)

Year	Amount
1–5	$20,000
6–10	25,000

20. What is the present value of the following cash flow stream? All cash flows are annual and received at the end of the period. Assume a 10% interest rate. $200 is received at the end of years 1–5, $300 is received at the end of years 6–10.

21. What is the future value of a 10-year ordinary annuity of $15,000 per year, assuming an interest rate of 10% per year?

*22. What is the future value of a 2-year ordinary annuity of $500 per month, assuming an annual interest rate of 12% per year?

23. What is the future value of a $1,000 deposit made today that will be left on deposit for 5 years earning an annual rate of 12%?

24. What is the present value of an ordinary annuity of $1,500 per year that will be received for 5 years, assuming an interest rate of 12%?

25. What is the present value of an annuity due of $1,500 per year that will be received for 5 years, assuming an interest rate of 12%?

26. What is the present value of a lump sum of $300 that will be paid at the end of the fifth year, assuming that the interest rate is 10%?

27. What is the future value at the end of year 3 of the following cash flow stream, assuming a 10% interest rate? $100 will be received at the end of year 1, $200 will be received at the end of year 2, and $300 will be received at the end of year 3.

28. What will be the present value of the cash flow in problem 27?

29. If the present value of a 5-year ordinary annuity is $500, assuming that the discount rate is 10%, what are the annual payments?

30. What is the future value after 5 years of $1,000 that is placed in a savings account today that pays interest quarterly, assuming an annual interest rate of 8%?

31. What is the effective annual interest rate for an account that pays interest quarterly at the annual rate of 8%?

32. In today's dollars you need $50,000 per year to retire. If you will retire in 30 years and if inflation will average 4% per year between now and when you retire, how much will you need during the first year of your retirement?

*33. What will be the monthly payment on a loan of $15,000 that is amortized over 2 years at an annual interest rate of 12%?

*34. What is the interest rate on a loan of $20,000 due in 5 years and requiring an annual payment of $5,686.29?

35. What is the present value of a perpetuity that pays $2 per quarter if the discount rate is 12% per year?

*Requires financial calculator or the use of equation method.

WEB EXPLORATION

1. There are many sites on the Web to help you compute whether you are properly preparing for your retirement. One of the better ones is offered by Quicken. You will find it at www.quicken.com/retirement/planner/.

    Have you set aside enough retirement money to last your lifetime? The earlier you start, the easier it will be. In general, your retirement funds will come from four sources:
    a. Pension Plans
    b. Social Security
    c. Tax-deferred savings
    d. Basic (taxable) savings

    Use the Retirement Planner to predict the income from the first two, and to determine how much you will need to save to make up the balance for your retirement goals.

2. An alternative to the financial goals calculation in problem 1 are sites that offer calculators that let you input figures to compute your goals. Go to library.thinkquest.org/10326/other_features/calc.html. Use both the financial calculator provided and your own financial calculator to answer the following questions.

    Solve for the length of time and total gains in the following problems (do not input $ or ,) by plugging in each number in the following sequence, as per part a below:
    a. Your Goals = $1,000,000; Initial Capital = $1,000; Monthly Invested = $400; ROI = 12%.
    b. $2,000,000; $1,000; $600; 15%.
    c. $1,500,000; $10,000; $0; 15%.

    Verify the calculator figures with your figures you have calculated manually. What have you observed? Why?

MINI CASE

You have graduated and obtained the job of your dreams. It is now time to evaluate what you must do to look out for your retirement. You consider contacting the financial planner provided by your firm but decide to make an initial stab at the calculations first. You decide to do the calculations on a spreadsheet program such Excel or Lotus 1-2-3 so that it will be easy to change your assumptions depending on what the financial planner advises. You try to be as complete as possible so that the results are useful to you and so that you will know what to ask the planner.

If you are married, use joint income and joint expenses. Be sure to consider Social Security and company pension plans.

a. Determine what your annual retirement expenses will be. Use current dollars. Show each major element. Include everything. Do not cut yourself short. Allow enough funds to pursue recreational activities. Do not forget that for most retired people medical expenses are a major expense.

b. Estimate what you believe inflation will average between now and when you retire. Determine how many years you will work between now and when you retire. Then estimate how long you will live after retirement. Clearly state these assumptions and justify them in your write-up. The Web Exploration assignments in Chapters 1 to 5 contain numerous references to sites that can be used to compute life expectancy and inflation.

c. Estimate what average rate of return you believe is possible given the types of investments you plan to make. Justify your estimate. This may require contacting brokerage firms. Be conservative.

d. Determine what alternative sources of funds are available to you to offset your retirement costs. Again be conservative. Do not count on anything unless it is assured.

e. Compute how much you will need each year during your retirement years. (Hint: Take the amount you need in current dollars and find the future value using the inflation rate as the discount factor.) Compute how large a retirement balance is needed to retire. Be sure to adjust for inflation. (Hint: This will be the present value of the stream of annual withdrawals you will need to make during your retirement years. Note that each year while you are retired the amount you need will continue to grow by the inflation rate.) Now compute the size of your retirement nest egg by computing the present value of the annual cash plans you need during retirement.

f. Compute how much must be saved every month to reach your retirement goal. (Hint: This will be a future value of an annuity calculation where the future amount is the nest egg needed from part e and you compute the PMT amount.)

g. Is the above reasonable? If not, devise an uneven savings retirement plan that is more rational. That is, design a savings program where you save less at the beginning, then increase your savings amount later when you can afford it more.

7

Risk and Return

Chapter Objectives

By the end of this chapter you should be able to:

1. Compute the annualized simple interest return
2. Calculate the expected return on a single asset
3. Figure the standard deviation of returns to a single asset
4. Determine the expected return for a portfolio of assets
5. Calculate the required return for a portfolio of assets
6. Discuss the computation and meaning of beta

Chapter 2 described many different financial instruments. Each had different levels of expected return and different probabilities that the expected return would be realized. This chapter investigates the relationship between risk and return. It will come as no surprise that increasing risk is sometimes accompanied by increasing return. What may be a surprise is that increasing the amount of some types of risk does not result in a larger return.

This chapter also develops the capital asset pricing model. This model provides a method of estimating the amount of return required by investors given the risk of an investment. This important model will be used extensively throughout the text.

EXAMINING THE RISK–RETURN RELATIONSHIP

Suppose that you have recently married. You and your new spouse are living in a small one-bedroom apartment. This is fine for the moment because you are just starting out in new careers and have no children. However, you

have decided that in about 5 years you would like to start a family and move into a house. The problem is that to buy a house you need to be able to afford a down payment and closing costs. Your parents have expressed sympathy but are too concerned with providing for their own pending retirement to feel comfortable lending any funds to you. What should you do?

The obvious answer is to save a little money each month until the required amount is sitting in your savings account. If you determine that you will need $10,000 to cover the initial costs of buying the house and the bank offers a 5% interest rate on savings accounts, you will have to save $147 per month.[1] You may find that this is very difficult to do, given all the other expenses of beginning married life. Is there a better way? Consider that over the last 65 years the stock market has returned an average of 12%. Given this average return, if you put $122 ($25.00 less than the $147 required at a 5% return) into stocks and the market returns 12%, you would have the $10,000 at the end of 5 years. This is better, but consider that the stocks of small firms have risen an average of 17% over the last 65 years. At this rate of return, you have to invest only $107 per month. Finally, your stockbroker tells you about a firm that has been earning a return of 25% for the last 2 years. If you invest in this security and it continues its high return, you can achieve your 5-year goal by investing only $85 per month. Which option should you choose?

To decide which investment best suits your needs, consider the features of each option. If you put the funds in the bank, the amount invested and the earnings are absolutely certain. The government guarantees funds in the bank against loss. You can be secure and comfortable with the knowledge that if you make your monthly $147 deposit, you will have $10,000 at the end of 5 years. The stock market is less certain. It has averaged 12% per year, but the actual annual return is not assured and varies substantially from year to year. Similarly, the returns on small stocks are even more variable than the returns on stocks in general. If you invest in the stock market, you may have the $10,000 at the end of 5 years, or you may have much more or much less. Finally, the 25% return hoped for on the high-risk stock offered by the stockbroker is extremely uncertain. If you want to reduce the amount you have to save each month, you will have to accept greater levels of risk. The point of this discussion is one of the most important and fundamental concepts in finance: *To earn a higher return, you must incur higher risk.* Figure 7.1 shows the assumed relationship between risk and return. With zero risk, some return is still expected. As risk increases, so does the expected return.

Investors study an asset's characteristics and develop expectations regarding the likelihood of the cash flows being as projected. The less certain the investor is about the projected cash flows, the riskier is the asset. What makes the investor uncertain about the projections? Often, uncertainty arises from factors that are difficult to predict and will influence the firm's future. For example, Sunbeam sells toasters in the Asian markets. If this region suffers a recession, Sunbeam will also suffer, but it is very hard to predict exactly how large the effect will be. Additionally, it is hard to predict the probability and length of a foreign country's recession. ***The point is that risk is determined by the uncertainty of future cash flows, and this uncertainty is the result of factors peculiar to each asset.***

---

[1]$10,000 = PMT(FVIFA_{60 mo,(5%,12)}), PMT = 147. Computed using financial calculator.

FIGURE 7.1
Risk–Return
Relationship

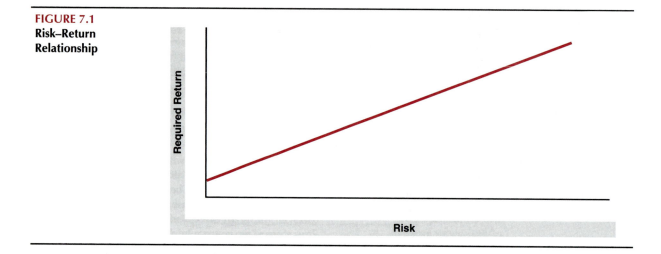

Once investors establish the riskiness of the asset, the market allows the price of the asset to adjust so the expected return on the asset fairly compensates investors for their perceived risk. ***Thus, we see that the perceived risk of the asset is determined first, and then the market establishes the price that will provide an expected return sufficient to induce investors to buy the asset.***

In this chapter we focus on how to measure return and risk. To simplify the presentation, the chapter breaks the discussion into four parts:

- How to compute the return on a single asset
- How to compute the risk of a single asset
- How to compute the expected return on a portfolio of assets
- How to compute the risk of a portfolio of assets

Computing the returns on investments is straightforward. It is also not too difficult to compute the risk of a single asset. The challenging part of this chapter is determining the risk of a *portfolio* of assets.

The relationship between risk and return is fundamental to the study of investments. As the example that introduced this chapter pointed out, there are many different investment vehicles to choose from and each offers a different risk–return combination. To invest properly, you must select investments that best suit your need for high returns while not exceeding your tolerance for risk.

The risk–return relationship is also of interest to financial managers of corporations. Their goal is to maximize the price of the firm's stock and, as we will see in the next chapter, the stock price depends on the risk of the firm. A thorough understanding of the types of risk that affect the return demanded by shareholders will help managers steer their firm on the right course.

COMPUTING THE RETURN ON A SINGLE ASSET

In this section we will compute the return on an asset held in isolation. Later we will show that the wise investor will not willingly invest in single assets by themselves. However, there are times when circumstances will require it. This section also provides a foundation for computing the return on a portfolio of assets.

Computing Simple Returns

Suppose you bought a share of Wal-Mart stock on January 1, 2001, at a price of $50.50 per share. A year later you want to evaluate this investment. After consulting the *Wall Street Journal,* you find that the current price of Wal-Mart shares is $61.00. Additionally, you remember that you were paid $0.20 per share in dividends.[2] The **holding period return (HPR)** consists of the earnings from dividends paid plus the return from appreciation in the price of the stock. The HPR is simply the percentage earnings during the time you have held the investment. The formula for calculating holding period return is

$$HPR_i = \frac{\text{Ending price} - \text{Beginning price} + \text{Dividends}}{\text{Beginning price}} \tag{7.1}$$

For your investment in Wal-Mart, the return is

$$HPR_i = \frac{\$61.00 - \$50.50 + \$0.20}{\$50.50} = 0.2119 = 21.19\%$$

The numerator of the HPR equation represents what you earned and the denominator is what you invested to achieve this income. Thus, the HPR—in this case, 21.19%—is the return on investment.

The above equation computes the return earned while you held Wal-Mart stock. Would you be impressed by an investor who reported earning 89% on an investment in Disney stock? Would you still be impressed if you learned that to get the 89% the investor had held the security for 25 years? To compare returns to one another we normally convert them into *annualized* returns. This is done by multiplying Equation 7.1 by the ratio that results from dividing 365 by the number of days the investment was held:

$$\frac{\text{Annualized}}{\text{Return}} = \frac{\dfrac{\text{Ending}}{\text{price}} - \dfrac{\text{Beginning}}{\text{price}} + \text{Dividends}}{\text{Beginning price}} \times \frac{365}{\dfrac{\text{Number of}}{\text{days held}}} \tag{7.2}$$

Two important points must be made about Equation 7.2. First, it provides the **simple interest** return, in which no interest is paid, not the compounded return. The **compounded return** reflects interest that is being earned on interest previously paid. In this example, no interest has been paid, so the simple interest calculation is correct.

---

[2] There are many sites that report the current prices of stock for free. The following are particularly easy to use: finance.yahoo.com/, quicken.excite.com/investments/markets/, and www.quote.com/layout/index.frames.html.

Study Tip

The most common mistake made applying Equation 7.1 is to divide by the ending price rather than by the beginning price. You must divide by the beginning price because that is what you have invested. Another common error is to subtract the ending price from the beginning price when the stock price has declined.

The second point to note about this equation is that it computes the *historic* return. In other words, it tells you what you earned in the past by holding Wal-Mart stock. *If you are considering an investment, you do not care what others earned last year; you want to know what you will earn during the next year. We call this the expected return.*

Self-Test Review Question*

You bought a stock for $75.00 and sold it after 2 years for $100.00. While you held the stock it paid $4.00 in dividends. What is the annualized return?

Study Tip

Be careful to note the difference between *expected* returns and *required* returns. Expected returns are what you expect to get; required returns are what you need to get to be satisfied that you have been compensated for risk.

Computing Expected Returns

The expected return reflects the investor's evaluation of the probable return an investment will yield. This is not the same as the historic return computed above, nor is it the required return that we will compute later in this chapter. The **expected return** is the weighted average of all the possible returns, where the weights reflect the probabilities of each possible return. This concept is best explained with the following example.

In June 1992, *Forbes* and other investment analysts were ready to write off McDonnell Douglas, a large commercial and military aircraft contractor. Amid decreasing government military spending, the firm lost $101 million in 1990. The jetliner business was crowded, with Boeing and Europe's Airbus Industries capturing most of the orders. Expected returns for McDonnell Douglas were low. How were these expected returns computed?

First, analysts predicted the possible outcomes for the firm in a variety of different economies and situations. They then predicted the return the firm would earn in each possible situation. Next, they assigned probabilities to each situation. Finally, they computed the expected return by summing the product of the probability times the projected return. Table 7.1 reflects what analysts may have been projecting early in 1992 for McDonnell Douglas.

For example, they may have felt there was a 30% chance that the firm would suffer from poor management decisions and that this would result in a return of −20%. Aver-

TABLE 7.1 Expected Returns for McDonnell Douglas

MD Management Quality	Probability	Projected Return	Prob × Proj Return
Poor management	0.30	−0.20	−0.06
Average management	0.60	−0.05	−0.03
Outstanding management	0.10	+0.10	+0.01
Expected return			**−0.08**

age management would provide −5% returns, and truly outstanding management would generate +10% returns.

Based on these projections, the expected return for MD was −0.08. What actually happened? By cutting costs aggressively and bringing in partners to help with development expenses, MD turned a profit in 1994 of $570 million. Meanwhile, the stock advanced from $40 in 1992 to $89.50 by 1996, including a 3:1 stock split. (In a stock split investors receive additional shares for every share they already own. For instance, in a 3-for-1 stock split, for every 1 share investors own, they receive two additional shares.) Investors who ignored the analysts and bought MD at $40 earned over 500% on their investment. Finally, investors benefited again when McDonnell Douglas merged with Boeing in August of 1997. Every share of MD was exchanged for 1.3 shares of Boeing, then valued at $57.25. Thus, an investor who bought one share of MD stock in 1992 received $223.27 worth of Boeing stock in 1997 after accounting for the stock split ($57.25 × 1.3 × 3 = $223.27).

The point of this example is to illustrate that the expected return is computed using the information that is available at the time the projection is made. The *expected* return and the *actual* return can differ, and they often do. MD's low stock price (in 1992) reflected the low probability that management could pull the firm out of its problems so quickly and effectively. What was the expected return for McDonnell Douglas in mid-1996? With MD stock at an all-time high, investors expected high returns in the future. The price MD shareholders received in the merger reflected the synergies that Boeing expected from ownership of MD.

In the above example, only three possible outcomes were listed: poor, average, and outstanding. Of course, there are an infinite number of possible states of the world to be considered and investors cannot evaluate all of them. The expectations concept is valid, however. Expected returns reflect investors' best projection of the future of the firm where the projection is based on the weighted average of the possible outcomes. Equation 7.3 shows the generalized equation for computing the expected return:

$$\text{Expected return } (\bar{k}) = k_1\text{Pr}_1 + k_2\text{Pr}_2 + \cdots + k_n\text{Pr}_n \qquad (7.3)$$

where

k_i = the return in ith state of nature
Pr_i = the probability of occurrence of the nth outcome

Self-Test Review Questions*

1. If the expected return on an asset is 12% and the required return is 11%, should you buy the asset?
2. What is the expected return for a security if there is a 40% probability of returning 10% and a 60% probability of returning 20%?

EVALUATING THE RISK OF HOLDING A SINGLE ASSET

We typically think of risk as the chance of loss. A risky investment is one in which you might lose money. In finance, there is another definition of *risk*: the variability in the cash flows. Suppose a firm earned constant cash flows for each of the last 20 years due to long-term government contracts to provide liners for arctic boots. The stock of this firm would have very little risk. Now suppose this same firm decided to bid on another government contract to make the soles for the boots as well. If the firm gets the new contract, its earnings and stock price will rise. If it does not get the contract, the earnings will be the same as during the last 20 years. This firm is now riskier than before it bid on the contract because investors cannot predict future earnings or cash flows as accurately. The firm is more risky now because there is a chance of variability in the cash flows. To define risk we need a statistic that captures the concept of varying cash flows over time. The standard deviation does this.

Computing the Risk of a Single Asset

The **standard deviation** is a measure of the risk of a single asset. Recall from your statistics class how the standard deviation is computed. First, you compute the *mean*. Then you subtract the mean (which we call the *expected return* in finance) from each observation to determine the *deviation* of the observations. You then square the deviations to remove any negative signs, sum them, and then divide by the number of observations

FIGURE 7.2
Using Standard Deviation to Measure Risk and Computing Standard Deviation

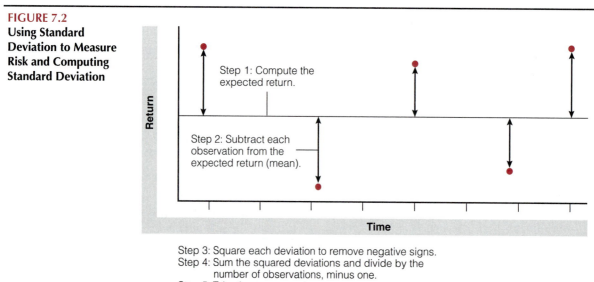

Step 3: Square each deviation to remove negative signs.
Step 4: Sum the squared deviations and divide by the number of observations, minus one.
Step 5: Take the square root.

minus 1. Finally, you take the square root of the sum to get the standard deviation. Figure 7.2 shows how the standard deviation measures risk. Greater deviations from the mean, whether positive or negative, result in a greater standard deviation. Thus the greater the standard deviation, the greater the risk. These characteristics make the standard deviation a viable method for computing the risk of an asset held by itself.

EXTENSION 7.1

Computing the Standard Deviation and the Coefficient of Variation

The method shown in Figure 7.1 for computing the standard deviation assumes that each observation occurs with equal probability. If we can assign more accurate probabilities, as we did for McDonnell Douglas, we can compute a more accurate standard deviation. This is done in Equation 7.4:

$$\text{Standard deviation} = \sqrt{\sum_{i=1}^{n}\left(k_i - \bar{k}\right)^2 \times \text{Pr}_i} \qquad (7.4)$$

where
  $\bar{k}$ = expected return as computed in Equation 7.3 (mean)
  k_i = return for the ith outcome
  Pr_i = probability of occurrence of the ith outcome
  n = number of outcomes evaluated

Study Tip

Your calculators and Excel will compute standard deviations using the method outlined above, not the method shown in Equation 7.4. You must compute standard deviation as shown and not rely on your calculator's functions.

E X A M P L E   7 . 1   Standard Deviation

The following table computes the standard deviation of the expected returns for McDonnell Douglas using the numbers from Table 7.1:

MD Management Quality	Probability (Pr)	Projected Return (k)	Expected Return ($\bar{k}$)	$(k - \bar{k})$	$(k - \bar{k})^2$	Pr × $(k - \bar{k})^2$
Poor management	0.30	−0.20	−0.08	−0.12	0.014	0.0042
Average management	0.60	−0.05	−0.08	0.03	0.001	0.0005
Outstanding management	0.10	0.10	−0.08	0.18	0.032	0.0032

$\sum_{i=1}^{n}(k_i - \bar{k})^2 \times \text{Pr}_i$

Variance = **0.0079**

σ = standard deviation = $\sqrt{0.0079} = 0.0889 = 8.89\%$

Solution
Using Equation 7.4,

$$\sigma^k = \sqrt{\sum_{i=1}^{n} \left(k_i - \bar{k}\right)^2 \times \text{Pr}_i} = \sqrt{0.0079} = 0.0889 = 8.89\%$$

If we assume that the returns to McDonnell Douglas follow a normal probability distribution, we can use the standard deviation to establish confidence intervals for the expected returns. Recall that for a normal probability distribution, 68% of the observations fall within one standard deviation above and below the mean. Because the mean expected return is −0.08 and one standard deviation is 0.0889, 68% of the time the return will fall between −0.1689 and 0.0089:

$$-0.08 + 0.0889 = 0.0089$$
$$\text{and}$$
$$-0.08 - 0.0889 = -0.1689$$

Figure 7.3 shows the distribution of expected returns for two securities. The standard deviation of security A is 10% and the standard deviation of security B is 5%. Security A, with the greater standard deviation, requires a greater spread to encompass 68% of the observations.

Coefficient of Variation: Comparing Assets with Different Returns

You cannot use standard deviation to compare the risk of one asset to another if their returns are very different. Suppose that expected earnings for one asset are $1 billion and expected earnings for another are $1,000. A standard deviation of $100 is not very large for the asset with a $1 billion return; however, a $100 standard deviation for an asset with a $1,000 return is large. *Usually, the standard deviation of the asset with the larger return is greater simply because the return is greater*.] To compare securities with different returns we compute the **coefficient of variation (CV).** The CV standardizes (or scales) the standard deviation to make assets with different returns comparable. The equation for computing CV is

FIGURE 7.3
Effect of Increased Dispersion on Standard Deviation

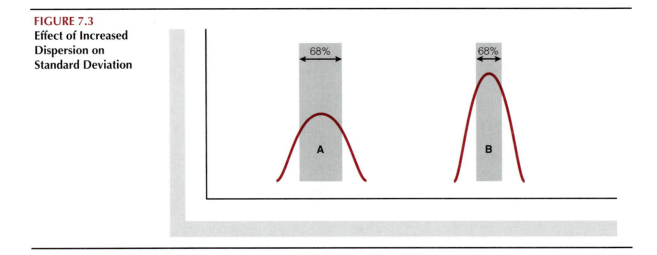

$$CV = \frac{\sigma_k}{k} \qquad\qquad (7.5)$$

The coefficient of variation converts the standard deviation into a percentage of the mean.

E X A M P L E 7.2   **Coefficient of Variation**

The standard deviation of the returns for Barrier Group is 0.04. If the expected return is 12%, what is the coefficient of variation?

Solution

The coefficient of variation for Barrier Group is

$$CV = \frac{\sigma_k}{k} = \frac{0.04}{0.12} = 0.33$$

Self-Test Review Questions*

1. How do you measure the risk of an asset held by itself and not as part of a diversified portfolio?
2. When do you use the coefficient of variation (Extension 7.1)?

COMPUTING THE EXPECTED RETURN FOR A PORTFOLIO OF ASSETS

The preceding discussion was about assets held by themselves. Occasionally, investors hold only one asset. For example, many firms invest employee retirement moneys in the firm's stock. If this is the employee's only asset, then the appropriate measures of risk are the standard deviation and coefficient of variation. Most of the time, however, investors hold more than one asset. This section shows how to compute the expected return on a group of assets.

A **portfolio** is a collection, or group, of assets held as an investment. An investment portfolio may contain a group of stocks, a group of bonds, or a combination of stocks and bonds. A portfolio also may include real estate, gold, options, and other income-producing assets.

Study Tip

We have had to compute a number of weighted averages already in this chapter. You will continue to need to compute them throughout the text. If you are not comfortable with the method already, review the examples carefully.

How to Compute the Expected Return on a Portfolio

The expected return for a portfolio is the weighted average of the expected returns for each individual security, where the weights are the percentage of wealth invested in each security. Equation 7.6 shows how the expected return for a portfolio is computed:

*1. By computing the standard deviation of the expected returns.
*2. To compare the risk of two assets held by themselves and having very different expected returns.

$$\text{Expected return on portfolio } (R_p) = \omega_1 k_1 + \omega_2 k_2 + \cdots + \omega_n k_n \qquad (7.6)$$

where

ω_i = proportion of the total investment in asset i

k_i = expected return on asset i

E X A M P L E 7.3   Expected Return on a Portfolio

Suppose that you hold a two-asset portfolio consisting of 100 shares of Caltron at $24.50 and 100 shares of Bisbee at $54.75. Assume that you have computed the expected return on Caltron and Bisbee to be 22.17% and 21.81%, respectively. What is the expected return from the portfolio?

Solution

The table below computes the expected return from the portfolio:

	Number of Shares	Price per Share	Total Investment	Percent (ω)	Expected Return (k)	$\omega_i \times \bar{k}_i$
Caltron	100	$24.50	$2,450.00	30.9%	22.17%	6.85%
Bisbee	100	54.75	5,475.00	69.1	21.81	15.07
Total			7,925.00	100		**21.92**

The expected return for this portfolio is 21.92%

The calculation of the expected return on a portfolio is a two-step process. You first must estimate the expected return on each asset in the portfolio. You then compute the weighted average of these returns.

The weight is found by dividing the amount invested in an asset by the total amount invested. Clearly, the accuracy of your computed portfolio return is only as accurate as your ability to estimate expected future returns. Example 7.3 used the returns earned by Caltron and Bisbee during the prior year as a *best guess* of future returns. Research is mixed about the validity of this method for estimating future returns. The two-step process required to compute a portfolio return is demonstrated in Example 7.4.

E X A M P L E 7.4   Expected Return, Two Step

You are evaluating securities for your portfolio. Kemple Inc. is expected to earn 10% if the economy is normal but it will earn 12% in a recession. Pander Inc. will earn 8% in a normal economy and 6% in a recession. Both firms are expected to earn 16% in a boom. The probability of a normal economy is 60%. The probability of a recession is 20% and the probability of a boom is 20%. What is the expected return on a portfolio composed of 50% Kemple and 50% Pander?

Solution

The first step is to compute the expected return for each security using Equation 7.3:

$$k_{\text{Kemple}} = (0.6 \times 10\%) + (0.2 \times 12\%) + (0.2 \times 16\%) = 11.6\%$$

$$k_{\text{Pander}} = (0.6 \times 8\%) + (0.2 \times 6\%) + (0.2 \times 16\%) = 9.2\%$$

The second step is to compute the expected return on the portfolio using Equation 7.6:

$$R_p = (0.5 \times 11.6\%) + (0.5 \times 9.2\%) = 10.4\%$$

A portfolio composed of 50% Kemple and 50% Pander would have an expected return of 10.4%.

Self-Test Review Question*

What is the expected return for a portfolio composed of 40% of asset A with an expected return of 10% and 60% of asset B with an expected return of 15%?

EVALUATING THE RISK OF A PORTFOLIO OF ASSETS

Before we attempt to compute the risk of a portfolio, let us review for a moment.

- To compute the *expected return* on an asset held by itself, we take the weighted average of the possible outcomes, where the weights reflect the probability of each outcome.

- To compute the *risk* of an asset held by itself, we compute the standard deviation of the expected returns.

- In the last section we computed the *expected return* on a portfolio of assets by finding the weighted average of the expected returns.

We now need to find the risk of a portfolio of assets. How would you guess we would do this?

Many students logically suggest that the risk of a portfolio can be found by finding the weighted average standard deviation. Let's look at that method. In Figure 7.4, asset A

Study Tip

Notice that the return to the portfolio that combines stocks A and B in Figure 7.4 is the average of the returns generated by each security. As we add more securities to a portfolio, the return continues to be the average of the returns expected on each security. The risk of the portfolio is the variation in these average returns over time. In Figure 7.4, there is no variation so there is zero risk.

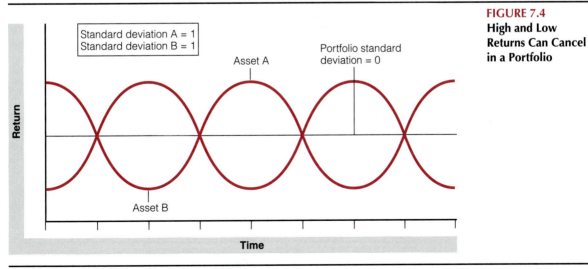

FIGURE 7.4
High and Low Returns Can Cancel in a Portfolio

Standard deviation A = 1
Standard deviation B = 1

Asset A

Portfolio standard deviation = 0

Return

Asset B

Time

and asset B both have a standard deviation of 1. If you invest 50% of your wealth in A and 50% of your wealth in B, the weighted average of the standard deviations is 1. In fact, any combination of A and B will produce a weighted average standard deviation of 1. Now look at the variation in the return to the holder of this portfolio. When A is high, B is low. When B is high, A is low. The variation in one asset exactly offsets the variation in the other. The resulting return is represented by the horizontal line. This portfolio actually has zero variation in returns over time, so it has no risk. *The standard deviation of the portfolio is 0, not 1.* What went wrong? Why did the weighted average method not work?

Correlation

The problem is that the returns to asset A and asset B are correlated. *Correlation* means there is a predictable relationship between two series of numbers. This relationship is measured by the correlation coefficient *r*. In Figure 7.4, the returns are *negatively* correlated because when one moves up, the other moves down. When returns are perfectly negatively correlated they have a correlation coefficient equal to −1.0. Figure 7.5 shows the relationship between perfectly *positively* correlated returns, where both returns move in exactly the same direction at all times. In this example, *r* = +1.0. The degree of correlation between different investments can vary between −1.0 and +1.0. Most securities have positively correlated returns, but not perfectly positively correlated returns. We discuss what this means to investors in the next section.

Diversification

Table 7.2 shows the correlation matrix for a sample of familiar companies. The table was prepared by computing the correlation between 10 years of quarterly returns. Most pairs of stocks have correlation coefficients between 0.2 and 0.5. For example, the correlation between the returns to Delta Airlines and United Airlines was found to be 0.48.

Because the stocks of different companies are not perfectly correlated, you can reduce risk by holding more than one stock, although risk cannot be completely

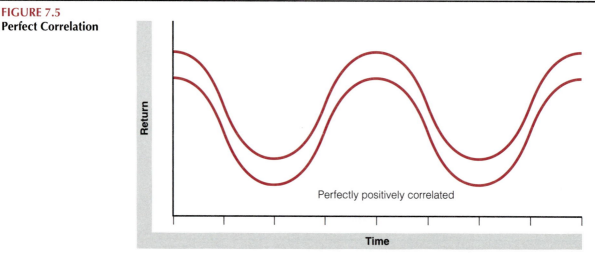

FIGURE 7.5
Perfect Correlation

Return

Perfectly positively correlated

Time

TABLE 7.2 Correlation of Returns Between Firms, Based on Quarterly Returns for 10 Years

	Delta	SWA	United	USAir	AT&T	Sprint	Fairchild	MCI	Motorola	Apple	Compaq	IBM	Lotus
Delta	1.00												
SWA	0.51	1.00											
United	0.48	0.31	1.00										
AT&T	0.20	0.36	0.45	0.27	1.00								
Sprint	0.50	0.22	0.40	0.38	0.39	1.00							
Fairchild	−0.20	−0.47	−0.17	−0.04	0.07	0.29	1.00						
MCI	0.25	0.31	0.37	0.30	0.41	0.68	0.26	1.00					
Motorola	0.26	0.28	0.24	0.31	0.34	0.53	0.09	0.43	1.00				
Apple	0.30	0.25	0.37	0.38	0.17	0.07	−0.09	0.11	0.24	1.00			
Compaq	0.33	0.28	0.34	0.29	0.35	0.14	−0.06	0.21	0.36	0.57	1.00		
IBM	0.21	0.07	0.14	0.11	0.03	0.07	0.11	0.05	0.21	0.36	0.27	1.00	
Lotus	0.37	0.25	0.37	0.39	0.47	0.36	0.16	0.22	0.43	0.37	0.46	0.18	1.00

eliminated. Figure 7.6 shows how two imperfectly correlated stocks combine to produce a portfolio with less risk than if either security were held by itself. The portfolio return goes neither as high nor as low as the returns of either individual stock. Table 7.3 shows the portfolio standard deviation achieved by incrementally increasing the number of securities in a portfolio.[3] Observe that as the number of securities in the portfolio increases, the standard deviation falls. This is a very significant observation. ***Holding more than one stock, even if the stocks are not negatively correlated, can reduce the total level of risk below that of any one stock in the portfolio***. As additional stocks are added to the portfolio, the level of risk continues to fall, though at a decreasing rate. We

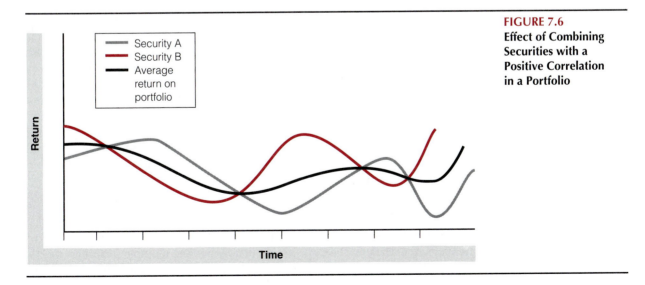

FIGURE 7.6
Effect of Combining Securities with a Positive Correlation in a Portfolio

---

[3]Table 7.3 was prepared using the same real-life data that were used to prepare Table 7.2, which consists of quarterly returns over a 10-year period.

TABLE 7.3 Standard Deviation of Increasingly Large Portfolio

New Security Added to Portfolio	Total Number of Securities in Portfolio	Standard Deviation of Portfolio
United	1	0.2325
Sprint	2	0.1559
Fairchild	3	0.1256
Motorola	4	0.1179
Apple	5	0.0981
CBS	6	0.1094
Disney	7	0.1012
K-Mart	8	0.1004
Lowe's	9	0.1030
Sears	10	0.1020
Wal-Mart	11	0.0992
Woolworth's	12	0.0973
MCI	13	0.0985
IBM	14	0.0954
Delta	15	0.0890

cannot completely eliminate risk by adding additional securities because securities are not perfectly negatively correlated.

What would be the effect on risk of combining two perfectly positively correlated stocks? Because this means the two securities move in lockstep with each other, no risk reduction occurs. In other words, there is no risk benefit to combining perfectly positively correlated stocks. The goal of diversification is to pick stocks that have the lowest possible level of correlation. Review Table 7.2 again. We see that stocks in the same industry have higher correlations than stocks in different industries. Thus, a lower-risk portfolio can be formed by combining the stocks of firms in different industries than by choosing all automotive stocks, for example.

What is remarkable about diversification is that by combining assets into a portfolio, risk is reduced *but expected returns are not*. It is close to getting something for nothing. This raises an important point. If diversification lowers risk, without lowering the expected return, would any investor choose to hold an undiversified portfolio? We will return to this important question later in this chapter. Box 7.1 discusses the risk of not diversifying your portfolio.

Types of Risk

Earlier in this chapter we established that the risk of a stock held by itself is measured by its standard deviation. Then we showed that by holding multiple securities, we can reduce this risk. We saw graphically in Figure 7.6 and numerically in Table 7.3 how this risk reduction occurs, and an example will help drive the point home.

Suppose two firms produce 100% of the widgets used in the world. You are an extremely wealthy investor and choose to buy all of the stock of both Widget A, Inc. and

Box 7.1   Failing to Diversify Could Delay Your Retirement

This chapter discusses at length the advantages of diversifying your investment portfolio. Sometimes, however, this is not as easy to do as it should be. Many employers require employees to put their retirement funds into the firm's stock. This has the advantage of closely tying the employee financially to the firm with the goal of aligning stockholder and employee interest.

While these plans may be effective motivators, they have a hidden risk. If the firm does poorly, the employees can lose their retirement nest eggs. Proctor and Gamble's profit-sharing plan is the oldest in the United States. The employees of P&G hold 20% of the stock. P&G stock accounts for fully 93% of the contents of its employees' retirement plans.

This arrangement was not a problem in the past, because P&G outperformed the market through the 1990s.

It gave high returns with lower volatility than the average market stock. Over the last 30 years P&G provided an annualized 13.3% return, compared with 9.7% for the S&P 500. That ended in 2000.

Between mid-January 2000 and December 2000, the stock dropped 52%. This drop in value deeply affects the 40,000 U.S. employees who have little to retire on other than P&G stock. Many employees have had to delay retirement plans while they hope that the stock price will recover.

P&G is not unique. Coca-Cola has 83% of its employees' retirement money in its stock. Wal-Mart stashes about 80% of its employee profit sharing in its own stock. Employees cannot count on their employers to properly diversify. This is the responsibility of the employee and one that should not be ignored.

Widget B, Inc. Despite the common ownership, these two firms compete furiously for market share and sales. Over time, the lead switches from firm to firm. Widget A, Inc. may have labor problems that lead to shipping delays. Widget B, Inc. may have an advertising campaign fall flat. As the owner of both firms, however, you do not really care which firm sells the most widgets. If the fortune of one firm falls, the other will increase, so you reap the benefit of the sales, regardless of which firm makes them. This illustrates the benefit of diversification. Events that affect individual firms tend to cancel over time because when one firm does poorly, an opportunity is created that permits another to do well.

Now suppose that the world demand for widgets falls. It does not help that you hold both firms. Total sales by both firms fall, so your fortunes diminish. Thus, we see that diversification does not help when the whole market falls. Figure 7.7 shows how Widget A, Inc. and Widget B, Inc. change position over time, but that as the whole market ebbs and flows, total returns rise and fall. The reason for this relationship is that there are two kinds of risk.

Firm-Specific Risk

The risk associated with factors peculiar to a particular firm is called **firm-specific risk.** Firm-specific risk depends on management quality, advertising campaigns, the success of research and development projects, and other factors that affect one specific firm. For example, Apple Computer was developing a new operating system called Copeland that it expected would propel the firm into the future. In August 1996, it abandoned its plan to release the new operating system as a complete package. This was bad news to investors, who were hoping the new program would increase revenues. Later, it introduced the iMac, which did very well. The success of research and development is a firm-specific factor. This type of risk can be diversified away. As in the example above, when one firm has a setback, another may have a breakthrough. Firm-specific risk is synonymous with the terms **unsystematic risk** (because it is independent of the market

FIGURE 7.7
**Diversification Cannot
Eliminate Market Risk**

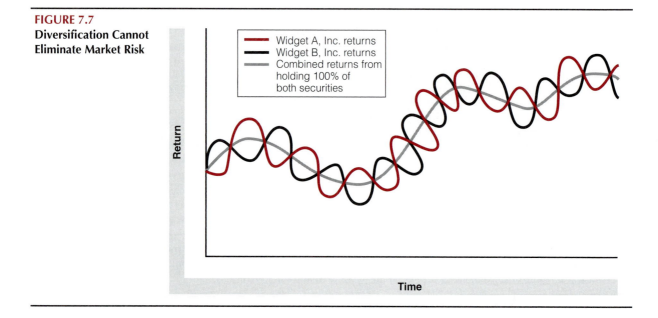

Legend:
— Widget A, Inc. returns
— Widget B, Inc. returns
— Combined returns from holding 100% of both securities

(y-axis: Return, x-axis: Time)

system), **diversifiable risk** (because it can be eliminated by diversification), and **business risk.**

Just as one firm may suffer a setback that does not affect other firms, one industry may have a setback that does not affect other industries. For example, when the airline industry was deregulated in the 1980s, many airline companies suffered declining profits. Problems in one industry are not necessarily transferred to another. For this reason, the investor must diversify not only among many different companies, but also among many different industries (see Box 7.2).

Market Risk

In contrast to firm-specific risk, **market risk** cannot be eliminated by diversification. It is the risk associated with the entire market. Changes in interest rates, natural disasters, business cycles, and the price of inputs to production (such as oil) all affect the whole

Study Tip

The point made in the pre-ceding paragraph is so important it bears repeat-ing. Because firm-specific risk can be removed by diversifying a portfolio, greater firm-specific risk in a security does not increase its required return.

Box 7.2 **Conglomerates Have Not Solved Need for Diversification**

Many firms have sought to eliminate the need for investors to diversify by diversifying themselves. These conglomer-ates run so many different businesses that it is unlikely that market conditions would make them all decline at the same time. To a certain extent this is true. However, in the last few years many conglomerates have spun off subsidiaries. For example, Dun & Bradstreet spun off its Nielsen rating group and its Reuben H. Donnelly Yellow Pages group as separate firms in 1996. Stockholders applauded these moves by bidding the price of Dun & Bradstreet Corp. stock up $1.63 when the news was made public. The rea-son for these breakups is that many firms find it difficult to manage very divergent subsidiaries effectively. Instead of each firm diversifying, it makes sense to let the investor diversify by simply holding the stock of multiple compa-nies. General Electric remains a notable exception to this rule, however. While successfully managing divergent units, GE has given investors unusually high returns.

market. Holding multiple firms is no help if the returns of all firms are falling together. Market risk is also called **nondiversifiable risk** and **systematic risk.**

Not every firm reacts the same to a particular event. For example, falling oil prices are good for Delta Airlines but bad for Exxon. Some firms' returns tend to fluctuate little when market conditions change, whereas others change substantially. For example, the earnings to grocery stores and utility companies may not change much when the economy slows down. Similarly, their earnings do not rise appreciably as the economy peaks. The amount of movement in a security's returns when the whole market moves is its market risk. Utilities usually have low market risk and automobile companies have high market risk.

Figure 7.8 shows the reduction in risk that results from diversification and represents a smoothed graph of Table 7.3. The first few securities added to the portfolio have a substantial effect on total risk. Most of the benefits have been realized by the time 15–20 securities have been added. No matter how many securities are held, however, market risk is not reduced.

Recall from Chapter 1 that one of the foundations of finance is that greater returns require greater risk. We then graphed the relationship between risk and return as an upward-sloping line. We now modify this maxim to be *greater returns require greater market risk.* ***Because we can remove firm-specific risk by diversifying, there is no reason to believe that the market will give higher returns for risk that could be avoided.*** Our measure of the risk of an asset held in a portfolio, then, must measure only the market risk of an asset. The firm-specific risk is eliminated by diversifying.

Total Risk

Earlier in this chapter we used standard deviation to measure risk. We can now more accurately identify what risk is represented by the standard deviation of individual stock returns. ***The standard deviation of an individual stock return measures total risk.*** **Total risk** is the sum of firm-specific risk and market risk. If an asset is held by itself, no benefits from diversification are realized and the correct measure of risk is total risk. When an asset is held in conjunction with other assets, firm-specific risk is reduced and market risk becomes important.

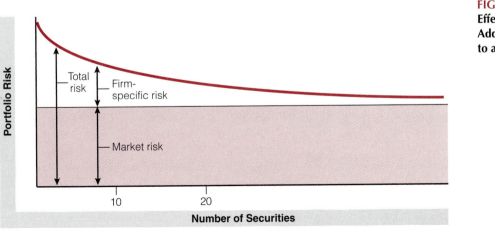

FIGURE 7.8
Effect on Risk of Adding Securities to a Portfolio

Study Tip

1. Remember that the point of this discussion is to identify a way to measure the risk of a portfolio of risky assets. The portfolio standard deviation does this accurately because the correlation between the assets is included in the equation. Correlation is not considered if you were to simply take the weighted average of the standard deviations of the individual assets.

2. Because Equation 7.7 becomes complex very quickly, it is not a useful model. It is presented here only to illustrate why a better model is required.

EXTENSION 7.2

Computing Portfolio Standard Deviation

Recall that our current goal is to determine how to compute the risk of a portfolio of assets. So far we have found that it is not appropriate to compute a weighted average of the individual standard deviations. We have also found that diversification reduces firm-specific risk. The reduction in risk depends on the correlation between the assets. Equation 7.7 shows the calculation of the standard deviation of a two-asset portfolio with correlated returns:

$$\sigma_p = \sqrt{\omega_A^2 \sigma_A^2 + \omega_B^2 \sigma_B^2 + 2\omega_A \omega_B r_{AB} \sigma_A \sigma_B} \qquad (7.7)$$

where

$\omega_{A,B}$ = the weight of asset A and B in the portfolio
σ_p = the standard deviation of the portfolio
$\sigma_{A,B}$ = the standard deviation of asset A and B
r_{AB} = the correlation coefficient between asset A and B

We can investigate the effect of diversification on risk by using Equation 7.7 to compute the risk of a portfolio when there is perfect positive correlation (so no benefit from diversification) and when there is less than perfect correlation.

EXAMPLE 7.5   Portfolio Standard Deviation

Compute the portfolio standard deviation for a portfolio composed of 45% Delta Airlines and 55% AT&T (a) assuming that the correlation between the two securities is equal to 1, then (b) assuming that the correlation is .2. Assume the standard deviation of returns for Delta is 17.1% and that the standard deviation of returns for AT&T is 20.8%.

Solution:
(a) Use Equation 7.7 to compute the portfolio return:

$$\sigma_p = \sqrt{\omega_A^2 \sigma_A^2 + \omega_B^2 \sigma_B^2 + 2\omega_A \omega_B r_{AB} \sigma_A \sigma_B}$$

$$\sigma_p = \sqrt{(.45)^2 (17.1)^2 + (.55)^2 (20.8)^2 + 2(.45)(.55)(1)(17.1)(20.8)}$$

$$\sigma_p = 19.135$$

Note that this is simply the weighted average of the two individual standard deviations:

$$(.45)(17.1) + (.55)(20.8) = 19.1350\%$$

When the correlation coefficient is equal to 1, there is no advantage from diversification.
(b) Again use Equation 7.7 to compute the standard deviation of the portfolio; this time the correlation coefficient is equal to .2:

$$\sigma_p = \sqrt{(.45)^2(17.1)^2 + (.55)^2(20.8)^2 + 2(.45)(.55)(.2)(17.1)(20.8)}$$

$$\sigma_p = 15.01$$

The portfolio standard deviation has fallen from 19.135% to 15.01% as a result of diversification.

In Example 7.5 we saw that the portfolio standard deviation fell about 24% when the correlation coefficient fell from +1 to +.2. If the correlation coefficient was −.2, the portfolio standard deviation falls to about 12.4%. With a −1 correlation coefficient, the portfolio standard deviation is 3.745%.

Another thing to notice about the results of Example 7.5 is that the portfolio standard deviation computed in part b is actually less than the standard deviation of either security held independently (15.01% versus 17.1% and 20.8%). This is a tremendously important finding. We can combine two risky securities and end up with a portfolio less risky than either security held outside of a portfolio.

If there were three stocks in the portfolio, the equation expands to include nine terms. Additionally, the analyst would also have to know the correlation between all three pairs of stocks.[4] This involves computing three correlation coefficients instead of only one as when there are two securities. With a 20-stock portfolio the equation has 400 terms, and you would have to track 190 different correlations. The standard deviation of a portfolio with 100 stocks would require 10,000 terms and the calculation of 4,950 separate correlation coefficients. This process becomes tedious when you realize that there are about 10,000 actively traded securities. Clearly, Equation 7.7 is not practically useful, and an alternative method of evaluating risk is required.

Self-Test Review Questions*

1. What type of risk is priced by the market?
2. Why can you not use the weighted average of the standard deviations of the securities in your portfolio to measure portfolio risk?

CAPITAL ASSET PRICING MODEL

Let us now return to the question raised earlier: Would anyone ever want to hold a non-diversified portfolio? This issue is addressed by the **capital asset pricing model (CAPM),** developed by Bill Sharpe (Stanford), John Lintner (Harvard), and Jan Mossin (Bergen) simultaneously and independently in 1965, based on earlier work by Harry Markowitz. In

---

*1. Market risk, also called nondiversifiable risk.
2. Because the correlation of the asset returns may reduce the variation in the portfolio returns.

---

[4]The number of correlation coefficients is found by using the formula $N(N − 1)/2$ where N is the number of stocks in the portfolio.

TABLE 7.4 Sample Betas

Company Name	Beta
Citation Computer Systems	3.1
First Essex Bancorp	2.7
K-Mart	1.5
Microsoft	1.4
Wal-Mart	1.2
Atlantic Richfield Corp.	0.5
Bell Atlantic	0.5
Sunshine Mining and Refining	−0.6

1990, Sharpe and Markowitz were awarded the Nobel Prize in Economics for their contribution to the theory of finance (by 1990 Lintner and Mossin were deceased). The theory postulates that because diversification allows constant returns with lower risk, we assume no investor would hold a nondiversified portfolio. The CAPM recognizes this and further assumes that there is *one* portfolio of assets that provides the highest return for the risk the investor must assume. Because this one portfolio provides the highest return for the risk, it is called the **efficient portfolio.** This efficient portfolio also is called the market portfolio and is theoretically composed of all possible investments. Because there is one best portfolio, it is assumed that everyone will hold it (remember, this is all just theory). After all, why would anyone hold one portfolio if there was another one that was better? Suppose now that we want to determine the risk of an asset. Because everyone holds the same portfolio, the relevant question is the relationship between that best portfolio and that asset. As a result, instead of having to compute the correlation between every asset with every other asset, we need only to compute the correlations between each asset and this best portfolio, the efficient or market portfolio.

So far, we know that the only relevant risk is market risk. High market risk implies that when the return on the market portfolio (the *best* portfolio discussed above) changes, the return on an asset changes in the same direction and by a large amount. To find a measure of this relationship, we can graph the returns on the market portfolio against the returns on an asset. The slope of the best-fitting line is **beta.** Beta measures the market risk of an asset. A beta of 1 means that the security has average risk. A beta of 2 means the security is twice as risky as the average. Table 7.4 reports the betas of several sample companies.

EXTENSION 7.3

Derivation of Beta

The quarterly returns to Sears and the market portfolio over a 10-year period are graphed in Figure 7.9. Each quarterly return for Sears is graphed against the return earned during that same quarter by the whole market. A line is drawn on the chart that best fits the data. This line relates the return on Sears to the return on the market and is called the **characteristic line.** The slope of the characteristic line is the beta of the security.

Note that there are many points that do not fall on the line. These variations result from firm-specific risk factors. If the security were held as part of a diversified portfolio, these variations would not be material to the overall return on the portfolio. All that would matter would be the variation in return due to the market risk.

The equation for the line is reported on the graph as $y = 0.1449 + 1.083x$. This equation means that the slope of the line is 1.083 and that the y-intercept is 0.1449. Over this period of time using these data, the beta of Sears is 1.083.[5]

E X A M P L E 7.6   Computing Beta

Given the following table of returns, plot the characteristic line and estimate beta:

Return on Zoro Inc.	Return on the Market Portfolio
10%	5%
7	3.5
0	0
5	2.5
−15	−7.5

Solution
Put the market returns on the x-axis and those of Zoro Inc. on the y-axis, as plotted here:

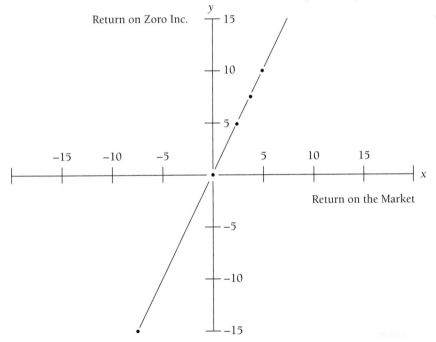

[5]You may wonder why the slope of the characteristic line is called beta. This term originated from the output of the statistical program that was used to plot the firm's returns against the market's returns. When giving the output of any regression, the program reported the intercept as alpha and the slope coefficient as beta. The term stuck and is now universally known as the measure of the market risk of an asset.

Estimate the slope as the rise over the run (for example, 10%/5% = 2). The simplest way to estimate the slope is to find a point where the line crosses one of the axes. In this example, the line crosses at (0,0). Next, pick a point on the x-axis (the run) and find its corresponding point on the line (the rise). If we pick 5% on the x-axis for our run, we get a rise of 10%. Of course, the most accurate way to find the slope of the line is to let Excel or some statistical program plot the data for you and compute the slope of the best-fitting line, as was done for Sears in Figure 7.9.

Portfolio Risk

Betas on individual firms can be computed as shown in Example 7.6 and are readily available from a number of sources, such as Standard & Poor's Stock Reports or Valueline. For example, Valueline reports the beta of Sears to be 1.1. Once the beta for each security in the portfolio has been collected, the risk of the portfolio can be computed by finding the weighted average of the individual betas. The general formula for finding portfolio betas is

$$Beta_{portfolio} = \omega_1\beta_1 + \omega_2\beta_2 + \cdots + \omega_n\beta_n \tag{7.8}$$

where

ω_i = percentage of the portfolio invested in asset i
β_i = beta of asset i

E X A M P L E 7.7   Portfolio Betas

Suppose you held a portfolio with 60% of your funds in Intel (beta=1.7) and 40% of your funds in Carolina Power and Light (beta = 0.5). Compute the risk of the portfolio (the portfolio beta).

FIGURE 7.9
Characteristic Line for Sears

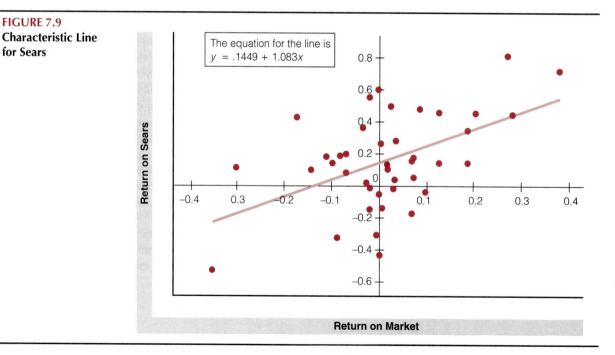

The equation for the line is
$y = .1449 + 1.083x$

Return on Sears

Return on Market

Solution

The portfolio beta would be $(0.60 \times 1.7) + (0.40 \times 0.5) = 1.22$.

Required Rate of Return

Investors have a choice of investing in risky stocks or investing in risk-free assets such as Treasury bills. Investors are assumed to demand higher returns for incurring higher risk. If the returns on Treasury bills and Intel stock were the same, investors would not be willing to give up the safety of the Treasury bill. Intel must pay a risk premium to induce investors to buy its stock. The *average* risk premium paid is the difference between the return on the market portfolio (R_m) and the return on the risk-free security (R_f). Equation 7.9 computes the market risk premium:

$$\text{Market risk premium} = R_m - R_f \tag{7.9}$$

The average return over the last 65 years on large stocks was 12.30%. The Treasury bill currently returns 5.05%. This gives a market risk premium of 7.25% (12.30% − 5.05% = 7.25%).

To find the risk premium associated with a particular security, we need to adjust the market risk premium by multiplying by beta. Low-risk firms have a smaller risk premium than high-risk firms. The risk premium for Intel is $1.7 \times (12.3\% - 5.05\%) = 12.325\%$. The risk premium for Carolina Power and Light is $0.5 \times (12.3\% - 5.05\%) = 3.625\%$.

The total **required rate of return** an investor demands is the sum of the return on the risk-free asset plus the market risk premium adjusted by beta.

CAPM

The CAPM theory states that the return needed to satisfy investors that they are being compensated for both giving up current consumption and for enduring risk is the sum of the risk-free rate of interest plus the market risk premium adjusted by beta. This relationship is given as follows:

$$R_i = R_f + \beta_i(R_m - R_f) \tag{7.10}$$

where

R_i = required return for asset i
R_f = risk-free rate of return
R_m = return on the market
β_i = beta for firm i representing the market risk for asset i

Look at Equation 7.10 carefully. It says that the required return on a risky asset (R_i) is equal to the return you would earn by investing in a riskless asset plus an additional return to compensate you for the risk of the investment. This additional return is the market risk premium multiplied by beta.

Another thing to notice about Equation 7.10 is that the only type of risk that contributes to the required return is the kind that is measured by beta. We know that beta only measures market risk. Firm-specific risk never enters into the calculation of the required return. This is consistent with the conclusion we reached earlier: If firm-specific risk can be eliminated by diversifying your portfolio, you will not be compensated with higher returns for enduring firm-specific risk.

Study Tip

Pay close attention to the terminology used in this section. The CAPM equation provides an estimate of the *required return*. This is neither the expected nor the actual return. The required return is the return that makes investors satisfied that they are being fully compensated for risk and delayed consumption.

Study Tip

It is tempting to think of beta as the slope of the security market line. This is incorrect. The x-axis is beta and the slope is the market risk premium.

E X A M P L E 7.8   Using CAPM

If the beta for Intel is 1.7, the risk-free rate of interest is 5.05%, and the return on the market portfolio is 12.30%, what return must Intel provide investors to compensate them for the risk of the security?

Solution

Substituting these figures into the CAPM equation,

$$R_i = 5.05\% + 1.7(12.30\% - 5.05\%)$$
$$R_i = 5.05\% + 12.325\%$$
$$R_i = 17.375\%$$

Investors in Intel should be satisfied if they receive a 17.375% return.

Security Market Line

The graph of the CAPM equation (Equation 7.10) is called the **security market line.** Remember that the graph of a straight line is $y = b + mx$ where b is the y-intercept and m is the slope of the line. The y-intercept of the CAPM is the risk-free rate of interest (R_f) and the slope is the risk premium ($R_m - R_f$). Figure 7.10 shows the security market line. The average stock beta is 1. In Figure 7.10 the required return on the average stock is 12.30%. Similarly, we find the required returns on Intel and Carolina Power to be 17.37% and 8.67%, respectively. Notice that when beta = 1, the required return is equal to the average return on the market portfolio [$R_i = 5\% + 1(12.3\% - 5\%) = 12.3\%$].

E X A M P L E 7.9   Using CAPM

Suppose that you are considering the purchase of shares in Gap, Inc., a chain of retail clothing stores. After studying the financials, you project the future return on investment to be 14%. Given that the beta of Gap, Inc. is 1.3, should you buy the stock?

FIGURE 7.10
Security Market Line

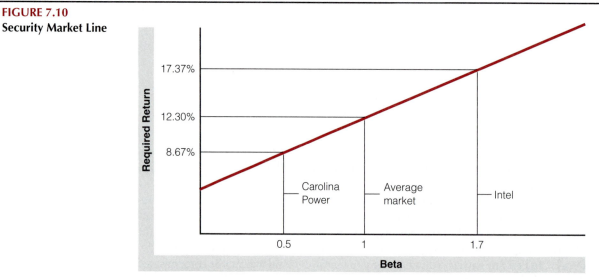

Solution

To answer this question you must first compute the required return using the CAPM and Equation 7.10:

$$R_{Gap} = 5.05\% + 1.3(12.30\% - 5.05\%) = 14.475\%$$

Because you need 14.475% (the required return) and expect the firm to return only 14% (the expected return), you should not invest.

Applying the Concepts

The CAPM is popular because it has many practical applications. The model answers the question, *What return is required from a given level of risk?* This question arises in many situations.

Investments: Estimating the Required Return on Stock

In Example 7.9, CAPM was used to make an investment decision regarding the purchase of a stock. Note from this example that only three pieces of information are needed to make the decision. The investor must estimate the return on the market over the investment period, the risk-free rate of interest, and the beta of the stock. With these three pieces of information alone, the CAPM lets the investor determine what return is fair for the level of risk of the security. This makes CAPM a highly useful theory.

Investments: Calculating the Riskiness of a Portfolio

Different investors have different levels of tolerance for assuming risk. Some investors are comfortable with high-risk portfolios. Others cannot sleep well if there is any chance that they may suffer a loss. The CAPM can help investors maintain the riskiness of their portfolios at their desired level.

Corporate: Using CAPM to Analyze Corporate Investments

Earlier examples demonstrated how CAPM could be used to estimate the required return on stocks. Another use for CAPM is to estimate the required return on projects being considered by a firm.

To make a decision about accepting a project, the firm can compute the beta of the project. They could then use this beta with the risk-free rate of interest and the return on the market to compute a required return. If the expected return on the project exceeds the required return, the firm should accept the project.

Recognize that a firm is made up of a bundle of projects that provides earnings for shareholders. In many ways, this bundle of projects can be likened to a portfolio of investments. The return to the firm is simply the weighted average of the returns on the projects it undertakes. The risk of the firm is the weighted average of the betas of the projects.

Applications of the CAPM

There is nothing in the CAPM theory to suggest that the security market line is stable over time. In fact, it is believed to shift with changing inflationary expectations and changing attitudes toward risk.

Study Tip

We have discussed several different lines in this chapter. Do not confuse the characteristic line with the security market line. The characteristic line graphs one firm's returns against the market and its slope is that firm's beta. The security market line is the graph of the CAPM. Its slope is the market risk premium and it relates risk to return. The characteristic line shows the risk characteristic of *one* security. The security market line shows the required return for *all* securities in the market.

Effect of Inflation

The risk-free rate of interest reflects the compensation you require to give up consumption today. If you expect inflation to diminish the purchasing power of your return, you will demand a higher return. Thus, the risk-free rate of interest is the sum of the real return you require (i.e., the additional consumption you demand) plus an inflation adjustment. Similarly, the return earned by the market portfolio includes the same inflation adjustment.

Now suppose that market participants believe inflation is going to fall in the future. The risk-free rate of interest will fall, as well as the market return. As a result, the security market line will make a parallel shift down from its original location. Figure 7.11 shows the effect of lowered inflationary expectations.

Effect of Changing Attitudes

Remember that the slope of the security market line is the market risk premium ($R_m - R_f$). This premium compensates investors for taking on risk. If investors' attitudes change so that they are less willing to incur risk, the risk premium must increase. Think of the risk premium as a bribe. Investors must be bribed into leaving the safety of the risk-free investment to take on a risky investment. The less willing investors are to take on risk, the higher the bribe must be. Consider the factors that influence investors' attitudes toward risk. If investors have confidence in the current political process, the effectiveness of the government to avert a recession, and the stability of the social structure, they will be less averse to incurring risk. On the other hand, if they believe the economy is in trouble, or that their lives may be disrupted, they will be very opposed to risk.

When risk preferences change, the risk-free rate may stay the same, but the slope of the security market line will pivot. Figure 7.12 shows the effect of increasing aversion to risk. The slope of the security market line has increased. As a result, a higher return is required on every risky investment.

FIGURE 7.11
Effect of Lowered Inflationary Expectations on the Security Market Line

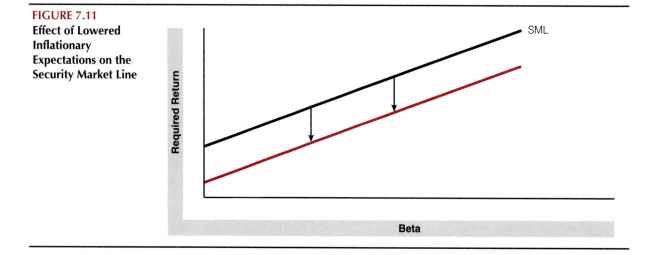

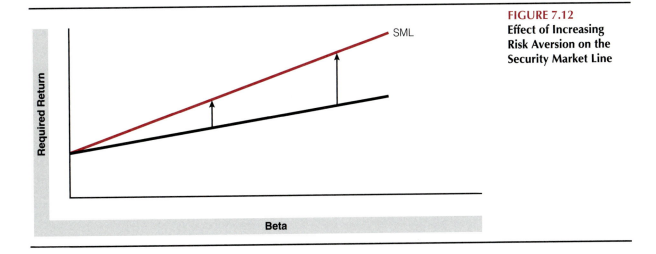

FIGURE 7.12
Effect of Increasing Risk Aversion on the Security Market Line

International Diversification

In our discussion of diversification, we assumed that market risk could not be reduced and that no matter how many stocks you held, you would still be subject to economic factors. Recently, more attention has been given to the possibility of reducing market risk by adding stocks from foreign countries. If you diversify internationally, no one economy can totally disrupt your income stream. For example, Japanese stock soared in the early 1990s, while American stocks languished. In the mid-1990s, when American stocks performed well, Japanese stocks sank. If an investor had held stock in both these markets, much of the variation in returns would have been eliminated.

The original CAPM theory assumes that investors are totally diversified, yet most research on the model has used proxies for the market portfolio that are, at best, limited to a few thousand stocks. Users of the model should remember that complete diversification is needed.

Are Investors Truly Diversified?

One of the tenets of CAPM is that all investors will diversify and security returns will not be sufficient to compensate poorly diversified investors. The fact is that most investors do not hold well-diversified portfolios. There are several reasons for this. First, some of our most important assets are our own personal skills and abilities. These personal skills represent assets in our investment portfolio. When we work for a firm for an extended period of time, often these skills become very centered on that one firm. They may be of little value to other firms. If that firm fails, we may not be as valuable to another firm. The more firm-specific our personal skills, the less well diversified we are.

A second reason many investors hold poorly diversified portfolios is that many firms require or strongly encourage employees to invest in company stock. The result is that not only are the employees' human assets centralized in the firm, but their cash assets are as well.

If the CAPM assumes that investors are fully diversified, yet we know that they often are not, is the model still valid? This question has troubled theorists and practitioners since the model was initially introduced. We will address whether the model works in the next section.

Self-Test Review Questions*

1. What is the slope of the security market line?
2. What is the slope of the characteristic line?
3. How do we compute the risk premium for a security?
4. What does the CAPM compute?
5. If the expected return on an asset is 10% and the required return as computed by CAPM is 9%, should you buy the asset?

DOES CAPM WORK?

We have just spent most of this chapter developing the CAPM theory. A fair question to pose at this juncture is whether the theory actually reflects what happens in the markets. Let us begin answering this question by demonstrating why theorists think it *should* work.

Why CAPM Should Work

The theory suggests that an army of professional, rational investors are carefully searching for any mispriced security. When a mispriced security is located, investors move huge quantities of funds into the security until the price adjusts and the mispricing disappears. The result of these activities is an efficient portfolio in which all securities are correctly priced and the expected return equals the required return. Any security that deviates from the security market line is mispriced, and its presence triggers the above transactions. The result is that all securities are constantly on the security market line.

The model has been embraced by the academic community because it provides important theoretical insights, and by the professional community because it provides practical solutions to difficult problems. However, one problem with the model is that it cannot be tested. For example, we cannot directly observe the inputs to the model. Betas change over time but must be computed using historic data. We cannot accurately estimate the market portfolio because no measure exists of the return on *all* investments.

Another issue is whether it is reasonable to assume that one measure of risk can capture all of the risk of an asset. Is the firm's sensitivity to the market the *only* risk of

5. Yes.
4. The required return on an asset.
3. Multiply the market risk premium by the firm's beta.
2. Beta.
*1. The market risk premium = $R_m - R_f$.

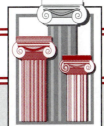

Careers in Finance

Financial Analyst

Each brokerage house and investment fund hires financial analysts who study firms and recommend companies to be purchased or sold. As discussed in this chapter, investors want to buy firms with expected returns that exceed their required returns. Financial analysts study the market looking for opportunities for investment. Usually, analysts specialize in a particular industry and become experts at analyzing how information about that industry will affect firms in it. Students interested in this field may choose to obtain the Certified Financial Analyst designation. This certification requires taking a series of exams over a period of time. Financial analysts should have strong computer and statistical skills as well as a thorough grasp of financial principles.

concern to investors and can this measure fully explain the required return? These questions have generated extensive research into CAPM and the efficiency of the markets.

Does the Evidence Support the Theory?

We address the question of whether the evidence supports the theory in more detail in Chapter 9. At this point it is fair to summarize by saying there is evidence on both sides. The theory states that the only type of risk that matters in pricing a security is market risk. It states that nothing else influences the required return. However, researchers have found that other factors seem to play a role. So far, finance theory has not progressed to a point where we clearly understand what these other factors are, nor why they are important to investors.

One of the studies most damaging to CAPM was published by Eugene Fama and Kenneth French in 1992.[6] These economists found that CAPM fails to fully explain stock returns over time. One reason this study was so widely read is because Fama was an early advocate of CAPM. The study showed that firm size and the book-to-value ratio were better predictors of returns than was beta.

Does all this controversy mean that we should reject CAPM or not use its conclusions in our investment analysis? No, at this point CAPM continues to provide a useful way of thinking about risk and return. Although CAPM is the best theory currently available and is widely used, it is very likely that the next generation of finance students will be taught a modified theory to explain how risk is priced by the market. Until this new theory is found, however, we will continue to use CAPM as the primary method of estimating required returns.

---

[6]Eugene Fama and Kenneth French, "The Cross-Section of Expected Stock Returns," *Journal of Finance,* June 1992.

CHAPTER SUMMARY

This chapter addressed one of the most important topics in finance: the relationship between risk and return. This topic was developed by reviewing four separate points.

- The return on an asset held by itself is found by computing the weighted average of the possible states of nature.
- The risk of an asset held by itself is the standard deviation of the returns. The advantage of the standard deviation as a measure of risk is that it measures both positive and negative deviations from the expected (mean) return.
- The expected return from a portfolio of assets is found by computing the weighted average return from each asset in the portfolio. The weights are the proportion of wealth invested in each asset.
- Finally, the risk of an asset held in a portfolio is measured with beta. We cannot use the standard deviation or the coefficient of variation because these measures of risk fail to adjust for correlation among the assets. The correlation causes firm-specific factors to cancel out. All that remains in a fully diversified portfolio is market risk. Market risk is measured by beta.

If you hold a one-stock portfolio, you will be exposed to a high degree of risk, but you will not be compensated for all of it. If the stock were priced low enough to provide a return high enough to compensate you for your high risk, it would be a bargain to diversified investors. They would rush into the market with buy orders and drive the stock's price up and its return down.

The required return is the amount an investor must earn to feel fully compensated for the risk of holding an asset. The required return is equal to the return you could earn on a riskless asset plus a market risk premium adjusted by beta. The market risk premium is the difference between the return on the market and the riskless asset. The theory that develops this relationship is called the capital asset pricing model. It is often summarized by the equation $R_i = R_f + \beta_i(R_m - R_f)$.

The CAPM allows us to compute the required return. Alternatively, we can estimate an expected return. We will make investments only where the expected return exceeds the required return.

Beta is found by graphing the return on a security against the return on a portfolio that represents the market. The line that results is called the characteristic line. The slope of the characteristic line is the firm's beta.

We can also graph the CAPM equation. The result is the security market line, which shows the required return for every level of market risk. The slope of the security market line is the market risk premium.

The evidence regarding the accuracy of the capital asset pricing model is mixed. Although early tests seemed to support its value for estimating required returns, more recent evidence has called its results into question. Despite these problems, CAPM remains the dominant risk–return theory in finance and it is valuable as a way to think about risk, diversification, and required returns.

KEY WORDS

beta 188	compounded return 171	market risk 184	simple interest 171
business risk 184	diversifiable risk 184	nondiversifiable	standard deviation 174
capital asset pricing model	efficient portfolio 188	risk 185	systematic risk 185
(CAPM) 187	expected return 172	portfolio 177	total risk 185
characteristic line 188	firm-specific risk 183	required rate of	unsystematic risk 183
coefficient of variation	holding period return	return 191	
(CV) 176	(HPR) 171	security market line 192	

DISCUSSION QUESTIONS

1. Why can you not compute the risk of a portfolio by finding the weighted average of the individual securities' standard deviations?
2. Demonstrate graphically how the expected returns for a portfolio will vary over time in each of the following situations. Draw a separate graph for each portfolio. On each graph draw the returns to both securities and then the return to the portfolio.
   a. Two perfectly positively correlated securities
   b. Two perfectly negatively correlated securities
   c. Two securities with a correlation coefficient of +0.5

3. Explain when diversification will lower risk and when it will not affect risk. Can diversification ever raise the risk of a portfolio?
4. Identify five events that would affect the returns to an individual firm, but not the whole economy. If you held a well-diversified portfolio, would these events be of great concern to you?
5. Identify five events that would affect the returns to a large number of firms in the economy. If you held a well-diversified portfolio, would these events be of great concern to you?
6. Discuss the following:
   a. How is total risk measured?
   b. What two types of risk make up total risk?
   c. What is the difference between firm-specific risk and market risk?
   d. Which type of risk can be eliminated by diversifying your portfolio?
   e. Which type of risk remains after a portfolio is diversified?
   f. Which type of risk is priced by the market?
   g. What does it mean to be priced by the market?
7. Review Equation 7.7. If the correlation coefficient between assets A and B were negative, would the portfolio's standard deviation increase or decrease? If your goal is to decrease the portfolio standard deviation, do you want the correlation coefficient to be large or small? (Extension 7.2)
8. What type of risk is measured by beta? Is this the type of risk an investor would be concerned about if the investor holds a diversified portfolio?
9. Explain the meaning of the required return as computed by the capital asset pricing model.
10. What equation is used to compute the security market line? Is the security market line stable over time?
11. What does the evidence say about the validity of the capital asset pricing model?
12. How will international diversification affect the riskiness of a portfolio? Will it reduce market risk or firm-specific risk?
13. Are most investors truly diversified?

PROBLEMS

1. You invested in a stock when it was selling for $10 per share. You just sold it for $17 per share. What was your holding period return? Can this return be compared with annual returns without making adjustments?
2. Assume that you buy a share of stock at $20.50, it pays $1.00 in dividends, and you sell it 90 days later for $21.00. What is your annualized return? Is the return you calculated a simple return or a compounded return?
3. Compute the expected return for the following stock:

State of Nature	Probability	Return
Boom	20%	18%
Average	50	12
Recession	30	5

4. Compute the expected return for a security with the following projected returns:

State of the Economy	Probability	Projected Return
Recession	10%	−15%
Moderate	20	0
Average	40	10
Good	20	15
Outstanding	10	20

5. The following data are available for Agness Corporation (assume an equal probability for each possible economy):

	Project 1	Project 2
Investment	$1,000	$1,000
	Expected Return	
Recession	3%	0%
Normal	5	5
Boom	7	10

   a. What is the expected return for each project?
   b. What is the range of return of each project?
   c. Which project is more risky?
   d. Which project would you choose?
6. Use the following table to answer this problem:

State of the Economy	Probability	Projected Return
Recession	10%	−15%
Moderate	20	0
Average	40	10
Good	20	15
Outstanding	10	20

   a. Compute the standard deviation of the returns. (Extension 7.1)

b. What kind of risk is measured by the standard deviation?

c. Is the standard deviation the appropriate measure of risk for an asset that is held by itself?

7. Assume that you have collected the following data on securities A, B, and C. You will select only one to be held in isolation.

Security	Standard Deviation	Expected Return
Security A	10%	20%
Security B	8	10
Security C	5	1

a. Compute the coefficient of variation for each of these securities. (Extension 7.1)

b. Which security is most risky when risk is measured by the standard deviation?

c. Which security is most risky when risk is measured by the coefficient of variation? (Extension 7.1)

d. Which measure of risk is most appropriate in this instance?

8. Compute the expected return for the following portfolio:

Security	Number of Shares in Portfolio	Price per Share	Expected Return on Security
A	20	$15	20%
B	30	10	18
C	50	12	5

9. What is the expected return for the following portfolio?

Security	Number of Shares	Price per Share	Expected Return
Winner	100	$25	12%
Loser	200	20	6

10. Assume that the standard deviation of security A is 0.2 and that the standard deviation of security B is 0.4. The correlation coefficient between A and B is 0.5. What is the standard deviation of a portfolio composed of 40% security A and 60% security B? Now compute the standard deviation assuming that the correlation coefficient between A and B is 0. What happens to the portfolio standard deviation as the correlation between the securities falls? (Extension 7.2)

11. Use the following data to plot the characteristic line for security J. Use this line to estimate the firm's beta. Is this firm more or less risky than the average firm in the market? Why? (Extension 7.3)

Month	Return on Stock J	Return on the Market
1	−10%	−5%
2	−5	−2.5
3	+5	+2.5
4	−2	−1
5	+10	+5
6	+12	+6
7	0	0

12. Plot the returns on Ajax Inc. and Borax Inc. (y-axis) against the return on the market (x-axis). Estimate the slope of the best-fitting line (remember rise over run). What is the beta of Ajax? Which stock is more risky?

Week	Return on Ajax	Return on Borax	Return on the Market
1	2%	1%	1%
2	−3	0.5	0
3	5	2	2
4	6	3	3
5	−4	−1	−1
6	8	4	4

13. If the risk-free rate of return is 5% and the average return on the market is 12%, what is the risk premium charged by the market? What happens to the risk premium if inflation increases? If investors became more risk averse, would the risk premium rise or fall?

14. If the risk-free rate of return is 5% and the return on the market is 12%, compute the rate of return that will be demanded by investors for a firm with beta equal to
   a. 0.5
   b. 1.0
   c. 1.5
   d. 2.0
   e. 2.5

15. You are considering an investment. After a great deal of careful research you determine that the expected return on the investment is 14%. You also estimate the beta to be 2. If the risk-free rate of interest is 5% and the return on the market is 10%, should you accept the project?

16. You are considering an acquisition of another firm. It is about one-fourth the size of your firm and has a beta of 2.5. You firm's beta is 1. The risk-free rate of interest is 5% and the return on the market is estimated to be 12%. If you complete the acquisition, what will the beta of

your firm be? What is your firm's required return before and after the acquisition?

17. Draw the security market line if the return on the market is 12% and the risk-free rate is 5%. Locate the average firm on the graph. Locate a firm with a beta of 1.5 on the graph. Read the required rate of return on this security off the graph.

*Now assume that the inflation rate increases by 3%, and that all interest rates rise by this amount as a result. Draw the new security market line on the same graph and locate the same two securities. Comment on what happens to the required rate of return when inflation increases.

SELF-TEST PROBLEMS

1. Compute the holding period return for a security you bought for $30.00 two years ago and sold last week for $35.00. You received $1.00 in dividends while you owned the stock.

2. You believe that next year there is a 30% probability of a recession and a 70% probability that the economy will be normal. If your stock will yield −10% in a recession and 20% in a normal year, what is your expected return?

3. What is the standard deviation of the security discussed in problem 2?

4. If the standard deviation of a security's returns is 14% and the expected return is 11%, what is the coefficient of variation?

5. You hold a portfolio composed of 20% security A and 80% security B. If A has an expected return of 10% and B has an expected return of 15%, what is the expected return from your portfolio?

6. Suppose you rebalance the portfolio discussed in problem 5 such that it is now composed of 80% security A and 20% security B. If A has an expected return of 10% and B has an expected return of 15%, what is the expected return from your portfolio?

7. If you were to choose two of the firms listed in Table 7.2 to combine in a portfolio and if your only goal was to minimize risk, which two would you choose?

8. Estimate the beta of a firm assuming that when the market goes up 5% this firm's returns rise 20% and when the market falls 10% this firm's returns fall 40%.

9. Estimate the beta of a firm assuming that when the market goes up 5% this firm's returns rise 2.5% and when the market falls 10% this firm's returns fall 5%.

10. What is the beta of a portfolio composed of 40% security A with a beta of 2 and 60% security B with a beta of 0.75?

11. What is the beta of a portfolio composed of 40% security A with a beta of 1.5 and 60% security B with a beta of −0.25?

12. If the average return on the market is 21% and the risk-free security has a return of 6%, what is the market risk premium?

13. Assume that the risk-free rate is 5%, the return on the market is 15%, and that a firm's beta is 0.5. What return must you earn to be satisfied that you are being fairly compensated for the risk of the firm?

14. Using the assumptions made above about the risk-free rate and the return on the market, what will be the required return for a security with a beta of 1.5?

15. You have analyzed the firm discussed in problem 14 and determined that its expected return is 19.5%. Would you choose to buy it?

16. If investors in general agree that the market is less likely to post a loss, are market risk premiums likely to rise or fall?

17. The risk-free rate of interest is 5%. The market risk premium falls from 10% to 8%. How much does the required return fall for a security with a beta of 1.5?

18. The risk-free rate of interest is 5%. The market risk premium falls from 10% to 8%. How much does the required return fall for a security with a beta of 0.75?

19. You have become convinced that inflation has been tamed. You have been using a real interest rate of 2% and an inflation rate of 4% to estimate the risk-free rate to be 6%. The market rate is also estimated using an assumed inflation rate of 4%. If you believe that inflation will be 3% in the future, how much will the required return on your portfolio change by if the return on the market is 10% and your portfolio's beta is 1.2? (Note that both the market rate and the risk-free rate will change.)

20. Refer to the data in problem 19. How much will the required return on your portfolio change by if your portfolio's beta is 0.5?

WEB EXPLORATION

1. Go to biz.yahoo.com/p/v/vrio.html. This site reports profiles on a large number of firms. These profiles include beta and return on equity. Look up 10 firms and plot the beta for each firm on the x-axis against the return on equity for each firm on the y-axis.
   a. Does beta appear to be correlated with the return on equity?
   b. Find the slope of the security line that you have prepared. Using this result, write down the equation you have found for the CAPM.

2. The CAPM relies on the idea the news is rapidly incorporated into stock prices. The Internet has greatly increased the speed with which such information can be made available. It has been argued that as typical investors become more and more aware of the Internet and its ability to keep them informed, the markets may become increasingly effi-cient. Students of finance should be aware of the news services that report financial information.
   a. Visit the following sites and make a brief list of the types of information available at each. Identify the one you prefer.
      quicken.excite.com/
      averages.dowjones.com/home.html
      news.lycos.com/headlines/business/
      www.nasdaq.com/
      moneycentral.msn.com/investor/home.asp
      www.quote.com/quotecom/
      www.spcomstock.com/
      finance.yahoo.com/?u
   b. Identify three sites that are not listed above that report current business information to the public without charge.

MINI CASE

In this exercise you will learn to compute the beta of a firm. Go to Yahoo finance at finance.yahoo.com/m1?u.

a. At the top of the page a number of indexes are listed. Choose S&P500 or DOW. When you are taken to a graph, choose "5 year" at the bottom of the graph. At the bottom of the 5-year table, choose Historical Data and Monthly. You will now see a table of monthly figures for the index. At the bottom of this table, choose Download Spreadsheet Format. Highlight the entire spreadsheet, copy it, and paste it into a new Excel spreadsheet.

b. Return to the Yahoo site above. Click on Symbol Lookup and type in the name of a company, for example, "Microsoft." Repeat the steps above and paste the 5 years of monthly stock prices into the same spreadsheet as the index values.

c. Compute the monthly returns for both the index and firm. [(Ending − Beginning)/Beginning]. The returns on the market should be to the left of the returns on the firm so that the charting wizard will put the R_m on the x-axis.

d. Graph the returns. Select the column of returns you computed for the market, and then press the control button and select the returns you computed for the individual stock. By pressing the control button, only the columns you select will be highlighted. Use the scatter-type chart. Do not connect the dots with lines. Click on one of the dots on the chart. All the dots will turn yellow. Right click and then choose Add Trendline from the drop-down menu. Under the Type tab, choose Linear. Under the Options tab, check that you want the equation displayed on the chart. Click OK.

e. The coefficient of x is the slope of the line and is the beta for the firm.

f. Go to biz.yahoo.com/p/v/vrio.html and look up the beta of the firm as published. How does this beta compare with the one that you found? List reasons why there may be a difference.

Asset Valuation: Bonds

Chapter Objectives

By the end of this chapter you should be able to:

1. Discuss the theory of valuation
2. Show how bonds are valued
3. Compute yields to maturity on bonds

In this chapter we will investigate how to value financial assets. We will learn that the theory behind asset valuation is the same for all financial assets. Although the theory is not difficult, the calculation of accurate market prices can be challenging. There is room for a great deal of error in the process of valuing many assets, which is why some security prices can be very volatile. An understanding of asset valuation is important for many financial decisions.

In this chapter we draw together many of the skills learned earlier in this text. In Chapter 7 we learned about risk and return. In Chapter 6 we studied the time value of money. In Chapters 2 through 5 we learned how the markets function and who the players are. In this chapter, we put all this information to work to show how financial asset values are established.

This chapter appears in the Investments section of this text. It could as easily have appeared in the Markets section, because that is where asset values are established. It also could have appeared in the section of the book dealing with corporate assets, because virtually all corporate decisions are made with an eye toward maximizing the firm's security prices. Assets are not valued in isolation. It is the interaction of market traders with each other that establishes prices. Asset valuation appears here because the pricing of investments is fundamental to the investment decision.

USE PRESENT VALUE TO PRICE
ANY BUSINESS ASSET

The value of all financial assets are found the same way. ***The current value is the present value of all future cash flows***. Recall the meaning of present value from Chapter 6. If you have the present value of a future cash flow, you can exactly reproduce that future cash flow by investing the present value amount at the discount rate. For example, the present value of $100 that will be received in 1 year is $90.91 if the discount rate is 10%. An investor is completely indifferent between having the $90.91 today and having the $100 in 1 year because the $90.91 can be invested at 10% to provide $100.00 in the future ($90.91 × 1.10 = $100). This represents the essence of value. The current price must be such that the seller is indifferent between continuing to receive the cash flow stream provided by the asset and receiving the offer price.

Valuing Investments

Suppose you are interested in investing in a Yeats painting called *Tinker's Encampment: The Blood of Abel*. If you think you can hold the painting for 2 years and then resell it for $1,200,000, how much would you pay for the painting today? The only cash flow from this investment is the final sales price. No periodic payments will be received. To compute the current price of the painting, you will first need to determine an appropriate discount rate to use for computing the present value of the cash flows. Investments in art are high risk and therefore require a high discount rate. Let us assume you require a 16% return to compensate you for the risk of the investment.

To find the current price of the painting, discount the future cash flow back to the present at 16%. This provides a present value of $891,795.48 [$1,200,000/(1.16^2)]. In fact, this painting actually sold recently for $883,123. The buyer must have expected a slightly lower future price or required a slightly higher return than assumed by our example.

A commercial building is valued using the same technique. An appraisal of commercial property is composed of several methods of valuation. Paramount among these is the income approach, which involves computing the present value of the building's cash flows and using this to estimate the property's value. Other methods used by appraisers include the cost of construction and the sales prices of similar properties. The property appraiser reconciles the income approach with the other valuation methods to arrive at a final price. Suppose that you wanted to find the value of a four-unit student apartment building. Assume that the revenues from rents total $2,000 per month and total expenses average $1,000 per month to pay for insurance, utilities, and damage (such as holes in walls and collapsed balconies). To find the value of the building we also have to estimate the useful life of the building. If we assume that it can be rented for 30 years before needing major renovation, then the current value is the present value of the net cash flows ($2,000 − $1,000 = $1,000/month) for 30 years. If a discount rate of 12% is appropriate, the value of the building is $1,000 × PVIFA$_{360,1\%}$ = $97,218.33 (note that the interest rate is 1% because of monthly compounding).

Why did the Yeats painting not sell for the present value of its expected cash flows and why might the apartment building sell for an amount other than $97,218.33? It is because competition for valuable investments in the market causes prices to adjust so that they represent the best estimate of value by market participants. Not everyone agrees about what the future cash flows are going to be. Assets will sell to the investor who either expects the largest cash flows or sees the least risk in the investment. We will return to this concept later in the chapter.

Let us summarize how to find the value of any business asset.

1. Identify the cash flows that result from owning the asset.

2. Determine what discount rate is required to compensate the investor for holding the asset.

3. Find the present value of the cash flows estimated in step 1 using the discount rate determined in step 2.

The rest of this chapter focuses on how one important asset is valued: bonds. In the next chapter we will study stock valuation. Later in the text we look at how to value businesses.

FINDING THE PRICE OF BONDS

Chapter 2 introduced bonds. Recall that a bond usually pays interest semiannually in an amount equal to the coupon interest rate times the face amount (or par value) of the bond. When the bond matures, the holder also receives a lump sum payment equal to the face amount. Most corporate bonds have a face amount of $1,000. Basic bond terminology is reviewed in Table 8.1.

The issuing corporation usually sets the coupon rate close to the rate available on similar outstanding bonds at the time the bond is offered for sale. Unless the bond has

TABLE 8.1 Bond Terminology

Coupon interest rate	The stated annual interest rate on the bond. It is usually fixed for the life of the bond.
Current yield	The coupon interest payment divided by the current market price of the bond.
Face amount	The maturity value of the bond. The holder of the bond will receive the face amount from the issuer when the bond matures. Face amount is synonymous with par value.
Indenture	The contract that accompanies a bond and specifies the terms of the loan agreement. It includes management restrictions, called covenants.
Market rate	The interest rate currently in effect in the market for securities of like risk and maturity. The market rate is used to value bonds.
Maturity	The number of years or periods until the bond matures and the holder is paid the face amount.
Par value	The same as face amount.
Yield to maturity	The yield an investor will earn if the bond is purchased at the current market price and held until maturity.

an adjustable rate, the coupon interest payment remains unchanged throughout the life of the bond.

The first step in finding the value of the bond is to identify the cash flows the holder of the bond will receive. The value of the bond is the present value of these cash flows. The cash flows consist of the interest payments and the final lump sum repayment.

In the second step these cash flows are discounted back to the present using an interest rate that represents the yield available on other bonds of like risk and maturity. We can now draw a time line to show the cash flows:

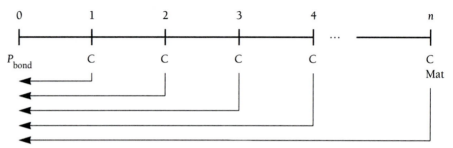

The equation for the value of a bond is provided by Equation 8.1:

$$P_{bond} = \frac{C_1}{\left(1 + k_d\right)^1} + \frac{C_2}{\left(1 + k_d\right)^2} + \cdots + \frac{C_n}{\left(1 + k_d\right)^n} + \frac{Mat}{\left(1 + k_d\right)^n} \qquad (8.1)$$

In summation form, this is

$$P_{bond} = \sum_{n=1}^{N} \frac{C_n}{\left(1 + k_d\right)^n} + \frac{Mat}{\left(1 + k_d\right)^n}$$

where

P_{bond} = current market value of the bond
C = coupon interest payment, equal to the coupon rate times the par value of the bond
Mat = maturity value of the bond (usually $1,000 for corporate bonds)
n = number of periods until the bond matures
k_d = the market interest rate (i.e., the interest rate that the market has set for bonds of similar risk and maturity)

Equation 8.1 becomes tedious to use if there are many cash flows. Because all of the coupon payments are the same, the equation for an annuity can be used. Using present value interest factor notation, Equation 8.1 is rewritten as Equation 8.2:

$$P_{bond} = C(PVIFA_{kdn}) + Mat(PVIF_{kdn}) \qquad (8.2)$$

A financial calculator can also be used to easily find bond values. Many financial calculators have bond value functions that allow input of the exact maturity date along with the current date to give very precise answers. We will demonstrate how to use the more typical calculators to solve bond valuation problems in the next example.

E X A M P L E   8.1   Bond Valuation: Annual Interest Payments

Suppose you found a bond in your great, great aunt's attic. It has 2 years before it matures (it has been in that shoebox for 28 years), a 10% coupon rate, and a $1,000 par value. If interest is paid annually and bonds with similar risk currently have an interest rate of 9%, what is the current value of this bond?

Solution: Numerical Equation

The coupon interest payment is $100 (0.10 × $1,000 = $100). Putting the numbers from the example into Equation 8.1 yields

$$P_{bond} = \frac{\$100}{\left(1 + 0.09\right)^1} + \frac{\$100}{\left(1 + 0.09\right)^2} + \frac{\$1,000}{\left(1 + 0.09\right)^2}$$

$$P_{bond} = \$91.74 + \$84.17 + \$841.68 = \$1,017.59$$

Solution: Financial Factors

Using Equation 8.2 results in the following:

$$P_{bond} = \$100(PVIFA_{2,9\%}) + \$1,000(PVIF_{2,9\%})$$

$$P_{bond} = \$100(1.7591) + \$1,000(0.8417)$$

$$P_{bond} = \$175.91 + \$841.70 = \$1,017.61$$

Solution: Financial Calculator

There are five keys on the financial calculator that deal with the time value of money. Bond valuation problems use all of them:

$$= -1017.59$$

If you do not get the right answer, make sure that your calculator is set to one payment per period. Note that the answer is *negative* $1,017.59. The negative number indicates a cash outflow. If you invest $1,017.59 (an outflow), you will receive two payments of $100 and one payment of $1,000 (inflows). It is important to keep track of the direction of your cash flows and to be consistent when you input the signs.

Your great, great aunt did not exactly make you rich. Maybe she should have bought General Electric stock instead.

Self-Test Review Question*

Suppose your great, great aunt had deposited the $1,000 in an account earning 10%. How much would be in this account and why is the value so different from the value of a bond?

*The future value of a $1,000 deposit earning 10% for 28 years is $14,420.99 [$1,000(1.10^{28}) = $14,420.99]. A bond pays interest, but the interest does not get added back to the balance to earn additional interest. In other words, bond interest is not compounded.

Pricing of Bonds with Semiannual Compounding

Let us look at a more realistic example. Most bonds pay interest semiannually. To adjust the cash flows for semiannual payments, divide the coupon payment by 2 because only half of the annual payment is paid each 6 months. Similarly, to find the interest effective during one-half of the year, the market interest rate must be divided by 2. The final adjustment is to double the number of periods because there will be two periods per year. With semiannual compounding, Equation 8.2 becomes Equation 8.3:[1]

$$P_{\text{semiannual bond}} = \sum_{n=1}^{2n} \frac{C/2}{\left(1 + \dfrac{k_d}{2}\right)^n} + \frac{\text{Mat}}{\left(1 + \dfrac{k_d}{2}\right)^{2n}} \tag{8.3}$$

E X A M P L E 8.2   Bond Valuation: Semiannual Payment

Let us compute the price of Safeway bonds recently listed in the Wall Street Journal. The bonds have a 10.95% coupon rate and a $1,000 par value (maturity value), and mature in 2021 (n = 20). Assume semiannual compounding and that the market rate of interest is 12%.

Solution

Begin by identifying the cash flows. Compute the coupon interest payment by multiplying 0.1095 times $1,000 to get $109.50. Because the coupon payment is made each 6 months, it will be half of $109.50, or $54.75. The final cash flow consists of repayment of the $1,000 face amount of the bond. This does not change because of semiannual payments.

Next, we need to know what market rate of interest is appropriate to use for computing the present value of the bond. We are told that bonds being issued today with similar risk have coupon rates of 12%. Divide this amount by 2 to get the interest rate over 6 months. This gives an interest rate of 6%.

Finally, find the present value of the cash flows. Note that with semiannual compounding the number of periods must be doubled. This means that we discount the bond payments for 40 periods.

Solution: Financial Factors

It is not reasonable to compute the present value of 40 separate cash flows using the numeric equation method. Below we find the value of the bond using financial factors, which take advantage of the fact that the constant interest payments are an annuity:

$$P_{\text{bond}} = \$54.75(\text{PVIFA}_{40,6\%}) + \$1,000(\text{PVIF}_{40,6\%})$$

$$P_{\text{bond}} = \$54.75(15.0463) + \$1,000(0.0972)$$

$$P_{\text{bond}} = \$823.78 + \$97.20 = \$920.98$$

---

[1]There is a theoretical argument for discounting the final cash flow using the full-year interest rate with the original number of periods. Derivative securities are sold in which the principal and interest cash flows are separated and sold to different investors. The fact that one investor is receiving semiannual interest payments should not affect the value of the principal-only cash flow. However, virtually every text, calculator, and spreadsheet computes bond values by discounting the final cash flow using the same interest rate and number of periods as are used to compute the present value of the interest payments. To be consistent, we will use that method in this text.

Solution: Financial Calculator

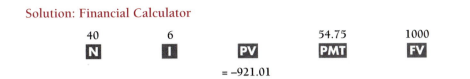

Note the small difference in value between the financial factors and the financial calculator approaches. The calculator is the most accurate. The market price of this bond should be $921.01. The value of the bond computed with annual compounding is $921.57.[2]

Notice that the market price is below the $1,000 par value of the bond. When the bond sells for less than the par value, it is selling at a **discount.** When the market price exceeds the par value, as in Example 8.1, the bond is selling at a **premium.** Notice that in the previous paragraph the price of the semiannual bond is less than the price of the annual bond. This is always true for *discount* bonds. The price of semiannual premium bonds is always above that of similar annual bonds.

EXTENSION 8.1

Computing Semiannual Bond Prices Using the Effective Annual Rate

In the last section we computed the price of semiannual bonds using a discount rate found by simply dividing the annual rate by 2. While this initially seems intuitive and easy to do, it results in bond prices that may not make sense. Consider the following example.

Suppose that you have an annual 10% coupon bond with 5 years to maturity and a $1,000 par value. What is the current market price if market rates are currently 12%? Solving this with a calculator where N = 5, I = 12%, PMT = $100, and FV = $1,000, we get a price of $927.90.

Now let us find the price of the bond if the interest payments are made semiannually. If we solve this as shown in the last section, we divide the interest payment and market interest rate by 2 and double the number of periods. Again, solving using the calculator method with N = 10, I = 6%, PMT = $50, and FV = $1,000, we get a price of $926.40.

When we compare the price of the bond with annual payments with the one with semiannual payments, we find that by using this method the price of the semiannual bond is *less* than that of the annual bond. Clearly, investors would rather have the semiannual bond and should therefore be willing to pay more for it. What went wrong?

---

[2]The method for computing semiannual bond prices shown here is a simplification that gives only an approximate answer. See Extension 8.1 for a more complex but accurate approach.

The problem is that by discounting the cash flows of the semiannual bond at an interest rate computed by simply dividing the annual rate in half, we have ignored the effect of compounding discussed in Chapter 6. To correctly adjust for semiannual compounding, we must compute the periodic interest rate by using the effective rate of return. We do this by manipulating Equation 6.3,

$$\text{Effective Rate} = \left(1 + \frac{i}{m}\right)^m - 1 \qquad (6.3)$$

We know that the effective rate is 12%, since the effective rate for the annual and semiannual bonds must be the same. Let us call the periodic rate i' and rearrange Equation 6.3 to solve for i':

$$\textit{Effective Rate} = (1 + i')^m - 1 \qquad (8.4)$$
$$i' = (1 + \textit{Effective Rate})^{1/m} - 1$$

Using Equation 8.4 solve for the periodic rate,

$$i' = (1 + 12)^{1/2} - 1$$
$$i' = .0583 \text{ or } 5.83\%$$

Now if we use i' as the periodic rate and compute the price of the semiannual bond as above (N = 10, I = 5.83, PMT = $50, and FV = $1,000), we find the semiannual bond worth $938.41. This is above the value of the bond that pays interest annually ($938.41 versus $927.90).

E X A M P L E   8 . 3   Bond Valuation of Semiannual Bonds Using Effective Annual Rate Calculation

Compute the price of a semiannual bond with a 10% coupon rate, 10 years to maturity, and a $1,000 par, assuming a 7.5% market rate. Use the effective rate method.

Solution
Begin by computing the period rate using Equation 8.4:

$$i' = (1 + \textit{Effective Rate})^{1/m} - 1$$
$$i' = (1 + .075)^{1/2} - 1$$
$$i' = .0368 = 3.68\%$$

Now solving using the calculator approach, with N = 20, I = 3.68, PMT = $50, and FV = $1,000, the value is $1,184.58. The price of the same bond paying interest annually would be $1,171.60.

Study Tip
The relationship between interest rates and value can be used to check your answers to bond value problems. If the market interest rate is above the coupon rate, your bond value should be less than $1,000. If the market interest rate is below the coupon rate, the bond value should be more than $1,000.

Interest Rate Risk

What determines whether a bond will sell for a premium or a discount? Suppose that you are asked to invest in an old bond that has a coupon rate of 10% and $1,000 par. You would not be willing to pay $1,000 for this bond if new bonds with similar risk were available yielding 12%. The seller of the old bond would have to lower the price on the 10% bond to make it an attractive investment. In fact, the seller would have to lower the price until the yield earned by a buyer of the old bond exactly equaled the yield on similar new bonds. This means that as interest rates in the market rise, the value of bonds with fixed interest rates falls. Similarly, as interest rates available in the market on new bonds fall, the value of old bonds with fixed interest rates rises.

Many investors think that bonds are a very low risk investment because the cash flows are fairly certain. It is true that high-grade bonds seldom default, but bond investors face price fluctuations due to market interest rate movements in the economy. In Chapter 7 we defined risk as fluctuations in the cash flows. As interest rates rise and fall, the value of bonds changes in the opposite direction. This does not cause a loss to investors who do not sell their bonds, but many investors do not hold their bonds until maturity. If they attempt to sell their bonds after interest rates have risen, they will receive less than they paid. The possibility of suffering a loss because of interest rate changes is called **interest rate risk.**

Review Table 8.2. This table shows the market price of 10% coupon bonds with 1, 10, and 20 years to maturity at three different market interest rates. Notice that when the market rate is the same as the coupon rate the bond is valued at par. In other words, the value of the bond does not change unless the market interest rate changes, regardless of how many years there are to maturity. The other important feature to note in Table 8.2 is that the change in the value of the bonds is much greater for bonds with longer maturities. A 1% drop in interest rates results in a $9.17 increase in price if the bond has 1 year to maturity. That same 1% drop in interest rates results in a $91.28 increase in price if there are 20 years to maturity. We can conclude from this that *interest rate risk increases with increasing maturity*.

Recall the discussion of the yield curve from Chapter 4. We found that bonds with longer maturities had higher interest rates and discussed several theories to explain the shape of the yield curve. Interest rate risk is one reason for the upward slope. Longer-term bonds are more risky because interest rate risk is greater the longer the term to maturity. Investors demand higher returns to compensate for the increased risk (see Box 8.1).

TABLE 8.2 Price of $1,000 Par, 10% Coupon Bond with Different Maturities and Market Interest Rates

	Market Rate		
Term	9%	10%	11%
1	$1,009.17	$1,000.00	$990.99
10	1,064.18	1,000.00	941.11
20	1,091.28	1,000.00	920.37

Box 8.1 Investors Can Select Desired Interest Rate Risk

Many investors in bonds want and expect low risk. When interest rates rise and fall the values of their bonds change, possibly for the worse. Some investment companies attempt both to educate investors about the perils of interest rate risk and to offer investment alternatives that match their investors' risk preferences.

Vanguard Group, for example, offers eight separate high-grade bond mutual funds. In its prospectus, Vanguard separates the funds by the average maturity of the bonds they hold. Three funds invest in bonds with average matu-

rities of 1 to 3 years, which Vanguard rates as having low interest rate risk. Three different funds hold bonds with average maturities of 5 to 10 years, which Vanguard rates as having medium interest rate risk. Two funds hold long-term bonds with maturities of 15 to 30 years, which Vanguard rates as having high interest rate risk.

The Vanguard prospectus demonstrates the effect on interest rates by computing the percentage change in bond value resulting from a 1% increase and decrease in interest rates.

Bond Price Changes over Time

In Table 8.2 we see that as the time to maturity falls, the closer the values of both the 9% and 11% bonds are to par ($1,000). In other words, as the maturity date approaches, the value of the bonds approaches the maturity value of the bond, regardless of whether it initially sold at a premium or a discount. To see why this occurs, consider what you would pay for a bond the day before it matures. You would pay almost $1,000, regardless of the coupon rate or the market rate, because you would know that the very next day you would be paid the face amount of $1,000.

The relationship between the time to maturity and the price of a discount bond (one with a coupon rate below market rates), a premium bond (one with a coupon rate above market rates), and a par value bond is graphed in Figure 8.1. All mature in the year 2003.

When you buy a bond at a discount, you will receive the benefit of price appreciation as the maturity date approaches. This is in addition to the interest payment you will

FIGURE 8.1
Price for Various Years of a 10% Coupon Bond at 9% and 11% Market Rates

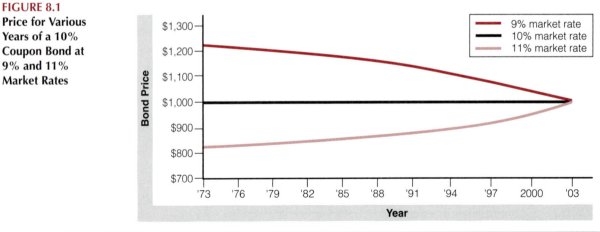

receive from the issuing firm. If you buy a premium bond, you will suffer a price decline as the maturity date approaches.

The 10% coupon bond shown in Figure 8.1 initially sold for $1,225.16 when market interest rates were 8%. The market price falls the closer to maturity in 2003. The 10% coupon bond initially sold for $838.90 when market interest rates were 12%. Its price rises the closer to maturity in 2003. The 10% coupon bond has a constant value of $1,000 when market rates are also 10%. The value of the bonds in all three situations is $1,000 at maturity.

Computing the Yield to Maturity

Study Tip

It is easy to confuse the market rate of interest and the YTM. In fact, they are the same thing. If you are given the current market price of the security, you can solve for the YTM. If you are given the current market interest rate, you can solve for the market price of the bond.

Does the coupon rate offered on a bond accurately reflect the yield an investor will receive from a bond? No, the coupon rate is only part of the return an investor earns. Remember that the issuer of a bond pays the holder the face amount of the bond when it matures. In Example 8.2, an investor pays $921.01 (calculator method) for a bond with a coupon rate of 10.95%. The investor receives semiannual interest payments equal to 10.95% of $1,000 *plus a capital gain from an increase in the price of the bond from $921.01 at purchase to $1,000 at maturity.* The total return consists of the interest income plus the capital gain:

Total return = Interest payment + Change in price of the bond

The total return an investor earns on a bond from both interest payments and a change in the price of the bond is called the **yield to maturity** (YTM). The YTM is computed by solving for the discount rate that sets the present value of the interest and principal payments equal to the current market price. In Example 8.2 the YTM is 12%. Equation 8.5 shows the role of YTM in the bond valuation equation:

$$P_0 = \frac{C}{\left(1 + YTM\right)^1} + \frac{C}{\left(1 + YTM\right)^2} + \cdots + \frac{C}{\left(1 + YTM\right)^n} + \frac{Mat}{\left(1 + YTM\right)^n} \quad (8.5)$$

If interest rates in the market are above the coupon rate, then the price of the bond must be below par so that investors will earn an extra return from the increase in price to make up for a low coupon rate. If interest rates in the market are below the coupon rate, then the price of the bond must be above par so that investors will incur a loss on the principal. In either case the price of the bond adjusts so that the YTM on the bond is exactly equal to the return available on similar bonds selling in the market. Box 8.2 discusses an unusual situation in which the YTM was negative.

Calculation of the YTM is most easily done on a financial calculator. Simply input the current market price as the PV, the face amount as the FV, the number of periods to maturity as N, and the coupon payments as PMT, and compute I.[3]

---

[3]On most calculators you must accurately input the signs of the cash flows. If you input all cash flows with a positive sign, you will get an error message. Input the current market price as a negative value and the interest payments and par value as positive values.

Box 8.2 Are Negative T-Bill Rates Possible?

We normally assume that interest rates must be positive. Negative rates mean that in the future investors get back less when their securities mature than was originally invested. Negative rates would seem impossible then—why would anyone invest when they could simply hold cash?

Despite this argument, in November 1998, interest rates on Japanese 6-month Treasury bills became negative, yielding an interest rate of –0.004%. This was an extremely unusual event; no other country has seen negative interest rates during the past 50 years.

Why did the Treasury rates go negative? We cannot look to the weakness of the Japanese economy nor to their negative inflation rate. These factors can explain low rates but not negative ones. The actual reason is because the convenience of holding large sums of money in bonds rather than in cash made T-bills more desirable than cash. Obviously, this convenience factor cannot justify taking the rates much below zero, but it did give rise to a seemingly impossible situation.

E X A M P L E 8.4   Yield to Maturity

What is the YTM of a $1,000 par bond with a 10% coupon, 2 years to maturity, and a current market price of $966.20?

Solution
The solution is found by solving the following equation for YTM:

$$\$966.20 = \frac{\$100}{\left(1 + YTM\right)^1} + \frac{\$100}{\left(1 + YTM\right)^2} + \frac{\$1,000}{\left(1 + YTM\right)^2}$$

There is no easy algebraic method to solve for YTM in this equation. There are three non-algebraic approaches.

Financial calculator: In this example PV = –$966.20, PMT = $100, FV = $1,000, and N = 2. I computes as 12%.

Plug and chug: Pick an interest rate and plug it in for YTM in Equation 8.5. Then calculate whether the right-hand side equals the current market price. If it does not, pick another interest rate and try again. You can use what you know about the price of bonds to help pick interest rates. If the price is below par, then we know that the yield to maturity is above the coupon rate. You might begin by trying 11%. If you plug 11% into the above equation and solve for the price, you get $982.87. Because this is still above the actual market price, try 12%.

Approximation equation: An estimation equation has been developed that gives reasonable approximations of the yield to maturity. Equation 8.6 can be used when calculators are not available:[4]

$$YTM = \frac{C + \dfrac{Par - Market}{n}}{\dfrac{Par + 2\,Market}{3}} \qquad (8.6)$$

Study Tip

A common mistake made when applying Equation 8.6 is to use the coupon interest *rate* in the numerator rather than the coupon interest *payment*.

---

[4]Equation 8.6 differs from the YTM estimation equation that is widely reported. Ricardo Rodriguez demonstrates in the *Journal of Financial Education,* Fall 1988, that the above provides consistently better results.

where

> C = coupon interest payment, equal to the coupon rate times the par value of the bond
> Par = face amount of the bond, usually $1,000
> $Market$ = current market price of the bond
> n = number of periods until maturity

Equation 8.6 is used here to solve for the YTM in this Example 8.4:

$$YTM = \frac{\$100 + \dfrac{\$1{,}000 - \$966.20}{2}}{\dfrac{\$1{,}000 + 2(\$966.20)}{3}} = 11.96\%$$

This is a reasonable approximation of the actual YTM of 12%.

Comparing Yield to Maturity to Current Yield

An investor earns the YTM in effect at the time the bond is purchased only if the bond is held until it matures. As interest rates rise and fall over time, the YTM changes. This does not matter to the investor as long as the bond is not sold. Because many investors do not know how long they will hold a bond, another measure of a bond's return is often quoted. The **current yield** is the coupon interest payment divided by the current market price of the bond and is computed using Equation 8.7:

$$Current\ yield = \frac{C}{Market} \tag{8.7}$$

where

> C = coupon interest payment, equal to the coupon rate times the par value of the bond
> $Market$ = current market price of the bond

The current yield is widely reported. Be aware that it only approximates the actual yield to maturity. It tells you what you will earn in interest payments, but it ignores the earnings from appreciation or depreciation in the price of the bond.

E X A M P L E 8.5   Current Yield

What is the current yield for the Safeway bond described in Example 8.2? The coupon interest rate is 10.95% and we computed the market price to be $921.01.

Solution
The coupon interest payment is found by multiplying the coupon interest rate times the $1,000 par value (0.1095 × $1,000 = $109.50). Substituting the factors into Equation 8.7, you obtain

$$Current\ yield = \frac{\$109.50}{\$921.01} = 11.89\%$$

The current yield is well above the coupon rate because investors pay less than $1,000 for the investment.

We can now put current yield together with the YTM and the **capital gain** (the percentage change in the price of the bond):

$$\text{Yield to maturity} = \text{Current yield} + \text{Capital gain} \qquad (8.8)$$

In Example 8.5 the yield to maturity is 12%, since the market rate of interest is given as 12%. The current yield is 11.89%. If we solve for the capital gain, we get the following:

$$12\% = 11.89\% + \text{Capital yield}$$
$$\text{Capital gain} = 12\% - 11.89\% = 0.11\%$$

We can verify this figure by computing the price appreciation of the bond. The bond price was originally computed with 20 years to maturity. The bond price with 19 years to maturity is $922.06. The price has increased by $1.05. The percentage increase is $1.05/$921.01 = 0.0011 = 0.11%, as computed above.[5]

Self-Test Review Questions*

1. What is the current market price of a $1,000 par bond with a 6% coupon paid semiannually and 5 years to maturity if current market rates on similar bonds are 8%?
2. What is the current yield on this bond?
3. If the price goes to $950, what is the yield to maturity?

INVESTING IN BONDS

Bonds are one of the most popular long-term alternatives to investing in stocks. Bonds are lower risk than stocks because they have a higher priority of payment. This means that when the firm is having difficulty meeting its obligations, bondholders get paid before stockholders. Additionally, should the firm have to liquidate, bondholders must be paid before stockholders.

Even healthy firms with sufficient cash flow to pay both bondholders and stockholders often have very volatile stock prices. This volatility scares many investors out of

---

*1. $P_b = \$30(PVIFA_{4\%,10\ yr}) + \$1,000(PVIF_{4\%,10\ yr}) = \$243.33 + \$675.60 = \$918.93$.

2. $CY = \$60/\$918.93 = 0.06529 = 6.53\%$.

3. Use the estimation equation:

$$YTM = \frac{\$30 + \dfrac{\$1,000 - \$950}{10}}{\dfrac{\$1,000 + 2(\$950)}{3}} = 0.0362 = 3.62\%$$

Because the bond is semiannual, the interest rate computed by the estimation equation must be multiplied by 2 to get the annual interest rate: 3.62 × 2 = 7.24%

---

[5]The bond price is found by computing the present value with $n = 38$, PMT = $54.75, $i = 6\%$, and FV = $1,000 because the bond has semiannual payments.

Careers in Finance

Credit Manager

Many firms sell their products on credit, giving their customers varying amounts of time to pay. The credit manager evaluates the customers and decides whether to extend them credit. Once credit has been given, the credit manager is responsible for making sure that payments are made as agreed and initiating collection efforts when problems arise. In some firms the amount of credit extended can be very large and evaluating customer creditworthiness is very similar to being a bank loan officer. The credit manager must balance the firm's desire to sell its products against the risk that the customer could fail to pay. Credit managers should earn between $30,000 and $65,000 depending on the firm's size.

the stock market. Bonds are the most popular alternative. They offer security and dependable cash payments, making them ideal for retired investors and those who want to live off their investment.

One important lesson in this chapter is that even though bonds may be less risky than stock, they are still subject to interest rate risk. Recall that this means that changing interest rates can result in changing bond prices. If an investor were to buy long-term bonds when interest rates were low, a loss may be suffered if rates rise. For this reason prudent investors match the maturity of their bond portfolios with their return and risk requirements. Box 8.3 discusses the importance of the yield curve when selecting bonds.

Box 8.3 Watch That Yield Curve

In Chapter 4 we introduced the yield curve and noted that it is usually upward sloping, meaning that long-term bonds provide higher returns than short-term bonds. We also learned that the yield curve changes its shape based on a number of factors. Investors in bonds should carefully examine the yield curve before buying bonds.

At times there is a large premium for investing in long-term bonds. At other times, such as when the yield curve is flat, there are very little additional earnings for taking the risk of buying a long-term security. For example, in December 1997, the yield curve was flat and investors earned only about 0.75% for investing in 30-year bonds rather than 1-year bonds. Yet with interest rates very low, those long-term bonds are subject to large losses in principal value if interest rates in the market were to increase. By contrast, in 1992, 30-year bonds paid 3.78% more than 1-year bonds, yet with the higher interest rates then offered, the chance of a principal loss was lower.

Bond investors should consider the level of interest rates in the market, the shape of the yield curve, and the likelihood that rates will rise in the future when deciding which bonds to purchase.

By December 2000, the yield curve was inverted. Short-term interest rates were high due to rate hikes by the Federal Reserve, but long-term rates were low due to expectations that rates would be dropped in the future to spur the economy. Investors at this time were actually penalized, rather than rewarded, for buying long-term bonds with their accompanying high interest rate risk.

CHAPTER SUMMARY

The values of all business assets are computed the same way: by computing the present value of the cash flows that will go to the holder of the asset. For example, a commercial building is valued by computing the present value of the net cash flows the owner will receive. We compute the value of bonds by finding the present value of the cash flows, which consist of periodic interest payments and a final principal payment.

The value of bonds fluctuates with current market prices. If a bond has an interest payment based on a 5% coupon rate, no investor will buy it if new bonds are available for the same price with interest payments based on 8% coupon interest. To sell the bond the holder will have to discount the price until the yield to the holder equals 8%. The amount of the discount is greater the longer the term to maturity.

The return a bond holder will earn if the bond is held until it matures is its yield to maturity. Because investors often do not plan to hold a bond this long, many prefer to look at the current yield, which ignores the final principal payment. The yield to maturity is the sum of the current yield and the percentage change in the price of the bond.

Bond values can be computed accurately because all of the inputs are known with a high degree of confidence. This is not the case for stock valuation. We explore this topic in Chapter 9.

KEY WORDS

capital gain 216
current yield 215

discount 209
interest rate risk 211

premium 209
yield to maturity 213

DISCUSSION QUESTIONS

1. How is any investment asset valued?
2. Explain why an investor is willing to pay a price equal to the present value of the cash flows for an investment.
3. What cash flows will an investor receive from the purchase of a bond?
4. If you buy a bond, are you borrowing money from a corporation or lending money to the corporation? Explain your answer.
5. Under what conditions will an investor actually receive a return on a bond equal to the yield to maturity?
6. What is interest rate risk?
7. Is interest rate risk more or less for long-term bonds than for short-term bonds?
8. What two points are made by Table 8.2?
9. As a bond approaches maturity, what happens to its market price?
10. What portion of the yield to maturity is measured by the current yield? What other return does the investor earn?

PROBLEMS

1. A firm is considering buying another company. The acquisition will increase revenues by $10,000 per year for 5 years. If the appropriate discount rate is 15%, what is the value of this acquisition? (Hint: Find the present value of the cash flows.)
2. What is the value of a building that will generate net revenues (after all costs and maintenance) of $15,000 per year for 20 years if the appropriate discount rate is 10%?
3. A bond pays $80 per year in interest (8% coupon). The bond has 5 years before it matures, at which time it will pay $1,000. Assuming a discount rate of 10% and annual payments, what should be the price of the bond?
4. A bond has a 10% coupon rate of interest (paid annually). If it matures in 4 years and market interest rates for similar bonds are 7%, what is the price of the bond?
5. A zero coupon bond has a par value of $1,000 and matures in 20 years. Investors require a 10% annual return on these bonds. For what price should the bond sell? (Note: Zero coupon bonds pay no interest. The entire return is from appreciation.)
6. Consider the two bonds described here:

	Bond A	Bond B
Maturity	15 yr	20 yr
Coupon rate (paid semiannually)	10%	6%
Par value	**$1,000**	**$1,000**

   a. If both bonds had a required return of 8%, what would the bonds' prices be?

   b. Describe what it means when a bond sells at a discount, at a premium, and at its face amount (par value). Are these two bonds selling at a discount, a premium, or par?

   c. If the required return on the two bonds rose to 10%, what would the bonds' prices be?

7. A bond sells for $1,525, matures in 10 years, has a par value of $1,000, and has a coupon rate of 10%, paid semiannually. What is the bond's yield to maturity?

8. A 10-year bond pays interest of $35 semiannually, has a par value of $1,000, and is selling for $737. What are its coupon rate and its yield to maturity?

9. A bond has 5 years to maturity, a coupon rate of 10%, and a par value of $1,000, and the market rate for similar bonds is 12% (yield to maturity = 12%). Assume annual compounding.

   a. What is the current price of the bond?

   b. What is the current yield?

   c. What is the capital gain?

   d. What will be the price of the bond when it has 4 years to maturity?

   e. What is the percentage increase in price during the first year? Is it the same as you found in part c?

10. A bond has 10 years to maturity, a coupon rate of 8%, and a par value of $1,000, and the market rate for similar bonds is 6% (yield to maturity = 6%).

   a. What is the current price of the bond? Assume annual compounding.

   b. What is the current yield?

   c. What is the capital gain?

   d. What will be the price of the bond when it has 9 years to maturity?

   e. What is the percentage decrease in price during the first year?

11. A bond pays interest semiannually, has a par value of $1,000, a coupon rate of 7%, and 6 years until it matures. Assuming a market rate of 6%, what is the value of the bond computed using the effective annual rate? (Extension 8.1)

12. A bond pays interest semiannually, has a par value of $1,000, a coupon rate of 5%, and 10 years until it matures. Assuming a market rate of 8%, what is the value of the bond computed using the effective annual rate? (Extension 8.1)

SELF-TEST PROBLEMS

1. A building has an expected life of 30 years. Its net cash flows are projected to be $120,500 per year. If a discount rate of 17% is appropriate, what is the value of the building?

2. If in problem 1 the discount rate were to increase to 23% because of a perception of increased risk in the real estate market, what would the value of the building become?

3. A bond's par value is $1,000. The bond has 5 years until maturity and its coupon rate is 7%. What is the value of the bond if the market rate is 10%, assuming annual compounding?

4. Given the bond in problem 3, what would the current value be if the market rate were 5%?

5. Again use looking at the bond in problem 3, what would the value be if it had 30 years to maturity instead

of 5 years, assuming all other features are as given in problem 3?

6. What is the price of a bond with features as given in problem 3 except that it matures in 1 year rather than in 5 years?

7. Review your solutions to problems 5 and 6. Which bond is subject to the greatest interest rate risk?

8. What would be the value of the bond discussed in problem 3 if interest payments made were semiannually rather than annually?

9. What would be the value of the bond discussed in problem 4 if interest payments were made semiannually rather than annually?

10. What will be the price of the bond discussed in problem 3 when there are 4 years before it matures?

11. What is the percentage change in price of the bond discussed in problem 10 between when there are 5 years before it matures and when there are 4 years before it matures?

12. What is the current yield of the bond discussed in problem 3?

13. Is the sum of the current yield and the change in price found in problem 11 the same as the market rate?

14. A bond has a current market price of $1,125. It has an annual coupon rate of 6%, its par value is $1,000, and it matures in 10 years. What is its yield to maturity?

15. A bond has a current market price of $825. It has an annual coupon rate of 6%, its par value is

$1,000, and it matures in 10 years. What is its yield to maturity?

16. What would be the yield to maturity for the bond discussed in problem 14 if the payments were made semi-annually rather than annually? If you use a calculator, remember to multiply your answer by 2.

17. What would be the yield to maturity for the bond discussed in problem 15 if the payments were made semi-annually rather than annually?

*Some of these problems require the use of a financial calculator since some of the interest rates are not in the tables.

WEB EXPLORATION

1. Investment companies attempt to explain to investors the nature of the risk they incur when buying shares in its mutual funds. For example, Vanguard attempts to carefully explain interest rate risk and to offer alternative funds with different interest rate risk. Go to majestic.vanguard.com/FP/DA.
   a. Select the bond fund you would recommend to an investor who has very low tolerance for risk and a short investment horizon. Justify your answer.
   b. Select the bond fund you would recommend to an investor who has very high tolerance for risk and a long investment horizon. Justify your answer.

2. *Saving bond redemption.* In this chapter we have discussed bonds as if there were only one type: long-term interest-paying corporate bonds. In fact there are also discount bonds. A discount bond is sold at a low price, and the whole return comes in the form of price appreciation. You can easily compute the current price of a discount bond using the financial calculator at app.ny.frb.org/sbr/.

   To compute the redemption values for savings bonds, fill in the information at the site and click on the Compute Values button. A *maximum* of 5 years of data will be displayed for each computation.

MINI CASE

Your favorite uncle learned that you have completed a course in finance. Uncle Bob has been investing in stocks for years through his company pension plan. He has also bought some stock outside the company plan. Bob does not think he is saving enough for his retirement and wants your help in choosing where he should put his extra funds. He wants to get together with you several times, and during the first session he wants to talk about bonds.

a. Explain how any financial asset is valued. Why is this method reasonable?

b. What is a bond? What are the primary features of a bond?

c. What cash flows will your uncle receive from investing in a bond?

d. Your Uncle Bob has become very excited about bonds because he sees that if he buys bonds issued by a solid company, there is no risk. Explain the concept of interest rate risk. Discuss when interest rate risk is greatest and lowest.

e. Your uncle tells you that he checked online and has found that he can buy a $1,000 face value bond for only $950. He thinks this sounds like a bargain and wants your opinion. What additional information would you need to accurately advise him about this bond? Why is the bond probably selling below par? What are the two sources of return from a bond?

f. Uncle Bob has a list of bonds he has found for sale. He asks you to compute what the return on each of the following bonds will be:

i. $1,000 par, 8.5% coupon, 10 years to maturity, current price $907.83

ii. $1,000 par, 7.75% coupon, 15 years to maturity, current price $828.86

iii. $1000 par, 12.5% coupon, 5 years to maturity, current price $1,094.77

g. What do the results you found in part f suggest about the relative risk among the three bonds?

h. Your uncle looks at what you computed for part f and wants to know how the current market prices were computed. Demonstrate how bond prices are found by computing the price of the following bonds:

i. $1,000 par, 8.5% coupon, 10 years to maturity, current YTM 8.5%

ii. $1,000 par, 8.5% coupon, 10 years to maturity, current YTM 6.8%

iii. $1,000 par, 8.5% coupon, 10 years to maturity, current YTM 9.25%

i. Explain to your uncle why the current yields to maturity reported in part h could be different.

j. Your uncle's last question is whether you think he should include some bonds in his investment portfolio. How would you respond?

Asset Valuation: Stock and Market Efficiency

Chapter Objectives

By the end of this chapter you should be able to:

1. Compute the price of preferred stock

2. Compute the price of a share of common stock using the constant growth dividend model

3. Compute the value of a share of common stock with either zero or nonconstant growth

4. Compute the value of a share of stock using the price/earnings ratio

5. Appreciate why stock prices are volatile

6. Understand the basic reasoning behind the efficient market hypothesis

7. Recognize the implications of the efficient market hypothesis with regard to financial decision making

In Chapter 8 we learned that any investment asset is valued by computing the present value of its future cash flows. We applied this method to the valuation of a variety of assets including a painting, rental property, and bonds. In each case we identified the cash flows, estimated a discount rate, and computed a present value. In this chapter we continue our study of investment valuation by learning to value stock. We begin by valuing preferred stock because the cash flows are easy to determine and the present value is straightforward to compute. Common stock valuation is not so easy.

To value common stock we must estimate its cash flows. We will learn in this chapter that common stock cash flows are very difficult to determine. We will also learn that it is this uncertainty that leads to so much volatility in the stock markets.

Once we have learned the methods required for stock valuation, we explore how good a job the markets do of establishing fair prices for securities. The idea that security prices are accurate is called the efficient market hypothesis. We examine whether the evidence supports this hypothesis.

COMPUTING THE PRICE OF PREFERRED STOCK

Preferred stock shares some of the characteristics of both bonds and common stock. Like bonds, preferred stock pays a fixed amount each period. Like common stock, preferred stock does not usually mature and the periodic payments are in the form of dividends rather than interest. Bond interest payments have a higher payment priority than do preferred dividends, but preferred dividends have a higher priority than common stock dividends. The board of directors of a firm can elect to suspend preferred dividend payments, but skipped preferred dividends usually must be paid before the firm can pay any common stock dividends.

Because most preferred dividend payments can be assumed to continue in perpetuity (forever), we use the formula for the present value of a perpetuity developed in Chapter 6 to value preferred stock. Equation 9.1 computes the value of preferred stock:

$$P_{preferred} = \frac{Div}{k_p} \tag{9.1}$$

E X A M P L E 9.1   Preferred Stock

Coca-Cola Bottling Company had $57 million of preferred stock outstanding in 1991. The firm repurchased this stock in 1992. If there were 4.75 million preferred shares outstanding, investors required a 12.5% return, and the stock paid $1.50 per year, what was the market price per share?

Solution

Use Equation 9.1 to find the market price per share:

$$P_{preferred} = \frac{\$1.50}{0.125} = \$12.00$$

We can easily adjust the equation to compute the required return if we know the dividend and the current market price:

$$k_p = \frac{Div}{P_{preferred}}$$

We will use this form of the preferred stock valuation equation in Chapter 12 when we learn how to find the average cost of funds to a firm.

COMPUTING THE PRICE OF COMMON STOCK

Common stock is the principal way in which corporations raise equity capital. Holders of common stock own an interest in the corporation consistent with the percentage of outstanding shares owned. This ownership interest gives **shareholders**—those who hold stock in a corporation—a bundle of rights. The most important are the right to vote and to be the **residual claimant** of all cash flows, meaning that the shareholder receives whatever remains after all other claims against the firm's assets have been satisfied. Shareholders are paid dividends from the net earnings of the corporation. **Dividends** are payments made periodically, usually every quarter to stockholders. The board of directors of the firm sets the level of the dividend, usually upon the recommendation of management. In addition, the stockholder has the right to sell the stock.

As with any asset, we value common stock as the present value of all future cash flows. As noted above, the cash flows a stockholder may earn from stock are either dividends, the sales price, or both. The simplest valuation model assumes that you buy the stock, hold it for one period to get a dividend, and then sell the stock. We call this the one-period valuation model.

One-Period Valuation Model

Suppose that you have some extra money to invest for 1 year. After a year you will need to sell your investment to pay tuition. After listening to *Wall Street Week* on TV you decide that you want to buy Intel Corp. stock. You call your broker and find that Intel is currently selling for $50.00 per share and pays $0.16 per year in dividends. The analyst on *Wall Street Week* predicts that the stock will be selling for $60 in 1 year. Should you buy this stock?

To answer this question you need to determine whether the current price accurately reflects the analyst's forecast. To value the stock today you need to find the present value of the expected cash flows. The cash flows consist of one dividend payment plus a final sales price. Equation 9.2 computes the price of the stock:

$$P_0 = \frac{\text{Div}_1}{(1 + k_e)} + \frac{P_1}{(1 + k_e)} \tag{9.2}$$

where

P_0 = the current price of the stock (the zero subscript refers to time period zero, or the present)

Div_1 = the dividend paid at the end of year 1

k_e = the required return on investments in equity

P_1 = the price at the end of the first period (this is the assumed sales price of the stock)

E X A M P L E 9.2   Stock Valuation

Find the price of the Intel stock given the figures reported here. You will need to know the required return on equity to find the present value of the cash flows. Because stock is more risky than bonds, you will require a higher return than that offered in the bond market. Assume that after careful consideration you decide that you would be satisfied to earn 12% on the investment.

Solution
Begin by preparing a time line:

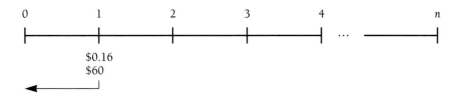

Putting the numbers into Equation 9.2 yields the following:

$$P_0 = \frac{\$0.16}{1 + 0.12} + \frac{\$60}{1 + 0.12} = \$0.14 + \$53.57 = \$53.71$$

Based on your analysis you find that the stock is worth $53.71. Because the stock is currently available for $50.00 per share, you would choose to buy it. Why is the stock selling for less than $53.71? It may be because other investors place a different risk on the cash flows or estimate the cash flows to be less than you do. Because your analysis indicates that the stock is currently undervalued, you would buy it. Only time will tell whether you or the rest of the market is correct.

Generalized Dividend Valuation Model

The one-period dividend valuation model can be extended to any number of periods. The concept remains the same. The value of stock is the present value of all future cash flows. The only cash flows that an investor will receive are dividends and a final sales price when the stock is ultimately sold. The generalized formula for stock can be written as in Equation 9.3:

$$P_0 = \frac{D_1}{\left(1 + k_e\right)^1} + \frac{D_2}{\left(1 + k_e\right)^2} + \cdots + \frac{D_n}{\left(1 + k_e\right)^n} + \frac{P_n}{\left(1 + k_e\right)^n} \tag{9.3}$$

If you were to attempt to use Equation 9.3 to find the value of a share of stock, you would soon realize that you must first estimate the value the stock will have at some point in the future before you can estimate its value today. In other words, you must find P_n in order to find P_0. How do we find P_n? It will be the present value of all future dividends plus a future sales price. That future sales price will also be the present value of all future dividends plus an even more distant sales price. This process continues so that the current price of the stock is found as the present value of a stream of dividends plus the present value of a very distant future stock price. Consider that the present value of a sum to be received far in the future is actually going to be *very* small. For example, the present value of a share of stock sold 75 years from now for $50.00 is just 1¢ if the discount rate is 12% [$50/(1.12^{75}) = \$0.01$]. This means that the current value of a share of stock can be found as simply the present value of the future dividend stream. The **generalized dividend model** is rewritten in Equation 9.4 without the final sales price:

$$P_0 = \sum_{t=1}^{\infty} \frac{D_t}{\left(1 + k_e\right)^t} \tag{9.4}$$

Stop and think about the implications of Equation 9.4 for a moment. The generalized dividend model says that the price of stock is determined only by the present value of the dividends and that nothing else matters. Many stocks do not pay dividends—so how do these stocks have value? The majority stockholder of Toys R Us has repeatedly stated that Toys R Us has never paid a dividend and never will, yet the company's stock continues to increase in price. Let us see how these issues can be reconciled with our model.

Suppose that a friend offers to sell you stock in a new company he is forming to produce and market his invention. He demonstrates an antigravity plate on which he holds the patent. Anything put on the plate becomes weightless. After only a few moments of reflection you realize that this invention will change the way the whole world works. You picture the new company dwarfing Microsoft in a few years. As you are pulling out your checkbook and considering where you can borrow more money to invest, your friend tells you there is one thing he thinks you should know before investing. He plans to retain 51% ownership in the firm and any earnings are going to be paid to him as salary to avoid the double taxation issue associated with dividends. He says the firm will *never, ever* pay a dime in dividends. He further explains that his will is set up so that his heirs can never pay dividends either (this story may be getting a little far-fetched here, but follow along for a moment). Will you still buy the stock? You might be tempted to say that you will be satisfied with just the increase in stock price over time without needing any dividends. The problem with this reasoning is that the stock price will not increase if there will never be any cash flows for the investors. Although this firm has tremendous value to the founder and majority stockholder, it would have no value to you.

Why do firms that pay no dividends have valuable stock that increases in price over time? *Buyers of the stock expect that the firm will pay dividends someday.* In the example above, the owner promised never to pay a dividend. Most of the time a firm institutes dividends as soon as it has completed the rapid growth phase of its life cycle. The stock price increases as the time approaches for the dividend stream to begin. Review the following time line:

Study Tip

Pay attention to this discussion since it is fundamental to the understanding of stock valuation and stock price changes.

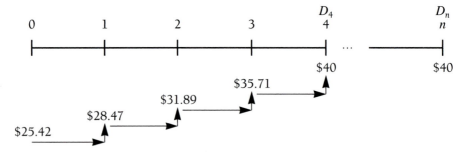

Assume that dividends will begin at the end of the fourth period and that based on the anticipated dividends the stock price then will be $40. At time 0 the price will be $25.42, assuming a 12% discount rate ($40/1.12^4 = $25.42). One year later, at time 1, the price will be $28.47 because it is one period closer to when dividends begin and the dividend stream is discounted for one less period ($40/1.12^3 = $28.47). Similarly, at time 2 the stock will have grown in value to $31.89 because now there are just two periods before dividends begin. The price will continue to rise until it reaches $40. If dividends are constant after the fourth period, the price from period 4 on will also stay constant.

The point is that stock prices will naturally increase just because the date of the expected dividend approaches, even if expectations about future cash flows or dividends do not change.

We are still left wondering whether the dividend model applies to firms such as Toys R Us and Ben & Jerry's Ice Cream, which claim they will never pay dividends. Investors must expect that eventually there will be cash flows generated by the company in some form. For example, maybe the firm will be purchased and holders of the stock will receive a premium price for their shares. Maybe the heirs of the founder will pay dividends once the growth opportunities have been exhausted.

The generalized dividend valuation model requires that we compute the present value of an infinite stream of dividends, a process that could be difficult, to say the least. Therefore, simplified models have been developed to make the calculations easier. One such model is the **Gordon growth model,** which assumes constant dividend growth.

Gordon Growth Model

Many firms strive to increase their dividends at a constant rate each year. For example, Proctor & Gamble dividends have grown at a constant 5% for many years. Equation 9.5 rewrites Equation 9.4 to reflect this constant growth in dividends:

$$P_0 = \frac{D_0 \times (1 + g)^1}{(1 + k_e)^1} + \frac{D_0 \times (1 + g)^2}{(1 + k_e)^2} + \cdots + \frac{D_0 \times (1 + g)^\infty}{(1 + k_e)^\infty} \tag{9.5}$$

where

D_0 = the last dividend paid
g = the expected constant growth rate in dividends
k_e = the required return on an investment in equity

Equation 9.5 has been simplified using some tricky algebra to obtain Equation 9.6:[1]

$$P_0 = \frac{D_0 \times (1 + g)}{k_e - g} = \frac{D_1}{k_e - g} \tag{9.6}$$

Study Tip

The most common error students make applying the Gordon growth model is to use the wrong dividend in the numerator. D_0 is the dividend just paid. It is assumed that the investor will not receive this dividend. It is only a benchmark to use for estimating the next dividend (D_1) that the investor will receive. If the problem gives you D_1, do not multiply by $(1 + g)$. If the problem gives you D_0, be sure that you compute D_1.

---

[1]To generate Equation 9.6 from Equation 9.5, first multiply both sides of Equation 9.5 by $(1 + k_e)/(1 + g)$ and subtract Equation 9.5 from the result. This yields

$$\frac{P_0 \times (1 + k_e)^1}{(1 + g)^1} - P_0 = D_0 - \frac{D_0 \times (1 + g)^\infty}{(1 - k_e)^\infty}$$

Assuming that the k_e is greater than g, the term on the far right will approach zero and can be dropped. Thus, after factoring P_0 out of the left-hand side,

$$P_0 \times \left(\frac{1 + k_e}{1 + g} - 1\right) = D_0$$

Next simplify by combining terms to

$$P_0 \times \left(\frac{(1 + k_e) - (1 + g)}{1 + g}\right) = D_0$$

$$P_0 \times (k_e - g) = D_0 \times (1 + g)$$

$$P_0 \times \frac{D_0 \times (1 + g)}{k_e - g} = \frac{D_1}{k_e - g}$$

This model is useful for finding the value of stock given a few assumptions:

- *Dividends are assumed to continue growing at a constant rate forever.* Actually, as long as they are expected to grow at a constant rate for an extended period of time, the model should yield reasonable results. This is because errors about distant cash flows become small when discounted to the present.
- *The growth rate is assumed to be less than the required return on equity, k_e.* Myron Gordon, in his development of the model, demonstrates that this is a reasonable assumption. In theory, if the growth rate were faster than the rate demanded by holders of the firm's equity, in the long run the firm would grow impossibly large.

The Gordon growth model relies on future growth rates. Box 9.1 discusses the significance of growth rates with respect to the value of Microsoft and Intel.

Self-Test Review Questions*

1. What is the current price of a share of stock if the last dividend was $3.00, the expected growth rate is a constant 5%, and the required return is 12%?
2. What is the current price of a share of stock if the next dividend is expected to be $3.15, the growth rate is a constant 5%, and the required return is 12%?

Let's see how this equation works when there is no growth expected in dividends.

Zero Growth

A special case of the constant dividend model occurs when the expected constant growth rate is zero. In this case Equation 9.6 becomes

$$P_0 = \frac{D_1}{k_e - 0}$$

$$P_0 = \frac{D_1}{k_e}$$

* 1. $\dfrac{\$3.00\,(1.05)}{0.12 - 0.05} = \$45.00$

2. $45.00, the same as for question 1, except that the future dividend is already calculated because you are given D_1 in the problem.

Box 9.1 New King of Stocks

In 1997 Microsoft and Intel had a combined stock market value of more than $224 billion. This exceeded the combined market value of General Motors, Ford, Boeing, Eastman Kodak, Sears, J.P. Morgan, Caterpillar, and Kellogg. What made this remarkable was that Microsoft and Intel had combined revenues of $30.3 billion, compared to the combined revenues of the other eight firms of $425.2 billion.

What made investors value Microsoft and Intel twice as highly as these other high-quality firms when revenues were substantially lower? The explanation lies in growth rates. Earnings at Microsoft and Intel had been growing much faster than at the traditional companies. Microsoft's earnings had grown about 36% a year for the past 4 years; Intel's had grown about 37% a year. Investors clearly expect their blistering growth pace to continue and this expectation was reflected in the firms' stock prices.

—————

Source: Wall Street Journal, March 24, 1997, p. c1.

This is the formula for a perpetuity that we use to value preferred stock. The constant dividend is simply divided by the required return for equity.

EXAMPLE 9.3 Stock Valuation, Stock Growth

What is the price of stock with a constant dividend of $2.00 if the required return is 12%?

Solution
Use Equation 9.6 with growth = 0:

$$P_0 = \frac{D_1}{k_e - g}$$

$$P_0 = \frac{\$2.00}{0.12 - 0} = \frac{\$2.00}{0.12} = \$16.67$$

The stock should sell for $16.67.

Constant Growth

A new firm may experience rapid growth during the early years of its life. It will be expanding into new markets and increasing its sales at a rapid rate. When it matures, its growth may level to a constant rate that reflects a healthy but not high-growth firm. In this case the constant growth model may accurately estimate the value of the firm's stock. The difficult part of valuing the stock is estimating the long-term average growth rate to use in the model. There are several methods to use. One would be to look at the past change in dividends and use this rate as an estimate of the future change. For example, assume the dividends paid by Coca-Cola Company over the 1996–2000 period were

Dividends by Coca Cola	
Year	Dividend
1996	$0.66
1997	0.70
1998	0.80
1999	0.88
2000	1.00

The average growth rate in dividends is computed by using the growth equation introduced in Chapter 6:

$$g = \sqrt[n]{\frac{FV}{PV}} - 1$$

PV is the earliest occurring dividend and FV is the most recently occurring dividend. n is the number of intervals during which the dividends can grow. For example, there is one interval between 1996 and 1997, a second between 1997 and 1998, and so on for a total of four intervals. To find the growth in dividends for Coca-Cola, substitute the dividends into the growth equation as follows:[2]

$$g = \sqrt[4]{\frac{\$1.00}{\$0.66}} - 1$$

$$g = \sqrt[4]{1.51} - 1$$

$$g = 1.1095 - 1 = 0.1095 = 10.95\%$$

Alternatively, the growth rate can be found on a calculator, with N = 4, PV = −0.66, FV = $1.00, and PMT = 0; we compute I = 10.95%. Note that either the PV or the FV must be entered as a negative number on most calculators.

In this example we used the change in the dividends to establish the firm's growth rate. Often the growth in the firm is not reflected in increased dividends. High-growth firms may be reinvesting all of their income rather than paying dividends. In these cases other measures of growth may be used. Such measures include the growth in sales, earnings per share, or earnings before interest and taxes (EBIT).

One method for computing the growth rate is the retention growth rate. This model is useful because the required data is generally available and it does not rely on the firm paying dividends. The retention growth rate is computed using Equation 9.7:

$$g = b \times r \tag{9.7}$$

where

g = growth rate
b = fraction of its earnings that a firm is expected to retain (computed as 1 − payout ratio)
r = expected future return on equity (ROE)

This model assumes that the firm's payout ratio and return on equity will remain constant in the future. The intuition behind the model is straightforward. Whatever the firm does not pay out in dividends (b) will be reinvested into the company. These reinvested dollars will earn a return that we estimate as equal to the future ROE (r). The product of b times r gives an estimate of the growth the firm could experience.

Suppose a firm pays out 20% of its net income as dividends to shareholders. Also assume that ROE is expected to be 6% in the future. The growth rate could be estimated using Equation 9.7 as (1−.2)(.06) = .048 or 4.8%.

We can now use Equation 9.6 to find the current market price of Coca-Cola stock.

E X A M P L E 9.4   Stock Valuation, Constant Growth

Find the current market price of Coca-Cola stock assuming that dividends grow at a constant rate of 10.95%, D_0 = $1.00, and the required return is 13%. Coca-Cola stock should sell for $54.12 if the assumptions regarding the constant growth rate and required return are correct.

---

[2]You can find roots on any calculator that has an exponent key. Finding the nth root of a number is the same as raising that number to 1 over n. For example, the 4th root of 1.51 is equal to $(1.51)^{1/4} = (1.51)^{0.25} = 1.1095$.

Solution

$$P_0 = \frac{D_0 \times (1 + g)}{k_e - g}$$

$$P_0 = \frac{\$1.00 \times (1.1095)}{0.13 - 0.1095}$$

$$P_0 = \frac{\$1.1095}{0.0205} = \$54.12$$

Self-Test Review Questions*

1. Dividends for ABC Corp. were $1.00 at the end of 1990 and $3.00 at the end of 1998. What is the average compounded growth rate?
2. If the required return is 20%, use the answer to question 1 to compute the price of ABC stock at the end of 1998.

Computing the Required Return on Stock

Before looking at more complex valuation problems, let us first review the dividend growth model more closely. In Chapter 7 we studied risk and return and learned that the required return on stock was equal to the market risk premium adjusted by beta plus the risk-free rate. The equation for the required return is called the CAPM and is repeated here.[3]

$$k_e = R_f + \beta(R_m - R_f)$$

This equation tells us what discount rate to use in the denominator of the constant growth model. The beta for Coca-Cola is 1.1. If we estimate the return on the market as 12.25% and the risk-free rate as 4.75%, we can solve for k_e:

$$k_e = 0.0475 + 1.1(0.1225 - 0.0475) = 0.13 = 13\%$$

Now we rearrange the terms in the constant growth model to solve for k_e:

$$P_0 = \frac{D_1}{k_e - g}$$

$$P_0(k_e - g) = D_1$$

$$(k_e - g) = \frac{D_1}{P_0}$$

$$k_e = \frac{D_1}{P_0} + g \qquad\qquad (9.8)$$

Study Tip

Notice the terminology used in the above paragraph. A high-yield stock is not one that offers unusually high returns. It is one for which a large *portion* of the return is paid as a dividend.

2.
$$g = \sqrt[8]{\frac{\$3.00}{\$1.00}} - 1 = 0.1472 = 14.72\%$$

*1. Draw a time line and count the periods during which the dividends can grow. There are 8 such periods.

---

[3]Equation 7.10 set R_i equal to the sum of the risk-free rate and the market risk premium. Here we replace R_i with k_e to show that we are computing the required return on *equity*.

Here we see that the required return on equity is equal to the **dividend yield** (D_1/P_0), plus the **capital yield**, g:

$$k_e = \text{Dividend yield} + \text{Capital yield}$$

The dividend yield is the amount paid to shareholders as a percentage of the firm's current stock price. The capital yield is the yield the stockholder receives due to the price of the stock increasing or from internal growth due to retaining earnings for investment.

A stock can provide a return to the investor by paying a dividend, by increasing in value, or by some combination of the two. **High-yield stocks** pay out a large portion of their net earnings as dividends. Alternatively, zero- or low-yield stocks retain all or most of their earnings and reinvest them in the company. Coca-Cola has a dividend yield of 2.05% ($1.11/$54.12) and a capital gains yield of 10.95% (13% − 2.05%). The sum of these returns equals the required return of 13%.

We now have two equations that compute k_e: the CAPM and the dividend growth model. The equations serve different purposes. The CAPM tells us what investors require to feel satisfied that they are being compensated for the risk they are incurring. The growth model tells us how that return is being generated by the firm.

EXTENSION 9.1

Nonconstant Growth

The constant dividend growth model is useful for finding the value of firms that have reached maturity and have exhausted most of their high-growth opportunities. It is fair to assume that these firms will maintain a constant growth rate into the foreseeable future. Alternatively, some firms may be experiencing an unusual dividend stream because of an aggressive expansion program or a difficult business environment. It is inappropriate to use the constant dividend model to value these firms. The uneven or variable growth model may be used when the first few dividends can be projected but they are not constant and are not anticipated to continue. For example, in 1996 Apple Computer posted a $740 million first-quarter loss. It suspended dividends and received a great deal of negative publicity. Analysts began projecting that Apple would either become a niche player (appealing to a narrow and specific application), fail altogether, or merge with another firm. Rumors even circulated that Microsoft might buy the firm. At this time analysts had to project future cash flows for Apple in order to make buy or sell stock recommendations. It would have been inappropriate to use the historic average growth in dividends to value this firm because it was undergoing drastic changes in its business structure. A superior approach would have been to project when dividends would resume and at what level. Let us examine how this might be done:

1. Determine the dividend expected at the end of each year during the nonconstant growth period. For example, Apple may be projected to have zero dividends for 2 years, then to establish a $1.00 dividend.

2. Estimate the constant growth rate and use it to price the dividend stream that begins after the nonconstant growth period.

3. Find the present value of the nonconstant dividends and add the sum to the present value of the price found in step 2.

An example should help make these steps clear.

E X A M P L E 9.5   Stock Valuation, Nonconstant Growth

Assume that Apple Computer pays no dividends for 2 years. At the end of the third year it pays a $1.00 dividend and then establishes a dividend growth rate of 5% per year from then on. Draw a time line and compute the current price of Apple stock assuming a 15% discount rate.

Study Tip

Be sure to compute the *present value* of the future price before adding it to the present value of the dividends. Many students forget this step, especially when they get rushed on exams.

Solution

Begin by drawing a time line:

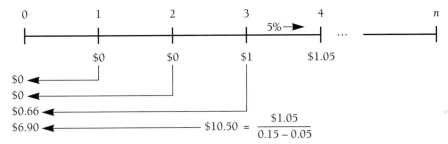

1 & 2. The relevant dividends are $0 paid for 2 years, then $1, followed by 5% growth.

3. The present value of the first two dividends is $0. The present value of the next dividend of $1 is $0.66 ($1/1.15^3 = \$.66$). The present value of the stream of dividends having a constant 5% growth rate following the $1 dividend is found using the Gordon growth model. Application of this model provides a stock price at the end of the third period, not at the end of the fourth. The Gordon growth model discounts the dividend stream back *one* period. The price as of time 3 must be discounted back three more periods and added to the present value of the other dividends to find the current price:

$$P_3 = \frac{\$1.05}{0.15 - 0.05}$$

$$P_3 = \frac{\$1.05}{0.10} = \$10.50$$

$$P_0 = \$0 + \$0 + \$0.66 + \frac{\$10.50}{(1.15)^3}$$

$$P_0 = \$0 + \$0 + \$0.66 + \$6.90 = \$7.56$$

The nonconstant growth model can be applied to firms that experience supernormal growth, such as Microsoft or Intel during the 1990s. Simply determine each dividend the firm will offer until it reaches a constant growth phase of its life cycle. Find the value of the firm at the time the constant growth phase is projected to begin, and then sum the present value of the nonconstant dividends and the present value of the future price. This is demonstrated by Example 9.6.

EXAMPLE 9.6   Stock Valuation, Supernormal Growth

The last dividend paid was $2.00 per share. The stock is expected to grow at 20% for the next 3 years, then to grow at a constant 10% thereafter. If the required return is 15%, what should the stock sell for today?

Solution

Begin by drawing a time line:

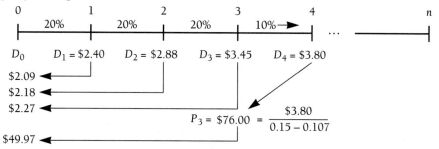

1. Compute the dividends and put them on the time line. The last dividend paid was $2.00. The next one will be 20% larger, which is computed by multiplying $2.00 × 1.20=$2.40. Each subsequent dividend is computed by multiplying by the appropriate growth rate.

2. Compute the price of the stock when the constant growth phase of the company's life cycle begins. In this example, the 10% constant growth rate begins at the end of the third period. We compute P_3 using the Gordon growth model and the dividend that will be paid one period later (D4):

$$P_3 = \frac{D_4}{k - g} = \frac{\$3.80}{0.15 - 0.10} = \frac{\$3.80}{0.05} = \$76.00$$

Study Tip

D_3 and P_3 could be added together to save time since both are divided by the same factor. They are kept separate in this example only to help show how the calculation is made.

3. Find the present value of all of the dividends, except D_0. We do not include D_0 in the pricing process because it is assumed to have already been paid to the current owner of the stock. The buyer will not receive this dividend, so it should not influence the price of the security. The present value of the dividends is computed as follows:

$$P_0 = \frac{\$2.40}{(1.15)^1} + \frac{\$2.88}{(1.15)^2} + \frac{\$3.45}{(1.15)^3} + \frac{\$76.00}{(1.15)^3}$$

$$P_0 = \$2.09 + \$2.18 + \$2.27 + \$49.97 = \$56.51$$

The stock should sell for $56.51 today.

Self-Test Review Question*

The next dividend for ABC Corp. is expected to be $1.00. It will rise to $2.00 the next year and then grow at a constant 6% from then on. The required return is 12%. What is the current price of the stock?

*Begin by drawing a time line and placing each dividend above the appropriate number. Next compute P_2 using D_3. Finally, compute and sum the present values of D_1 and D_2:

$$P_2 = \frac{\$2.12}{0.12 - 0.06} = \$35.33. \quad P_0 = \frac{\$1}{(1.12)^1} + \frac{\$2}{(1.12)^2} + \frac{\$35.33}{(1.12)^2} = \$30.65.$$

Price Earnings Valuation Method

Theoretically, the best method of stock valuation is the dividend valuation approach. Sometimes, however, it is difficult to apply. If a firm is not paying dividends or has a very erratic growth rate, the results may not be satisfactory. Other approaches to stock valuation are sometimes applied. Among the more popular is the price/earnings multiple.

The **price/earnings ratio** (PE) is a widely watched measure of how much the market is willing to pay for $1 of earnings from a firm. The PE ratios for a variety of firms are reported in Chapter 14. You will see that PEs vary substantially across firms and industries. A high PE has two interpretations:

Study Tip

Notice that the *E* in the PE ratio is earnings per share, not total earnings. Earnings per share are found by dividing total earnings by the number of shares outstanding.

- A high PE may mean that the market expects earnings to rise in the future. This would return the PE to a more normal level.

- A high PE may indicate that the market feels the firm's earnings are very low risk and is therefore willing to pay a premium for them.

The PE ratio can be used to estimate the value of a firm's stock. Note that algebraically the product of the PE ratio times expected earnings is the firm's stock price:

$$\frac{P}{E} \times E = P \qquad (9.9)$$

Firms in the same industry are expected to have similar PE ratios in the long run. The value of a firm's stock can be found by multiplying the average industry PE times the expected earnings per share.

E X A M P L E 9.7   Stock Valuation, PE Ratio Approach

The average industry PE ratio for restaurants similar to Applebee's, a pub restaurant chain, is 23. What is the current price of Applebee's if earnings per share are projected to be $1.13?

Solution

Using Equation 9.9 and the data given, we find

$$P_0 = PE \times E$$
$$P_0 = 23 \times \$1.13 = \$26$$

The PE ratio approach is especially useful for valuing privately held firms and firms that do not pay dividends. The weakness of the PE approach to valuation is that by using an industry average PE ratio, firm-specific factors that might contribute to a long-term PE ratio above or below the average are ignored in the analysis. The PE method is applied to a case in Chapter 18.

HOW THE MARKET SETS SECURITY PRICES

As noted at the beginning of this chapter, we could have discussed asset valuation under a number of different headings. Although it appears in the Investments section of this text, in the end, the markets set security prices. Let us investigate how this occurs.

Suppose you went to an auto auction. The cars are available for inspection before the auction begins, and you find a little Mazda Miata that you like. You test drive it in the parking lot and notice that it makes a few strange noises, but you decide that you would still like the car. You decide $5,000 would be a fair price that would allow you to pay some repair bills should the noises turn out to be serious. You see that the auction is ready to begin, so you go in and wait for the Miata to enter.

Suppose there is another buyer who also spots the Miata. He test drives the car and recognizes that the noises are simply worn CV joints that he can fix himself at a nominal cost. He decides that the car is worth $7,000. He also goes in and waits for the Miata to enter.

Who will buy the car and for how much? Suppose only the two of you are interested in the Miata. You begin the bidding at $4,000. He ups your bid to $4,500. You bid your top price of $5,000. He counters with $5,100. The price is now higher than you are willing to pay, so you stop bidding. The car is sold to the more informed buyer for $5,100.

This simple example raises a number of points. First, the price is set by the buyer willing to pay the highest price. The price is not necessarily the highest price the asset could fetch, but it is greater than what any other buyer is willing to pay.

Second, the market price is set by the buyer who can take best advantage of the asset. The buyer who purchased the car knew that he could fix the noise easily and cheaply, so he was willing to pay more for the car than you were. The same concept holds for other assets. For example, a piece of property or a building will sell to the buyer who can put the asset to the most productive use. Consider why one company often pays a substantial premium over current market prices to acquire ownership of another (target) company. The acquiring firm may believe it can put the target firm's assets to work better than they are currently and this justifies the premium price.

Finally, the example shows how superior information about an asset can increase its value. When you consider buying a stock, there are many unknowns about the future cash flows. The buyer who has the best information about these cash flows will discount them at a lower interest rate than will a buyer who is very uncertain.

Now let us apply these ideas to stock valuation. Suppose that you are considering the purchase of stock expected to pay dividends of $2.00 next year. The firm is expected to grow at 3% indefinitely. You are quite *uncertain* about the constancy of the dividend stream and the accuracy of the estimated growth rate. To compensate yourself for this risk you require a return of 15%.

Now suppose Bud, another investor, has spoken with industry insiders and feels more confident in the projected cash flows. Bud requires only a 12% return because his perceived risk is lower than yours. Jamie, on the other hand, is dating the CEO of the company. She knows with near certainty what the future of the firm actually is. She thinks that both the estimated growth rate and the estimated cash flows are lower than what they will actually be in the future. Because she sees almost no risk in this investment, she only requires a 7% return.

What are the values each investor will give to the stock? Applying the Gordon growth model yields the following stock prices:

Investor	Discount Rate	Stock Price
You	15%	$16.67
Bud	12	22.22
Jamie	7	50.00

You would be willing to pay $16.67 for the stock. Bud would pay up to $22.22, and Jamie would pay $50.00. The investor with the lowest perceived risk is willing to pay the most for the stock. If there were no other traders, the market price would be just above $22.22. If you already held the stock, you would sell it to Jamie.

The point of this section is that the players in the market, bidding against each other, establish the market price. When new information is released about a firm, expectations change and with them, prices change. New information can cause changes in expectations about the level of future dividends or the risk of those dividends. Because market participants are constantly receiving new information and constantly revising their expectations, it is reasonable that stock prices are constantly changing as well.

ERRORS IN VALUATION

At the beginning of this chapter we learned several asset valuation models. An interesting exercise is to apply these models to real firms. Students who do this find that computed stock prices do not match market prices much of the time. Students often question whether the models are wrong or incomplete or whether they are simply being used incorrectly. There are many opportunities for errors in applying the models. These include problems estimating growth, estimating risk, and forecasting dividends. Box 9.2 discusses a case in which investors were purposely led to make incorrect estimates of a firm's cash flows.

Problems with Estimating Growth

The constant growth model requires the analyst to estimate the constant rate of growth the firm will experience. Earlier in the chapter we noted that no one method always yields acceptable results. You may estimate future growth by computing the historical growth rate in dividends, sales, or net profits. This approach fails to consider any changes in the firm or the economy that may affect the growth rate. Robert Haugen, a professor of finance at the University of California, writes in his book, *The New Finance,* that competition will prevent high-growth firms from being able to maintain their historical growth rate. However, he demonstrates that the stock prices of historically high-growth firms tend to reflect

---

Box 9.2 How Bre-X Gave Shareholders the Golden Shaft

In 1994 Bre-X's stock was priced at pennies per share. The gold exploration firm was little known and had few good prospects; then it struck gold, or at least the firm's managers led the market to believe so. By "salting" ore samples from gold claims in a remote part of Indonesia, Bre-X led the world to believe it had discovered not just gold, but possibly the largest gold vein on earth (worth as much as $70 billion). The discoverer, Michael de Guzman, a Philippine geologist who battled snakes, mosquitoes, tropical fatigue, and 14 bouts with malaria, was well rewarded for his efforts when the stock price rose to a high of over $200 per share. The cofounder and president, David Walsh, raked in $20 million and John Felderhof, the chief geologist, made $29 million before independent investigators determined in 1997 that the Bre-X claim was an elaborate scam. The stock price has once again fallen to pennies per share and the principals of the company have disappeared.

TABLE 9.1 **Stock Prices for a Security with D_0 = $2.00, k_e = 15%, and Constant Growth Rates as Listed**

Growth	Price
1%	$ 14.43
3	17.17
5	21.00
10	44.00
11	55.50
12	74.67
13	113.00
14	228.00

a continuation of the high growth rate. The result is that investors in these firms receive lower returns than they would by investing in mature firms. This just points out that even the experts have trouble estimating future growth rates. Table 9.1 shows the stock price for a firm with a 15% required return, a $2 dividend, and a range of different growth rates. The stock price varies from $14.43 at 1% growth to $228 at 14% growth rate. Estimating growth at 13% instead of 12% results in a $38.33 price difference.

Problems with Estimating Risk

The dividend valuation model requires the analyst to estimate the required return for the firm's equity. This is usually done using the CAPM, where beta reflects the market risk of the firm. As noted in Chapter 7, CAPM may not capture all of the risk that affects firm value. Although modern finance acknowledges the valuable contribution the CAPM has made to our understanding of the risk–return tradeoff, few practitioners or academics believe that the model is complete. Even if it were accurate, beta can only be estimated using historical information. The calculated beta may not reflect the true current risk of the firm. Table 9.2 shows how the price of a share of stock offering a $2 dividend and a 5% growth rate changes with different estimates of the required return. Clearly, stock price is highly dependent on the required return, despite our uncertainty regarding how this return is found.

TABLE 9.2 **Stock Prices for a Security with D_0 = $2.00, g = 5%, and Required Returns as Listed**

Required Return	Price
10%	$42.00
11	35.00
12	30.00
13	26.25
14	23.33
15	21.00

Problems with Forecasting Dividends

Even if we are able to accurately estimate a firm's growth rate *and* its required return, we are still faced with the problem of determining how much of the firm's earnings will be paid as dividends. Clearly, many factors can influence the dividend payout ratio. These include the firm's future growth opportunities and management's concern over future cash flows.

Putting all of these concerns together, we see that stock analysts are seldom very certain that their stock price projections are accurate. This is why stock prices can fluctuate so widely on news reports. For example, information that the economy is slowing can cause analysts to revise their growth expectations. When this happens across a broad spectrum of stocks, major market indexes can change. For example, on December 5, 2000, Allen Greenspan, the Chairman of the Board of Governors of the Federal Reserve, mentioned in a speech that he felt the Fed should back off its efforts to reduce the threat of inflation. The NASDAQ soared 274 points for a record gain of 10.48% in one day. Had investors been more certain of the cash flows and discount rates to use in valuing the firms in the NASDAQ, they would not have been so willing to change their price estimates.

Does all this mean that you should not invest in the market? No, it means only that short-term fluctuations in stock prices are expected and natural. Over the long term, the stock price adjusts to reflect the true earnings of the firm. If high-quality firms are chosen for your portfolio, they should provide fair returns over time. We investigate this issue further in the next section. Box 9.3 discusses changing expectations in tech stocks during 2000.

EXTENSION 9.2

What Is the Efficient Market Hypothesis?

Webster's defines *efficient* as acting or functioning competently, with minimum waste or extra motion. The term retains this meaning in the context of efficient markets. An **efficient market** must function competently, without waste or extra movement. What do we mean by functioning competently? One way to address this question is by looking at examples of markets that do *not* function efficiently. For example, most long-distance interstate (from one state to another) phone rates are lower than long-distance intrastate (within one state) rates. Although we know that this is a result of competition and government regulation, it still defies what most people believe to be rational pricing. If these rates were set by the market instead of regulators, we would say that the market is functioning *in*efficiently.

An efficient market also has prices adjusting rapidly and accurately. Before grocery stores used bar codes and computer networks to price inventory, each item had to have a price sticker attached. When an item's price changed, clerks had to put new price stickers on all of the items on the shelf. Time constraints sometimes restricted price changes to only adjusting prices on new inventory as it was tagged. College students on tight budgets regularly searched items on the back of the shelf to see whether any had old tags with lower prices still attached. This is another example of an *in*efficient market in that prices adjusted slowly, and not every unit of a particular type was priced the same.

Box 9.3   The NASDAQ Disappoints Investors

In the late 1990s the prices of tech stocks and the NASDAQ soared. For example, Amazon.com hit $103 per share in December 1999 even though it had never earned a profit and publicly acknowledged that it was not going to do so for several more years. How did investors arrive at this price? They were betting that the firm and other technology-oriented firms like it would grow very rapidly in the future. Investors were unconcerned about the lack of earnings. They reasoned that the company's rapid expansion prevented it from realizing earnings.

By the end of 2000 Amazon.com's stock price had fallen to $24. During 2000 the economy entered a mild slowdown. Additionally, investors became skeptical about the ability of tech firms to live up to the lofty growth expectations underlying their stock prices. The result was that investors reevaluated the assumptions that had led to the high stock prices and sharply lowered them. This happened across a broad spectrum of securities. The chart below shows the NASDAQ between December 1997 and December 2000. We can observe the increase in price as the raging economy led investors to project high growth rates, then the rapid fall as these expectations were adjusted. The NASDAQ lost nearly half its value between March 2000 and December 2000.

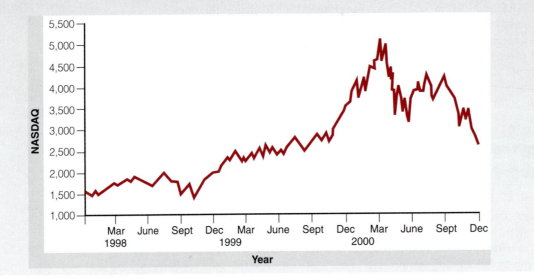

Now that we have explored a few examples of inefficient markets, let us define what an *efficient* market is. ***In efficient markets all prices accurately and rapidly adjust to reflect the true intrinsic value of securities***. Note several features about this definition. First, we say that prices are set accurately. This precludes situations such as interstate long-distance rates being lower than intrastate rates. Second, the definition includes a time component. Prices must adjust quickly to changes in the environment. This precludes situations such as those we used to find in grocery stores.

Consider what it means to investors if the financial markets are really efficient. If every stock is correctly priced, then it makes absolutely no difference which stock you buy because every one is fairly priced. It is a waste of time and energy to research the stock market because no amount of study will identify one security that will perform better than another.

Does this mean you will be as well off buying Wal-Mart stock as K-Mart stock? The surprising answer is *yes*. If the financial markets are efficient, the price of K-Mart will have adjusted down to reflect the risk inherent in the company's future and the price of Wal-Mart will have adjusted up to reflect its expected future cash flows. "Bad" stocks will be cheap. "Good" stocks will be expensive. Both will be priced fairly for what the investor gets.

Students of finance are often disappointed to hear that the stock market may be efficient. They hope that by taking a course in finance they will learn some secret of how the markets function that will allow them to get fabulously wealthy by investing a little of their pocket change. This will not happen if the markets are efficient. Furthermore, if the markets are efficient, there is no point in watching those investment gurus who provide stock advice on TV or reading the *Wall Street Journal* for investment tips.

Although it may be disappointing that in efficient markets no great deals exist, it also can be considered good news. Put another way, if the markets are efficient, no matter what investment you choose, you will be getting a good deal. You cannot make a stupid investment. You do not need to waste time searching for the right stocks; simply pick one that appeals to you for any reason and rest assured that you have selected a security that will provide a fair return for your investment. Of course, this is true only if the markets are really efficient.

Before we look at the evidence supporting efficient markets, let us review why anyone would believe that the markets are truly efficient.

What Makes the Markets Efficient?

Suppose that you go into McDonald's this afternoon for lunch. As you enter, you note that the restaurant is busy and that there are four registers open. What are the chances that you will be able to walk directly up to the counter and place your order? Virtually none. The reason is that everyone there has the same goal: to get waited on as quickly as possible. Customers, acting rationally in their own best interest, will seek out the shortest line. When you review your options, you will usually find that it does not make much difference which line you choose. They will all appear to provide about the same wait.

Does this mean that it really makes no difference which line you choose? Actually, they will not all move at the same speed. The guy in line 2 may be ordering lunch for a whole construction crew. Until you observe this order being placed, line 2 may have appeared to be a good option. Once this new information becomes available, you may choose to move to another line. The point is that when you initially picked a line, they all appeared to be equal given the information available to you at the time. Only the arrival of new information changes this.

Now suppose that line 3 unexpectedly shortens because two people in a row order only soft drinks. Now line 3 is a good deal. Anyone who gets in that line will have a shorter wait than if they get in any of the other lines. Who will get to take advantage of this good deal? The shorter wait will go to the customer who is alert to the opportunity and who moves most quickly to take advantage of it. The guy daydreaming at the end of line 4 never stands a chance. Line 3 rapidly adjusted and the opportunity disappeared before he even knew a good deal existed.

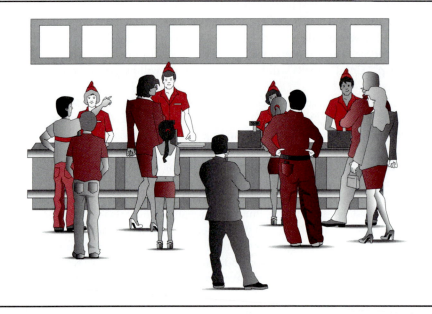

Let us review what makes the lines at McDonald's efficient:

- Everyone has the same goal.
- There are a large number of customers competing for good deals.
- Some of the customers are alert to changes and new information.
- Some of the customers react quickly to changes and new information.

The security markets share these characteristics. Everyone who participates in the financial markets has the *same goal:* to earn the greatest return possible for a given level of risk.

Additionally, there are a *large number of investors* in the market. Currently, there are over 6,000 separate mutual funds, each with a manager searching for good deals for his or her clients. In addition, there are millions of individual investors who actively participate in the security markets, again, each looking for good deals. It is hard to find an example of an asset with more prospective buyers than common stocks.

Many investors and investment managers *actively search for new information* about the companies in which they invest. Larger investment funds have industry specialists who devote all of their time to studying one particular industry, such as steel, oil, or automobiles. They are constantly alert to any news reports that bear on the firms in their industry. These specialists have access to news as soon as it is released through industry contacts and costly news sources. Some even have access to industry insiders who will help them analyze information as it is released.

Finally, many participants in the security markets are willing and able to *quickly react to new information.* It is generally believed that most investors have little long-term firm loyalty. This means that they will not continue to hold a stock simply because they have had it for several years if another stock is available that is expected to provide a higher risk-adjusted yield.

The efficient market hypothesis is based on the combined effect of many competitive investors, all with the same goal of locating securities that provide the highest risk-adjusted return and all willing and able to take advantage of new, changing conditions.

Price Adjustments with the Security Market Line   We can look to the security market line first introduced in Chapter 7 for another explanation for why we think the markets may be efficient. Review Figure 9.1. Security A is providing a higher risk-adjusted return than other securities. Alert investors will identify this security and attempt to buy it. As demand pressure mounts for security A, its price will rise. Because the market price of the security will not affect its cash flows or dividends, a rising price means that the return will fall, the opposite of what we demonstrated with Example 7.9 in Chapter 7. The demand for security A will continue as long as its return is better than is available on other securities with similar risk. Eventually, the price will rise until the return falls from R′ to R. At this point, demand for the stock will dissipate and the price will stabilize. At its new price, security A provides a fair return to any investor who chooses to buy it. Investors who purchased it for less than its equilibrium price received a good deal in the form of excess returns.

How many investors does it take to cause the price of security A to adjust to its proper level? Only one, if that investor has sufficient wealth to buy the security until its price adjusts. With thousands of well-informed investors, all looking for any firm whose return deviates from the security market line, any deviation is expected to disappear very quickly.

Stocks Follow a Random Walk in Efficient Markets

If the financial markets are indeed efficient, then past trends in stock prices should have no bearing on future price changes. For example, just because a stock's price has had a series of price increases, as shown in Figure 9.2, we cannot assume that tomorrow's price

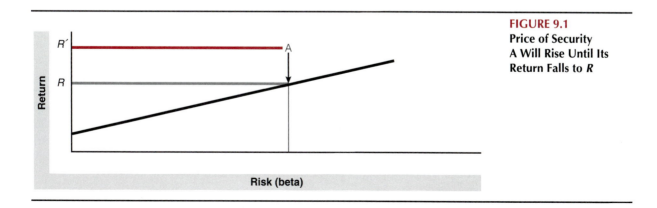

FIGURE 9.1
Price of Security A Will Rise Until Its Return Falls to *R*

FIGURE 9.2
Historical Trends Do Not Predict Future Prices

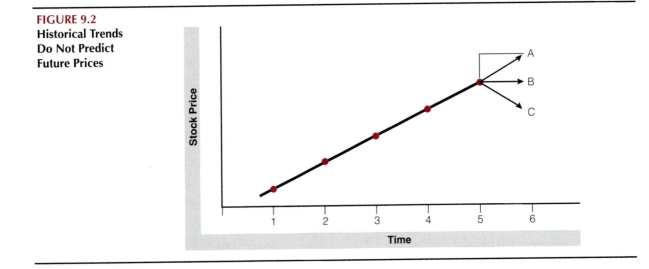

will be A. This is because everyone in the market has access to past stock prices. Suppose that if the stock price increases 5 days in a row there will be an increase on the sixth day as well. Investors would bid the price up on the fifth day instead of waiting for the sixth (the vertical line in Figure 9.2). As a result, the increase on the sixth day would disappear. In an efficient market, investors could not predict on day 5 whether the stock price on day 6 would be A, B, or C. If they could, an investment opportunity would exist that would provide superior returns.

The implication of Figure 9.2 is that the best prediction of tomorrow's price is today's price. For this reason the efficient market hypothesis is sometimes called the random walk hypothesis. Suppose that you deposit a drunk friend in a field of corn. You give him a little shove and he staggers off. If you leave and come back to search for him the next day, where would you begin your search? Where you left him. He probably will not be there, but in the absence of any additional information, that is the best place to start looking. In an efficient market, stocks will follow this same random walk. The price will change from one day to the next, but you cannot predict the direction of consecutive movements.

There is an old joke that has a financial academic walking down the street with a financial practitioner. They both spot a $1 bill lying on the sidewalk. The academic begins to walk past it, but is stopped by the practitioner, who asks, "Aren't you going to pick that up?" The academic replies, "No, if it were really there, someone else would have already taken it." At this point the practitioner shrugs, picks up the dollar, and walks on. Though not an especially great joke, it points out that some people do not believe the markets are efficient and choose instead to pick up the dollars while the academic community debates the point. Are the markets really efficient, or is this theory, which sounds so rational when explained, simply wrong? Let us next review the evidence.

Evidence for Market Efficiency

A famous financial economist named Eugene Fama conducted the first major, comprehensive examination of the market efficiency question.[4] He recognized that there may be degrees of market efficiency ranging between a market that is not efficient to one that is perfectly efficient. To test just how efficient the market is, he looked first at whether the markets were even slightly efficient. He called this level of efficiency **weak form market efficiency.**

If the markets were weak form efficient, then all historical information would be reflected in stock prices. Put another way, no unusually high earnings would be possible by using historical information, such as past prices, old news articles, or last month's annual report. Fama deemed this the weakest test of market efficiency because historical information is readily available to everyone at little cost. If an investor could profit from using this type of information, the markets could not be very efficient at all.

After studying the results of dozens of research projects, Fama was unable to find any evidence that superior returns could be earned by using historical information. This rejected the entire field of **technical analysis,** which refers to investing based on studying the patterns of past prices. For example, a technical analyst may load a high-speed computer with all of the stock returns for the last 60 years and program it to search for any patterns that repeat themselves. For example, if two upticks followed by three downticks is usually followed by an uptick, then a trading rule is established. The computer is then programmed to search current stock returns for the pattern and to issue a buy order whenever the pattern is located. Even using the most sophisticated programs and most complicated data searches, Fama could uncover no convincing evidence of profits. He then proclaimed that the markets were at least weak form efficient.

Fama next examined whether any public information could be used to earn superior returns. If no unusual profits could be earned using public information, the markets would be **semi–strong form efficient.** Fama reviewed studies looking at the impact of earnings announcements, stock splits, and other events for evidence that stock prices quickly adjusted to their news content. He concluded that investors could not earn unusual returns by trading on public information. This supported the idea that the markets are at least semi–strong form efficient.

In a **strong form efficient market** *all* information, both public and private, is reflected in the price of the stock. In Fama's original research, he examined strong form market efficiency by looking at the performance of mutual funds. He hypothesized that mutual fund managers should have access to insiders who would provide them with inside, nonpublic information. Many studies have been conducted attempting to show whether these managers are able to earn superior returns. *To date, there is no convincing evidence that fund managers are able to outperform a random selection of stocks over the long run.* A well-respected researcher named Michael Jensen looked at mutual fund performance.[5] Jensen evaluated the risk and return of mutual funds and plotted them on the

---

[4]Eugene F. Fama, "Efficient Capital Markets: A Review of Theory and Empirical Work," *Journal of Finance,* May 1970, pp. 383–417.

[5]Michael Jensen, "Risks, the Pricing of Capital Assets, and the Evaluation of Investment Performance," *Journal of Business,* April 1969.

security market line. He found that more of them were below the line than above. This indicates that investing in a mutual fund results in about a 1% lower return than would be earned with a random pick of stocks. Later in this same research paper Jensen demonstrated that the negative returns are approximately equal to the cost of staff salaries, office space, advertising, data acquisition, and commissions that mutual fund managers must pay. Thus, the source of the underperformance is the expenditure of funds associated with the management of the funds.

Most people do not consider this as supporting strong form market efficiency because there is no proof that fund managers actually have insider information. Instead, the failure of fund managers to earn better returns than a random draw of stocks is viewed as additional support for semi–strong form efficiency.

The *Wall Street Journal* has been running a contest for years in which mutual fund managers are challenged to pick stocks that perform better than those selected by *Wall Street Journal* staff who throw darts at the stock page of the *Journal*. So far the pros are ahead of the darts, but not by much.

For the market to be strong form efficient, no superior earnings would be possible, even with inside information. In fact, there is a great deal of evidence that tremendous profits *are* possible when insider information is used. Despite insider trading being against the law and the severe penalties imposed for infractions, the profits often prove too tempting to pass up. In one of the most famous insider trading scandals, Ivan Boesky, a fund manager, conspired with Michael Milken, an investment banker with Drexel Lambert Securities, to earn millions of dollars in insider trading profits. With this in mind we can safely reject strong form market efficiency.

But What About Those Ads?   If you read the financial press, you will be inundated with ads explaining how one fund or another has outperformed the market for extended periods of time. How is this possible if the markets are efficient and why does academic research show that fund managers do not outperform other investors? Suppose that you know nothing about football, but want to convince people that you do. One way would be to mail 10,000 letters to different people, with half of them saying the Dallas Cowboys will win their next game and the other half saying the Cowboys will lose. Next week do the same thing, but mail only 5,000 letters to those who received the letter with the correct prediction the previous week. You will now have correctly predicted the outcome of two games to 2,500. Continue this process throughout the season. After 10 games you will have correctly predicted the winner of every game to 20 people. You can now offer to tell them the winner of the eleventh game for a huge fee.

There are thousands of investment fund managers. By pure chance, every year some emerge as beating the market and some are losers. Similarly, each successive year some win and some lose. A few emerge as winners over an extended period of time, again, all by pure chance. These winners are hired by the big funds and promoted as financial experts with insights into the market that will yield extraordinary profits to those who trust them with their funds.

For example, the Fidelity Magellan Fund has attracted $56 billion in investments because of its exemplary performance over a 13-year period. However, since 1990 it has had three managers who have failed to match its previous performance. Academic research tries to separate superior performance that is the result of truly exceptional ability from that due to chance. This is not an easy task. For a fund to show statistical superiority it must outperform the market by a significant level over many years. With the difference between doing well and doing poorly being only a few percentage points, it is possible that our research has simply failed to identify a good performer as being a *statistically significant* good performer. This is the position taken by many practitioners on Wall Street.

Evidence Against Market Efficiency: The Theory Shows a Few Cracks

Through the 1960s, 1970s, and early 1980s, most research seemed to support the notion that the financial markets were at least semi–strong form efficient. Technical analysis was largely out of favor and investments grew in funds that simply mirrored some popular index such as the S&P 500 (these are called **index funds).** Index funds were popular because they had lower fees since they were not actively managed. They generally provided returns at least as high as actively managed mutual funds. However, in the late 1980s a small body of research began emerging that identified situations in which the market did not seem to be behaving efficiently. These situations were so rare that they were called **anomalies** and did little to shake anyone's faith in the concept of efficient markets or in the theories that relied on them. However, by the 1990s the evidence against market efficiency was becoming difficult to ignore.

One of the first and most widely publicized anomalies was called the small firm effect. Studies showed that small firms had outperformed large firms during most of the last 30 years. This performance advantage existed even when the returns were adjusted for the risk of small stocks, as measured by beta. Various theories suggest that the small firm effect is due to either portfolio rebalancing by institutional investors or to tax issues. Alternatively, it could be that there is some risk component of small firms that is not captured by beta and that justifies greater returns to those who hold small firms.

In another blow to market efficiency, research conducted that earnings have increased or fallen by large amounts by Debont and Thaler showed that the market may overreact to news announcements and that it may correct its errors slowly. This violates market efficiency because a profitable trading rule can be devised to take advantage of the slow price adjustment of stocks subject to earnings shocks. For example, whenever a firm announces that earnings have declined more than 40% below last year's level, wait until the stock price falls, then buy. The returns over the next few weeks should be greater than normal. It appears that the market is almost emotional in its overreaction to these surprise earnings announcements.

An important study by Jedadeesh and Titman[6] also suggests that the markets may not be as efficient as once thought. They show that markets fail to recognize that good news has a tendency to follow more good news and that the same happens with bad news. When a firm announces earnings that are above expectations, the firm's stock goes up, as you might predict. However, it does not go up as far as it should. Subsequent good

---

[6]N. Jedadeesh and S. Titman, "Returns to Buying Winners and Selling Losers: Implications for Stock Market Efficiency," *Journal of Finance,* March 1993.

reports catch the market by surprise, and the price continues to climb. A rational, efficient market would be aware of this tendency. It would anticipate the good reports in advance and would not have to react upon their arrival.

Jedadeesh and Titman show that the market continues to be confused. When a firm makes several good reports the market seems to become convinced that these are the precursors of *many* more to follow. Unfortunately, winners tend not to remain winners and losers tend not to remain losers. Both tend to revert to the average. Why does the market not learn this pattern and price stocks appropriately? Robert Haugen, a professor of finance and author of the book *The New Finance: The Case Against Efficient Markets,* says it is because the markets are not efficient at all.[7]

Is Beta Really Dead?

Eugene Fama and Kenneth French wrote a paper that was voted the best article published in the *Journal of Finance* in 1992 by the widest margin in history.[8] Given that the *Journal of Finance* is the oldest and most prestigious journal in academic finance, this article may forever change traditional views about financial theory.

Fama and French look at the returns accruing to value stocks and growth stocks. **Value stocks** are defined as those for which the stock price is low compared with earnings or with the accounting value of the firm's assets. These are firms that are somewhat out of favor in the market. Usually they have had low earnings, and their low PE ratio suggests that the market expects these low earnings to continue. **Growth stocks,** on the other hand, have high PE ratios and a high market-to-book ratio (low book-to-market ratio). These are the market favorites, such as Microsoft and Wal-Mart. Fama and French sorted stocks into 10 groups each year by their book-to-market ratio and computed the annualized return. The results are shown in Figure 9.3. The out-of-favor value stocks have much higher earnings than the popular growth stocks. Value stocks earned an average annualized return of 21.4% per year, whereas the growth stocks earned only 8%. Keep in mind that each group contained more than 200 stocks and that not all of those in the first group of value stocks performed well. On average, however, they significantly outperformed the growth stocks. Although this is interesting research, so far it is not earth-shaking.

The next contribution of the Fama and French paper was to plot beta against the book-to-market ratio. Remember that beta is the way risk is measured by the capital asset pricing model. In fact, according to CAPM, it is the only relevant measure of risk and should accurately predict returns. The higher the beta, the higher should be the returns. See Figure 9.4, which shows the relationship between beta and the book-to-market ratio. The popular growth stocks have high betas and the value stocks have low betas. In other words, the high-risk stocks, as measured by beta, have lower returns than the low-risk stocks. The riskiest stocks can be expected to produce the lowest future returns and the safest stocks the highest. These findings by such eminent financial economists shake the very foundation of market efficiency, the capital asset pric-

---

[7]Robert A. Haugen, *The New Finance: The Case Against Efficient Markets.* Englewood Cliffs, NJ: Prentice Hall, 1995, p. 22.

[8]Eugene Fama and Kenneth French, "The Cross-Section of Expected Stock Returns," *Journal of Finance,* June 1992.

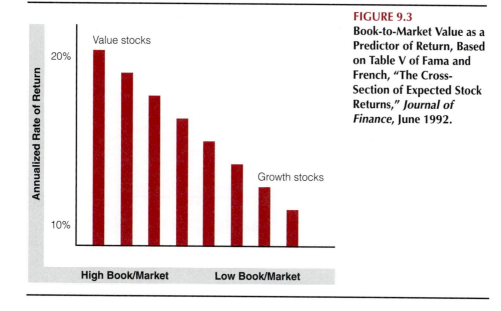

FIGURE 9.3
Book-to-Market Value as a Predictor of Return, Based on Table V of Fama and French, "The Cross-Section of Expected Stock Returns," *Journal of Finance*, **June 1992.**

ing model, and all that is based on it. David Dreman, a regular columnist for *Forbes* and the manager of a large mutual fund, claims that Fama and French have caused the death of beta.[9]

Fama and French demonstrated that the book-to-market ratio can better predict stock returns than can beta. Proponents of market efficiency argue that this does not necessarily spell the death of either beta or of market efficiency. Beta measures how much a company's stock price bounces around, compared with the market as a whole. Small firms and value companies are distressed. Their earnings may not be very volatile, but there is certainly the chance that something will go wrong. Investors may very properly demand additional compensation for incurring this risk in the form of higher returns. The market may not be inefficient; we just may not yet have developed the tools needed to properly measure all of the risk of an investment. Future models may include other factors, in addition to beta, that measure firm risk.

So, Are Financial Markets Efficient or Not?

We do not really know the answer to this question. On one hand, the reasoning behind the efficient market hypothesis is very appealing. Consider that our whole capitalistic society is based on the idea that many rational people, all working in their own self-interest, will provide the best mix of products at the best prices possible. Why should this not apply to financial markets, where the goals are clear and the competition is keen? If a security is priced too cheap, someone should recognize the error and take advantage of it to his or her own benefit. This activity should eventually correct the mispricing.

---

[9]"Value Will Out," *Forbes*, June 17, 1996, p. 146.

FIGURE 9.4
Book-to-Market Value of Portfolios Ranked by Beta, Based on Table II of Fama and French, "The Cross-Section of Expected Stock Returns," *Journal of Finance*, June 1992.

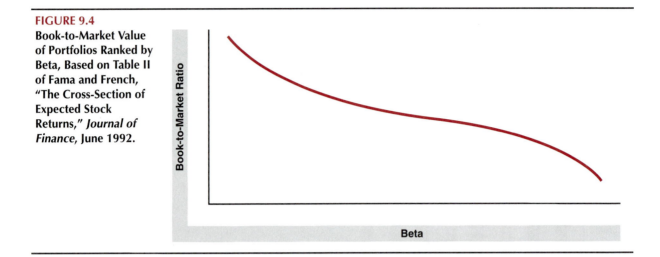

On the other hand, we are continuing to identify situations in which the markets fail the market efficiency test. We must determine whether it is market efficiency or the tests that fail. Financial economists will be working on these questions for many years as they attempt to nail down the answer.

What can we say about market efficiency today? First, sufficient research has been conducted in enough different arenas to establish that the markets function reasonably well. Although we may question whether beta is the best measure of risk or whether small or troubled firms have some form of risk so far unidentified, we can continue making decisions assuming that security prices are fair and that it is very hard to outguess the market.

There are many stories about financial managers who believed that they could outsmart the market. Few succeed in the long run. For example, in 1994 Robert Citron lost $1.7 billion for the Orange County, California, investment fund by betting on interest rates. This put Orange County, one of the wealthiest counties in the country, into bankruptcy until 1996. Another example occurred in 1995, when many universities suffered losses in their endowment funds because they invested in the College Equities Fund. They used financial derivatives to gamble that they could outsmart the market. Similarly, the Singapore manager of Lyons Bank in England gambled that he could beat the market. His losses also amounted to billions of dollars. Again, we see that even the professionals cannot outsmart the market.

Let us next review the implications of market efficiency on financial decision making.

What Market Efficiency Means to Financial Decision Making

If the financial markets are even reasonably efficient, most of the time most securities will be correctly priced. What does this mean to the investor and to the financial manager?

Do Not Try to Outsmart the Market   If markets are efficient, security prices impound all available information about the value of each security. This means that to outsmart the market you not only have to know more than *someone* else; you need to know more than *everyone* else. Only when you believe this to be true can you justify trading to beat the market.

Do Not Waste Money or Time Looking for Good Deals   Many investors spend great amounts of time and energy searching for good deals in the market. There was a graduate student in finance who saved for years to bring his family over from India so that he could get his Ph.D. from an American school. After studying finance for several years he believed that he could beat the market. He began trading daily. He was constantly buying and selling stocks in an attempt to earn abnormal returns. How do you suppose this intelligent, well-informed investor did? After the first year of trading he had to send his family back to India to live with his parents. By the second year he had to leave, too.

What went wrong? If the market is efficient, he should have just done as well as you would with a random pick of stocks, right? The problem was the transaction costs. Full-service brokers charge about 3% to buy stocks, depending on the cost of the stock and the size of the trade. Buying and then selling a stock costs about 6%. If this is done once per month, then you need to earn $12 \times 6\% = 72\%$ just to break even. Clearly our friend could not do this.[10]

The moral of the story is that the current evidence on market efficiency suggests that the best investment strategy to follow is one in which you buy securities with the intention of holding them for long periods of time. Do not invest short term. Invest for the long term. This will minimize your transaction costs.

---

[10]Discount brokers and online trading services can reduce transaction costs well below what they were when this graduate student was losing money. Lower costs simply mean it will take longer to lose your money.

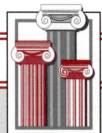

Careers in Finance   Stockbroker

Many investors prefer to use a stockbroker to help them invest in securities. Stockbrokers are usually employed by brokerage houses such as Merrill Lynch and Paine Webber. A new stockbroker will begin by studying to pass several exams required before being allowed to sell securities to the public. Most brokerage houses have in-house training programs to help prepare for these exams. During the training phase, stockbrokers will work with established brokers and will begin developing a client base. Brokers advise clients about which securities or mutual funds best suit the clients' risk and return requirements, and they initiate securities transactions.

Most brokerage firms provide a relatively small initial salary during training. This salary is phased out as com-

mission income increases. After 2 or 3 years, the broker is expected to be earning enough to not need a supplemental salary. After 5 or 6 years developing a client base, a stockbroker is expected to be earning at least $70,000. Successful brokers often earn well over $100,000.

The difficult part of becoming a stockbroker is surviving the first 5 years until your income rises to a level that compensates you for the many hours that are required. Less than 50% of those who begin as brokers are able to stick with it long enough to make it their career. Those who do survive find stockbroking to be exciting, rewarding, and lucrative.

Remember That History Does Not Matter   If you flipped heads on a coin five times in a row, what is the probability that you will flip heads on the sixth attempt? The probability is still 50%. This lesson is emotionally hard to follow sometimes, but the best evidence suggests that it is true for the financial markets. Just because a stock has risen 10 days in a row, it will not necessarily continue to rise. In fact, the evidence suggests just the opposite.

Many studies have shown that it is nearly impossible for analysts to accurately predict future growth more than a few quarters into the future.[11] Yet the market tends to price stocks as if historical growth will continue unabated indefinitely. Buying stocks with very high PE ratios has been shown to provide lower returns than buying value stocks, which have low PE ratios.

Final Note: What If the Markets Are Not Efficient?

There is a growing contingent of academics and practitioners who do not believe that the markets are efficient. T. Boone Pickens, a well-known corporate raider, has made a fortune buying firms and subsequently selling them. He has scoffed at the idea of market efficiency for years, while earning vast sums doing what academics said was impossible. Similarly, Robert Haugen has written a book that he feels refutes the market efficiency argument. Although most people who have studied the evidence feel that the market is probably reasonably efficient, we might still ask, What if it is not? This would have a serious effect on many of our financial theories and decisions.

---

[11]See G. Foster, "Quarterly Accounting Data: Time Series Properties and Predictive Ability Results," *Accounting Review,* Spring 1977; L. D. Brown and M. S. Rozeff, "The Superiority of Analysts' Forecasts as Measures of Expectations: Evidence from Earnings," *Journal of Financial Economics,* June 1978.

CHAPTER SUMMARY

Stocks are valued as the present value of the dividends. Unfortunately, we do not know precisely what these dividends will be. This introduces a great deal of error into the valuation process. The Gordon growth model is a simplified method of computing stock value that depends on the assumption that the dividends are growing at a constant rate forever. Given our uncertainty regarding future dividends, this assumption is often the best we can do.

The interaction between traders in the market is what sets prices on a day-to-day basis. The trader who values the security the most, either because of less uncertainty about the cash flows or because of greater estimated cash flows, is willing to pay the most. As new information is released, investors revise their estimates of the true value of the security and either buy or sell it depending on how the market price compares with their estimated valuation. Because small changes in estimated growth rates or required return result in large changes in price, it is not surprising that the markets are often volatile.

The efficient market hypothesis states that because of intense competition among traders who have similar motives and the ability to react quickly, all securities are always correctly priced. No amount of study or investigation will allow one investor to consistently earn higher risk-adjusted returns than another. If all securities are correctly priced, then historical, public, or even private information should not be useful for increasing an investor's returns. Stocks would follow a random walk, where previous stock price movements would not predict future movements.

The evidence for market efficiency is mixed. Most research shows that the markets are at least weak form and semi–strong form efficient (i.e., no historical or public information will result in unusually large profits). However, there is little evidence to support strong form market efficiency; insider information does appear to be useful to traders. Additionally, there are a number of specific instances in which even public information may allow for high profits.

Although most practitioners and academics do not believe that CAPM tells the whole story about the risk–return relationship, it continues to be used. One reason that CAPM continues to be popular is because no other idea has been advanced that is as theoretically appealing and easy to apply as CAPM. Unquestionably, new theories and methods will emerge as our understanding of the financial markets increases. In the meantime, we will continue to apply our theories judiciously while staying open to new approaches.

KEY WORDS

anomalies 247
capital yield 232
dividend 224
dividend yield 232
efficient market 239

generalized dividend
   model 225
Gordon growth
   model 227
growth stocks 248
high yield stocks 232

index funds 247
price/earnings ratio 235
residual claimant 224
semi–strong form
   efficient 245
shareholders 223

strong form efficient
   market 245
technical analysis 245
value stocks 248
weak form market
   efficiency 245

DISCUSSION QUESTIONS

1. Discuss the factors that may cause estimates of prices to be inaccurate.
2. How does the interaction of traders in the market cause security prices to adjust?
3. Is the market price of a security the highest price the trader who places the greatest value on stock is willing to pay? Why not?
4. Describe how traders, each motivated to find good deals, keep stock prices accurately reflecting firm value. (Extension 9.2)
5. On January 12, a firm announces it will replace its CEO. Over the next 2 weeks the stock of the firm gradually rises. Is this consistent with what would be expected to happen in an efficient market? Why or why not? (Extension 9.2)
6. A printer for the *Wall Street Journal* who has access to columns before they are published figured out that he could earn a profit by buying firms recommended by the paper before the paper became public. Is this consistent with an efficient market? What form of market efficiency does it support or violate? (Extension 9.2)
7. A firm has dividends of $1 per year. It is not growing and the stock currently sells for $10. After analysis you decide that because of increased risk investors will demand that the return increase to 15% in the near future. What is the most you would pay for the stock, assuming dividends are unchanged? (Extension 9.2)

8. Explain how some mutual fund managers are able to report above-average performance year after year if the markets are really efficient. (Extension 9.2)
9. Why would you not want to follow the advice of a technical analyst if you believe the markets to be efficient? (Extension 9.2)
10. Research has shown that when a firm makes several good reports about earnings, the market acts as if many more such reports are to follow. Is this likely to happen in an efficient market? Why or why not? (Extension 9.2)
11. Research has shown that value stocks are less risky than growth stocks. (Extension 9.2)
    a. What is a value stock and what is a growth stock?
    b. Do value stocks or growth stocks have the larger returns?
    c. Consider your answer to part b. What does this say about beta and market efficiency?
12. If you believe that the markets are reasonably efficient, what investment strategy should you follow (i.e., what general rules should you follow)? (Extension 9.2)
13. Given the evidence on market efficiency, should we continue to use CAPM? (Extension 9.2)

PROBLEMS

1. A share of preferred stock pays a dividend of $4 annually. The required rate of return is 8%. What is the preferred stock's price per share?

2. A share of preferred stock has a par value of $10. It pays a 10% dividend. If the required return is 12%, what is the price of the stock?

3. If preferred stock sold for $67 a share and $4 dividends were paid annually, what would be the required rate of return?

4. An investor plans to buy a share of stock today. It will be held for 1 year. The stock will pay a $2.00 dividend and should sell for $20. If the required return is 15%, how much should the investor pay for the stock?

5. You are contemplating the purchase of a stock that you will hold for 2 years. You will receive $1.50 per year in dividends, and then you expect to sell it for $35. If the required return is 12%, what is the most you would pay for the stock?

6. Investors expect Bozo Inc. to grow at a constant 5% indefinitely. If the next dividend is expected to be $3.00 and the required return is 10%, what is the market price of Bozo?

7. Carlson Enterprises' common stock dividend is expected to grow at 4% per year. The dividend recently paid was $2.00 per share and the required return is 10%.
   a. What is the estimated value of the common stock?
   b. If the value of a common stock was $50 per share and dividends were currently $1.50 but were expected to grow at 6% per year, what would be the required rate of return?
   c. If Carlson's dividends grew at 7% instead of 4%, what would be Carlson's price?
   d. If investors' required rate of return increased from 10% to 12% and dividends grew at 7%, what would be Carlson's price?

8. Bryson Industries paid $2.50 per share in dividends yesterday. Its dividends are expected to grow steadily at 7% per year.
   a. What are Bryson's dividends expected to be for each of the next 3 years?
   b. If the required return is 11%, what is the current price (P_0)?

   c. What is the estimate of the stock's price 1 year from now (P_1)?
   d. If you buy the stock today (and pay P_0 for it) and hold the stock 1 year, selling it for P_1, what return do you realize?

9. Company Y's dividend is expected to grow at a 20% rate for the next 3 years. It is then expected to grow at 8% annually for the foreseeable future. Company Y just paid $1.50 in dividends, and the investors require a 16% return on the company's stock. (Extension 9.1)
   a. What is the forecasted dividend for each of the next 3 years (D_1, D_2, D_3)?
   b. What is the dividend expected to be 4 years from now?
   c. At what price do you expect Company Y's stock to be selling 3 years from now (forecasted P_3)?
   d. What is the present value of D_1, D_2, D_3, and P_3?
   e. What is your estimate of today's price?

10. Hayworth Industries does not currently pay dividends. However, investors expect that in 4 years Hayworth will pay its first dividend of $7 per share, and it will continue to grow at an 8% annual rate forever. If investors require a 12% annual return on the stock, what is the current price? (Extension 9.1)

11. An analyst has made the following estimate of Company Z's future dividends. After 5 years, Company Z is expected to quit growing and pay a constant dividend of $1.50. If the required rate of return is 10%, what is the stock's price? (Extension 9.1)

Year	1	2	3	4	5
Dividend	1.00	1.05	1.22	1.37	1.50

12. The last dividend paid by Abbot Company was $2.00. Dividends are expected to grow at 15% for the next 2 years, then to grow at a constant 5% indefinitely. If the required return is 12%, what should the stock of Abbot sell for today? (Extension 9.1)

13. Teal Corp. has been having trouble. The last dividend was $3.00, and it is projected to fall 3% per year indefinitely. If the required return is 10%, what is Teal Corp.'s stock price? (Extension 9.1)

SELF-TEST PROBLEMS

1. What is the price of a share of preferred stock that has a dividend of $3 if the return required on preferred stock (k_p) is 15%?

2. What is the return required on preferred stock if the dividend is $3 and the price is $30?

3. What would you pay for a share of common stock if you expect the next dividend to be $2 and you expect to sell it in one year for $20, assuming the cost of equity (k_e) is 10%?

4. What would you pay for a share of common stock if you expect the next dividend to be $2 and you expect to sell it in one year for $20, assuming the cost of equity (k_e) is 15%?

5. What would you pay for a share of stock if the next dividend was $2, the one after that was $2.50, and after two years you expected to sell the stock for $15, assuming a cost of equity of 15%?

6. What would you pay for a share of common stock with a $3 dividend that was not expected to grow in the future, assuming a 15% cost of equity?

7. What would you pay for a share of common stock where the last dividend was $3 and that was expected to grow at 5% per year indefinitely, assuming a 15% cost of equity?

8. What would you pay for a share of common stock where the last dividend was $3 and that was expected to grow at 8% per year indefinitely, assuming a 15% cost of equity?

9. What would you pay for a share of common stock where the last dividend was $3 and that was expected to grow at 5% per year indefinitely, assuming a 25% cost of equity?

10. What would you pay for a share of common stock where the last dividend was $3 and that was expected to grow at −5% per year indefinitely, assuming a 25% cost of equity?

11. You do not expect there to be a dividend paid on a share of common stock next year. After that, however, you expect a $2 dividend that will grow at a constant 6% thereafter. How much would you pay for the stock assuming a cost of equity of 10%?

12. One year from now, what will be the price of the stock discussed in problem 11?

13. What is the percentage increase in price between now and 1 year from now for the stock discussed in problems 11 and 12?

14. A stock currently sells for $25 and pays a $3 dividend. What is the current yield?

15. Suppose the current yield on a stock was 3% and the cost of equity was 15%. What would you expect the appreciation in the stock's price to be?

16. The beta of a stock is 1.5. The required return on the market is 12% and the risk-free rate is 5%. What is the cost of equity?

17. What is the price of a share of stock if the beta is 2, its next dividend is projected to be $3, and its growth rate is expected to be a constant 7%, assuming the market return is 15% and the risk-free rate is 6%?

18. The PE ratio for a firm is 20. Expected earnings per share are $1.50. What is the current price of the firm's stock?

19. You wish to estimate the value of a company that has not yet issued stock. The PE ratio of similar firms is 16. You expect earnings to be $200,000. What is the total value of the firm?

20. Given the data in problem 19, what would be the price per share if the company issues 100,000 shares?

WEB EXPLORATION

1. Investing in stocks is often compared to playing a high-risk game. You are buying stocks even though you do not know how they will perform in an uncertain future. This exercise allows you to allocate funds among four stocks and to track their performance when various news events occur. You may reallocate your investment funds

after each news event. This game allows you to observe the benefits of various investment strategies. It should take less than 30 minutes.

   a. Go to www.pbs.org/wgbh/nova/stockmarket/ virtual.html and read the opening discussion. Click on Trade Traditional Stocks.

   b. Read the next screen and again click on Trade Traditional Stocks. You may be prompted to download Shockwave.

   c. Under each of the four companies is a company profile. Read each profile.

   d. Allocate $100,000 into each of the four stocks. Note that the game can only be played once, since the stocks behave the same way each time. Be careful that you are making your best effort the first time.

   e. Click Advance Two Weeks.

   f. Click News Flash. After reading the news flash, reallocate your investment in each firm as you see fit.

   g. Continue advancing and reallocating until the game in completed and your performance is evaluated.

   h. Compare your strategy and performance with those of your classmates.

2. The game identified in exercise 1 takes only a few minutes to play and gives you a flavor what investing in stocks is like. The game discussed in this exercise will take the rest of the semester and is much more realistic. As opposed to many of these games, this one is free to play.

The *Invest Smart Stock Game* is a great place to learn about trading stocks. You will to decide how to invest 100,000 virtual dollars. You may buy stock on the New York Stock Exchange (NYSE), NASDAQ, or the American Stock Exchange (AMEX). The stock quotes used are actual 20-minutes-delayed data from the exchange. (The delay is due to SEC regulations.)

You will start out with 100,000 virtual dollars in your cash account. Then, you may research companies and decide which stocks you want to buy or sell. We suggest that you invest in not more than five stocks and that each of the companies be in different industries. There will be a $15–30 virtual commission for every transaction, depending on which brokerage firm you use.

You may sign up for this game more than once with different login names and trade different stocks in each account to test out various investing strategies. A players' ranking will be generated daily. This ranking will see who can build up a stock portfolio with the greatest value.

To begin go to library.thinkquest.org/10326/market_simulation/index.html. Go to the Invest Smart Stock Game and login. You may click on the Stock Market Basics hyperlink to read about possible investment strategies. Note that you can click on the Research tab on the left to look up specifics about various companies. Go ahead and register and begin the game.

MINI CASE

You have been hired as an analyst for Brunswick Brokerage Incorporated, a firm that manages several stock mutual funds. On your first day of work you meet with your new boss, who wants to put you to work on a meaningful task. He tells you that he has been reading about Shazam Inc., a maker of computer peripherals, and thinks they may currently be underpriced. He would like you to do an analysis to determine whether they should be acquired by Brunswick's high tech mutual fund. Your preliminary report is due tomorrow.

You immediately return to your office and begin collecting information. Shazam has not yet paid any dividends. It has been turning a profit. Sales in 1998, 1999, 2000, and 2001 were $2 million, $2.25 million, $3 million, and $4 million respectively. Net income was $200,000, $250,000, $300,000, and $350,000 over that period. Total equity was $0.769 million in 1998. It increased to $0.925 million in 1999, to $1.25 million in 2000, and to $1.35 million in 2001. There are 600,000 shares of stock outstanding. The current market value of the stock is $15.50 per share.

The firm's beta is 2.25 and you feel that a market return of 15% is realistic. The Treasury bill rate is 5.5%.

The industry PE ratio is 27. You judge this to be a little too high for Shazam since it competes against some very strong firms. You decide that a PE of 24 is more appropriate for valuing its stock.

You read the report from the president that is included in Shazam's latest annual report and learn that the firm believes it can begin paying dividends next year of $1.00 per share.

a. Compute the growth rate in sales and net income. Which do you feel is most appropriate to use as the firm's growth rate?

b. Compute the return on equity for each year. What ROE do you feel the firm is likely to have next year?

c. Compute the required return for the firm using the CAPM. Is this consistent with the results of part b?

d. Compute the earnings per share for each year and project next year's EPS using the growth rate in net income.

e. Using the growth rate in net income, compute the price of the firm's stock with the Gordon growth model. (Equation 9.6)

f. Compute the price of the firm's stock using the PE valuation method. (Equation 9.9)

g. If you assume that the firm will pay dividends next year as suggested by its president, what is its dividend yield?

h. Would you recommend that Brunswick buy shares in Shazam? Why? Discuss sources of errors in your analysis and whether they make the stock look more or less attractive.

Capital Budgeting: Introduction and Techniques

S imply put, investment decisions have a greater impact on a business's future than any other decision it makes. Businesses that invest profitably make money and provide a fair return for their owners. Those that fail to invest profitably are unlikely to survive in the competitive business world. Businesses must invest constantly. Vail Associates, the ski resort operator, invested $1 million in 1996 in a snowmobile and horseback riding center. Beaver Creek ski area invested $20 million in a retail complex. Both were hoping to attract an increasingly elusive ski customer. Were these wise investments? No matter how sophisticated the analysis, a firm is seldom sure. However, we can develop methods that increase the chance that investments yield more than they cost.

The purpose of this chapter is to investigate methods for evaluating investment decisions. We will use many of the tools developed so far in this text. For example, we must adjust an investment's cash flows to take into account the time value of money. Additionally, we must be able to adjust for the risk of those cash flows.

We begin this discussion by defining capital budgeting.

Chapter Objectives

By the end of this chapter you should be able to:

1. Introduce TVM concepts to investment analysis
2. Develop project evaluation models
3. Compare NPV to IRR
4. Select projects under capital rationing

WHAT DOES *CAPITAL BUDGETING* MEAN?

Chapter 2 introduced the capital markets. The term *capital* referred to long-term securities and investments. The term retains the same meaning in this chapter. **Capital budgeting** is the process of deciding which long-term investments or projects a firm will acquire using the long-term funds it has available. The term *budgeting* is appropriate because most firms have more ways to spend money than they have available funds. They must allocate these limited funds in such a way as to provide the most long-term profits. Keep in mind that the goal of the financial manager is to increase shareholder wealth. The purpose of this chapter is to provide techniques for selecting projects that accomplish this.

Summary of Capital Budgeting

Once a possible project has been identified, a firm's management must evaluate whether firm value will be increased if the project is accepted. There are a number of steps to this evaluation.

1. All relevant cash flows must be identified. Surprisingly, this is where the firm will make the greatest errors. Although it is often possible to estimate the initial cost of the project or investment accurately, estimating the cash inflows that follow is very difficult. For example, Robert Harshaw quit his job with Texas Instruments in 1987 to market a device he had invented to help pilots go through their safety checklist without making errors. He thought that he was going to get rich selling his product to the airlines. What he had failed to appreciate was that airlines are extremely reluctant to spend money on products not required by the Federal Aviation Administration. Sales were poor and losses mounted. Harshaw's company did not earn a profit until he won a contract from Cessna in 1993 to develop a digitized voice system to alert pilots of equipment malfunctions. Because estimating cash inflows may require estimating the success of new products, errors are almost inevitable.

2. Once all of the cash flows have been identified, they must be analyzed. We will learn one method that does not require the use of time value of money (TVM) and four methods that do.

    *   The non-TVM method is the *payback period*. Although this method has many faults, it continues to be widely reported and used. A project's payback is simply the number of years until the investment is recovered.

    *   The most widely used capital budgeting method is the *net present value* (NPV). The NPV is computed by subtracting the present value of cash outflows from the present value of cash inflows. If inflows exceed outflows on a present value basis, the project is acceptable.

    *   The *profitability index* (PI) is closely related to NPV. It converts NPV to a ratio that is often easier to interpret than NPV.

    *   The fourth method we will learn is the *internal rate of return* (IRR). The IRR is the average compounded annual return earned by a project. If the return exceeds the firm's cost of capital, the project is accepted.

- Finally we will learn how to compute the *modified internal rate of return*. This method is similar to the internal rate of return, but it is modified so that it is more theoretically sound and in some ways easier to calculate (see Extension 10.1).

3. Finally, the results of the cash flow analysis must be interpreted. We will see that one important advantage of the TVM-based methods is that they have a clear interpretation. This is not the case with the payback method.

Finding Investment Opportunities

Riches and wealth go to those who are able to see investment opportunities before others. Consider Duffy Mazan and his partners at Electric Press. In 1994 they formed a company to set up and maintain Internet Web sites. When they first began marketing their services they had to explain to their potential customers what the Internet was. Now they receive calls from customers who are eager to get on the Web. It takes foresight, an understanding of the market in which you are interested, and some luck to pick growth areas such as this.

On the other hand, consider IBM's investment in OS/2 Warp. Despite huge expenditures, the operating system remains unpopular and not widely distributed. Similarly, Steve Jobs, one of the founders of Apple Computer, has spent an estimated $130 million, including $12 million of his own money, on Next Computer (a new computer company). There has been little payoff from these investments to date.

Most firms are constantly seeking new investment ideas and opportunities. These ideas may be as simple as replacing two low-output copiers with one high-speed unit. Alternatively, an investment may change the whole face of a firm. In this chapter we assume that management has investment ideas to evaluate. ***Do not lose sight of the fact that the collection of these ideas spells the success and failure of the firm***.

Steps in the Capital Budgeting Process

The capital budgeting process is so critical to the survival of a firm that it is worth discussing the full scope of the capital budgeting process, rather than simply how the evaluation tools are computed. We can identify five steps that a firm should follow.

1. *Identification of opportunities:* Initially, the firm must have some method in place by which new opportunities are identified and brought to the attention of management. For example, when First National Bank of Fairbanks offered a $100 reward to employees who sent in ideas that were implemented, a vault teller in a small branch suggested a cash counting machine. Management found that this branch received large commercial deposits and that the teller was counting each bill separately. Without the reward offer, management would never have learned of the opportunity to save substantial amounts of teller time with a small capital investment. Management is often removed from the factory floor or direct customer contact. Employees on the front lines must have both the incentive and the means to communicate ideas to those who have the authority to implement them.

2. *Evaluation of opportunities:* Once the firm identifies an opportunity, it must be evaluated. This requires that all of the costs and benefits be tabulated. These data are

then subjected to analysis. In this chapter we focus on how to analyze data once they have been prepared. In the next chapter we learn how to organize the cash flows from an investment opportunity.

3. *Selection:* Often firms have more good projects than they can accept in any given year. This may be because of limited funds or because of human or physical constraints facing the firm. In this chapter we look at how a firm might rank projects to facilitate selecting among them.

4. *Implementation:* Once a project has been selected, it must be implemented. The machines will be purchased, people hired, or investments made. Management must be vigilant at this stage to ensure that the costs reflect what was initially proposed and evaluated. For example, Twentieth-Century Fox decided to produce the movie *Titanic* in 1995. They projected costs to be about $100 million and decided that the project would be profitable. Unfortunately, by 1997 cost overruns brought the total cost to over $200 million. Total movie revenues would have to exceed $350 million for the project to be profitable. Although this did happen, the risk of the project was much greater than originally anticipated.

5. *Post audit:* Once the project has been completed, management must compare the costs and revenues with the original projections. This is a critical step that is often overlooked. Holding employees responsible for errors in their projections gives them an incentive to make more accurate future cost and revenue projections. Employees who know that they must later explain deviations from projections will study the results of their last estimates diligently so as to improve in the future.

Taken together, these steps can dramatically improve a firm's ability to select wealth-increasing projects, bring them to fruition, and learn from each experience. In the next section we study methods of evaluating a project once it has been identified as a possible candidate for capital spending.

EVALUATING THE CASH FLOWS

The financial analyst first estimates the cash inflows and outflows that an investment will generate. Then these cash flows are evaluated to determine whether the project should be accepted. In this chapter we investigate methods for evaluating the cash flows, and in Chapter 11 we will learn how to estimate the cash flows and to handle special situations that arise in evaluating them.

Businesses and investors commonly use the investment evaluation methods discussed earlier. Each suffers from at least one drawback. Some have many problems but continue to be used because they are simple. We will learn all of the common techniques. Summarized, they include the following:

- Payback period
- Net present value
- Profitability index

- Internal rate of return
- MIRR (Extension 10.1)

Payback Period Method

The **payback period** method is the easiest investment evaluation method to perform, but the theoretically worst method available. The payback is simply the number of years it takes to recover the initial investment. The timing and riskiness of the cash flows are ignored. The reason it continues to be used is that it is easy to understand and explain to others. Small businesses are especially likely to use the payback method if the owners or managers are not well versed in financial principles. The method is also used to supplement more sophisticated techniques.

Computation

The calculation of the payback is very easy if the annual cash flows are annuities (remember that annuities are equal payments received at equal intervals). The payback is found by dividing the initial investment by the annual annuity.

If the cash flows vary from year to year, they must be accumulated until the sum equals the initial investment. Partial years can be estimated. In Example 10.1 we use payback to evaluate an annuity.

E X A M P L E 10.1   Payback Period: Annuity

In 2000 *Consumer Reports* listed Lindeman's Bin 40 Cabernet Sauvignon as a best buy in its taste test. If Lindeman's wants to expand production to take advantage of the increased sales this report may generate, it will have to expand its facilities. Assume that expansion of its winery will cost $1,000,000. If this will generate after-tax cash inflows of $235,000 for 8 years, what is the payback? It will take about 4 years and 3 months for the firm to recover its initial investment.

Solution

Because the annual cash inflows are equal, simply divide them into the initial investment:

$$\text{Payback} = \frac{\text{Initial investment}}{\text{Annual cash inflow}}$$

$$\text{Payback} = \frac{\$1,000,000}{\$235,000} = 4.25 = 4 \text{ years, 3 months}$$

The calculation is somewhat more complicated if the cash inflows are not equal. An accumulation table can be constructed to compute payback in this case. We evaluate an investment with unequal cash flows in Example 10.2.

E X A M P L E 10.2   Payback Period: Unequal Cash Flows

Suppose after reviewing its cash flow estimates, Lindeman's decides that the publicity provided by the *Consumer Reports* article will wear off over time. As a result, cash inflows would decline 10% the first year and then 15% per year thereafter. What is the payback?

Solution

Set up a table, as presented here. The initial investment and cash inflow are given in the problem. The next column is the sum of the cash inflows. The last column is computed by subtracting the accumulated inflow column from the initial investment.

Year	Initial Investment	Cash Inflow	Accumulated Inflow	Balance
0	−$1,000,000	0	0	−$1,000,000.00
1		$235,000.00	$235,000.00	−765,000.00
2		211,500.00	446,500.00	−553,500.00
3		179,775.00	626,275.00	−373,725.00
4		152,808.75	779,083.75	−220,916.25
5		129,887.44	908,971.19	−91,028.81
6		110,404.32	1,019,375.51	+19,375.51

The final year can be estimated by dividing the remaining balance by the cash inflow and then multiplying the product by 12:

$$\frac{\$91,028.81}{\$110.404.32} = 0.824 \times 12 = 9.89 \text{ months}$$

It will take Lindeman's about 5 years and 10 months to recover its initial investment if the cash flow estimates are correct (5 years + 9.89 months).

Self-Test Review Question*

What is the payback for an investment that requires a $10,000 initial investment and returns $3,000 per year thereafter?

Advantages

The principal advantage of the payback method is its simplicity. It also provides information about how long funds will be tied up in a project. The shorter the payback, the greater the project's liquidity.

Disadvantages

There are many problems with the payback method.

- *No clearly defined accept/reject criteria:* Is a 4-year payback good or bad? We do not have a method to determine this. Often a payback of 2 or 3 years is required, but clearly this is arbitrary.

- *No risk adjustment:* Risky cash flows are treated the same way as low-risk cash flows. The required payback period could be lengthened for low-risk projects, but the exact adjustment is still arbitrary.

*$10,000/$3,000 = 3.33. This means it will take 3.33 years to recover the initial investment. One-third of a year is 4 months. The payback is then 3 years and 4 months.

TABLE 10.1 Cash Inflows, $1 Million Over 3 Years

Year	Cash Inflow A	Cash Inflow B	Balance
0	0	0	−$1,000,000
1	$500,000	$200,000	
2	300,000	300,000	
3	200,000	500,000	0

- *Ignores cash flows beyond the payback period:* Any cash inflows that occur after the payback period are excluded from the analysis. This is clearly a short-sighted way to view investments.

- *Ignores time value of money:* Consider Table 10.1. The payback is the same, 3 years, but cash inflow A is clearly preferred because of the time value of money.

To properly evaluate investment projects we need a method that does not suffer from the above problems. One such method is the net present value. One reason for learning the payback method was to demonstrate a poor method of analysis so that you will be able to appreciate a theoretically sophisticated method. Pay attention to how the net present value approach differs from the payback method.

Study Tip

Do *not* simply add together cash flows that occur at different points in time. This will never be correct. Always adjust the cash flows by computing the value they have at a common point in time, usually the present. *You must always adjust for the time value of money before combining cash flows.*

Net Present Value

The **net present value (NPV)** is the most popular and theoretically sound evaluation tool available to analysts. NPV has grown in use among corporations as more students are exposed to the method in their finance or MBA coursework. Its interpretation requires a fundamental understanding of the time value of money. Surveys of large national corporations find that over 70% now apply NPV to project evaluation, although most companies continue to use other methods as well.

Theory

Most investments have some funds being spent today in the hope that greater amounts will be received in the future. Because the cash inflows and the cash outflows occur at different times, they cannot be compared directly. Instead, they must be translated into a common time period. It is usually easiest to convert all of the cash flows into *current* dollars because at least some expenditure is probably made at time zero. After the conversion into present values, the cash inflows are compared with the cash outflows. If inflows exceed outflows, the project is acceptable. The difference between the cash outflows and the cash inflows is the NPV.

Computation

The formula for calculating NPV can be written several ways. Equation 10.1 uses summation notation:

$$\text{NPV} = \sum_{t=1}^{n} \frac{\text{CF}_t}{\left(1 + i\right)^t} - \text{Initial investment} \quad \quad (10.1)$$

The first term on the right-hand side of the equation computes the present value of the cash inflows where i is the discount rate. This discount rate is equal to the firm's cost of capital when evaluating projects similar in risk to others in the firm's portfolio. The initial investment is assumed to be paid at time zero, so no discounting is required. If the initial investment is actually paid out over a period of time, the present value of the initial investment must be found. Each year's cash outflows would have to be discounted back to the present before subtracting from the present value of the inflows.

An alternative equation for NPV is

$$NPV = PV(\text{Cash inflows}) - PV(\text{Cash outflows}) \tag{10.2}$$

You can interpret a positive NPV as meaning that the current value of the income exceeds the current value of the expenditure, so the project should be accepted. A negative NPV means the project costs more than it will bring in and so should be rejected. *The decision criteria for NPV can then be summarized as follows: Accept the project if NPV is positive or equal to 0; reject the project if NPV is negative.*

E X A M P L E 10.3   Net Present Value Calculation

The owner of a Texaco gas station in Nevada is considering buying a slot machine to put in his small convenience store. The slot machine will sell for $6,000 and is expected to bring in about $10 per day after expenses. Slot machines in casinos have an average take of about $150 per day after expenses, so the owner believes his cash flow estimate is conservative. If the average cost of funds to the gas station is 15%, should the slot machine be installed? The machine is expected to last 3 years before a newer model will be needed to attract gamblers.

Solution
We can simplify the calculations by using the annual projected cash inflow rather than the daily cash inflow ($10 \times 365 = \$3,650$). Putting the numbers into Equation 10.1 yields the following:

$$NPV = \sum_{t=1}^{n} \frac{CF_t}{(1 + i)^t} - \text{Initial investment}$$

$$NPV = \frac{\$3,650}{(1.15)^1} + \frac{\$3,650}{(1.15)^2} + \frac{\$3,650}{(1.15)^3} - \$6,000 = \$2,333.77$$

Because the NPV is positive, the gas station owner should install the slot machine. The problem could also have been worked using the annuity tables to find the present value of the equal cash inflows.[1]

How would you explain what an NPV of $2,333.77 means to someone who has not taken an introductory finance course? One accurate interpretation is that the project has returned the cost of capital (15%) plus $2,333.77. In other words, the value of the firm will increase by $2,333.77 as a result of accepting the project.

Suppose that you had completed the analysis of an investment for a very large firm. The initial investment is $1 billion and the NPV is $1. Assuming you are absolutely

---

[1]For example, NPV = $3,650(PVIFA$_{15\%, 3\text{ yr}}$) − $6,000 = $2,333.68.

positive of all of your calculations and estimates (this will probably never be true), do you recommend that the firm make the investment? In other words, do you invest $1 billion to get an NPV of $1? The decision criterion says to accept the project if the NPV is positive. Many students want to abandon the NPV decision criteria of accepting all positive-NPV projects when faced with this example. You *should* recommend acceptance. The reason is that the project is returning much more than $1. It is returning the required return (the cost of capital) *plus* $1. In other words, the firm is getting all that it needs to be satisfied that it is receiving a fair return, plus a $1 bonus. ***The point is that a positive NPV is the amount the investor is receiving above what is required valued at time = 0.***

E X A M P L E 10.4   Net Present Value Calculation

Not all investments are made in one lump sum. Sometimes the initiation of the project takes several years. For example, the Trans-Alaska Pipeline took 4 years to complete, at a total cost of $8 billion. Suppose $1 billion was spent the first year, $1 billion the second year, $2 billion the third year, and $4 billion the last year (assume all investments are made at the beginning of the year). If the revenues are expected to be $1 billion per year for 20 years and the discount rate is 15%, should the pipeline have been built (assume all cash inflows occur at the end of the year and begin at the end of year 1)?

Solution

We will first compute the present value of the cash outflows, and then we will compute the present value of the cash inflows. Finally, we will compute NPV by subtracting the present value of the outflows from the present value of the inflows.

$$\text{Step 1: PV(outflows)} = \frac{\$1 \text{ billion}}{1} + \frac{\$1 \text{ billion}}{(1.15)^1} + \frac{\$2 \text{ billion}}{(1.15)^2} + \frac{\$4 \text{ billion}}{(1.15)^3}$$

$$\text{PV(outflows)} = \$1 \text{ billion} + \$0.87 \text{ billion} + \$1.51 \text{ billion} + \$2.63 \text{ billion}$$

$$\text{PV(outflows)} = \$6.01 \text{ billion}$$

$$\text{Step 2: PV(inflows)} = \$1 \text{ billion} \times \left(\text{PVIFA}_{20 \text{ yr, } 15\%}\right)$$

$$\text{PV(inflows)} = \$1 \text{ billion} \times 6.259 = \$6.259 \text{ billion}$$

$$\text{Step 3: NPV} = \text{PV(inflows)} - \text{PV(outflows)}$$

$$\text{NPV} = \$6.259 \text{ billion} - \$6.01 \text{ billion} = \$0.248 \text{ billion}$$

Because the NPV is greater than zero, the pipeline should have been built.

Advantages

The net present value method solves the problems listed with the payback period approach.

- *Uses time value of money concept:* The cash flows are discounted back to the present so that all cash flows are compared on an equal basis.
- *Clear decision criterion:* Accept the project if the NPV is zero or greater. Reject if less than zero.

- *Discount rate adjusts for risk:* By increasing or decreasing the discount rate, the firm can adjust for the riskiness of the cash flows. We will investigate how to do this in a later section. The discount rate used to evaluate capital budgeting projects is the firm's **cost of capital,** which is the average cost of its debt and equity. The cost of capital reflects the risk of the firm and the firm's average required rate of return on its investments. In Chapter 12 we will learn how to compute the cost of capital. For now it is best described as the return the firm must earn on its investments to satisfy investors.

Disadvantages

The primary disadvantage to NPV is that it may be difficult for someone without a background in financial theory to understand. This problem sustains the popularity of other methods we will study.

A second problem with NPV is that it can be difficult to use when available capital or resources are limited. If a company must select among a group of positive-NPV projects, it may want to know which projects provide the highest return for the amount invested. NPV does not provide this information. We will point out alternative methods that can be helpful when the firm must rank projects.

Self-Test Review Question*

The investment required to obtain a new machine is $2,500. The cash flows are estimated to be $500 per year for 8 years. If the firm's cost of capital is 12%, should it buy the machine? (Compute NPV)

NPV Profile

An **NPV profile** graphs the NPV at a variety of discount rates. The NPV profile demonstrates how sensitive the NPV is to changes in the discount rate. We will learn in Chapter 12 that it is very difficult to accurately and confidently estimate the cost of capital for a firm. At best we can determine an approximate value. Before we recommend that a firm accept or reject a project, we should determine whether a small error in our cost of capital estimate is important. We can do this by preparing an NPV profile. Once the profile is prepared, we can note whether small changes in the cost of capital will result in major changes to the NPV.

Let us prepare an NPV profile for the cash flows given in Table 10.2.

Study Tip

Many students get confused about which discount rates should be used to construct an NPV profile. *Any* interest rate works. Simply pick ones that are above and below the crossover point. You will not know where this occurs until you begin computing some NPVs.

TABLE 10.2

Year	Cash Flow
0	−$1,000
1	250
2	250
3	250
4	250
5	250

*No: NPV = $2,483.82 − $2,500 = −16.18. Because the NPV is negative, do not buy the machine.

FIGURE 10.1
NPV Profile

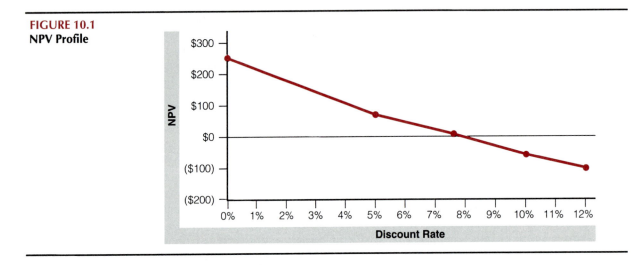

To compute the NPV profile, select a number of different discount rates and compute the NPV for each. You may use any discount rates you choose, although it is usually easiest to begin at 0% because the NPV is found simply by summing the cash flows. Continue using increasingly larger discount rates until the NPV turns negative. The NPVs for five interest rates using the cash flows from Table 10.2 are reported below.

Discount Rate	NPV
0%	$250.00
5	82.37
7.5	11.47
10	−52.30
12	−98.81

These numbers are graphed in Figure 10.1. We can read the point where the graph crosses the horizontal axis. This occurs at about 8%. This is where NPV = 0. To the left of this point NPV is positive and the project is acceptable. To the right of this point NPV is negative and the project should be rejected. If you are confident that the cost of capital (the average cost of funds to the firm) is less than the crossover point, accept the project.

E X A M P L E 10.5   Preparing an NPV Profile

You are contemplating an investment in a Putt-Putt miniature golf course. If you invest $50,000 today, you expect to receive annual cash flows of $15,000 for the next 5 years. You are not certain of your cost of capital but expect it to be around 15%. Prepare an NPV profile and discuss whether the investment should be made.

Solution

We will need to compute the NPV at a variety of different discount rates. We do not know which ones until we actually begin computing a few to see how the NPV profile develops. We will begin with the discount rate equal to zero and will compute the NPV using increasingly large discount rates until the NPV is negative. The formula for computing NPV is

$$NPV = \$15,000 \times (PVIFA_{5\ yr,i}) - \$50,000$$

When i = 0%,

$$NPV = \$15,000(5) - \$50,000$$
$$NPV = \$75,000 - \$50,000 = \$25,000$$

When i = 5%,

$$NPV = \$15,000(4.329) - \$50,000$$
$$NPV = \$64,935 - \$50,000 = \$14,935$$

We continue computing the NPV at different discount rates until NPV is negative. The results are reported in this table:

Discount Rate	NPV
0%	$25,000
5	14,935
10	6,862
15	282
20	(5,141)

We now graph the results to obtain our NPV profile:

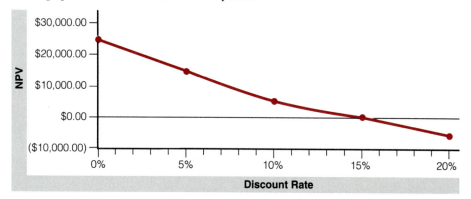

From the NPV profile we see that we would accept the project as long as the cost of capital was less than about 15¼% because the NPV is positive in that range. Alternatively, we would reject the project if the cost of capital was greater than about 15¼%. In this example, since the cost of capital is 15%, you would make the investment.

   In the next section we will introduce a method that converts NPV into a ratio that is easier for some to interpret.

Profitability Index (Cost–Benefit Ratio)

The **profitability index (PI)** uses the same inputs as the NPV, but by converting the results to a ratio, it provides additional information. Equation 10.3 computes the PI:

$$PI = \frac{PV\left(Cash\ inflows\right)}{PV\left(Cash\ outflows\right)} \tag{10.3}$$

$$PI = \frac{PV\left(Cash\ inflows\right)}{Initial\ investment}$$

The numerator is the present value of the benefits of taking the project. The denominator is the present value of the cost of taking the project. The PI is the benefit relative to the cost, on a present value basis. An easier interpretation is that the PI is the *bang for the buck* provided by the project. When NPV is zero, the PV(Cash inflows) will equal the PV(Cash outflows) and the PI will be 1. ***Thus, our decision criterion is to accept the project if the PI is greater than or equal to 1***.

Computation

To compute PI simply find the present value of the cash inflows and divide by the PV of the cash outflows. If you are also computing an NPV, these values should be readily available. We can use the figures provided by Example 10.3 to illustrate the process.

E X A M P L E   10.6   Profitability Index

Suppose that a $6,000 investment will yield three cash inflows of $3,650 each. With a discount rate of 15%, what is the PI?

Solution

The PV of the cash outflow is $6,000 because the entire investment is made today. The PV of the cash inflows is $3,650(PVIFA$_{15\%,3\,yr}$), which is $3,650(2.2832) = $8,333.68. Put these figures into Equation 10.3:

$$PI = \frac{PV\left(\text{Cash inflows}\right)}{PV\left(\text{Cash outflows}\right)}$$

$$PI = \frac{\$8,333.68}{\$6,000}$$

$$PI = 1.39$$

Study Tip

Because PI gives the return per dollar invested, it is said to give the "bang per buck."

The profitability index is 1.39. Because it is greater than 1, we would accept the project. Notice that this is the same decision we reached in Example 10.3. ***In fact, PI and NPV will always provide the same answer to the accept/reject question***.

Advantages

The PI is useful as an aid in ranking projects from best to worst. It may be necessary to rank projects if the firm does not have sufficient funds or capacity to accept all positive-NPV projects. Consider two positive-NPV projects, one small and one large. The large one may have the largest NPV even though the smaller one has a greater return on the dollars invested. The profitability index will highlight this difference by computing the return per dollar invested, on a present value basis. The firm may be better off taking several small high-PI projects instead of one large positive-NPV project.

Self-Test Review Question*

A machine will cost $2,500 to buy and is expected to yield profits of $500 per year for 8 years. What is the profitability index? Assume a cost of capital of 12%.

E X A M P L E 10.7   Using PI to Rank Projects

Suppose that you have collected the following data on four possible projects. Rank the projects using PI. If your capital budget was $1,000, which project(s) would you select?

Project	Net Investment	PV (cash inflows)	NPV
A	$ 500	$ 550	$50
B	100	90	−10
C	1,000	1,052	52
D	20	25	5

Solution

Begin by computing the profitability index for each project:

Project	Net Investment	PV (cash inflows)	PI
A	$500	$550	$550 ÷ $500 = 1.1
B	100	90	$90 ÷ $100 = .9
C	1,000	1,052	$1,052 ÷ $1,000 = 1.052
D	20	25	$25 ÷ $20 = 1.25

Now review the PI ratios to see which projects are acceptable. Because project B has a PI less than 1, it is immediately rejected. Next, rank the projects in order from highest PI to lowest. Project D has the highest PI, A is next, and C is third. This analysis suggests we should accept projects A and D, for a total capital budget of $520. The combined NPV of these two projects is $55, which is greater than the NPV of project C by itself.[2]

Disadvantages

Although there are no theoretical problems with PI, it should not replace NPV. Ultimately, the goal of the financial manager is to maximize shareholder wealth. PI may be used as a supplement to NPV, but not as a replacement.

In the next section we will discuss the most frequently used alternative to the net present value: the internal rate of return.

Internal Rate of Return

The **internal rate of return (IRR)** is the discount rate that sets the present value of the cash inflows equal to the present value of the cash outflows. Alternatively, *IRR can be defined as the discount rate that sets NPV equal to zero.* If the IRR is greater than the cost of capital, the project is accepted. If the IRR is less than the cost of capital, the project is rejected.

IRR is more difficult to calculate than NPV and often requires the use of a financial calculator or computer. However, it is far easier to interpret. For this reason it continues to be used almost as often as NPV.

---

[2]The NPV is computed by subtracting the net investment from the PV(inflows). The NPV of A = $50, B = −$10, C = $52, and D = $5.

Theory

Suppose that your roommate offers you an opportunity to invest in his mail-order computer parts business. If you invest $100 today, you will receive $110 in 1 year. What is the return on this investment? You probably answered 10% without needing paper and pencil. The return on this investment is independent of what else is happening to market returns, so we call it an *internal* return.

Would you accept your roommate's offer? That depends on what your required rate of return is. If your cost of capital is 12%, you would reject the proposal.

Let us continue with this example by demonstrating how we would compute the NPV. The figures are initially put into Equation 10.3:

$$NPV = \frac{\$110}{1 + i} - \$100$$

If we know the discount rate (i), we can compute NPV. The IRR approaches the problem from a slightly different angle. Rather than inputting a discount rate and computing NPV, we ask how high the discount rate can be before NPV becomes negative and the project is unacceptable. We find this *breakeven* discount rate by setting NPV equal to zero and solving for i. For example,

$$NPV = 0 = \frac{\$110}{1 + i} - \$100$$

$$\$100 = \frac{\$110}{1 + i}$$

$$1 + i = \frac{\$110}{\$100} = 1.10$$

$$i = 0.10 = 10\%$$

The 10% interest rate is the value of the discount rate that sets the present value of the cash inflows equal to the present value of the cash outflows. If the 10% return is acceptable, the project should be taken. In this example, because capital cost 12%, we reject the project. ***Thus, the decision criterion for IRR can be summarized as follows: Accept the project if the IRR is greater than or equal to the cost of capital***.[3]

Review Figure 10.1. We can read the IRR directly off the NPV profile. The IRR is the discount rate where NPV = 0. This is where the profile crosses the horizontal axis.

Computation

In the preceding example we saw that the calculation of the IRR was fairly straightforward when there was a single cash inflow. It becomes much more complicated when there are multiple cash flows. There are three methods to use depending on the nature of the cash flows and the availability of a financial calculator. They involve using financial tables, trial and error, and a calculator. We will discuss each of the methods below and illustrate them with examples.

---

[3]When used in this context, the cost of capital is often referred to as the hurdle rate. It is the rate the IRR must exceed to be acceptable.

The first method involves using financial tables: If there is only one cash inflow or if the cash inflows are equal, the financial tables may be used to find an approximation of IRR. The steps are listed here:

1. Set up the problem as if you were solving for NPV.

2. Set NPV equal to zero.

3. Solve for PVIF or PVIFA.

4. Look up the interest rate that corresponds to the factor found in step 3 in the PVIF or PVIFA table.

E X A M P L E 10.8   Computing IRR: Factor Method

If the initial investment is $500 and the cash inflows are $200 for 3 years, what is the IRR?

Solution

$$\text{NPV} = 0 = \$200(\text{PVIFA}_{IRR,3\,yr}) - \$500$$

$$\$500 = \$200(\text{PVIFA}_{IRR,3\,yr})$$

$$\$500/\$200 = \text{PVIFA}_{IRR,3\,yr}$$

$$2.500 = \text{PVIFA}_{IRR,3\,yr}$$

Look in the PVIFA table for the factor equal to 2.5 with 3 periods. We find that the interest rate falls between 9% and 10%. We could estimate the IRR to be 9.5%.

The second method involves trial and error. This method is used if the cash flows are not equal. The problem is again set up as if you were setting NPV equal to zero. Select an interest rate and determine whether NPV computes to zero. If not, try another. (If the computed NPV was positive, try a higher interest rate; if it was negative, try a lower rate.) Keep trying interest rates until NPV is equal to zero.

E X A M P L E 10.9   IRR by Trial and Error

Use the cash flows from Example 10.8 and compute the IRR by trial and error.

Solution

To solve this example by trial and error we would set it up using Equation 10.3:

$$\text{NPV} = 0 = \frac{\$200}{\left(1 + i\right)^1} + \frac{\$200}{\left(1 + i\right)^2} + \frac{\$200}{\left(1 + i\right)^3} - \$500$$

If the discount rate is set equal to 9%, NPV = 6.26. If the discount rate is set equal to 10%, NPV = −2.63. The internal rate of return is between 9% and 10%.

The third method involves using a financial calculator. Many financial calculators have built-in IRR formulas. The cash flows must be entered before the IRR can be calculated.

(Refer to the owner's manual to find out how to do this because each brand of calculator is different.) Solving this example using a financial calculator yields an IRR of 9.70%.

Advantages

The primary advantage of the IRR method of investment analysis is that it is easy to interpret and explain. Investors like to speak in terms of annual interest rates when evaluating investment options. For this reason, many firms that use NPV also compute IRR.

Study Tip

Note that we also make an assumption about reinvestment of periodic cash flows when computing NPV. We assume that those cash flows are reinvested at the firm's cost of capital.

Disadvantages

There are several serious problems with IRR that must be understood. They do not necessarily invalidate the model, but must be considered before its application.

Reinvestment Rate Assumption   The IRR assumes that the cash flows are reinvested at the internal rate of return when they are received. In Example 10.8, three payments of $200 are received. The first payment is reinvested for two periods and the second payment is reinvested for one period. IRR assumes that these payments earn 9.70% when reinvested until the project is over. We consider this reinvestment rate assumption to be a disadvantage because there may not be any other investments available with returns equal to high-IRR projects, so it may not be possible to reinvest at the IRR.

The reinvestment rate assumption is a problem only when you are attempting to rank mutually exclusive projects. If you are just attempting to reach an accept/reject decision on a project, the reinvestment rate assumption is not relevant. On the other hand, it may cause incorrect ranking of projects. If you depend on IRR to select among projects, you may select the wrong one. Review Table 10.3. The initial investment is $1,000 for projects A and B, but we get conflicting rankings from NPV and IRR. NPV is higher for project A, but IRR is greater for project B. Which project do we accept? Because the NPV is computed using the firm's cost of capital, we can assume that other projects are available at that rate. We do not know whether any more investments are available that yield 20%. For this reason, we favor NPV when ranking projects. Note that both methods gave the same accept/reject decision. This will *always* be true. *A project that is found acceptable with NPV will also be acceptable with IRR*.

To better understand the ranking problem, review Figure 10.2, which graphs the NPV profiles of projects A and B. Project A has the highest NPV for all discount rates

TABLE 10.3

	Cash Flows	
Year	**Project A**	**Project B**
0	−$1,000	−$1,000
1	0	$1,200
2	0	0
3	$1,500	0
NPV@5%	$295.76	$142.86
IRR	14.47%	20%

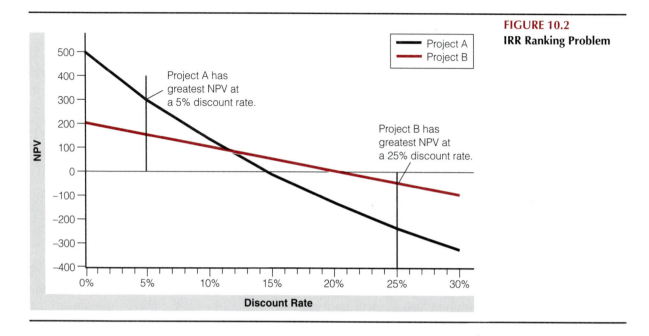

FIGURE 10.2

IRR Ranking Problem

less than 12%. Project B is superior for all discount rates greater than 12%. ***The pro-ject's rank depends on the discount rate***. Because the IRR method does not evaluate the project at a particular discount rate, it cannot be used for ranking mutually exclusive projects.

There May Not Be a Solution to an IRR Problem   In some instances there is more than one solution to an IRR problem. Because computer programs and calculators cannot tell which is correct, they return an error message. This usually happens when there are changing signs on the cash flows (most periods having positive cash flows and some having negative cash flows). The multiple IRR problem can be shown graphically with the NPV profile.

Suppose a mining operation will spend $120 million to begin operation, will receive $310 million the second year, and will spend $200 million to clean up. The NPV profile is shown in Figure 10.3.

The NPV is initially negative, becomes positive, then becomes negative again. Because it crosses the zero NPV line twice, there are two IRRs. Because cash flows often alternate signs, this can be a serious problem.

Accurate Calculation Often Requires a Financial Calculator   It becomes very tedious to find the IRR by trial and error. You will probably not want to attempt many IRR calculations without the help of a financial calculator or spreadsheet program. However, with financial calculators available for less than $30, this is less of a problem than it used to be.

FIGURE 10.3

Multiple IRRs

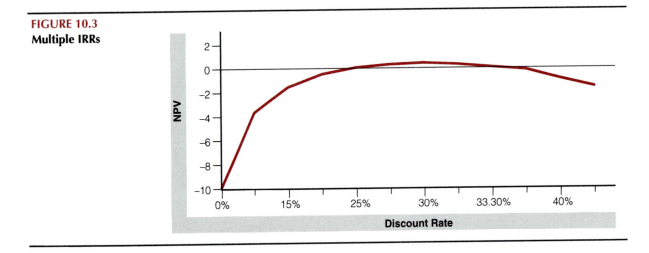

IRR Ignores Differences in Scale   Suppose you had the choice of buying the Kinston Indians (a small-town baseball team) or the Atlanta Braves. You can buy the Indians for $10,000. The Atlanta Braves cost $10 million, but contractual provisions limit you to owning only one baseball team of any kind. If both have an IRR of 25%, which would you take if you could afford either? The IRR does not give you any help because it converts the cash flows to percentages and ignores differences in the size or scale of projects being considered. Clearly anyone of sound mind would go with the Braves.

NPV Versus IRR

Which method should you use to evaluate a project? It depends on who your audience is, whether you are ranking projects or just trying to determine which are acceptable, and whether the project has alternating signs on the cash flows.

If you are a small business owner doing calculations for your own business, you do not have to worry about the sophistication of your audience. However, most of the time you will be presenting your analysis to other investors. How successful would you be in convincing your art major roommate to invest in your new mail-order pizza business if you spoke only of net present values, cost of capital, risk-adjusted discount rates, and the like? Once you were convinced your numbers were correct by using NPV, a simplified presentation using IRR and payback may be more successful.

The choice of analysis methodology also depends on whether you are attempting to select among many good projects or just determining the acceptability of a single project. Remember that IRR cannot be used to rank projects.

Finally, if your project has cash flow sign changes, you may not be able to compute an IRR. This will force you to focus on NPV. Never rely wholly on the payback method because it leaves so much out of the analysis.

Some analysts have attempted to save the IRR method by developing an alternative calculation that reinvests funds at the cost of capital. This method, known as the modified internal rate of return, is often used in real estate analysis.

EXTENSION 10.1

Modified Internal Rate of Return (MIRR)

Because of the problems listed above for the internal rate of return, analysts have developed an alternative evaluation technique that is similar to IRR, but attempts to improve on it. The cash outflows are discounted back to the present at the cost of capital and the cash inflows are compounded at the cost of capital to the end of the project's life. The future value of the cash inflows is called the terminal value. The **modified internal rate of return (MIRR)** is the interest rate that sets the PV of outflows equal to the terminal value.

The calculation of MIRR, though it takes several steps, is not difficult.

1. Find the present value of all cash outflows at the firm's cost of capital. Often the only cash outflow is the initial investment. If any subsequent cash outflows are required, such as a future modification, compute the present value of these outflows as well.

2. Find the future value of all cash inflows at the firm's cost of capital. All positive cash flows are compounded to the point in time at which the last cash inflow is received.

3. Compute the yield that sets the present value of the inflows equal to the present value of the outflows. This yield is the modified internal rate of return.

An example will help explain this method.

E X A M P L E 10.10   Modified Internal Rate of Return

Compute the MIRR for the following cash flow stream. Assume a cost of capital of 10%. The initial investment is $500. The cash inflows are $300 per year for 2 years, followed by a $200 expenditure and then one more $300 inflow.

Solution

Prepare a time line to better visualize the process:

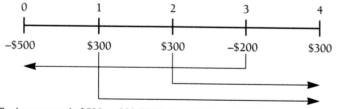

1. The investment is $500 + 200(PVIF 3 yr, 10%) = $650.26.

2. There are three positive cash inflows that must be compounded to the end of the fourth period. The first $300 cash flow is compounded for three periods. The second $300 cash flow is compounded for two periods, and the last $300 earns no interest. The sum of the future value of the cash flows is the terminal value:

   Terminal value = $300(1.10^3) + $300(1.10^2) + $300
   Terminal value = $399.30 + $363.00 + $300
   Terminal value = $1,062.30

3. In this step we compute the interest rate that will set the investment of $650.26 equal to the terminal value of $1,062.30. This is most easily done using a financial calculator.

Calculator solution:

$$PV = -650.26, \quad FV = \$1,062.30, \quad N = 4, \quad PMT = 0, \quad \text{compute } I = 13.05\%$$

Factor table solution:

$$PV = FV\left(PVIF_{n,i}\right)$$

$$650.26 = 1,062.30\left(PVIF_{n,i}\right)$$

$$PVIF_{n,i} = \frac{650.26}{1,062.30} = 0.6121$$

Now go to the PVIF table and find the factor closest to 0.6121 in the row corresponding to four periods. We find that the factor falls close to 13%, so we estimate the MIRR as about 13%.

The MIRR solves the reinvestment rate assumption problem because all cash flows are compounded at the cost of capital. It also solves the problem of changing cash flow signs resulting in multiple IRRs. It still suffers from scale problems. Remember that one problem with IRR is that it does not distinguish between large and small projects effectively. MIRR suffers from this same limitation. As a result, it cannot be used to rank projects. Hence, it can only be used to make the accept/reject decision, which is accurately done by IRR. Again we reach the same conclusion: Because NPV is easy to calculate and provides a correct wealth-maximizing decision, it is the preferred method.

Self-Test Review Question*

The initial investment for a project is $706.80. It will generate cash inflows for each of the next 3 years of $300. What is the MIRR, assuming a cost of capital of 10%?

---

*Terminal value is $300(1.1^2) + \$300(1.1) + \$300 = \$993$. The initial investment is $706.80. The MIRR is found using a financial calculator with N = 3, PV = $-\$706.80$, FV = 993, and PMT = 0; we compute I = 12%. Alternatively, the PVIF = $\$706.80/\$993 = 0.7118$, which corresponds to 12% at 3 periods.

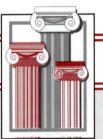

Careers in Finance

Financial Analyst

Large corporations employ financial analysts whose primary responsibility is to evaluate capital spending projects of interest to the firm. A financial analyst collects information from throughout the firm to prepare cash flow estimates. These estimates are then analyzed to determine whether the firm should pursue the projects. The financial analyst is often also employed in reviewing projects as they are implemented and post completion.

Financial analysts' salaries range from $23,000–$27,000 for new hires by small firms to $50,000 or $60,000 for seasoned analysts employed by larger firms. Many financial analysts use the skills they learn analyzing individual projects to advance into into positions of chief financial officer, where salaries can reach several hundred thousand dollars per year.

CHAPTER SUMMARY

Capital budgeting is the process of evaluating the cash flows from investment opportunities and deciding which investments should be accepted or rejected by the firm. The capital budgeting process requires two distinct steps. First, the cash flows from the project must be accurately estimated. Second, the cash flows must be evaluated to determine whether they provide a return sufficient to cover the firm's cost of capital. This chapter introduced five methods to evaluate potential investment opportunities. In Chapter 11 we will investigate how cash flows are estimated.

The payback period method simply computes the number of years required to recapture the initial cash outflows. This method is used primarily because of its simplicity. It can also provide an indication of the project's liquidity because it tells the analyst how long the firm's funds will be tied up in the project. However, it fails to adjust for risk or for the time value of money. Additionally, any cash flows that occur after the payback period are ignored.

The net present value (NPV) method is the preferred way of evaluating cash flows. It adjusts for risk and for the time value of money by evaluating all cash flows in the present. It is theoretically accurate and is easy to compute. Accepting all positive-NPV projects will lead to maximizing the value of the firm. It can also be used to rank projects if the firm is unable to accept all positive-NPV opportunities.

The profitability index (PI) is the ratio of the present value of the cash inflows to the present value of the cash outflows (initial investment). If the PI is greater than 1, the project should be accepted. Although the PI always gives the same accept/reject decision as NPV, it has the advantage of providing an indication of the return per dollar invested (the bang for the buck). This can be useful in attempting to rank projects.

The internal rate of return (IRR) is popular because it provides a percentage return on the project that is easy to interpret and to explain to others. It suffers from several problems, however. First, there is a fundamental theoretical problem in that the cash flows are assumed to be reinvested at the IRR instead of at the cost of capital. Second, when there are alternating signs in the cash flows, no single solution may be available. Third, the IRR is difficult to compute. It usually requires a financial calculator. Finally, it cannot be used to rank projects because it does not adjust for differences in scale.

The IRR and the NPV always provide the same accept/reject decision. This means that as long as IRR is not being used to rank the merits of projects, it can be used to evaluate potential investment opportunities.

The modified IRR (MIRR) attempts to solve some of the problems of the IRR. All cash flows are assumed to be reinvested at the cost of capital. The MIRR is the rate that sets the present value of the initial investment equal to the future value of the periodic cash flows.

In Chapter 11 we will learn to estimate cash flows and some refinements to capital budgeting techniques that are often required.

KEY WORDS

capital budgeting 261
cost of capital 269
internal rate of return
  (IRR) 273
modified internal rate of
  return (MIRR) 279
net present value
  (NPV) 266
NPV profile 269
payback period 264
profitability index (PI) 271

DISCUSSION QUESTIONS

1. Why is *capital* an appropriate word to use to describe the process of evaluating possible investment projects?
2. What steps should a firm take to maximize its chance of successfully identifying and implementing investment projects?
3. What is the purpose of the post audit?
4. What are the advantages and disadvantages of the payback method, NPV, IRR, PI, and MIRR?
5. What is the decision criterion for NPV, PI, IRR, and MIRR?
6. What is the purpose of the NPV profile? Where is the IRR on the profile? Which region of the profile shows acceptable projects?
7. Why would you choose to use the PI over the NPV? (What does the PI tell you that the NPV does not?)
8. What is the reinvestment assumption for the NPV and for the IRR? Which is more theoretically sound?
9. When is the IRR as good a method to use as the NPV? When should IRR not be used?
10. What problems with the IRR are fixed by the MIRR? (Extension 10.1)

PROBLEMS

1. Consider the cash flows for the following two investments:

Year	Investment 1	Investment 2
0	-$150	-$150
1	20	30
2	50	40
3	70	100
4	120	110

  a. What are the payback periods on these two investments?
  b. What are the NPV and PI for each project if the required rate of return is 8%?
  c. If these two investments were mutually exclusive, which would you choose?

2. Consider the following cash flows:

Year	Project 1	Project 2
0	-$200	-$300
1	0	100
2	50	100
3	100	100
4	150	100

  a. Calculate the NPV and PI for each project. There is a 10% required return.
  b. Calculate the IRR for project 2.

3. Using the data from problem 2,
  a. Use the cash flows from project 2 to prepare an NPV profile.
  b. On the graph prepared in step a, identify the range of discount rates at which the project is acceptable.
  c. On the graph prepared in step a, identify the range of discount rates at which the project is not acceptable.
  d. On the graph prepared in step a, locate the IRR.

4. Compute the NPV, PI, and IRR for the following projects. Which projects should be accepted?
  a. The project requires an initial investment of $1,200 and provides five annual cash inflows of $350. Assume a cost of capital of 13%.
  b. The project requires an initial investment of $12,000 and provides five annual cash inflows of $3,500. Assume a cost of capital of 13%.
  c. The project requires an initial investment of $12,000 and provides 10 annual cash inflows of $1,750. Assume a cost of capital of 13%.

  d. The project requires an initial investment of $12,000 and provides 10 annual cash inflows of $1,750. Assume a cost of capital of 8%.
  e. The project requires an initial investment of $12,000 and provides 10 annual cash inflows of $1,750. Assume a cost of capital of 6%.

5. Project L has a cost of $40,000, and its expected net cash inflows are $9,000 per year for 8 years.
  a. What is the project's payback period?
  b. The cost of capital is 12%. What are the project's NPV and PI?
  c. What is the project's IRR?

6. A factory costs $550,000. You forecast that it will produce cash inflows of $100,000 in year 1, $200,000 in year 2, and $300,000 in year 3. The cost of capital is 12%. What is the NPV of the factory?

7. You are presented a proposal for a project. Project Iron costs $5,000 and will bring in $25,000 in the first year. The next year you will have to pay out $20,000. With a 10% cost of capital, calculate the NPV for the project. Do you accept the project?

8. Rollins Supplies Company is considering an expansion project. The cash flows are shown in the following table. The cost of capital is 20%.

Year	Cash Flow
0	-$2,500
1	1,500
2	1,700
3	1,000
4	1,000
5	1,000

  a. Calculate the NPV and PI for the expansion project.
  b. What is the IRR of the project?

9. You are considering building a shopping mall. The initial investment for the mall is $1 million. The cash flows are $500,000 for year 1, $400,000 for year 2, $300,000 for year 3, and $100,000 for year 4.
  a. What are the NPV and PI of the project if the cost of capital is 10%?
  b. Compute the IRR for the project.
  c. Construct an NPV profile for the project.

10. Consider the following two projects. All cash flows shown are on an after-tax basis.

Year	Project A	Project B
0	−$75,000	−$55,000
1	30,000	22,000
2	18,000	13,200
3	50,000	37,000

a. If the discount rate is 16%, what are the PI and NPV of project A?

b. If the discount rate is 16%, what are the PI and NPV of project B?

c. Find the IRR of project A.

d. Find the IRR of project B.

e. Which project would you prefer?

f. If the cost of capital for project A is 13% and the cost of capital for project B is still 16%, which project would you prefer?

11. A firm has a project with a cost of $65,000 that is expected to produce benefits of $14,000 per year for 10 years. Calculate the project's payback period, NPV, PI, and IRR. Assume a cost of capital of 14%.

12. Eastern Building is considering two mutually exclusive projects. With a 12% cost of capital, evaluate the given net cash flows to determine which project, if any, should be accepted, and why. Comment on any differences in NPV, MIRR (Extension 10.1), and IRR (if any exist). The IRR is 17.28% for Rivergate and 17.12% for Treywood. The initial cost of Rivergate is $445,000, whereas the cost of Treywood is $1,400,000.

Years	Rivergate Net Cash Flows	Treywood Net Cash Flows
1	$160,000	$275,000
2	160,000	275,000
3	160,000	600,000
4	95,000	600,000
5	95,000	600,000

13. The Renn project cost $55,000 and its expected net cash inflows are $12,000 per year for 8 years.

a. What is the project's payback period?

b. The cost of capital is 12%. What is the project's NPV?

c. What is the project's IRR?

d. Calculate the project's MIRR assuming a 12% cost of capital. (Extension 10.1)

14. Lacey Industries Co. has been evaluating a project with a cost of $700,000. Estimated net cash flows of $180,000 are expected for a 7-year period. The cost of capital is 14%. Find the NPV and IRR.

15. The Fitness Center is considering including two pieces of equipment, a treadmill and a step machine, in this year's capital budget. The projects are independent. The cash outlay for the treadmill is $1,700 and for the step machine it is $2,200. The firm's cost of capital is 14%. After-tax cash flows, including depreciation, are as shown in the following table. Calculate the NPV, the IRR, and the MIRR (Extension 10.1) for each project, and indicate the correct accept/reject decision for each.

Years	Treadmill	Step Machine
1	$510	$750
2	510	750
3	510	750
4	510	750
5	510	750

SELF-TEST PROBLEMS

1. XYZ Company wants to know the payback period for a project with an initial investment of $4 million and annual cash flows of $800,000. What is it?

2. Suppose the annual cash flows listed for problem 1 start at $800,000 and then decrease by 15% each year. What is the payback period?

3. A firm is evaluating a project with an initial cost of $3.35 million and annual cash flows of $1.15 million for 4 years. If the cost of capital for the firm is 14%, what is the NPV? Should the firm accept or reject the project?

4. Suppose the cost of capital for the firm in problem 3 increases to 15%. What is the NPV? Should the firm accept or reject the project?

5. Evergreen Inc. is evaluating a project with an initial cost of $6 million. Cash flows would start at $1 million and increase by $750,000 annually for the next 3 years. If the cost of the capital for the firm is 12%, what is the NPV? Should the firm accept or reject the project?

6. A project has projected cash outflows of $2 million in the current time period. Additional cash outflows of $1 million, $1 million, and $2 million are projected during the next 3 years of operation. Cash inflows of $1.3 million are expected in years 4 through 13 (10 cash inflows). Should the project be accepted if the company has a cost of capital of 14%? (What is the NPV?)

7. Would the accept/reject decision change for the project described in problem 6 if the costs of capital fell to 12%?

8. Suppose that a $10,000 investment will yield three annual cash flows of $4,000 each. With a discount rate of 12%, what is the PI? What is the accept/reject decision?

9. Rank the following projects by PI:

Project	Net Investment	PV (cash inflows)	NPV
A	$ 400	$480	$80
B	700	735	35
C	150	225	75
D	1,000	950	(50)
E	250	275	25

10. If the initial investment for a project is $500 and the cash inflows are $300 for 3 years, what is the IRR?

11. If the initial investment for a project is $500 and the cash inflows are $300 for year 1, $250 for year 2, and $150 for year 3, what is the IRR?

12. If the initial investment for a project is $1,500 and the cash inflows are $300 for 4 years, what is the IRR?

13. Suppose Project A has an NPV of $350 with an IRR of 12% and Project B has an NPV of $300 with an IRR of 20%. If these projects are mutually exclusive, which project should you accept? Why?

14. Compute the MIRR for a project with a $10,000 investment and cash flows of $3,000 for 4 years. Assume of the cost of capital is 12%.

15. Compute the IRR and MIRR for a project with a $5,000 investment and cash flows of $1,500 for 4 years. Assume the cost of capital is 13%.

16. Compute the MIRR for a project with a $6,000 investment and cash flows of $1,000 in year 1, $2,000 in year 2, $3,000 in year 3, and $4,000 in year 4. Assume the cost of capital is 10%.

17. Compute the MIRR after reversing the cash flows in problem 16. (Cash flows of $4,000 in year 1, $3,000 in year 2, etc.) Assume the investment and cost of capital do not change.

18. Compute the IRR for problem 16.

19. Compute the IRR for problem 17.

20. What is the NPV of a project with initial investments of $3 million at the beginning of years 1 and 2, and cash inflows of $1.5 million at the beginning of years 2 through 6? Assume the cost of capital is 10%. Should the project be accepted? (Hint: At the beginning of year 2, the net cash flow is −1.5 million.)

WEB EXPLORATION

1. The concepts behind NPV and IRR apply equally to investing in capital projects or in securities. Go to www.financenter.com/calculate/all_calculate.fcs and choose the calculator titled What Selling Price Provides My Desired Return? This site allows you to input a variety of variables and to look at the rate of return the investment provides. It also allows you to view graphs of the answers. Relate the results you find using this calculator to IRR and NPV.

2. There are many instructional sites on the Web that are sponsored by educational institutions. One particularly good one sponsored by the University of South Carolina is available at hadm.sph.sc.edu/courses/econ/invest/invest.html. Review this site and investigate any of the links that you feel may improve your understanding of the concepts behind NPV and IRR. The calculators attached can be very helpful.

MINI CASE

You have recently gone to work for a development/construction firm. This company does contract and bid construction work as well as real estate development. You work on the development side helping to select projects that will be profitable. The development company is organized as a separate entity from the construction firm. This requires that both firms be independently profitable.

The company founder, Jerry Hammer, is primarily responsible for identifying development opportunities. Once an opportunity is identified, Hammer turns it over to his staff for analysis. Jerry began as a carpenter and has built the firm into a multi–million dollar enterprise mostly based on good intuition and street smarts. He has no college education.

Last week Jerry called the staff of the development firm together to discuss his latest idea. He would like to build a new strip mall on a corner of property near the university. He visualizes a group of tenets that would service the needs of college students. He directed you to let him know if the project was feasible.

Your first step was to collect cost and revenue estimates. The proposed mall is a duplicate of one built last year for $3,750,000 with minor cosmetic changes. The mall will have 30,000 square feet, all of which can be leased. You contact the owner of the property and find it can be purchased for $500,000.

The revenues are more difficult to estimate. You decide the most practical approach is to assume the mall will lease for $2.75 per square foot per month. The mall will take about 10 months to build and you think the mall will be 10% leased by the end of the first year. You will get 10% of the

possible revenues for 2 months. Thus, the first year revenues will be computed as $16,500 (30,000 × $2.75 × .1 × 2). You project to get about 60% of the possible revenues during the second year (i.e., 30,000 × $2.75 × 12 × .6). This will rise to 90% by the end of the third year. During the fourth year you project the mall to be fully leased. It is the intent of the company to sell the property once it is fully leased. You think it reasonable to project a sale by the end of the fifth year for $150 per square foot.

You decide a 15% discount accurately reflects the firm's cost of capital.

a. Project the annual cash flows. Remember that the lease revenues will be received until the property is sold. Assume the initial cash flow occurs at the beginning of the first year and that all other cash flows occur at the end of the year. Ignore taxes and depreciation.

b. Put the cash flows onto a time line.

c. Compute the payback period. Is this any help in making an accept/reject decision?

d. Compute the NPV.

e. Prepare an NPV profile. Identify the IRR on the graph. Identify on the graph the discount rates that make the project acceptable and those that make it unacceptable.

f. Compute the IRR.

g. Compute the PI.

h. Compute the MIRR. (Extension 10.1)

i. Do all of the methods (except payback) give the same accept/reject result? Is this surprising?

j. Discuss how you would present your results to Jerry Hammer.

Estimating Cash Flows and Refinements to Capital Budgeting

The first step in the capital budgeting process is to estimate the cash flows. Even the most well-funded firms can make huge errors determining costs and income. Alyeska Pipeline Company was formed in 1970 to build the Trans-Alaska Pipeline from Prudhoe Bay to Valdez, Alaska, a distance of nearly 800 miles. Alyeska was a joint venture composed of seven large oil companies. The firm initially estimated the cost of constructing the pipeline to be just under $800 million. The problem was that no one had built a pipeline under the conditions posed by northern Alaska. The extreme cold, lack of roads, and permafrost (frozen ground) caused the final cost of the pipeline to exceed $8 billion. Not many companies can afford errors of this magnitude.

In a similar case, the Chunnel is a tunnel built under the English Channel linking Great Britain and France. The final $17.5-billion cost was two and one-half times the initial estimate. Construction was halted several times while additional funds were raised. In many situations, far smaller errors than these cause firms to fail. The point cannot be made too strongly. Bad input into the models developed in Chapter 10 will result in bad output. The most sophisticated method is worthless if it is based on poorly estimated numbers.

> ### Chapter Objectives
>
> By the end of this chapter you should be able to:
>
> 1. Show how cash flows are estimated
> 2. Rank investment options
> 3. Adjust evaluation methods for differing risk levels
> 4. Evaluate projects with very different lives
> 5. Use sensitivity analysis to help evaluate projects

In this chapter we must assume that we have access to correct cost and income estimates. We use these to construct the cash flows. We first compute the *initial cash flow,* the cash flows associated with project startup. This may be as simple as determining the purchase price of a security or it may be more complex if new machinery is replacing old. The next step is to estimate the *annual cash inflows.* These are not the same as the accounting earnings. Annual cash inflows adjust the accounting earnings for accruals and depreciation. Finally, we must compute the *terminal cash flow.* The final year of the project may differ from previous years due to selling equipment, recapturing working capital, or other project completion expenses.

Once all of the cash flows have been estimated we can apply the capital budgeting techniques learned in Chapter 10. In this chapter we also investigate how to adjust for risk, how to evaluate projects with unequal lives, and how to select projects under capital rationing.

RULES FOR ESTIMATING CASH FLOWS

There are some rules you should always follow when estimating cash flows:

- *Include only incremental costs:* Incremental costs are those that change as a result of accepting a project. Suppose that you add a new machine to the production line. Do not worry about the cost of operating the whole line. Just compute the costs that change because of the new machine. The analysis is often substantially simplified by considering only incremental costs.

- *Aggressively seek and include indirect costs:* In 1979 the author of this text was working for First National Bank of Fairbanks, Alaska, and was analyzing whether the bank should install an automated teller machine system. It was easy to find the direct costs of buying and installing the machines because advance bids were gathered on the purchase price and construction. However, the indirect costs were much more difficult to judge. For example, because of the cold climate, all of the machines had to be in heated kiosks. Additional parking lot lights were required because of the long hours of darkness in the winter. Because those first-generation machines required new currency, the bank had to buy new cash from the Federal Reserve and pay to return used bills. The machines could not hold enough cash to last over long weekends, so armored car services were required to replenish the machines. The indirect costs dwarfed the direct costs in this case.

- *Disregard sunk costs:* Sunk costs are costs that have already been paid and cannot be recovered. Sunk costs are not relevant because accepting or rejecting the project does not change them. One of the largest examples of disregarding sunk costs involved Washington Water and Power Service (WWPS). The utility sold income bonds to finance the construction of nuclear power plants in Washington state. The holders of income bonds are paid from the revenues generated by the project. Builders of the power plants ran into problems and costs far exceeded the initial estimates. After spending over $1.5 billion, WWPS reevaluated the power plants. It found that the electricity would not sell for enough to justify the projected cost of finishing the plants. This analysis ignored the vast sums already spent. Since then, WWPS, locally called Whoops, has abandoned construction and defaulted on the bonds. This remains one of the largest public bond defaults ever.

- *Include opportunity costs:* An opportunity cost is a benefit that is given up when another alternative is chosen. The most common opportunity cost occurs when an asset that the firm already owns has multiple possible uses. For example, Weyerhaeuser has a lumber mill in eastern North Carolina that is surrounded by land also owned by the firm. Suppose that Weyerhaeuser is considering expanding its facility to include a paper plant. Should the value of the land already owned be included in the analysis? Because the land has alternative uses, its value should be included. If the plant is not constructed, the land could be leased to farmers or sold to developers. The correct opportunity cost to use is the most valuable alternative use of the asset.

- *Always adjust for taxes:* As we develop the equations for computing cash flows, you will see that taxes add complexity to the calculations. It may be tempting to ignore the tax impact of a proposed project. However, the total of state, local, and federal taxes often exceeds 40% for corporations. The tax effect of a project can clearly be a deciding factor in whether it will be accepted.

- *Ignore financing cost:* One of the most common mistakes students make when estimating cash flows is to include interest cost. You would be less tempted to include financing cost if a project were financed with retained earnings. The financing decision (whether to use debt or equity) is separate from the capital budgeting decision. NPV and IRR include the cost of funds by using a discount rate that reflects the required return. If we were to include interest expense in the cash flow estimate, we would be, in essence, double charging the project for financing.

Let us summarize the rules you should follow for evaluating cash flows:

- Include only incremental costs.
- Include indirect costs.
- Disregard sunk costs.
- Include opportunity costs.
- Adjust for taxes.
- Ignore financing costs.

Self-Test Review Questions*

1. Should a consulting fee paid to a finance professor to evaluate a project be included in the analysis?
2. Should interest paid on debt solely to finance a project be included in the analysis?
3. Should lease revenues that are lost because property is used for a project be included in the analysis?

ESTIMATING CASH FLOWS

In this section we investigate how the cash flows that are used to calculate NPV and IRR are computed. To simplify the discussion, we break the analysis into three parts. In the first part we compute the initial cash flow. This cash flow typically occurs at the time the project is started. We then compute the annual cash flows. These span the time during which the project is actually under way. Finally, we discuss the terminal cash flow. This cash flow occurs at the time the project is concluded. The cash flows are shown on the following time line:

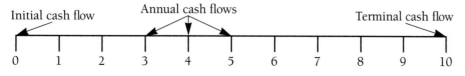

Once we have studied all of the parts to estimating cash flows, we can put them together to perform capital budgeting analysis.

We can classify projects as either expansion or replacement projects. An **expansion project** is one in which some aspect of the company grows. This may be as simple as adding a new machine to the assembly line or as significant as acquiring a competitor. Expansion projects do not involve selling any existing company assets.

In contrast to expansion projects, a firm may want to analyze replacement projects. A **replacement project** is one in which an asset of the firm is replaced by a new one. For example, a firm may want to replace an old computer system with a newer one with higher speed and lower operating costs.

The reason we need to identify which type of project we are analyzing is because we treat them somewhat differently. Replacement projects involve an old asset that may be sellable, and there may be changes in costs and revenues to consider. In expansion projects, only the cost of the new assets must be considered; there are no old costs and revenues to complicate the analysis. In the discussion that follows, we will identify how each type of project should be handled and we will review examples of each.

Estimating the Initial Cash Flow

The **initial cash flow** includes the acquisition, installation, and setup of a new investment or project. A firm usually incurs one-time expenses and costs when initiating a new investment. These one-time costs are the initial cash flow. If the investment involves replacing an existing machine or asset, there may be salvage on this asset that can offset the cost of the new machine.

The basic approach to estimating the initial cash flow in a project is shown by Table 11.1.

The initial cash flow consists of the initial purchase price (a cash outflow) minus shipping and installation (more cash outflows), plus the tax-adjusted proceeds from selling the old machine (if the new asset is replacing an old one), plus or minus any change in net working capital. Let us discuss these factors separately.

Initial Purchase Price

The initial purchase price is often the easiest and most accurate number to obtain. Include any taxes, tariffs, or other expenses that are part of the cost. Notice that the

Study Tip

Students often find the calculation of the initial cash flow confusing because there are so many pieces to keep track of. Keep your focus on the idea that you are simply trying to determine how much *cash* will go out the door when the new asset is acquired. Pay particular attention to adjusting for taxes because this is where most errors are made.

TABLE 11.1 Calculation of Initial Cash Flow

−	Initial purchase price of new asset
−	Installation/shipping cost of new asset
=	Net purchase price
+	Proceeds from sale of old asset
+/−	Tax on sale of old asset
+/−	Change in net working capital
=	Initial cash flow

initial purchase price has a minus sign in front of it. This is because it is a cash *outflow*. By giving all cash outflows minus signs and all cash inflows plus signs, we will be sure to correctly account for them.

One reason the initial purchase price is easy to estimate is that it can often be established by a contract with suppliers and contractors. Unlike later annual cash inflows, the initial purchase price may be quite accurate. This is not always the case, however. Recall the grievous errors made by Alyeska when it estimated the cost of building the Trans-Alaska Pipeline.

Installation/Shipping

Installation and shipping are considered part of the initial cost of acquiring the asset and must be included in the initial cash flow. This is because these items are usually added to the purchase price on the firm's balance sheet and are depreciated as if they were included in the initial cost of the item. Installation costs can include any construction costs, employee training, and other miscellaneous expenses associated with putting the equipment into service. The net purchase price is the total of the initial purchase price and the installation and shipping. This figure is the amount used for computing the annual depreciation expense in the next section. The appendix to this chapter reviews depreciation methods.

Self-Test Review Question*

You are evaluating the purchase of a new plastic molding press. The sales representative has quoted you a price of $25,500. You contact the shipper and learn it will cost an additional $1,500 to get it to your factory. It will cost $750 to set it up for production. What is the net purchase price? What amount would you use as the basis for computing depreciation?

Proceeds from the Sale of the Old Asset

The two types of equipment acquisitions require different treatment. If the project is an expansion project in which new assets are being acquired but no old assets are being replaced, this line is zero. However, in replacement projects an old machine may be sold. The proceeds of this sale can be added to reduce the overall initial cost. Put the amount for which the old asset is sold on this line. We will adjust for taxes on the next line.

*Simply add the costs together: $25,500 + $1,500 + $750 = $27,750. This is the amount that you would use as the basis for computing depreciation.

Taxes on the Sales of the Old Machine

Taxes are based on whether the old machine is sold for more or less than its book value. The **book value** is the initial purchase price minus accumulated depreciation. The calculation of book value is shown by Equation 11.1:

$$\text{Book value} = \text{Initial cost} - \text{Accumulated depreciation} \qquad (11.1)$$

Accumulated depreciation is the sum of the annual depreciation expenses. Most assets are depreciated using the modified accelerated cost recovery system (MACRS). The MACRS depreciation table appears in the appendix to this chapter.

E X A M P L E 11.1   Computing Book Value

Suppose you bought a dump truck 2 years ago at a price of $18,500. What is the current book value of the truck?

Solution

You must first establish what life the asset will have for depreciation purposes. The IRS specifies asset classes and their associated lives. A sample of IRS asset classes is included in the chapter appendix. There we find that a truck is to be depreciated over 5 years.

We next need to sum the accumulated depreciation. Refer to the MACRS depreciation table in the appendix under the 5-year investment class. Depreciation is 20% the first year and 32% the second year, so total accumulated depreciation is 52% of the initial asset value, or $9,620 ($18,500 × 0.52 = $9,620). Apply Equation 11.1 to compute the book value:

$$\text{Book value} = \text{Initial cost} - \text{Accumulated depreciation}$$
$$\text{Book value} = \$18,500 - \$9,620 = \$8,880$$

The book value of the truck is $8,880 after 2 years.

Once the book value of the old asset is computed, the gain or loss on its sale is found by subtracting the book value from the sales price.

The tax effect from selling an old asset is then computed by multiplying by the annual tax rate. Equation 11.2 computes the tax due on the sale of the old machine:

$$\text{Tax on sale} = (\text{Sales price} - \text{Book value}) \times \text{Tax rate} \qquad (11.2)$$

If the sales price is *greater* than the book value, then a taxable gain has occurred, and the tax is *subtracted* from the total initial cash flow. If the sales price is *below* the book value, a tax loss has occurred, and the tax is *added* to the initial cash flow. This assumes that there is other income that can be offset by this tax loss.

Self-Test Review Question*

Suppose the truck used in Example 11.1 was sold after 2 years for $10,000. What would be the tax on the sale? Assume a 40% tax rate.

---

*Tax = (Sales price − Book value) × Tax rate, so Tax = ($10,000 − $8,880) × 0.40 = $448. Because the car was sold for more than the book value, the firm owes a tax of $448 on the sale. This is a cash outflow.

Change in Working Capital

Expansion projects may require increases in net working capital. For example, if The Gap clothing chain opens a new store, it will have to increase its inventory. This will require an increase in The Gap's net working capital. It is also possible that a new asset will result in a reduction in the net working capital if it allows for increased efficiency in inventory management. Increases in net working capital are subtracted from the initial cash flow and decreases are added. The change in net working capital is computed with Equation 11.3:

$$\text{Change in net working capital} = \text{Change in current assets} \\ - \text{Change in current liabilities} \tag{11.3}$$

Look at Equation 11.3 carefully. If current liabilities did not change and current assets increased, then there would be a change in net working capital. This amount would have a *minus* sign in the calculation of the initial investment. To understand why, recognize that the increase in net working capital results from the company buying more assets. Just as the purchase of the new machine is entered with a minus sign, the purchase of additional current assets required to make the machine work is also entered with a minus sign.

E X A M P L E **11.2**   **Changes in Net Working Capital**

As a result of a new machine, your production process has changed. This change requires that you keep $12,000 worth of additional widgets on hand. Accounts payable are expected to increase by $3,000 because you will rely on vendor financing as much as possible. What is the change in net working capital?

Solution

The increase of $12,000 in widgets means that you have to increase inventory. Because inventory is a current asset, this increase affects net working capital. Similarly, accounts payable are current liabilities that also affect net working capital. Using Equation 11.3 we get the following:

$$\text{Change in net working capital} = \text{Change in current assets} - \text{Change in current liabilities}$$
$$\text{Change in net working capital} = \$12,000 - \$3,000 = \$9,000$$

Current assets go up by $12,000. This increased need for assets is funded partly by an offsetting increase in current liabilities of $3,000. The change in the net working capital is $9,000. This amount would be entered with a minus sign in the initial cash flow.

Study Tip

In a long, complex problem it can be difficult to isolate the initial cash flows from the annual cash flows. The initial cash flows include items that occur only *once* and at the beginning of the project.

E X A M P L E **11.3**   **Initial Cash Flows: Comprehensive Example**

Suppose that K-Mart is contemplating upgrading its computers at a cost of $1 million to allow for increased inventory control systems. It will cost $250,000 to install the computers. Assume the old computer system that originally cost $500,000 has been in service for 3 years and has a MACRS depreciable life of 5 years. If the old system can be sold for $200,000 and net working capital decreases by $40,000, what is the initial cash flow?

Solution

	Calculation of Initial Cash Flow	
−	Initial purchase price of new asset	−$1,000,000
−	Installation/shipping cost of new asset	−$250,000
=	Net purchase price	−$1,250,000
+	Proceeds from the sale of old asset	+$200,000
+ / −	Tax on sale of old asset (see below)	−$22,000
+ / −	Change in net working capital	+$40,000
=	Initial cash flow	−$1,032,000

The initial purchase price and installation/shipping are added together to obtain the net purchase price of the asset. Offsetting this cost are the proceeds of selling the old computer for $200,000. The tax on the sale of the old computer is figured as follows.

$$\text{Accumulated depreciation} = \$500,000 \times (0.20 + 0.32 + 0.19) = \$355,000$$

The depreciation percentages come from the MACRS table in the appendix to this chapter.

Continuing:

Book value = Initial cost − Accumulated depreciation
Book value = $500,000 − $355,000
Book value = $145,000

and

Tax on sale = (Sales price − Book value) × Tax rate
Tax on sale = ($200,000 − $145,000) × 0.40
Tax on sale = $55,000 × 0.40 = **$22,000**

A tax of $22,000 must be subtracted from the initial cash flow because the old machine was sold for a taxable gain, which required that additional taxes be paid.

The last line in the calculation of the initial cash flow is the change in net working capital. The problem states that net working capital decreases by $40,000. A decrease in working capital means that the firm holds less working capital than it did before. For example, the firm may hold less inventory with the new asset than it had to with the old asset. This reduction in net working capital is treated as a cash inflow and is given a positive sign, just as if the firm had received a check in the mail. By lowering the required net working capital, the firm frees up assets that can be used elsewhere. If the net working capital had increased, we would have subtracted rather than added it to the initial cash flow.

The initial cash flow for this new computer is $1,032,000. It is substantially less than the initial net purchase price because the sale of the old machine resulted in a positive net cash flow and because net working capital decreased.

Estimating the Annual Cash Inflows

In return for making an investment in plant, machinery, or equipment, the firm expects to receive a series of cash inflows. Only when the present value of the inflows exceeds the present value of the investment will the project be accepted. In this section we determine how the annual cash inflows are estimated.

TABLE 11.2 Calculation of Annual Cash Flows

+	(New sales revenue − Old sales revenue)
−	(New operating expenses − Old operating expenses)
=	Gross profit
−	(New depreciation − Old depreciation)
=	Net profit before taxes
−	Taxes
=	Net profit after taxes
+	(New depreciation − Old depreciation)

Study Tip

Many students are confused by the calculation of the incremental depreciation. It may seem reasonable that because the old machine has been sold, there should not be any depreciation on it. Stay focused on the idea that we are computing changes that result from replacing the machine. One of the changes is in the depreciation amount. If the new machine was not purchased, the old depreciation amount would have continued.

The **annual cash inflows** adjust accounting earnings for accruals and depreciation and are computed using a modified income statement, as shown in Table 11.2.

Review this income statement. Remember that only *incremental* changes are relevant to capital budgeting analysis. Incremental changes are computed by subtracting the old level of revenues, expenses, and depreciation from the new level. Obviously, *if the project is an expansion project, there will not be any old cash flows*.

Notice that depreciation is subtracted from gross profit in the fourth line but added back to net profit in the eighth line. The reason why depreciation is first subtracted and then added back is to adjust net profit so that the correct tax amount will be computed. If we did not need to adjust for taxes, these steps could be eliminated.

Note that the sign on taxes will always be the opposite of the sign on net profit before taxes. If the net profit is negative, indicating a loss, this loss will offset other income and result in a tax savings.

The calculation of cash inflows is an excellent application for spreadsheets. By putting the figures into an Excel or Lotus spreadsheet, it becomes easy to adjust numbers and to perform what-if calculations.

Example 11.4 demonstrates the calculation of annual cash flows.

E X A M P L E 11.4   Computing Annual Cash Flows: Expansion Project

Logan's Roadhouse Inc. owns a chain of restaurants that competes with Outback and Lone Star steakhouses. Its rapid growth earned it the ninth position on *Business Week's* 1996 list of hottest growth companies. By offering smaller portions than the other restaurants, it can price meals so that the average customer check is $11.25 instead of about $16 at its competitors. If a new Logan's restaurant will have revenues of $2.5 million and revenue growth of 15% per year, and if the total expenses are 90% of revenues, what are the annual cash inflows over the next 5 years (2001–2005)? Assume straight-line depreciation over 39 years on an initial cost of $2.73 million and a 40% marginal tax rate.

Solution

Logan's Roadhouse Inc. (millions)					
	2001	**2002**	**2003**	**2004**	**2005**
New revenues – Old revenues	$2.500	$2.875	$3.306	$3.802	$4.373
New expenses – Old expenses	2.250	2.588	2.976	3.422	3.935
Gross profit	0.250	0.287	0.330	0.380	0.438
– (New depr. – Old depr.)	0.070	0.070	0.070	0.070	0.070
Net profit before tax	0.180	0.217	0.260	0.310	0.368
– Taxes (40%)	0.072	0.087	0.104	0.124	0.147
Net profit	0.108	0.130	0.156	0.186	0.221
+ Depreciation	0.070	0.070	0.070	0.070	0.070
Net cash flow	0.178	0.200	0.226	0.256	0.291

Because this is an expansion project, as opposed to a replacement project, no *old* revenues, expenses, or depreciation exist. This spreadsheet was prepared using formulas wherever possible so that as estimates change, new cash flows can be computed easily. For example, the new revenues for the year 2002 are computed as the new revenues from 2001 × 1.15. Similarly, new expenses are computed as new revenues × 0.9.

Because a restaurant is commercial property, it is straight-line depreciated over 39 years (see the appendix to this chapter):

$$\$2.73 \text{ million}/39 = \$70,000, \text{ or } \$0.07 \text{ million}$$

In Example 11.4, there was no old asset being replaced. The restaurant chain was expanding, so it was an expansion project. When a firm contemplates replacing an existing asset, the analysis becomes slightly more complex because we consider incremental cash flows. The incremental cash flows are found by subtracting the old cash flows from the new ones. In the next example we demonstrate how this changes the calculation.

E X A M P L E 11.5   Computing Annual Cash Flows: Replacement Project

As the manager of a movie theater, you were impressed at a local trade show with a new-generation popcorn machine. Despite being smaller than your old model, it pops corn faster. To help you decide whether you should buy the new machine, you collect the following information.

The old machine generates revenues of $50,000 per year. It costs $10,000 to operate. Two years ago it cost $15,000 and it is being depreciated over 3 years using MACRS. The new machine costs $25,000 and will also be depreciated over 3 years. Revenues will increase to $65,000 and costs will rise to $11,000. Assume a 40% tax rate and compute the annual cash flows for the next 3 years.

Solution

The revenues are found by subtracting the old revenues from the new projected revenues. Similarly, the expenses are found by subtracting the old expenses from the new expenses.

Study Tip

Students tend to make mistakes when computing depreciation. Study the appendix to this chapter and the calculation of depreciation in Example 11.5 carefully.

	Popcorn Machine Analysis (thousands)		
	2001	2002	2003
New revenues – Old revenues	$65 – $50 = $15	$65 – $50 = $15	$65 – $50 = $15
New expenses – Old expenses	$11 – $10 = $1	$11 – $10 = $1	$11 – $10 = $1
Gross profit	$14	$14	$14
– (New depr. – Old depr.)	$8.25 – $2.25 =	$11.25 – $1.05 =	$3.75 – 0 =
	$6.00	$10.20	$3.75
Net profit before tax	$8.00	$3.80	$10.25
– Taxes (40%)	– $3.20	– $1.52	– $4.10
Net profit	$4.80	$2.28	$6.15
+ Depreciation	$6.00	$10.20	$3.75
Net cash flow	$10.80	$12.48	$9.90

The depreciation calculations require that you compute the depreciation on both the new and old machines and figure the difference. For the first year the new machine will be depreciated at 33% of its initial cost of $25,000. Thus, the new depreciation for the first year will be $8,250 (0.33 × $25,000 = $8,250). The depreciation for the old asset during its third year (2001) is $2,250 ($15,000 × 0.15 = $2,250). The depreciation during subsequent years is found the same way. Note that by the third year depreciation for the old asset is zero.

In 2001, a net profit results, so a tax of $3.2 thousand ($3,200) is due the IRS. We still cannot determine whether we should buy the popcorn machine. We must first compute the terminal cash flow.

Estimating the Terminal Cash Flow

The final year of a project often involves additional costs or inflows, called **terminal cash flows.** For example, once all of the ore has been removed from a mine, the company may have to return the land to its original condition. Alternatively, there may be equipment that can be salvaged or resold once it is no longer needed. If any additional working capital has been used, it may be recaptured.

The terminal cash flows are added to the regular annual cash inflows. Table 11.3 shows how to compute the terminal cash flow.

TABLE 11.3 Calculation of Terminal Cash Flow

+	(New sales revenue – Old sales revenue)
–	(New operating expenses – Old operating expenses)
=	Gross profit
–	(New depreciation – Old depreciation)
=	Net profit before taxes
–	Taxes
=	Net profit after taxes
+	(New depreciation – Old depreciation)
=	Operating cash inflows
+	*Sale of new asset*
+ /–	*Tax on sale of new asset*
+ /–	*Change in net working capital*
=	Terminal cash flow

The first part of the analysis is unchanged from Table 11.1. At the end of the project, however, we must account for salvage of the machine and recapturing the working capital. The tax on the sale of the new asset is computed in the same way as the tax on the sale of the old asset. The book value must first be found by subtracting the accumulated depreciation from the initial purchase price. The gain or loss on the sale is computed by subtracting the book value from the salvage price. The tax is computed by multiplying the marginal tax rate times the gain or loss on the sale.

E X A M P L E 11.6   Terminal Cash Flow

Return to the Logan's Roadhouse example (Example 11.4). Suppose that the company plans to sell the restaurant to the manager after 5 years to be operated as a franchise. This frees up additional capital to continue expansion. If the restaurant will sell for $3 million, what is the terminal cash flow?

Solution

The terminal cash flow is computed as follows:

Calculation of Terminal Cash Flow	
Net cash flow (year 2005 from solution to Example 11.4)	+$291,000
+ Proceeds from the sale of new asset	+$3,000,000
+/− Tax on sale of new asset (see below)	−$248,000
+/− Change in net working capital	0
= Terminal cash flow	+$3,043,000

The tax on the sale of the restaurant is computed later in this example.

The depreciation is computed as the number of years depreciation has been charged against the asset times the annual depreciation amount:

$$\text{Accumulated depreciation} = \$70,000 \times 5 = \$350,000$$

Note that this method is appropriate only where straight-line depreciation is used. For MACRS, the accumulated depreciation is found by summing the percentages off the MACRS table and multiplying this percentage by the initial value of the asset.

Continuing:

$$\text{Book value} = \text{Initial cost} - \text{Accumulated depreciation}$$
$$\text{Book value} = \$2,730,000 - \$350,000$$
$$\text{Book value} = \$2,380,000$$

and

$$\text{Tax on sale} = (\text{Sales price} - \text{Book value}) \times \text{Tax rate}$$
$$\text{Tax on sale} = (\$3,000,000 - \$2,380,000) \times 0.40$$
$$\text{Tax on sale} = \$620,000 \times 0.40 = \$248,000$$

The net terminal cash flow is $3,043,000, which is composed of the $291,000 cash flow from the year 2005 computations and $2,752,000 additional cash flow due to terminating the project.

Once all of the cash flows associated with a project have been identified, the project can be analyzed to determine whether it will increase the value of the firm. In the following example we combine all of the pieces into one comprehensive problem.

E X A M P L E   11.7   Comprehensive Example of Computing Cash Flows

Due to unexpectedly high demand, Pizzas-by-Mail finds that it may need a larger oven. The old oven cost $20,000 new and has been in use for 1 year. It has a 3-year life for depreciation and can be sold today for $12,000. The new oven costs $30,000 but will require $5,000 in remodeling to fit the restaurant. Shipping costs are $1,000. The new oven also has a 3-year class life. The larger oven will require that an additional inventory of $500 be held.

Revenues will increase $5,000 (from $25,000 per year to $30,000 per year) and costs will increase $2,000. Management expects to replace the larger oven after 5 years. It will have a salvage value of $4,000. Assume a 40% tax rate and discount rate of 15% and compute the NPV.

Solution

To compute the NPV we will need to first compute the cash flows that the new pizza oven will generate.

Computing the initial cash flow:

Calculation of Initial Cash Flow	
− Initial purchase price of new asset	−$30,000
− Installation/shipping cost of new asset	−$6,000
= Net Purchase Price	−$36,000
+ Proceeds from the sale of old asset	+$12,000
+/− Tax on sale of old asset (see below)	+$560
+/− Change in net working capital	−$500
= Initial cash flow	−$23,940

Accumulated depreciation = $20,000 × 0.33 = $6,600

The depreciation percentages come from the MACRS table in the appendix to this chapter. Continuing:

$$\text{Book value} = \text{Initial cost} - \text{Accumulated depreciation}$$

$$\text{Book value} = \$20,000 - \$6,600$$

$$\text{Book value} = \$13,400$$

and

$$\text{Tax on sale} = (\text{Sales price} - \text{Book value}) \times \text{Tax rate}$$

$$\text{Tax on sale} = (\$12,000 - \$13,400) \times 0.40$$

$$\text{Tax on sale} = \$-1,400 \times 0.40 = -\$560 \text{ (tax savings from the loss on sale)}$$

We add $560 in the cash flow estimate because we are reducing our taxes as a result of taking a loss on the sale. Note that the sign is negative in the equation and positive in the table. We are subtracting a negative amount, so the result is a positive cash flow.

Computing the Annual Cash Flows

This is an expansion project because a new oven is replacing an old oven. However, we do not need to subtract the old cash flows from the new because the figures given in the problem are *already incremental*.

	Pizza Oven Analysis				
	1999	*2000*	*2001*	*2002*	*2003*
New revenues – Old revenues	$5,000	$5,000	$5,000	$5,000	$5,000
New expenses – Old expenses	$2,000	$2,000	$2,000	$2,000	$2,000
Gross profit	$3,000	$3,000	$3,000	$3,000	$3,000
– (New depr. – Old depr.)	$2,880	$13,200	$4,000	$2,520	0
Net profit before tax	$120	–$10,200	–$1,000	$480	$3,000
– Taxes (40%)	–$48	+$4,080	+$400	–$192	–$1,200
Net profit	+$72	–$6,120	–$600	+$288	+$1,800
+Depreciation	$2,880	$13,200	$4,000	$2,520	0
Net cash flow	$2,952	$7,080	$3,400	$2,808	$1,800

Notice that the taxes have a positive sign in years 2000 and 2001, but they are negative in the other years. If the net profit before tax is positive, taxes are owed, so the sign is negative. If the net profit before tax is negative, a loss has occurred that can offset other income, so a tax savings results in a positive sign.

Computing the Terminal Cash Flow

Calculation of Terminal Cash Flow	
Net cash flow (year 2003 from solution to annual cash flow table)	+$1,800
+Proceeds from the sale of new asset	+$4,000
+/– Tax on sale of new asset (see below)	–$1,600
+/– Change in net working capital	+$500
= Terminal cash flow	+$4,700

The first entry in this table is the last entry from the annual cash flow table. We append this figure with the additional cash flows that apply only to the final year. The larger oven is sold for its $4,000 salvage value. Because it is fully depreciated, the sales amount is fully taxable. The increase in net working capital that was subtracted when we computed the initial cash flow is now added back. The terminal year cash flow is $4,700.

Computing NPV

Now that we have computed all of the relevant cash flows, we can compute the net present value:

$$NPV = \frac{\$2,952}{(1.15)^1} + \frac{\$7,080}{(1.15)^2} + \frac{\$3,400}{(1.15)^3} + \frac{\$2,808}{(1.15)^4} + \frac{\$4,700}{(1.15)^5} - \$23,940$$

$$NPV = \$14,098.22 - \$23,940 = -\$9,841.78$$

Because the NPV is negative, Pizzas-by-Mail should keep its old oven.

CAPITAL BUDGETING REFINEMENTS

In Chapter 10 we learned to apply a number of capital budgeting techniques to analyze the cash flows from an investment opportunity. In this chapter we have learned to estimate those cash flows. We complete our study of capital budgeting by reviewing some specific problems that often arise in the process. These include the following:

- Selecting investments when there are limited funds available
- Adjusting for risk when projects out of the ordinary are contemplated
- Adjusting the analysis to compare projects with very different lives
- Using sensitivity analysis to test the stability of our analysis

EXTENSION 11.1

Selecting Investments with Capital Rationing

In a theoretically perfect world, a firm would accept every positive-NPV project or investment. Of course, in this same world we would also look like supermodels, be sports stars, and sing in tune. Unfortunately, the world is not perfect, many of us cannot sing, and many firms cannot accept every good investment they identify. There are many reasons for this. The firm may not have the personnel available to properly manage a rapidly expanding firm. More often, the firm does not have sufficient funds available. Although theoretically the firm can raise more money, often managers are unwilling or unable to return to the capital markets. This means that the firm must select between a number of good projects.

Capital rationing occurs when the firm has more positive-NPV projects than it has funds available. Theoretically, as long as the NPV is positive, a firm should be able to borrow money or sell stock to raise the required funds. Realistically, however, many firms face constraints that limit their ability to accept all good opportunities. For example, management may want to hold some reserve borrowing capacity to meet emergencies or management may feel that it cannot properly control multiple projects. Whatever the reason, it may be necessary to select among many good projects.

Two methods of selecting projects under capital rationing are the investment opportunity approach and the net present value approach.

Investment Opportunity Schedule Approach

In Chapter 10 we introduced the investment opportunity curve in conjunction with the marginal weighted average cost of capital. We selected all projects with returns greater than the marginal cost of capital. Notice in Figure 11.1 that the projects are ranked by IRR. However, we established in Chapter 10 that IRR is not an appropriate tool to use for ranking projects. This means that the investment opportunity schedule approach to selecting projects should not be used exclusively. It may be a convenient starting point, but NPV should be used to make the final decision.

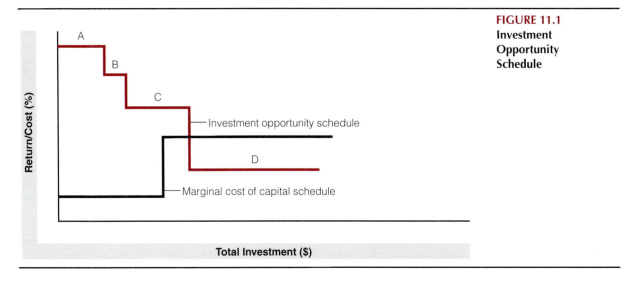

FIGURE 11.1
Investment Opportunity Schedule

Net Present Value Approach

The net present value approach to selecting investments involves selecting the mix of projects that maximizes the total net present value. Recall that the goal of the financial manager is to maximize the value of the firm. The net present value is the amount by which the project increases firm value. As we discussed in Chapter 10, by choosing the combination of projects with the greatest NPV, firm value is maximized. It is often helpful to compute the profitability index as well as the NPV of all projects under consideration. First, order the projects by PI and then select the projects with the highest PI until all funds are committed. Next, sum the NPV of all accepted projects. We can refine our technique introduced in Chapter 10 by substituting other projects to see whether a greater total NPV can be achieved. Example 11.8 illustrates the process.

E X A M P L E   11.8   Project Selection Through NPV Maximization

Department heads have submitted a number of proposed projects for management approval. Management has determined that only $5 million can be spent on this year's capital budget. Which of the projects listed in this table should be accepted?

Project	Cost (millions)	NPV (millions)	PI
A	$1.50	$0.20	1.13
B	1.50	0.30	1.20
C	2.00	0.10	1.05
D	2.50	0.25	1.10
E	0.75	0.15	1.20
F	0.50	0.10	1.20

Solution

The following steps result in maximizing NPV:

1. Order the projects by PI.

2. Cumulate the NPV and cost.

3. Select projects until all available funds are committed.

4. Verify your choices by substituting alternatives and determining whether NPV increases.

This has been done in the following table:

Project	Cost	Total Cost	NPV	Total NPV	PI
B	$1.50	$1.50	$0.30	$0.30	1.20
E	0.75	2.25	0.15	0.45	1.20
F	0.50	2.75	0.10	0.55	1.20
A	1.50	4.25	0.20	0.75	1.13
D	2.50	6.75	0.25	1.00	1.10
C	2.00	8.75	0.10	1.10	1.05

The "Total Cost" column is the cumulative cost of the projects listed. Similarly, the "Total NPV" column is the cumulative NPV of the projects accepted.

Our budget will allow us to accept projects B, E, F, and A. This will provide a total NPV of $0.75 million. If we were to drop A and add D, we would exceed our budget. If we were to drop A and add C, we would still be within budget but total NPV would drop to $0.65 million. Our first pass has maximized total NPV and hence shareholder wealth.

We see by this example that the process of selecting projects under capital rationing requires flexibility. Management will want to consider other soft issues in the process, such as whether one project opens future opportunities or whether another project requires less management involvement.

EXTENSION 11.2

Risk Adjustment Methods

Throughout this chapter we have used the weighted average cost of capital for the firm as the discount rate in NPV calculations and as the hurdle rate for IRR. This is appropriate for projects that are very similar to the firm's normal projects. Suppose, however, that a firm is contemplating a project very different from its usual type of business. For example, say your local telephone company is evaluating entering the cellular phone business. The phone company currently enjoys a monopoly on local service, but would be in heavy competition with other cellular phone providers. It would be inappropriate to discount the cellular phone business cash flows at the same rate used to evaluate projects such as extending regular phone service to a new subdivision. The cellular phone cash flows are much riskier. There are two alternative approaches to dealing with this problem: the certainty equivalent method and the risk-adjusted discount rate approach.

Certainty Equivalent Method

One common approach to dealing with risky cash flows is to determine the level of cash flows that we believe will be received with near certainty. This is called the **certainty equivalent approach.** For example, we may think a project's first-year cash flow will most likely be $100. However, for the purposes of the analysis we are *sure* that cash flows will be at least $60.

Once the certain cash flows have been determined, the NPV is computed using the risk-free rate of interest as the discount rate. The name for the method comes from the idea that *certainty equivalents* are substituted for the actual projected cash flows. The risk-free rate is used because virtually all risk has been removed from the analysis by using certainty equivalent cash flows.

The problem with the certainty equivalent method for risk adjustment is determining the certain cash flows. If they are estimated too low, the project will be rejected when it really should have been accepted.

Risk-Adjusted Discount Rate

An alternative approach, which may be easier to apply, is the **risk-adjusted discount rate method.** Instead of adjusting the cash flows, the discount rate is adjusted. If the firm is considering a risky project, the discount rate is adjusted up. If the project is less risky than usual, say a cost-plus contract with the government, the discount rate is reduced.

The question that must immediately be addressed is how much of an adjustment should be made. One way to determine this is to use a **pure play beta.** A pure play beta is the beta of a firm that is only in the business being evaluated. For example, the beta of U.S. Cellular would be a pure play beta. By plugging this beta into the CAPM, a firm analyzing the cellular phone business can compute a required return. Because the level of debt a firm holds affects its beta, adjustments for leverage may be required. We leave the calculation of levered and unlevered betas to intermediate texts.

The risk-adjusted discount rate method is generally considered more flexible and useful than the certainty equivalent method. It can be very difficult to estimate certain cash flows without being overly pessimistic. For this reason we see the risk-adjusted discount rate method used much more frequently in actual practice.

E X A M P L E 11.9   Adjusting the Discount Rate

Suppose that you are evaluating a project with a cost of $1,000 and five annual cash inflows of $325 each. The return on the market is 13%, the risk-free rate of interest is 6%, and the firm's beta is 1. The project you are evaluating is very different from those usually undertaken by the firm. Another firm, which is exclusively in the business of doing projects like the one under consideration, has a beta of 2. Should you recommend that the firm accept the project? Assume that the firm is all equity financed.

Solution

Before we can compute the NPV we need to compute the firm's required return. We cannot use the firm's beta because the risk of the project is not consistent with the risk of most projects done by the firm. Instead, we use the beta of the surrogate firm to compute the required return:

$$R_i = R_f + \beta(R_m - R_f)$$
$$R_i = 0.06 + 2(0.13 - 0.06)$$
$$R_i = 0.20$$

Now, using 20% as the discount rate, we can compute the NPV of the project:

$$NPV = \$325(PVIFA_{20\%,5\ yr}) - \$1,000$$
$$NPV = \$325(2.9906) - \$1,000$$
$$NPV = \text{-}28.05$$

Because NPV is less than 0, we reject the project. If the firm's beta of 1 had been used in the analysis, a positive NPV would have resulted (+$143.10). In this case, adjusting for risk changed the decision about the project.

EXTENSION 11.3

Evaluating Projects with Different Lives

Suppose that you are evaluating two projects. One will be completed in 3 years, but the other will not conclude for 10 years. Is it still reasonable to choose the one with the greatest NPV? The longer-term project may have the largest NPV because it consumes company resources for a long time. It may be that a series of shorter-term projects would have a larger total NPV than one long-term project. Accepting the long-term project may preclude the firm from accepting other shorter-term projects that become available later. The validity of this concern depends on the firm, its market, its size, and the probability of future opportunities surfacing.

There are two methods for comparing projects with different lives. They both assume that when the short-term project concludes, another similar project will be available. If this assumption is not realistic for your firm, these methods will not yield reliable results.

Replacement Chain Approach

The **replacement chain approach** requires the analyst string together as many short-term projects as necessary to equal the life of the long-term project. For example, if you are comparing a 5-year project with a 10-year project, the short one is doubled, so that it will take the same amount of time as the long one. The net present values are then computed and compared in the usual way.

E X A M P L E 11.10   **Project Evaluation: Replacement Chain Approach**

Disney built Epcot Center in Florida partly to display the world as it may be in the future. However, a recent editorialist noted that in one supposedly futuristic scene he spotted a rotary dial telephone. In 1996, Disney closed part of Epcot to remodel and update the displays. We can only speculate about the options the firm considered before beginning construction. Let us suppose that one option involved a $10 million alteration to the exhibits that would allow quick and efficient updates as new technology became available. The flexibility of this option would postpone future updates for 10 years. The alternative is less costly, but requires a total reconstruction in 5 years. Assume for simplicity that both options initially cost $10 million. The flexible option takes more space, so fewer visitors can be accommodated at one time. As a result, cash inflows are $2.5 million per year. The alternative has cash inflows of $3.75 million per year. Which option should Disney choose? Assume a cost of capital of 12%.

Solution
Begin by computing the NPV for each option, ignoring the difference in lives:

$$NPV_{inflex} = \$3.750(PVIFA_{5yr,12\%}) - \$10 = \$3.518 \text{ million}$$
$$NPV_{flex} = \$2.5(PVIFA_{10 \text{ yr},12\%}) - \$10 = \$4.123 \text{ million}$$

Because the NPV of the long-term flexible project is greater than that of the short-term inflexible approach, we may be tempted to conclude that the long-term project should be accepted. Let us continue the analysis, however, by assuming that after 5 years the inflexible project will be repeated. The extended project is shown on the following time line:

	3.75	3.75	3.75	3.75	3.75	3.75	3.75	3.75	3.75	3.75
−10					−10					
0	1	2	3	4	5	6	7	8	9	10

After 5 years, an additional $10 million must be invested to continue the cash inflows. We now compute the NPV of this extended project:

$$NPV_{inflex} = \$3.75(PVIFA_{10 \text{ yr},12\%}) - \$10(PVIF_{5 \text{ yr},12\%}) - \$10$$
$$NPV_{inflex} = \$21.188 - \$5.674 - \$10 = \$5.514 \text{ million}$$

The NPV of the shorter-term project done twice is greater than the NPV of the longer-term project done once. In this example, because Disney is assured of being able to redo the project at the end of the first 5 years, it should choose the short option.

The short-term project can be repeated any number of times to equal the length of the longer-term project. If one project would last 6 years and another 18 years, the short one could be repeated three times. The replacement chain approach can become tedious if the projects are not even multiples of each other. For example, if one project is 4 years and another was 18 years, the short one would have to be duplicated nine times and the longer one duplicated twice before a common length would be achieved. The next method avoids this problem.

Equal Annual Annuity Method
The **equal annual annuity (EAA) approach** assumes that both the short-term and the long-term project can be repeated forever. The cash flows from each of these projects are converted into annuities, which can be compared with each other. This is actually easier in practice than it sounds and is best explained with an example.

E X A M P L E 11.11   Project Evaluation: EAA

Use the numbers from the solution to Example 11.10 to compute the equal annual annuity (EAA) for each project.

Solution

Step 1: Compute the NPV for each project. In the last example we found NPV_{flex} to be $4.123 million and NPV_{inflex} to be $3.518 million.

Step 2: Find the annuity that has the same present value as the NPV and the same number of periods as the project. The flexible project has a life of 10 years and an NPV of $4.123 million. Using the firm's cost of capital of 12% and the factors approach yields

$$NPV = EAA(PVIFA_{10\ yr,12\%})$$
$$\$4.123 = EAA(5.6502)$$
$$EAA = \$4.123/5.6502$$
$$EAA = \$0.7297\ million$$

To find the EAA using a financial calculator, enter 4.123 as PV, 10 as N, 12% as I, and 0 as FV and compute PMT.

Review for a moment how this result is interpreted. An NPV of $4.123 million is the same as having a 10-period annuity of $0.729 million if the discount rate is 12%. We often convert annuities into present values. What we have done here is convert a present value back into an annuity.

Repeat this step for the other project:

$$\$3.518 = EAA(PVIFA_{5\ yr,12\%})$$
$$\$3.518 = EAA(3.6048)$$
$$EAA = \$3.518/3.6048$$
$$EAA = \$0.9759\ million$$

Study Tip

Since converting the EAA to a perpetuity involves dividing both EAAs by the same value, the results are never changed by this step. It is only included to demonstrate that we are now comparing projects of equal (perpetual) length.

To find the EAA using a financial calculator, enter 3.518 as PV, 5 as N, 12% as I, and 0 as FV and compute PMT.

Step 3: We now assume that these annuities continue forever because the projects, or similar projects, could be repeated over and over. To find the value of a perpetuity, divide each annuity by the discount rate:

$$Project_{flex} = \$0.7297/0.12 = \$6.0808\ million$$
$$Project_{inflex} = \$0.9759/0.12 = \$8.1325\ million$$

We again find that the shorter-term inflexible project is preferred to the longer-term one.

Be aware of several problems with attempting to correct for unequal lives. First, similar replacement jobs may not be available, as assumed by both methods. Second, because of inflation, subsequent costs may be higher than initially projected. Third, all of the errors we have discussed with estimating cash flows are compounded when we assume the cash flows will repeat. Despite these problems, it is often better to correct for unequal lives than to ignore the issue entirely.

Sensitivity Analysis

Project ideas may originate from anywhere within a firm. Once identified, many different individuals may participate in the evaluation exercise. Marketing will estimate sales and pricing. Production will estimate the cost of producing the new product. Accounting may provide historical numbers to help with these estimates. Finally, the financial manager gets the opportunity to evaluate the numbers. The financial manager often knows that many of the estimates are merely educated guesses. This does not imply incompetence, only that it can be extremely difficult to make estimates about costs and revenues for a product or activity that has never been attempted before.

In the early 1980s, IBM introduced a small, inexpensive home computer called the PC Junior to compete against the wildly popular Apple. The PC Junior was a resounding failure, largely because of a design that made the keyboard difficult to use. The small

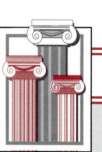

Careers in Finance

Chartered Financial Analyst

Many students who graduate with degrees in finance choose to continue their education by taking courses that lead to the Chartered Financial Analyst certification. This certification is very well respected. The CFA certification is often required by firms that employ people to analyze stocks. For example, Merrill Lynch employs CFAs to pick stocks that brokers will recommend to clients.

The Chartered Financial Analyst (CFA) certification dates back to 1963 when it was originally administered by an Association for Investment Management and Research (AIMR) predecessor. Since that time, the program has experienced great success, and in June 2001 AIMR expects to test as many as 80,000 candidates. The purpose of the CFA program is to act as a supplement to the education and work experience of individuals in the investment fields. The test focuses most strongly on the areas of portfolio management and financial analysis, but it also covers topics applicable to a wide range of investment specialists.

The CFA program is broken into three distinct levels, each requiring an estimated 250 hours of individual exam preparation. Exam candidates are allowed to participate in only one exam per year, and the exams must be taken in chronological order.

The CFA Level I exam is completely multiple choice. Its primary focus is on the methods and theories of investment valuation, portfolio management, and ethics. The second exam, CFA Level II, is half essay and half "item-set" questions. Item-set questions are case study investigations with multiple-choice questions. This exam is primarily focused on asset valuation and ethics. The final level (CFA Level III) is structured like the Level II exam and concentrates on portfolio management, asset allocation, and ethics.

More details about the precise content of each exam can be found at the Web site listed below.

Source: www.financialprep.com/cfa-about.html.

keys, similar to those found on calculators, prevented real typing. Likewise, the Cabbage Patch doll craze in the late 1980s was equally unpredictable. How is the financial manager supposed to deal with the uncertainty behind these estimates? One way is to produce a series of analyses that reflect the effects of different assumptions. This approach, called **sensitivity analysis,** tells the analyst how sensitive the results are to changes in the estimates. If a very small change in the sales projection makes a large difference in the NPV, the estimates may require additional review.

The ability to play what-if games with the cash flow estimates is one reason capital budgeting should be done using spreadsheets. By changing any of the inputs, new NPVs can be easily computed. The following steps help produce the data needed to make difficult capital budgeting decisions:

1. Prepare a complete cash flow estimation schedule using an electronic spreadsheet.

2. Use the formulas and built-in functions to compute the NPV of the cash flows.

3. Vary each of the uncertain estimates over its reasonable range and record the resulting NPV from each change in a table.

4. Graph the results of step 3.

5. Prepare additional evaluations by changing more than one input. For example, evaluate the effect on NPV if sales are below projections and costs are above projections.

After many such iterations, the analyst will garner a clearer view of the project and will better understand the risk involved.

For example, review Figure 11.2. A spreadsheet analysis of two projects was prepared. The level of sales was allowed to vary between 100 and 800. The NPV of each project was computed for each level of sales and the results graphed. Both projects have positive NPVs when sales are estimated to be 450 units. However, project 2 is much more

FIGURE 11.2
Sensitivity Analysis

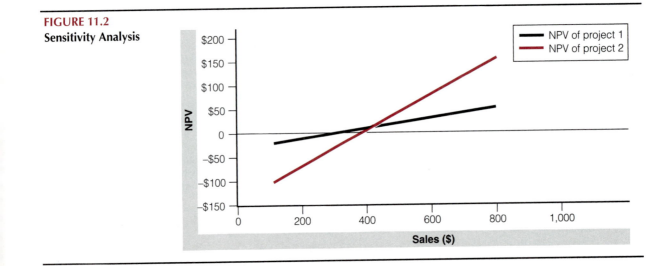

sensitive to the sales estimate. A small error estimating sales has a much larger effect on its NPV than on project 1's NPV. If sales turn out to be 350 units, project 1 still has a positive NPV but project 2 will have a negative NPV.

Sales is only one of many variables that can be evaluated when performing sensitivity analysis. You can also look at how cost estimates, sales growth rates, or interest rates affect the NPV of projects. Sensitivity analysis is an essential and critical part of the capital budgeting process.

APPENDIX: DEPRECIATION

Book value is computed by subtracting the accumulated depreciation from the original value. The amount that is subtracted each year is the annual depreciation. The sum of the annual depreciation charges is the accumulated depreciation. There are two common ways to compute depreciation: straight line and accelerated. The straight-line method requires that the same amount be subtracted each year. Often the straight-line method is used for a company's own books and another method is used for tax reporting.

Straight-line depreciation is easy to compute. Subtract the expected salvage value of the asset from the original purchase price and divide by the economic life of the asset:

$$\text{Annual depreciation} = \frac{\text{Original cost} - \text{Salvage}}{\text{Economic life}}$$

Accelerated depreciation expenses a larger portion of the asset in the early years, which postpones taxes. The currently used accelerated depreciation method is the modified accelerated cost recovery system (MACRS). The following table reports the annual percentage allowances under MACRS:

Percentage Allowances Under MACRS				
Ownership Year	Investment Class			
	3-Year	5-Year	7-Year	10-Year
1	33%	20%	14%	10%
2	45	32	25	18
3	15	19	17	14
4	7	12	13	12
5		11	9	9
6		6	9	7
7			9	7
8			4	7
9				7
10				6
				3
	100%	100%	100%	100%

Note that the 3-year class of investment is actually depreciated over 4 years. This is because of the half-year convention. The IRS assumes for tax purposes that every asset is put into service halfway into the initial year. The first-year depreciation is for 6 months. That leaves 6 more months to be depreciated during the final year.

The IRS assigns assets to classes for the purpose of depreciation; consult the IRS if you are uncertain about how to assign a particular asset to a class. The following table provides some examples:

MACRS Asset Classes	
Type of Asset	**Life**
Manufacturing tools	3-year
Cars, light trucks, computers	5-year
Industrial equipment, office furniture	7-year
Heavy-duty types of equipment	10-year
Residential rental property	27.5-year
Nonresidential real property	3-year

CHAPTER SUMMARY

The first step in the process of evaluating projects and investment opportunities is to compute the cash flows that will be generated. The initial cash flow is the amount spent (net of salvage, net working capital, and taxes) on initiating the project. All shipping and installation costs are included. If an old machine is being replaced, the funds received from its sale can be used to offset a portion of the initial purchase price. If there is a tax gain or loss from the sale of the old asset, this also must be included in the analysis.

Once the initial cash flow has been computed, the annual cash flows are determined. These are found using a typical income statement format that adds noncash charges (depreciation) back at the end. The annual cash flows are best computed using an electronic spreadsheet so sensitivity analysis can be conducted on the results.

The terminal cash flow is computed for the final year of the project. It differs from the annual cash flow in that there may be salvage of the equipment used in the project or recapture of net working capital. Once all of the cash flows have been found, they can be put on a time line and analyzed using the capital budgeting techniques learned in Chapter 10.

Many firms face capital rationing. Capital rationing refers to limiting the number of projects that are accepted for one reason or another. Under capital rationing the firm selects the projects that will maximize its shareholders' wealth. Shareholder wealth is maximized by accepting the group of projects that has the largest combined NPV possible. One way to simplify this is to first rank projects by their profitability index.

Accept those with the highest PI first and work down until the entire capital budget has been spent. There are times when this method does not yield the best possible selection of projects. Therefore, always check by substituting alternative projects to make sure some other mix is not marginally better.

Not all projects a firm evaluates have the same risk as the usual projects and investments in a firm's portfolio. When this occurs, there are two ways to adjust the evaluation. First, the cash flows can be reduced to a level you are certain can be achieved and the risk-free rate of interest can be used as the discount rate. Alternatively, the discount rate can be increased to compensate for the increased risk. The beta of a surrogate firm that is primarily in the business of doing projects such as the one under consideration can be used to compute a new required return. This new required return can then be used to evaluate the cash flows.

A final adjustment to capital budgeting analysis is required for ranking projects with very different lives. A longer-term project has a longer period of time to accumulate earnings, so naturally it has a larger NPV than an equivalent, shorter-term project. To evaluate two projects with very different lives, use either the replacement chain approach or the equal annual annuity approach. The replacement chain approach requires you to string together multiple cash flows until both projects are of equal length. The equal annual annuity approach requires you to find the annuity that has a value equivalent to the NPV. The sizes of the annual annuity payments are then compared.

KEY WORDS

DISCUSSION QUESTIONS

1. What does it mean that only incremental cash flows should be used in estimating cash flows? Is the total electric bill or the change in the electric bill an incremental cost?
2. What indirect cost may be involved in a project to change all of a company's Apple computers to IBM computers?
3. A consultant will be hired to provide support if a new project is accepted. The consultant has already provided valuable assistance with information used in the analysis. Which fees would be included in the project analysis and which would be considered sunk costs?
4. A new machine will occupy space in the plant that has been empty since the plant was constructed 40 years ago. It will also take up space currently leased to another manufacturer. Which of these costs will be included in the analysis as opportunity costs and which will be disregarded?
5. Is it true that if a firm has suffered losses for the last several years and projects that losses will continue, no tax adjustment should be made to the cash flows?
6. What are the three phases of the cash flow analysis? Briefly describe what cash flows are included in each phase.

7. Describe in words (no mathematical equations) how the tax on an asset being sold in a replacement analysis is calculated.
8. Can the change in net working capital ever be positive? If net working capital increases, is the sign on net working capital in the initial cash flow analysis positive or negative?
9. Why are depreciation expenses first added to gross profit and then subtracted from net profit after tax?
10. Explain why the sign on the change in net working capital is reversed when the terminal cash flow is computed.
11. When will capital rationing occur? What is capital rationing? (Extension 11.1)
12. Describe the process you would follow to select projects under capital rationing using the PI method. (Extension 11.1)
13. Why do we need to modify our analysis method when two projects have very different lives? (Extension 11.3)
14. What is sensitivity analysis? How would you perform sensitivity analysis on a project?

PROBLEMS

1. The initial purchase price of a new stamp press is $15,000. The firm will spend $5,000 on shipping and installation. Training of new employees will cost $3,000. As a result of the purchase, inventory must increase $1,000. What is the net initial cash flow?
2. A new tire balancing machine is available to replace an existing one. The new one will cost $5,000. The old one originally cost $4,000 and was being depreciated over its 3-year life using MACRS. Two years have passed since the old one was purchased. Shipping of the new machine will cost $500. Assume a 40% tax rate. What is the net initial cash flow? (Assume the old machine cannot be sold.)

3. You estimate that if a new computer graphic display product is launched by your firm, revenues will increase $2,500 the first year and 10% each year for the next 3 years. Expenses will be 50% of revenues. Depreciation is computed using MACRS for an asset with a 3-year life and a basis of $10,000. The tax rate is 40%. Compute the first 4 years' annual cash flows.
4. You have been asked by the president of your company to evaluate the proposed acquisition of a new project for the firm. The equipment needed for this project would cost $100,000 and the installation cost would be $35,000. This equipment would be depreciated using

straight-line depreciation with a 5-year life (do not assume any salvage value when computing the annual depreciation). It will be sold for $40,000 at the end of year 5. The use of the new equipment would require an increase in net working capital of $3,000. There would be an increase in revenue of $2,000 and the new project would save the firm $30,000 per year in before-tax operating costs. The firm's marginal federal-plus-state tax rate is 40%.

   a. What is the initial cash flow of the new project?
   b. What are the net operating cash flows in years 1–5?
   c. What is the terminal cash flow in year 5?
   d. What is the NPV for the project if the discount rate is 12%?

5. Jones Company is evaluating the proposed acquisition of a new machine. The machine will cost $200,000, and it would cost another $30,000 to modify it for special use by the firm. The machine falls into the MACRS 3-year class, and it would be sold after 3 years for $100,000. The machine would require an increase in net working capital of $10,000. The machine would have no effect on revenues, but it is expected to save the firm $120,000 per year in before-tax operating costs, mainly labor. The company's marginal tax rate is 40%.

   a. What is the initial cash flow for the project?
   b. What are the cash flows for years 1 and 2?
   c. What is the terminal cash flow?
   d. What is the NPV for the proposed acquisition if the discount rate is 12%?

6. The Kurston Company purchased a machine 5 years ago for $80,000. It has an estimated life of 10 years from the time of purchase and is expected to have zero salvage value at the end of year 10. The depreciation method used for the machine is straight line. A new machine can be purchased for $100,000. It has a 5-year life and is expected to reduce operating expenses by $60,000 per year. Sales are not expected to change. The machine after 5 years will have no salvage value. The straight-line method is used for the new machine. The old machine can be sold today for $70,000. The tax rate is 40%.

   a. What is the initial cash flow of the new machine?
   b. What is the cash flow for year 1?
   c. What is the NPV if the discount rate is 12%?

7. Meals on Wings Inc. supplies prepared meals for corporate aircraft and it needs to purchase new broilers. If the broilers are purchased, they will replace old broilers purchased 10 years ago for $105,000 that are being depreciated on a straight-line basis to a zero salvage value (15-year depreciable life). The old broilers can be sold today for $60,000. The new broilers will cost $200,000 installed (not counting funds already spent) and will be depreciated using straight-line depreciation with no salvage over their 5-year class life; they will be sold at their book value at the end of the fifth year. The firm expects to increase its revenues by $18,000 per year if the new broilers are purchased, but cash expenses will also increase by $2,500 per year. Annual interest expense will be $2,000. Net working capital will increase by $5,000. The new broilers will occupy space currently leased to another firm for $500 per month, and $5,000 has already been spent preparing the building for the new broilers. The firm's tax rate is 40%.

   a. What is the firm's initial cash flow?
   b. What is the firm's first-year annual cash flow?
   c. What is the firm's terminal year cash flow?

8. Given the following data, select which projects would maximize firm value by using the profitability index. Assume that the firm has a $500,000 capital budget. (Extension 11.1)

Project	Cost	NPV	PI
B	$60,000	$1,200	
E	50,000	1,300	
F	100,000	2,000	
A	250,000	3,000	
D	300,000	4,000	
C	75,000	1,750	

9. You are evaluating a project to develop an exclusive subdivision for residential housing. In the past you have developed apartments only for college students. You view the new subdivision as substantially more risky than your past endeavors. After doing some research you have learned that firms similar to yours doing this type of development have a beta of 2.5. The market return is 12% and the risk-free rate is 5%. The initial investment will be $3,500,000. You expect annual cash inflows of $1,300,000 for 5 years as the property is sold. (Extension 11.2)

   a. Should you accept the project if you compute the NPV at the firm's 15% cost of capital?
   b. Should you accept the project if you risk adjust the discount rate?

10. You are evaluating two projects. You may only accept one of them. One will cost $400,000 initially and will pay $125,000 each year for the next 5 years. The other will cost $475,000 initially but will pay $100,000 for the next 10 years. The firm's cost of capital is 15%. (Extension 11.3)

  a. Compute the NPV of each project. Which project has the highest NPV?

  b. Use the replacement chain approach to compute the NPV of each. Which project now appears best?

  c. Use the equal annual annuity method to select between the two projects. Does this result agree with what you found in part b?

SELF-TEST PROBLEMS

1. Your company has decided to purchase a new computer system for $150,000. Installation and training will cost an additional $40,000 and $25,000, respectively. What is the net purchase price?

2. In problem 1, what amount would you use as the basis for computing depreciation on the new computer system?

3. The computer system your company is currently using was purchased 3 years ago for $140,000 and has a MACRS depreciable life of 5 years. What is the book value of the old computer system?

4. Your company is selling the old computer system in problem 3 for $25,000. Using the information given in problem 3, what is the taxable gain (loss) on the sale of the old computer system? Assuming a 40% tax rate, what is the tax on the sale? Is this amount added to or subtracted from the net purchase price when computing the initial investment?

5. Using the information from problems 1 through 4, what is the initial cash flow, assuming the computer system will reduce net working capital by $32,000?

6. Using the straight-line depreciation method, what is the annual depreciation of commercial property that cost $2.5 million? Assume a 39-year depreciable life.

7. Suppose you owned a sporting goods store and decided to expand your operations by opening a new store. You project that revenue will reach $250,000 for the new store in the first year and increase by 20% over the next 3 years. Expenses are estimated at 75% of sales, the initial cost of the expansion was $400,000 (depreciable over 39 years using the straight-line method), and your tax rate is 40%. What are the annual cash flows from 2001 to 2004?

8. As the manager of a printing company, you were impressed at a local trade show with a next-generation printing machine. It occupies less space, is more efficient, and provides a better-quality product. This machine costs $260,000 and has annual operating costs of $15,000. However, 2 years ago you purchased a printing machine for $190,000 that has annual operating costs of $29,000. You are depreciating the old printing machine over 3 years using MACRS, as you would for the new printing machine. Revenues will increase from $760,000 to $790,000 with the replacement of the old printing machine. Note that the change in operating cost is $15,000 − $29,000. Assume a 40% tax rate and compute the annual cash flows for the next 4 years.

9. You plan to sell the new printing machine in problem 8 after 4 years for $60,000. Using the information from problem 8, what is the terminal cash flow?

10. The initial cash flow for a project is −$250 million. Cash flows are projected to be −$150 million in 2001, $300 million in 2002, $450 million in 2003, and $250 million in 2004. If the cost of capital is 12%,what is the NPV?

11. Suppose the initial cash flow for a project is −$500 million. Cash flows are projected to be −$300 million in 2001, −$200 million in 2002, $250 million in 2003, $500 million in 2004, $600 million in 2005, and $675 million in 2006. If the cost of capital is 14%, what is the NPV?

12. Suppose the cash inflow in the last year of a project is $22 million. The new asset is to be sold for $5 million, resulting in a tax of $450,000. If net working capital was initially decreased by $400,000, what is the terminal cash flow?

13. As a top manager, you must decide which of the proposed projects should be accepted for the upcoming year since only $6 million is available for the next year's capital budget. What is the total NPV of the projects that should be accepted?

Project	Cost (millions)	NPV (millions)	PI
A	$3.25	$0.80	1.25
B	1.75	0.52	1.30
C	4.50	0.69	1.15
D	3.75	0.95	1.25
E	1.25	0.25	1.20
F	0.50	0.25	1.50

14. Suppose that you are evaluating a project with a cost of $15,000 and five annual cash inflows in $6,500 each. The return on the market is 12%, the risk-free rate of interest is 6%, and the firm's beta is 1.2. The project you are evaluating is very different from those usually undertaken by the firm. Another firm, which is exclusively in the business of doing projects like the one under consideration, has a beta of 2.0. Should you recommend that the firm accept the project? Assume the firm is all equity financed.

15. Your company must decide between two positive-NPV projects with unequal lives. The 3-year project has an initial cash flow of −$2 million, with cash inflows of $4 million per year. The 6-year project has an initial cash flow of −$6 million, with cash inflows of $3 million per year. Assume a cost of capital of 12% and that neither project has additional end-of-project costs. What is the NPV for each project using the replacement chain approach? Which project should your company accept?

16. Refer to the information from problem 15 and give your accept/reject decision using the equal annual annuity method.

17. Use the replacement chain approach to evaluate the following projects. Project A has a 2-year life, an initial cost of $2.25 million, and cash inflows of $1.5 million per year. Project B has a 4-year life, an initial cost of $5 million, and cash inflows of $2 million per year. What is the NPV for each project and which should you accept? Assume a 15% cost of capital.

18. Refer to the information from problem 17 and give your accept/reject decision using the equal annual annuity method.

WEB EXPLORATION

1. Go to www.toolkit.cch.com/text/P06_6500.asp, "Financial Analysis of Major Projects." This site includes a tutorial on capital budgeting with many links to additional information about the various methods. This site is part of the CCH Business Owner's Toolkit, http://www.toolkit.cch.com, which contains a wealth of information on financing, taxes, regulations, laws, and marketing. Visit Deciding to Make a Major Purchase, http://www.toolkit.cch.com/text/p06.6100.asp, and click on Capital Budgeting. Identify two factors mentioned in these articles not discussed in the text.

2. Go to www.gleim.com/Accounting/CMA/UpdateQuestions.html#capitalbm. This site is sponsored by Gleim and offers a free online study guide for the CPA exam with multiple-choice questions fully answered. You can search this site for other topics being covered in your finance class.

MINI CASE

Phonemate, a manufacturer of telephone accessories, recently hired you as a financial analyst. A group of engineers reported to Phonemate's senior management that in their spare time they had developed an intelligent phone answering machine that could respond to simple questions. Businesses or individuals could load it with answers to the 20 most frequently asked questions, such as When do you close? What is your address? and so on, and the machine could then respond to those questions. Better yet, this machine could be produced for about $100. You have been asked to evaluate the viability of bringing this product to market.

Your first task is to gather data. From marketing you learn that Phonemate should be able to sell 43,000 units the first year if they are priced at $225 each. You expect sales to increase 10% per year for 5 years, then to stop when a new product will be introduced.

The firm will have to set up a new production line to make the machines. This is projected to cost $1.5 million. The line will be depreciated using the 5-year MACRS. Inventories will increase by $125,000. You learn that the engineers' cost to develop the machine was $75,000, including time and parts. When this project is over, the production line will be sold for book value.

If this project is accepted, the firm will discontinue production of the old answering machines it currently sells. This will require the removal of its production line. This line was set up 2 years ago at a cost of $750,000 and is being depreciated using 5-year MACRS. The old line can be sold for $100,000. Revenues from the old answering machine are currently $2.5 million per year and costs are $0.5 million.

Advertising for the new answering machine is projected to be $2 million per year. Repairs and returns should be $1.5 million per year. The $100 per unit engineers' estimate of production costs includes wages, electrical utilities, and all other costs of manufacturing.

The firm's tax rate is 40% and its cost of capital is 13%. Since this is a new technology, management feels that the cash flows should be discounted at 15%. This project will be financed with bank debt estimated to cost 10%.

a. Prepare a cash flow analysis.
b. Calculate the NPV and IRR.
c. Prepare an NPV profile.
d. Prepare a graph with NPV on the y-axis and various levels of initial sales on the x-axis. Does it appear this project is very sensitive to the estimate of the level of sales? (Continue to assume a 10% growth rate in sales.)

The Cost of Capital

I n Chapters 8 and 9 we learned how to compute the price of a variety of financial assets. To compute these prices we assumed there was a cost for each asset. For example, the cost of debt was given as k_d. The cost of preferred stock was given as k_p and the cost of equity was k_e. Financial managers use all three sources of funds to finance their firms' growth. In those earlier chapters we assumed that financial managers had the costs of the components available to them to use in the valuation process. Similarly, in Chapters 10 and 11 we learned various methods of capital budgeting. Again, we had to assume that the cost of capital was available to financial managers who were engaged in the analysis. In this chapter we learn how to compute the component cost of each type of financial asset and how to blend them together to form an average cost of capital.

Capital structure is the amount of permanent short-term debt, long-term debt, preferred stock, and common stock used to finance a firm's assets. Permanent short-term debt refers to that portion of current liabilities that is not seasonal and remains constantly on the balance sheet. For many firms this is an inconsequential figure. It can also be impossible for an outsider to determine.

Capital structure thus refers to the long-term sources of funds. The costs of these long-term funds are what we use to evaluate long-term investments.

Chapter Objectives

By the end of this chapter you should be able to:

1. Compute the cost of debt
2. Compute the cost of preferred stock
3. Compute the cost of equity
4. Compute the weighted average cost of capital

WHY COMPUTE A WEIGHTED AVERAGE COST OF CAPITAL?

Suppose that you are deciding whether to open a Sunglass Hut that you have determined will yield a 12% return. You know that you will finance this investment by borrowing the money at 10% from the local bank. Does this mean that you should go ahead and open the store? In Chapter 11 we saw that as a general rule we accept projects that earn more than our cost of funds. Because the Sunglass Hut is expected to yield more than the cost of the funds used to finance it, the store may appear to be a good investment.

Assume that you decide to open the Sunglass Hut at your local mall and it performs as expected. As an aggressive entrepreneur, you soon discover another investment opportunity. A new franchise for custom-fit shoes is available. By digitally scanning a foot, employees can give customers a perfect fit every time at a very reasonable cost. You are sure that this is the future of footwear. After careful financial analysis, you determine that this investment will yield a 16% return and that it has the same risk as your Sunglass Hut. You go to your bank for the startup capital but find that it refuses to lend you any more money. All of your assets have been pledged as security for the first loan. Not one to give up easily, you continue searching for funds and find that you can sell stock in your small conglomerate, but the investors demand that you pay a 20% return. Failure to pay the 20% would mean that investors would be disappointed and sell your stock, which would drive its price down, making future expansion impossible.

Do you open the custom-fit shoe store? The equity component of your **capital structure** costs 20% but the store is projected to earn only 16%, so you reject it. Consider what you have done. You accepted a 12% return in a Sunglass Hut but rejected a 16%-return investment opportunity that followed. Clearly there must be a better way to evaluate investments. There is. Use an *average cost of funds* rather than the cost of the capital raised to finance a particular investment. Suppose that over the long run you plan to raise money in equal parts debt and equity. What is your average cost of funds? The average is simply 10% plus 20% divided by 2, which equals 15%. If you had evaluated the Sunglass Hut using a 15% cost of funds, you would have rejected it. On the other hand, you would continue to find the custom shoe franchise attractive. This is demonstrated in Table 12.1.

From this example we see that it is clearly a mistake to evaluate an investment using the cost of funds that will be used to finance that particular investment. The reason is that you may accept poor projects before better ones become available. ***The better approach is to compute an average cost of funds and use this to evaluate every project***. The cost of capital for a number of industries is reported in Table 12.2.

TABLE 12.1 Choosing Investment Projects

Business Opportunity	Expected Return	Cost of Borrowing	Cost of Equity	Average Cost of Money
Sunglass Hut	12%	10%		15%
Custom Shoe	16		20%	15

TABLE 12.2 Cost of Capital for Various Industries

Industry Name	Number of Firms	Cost of Equity	After-Tax Cost of Debt	D/(D + E)	Cost of Capital
Air transport	37	11.32%	4.75%	43.83%	8.44%
Apparel	46	9.81	4.83	34.50	8.09
Bank	177	9.64	4.05	35.89	7.63
Beverage (alcoholic)	22	8.60	4.14	20.03	7.71
Building materials	40	10.10	4.32	33.08	8.18
Computer software & svcs	413	11.06	5.82	2.16	10.95
Drug	272	10.08	6.16	3.17	9.95
Grocery	27	9.20	4.17	27.85	7.80
Internet	307	16.38	6.26	1.22	16.26
Retail store	31	11.10	4.17	17.02	9.92
Securities brokerage	32	11.99	5.57	51.88	8.66
Tobacco	12	8.68	4.15	22.59	7.66
Toiletries/cosmetics	20	10.39	5.09	13.56	9.67
Trucking/transp. leasing	50	9.91	4.16	59.06	6.51
Water utility	15	8.54	3.98	46.00	6.44
Market	**5,903**	**10.02%**	**5.68%**	**19.30%**	**9.18%**

Source: www.stern.nyu.edu/~adamodar/New_Home_Page/datafile/wacc.htm.

Before you can compute an average cost of funds, you must first compute the cost of each type of capital. You then compute an average based on what proportion of the optimal or target capital structure each component occupies.

COMPUTING COMPONENT COSTS

Funds are raised from a number of sources. For example, a firm may borrow from a bank, issue bonds, or sell stock. It may also issue preferred stock or finance new projects from retained earnings (earnings held from prior periods). Each of these sources of funds has a unique cost. Consider that while retained earnings and a new issue of stock are both forms of equity financing, a new stock issue requires additional expenditures that raise the cost. In this section, we will discuss how the cost of each type of financing is computed; then we will put them all together to compute a weighted average cost.

One pleasant surprise is that you have already learned how to do the calculations required by this section. In Chapters 8 and 9 we noted how the cost of each type of capital could be found by rewriting the valuation equations. We will review these equations here.

After-Tax Cost of Debt

In Chapter 8 the equation for the price of a bond was given by Equation 8.1:

$$P_{bond} = \frac{C_1}{\left(1 + k_d\right)^1} + \frac{C_2}{\left(1 + k_d\right)^2} + \cdots + \frac{C_n}{\left(1 + k_d\right)^n} + \frac{Mat}{\left(1 + k_d\right)^n}$$

where

P_{bond} = current market value of the bond
   C = coupon interest payment, equal to the coupon interest rate times the par value of the bond
  Mat = maturity value of the bond, usually $1,000 for corporate bonds
   n = number of periods until the bond matures
   k_d = required return on debt

k_d is the *before-tax* cost of debt. In Chapter 8 we solved for k_d when computing the yield to maturity. Often, k_d is published in the firm's annual reports or by bond services such as Moody's Bond Record. For example, the cost of debt is reported in Wal-Mart's annual report (see Box 12.1). However obtained, k_d is not the true cost of debt to a company. *Interest on debt is tax deductible.* The tax deductibility of debt lowers the cost of debt financing because the government is paying a portion of the debt expense by reducing the taxes due from the company. Review Table 12.3. The first column shows the taxes and net income due for a debt-free company. The second column shows the interest, taxes, and net income for a firm with $100 of 10% debt. The net income for the debt-free company is $60 versus $54 for the company with $100 of debt. *The $10 interest expense lowers net income by only $6.* The cost of debt is then 6%, not 10%. The tax deductibility of interest reduces the cost of debt by $(1 - T)$, where T is the firm's tax rate. For example, if the pretax cost of debt is 10% and the tax rate is 40%, the after-tax cost is 6% [10% × (1 − 0.4) = 6%].
   The cost of debt is stated in the following equation:

$$\text{Cost of debt} = k_d(1 - T) \tag{12.1}$$

The cost of debt reflects the cost of borrowing at current market interest rates. That is, the cost of debt is the rate at which new debt could be issued. This means that the cost of debt rises and falls with market rates regardless of whether any new debt is being issued. The cost of debt should also reflect any **flotation costs**, the fees and expenses a firm incurs issuing securities. These include items such as brokers' fees, SEC registration costs, and labor expenses. A bond that sells for $1,000 may net the firm only $980 after the costs of issuing the bond are subtracted. The cost of debt should be computed using the net proceeds from the bonds.

TABLE 12.3

Debt-Free Company		Company with $100 of Debt	
EBIT	$100	EBIT	$100
− Interest	− 0	− Interest	− 10
EBT	$100	EBT	$ 90
− Tax (40%)	40	− Tax (40%)	36
Net income	$ 60	Net income	$ 54

Box 12.1 Excerpt from Wal-Mart's Annual Report

Information on short-term borrowings and interest rates is as follows (dollar amounts in millions):

Fiscal years ended January 31,

	2000	1999	1998
Maximum amount outstanding at month-end	$6,588	$1,976	$1,530
Average daily short-term borrowings	2,233	256	212
Weighted average interest rate	5.4%	5.1%	5.6%

At January 31, 2000, short-term borrowings consisting of $3,323 million of commercial paper were outstanding. At January 31, 1999, there were no short-term borrowings outstanding. At January 31, 2000, the Company had committed lines of $4,872 million with 85 firms and banks and informal lines of credit with various banks totaling an additional $1,500 million, which were used to support commercial paper.

Long-term debt at January 31, consists of (amounts in millions):

Fiscal years ended January 31,

	2000	1999
6.875% Notes due August 2009	$3,500	—
6.550% Notes due August 2004	1,250	—
6.150% Notes due August 2001	1,250	—
8.625% Notes due April 2001	750	750
5.875% Notes due October 2005	597	597
7.500% Notes due May 2004	500	500
6.500% Notes due June 2003	454	454
7.250% Notes due June 2013	445	445
7.800%–8.250% Obligations from sale/leaseback transactions due 2014	398	427
6.750% Notes due May 2002	300	300
7.000%–8.000% Obligations from sale/leaseback transactions due 2013	275	292
8.500% Notes due September 2024	250	250
6.750% Notes due October 2023	250	250
8.000% Notes due September 2006	250	250
6.375% Notes due March 2003	228	228
6.750% Eurobond due May 2002	200	200
5.850% Notes due June 2018 with biannual put options	—	500
5.650% Notes due February 2010 with biannual put options	—	500
9.100% Notes due July 2000	—	500
6.125% Eurobond due November 2000	—	250
7.290% Notes due July 2006	435	—
4.410%–10.880% Notes acquired in ASDA acquisition due 2002–2015	1,026	—
Commercial paper classified as long-term debt	993	—
Other	321	215
	$13,672	$6,908

E X A M P L E 12.1   Cost of Debt

Vocaltec is a software producer that offers I-phone, a software product that lets Internet users communicate over the Internet by voice without incurring long-distance toll charges. The managers of this firm want to issue bonds to finance research and development of methods including high-quality Internet fax communication. After the flotation costs, the bonds will net the firm $980 each. If the coupon rate is 10% and the bonds mature in 20 years, what is the cost of debt to Vocaltec? Assume annual compounding and a 40% tax rate.

Solution (Calculator Solution)

By far the easiest way to solve for k_d is to use a financial calculator. Input the price the firm receives for the bond after flotation costs have been deducted. Be sure to keep track of whether you are inputting cash inflows or outflows and use the correct sign.

=10.24%

The pretax cost of debt is 10.24%. The after-tax cost of debt is found by multiplying by $(1 - T)$:

$$\text{Cost of debt} = k_d(1 - T)$$

$$\text{Cost of debt} = 10.24\%(1 - 0.4) = 6.14\%$$

The after-tax cost of debt is 6.14%.

Estimation Equation Approach

If a financial calculator is not available, you can use the equation presented in Chapter 8 for estimating the yield to maturity. Using Equation 8.5, substitute the price per share the firm receives after flotation costs for the market price into

$$\text{YTM} = \frac{C + \dfrac{\text{Par} - \text{Market}}{N}}{\dfrac{\text{Par} + 2\text{Market}}{3}}$$

This gives

$$k_d = \frac{\$100 + \dfrac{\$1,000 - \$980}{20}}{\dfrac{\$1,000 + 2(\$980)}{3}} = 0.1024 = 10.24\%$$

The after-tax cost of debt is computed as before and equals 6.14%.

Self-Test Review Question*

A $1,000 par bond is currently selling for $1,200. It has an 8% coupon and 10 years to maturity. If the firm's tax rate is 40%, what is the after-tax cost of this debt?

The after-tax cost is $5.29\%(1 - 0.40) = 3.17\%$. The calculator solution is $5.36\%(1 - 0.4) = 3.22\%$.

$$k_d = \frac{\$80 + \dfrac{\$1,000 - \$1,200}{10}}{\dfrac{\$1,000 + 2(\$1,200)}{3}} = 0.0529 = 5.29\%$$

*Use either a calculator or the estimation equation:

Cost of Preferred Stock

About 5% of the average firm's capital is raised from issuing preferred stock. Although it does not constitute a large portion of the capital structure, it is a significant amount. Do not be surprised if you find a firm that has no preferred stock outstanding. This is not unusual. Even though preferred stock has many of the characteristics of bonds, dividends are paid instead of interest. *Dividends are not tax deductible.* This makes the after-tax cost of preferred stock higher than the after-tax cost of similarly risky debt. This higher cost is one reason why firms are reluctant to issue preferred stock. Given its close similarity to debt, most firms choose to sell bonds rather than issue preferred stock. What little preferred stock has been issued in recent years has usually been part of merger packages or convertible into the common stock of the company.

The cost of preferred stock (k_p) is found by rearranging Equation 9.1:

$$P_{preferred} = \frac{Div}{k_p}$$

This becomes

$$k_p = \frac{Div}{P_{preferred}} \tag{12.2}$$

where Div is the annual dividend paid per share and $P_{preferred}$ is the price per share.

E X A M P L E 12.2   Cost of Preferred Stock

Suppose that K-Mart tries to make the firm more competitive with Wal-Mart by issuing additional shares of preferred stock to finance upgrading its inventory control and ordering systems. What is the cost of preferred stock if the stock pays a $1.00 dividend and sells at a price that will net the firm $12 after deducting flotation costs?

Solution

Plug the factors into Equation 12.2:

$$k_p = \frac{\$1.00}{\$12.00} = 0.0833 = 8.33\%$$

The cost of preferred stock is 8.33%. *Note that there is no tax adjustment for the cost of preferred stock.*

Self-Test Review Question*

If a share of preferred stock pays $3.50 per year and the stock is currently selling for $25.00, what is the cost of the preferred stock?

Cost of Equity

The cost of equity is the return on investment required by investors in the stock of a company. Finding the cost of equity is far more difficult than finding the cost of either

$$^* \quad \frac{\$3.50}{\$25.00} = 0.14 = 14\%$$

Box 12.2 Surviving as CEO Requires Attention to Stock Price

Woe be to the CEO who fails to recognize the importance of the shareholder. Current shareholders tend to be very impatient with CEOs who do not work aggressively to maximize their wealth. In a recent article on CEO turnover, *Business Week* reported that "the fundamental task of today's CEO is simplicity itself: Get the stock price up. Period."

CEOs who fail to increase stock price have little time in today's corporate environment to make amends. Two-thirds of all major companies worldwide have replaced their CEO at least once since 1995, according to a survey by Drake Beam Morin Inc. More than 1,000 U.S. CEOs left office during the year 2000 alone.

Corporate boards are becoming very impatient with CEO performance, replacing them after only a short time if stock prices do not increase. For example, Richard Thoman of Xerox was replaced after only 13 months at the helm. Lloyd Ward lasted only 15 months at Maytag. Durk Jager led Proctor & Gamble for 17 months, and Michael Hawley was fired after only 17 months with Gillete.

The message being sent by these boards is unmistakable. Managers must constantly work to keep shareholders happy. Holders of equity demand a fair return, and they will fire any manager who does not deliver it.

Source: *Business Week*, December 11, 2000, pp. 86–92.

debt or preferred stock. Consider that the cash flows to bonds are very predictable. We know what the interest payments and final payment are going to be with a high degree of confidence. Similarly, we know what the promised dividend is for preferred stock. No such assurances are available for common stock. Dividends will be paid and grow in the future only if the board of directors so chooses. Because there is more uncertainty with the cost of equity, we use several different methods to compute its cost. If the cost of equity found by all of the methods is similar, we can be more confident that we have computed the correct cost. On the other hand, as often happens, the cost computed by the different methods may not be very similar at all. When this happens, we must reconcile the costs. This reconciliation involves analyzing the inputs to each equation and attaching weights that represent your confidence in these inputs.

Before we dive into evaluating the cost of equity, let us make one important point. Many students assume that equity has no real cost. After all, the firm does not *have* to pay interest or dividends on equity capital. ***In fact, equity is the most expensive type of capital available***. Recall that the capital asset pricing model (CAPM) was introduced in Chapter 7, "Risk and Return." The CAPM computes the return investors require to feel compensated for the risk they incur from holding a firm's equity. If investors require a given return, managers must earn that return or investors will sell the stock. When investors sell stock, its price falls and falling stock prices often result in the replacement of managers. The threat of losing a job is not an idle one. In recent years the chief executive officers of Coca-Cola, Maytag, Proctor & Gamble, and many others all have been replaced. See Box 12.2 for a discussion of CEO turnover. Just since 1993, the median number of years a chief executive stays in his or her job has shrunk from 5 years to 3 in the Dow Jones industrial companies. Furthermore, when a chief executive is terminated, he or she may find it very difficult to find a new position. Firms want to hire winners, not losers. No executive can ignore shareholders or fail to compensate them fairly. ***Equity has a cost that must be paid***.

Clearly it is important to attach a cost to equity. The question is, what does equity cost? Let us review the three popular methods for computing the cost of equity.

Study Tip

Remember that retained earnings are part of the total equity of the firm. Retained earnings are profits that have not been distributed to shareholders. Shareholders expect the firm to earn as much on these funds as the shareholder could had they been distributed.

CAPM

We already noted that the CAPM computes the required return on equity. The required return is the same as the cost to the firm. Therefore, one way to determine the cost of equity is by using the CAPM equation:

$$k_e = R_f + \beta(R_m - R_f)$$

To compute the cost of equity the financial manager must estimate the beta of the firm, the return on the market, and the risk-free rate of interest. In Chapter 7 and again in Chapter 9 we discussed the difficulty investors face when estimating these factors. The financial manager will encounter the same problems. For example, which market index and which period should be used to estimate R_m? Usually, the broader the index and the longer the time period, the better is the estimate. Remember that the goal is to estimate the future long-term return on the market. The past gives only clues, not definitive answers. If the risk of the firm has changed, the historical beta should be adjusted to reflect these anticipated changes.

E X A M P L E   12.3   Cost of Equity Using CAPM

The risk-free rate is 5.5% and the expected return on the market portfolio is 12.5%. What is the cost of equity for a firm with a beta equal to 1.5?

Solution
Using the CAPM equation,

$$k_e = R_f + \beta(R_m - R_f)$$
$$k_e = 0.055 + 1.5(0.125 - 0.055) = 0.16 = 16\%$$

Study Tip

Be sure to use D_1 in the numerator rather than D_0. D_1 is the next dividend paid and may have to be computed by multiplying D_0 by $(1 + g)$, where g is the expected growth rate in dividends.

Gordon Growth Model

Equation 9.7, developed in Chapter 9, shows that the cost of equity can be found as the sum of the dividend yield plus the capital gain:

$$k_e = \frac{D_1}{P_0} + g$$

Equation 9.7 computes the cost of equity given the current market price of the stock, an estimate of next period's dividend (D_1), and the constant growth rate the firm is expected to experience over the long run. In Chapter 9 we noted the difficulty of determining these inputs accurately. This is an especially hard task for firms that do not pay dividends or are experiencing fluctuating growth.

If a firm is paying dividends, then D_0 is known. Because D_1 is equal to $D_0(1 + g)$, the difficult part of applying the Gordon growth model is estimating the growth rate. There are a number of sources of analysts' estimates of growth rates that you can collect. *Valueline* is available in most libraries and has been shown to make better than average growth estimates. *Disclosure,* a CD-ROM–based data source, also reports analysts' growth estimates. A firm's management may predict an entirely different growth rate because of the expanded information set available on which to base its estimate.

E X A M P L E 12.4   **Cost of Equity Using the Gordon Growth Model**

The current stock price of HighTec, Inc. is $25.00. The dividend in 2002 is expected to be $3.00. The dividends for the last 5 years are listed in the following table. What is the cost of equity?

Year	Dividend
2001	$2.75
2000	2.50
1999	2.00
1998	2.30
1997	2.10

Solution

The first step will be to compute the average compounded growth rate in dividends using the method introduced in Chapter 6. Use the equation

$$PV = FV(PVIF)$$

$$\$2.10 = \$2.75(PVIF_{4,g})$$

$$\$2.10 \div 2.75 = 0.7636 = PVIF_{4,g}$$

Go to the PVIF tables and look up the factor on the row corresponding to 4 periods that is closest to 0.7636. This corresponds to a growth rate of 7%.

The second step is to plug the figures into Equation 9.7:

$$k_e = \frac{D_1}{P_0} + g$$

$$k_e = \frac{\$3}{\$25} + 0.07$$

$$k_e = 0.19 = 19\%$$

Bond Yield Plus Premium

A third method used to compute the cost of equity involves adjusting the cost of debt by adding a risk premium. This method is based on the fact that bond yields can be computed with a reasonable degree of accuracy because all of the inputs are known. The bond yield captures certain elements of the risk of the firm. By adding a risk premium that captures the risk particular to equity, a good estimate of the cost of equity is achieved. This method is specified in Equation 12.3:

$$k_e = k_d + \theta \qquad\qquad (12.3)$$

where θ is the equity risk premium.

Most analysts think that the risk premium is usually 3 to 5%. Use 5% for more risky stocks and 3% for less risky ones. A better method for estimating θ is to use historical data to compute k_e and k_d at different points in the past. You should find that θ is fairly stable and the historical risk premium can be used to compute the current cost of equity.

Study Tip

Remember to use the pre-tax cost of debt, not the after-tax cost, in Equation 12.3. This is because the cost of equity is not tax deductible.

E X A M P L E 12.5   Cost of Equity Using the Bond Yield Plus Premium Approach

The pretax cost of debt (k_d) is 8%. If a 3% premium for the risk of equity over debt is appropriate, what is k_e?

Solution

Use Equation 12.3 and plug in values for k_d and θ:

$$k_e = k_d + \theta$$

$$k_e = 8\% + 3\% = 11\%$$

Self-Test Review Question*

The return on the market is 12%. A firm's beta is 1.5 and the risk-free rate is 5%. The stock is currently selling for $20 and the next dividend is expected to be $2.00. The firm's growth rate is 6%. The cost of debt is 12%. Assume that the equity risk premium is 4%. Estimate the cost of equity three ways.

Reconciling the Costs of Equity

In this section we have discussed three methods for accomplishing the same task: computing the cost of equity. These methods are summarized here:

Method	Equation
CAPM	$k_e = R_f + \beta(R_m - R_f)$
Gordon growth model	$k_e = \dfrac{D_1}{P_0} + g$
Bond yield + Premium	$k_e = k_d + \theta$

Suppose that you are interested in computing the cost of equity for a firm. Which method do you use? The answer is to use all of the ones for which you have the required data. *Because each method has inputs that are difficult or impossible to estimate accurately, the more methods we can use, the more confidence we will have in the final result.*

Once you have computed k_e using each technique, we next need to reconcile the results. It is unlikely that each method will yield the same result. In fact, when real company data are applied, very different results are common. We need to determine *one* rate that best represents the true cost of equity capital. There is no clearly established approach to selecting this true cost. One obvious method would be to average the cost of equity as computed by each method. At times, this may be the best approach. However, the analyst might be able to weight one method more highly than another because of more confidence in the inputs to the equation. For example, if the growth rate and dividend stream have been very stable, the analyst may have greater faith in the Gordon

Note that it is not necessary that every method yield exactly the same result.

*(a) 0.05 + 1.5(0.12 − 0.05) = 0.16. (b) ($2/$20) + 0.06 = 0.16. (c) 0.12 + 0.04 = 0.16.

growth model than in the others. Similarly, if the analyst knows that the beta used in the CAPM reflects the historical risk of the firm, but that the firm is now much less risky, she may want to reject the CAPM results.

Retained Earnings Versus New Equity

Eighty percent of all new projects are financed with retained earnings, income that is earned by the firm but not distributed to shareholders. Retained earnings have a different cost than new equity because no flotation costs are incurred. For this reason it is a cheaper source of money than issuing new stock.

To compute the cost of retained earnings, use the current market price of the firm's stock in the Gordon growth model rather than the price minus flotation cost. Note that we used the CAPM and the bond yield plus premium as alternative methods for computing the cost of equity. These models are not helpful when we are attempting to adjust for flotation costs because the price of the security (which we need to be able to adjust) is not part of either equation. For this reason, when adjusting for flotation costs we use the Gordon growth model.

E X A M P L E 12.6   Cost of Retained Earnings Versus New Equity

The current market price of a share of LowTec, Inc. is $25. The firm is expected to continue growing at 5% in the foreseeable future. Flotation costs on new issues of stock will run $2 per share. If the next dividend is expected to be $3, what is the cost of retained earnings and new equity?

Solution

The cost of *retained earnings* is found using the Gordon growth model and the current market price of the stock, not adjusted for flotation costs:

$$k_e = (\$3.00 \div \$25.00) + 0.05 = 0.17 = 17\% \qquad (6.1)$$

The cost of *external equity* is found using the Gordon growth model and the market price of the stock, adjusted for flotation costs:

$$k_e = [\$3.00 \div (\$25.00 - \$2)] + 0.05 = 0.18 = 18\%$$

As a result of the costs associated with selling new stock, new equity costs 18% and retained earnings only cost 17%.

WEIGHTED AVERAGE COST OF CAPITAL (WACC)

In the last several sections we computed the cost of debt, preferred stock, and equity. We now need to combine these cost estimates to find a single cost of capital for a firm. The first step is to determine the firm's target mix of debt, equity, and preferred stock. The target mix is the proportion of each type of financing that results in the lowest average cost of funds. We discuss how the target mix is found in Chapter 13. For now assume that it has already been established.

To find the **weighted average cost of capital (WACC)**, multiply each component's cost by the proportion it occupies in the target mix. This method is specified by Equation 12.4:

$$\text{WACC} = \omega_d k_d (1 - T) + \omega_p k_p + \omega_e k_e \tag{12.4}$$

where

ω_d = proportion of debt in the target capital structure
k_d = cost of debt
ω_p = proportion of preferred stock in the target capital structure
k_p = cost of preferred stock
ω_e = proportion of equity in the target capital structure
k_e = cost of equity
T = the firm's tax rate

Note that the sum of the weights must equal 100% ($\omega_d + \omega_p + \omega_e = 100\%$). A **weighted average** is found by multiplying each cost component by its weight.

Study Tip

Do not include any short-term liabilities when computing the weights to use for the WACC.

E X A M P L E   **12.7**   **Computing Capital Structure Weights**

Use the following data to determine which weights to use when computing the weighted average cost of capital:

Long-term debt = $500,000

Preferred stock = $20,000

Common stock = $600,000

Solution

First, sum components of the firm's capital to compute the total capital in the firm:

Total capital = $500,000 + $20,000 + $600,000 = $1,120,000

Next, divide each component by the total capital:

ω_d = $500,000 ÷ $1,120,000 = 44.64%
ω_p = $20,000 ÷ $1,120,000 = 1.79%
ω_e = $600,000 ÷ $1,120,000 = 53.57%

Now, verify that the percentages are correct by testing whether they sum to 100%:

44.64% + 1.79% + 53.57% = 100%

It is often difficult for firm outsiders to determine a firm's target capital structure. The proportions of different types of capital may change frequently over time. Certainly no firm raises all types of funds at one time. Instead, a firm will raise one type at a particular time, then, when additional funds are needed, another type of security will be issued so that the target capital structure is approximately maintained. Firm management will know what this target mix is; however, outside analysts must guess. The usual method for outsiders to estimate the target capital structure is to look at the average capital mix over the last several years. Target weights could be based on either the accounting values shown on the firm's balance sheet or the market values of the different securities. Although the market value approach is theoretically more accurate, book value weights may be used if security prices have not changed substantially.

Remember that the preferred method of computing the weighted average cost of capital is to use weights based on the firm's *target* capital structure. Only when target weights are unavailable should other methods be substituted. The reason for this preference is that the WACC is a rate to use in evaluating long-term projects. We need to develop it using the mix of securities that will make up the firm's capital structure over this same period of time. In the long run the firm can be expected to achieve its targets.

In the next example we put everything together to compute the WACC.

E X A M P L E 12.8   Computing the WACC

The pretax cost of debt is 10%. The cost of preferred stock is 11% and the cost of equity is 13%. The firm's capital structure is composed of 40% debt, 10% preferred stock, and 50% equity. The tax rate is 40%. What is the firm's weighted average cost of capital after tax?

Solution
Plug the given figures into Equation 12.4 as shown here:

$$\text{WACC} = \omega_d k_d (1 - T) + \omega_p k_p + \omega_e k_e$$

$$\text{WACC} = 0.40 \times 0.10 \times (1 - 0.4) + 0.10 \times 0.11 + 0.50 \times 0.13$$

$$\text{WACC} = 0.10 = 10\%$$

The weighted average cost of capital after tax is 10%.

Self-Test Review Questions*

1. A firm has long-term debt of $50,000, common equity of $100,000, and preferred stock of $15,000. What is its current capital structure?
2. If debt costs 10% pretax, preferred stock costs 13%, and equity costs 15%, what is the WACC (assuming a 40% tax rate)?

USING THE WACC

In Chapters 10 and 11 we learned how to compute net present values and internal rates of return. To compute a net present value you discount the future cash flows back to the

Box 12.3 Cost of Capital Is Not Always a Factor

In a recent article in *CFO* magazine, Hans Storr, the CFO of Philip Morris, admitted that his firm virtually ignored the cost of capital when evaluating the largest acquisition in its history. In 1985, the company decided to diversify by purchasing General Foods. When asked why the cost of capital was not an issue, Hans Storr responded that the acquisition was a strategic decision. "We looked at the businesses where we would want to perform and where there were opportunities. The opportunities were very limited. So the question of what was available was a big factor. When we zeroed in on General Foods, we went through a detailed analysis of market share, their strategic decisions, the products they have, their cash flow, their related businesses, how they are structured, how they are internationally, what businesses they had in our core area. In the final analysis, cost of capital was not a factor."

Stephen Ross, a leading finance theorist at Yale University, responds that he is not surprised. "I used to tell people that whenever a company called a particular decision 'strategic,' it was because it was a negative net present value decision that they wanted to undertake. But I think, in fact, strategic decisions are extraordinarily difficult to make."

Source: "Capital Ideas: A Conversation with Hans Storr and Stephen Ross," *CFO*, April 1996.

present and subtract the present value of the cost of the project. The calculation of NPV requires that we have a discount factor. Up to now we simply assumed that we knew the required return to the firm and used this rate. Similarly, the decision criterion for the internal rate of return required that the project's IRR exceed the firm's required rate of return to be acceptable. We now have the ability to compute the required return. A firm must earn at least the WACC or the value of the firm will fall. ***Thus, the WACC is the firm's required return.***

We should recognize that when firms make decisions, not all factors can be quantified easily. At times, even sophisticated companies have to abandon NPV and the cost of capital in their decision-making processes. Box 12.3 discusses one such example.

EXTENSION 12.1

Marginal Cost of Capital Schedule

In the preceding discussion of the cost of capital, we assumed that the costs of each component remained constant regardless of how much capital was raised. This is not always true. In the early 1980s, for example, Drexel Securities earned tremendous fees by selling high-risk bonds, called junk bonds, to finance acquisitions. Firms with low levels of debt would borrow large amounts of capital by selling these junk bonds. The resulting high debt–equity ratio made these bonds more risky and increased their cost to the borrower substantially. The issuers of these securities usually tried to pay them off as rapidly as possible by selling portions of the acquisition or by otherwise recapitalizing the firm. The point is that as the debt ratio increased, the cost of debt also increased. The reason for this increase in cost is that as additional dollars of a particular type of security are raised, the risk to the buyer of the security increases. This increased risk is reflected in a higher required return.

Debt is not the only type of capital that increases in cost as more is used. Consider Applebee's International, a slightly upscale restaurant chain. It has about $100 million in equity and $30 million in debt. Suppose the firm chose to undertake an aggressive expansion plan and wanted to maintain its current debt–equity ratio. Suppose for simplicity that all of the firm's equity is retained earnings held as cash. $100 million can be spent without changing the firm's debt–equity ratio. Now suppose that the expansion program will cost the firm $150 million. With only $100 million in the bank, the firm is $50 million short of what it needs. To maintain its target capital structure it will have to sell new equity as well as issue bonds.

We must first compute the percentage of the firm's capital it has in debt and equity. The firm's total capital is the sum of its debt and its equity, $130 million ($100 million + $30 million = $130 million). The percentage in debt is $30/$130 = 23.08%. The percentage of its capital coming from equity is $100/$130 = 76.92%.

If Applebee's is $50 million short, we must next determine how much of the $50 million it will raise from equity and how much it will raise from debt. To maintain its capital structure, 23.08% must come from debt or $11.54 million ($50 × 0.2308 = $11.54) and 76.92% must come from equity or $38.46 million ($50 × 0.7692 = $38.46).

Since new stock must be sold to the public and this sale will require the services of investment banks, new stock will have a higher cost than retained earnings. The costs of issuing new equity are called *flotation costs* and they can increase the cost of capital to the firm.

If a firm's **capital budget** (the total of what it plans to spend on new capital projects) can be financed without any increase in the cost of financing, then the WACC calculated in the last section should be used to evaluate the new project and investment ideas. On the other hand, if an increase in cost will result, as with Applebee's, then a **marginal cost of capital** must be calculated.

Marginal Cost

The marginal cost refers to the cost of the last dollar. For example, the marginal tax rate is the tax paid on the last dollar earned. The marginal cost of capital is the cost of the last dollar raised. As more dollars are raised they become increasingly risky and therefore more costly.

In Figure 12.1 a marginal cost of capital schedule is put on the same graph with an investment opportunity schedule. The **marginal cost of capital schedule** shows the cost of capital as additional dollars are raised, whereas the **investment opportunity schedule** shows the return available on various investments. The firm must decide which of these investments to accept. Shareholder wealth is increased only if the cost of capital is less than the expected return on investments. Projects A, B, and C are acceptable because their expected return exceeds the cost of capital. Projects D and E are not acceptable because the cost of capital exceeds the expected return. If only projects A and B were being considered, we would simply use the WACC computed in the last section. But because the firm has investment opportunities that would require raising funds from more expensive sources, a marginal cost schedule is needed. Notice that Project D is acceptable using the WACC, but not when the marginal cost of capital is considered. In

FIGURE 12.1
Marginal Cost of Capital and Investment Opportunity Schedules

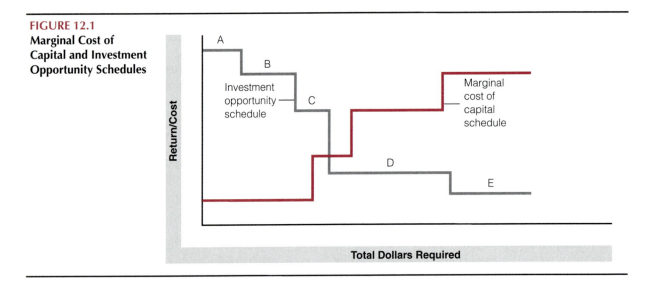

the next section we see how marginal cost of capital schedules are prepared. We first find the points at which the cost of capital increases, and then we compute the cost of capital at each new level of financing.

Finding Break Points

The point in Figure 12.1 where the cost of capital increases is called the **break point**. The break point is found by dividing the amount of funds of a particular type available before costs increase by the weight in the capital structure of that type of capital. The following equation can be used to compute the break points:

$$BP_i = \frac{TC_i}{\omega_i} \qquad (12.5)$$

where

> **Study Tip**
>
> Note that the percentage in the denominator of Equation 12.5 is in decimal form. You will not get the right answer if you use the percentage form of the weight.

BP_i = break point for a particular type of capital i
TC_i = amount of funds of a particular type of capital available at a particular cost
ω_i = weight of capital of type i in the capital structure (in decimal form)

The break point (BP) is the point where total financing will use up one type of capital. For example, if debt and equity are used in equal amounts and the firm has $1,000 of retained earnings, the break point will be at $2,000 ($1,000/0.5 = $2,000). This is because $1,000 will come from debt and the other $1,000 will be the retained earnings.

E X A M P L E   12.9   Computing Break Points

Compute the break point for retained earnings for Harley-Davidson. The firm has $57.355 million in long-term debt and $238 million total equity. Retained earnings from last year that are available for investment are $5 million.

Solution

The first step is to compute the weights of debt and equity in the capital structure. We will use the book value because we do not know either the target or market value of the debt and equity. The weights are computed here:

Capital Structure

	Millions	Percent
Long-term debt	$57.355	19.42%
Total equity	238.000	80.58
Total of debt and equity	$295.355	100.00%

The weight of retained earnings is 80.58%. The next step is to determine how much in total could be spent before new stock would have to be sold. This is done using Equation 12.5:

$$BP = \frac{\$5 \text{ million}}{0.8058} = \$6,205,013.65$$

Harley-Davidson can spend a total of $6,205,013 before it will have to issue additional equity if it wants to maintain its current capital structure. The $6,205,013 is composed of $5 million from retained earnings ($6,205,013 × 0.8058 = $5 million) plus $1,205,013 from new debt that will be issued. The break point is shown in Figure 12.2.

Break Point Calculation

Long-term debt	$1,205,013	19.42%
Retained earnings	5,000,000	80.58
New debt and equity	$6,205,013	100.00%

There may be many break points, as demonstrated in Figure 12.1. To find more than one break point, simply repeat the steps shown in Example 12.9. Divide the amount of each form of capital that is subject to increasing cost by its weight in the firm's capital

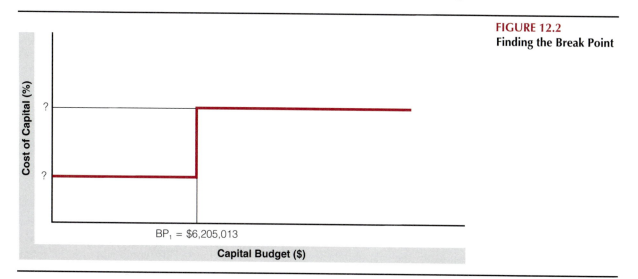

FIGURE 12.2
Finding the Break Point

structure. If the same type of capital has multiple break points, add previous BPs together to find subsequent ones.

Calculating the Weighted Marginal Cost of Capital (WMCC)

Once the break points have been found, we need to compute the **weighted marginal cost of capital (WMCC)**. The WMCC is the weighted average cost of capital at each break point. The first WMCC is found by computing the weighted average cost of capital between $0 and the first BP. The next WMCC is computed for the cost of capital between the first BP and the second. This continues until all WMCCs have been computed. In our Harley-Davidson example, there is only one break point. Therefore, two costs must be computed: one for capital expenditures below the break point, and one for expenditures above the break point.

Compute the cost of capital from $0 to the first BP by computing the WMCC using all of the lowest component costs. Find the WMCC between the first break point and the second by using the component costs from the first step and substitute in the cost of the component that has increased. An example should make this clear.

E X A M P L E 12.10   Computing the WMCC

In Example 12.9 we found the weights for debt and equity in the capital structure to be 19.42% and 80.58%, respectively. We also determined that after a total of $6,205,013 was spent, new equity must be issued. Assuming that the cost of debt is 7%, retained earnings are 12%, and the cost of new equity after flotation costs is 13%, compute the WMCC for Harley-Davidson. Assume a 40% tax bracket.

Solution
The WMCC from $0 to $6,205,013 is computed using Equation 12.4:

$$\text{WACC} = \omega_d k_d (1 - T) + \omega_p k_p + \omega_e k_e$$

$$\text{WMCC}_{0 \text{ to BP1}} = 0.1942(0.07)(1 - 0.40) + (0.8058)(0.12)$$

$$\text{WMCC}_{0 \text{ to BP1}} = 0.1049 = 10.49\%$$

Notice that the cost of capital below the first break point is computed using all of the lowest costs of each component.

The WMCC *above* $6,205,013 is also computed using Equation 12.4. The cost of equity must be increased to reflect the added cost of issuing new equity:

$$\text{WMCC}_{\text{above } \$6,205,013} = 0.1942(0.07)(1 - 0.40) + (0.8058)(0.13)$$

$$\text{WMCC}_{\text{above } \$6,205,013} = 0.1129 = 11.29\%$$

Figure 12.3 shows the WMCC schedule for Harley-Davidson. If the firm's capital budget was significantly more than $6,205,013, additional WMCCs would be required. Presumably, the cost of debt would rise at some point. This would add another break point and another WMCC.

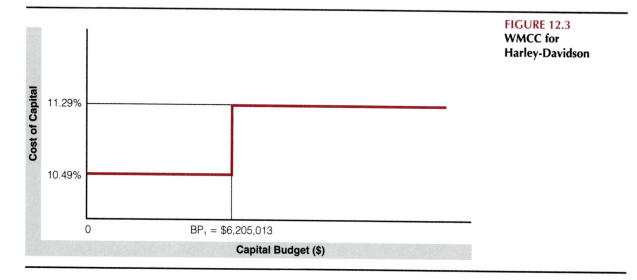

FIGURE 12.3
WMCC for Harley-Davidson

Calculating the Cost of New Equity

When new equity must be issued, the issuing firm will have to pay flotation costs. These costs reduce the amount the firm will receive from the issue and increase its cost of equity. We have three methods that we use to compute the cost of equity, the CAPM, the bond yield plus premium, and the Gordon growth model. Only the Gordon growth model (discounted cash flow method), however, allows the price to be adjusted to reflect

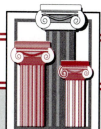

Careers in Finance

Personal Financial Planner

Personal financial planners help individuals determine whether and how they can meet their life goals through the proper management of their financial resources. In addition to the opportunity to earn a good income, a personal financial planner has the satisfaction of helping people from all walks of life solve their financial problems and reach their financial goals. A financial professional in planning often chooses to become a Certified Financial Planner (CFP).

Before applying for the Certification Examination, a candidate must first study financial planning topics. Typical college course titles covered by the curriculum include investments, estate planning, individual income tax, retire-

ment planning, risk management, insurance, and finance. Completion of the education requirement is available through three educational paths: CFP Board Registered Program, Transcript Review, or Challenge Status.

When you have successfully fulfilled the education requirement, you are eligible to apply for the CFP Certification Examination. The Certification Examination is designed to assess your ability to apply your financial planning education to financial planning situations in an integrated format, thereby protecting the public by assuring that you are at the level of competency required for practice. To learn more about becoming CFP certified, go to www.cfp-board.org/index.html.

the costs incurred from paying investment bankers. This causes a problem. In using all of the methods to compute an average cost of equity, the firm can only adjust one method for flotation costs. The problem is solved by finding how much flotation costs increase the cost of equity. Use the discounted cash flow method, and then add this increase to the average of the three methods found without flotation costs.

E X A M P L E   12.11   Computing the Cost of Equity with Flotation Costs

The cost of equity found using the CAPM is 11%. The cost of equity found using the bond yield plus a premium is 12.5%. The current price of the stock is $25 and the next dividend is expected to be $2. The growth rate is 4%. Flotation costs are expected to be $2 per share. What is the cost of equity before and after adjusting for flotation costs, assuming equal weighting of the three methods?

Solution
The cost of equity using the Gordon growth model is

$$\frac{\$2}{\$25} + 0.04 = 0.12 = 12\%$$

The average cost of equity, assuming equal weights, is

$$\frac{11\% + 12.5\% + 12\%}{3} = 11.83\%$$

The cost of equity after flotation costs using the Gordon growth model is

$$\frac{\$2}{(\$25 - \$2)} + 0.04 = 0.127 = 12.7\%$$

To find the increase in cost due to flotation, compare the cost with and without flotation when computed using the discounted cash flow method:

$$12.7\% - 12\% = 0.7\%$$

Now add this difference to the average cost of equity:

$$11.83\% + 0.7\% = 12.53\%$$

The cost of equity after allowing for the cost of flotation is 12.53%.

Once you have computed all of the break points and WMCCs, you superimpose the investment opportunity schedule on the marginal cost of capital schedule. Select the investments that have a higher return than the cost of funds at that level of expenditure.

Self-Test Review Questions*

A firm is 40% debt and 60% equity. The after-tax cost of debt is 6% and the cost of retained earnings is 12%. New equity will cost 14%.
1. If the firm has $100,000 in retained earnings, what is the break point?
2. What is the WACC above and below the break point?

CHAPTER SUMMARY

If investment decisions were made based on what the next increment of funds would cost, it is possible that bad projects would be accepted and good ones that occur later would be rejected. To avoid this problem, we compute an average cost of funds. This average cost is found in a three-step process:

1. Compute the cost of each component of the firm's capital (i.e., the cost of debt, the cost of equity, and the cost of preferred stock).
2. Determine the firm's target capital structure.
3. Compute a weighted average assuming that over the long run the target capital structure will be maintained.

The cost of debt is found by computing the yield to maturity, as was done in Chapter 8. This yield to maturity is multiplied by $(1 - T)$ to give the firm's after-tax cost of borrowing. The cost of preferred stock is computed by rearranging the preferred stock valuation equation so that we can solve for k_p. It is more difficult to solve for the cost of equity because we do not have confidence in any of our valuation models. As a result, we compute the cost of equity using three methods: the CAPM, the Gordon growth model, and the bond yield plus a premium. The analyst will evaluate which method

has the best inputs in a given situation to determine the reconciled cost of equity.

The percentage of each type of capital is found by computing the percentage of each component in the firm's target capital structure. Firm managers know what the percentages are. Outsiders must estimate them based on the firm's balance sheet.

Once the cost of each component and the target weights are known, the weighted average cost of capital after tax is found by computing a weighted average. This is the figure that is used in capital budgeting decision making.

As additional funds are raised, their costs often increase. If the firm is evaluating a capital budget that will require it to raise large amounts of capital, it may need to compute a weighted marginal cost of capital after tax. This technique requires that the analysis estimate when break points will occur and what cost will be associated with each new level of financing.

In this chapter we used the existing distribution of debt and equity as representative of the firm's target capital structure. We address how the firm may choose its capital structure in Chapter 13.

KEY WORDS

break point 332	investment opportunity	marginal cost of capital	weighted average cost of
capital budget 331	schedule 331	schedule 331	capital (WACC) 328
capital structure 317	marginal cost of capital 331	weighted average 328	weighted marginal cost of
flotation costs 319			capital (WMCC) 334

DISCUSSION QUESTIONS

1. Why is it incorrect to use the cost of financing that will apply to a particular project when evaluating whether to accept that project?
2. Explain the advantage to using an average cost of funds to evaluate whether to accept a project.
3. What types of funds make up the capital of a firm? (Hint: What is firm capital?)
4. How do you compute the cost of debt?
5. Why do you multiply the cost of debt by $(1 - T)$, without so adjusting the other sources of capital?
6. What model is used to compute the cost of preferred stock? Is it adjusted for taxes?
7. The chapter introduces three methods for estimating the cost of equity. Why not use just one of the methods?

8. What are the three methods for computing the cost of equity? Which is preferred? How would you reconcile the different methods?
9. What are flotation costs and what do they do to the cost of new equity?
10. What is a weighted average cost of capital? How is it computed? Where do you obtain the weights to use when computing the weighted average?
11. What happens to the cost of capital as additional funds are raised? (Extension 12.1)
12. What is the difference between the weighted marginal cost of capital and the weighted average cost of capital? (Extension 12.1)
13. What is a break point and how do you find it? (Extension 12.1)

PROBLEMS

1. Calculate the after-tax cost of debt under each of the following conditions:
   a. Interest rate = 10%; tax rate = 10%
   b. Interest rate = 8%; tax rate = 20%
   c. Interest rate = 12%; tax rate = 10%

2. National Bank just issued a new 20-year, noncallable bond at par. This bond requires a 15% coupon rate with semiannual payments and has a par value of $1,000. The tax rate is 40%. What is the cost of debt?

3. Tiny Tots has debt outstanding currently selling for $1,100. It matures in 10 years, pays interest annually, and has a 10% coupon payment. Par is $1,000 and the firm's tax rate is 40%. What is the cost of debt?

4. Rover's Dog Care has outstanding debt currently selling for $890. It matures in 5 years, pays interest semiannually, and has an 8% coupon payment. If par is $1,000 and the tax rate is 40%, what is the cost of debt?

5. Growfast Construction has preferred stock outstanding that pays $2.00 per year. The current market price of the preferred stock is $15. What is the cost of preferred stock to Growfast?

6. MCG Company decided to sell perpetual (never matures) preferred stock with an 8% yield (pays out 8% of par as dividend). If the stock had a par value of $150 and the stated flotation costs would amount to 2% of the par value, what is the component cost of perpetual preferred stock?

7. The Treasury bond rate is currently 6% and the market return was last reported to be 12%. National Bank has a beta of 1. What is the cost of retained earnings?

8. Fred's Lawn and Garden's last dividend per share was $1.10. The stock sells for $30 per share. The expected growth rate for the company is 5%. Calculate the company's cost of retained earnings.

9. Sam's Manufacturing projects net income to be $12,000, and its payout ratio is 35%. (Recall that a payout ratio is the percentage of net income that is distributed as dividends to shareholders.) The company's earnings and dividends are growing at a 4% constant rate, the last dividend was $1.00, and the current stock price is $8.00. Sam's Manufacturing can raise debt at a 10% before-tax cost. If Sam's Manufacturing issues new common stock, a 10% flotation cost will be incurred. Sam's target structure is 30% debt and 70% equity, and the firm's tax rate is 40%.
   a. What is the firm's cost of equity when it uses retained earnings?

b. What is the firm's cost of new common equity?
   c. What is the weighted average cost of capital using the retained earnings?
   d. What is the weighted average cost of capital using the new common stock?
   e. What is Sam's break point for retained earnings? (Extension 12.1)
   f. Graph the marginal cost of capital schedule. (Extension 12.1)

10. Braxton Company's long-term debt yields 12%. It could sell preferred stock with an $8 annual dividend for $80, but flotation costs would be 5%. The firm's beta is 1.1, the risk-free rate is 7%, and the required rate of return on the market is 12%. Braxton's next dividend is estimated to be $2.00, and it is growing at a constant rate of 4%. The firm's stock is selling for $25 per share. Its estimate of the risk premium for stocks versus bonds is 1%. Braxton's target capital structure is 30% debt, 10% preferred stock, and 60% common stock. The firm expects $50,000 in retained earnings and must incur flotation costs of 10% on new common stock sales. Its tax rate is 40%.
    a. What is the firm's after-tax cost of debt?
    b. What is Braxton's cost of preferred stock?
    c. What is the firm's cost of retained earnings? (Use all three methods.)
    d. What is the firm's weighted average cost of capital using retained earnings as the equity component?
    e. What is the cost of new common equity?
    f. What is the weighted average cost of capital using common stock?

11. Bilge Brothers has $50,000 of retained earnings. Their target capital structure calls for 30% debt and 70% equity. (Extension 12.1)
    a. How much can Bilge Brothers raise in total before they will need to sell additional equity? (Hint: What is the break point?)
    b. Show how much of the capital raised in part a comes from retained earnings and how much comes from debt financing.

12. Skipper's Sea Salvage has $100,000 of retained earnings. The current market price of its stock is $20 and it pays a dividend of $2.00. The firm's growth rate equals 0. If new stock must be sold, it will cost $3.00 per share in flotation costs. The target capital structure calls for 40% debt and 60% equity. (Extension 12.1)

a. What is the break point?
b. What is the cost of equity below the break point and above the break point?

13. Watson Company uses only debt and equity in its capital structure. It can borrow unlimited amounts at an interest rate of 12% as long as it finances at its target capital structure, which calls for 60% debt and 40% common equity. Its last dividend was $1.00; its expected constant growth rate is 5%; its stock sells for $8; and new stock would net the company $7 per share after flotation costs. Watson's tax rate is 40%, and it expects to have $10 million of retained earnings this year. (Extension 12.1)

a. What is Watson's cost of equity from newly issued stock?
b. What is Watson's cost of equity from retained earnings?
c. Prepare Watson's marginal cost of capital schedule showing at what expenditure the break point occurs and what the WACC is above and below the break point. Add projects A and B to the schedule and identify which would be accepted.

SELF-TEST PROBLEMS

1. The current market price of a $1,000 par bond is $925. Its semiannual coupon rate is 7% and it matures in 5 years. What is the pretax cost of debt (k_d)?

2. The current market price of a $1,000 par bond is $1,025. Its semiannual coupon rate is 7% and it matures in 5 years. What is the pretax cost of debt (k_d)?

3. What is the after-tax cost of debt using the data from problem 1 and assuming a 40% marginal tax rate?

4. What is the after-tax cost of debt using the data from problem 2 and assuming a 40% tax rate?

5. What is the cost of preferred stock financing if it pays a constant dividend of $3.00 and is currently selling for $35.00 per share?

6. What is the after-tax cost of preferred stock using the data from problem 5?

7. Use CAPM to compute the cost of equity given that the firm's beta is 1.1, the risk-free rate is 6%, and the return on the market is 13%.

8. Use the Gordon growth model to compute the cost of equity given that the next dividend is expected to be $2.00, the current price is $30.00, and the expected growth rate is 8%.

9. The *last* dividend paid was $1.50. What is the cost of equity using the Gordon growth model assuming a current price of $25.00 and an expected growth rate of 7%?

10. Use the data from problem 2 and assume the bond yield premium is 4% to compute the cost of equity.

11. Assume you have equal faith in each method used to compute the cost of equity. Use the results from problems 7, 8, and 10, assuming that these problems all discuss the same firm, to compute the cost of equity.

12. Again using the solutions to problems 7, 8, and 10, find the cost of equity assuming you are twice as confident in the CAPM approach as you are in either of the other two approaches to finding the cost of equity. (Weights are therefore 50%, 25%, and 25%.)

13. A firm currently has long-term debt totaling $1,500,000, preferred stock totaling $250,000, and equity outstanding of $3,000,000. Using the answers to problems 4, 5, and 12, assuming that these problems all discuss the same firm, compute the weighted average cost of capital.

14. If the firm discussed in problem 13 had outstanding current debt of $100,000, would the WACC change?

15. If the firm discussed in problem 13 has $125,000 of retained earnings this year, what is the break point for equity? (Extension 12.1)

16. If the firm discussed in problem 13 can sell $100,000 in bonds before the cost of debt will rise, what is the break point for debt? (Extension 12.1)

17. If the firm discussed in problem 13 can sell $50,000 of preferred stock before the cost of preferred stock rises, what is the break point for preferred stock? (Extension 12.1)

18. How much in total capital can be raised, using the assumptions discussed in problems 15, 16, and 17, before the WACC will increase? (Extension 12.1)

19. What is the WACC before the break point using the results of problem 13 and 15–17? (Extension 12.1)

20. What is the WACC after the break point using the results of problems 13 and 15–18 and assuming that new equity can be sold at a cost of 15%? (Extension 12.1)

WEB EXPLORATION

1. There is help available on the Web for computing the cost of capital for a firm. Go to www.valtechs.com/costofcapital.html. This site has a number of cost of capital calculators. After reviewing the site, choose section I and vary the Percent of Total Capital until you obtain the lowest average cost of capital.

2. Go to www.stern.nyu.edu/~adamodar/New_Home_Page/datafile/wacc.htm. This site contains a listing of the cost of capital for a large number of industries. Which industry has the highest cost of capital? Which has the lowest? What is the average cost of capital for the whole market?

MINI CASE

As a management consultant for Anderson Consulting, you have been retained by Weems and Plath to compute their cost of capital. You are surprised to learn that they have never bothered to determine this for themselves. They have been using 15% in their capital budgeting analysis but did not know if this was correct. You gather the following information:

Current liabilities	$200
Notes payable	400
Long-term debt	1,000
Preferred stock	100
Retained earnings	400
Common stock	1,200
Total liabilities and equity	$3,300

Bonds currently sell for $1,150. They have a 10% coupon paid semiannually, a $1,000 par, and 15 years to maturity. Preferred stock has a $3 dividend and is currently selling for $35. The beta of the company is 1.25 and the risk-free rate is 4%. The market has an expected return of 10%. The current price of the stock is $20. Its next dividend is expected to be $1.75 and its expected growth rate is 3%. Common stock sells at a premium of 3% over bonds. The firm's tax rate is 40%.

a. Using the data given:
  i. Compute the cost of debt.
  ii. Compute the cost of preferred stock.
  iii. Compute the cost of equity using CAPM.
  iv. Compute the cost of equity using the Gordon growth model.
  v. Compute the cost of equity using the bond yield plus premium approach.
  vi. Compute a single cost of equity by equally weighting the three costs of equity found above.
b. Compute the firm's capital structure weights.
c. Compute the WACC given the above information.
d. Now assume that the firm will have to issue new stock to fund its capital budget and that flotation costs will be 4% of the firm's stock price. Compute the new WACC.

The Theory of Capital Structure

Chapter Objectives

By the end of this chapter you should be able to:

1. Understand why leverage affects stockholder wealth
2. Discuss the different types of leverage
3. Perform breakeven analysis
4. Discuss the principal theories of capital structure
5. Compute the EBIT–EPS indifference point

An important question to managers is, What proportion of each source of funds will result in the lowest average cost of funds? When funds are less costly, the denominator in the dividend growth model equation is smaller and the price of the stock is higher. Because the goal of financial managers is to maximize stockholder wealth, determining the optimal mix of debt and equity is important. The mix of debt, equity, and preferred stock is the **capital structure** of the firm. In Chapter 12 we began our study of how a firm optimizes its capital structure by determining how to compute the average cost of capital. We now continue this discussion by studying the theories and techniques for optimizing a firm's capital structure.

DETERMINANTS OF THE DEBT–EQUITY DECISION

In Chapter 12 we learned to compute the cost of capital given a target capital structure. The target capital structure is the one that minimizes the firm's cost of capital. When the cost of long-term funds is at its lowest, the value of the firm will be maximized. The purpose of this chapter is to examine how that target capital structure is determined. You will find that this is an area of finance in which exact calculations are not possible. Both academics and practitioners agree that many unanswered questions remain about how the capital structure question should be addressed. Following a brief discussion of leverage, we will review the early theories of capital structure. We will then modify these theories to reflect current ideas on the topic. We then look at different types of leverage and how the level of one type may affect the level of another. Finally, we look at a variety of other factors that may affect the capital structure decision within a firm.

Leverage Is Important

Suppose that you are considering opening a chain of mail-order pizza restaurants. You have two ways to finance this investment. You could use all of your inheritance and have an all-equity firm, or you could finance it with 50% debt and 50% equity. What impact does this have on the earnings per share and return on equity? Table 13.1 reports the two alternatives in Panel A. Panel B reports the earnings per share (EPS) and return on equity (ROE) for three possible sales forecasts assuming the firm is financed entirely with equity. Panel C reports the EPS and ROE for three possible sales forecasts assuming the firm is financed with 50% debt and 50% equity.

TABLE 13.1 Effect of Leverage on EPS and ROE

Panel A

	All Equity	50% Equity
Assets	$1,000	$1,000
Debt	–0	–$500
Equity	$1,000	$500
Debt–equity ratio	0%	100%
Shares outstanding	100	50
Share price	$10	$10
Interest rate on debt	NA	10%

Panel B: All Equity Financing

	Weak Sales	Most Likely Sales	Strong Sales
EBIT	$25	$200	$400
Less interest	–0	–0	–0
Net income	$25	$200	$400
EPS	$0.25	$2	$4
ROE	2.5%	20%	40%

Panel C: 50% Debt Financing

	Weak Sales	Most Likely Sales	Strong Sales
EBIT	$25	$200	$400
Less interest	–$50	–$50	–$50
Net income	($25)	$150	$350
EPS	($0.50)	$3.00	$7.00
ROE	(5%)	30%	70%

We see in Panel B that even with weak sales the all-equity firm earns a profit and reports an ROE of 2.5% ($25 ÷ $1,000 = 2.5%). With strong sales the all-equity firm has an ROE of 40%. In contrast, we see in Panel C that the 50% debt-financed firm suffers a loss of $25 if sales are weak. The ROE is −5%. However, as sales improve the returns rise well above those reported by the all-equity firm.

This table demonstrates both the advantage and disadvantage of using financial leverage. When sales are low, you may not be able to pay your interest expense and could be forced out of business by creditors. This cannot happen to the all-equity firm, because there are no creditors to satisfy. On the other hand, leverage allows the debt-financed firm to take advantage of strong sales more effectively than the all-equity firm. In effect, by using debt, the firm is able to earn money by using someone else's money.

Recall from Chapter 7 that increased variability implies more risk. Table 13.1 demonstrates that increased leverage leads to increased variability in ROE, which explains why firms are considered to be more risky when they are leveraged.

The effect of leverage is also demonstrated by Figure 13.1. The relationships between earnings before interest and taxes (EBIT) from different levels of sales are plotted against the resulting EPS. The debt firm has greater EPS above EBIT = $100, but the equity firm has higher EPS below EBIT = $100. The steep slope of the leverage option reflects the greater variability leverage causes. The management of the firm graphed in Figure 13.1 would rather be leveraged if sales are over $100. However, it would rather be debt-free if sales are lower than $100.

This example dramatically demonstrates how the capital structure decision requires a tradeoff between returns and risk. Increasing financial leverage improves returns when times are good, but increases losses when times are bad. We should keep in mind that the goal is not really to maximize earnings per share, but rather to maximize share value. It is possible that as debt increases the risk of the firm will cause the stock price to fall despite increasing EPS. We will return to this discussion in the last section of this chapter.

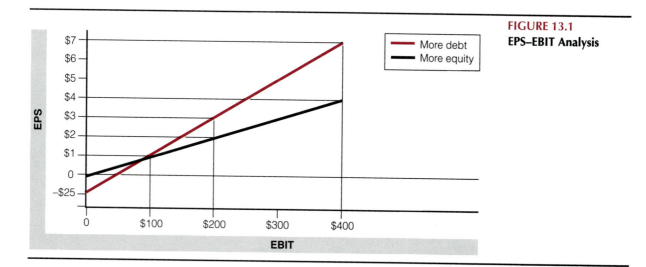

FIGURE 13.1

EPS–EBIT Analysis

Target Capital Structure

Financial managers want to know what specific capital structure is best for their firm. Even within industries we sometimes see very different capital structures. What factors influence the debt–equity decision? Before discussing this question further, let us look at the goal of the optimal capital structure.

Optimal Capital Structure Maximizes the Firm's Value

In Chapter 1 we developed the idea that the goal of the financial manager is to maximize firm value. When the WACC is minimized, the value of the firm is maximized. This is because the WACC is the appropriate discount rate for the firm's cash flows. As the discount rate falls, the present value of the cash flows increases. As we learned in Chapter 8, the value of the firm is the present value of the cash flows.

Because the goal of management is to maximize the value of the firm, we conclude that the goal of management includes finding the combination of debt, equity, and preferred stock that minimizes the weighted average cost of capital. This optimal combination is presumed to be the firm's target capital structure.

Why Not All Debt?

In Chapter 12 we computed the component costs of capital. We found that the cost of debt is multiplied by 1 minus the tax rate because interest payments are tax deductible. Additionally, because debt has a higher priority and more predictable cash flows than equity, its pretax cost is less. If debt is so much less expensive to the firm, why not finance 100% with debt?

Table 13.2 illustrates the complexity a firm faces in setting its target capital structure. At zero debt, the WACC is simply the cost of equity. As the proportion of debt increases, the WACC initially decreases. However, at some point the increased debt causes investors to perceive the firm as riskier, and the cost of debt and equity both rise. Eventually, the increased risk overwhelms the tax benefit of debt and the cost of capital rises. In Table 13.2 the optimal capital structure is 40% debt and 60% equity because this provides the lowest possible weighted average cost of capital.

TABLE 13.2 Selecting the Optimal Capital Structure

Percentage of Capital from Debt	Cost of Debt (k_d)	Cost of Equity (k_e)	WACC ($T = 40\%$)
0%	NA	11%	11.00%
10	3%	11	10.08
20	3	11	9.16
30	4	12	9.12
40	5	13	9.00
50	7	15	9.60
60	9	16	9.64
70	11	18	10.02
80	13	20	10.24
90	15	23	10.40
100	18	25	10.80

If each firm knew exactly how increases in debt would affect its component costs, it would be easy to select the correct capital structure. We would prepare a table similar to Table 13.2 and choose the proportion of debt that resulted in the lowest overall cost of capital to the firm. Unfortunately, firms cannot easily prepare such tables. It is time-consuming and costly to alter a firm's capital structure. Additionally, other factors affect the firm simultaneously, making it difficult to isolate the effects of capital structure changes. Given these problems, let us see whether theory can help with the decision.

Self-Test Review Question*

Suppose that your firm was financed with 60% debt and that you were able to prepare statistics about the firm that matched what appears in Table 13.2. What would you recommend regarding changes to the firm's capital structure?

Early Theories

Few topics in finance have received as much attention over the years as the question of what capital structure maximizes firm value. We will start our discussion by reviewing the earliest theories. Unfortunately, these theories assume away many of the complexities that actually exist in the real world. Their value is in establishing a beginning framework on which to build more meaningful theories.

Irrelevance

Merton Miller and Franco Modigliani earned the Nobel prize in economics for their early work on capital structure theory. M&M, as they are commonly called, argued that the capital structure decision is entirely irrelevant in a world without taxes and other costs. ***Their carefully explained theory says that the value of the firm will not be changed by how assets are distributed between bondholders and stockholders***. Rather, the value of the firm is based on the earning power of its assets. Merton Miller explained his theory with an analogy to a pizza. You would not go into a pizza parlor to order a pizza and say, "I'm especially hungry today; slice it a few more times." The size of the pizza does not change with how it is sliced. Similarly, the size or value of the firm does not change with who has claims on it. Figure 13.2 illustrates the irrelevance theory. At every level of debt, the value of the firm is constant.

Capital structure is irrelevant because the cost of equity rises as more debt (and hence more risk) is used. The increase in the cost of equity exactly offsets the increased use of low-cost debt. The result is that at every level of debt, the combined cost of funds is constant, as is the value of the firm.

This concept is also illustrated in Table 13.3. Notice that as the percentage of debt and the cost of debt rise, according to M&M the cost of equity increases by just enough to maintain a constant WACC.

Although the irrelevance theory established a beginning point for discussion, the world is actually more complex than in the M&M simplified model. Specifically, firms do face taxes. M&M next addressed this issue.

FIGURE 13.2
Effect of Leverage on Firm Value Without Taxes

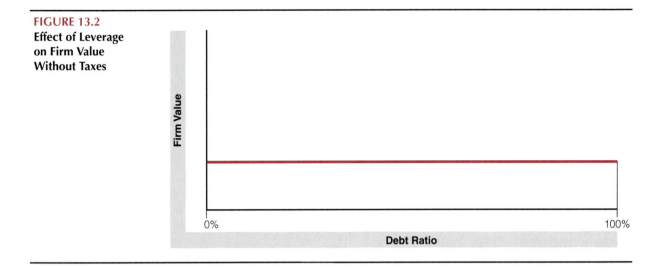

Taxes Favor All Debt

In M&M's second paper they relaxed their assumptions to include taxes. Other costs continued to be assumed away. The result was that, in the presence of taxes, optimal firm value is achieved when the firm is all debt financed. In essence, the government pays a portion of the cost of debt financing but none of the cost of equity financing. This suggests that firms should use as much debt in their balance sheet as possible. Figure 13.3 shows that as additional debt is used, firm value increases.

Self-Test Review Questions*

1. Figure 13.2 graphs the relationship between firm value and debt as a horizontal line. Interpret this graph.
2. Figure 13.3 shows the relationship between firm value and debt as a constantly upward-sloping line. Interpret this graph.

TABLE 13.3 Cost of Capital Without Taxes

Percent Debt in Capital Structure	Cost of Debt	Cost of Equity	WACC
10%	0.06	0.16	0.15
30	0.06	0.19	0.15
50	0.08	0.22	0.15
70	0.10	0.27	0.15
90	0.12	0.42	0.15

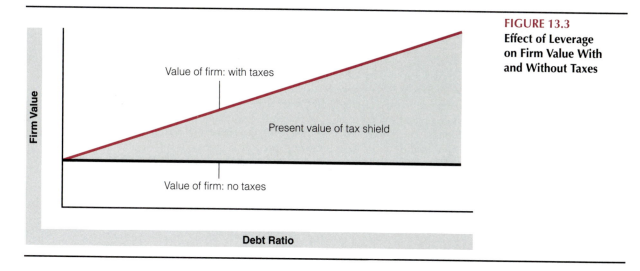

FIGURE 13.3
Effect of Leverage on Firm Value With and Without Taxes

The shaded area shows the value provided by the interest tax shield of debt. Similarly, Table 13.4 demonstrates how the cost of capital can fall when the tax shield reduces the cost of debt to the firm. Because more debt increases this tax shield, why are firms not financed with 100% debt? This question suggests that there must be other issues at work. Table 13.4 shows that the costs of debt and equity rise as additional debt is used. Next, let us investigate why this may happen.

Effect of Agency Costs

As the level of debt increases, the amount of equity shareholders stand to lose falls. This may result in the firm increasing its risk beyond what is acceptable to bondholders. Remember that the goal of the financial manager is to increase *stockholder* wealth. Bondholders may suffer as managers attempt to fulfill this goal. Consider the following example. Suppose that your firm drills wildcat (speculative) wells searching for oil. One in 100 wells is expected to pay. The payoff for a successful well is $1,000,000. First, what is the expected payoff for drilling 100 wells?

$$\text{Expected payoff} = 0.99(0) + 0.01(\$1,000,000) = \$10,000$$

So if thousands of wells are drilled, on average each one will yield $10,000.

TABLE 13.4 Cost of Capital with Tax Shield

Percent Debt in Capital Structure	After-Tax Cost of Debt	Cost of Equity	WACC
10%	0.06(1 − 0.4) = 0.036	0.16	0.148
30	0.06(1 − 0.4) = 0.036	0.19	0.144
50	0.08(1 − 0.4) = 0.048	0.22	0.134
70	0.10(1 − 0.4) = 0.06	0.27	0.123
90	0.12(1 − 0.4) = 0.072	0.42	0.107

Box 13.1 Who's Watching the Managers?

In the late 1970s interest rates rose to record levels. For investors who bought bonds this was great, but to S&Ls that had portfolios full of low-interest-rate mortgage loans, it was terrible. The S&Ls were forced to pay high interest rates to keep deposits, but could earn only low rates on their portfolio of loans. As a result, over 80% of S&Ls were technically bankrupt by 1980. This meant that the institutions had lost all their paid-in equity. Only emergency accounting rules passed by the regulating agencies allowed the S&Ls to stay open. At the same time as the equity levels were falling, the Reagan administration reduced the number of examiners. What was the result?

Because many S&Ls were already bankrupt, shareholders were not concerned with monitoring the actions of managers. After all, shareholders had nothing to lose at this point. If by taking on high-risk, high-return loans there was

a chance to bring the S&L back to profitability, the shareholders would be supportive. Additionally, the government was not adequately staffed to prevent risk taking. In most firms, the debtholders would step in and demand that managers reduce risk taking. The debtholders would be concerned with the firm being unable to pay them back. In the case of S&Ls the debtholders were silent.

To understand why debtholders did not restrict managers we must first determine who the debtholders to an S&L are. They are the depositors. When you make a deposit at a bank or savings institution, that firm owes the money to you. Why were depositors not worried about risk taking by the S&L managers? The reason is because the government insured the deposits against loss. The bottom line was that no one was watching managers and risk taking by S&Ls increased. This eventually led to the $150 billion loss the industry suffered.

Now suppose that an all-equity firm is considering drilling a well. If the cost of drilling is $15,000, it will decide to forgo the effort. On the other hand, suppose that the firm is 90% debt financed. In this case the equity holders will contribute only $1,500, which is 10% of the $15,000 cost. Now the equity holders are risking $1,500 for an investment with an expected value of $10,000. This investment would be accepted. Do bondholders agree with this risky investment? Absolutely not. They stand to lose the most since they will receive their contracted interest payments only if the oil well pays the $1,000,000. The situation exists because managers are the agents of stockholders.

One way to understand a theory is to consider what happens when it is taken to the limit. Suppose a firm had *no* equity. In this case the shareholders would have nothing to lose and everything to gain by taking risk. An example of this occurred when many S&Ls were technically bankrupt. The managers knew that they had nothing to lose by making high-profit high-risk loans. The effect on S&Ls of reduced equity is discussed in Box 13.1.

Bondholders have to expect high risk taking by managers because of the agency relationship as the equity portion of the capital structure falls. To protect themselves, bondholders require the borrowing firm to accept covenants that restrict managers. Additionally, because of the increased chance that the firm will take on risky projects despite their instructions, bondholders demand higher interest rates as equity levels fall.

Effect of Bankruptcy Costs

A firm does not have to declare bankruptcy to incur bankruptcy costs. As the debt–equity ratio increases, so does the probability of bankruptcy. Technically, bankruptcy occurs when the value of a firm's assets is less than its debts. The formal cost of filing with the bankruptcy court, paying attorneys, and so forth are the direct bankruptcy costs. These have been estimated to be small compared with the indirect costs. Indirect bankruptcy costs arise because a firm facing financial distress must work to recover its economic health. ***In addition to the managerial time and effort that will be extended dealing with creditors and attorneys, there may be a loss of customers and key employees***.

Customers tend to avoid buying durable goods from financially weak firms. Chrysler Motor Co. was in danger of failing in the early 1970s. Sales suffered because customers did not want to buy a car from a company that might not survive to perform warranty work and supply parts. In the late 1990s, Apple Computer faced the same problem. Even die-hard Apple fans were reluctant to buy Apple computers out of concern that the firm might not survive to service the units.

An additional indirect cost of bankruptcy is that key employees tend to seek new employment when a firm's probability of bankruptcy increases. It is widely believed that it is more difficult to find a job if you are currently unemployed. To reduce the risk of unemployment, the people most able to find other jobs often leave. Because these are often the most valuable employees, this can be very costly for a firm.

Putting the Costs and Benefits Together

As debt increases, the WACC initially falls because the firm benefits from the interest tax shield. However, as debt continues to increase, agency costs and bankruptcy costs increase as well. At some point these costs exceed the benefit of the tax shield. After this point, increased debt causes firm value to fall. ***The optimal capital structure occurs when the costs of the agency and bankruptcy costs just equal the benefits of using debt***. Figure 13.4 shows the optimal capital structure with taxes, agency costs, and bankruptcy costs. Maximum firm value occurs at the apex of the curve that includes taxes, agency, and bankruptcy costs.

Not all firms have the same optimal capital structure, because different firms are affected differently by the costs. For example, a motel chain has small indirect bankruptcy costs because its customers do not care about the firm's continued survival.

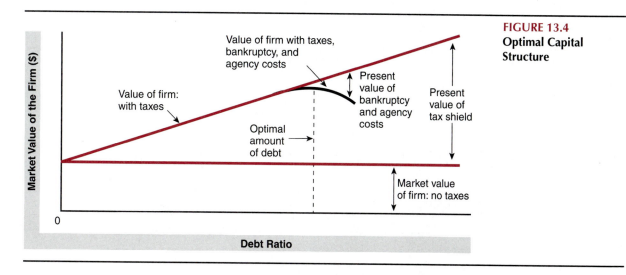

FIGURE 13.4
Optimal Capital Structure

Utilities have lower agency costs than other firms because they are so heavily regulated that managers have little opportunity to engage in risky investments. This is one more reason why firms within an industry often have similar capital structures.

What have we learned from this discussion? First, there is a tradeoff between the benefits of debt and the cost of the increased risk that comes with it. The amount of the increase in risk varies from one firm to another and from one industry to another. Analysts tend to rate firms based on how they compare with other similar firms. A poor investment rating can result for firms that deviate too far from the norm.

Self-Test Review Question*

Why does the curve in Figure 13.4 reach a maximum and then head back down?

There Is More Than One Type of Leverage

In the above discussion we examined one type of leverage, financial leverage. **Financial leverage** is increased by having greater amounts of debt in the capital structure of the firm. In fact, there are different types of leverage. Another type of leverage is called **operating leverage**. Operating leverage increases with the level of fixed assets. **Total leverage** is the product of financial leverage and operating leverage. The total risk of the firm is determined by total leverage. A firm can lower its risk by reducing either financial or operating leverage. Let us discuss each type of leverage in greater detail.

Financial Leverage

Study Tip

The percentage change is computed by subtracting the beginning level from the ending level, dividing this amount by the beginning level, and multiplying by 100.

The degree of financial leverage (DFL) is computed by Equation 13.1:

$$\text{DFL} = \frac{\text{Percent change in EPS}}{\text{Percent change in EBIT}} \tag{13.1}$$

Suppose that EBIT increases by 10%. If EPS increases by 20%, the DFL is 2 (0.20/0.10 = 2). The greater the change in EPS given a change in EBIT, the greater the

---

TABLE 13.5 Income Statement for Three Sales Levels

Unit sales	50	100	150		
Sales	$ 50.00	$100.00	$150.00		
Less variable cost	−$25.00	−$50.00	−$75.00	DOL	
Less fixed cost	− 10.00	− 10.00	− 10.00		
EBIT	$15.00	$40.00	$65.00		DTL
Less interest	−$10.00	−$10.00	−$10.00		
Net profits before taxes	$ 5.00	$30.00	$55.00		
Less taxes	−$ 2.00	−$12.00	−$22.00	DFL	
Net profits after taxes	$ 3.00	$18.00	$33.00		
EPS (1 share outstanding)	$ 3.00	$18.00	$33.00		

---

*At the maximum, bankruptcy and agency costs just equal the value of the tax shield. Beyond this maximum, the value of the firm is decreased as more debt is used.

financial leverage. Observe in Table 13.5 that the DFL deals with the bottom half of the income statement. As debt increases, the DFL increases.

$$\text{Percent change} = \frac{\text{End} - \text{Begin}}{\text{Begin}} \times 100$$

Self-Test Review Question*

What is the degree of financial leverage computed for a sales increase from 50 units to 100 units based on the data in Table 13.5?

As demonstrated in the last section, increasing the DFL leads to greater firm risk.

Operating Leverage

The degree of operating leverage (DOL) is computed by Equation 13.2:

$$\text{DOL} = \frac{\text{Percent change in EBIT}}{\text{Percent change in sales}} \tag{13.2}$$

Suppose that the percentage change in sales is 10%. If EBIT increases by 30%, the DOL is 3 (0.30/0.10 = 3). The greater the change in EBIT given a change in sales, the greater the operating leverage. Note Table 13.5 once again. The DOL deals with the top half of the income statement. As fixed costs increase, the DOL increases.

We can demonstrate how increased fixed costs increase risk by showing what happens to the breakeven sales quantity when fixed costs increase.

Self-Test Review Question**

What is the degree of operating leverage computed for a sales increase from 50 units to 100 units based on the data in Table 13.5?

Breakeven Analysis   Breakeven analysis is a valuable technique for analyzing the effects of operating leverage. As *operating leverage* increases, a firm's breakeven sales also must increase.

The breakeven equation can be derived easily. The breakeven point occurs when total revenues equal total costs. Total revenues are the product of the sales price (P) and the number of units sold (Q). Total costs are found by adding fixed costs (F) to variable costs. Variable costs are the product of Q and the variable cost per unit (V). This is demonstrated in Equation 13.3:

$$P \times Q = F + (V \times Q)$$

or

$$PQ = F + VQ \tag{13.3}$$

By rearranging Equation 13.3 you can solve for the quantity of units that must be sold to break even given the sales price, fixed costs, and variable costs, or you can solve for the sales price needed to break even given Q, F, and V.

EXAMPLE 13.1   Breakeven Analysis

A number of years ago the Payless Car Rental agency in Fairbanks, Alaska called the local university for help. The owner said she was losing money on the business and wanted to understand why. A group of MBA students was assigned to investigate. During the initial meeting with the owner, the team decided to compute a breakeven sales quantity. With the owner's help, they determined that fixed costs consisted of salaries, airport space rent, and lease payments on the cars. Total fixed costs were $15,000 per month. This is a daily fixed cost of $500 ($15,000/30). Variable costs consisted of franchise fees, mileage cost on the cars, and a portion of the cleaning cost of the cars. The total variable cost was $15 per day per car. The average daily rental rate was $40.

Solution

Putting the figures into Equation 13.3 yields the following breakeven sales quantity:

$$P(Q) = F + V(Q)$$
$$\$40(Q) = \$500 + \$15(Q)$$
$$\$25(Q) = \$500$$
$$Q = 20$$

This result means that the agency must rent 20 cars per day to break even. The students noticed that the business owner was not pleased with this information. It turned out that she had only 17 cars in her fleet.

What would happen to the breakeven number of cars rented if the owner of the firm reduced fixed costs by making arrangements to lease some of her cars from the local Ford dealership on an as-needed basis? What would be the breakeven point if fixed costs fell to $350 but variable costs rose to $18 as a result?

$$P(Q) = F + V(Q)$$
$$\$40(Q) = \$350 + \$18(Q)$$
$$\$22(Q) = \$350$$
$$Q = 15.9$$

The breakeven point has dropped because the level of fixed costs has been reduced. By reducing fixed costs, the firm has lowered its risk. As the DOL falls, the risk of the firm also falls.

Total Leverage

The degree of total leverage (DTL) is computed by Equation 13.4:

$$\text{DTL} = \frac{\text{Percent change in EPS}}{\text{Percent change in sales}} \tag{13.4}$$

Suppose that sales increase 10% and EPS increases 60%. The DTL is 6 (0.60/0.10). The greater the change in EPS given a change in sales, the greater is total leverage. See Table 13.5. The DTL deals with the entire income statement. As either fixed costs or debt increase, the DTL increases.

An alternative way to compute the DTL is to multiply the DFL times the DOL. Notice that %ΔEBIT cancels. Equation 13.5 and the equation for DTL results:

$$DFL \times DOL = DTL$$

$$\frac{\%\Delta EPS}{\%\Delta EBIT} \times \frac{\%\Delta EBIT}{\%\Delta Sales} = \frac{\%\Delta EPS}{\%\Delta Sales} \tag{13.5}$$

where %Δ = the percentage change

Besides pointing out that there is more than one way to leverage a firm, the reason for presenting this discussion of leverage is to show one factor that will bear on the capital structure decision. Some firms, by virtue of the industry in which they operate, have high operating leverage. A steel mill, for example, must invest substantial sums in expensive plant and equipment. Similarly, automobile manufacturers, railroads, and the producers of computer chips must invest heavily before producing products. In these industries the degree of operating leverage is high, so small changes in sales result in large changes in earnings per share. If these firms were to have high financial leverage as well, they might be too risky to be attractive to investors. *For this reason, firms with high operating leverage often have low financial leverage and vice versa.*

Review Equation 13.5. Financial leverage and operating leverage are multiplied together, not summed. This means that an increase in either type of leverage has a large impact on total risk.

We often see that firms within an industry tend to have similar capital structures. One reason is because firms within an industry often have similar operating leverage. To keep risk within acceptable limits, they adjust their financial leverage. Thus, one determinant of capital structure is the level of fixed assets.

Some academics argue that firms often miss an opportunity to increase firm value by holding too little debt. Hans Storr, the CFO of Philip Morris Co., and Stephen Ross, a leading finance theorist from Yale, debated the use of debt in an interview with *CFO* magazine.[1] Ross argued that the firm's value could be raised and hundreds of millions of dollars saved for shareholders if the firm would increase its debt ratio. Storr responded by saying the flexibility provided by a low debt ratio made up for the cost savings. Clearly, the capital structure debate is not over.

Other Considerations (FRICTO)

As the CFO of Philip Morris noted, other considerations bear on the financing decision. One way to discuss these other considerations is under the acronym FRICTO (which stands for *flexibility, risk, income, control, timing,* and *other*).

Flexibility

A fully leveraged firm may give up its flexibility to raise additional funds easily and quickly if it consistently operates with a high debt ratio. Debt capital is often faster to obtain than equity capital because banks can disburse funds almost overnight. Firms that have unexpected or unpredictable investment opportunities may choose to have lower debt than other firms in order to maintain their option to raise additional debt.

---

[1]"Capital Ideas: A Conversation with Hans Storr and Stephen Ross," *CFO,* April 1996.

Risk

We have discussed at some length the increase in risk that results from additional debt. The capital structure decision process must carefully evaluate the effect of any restructuring on the risk of the firm. Is the change in risk consistent with the desires of the shareholders? Will it cause an increase in the cost of financing? Is the probability of bankruptcy being substantially increased? Recognize that the answers to these questions depend on the business risk of the firm, its industry, its operating leverage, and its growth rate.

Income

Does the firm have the income to support the proposed debt? Is this income stable and predictable? Firms that have wide variations in their year-to-year income cannot support as much debt as firms with very stable cash flows. Even if *long-term* earnings are sufficient to make the principal and interest payments, there must be sufficient funds available *every period* or its creditors may force the firm into bankruptcy.

Control

The issue of maintaining corporate control while raising additional capital often governs the capital structure decision. A stockholder who has a controlling interest in a firm may refuse to allow additional issues of stock because this would dilute existing stockholders' ownership interest. An alternative to debt when the firm is concerned about dilution is nonvoting common stock.

Timing

In 1981 interest rates on high-grade bonds exceeded 15%. These rates are normally under 8%. This was not a good time to sell bonds. In fact, bond sales were very low. If a firm required capital at this time, it probably chose to issue stock. Alternatively, in 1993 bond interest rates approached 6%. This was a 20-year low. A record number of bonds were sold that year as firms chose to take advantage of the low cost of debt.

In addition to considering market conditions, firms must consider their internal conditions. For example, managers will not issue stock if they feel the market undervalues the firm's stock because the market does not yet know about the success of an R&D project. Alternatively, the firm is much more likely to issue stock if the market is overvaluing the firm.

Other

There are other important issues to consider when making the debt–equity choice. These issues include taxes, management attitudes and risk preferences, projected firm profitability, lender attitudes, and investment opportunities.

Did We Answer the Question?

After wading through a number of different theories you still may feel less than comfortable with how to set a firm's optimal capital structure. Despite the many years of research and effort put into answering the question of how to maximize firm value by using the best combination of debt and equity, no concrete answer has been provided. Ideally, we could develop an equation that would provide a definitive answer. No such equation exists. In fact, there is much we do not yet understand about capital structure. Let us review what we *do* know.

Debt is often the least costly form of financing because a portion of the cost is paid by the government through reduced taxes. This implies that firms should use some debt in their capital structure.

Second, as debt increases, so does the risk associated with bankruptcy and agency costs. The optimal debt level balances these costs against the tax benefit of using debt. Because different firms have different levels of bankruptcy and agency costs for each level of debt, we cannot specify one particular debt ratio that will be optimal. Each firm must be aware of how the market is reacting to its debt and adjust its capital structure appropriately.

Third, different firms are subject to different levels of risk. If the operating leverage of the firm is high because of the need for extensive fixed costs, small changes in sales can have a large impact on the earnings. Firms with high operating leverage are likely to maintain low debt ratios to keep total risk reasonable.

Many other considerations also are pertinent. Some firms may value the flexibility provided by low debt more than do other firms. Some owners and managers are more concerned about risk than are others. If a firm's cash flows are irregular, it cannot support as much debt as a firm with stable cash flows. There are situations in which control issues may take precedence over all other considerations.

What do managers of the country's largest corporations think about capital structure? In a survey of the Fortune 1,000 firms, financial managers generally agreed that prudent use of debt can lower their cost of capital. These managers reported that their firm's target long-term debt to total capitalization[2] ratio ranged between 26 and 40%. Most had a target ratio between 26 and 30%.[3]

One final point. We might reasonably ask how serious an error is being made if a firm has the wrong capital structure. The good news here is that it may not cost the firm very much. This is because most experts believe that the relationship between capital structure and firm value is flat. Review Figure 13.5. The optimal capital structure is shown where the value of the firm is maximized. The curve relating the debt ratio to firm value is flat, so deviations from the optimal have little effect on the value of the firm. We should still be concerned with determining the best capital structure for our firm. However, if we are not exactly right, the damage may not be too great. It also helps explain why researchers have so much trouble determining which capital structure is best. It is hard to observe the effects on firm value of capital structure changes in the real world because they may be very subtle.

---

[2]Total capitalization is defined as Long-term debt + Preferred stock + Common equity.
[3]David Scott and Dana Johnson, "Financing Policies and Practices in Large Corporations," *Financial Management,* Summer 1982, pp. 51–59.

FIGURE 13.5
Effect on Firm Value of Different Debt Levels

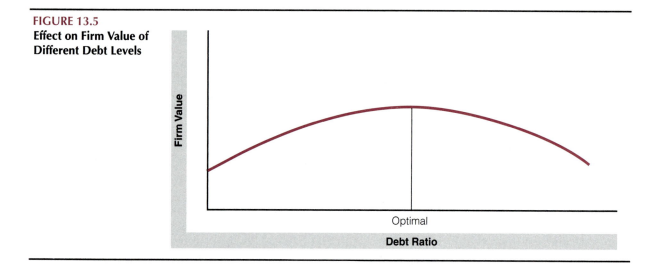

Despite the uncertainty that surrounds capital structure theory and the lack of definitive answers to what the optimal debt ratio should be, there is a method to help us choose between two financing alternatives. This method is explained in the next section.

EXTENSION 13.1

EBIT–EPS Analysis: A Capital Structure Choice Tool

EBIT–EPS analysis is a method for selecting between two alternative methods of financing. The goal of the approach is to pick the financing alternative that maximizes the firm's earnings per share. We know that the goal of the financial manager is to maximize the value of the firm, so the validity of this method depends on there being some correlation between earnings per share (EPS) and firm value.

Suppose that you need to raise additional capital. You have checked with the bank and found what debt will cost. You also know what equity will sell for. How do you go about choosing which to use? One method is to find the **EBIT–EPS indifference point**.

Recall from Table 13.1 that as financial leverage increases, a change in earnings before interest and taxes (EBIT) has an increasing effect on EPS. If EBIT is projected to be high, you want to use the debt alternative. However, if EBIT is low, you will want to use equity.

Review Figure 13.6. This graph plots the relationship between EPS and EBIT for two financing options. The goal of the firm is to pick the financing option that maximizes firm value. Because we cannot measure how a method of financing affects firm value directly, we use EPS as a substitute. We want to choose the financing option that provides the greatest EPS possible.

The relationship between EPS and EBIT is steeper when the firm is leveraged. This causes the two financing options to cross at an indifference point. At the indifference

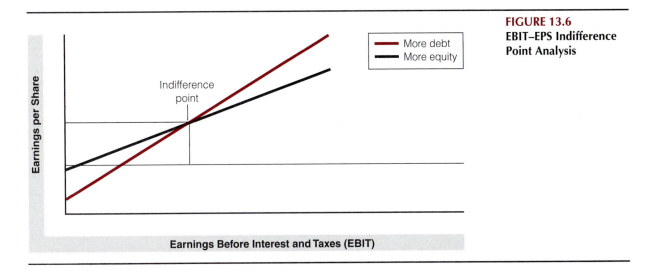

FIGURE 13.6
EBIT–EPS Indifference Point Analysis

point, both financing options provide the same EPS. To the right of the indifference point, the debt option results in a greater EPS. To the left of the indifference point, the equity option is preferred.

EBIT–EPS analysis can be a valuable tool for selecting between alternative financing options. The analysis takes three steps:

1. Compute the EBIT–EPS indifference point by setting EPS from one financing option equal to EPS from the alternative option and solving for EBIT.

2. Estimate the firm's EBIT. This must be done by management using projected sales and expected costs.

3. Select the option that yields the greatest EPS at the projected EBIT.

Computing the EBIT–EPS Indifference Point

EPS is computed by subtracting interest due and taxes from EBIT and dividing by the number of shares outstanding. EPS from financing with a debt option is computed as follows:

$$\text{EPS}_{\text{debt}} = \frac{\left(\text{EBIT} - \text{Interest}\right)\left(1 - T\right)}{n}$$

EPS from financing with an equity option is computed the same way. The interest amount will be less and the number of shares may be more. The indifference point is found by setting $\text{EPS}_{\text{debt}} = \text{EPS}_{\text{equity}}$. This results in Equation 13.6[4]:

$$\frac{\left(\text{EBIT} - \text{Interest}_{\text{debt}}\right)\left(1 - T\right)}{n_{\text{debt}}} = \frac{\left(\text{EBIT} - \text{Interest}_{\text{equity}}\right)\left(1 - T\right)}{n_{\text{equity}}} \qquad (13.6)$$

Study Tip

Students often want to plug a number for EBIT into Equation 13.6. Note that EBIT is what you are solving for in this equation. You will not have a number to plug in. You should have values for every other variable.

---

[4]Preferred dividends, if any, should be subtracted from the numerator.

Careers in Finance

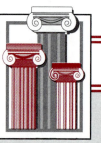

Real Estate Appraiser

Financial professionals work in many areas of real estate. One area that applies many of the lessons learned in this course is real estate appraising.

Banks require that borrowers have their property professionally appraised before accepting it as collateral for loans. For example, before you obtain a mortgage loan to finance a home purchase, you will be required to get the home appraised.

Commercial borrowers also require the services of appraisers. Commercial appraising is much more complex

and involves estimating required returns, revenues, cost, and risk. It also requires the calculation of present values.

Many appraisers work in small offices or by themselves. They can earn substantial salaries, especially once they establish a reputation at commercial work.

To become an appraiser, you will usually need to work for an appraiser as an apprentice while studying and taking classes in preparation for the certification exam.

Study Tip

If the firm has debt outstanding, be sure to include that interest when computing the interest due under the two options. For example, if Right Start had $1 million of 10% debt outstanding, $100,000 would be added to the interest figures used for both debt and equity.

where

$$\begin{aligned}
\text{Interest}_{\text{debt}} &= \text{the interest due if the debt option is selected} \\
\text{Interest}_{\text{equity}} &= \text{the interest due if the equity option is selected} \\
n_{\text{debt}} &= \text{the number of shares outstanding if the debt option is selected} \\
n_{\text{equity}} &= \text{the number of shares outstanding if the equity option is selected} \\
T &= \text{the firm's tax rate}
\end{aligned}$$

This is an admittedly messy looking equation, but it is easy to understand. The term on the left side of the equal sign computes the EPS if debt financing is selected. The term on the right computes the EPS if equity financing is selected. By setting the terms equal to each other, we can compute the EBIT where the two methods of financing give the same EPS. This is the indifference point shown in Figure 13.6. If expected EBIT is greater than this indifference point, choose the debt option. If EBIT is less than the indifference point, choose the equity option.

E X A M P L E 13.2   EBIT–EPS Indifference Point

The Right Start is a small firm that started out selling educational toys, strollers, and baby car seats for the toddlers of wealthy baby boomers. In 1993 it opened its first mall store in California. Another mall store opened in 1996 in Novi, Michigan. Suppose this firm wants to open 10 new mall stores in the next few months before competitors move in on its market. Right Start projects EBIT of $3,000,000 if the expansion is successful. Assume that the projected total funds needed for this expansion are $5 million. Also assume that Right Start could finance this $5 million by selling bonds with a pretax interest cost of 8% or by selling equity at $20 per share. If there are a million shares outstanding and the firm's tax rate is 37%, which option should Right Start choose?

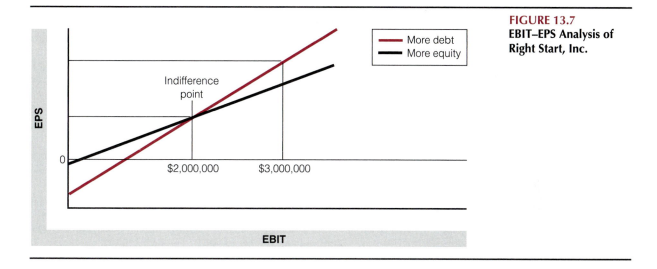

FIGURE 13.7
EBIT–EPS Analysis of Right Start, Inc.

Solution

The interest on the debt is $400,000 [$5,000,000(0.08) = $400,000]. If the equity option is used, 250,000 shares would have to be issued ($5,000,000/$20 = 250,000). There are already 1 million shares outstanding. Putting the values into Equation 13.6 yields the following:

$$\frac{(\text{EBIT} - \text{Interest}_{\text{debt}})(1 - T)}{n_{\text{debt}}} = \frac{(\text{EBIT} - \text{Interest}_{\text{equity}})(1 - T)}{n_{\text{equity}}}$$

$$\frac{(\text{EBIT} - \$400{,}000)(1 - 0.37)}{1{,}000{,}000} = \frac{(\text{EBIT} - \$0)(1 - 0.37)}{1{,}250{,}000}$$

$$\frac{(0.63\,\text{EBIT} - \$252{,}000)}{1} = \frac{0.63\,\text{EBIT}}{1.250}$$

$$(1.25)(0.63\,\text{EBIT} - \$252{,}000) = 0.63\,\text{EBIT}$$

$$0.7875\,\text{EBIT} - \$315{,}000 = 0.63\,\text{EBIT}$$

$$0.1575\ \text{EBIT} = \$315{,}000$$

$$\text{EBIT} = \$2{,}000{,}000$$

Because the expected EBIT of $3,000,000 is greater than the indifference point, Right Start should finance its expansion using debt rather than by selling stock. This results in the highest EPS. This solution is shown graphically in Figure 13.7.

Although EBIT–EPS analysis does not tell us which capital structure is optimal, it can be a useful tool for choosing between specific alternatives. However, it does not consider the effect on the firm's overall cost of capital, nor does it consider any changes in risk that may result. These qualitative issues must be considered separately.

CHAPTER SUMMARY

This chapter's purpose is to help financial managers select the combination of debt, equity, and preferred stock to use for financing the firm's assets. The optimal combination will provide the lowest weighted average cost of capital and will maximize the value of the firm.

There are three different types of leverage. Financial leverage increases as a firm uses a greater percentage of debt in its capital structure. The degree of financial leverage provides a means of measuring financial leverage. Operating leverage increases as a firm uses more fixed cost to generate revenues. The degree of operating leverage provides a means of measuring operating leverage. Breakeven analysis is useful for determining sales required to cover the firm's fixed costs. The greater the firm's operating leverage, the greater will be the firm's breakeven point.

Total leverage is the product of operating leverage and financial leverage. Firms with high operating leverage often use low financial leverage so that total leverage is kept within acceptable limits.

Miller and Modigliani began the capital structure debate by demonstrating that in a world without taxes or other expenses, the capital structure decision is irrelevant. When taxes are added to the model, they show that optimal firm value occurs with 100% debt. As we review the costs of the components, we see that the cost of debt is often

the lowest because it benefits from a tax shield; interest expense is tax deductible. Despite the research of Miller and Modigliani, firms are not actually 100% debt financed. The reason is that firms are subject to agency and bankruptcy costs.

Agency costs occur because managers run a firm to satisfy shareholders, not bondholders. As a result, as the debt level rises, the proportion of funds at risk by shareholders falls. This encourages managers to take greater risks than bondholders would prefer. To protect themselves, bondholders must increase the interest rate on the debt.

In addition to agency costs, bankruptcy costs increase when debt rises. The indirect costs of bankruptcy include the loss of customers and employees because they fear that the firm may not exist long.

The bankruptcy costs and agency costs offset the tax benefit from increasing debt. At some point the cost of debt is exactly offset and the firm's optimal value is achieved.

We do not have theories or equations that let the firm manager exactly determine the firm's optimal capital structure. However, we can evaluate two alternative financing methods. EBIT–EPS analysis finds the level of EBIT where EPS is equal under both financing plans. The firm then estimates its expected EBIT and selects the plan that optimizes EPS.

KEY WORDS

capital structure 341	financial leverage 350
EBIT–EPS indifference	operating leverage 350
point 356	total leverage 350

DISCUSSION QUESTIONS

1. Review Table 13.1 and explain why the all-equity firm does not suffer a loss when sales are weak but the leveraged firm does.
2. Review Table 13.1 and explain which firm you would rather own if sales are expected to exceed $200 and which firm you would rather own if sales are expected to be less than $50.
3. What is the difference between financial leverage and operating leverage? Which one is the financial manager more likely to have control over?
4. If a firm has few fixed assets, is it more likely to use debt financing or not? Why?
5. Will the breakeven level of sales increase or decrease if a firm increases its use of fixed costs?
6. What is the target capital structure?

7. In Chapter 12 we learned that debt benefits from a tax shield because interest is tax deductible. If debt is less expensive than other forms of financing, why do most firms not finance most of their operations exclusively with debt? (Hint: Refer to Table 13.2.)

8. Summarize Miller and Modigliani's conclusions when they assumed taxes did not exist.

9. What capital structure did Miller and Modigliani predict when taxes were added to their model?

10. How do agency costs and bankruptcy costs alter the prediction made by Miller and Modigliani?

11. What other factors should be considered by the financial manager when making the capital structure decision?

12. Are small errors in setting the firm's capital structure likely to significantly affect firm value?

13. What is the EBIT–EPS indifference point and how can it be used to select between alternative sources of financing? (Extension 13.1)

PROBLEMS

1. Consider two firms that are identical in every way except that one firm has $10,000 of debt and 50 shares of stock outstanding while the other firm is debt free and has 100 shares of stock outstanding. Interest on the debt is 10%. The firms' tax rate is 40%.
    a. What will be the firms' earnings per share if EBIT is $4,000?
    b. What will be the firms' earnings per share if EBIT is $1,500?
    c. Which firm would you rather own at each level of EBIT?

2. The percentage change in sales is 20%. The percentage change is EBIT is 40%. What is the firm's degree of operating leverage?

3. The percentage change in EPS is 200%. The percentage change is EBIT is 40%. What is the firm's degree of financial leverage?

4. If the degree of financial leverage is 3 and the degree of operating leverage is 4, what is the degree of total leverage?

5. Use the data in the following table to compute the DOL, the DFL, and the DTL.

Unit sales	1,000	5,000
Sales	$5,000	$25,000
Less variable cost	−$1,000	−$5,000
Less fixed cost	−2,000	−2,000
EBIT	2,000	18,000
Less interest	−$1,000	−$1,000
Net profits before taxes	$1,000	$17,000
Less taxes	−$400	−$6,800
Net profits after taxes	$600	$10,200
EPS (1,000 shares outstanding)	$0.60	$10.20

6. Fixed costs are $10,000. Variable costs are $4 per unit. Each unit sells for $5. How many units must be sold to break even?

7. Fixed costs are $1,000. Variable costs are $4.50. The price per unit is $5.00. How many units must be sold to break even?

8. You have two financing alternatives available and want to choose between them. In option A you will borrow $100,000 at 10%. No new equity will be issued. In option B you will sell stock for $20 per share. There are currently 10,000 shares outstanding and the firm is debt free. The tax rate is 40%. (Extension 13.1)
    a. What is the EBIT–EPS breakeven point?
    b. Prepare a graph showing the indifference point.
    c. Which option would you select if EBIT is projected to be $20,000?
    d. Which option would you select if EBIT is projected to be $35,000?

9. You are attempting to select between two financing options. Option 1 is to issue an additional $1,000,000 in debt at 8%. The second is to issue $1,000,000 of stock at $25 per share. The firm currently has $250,000 of 7% debt and 100,000 shares outstanding. Its tax rate is 40%. (Extension 13.1)
    a. What is the EBIT–EPS indifference point?
    b. Prepare a graph showing the indifference point.
    c. Which option would you choose if EBIT is projected to be $100,000?
    d. Which option would you choose if EBIT is projected to be $350,000?

10. Two options are available for financing a new project. With the first option, you will issue an additional $250,000 of debt at 12%. In the second option, you will issue $175,000 of debt and $75,000 of equity at $25 per

share. The cost of debt is lower in the second option because the firm will not be as leveraged due to issuing equity. The cost of debt in the second option is 9%. The firm currently has $50,000 of 8% debt outstanding and 20,000 shares have been issued. Assume a 40% tax rate. (Extension 13.1)

a. What is the EBIT–EPS indifference point?
b. Prepare a graph showing the indifference point.
c. Which option would you choose if EBIT is projected to be $100,000?
d. Which option would you choose if EBIT is projected to be $150,000?

WEB EXPLORATION

1. Go to www.quote.com/quotecom/stocks/. Here you can look up the debt–equity ratio for a firm by inputting the company name in the Get Quote box and then clicking on Snapshot to obtain details about the firm. Find the debt–equity ratio for ten firms, choosing five of the ten from one industry and five from another. Compare the debt–equity ratios for firms in the two industries. Address the following questions.
   a. Do firms within the same industry tend to have similar debt–equity ratios?
   b. Are the debt–equity ratios different between the two industries?

   c. Are the debt–equity ratios in the two industries consistent with the lessons discussed in this chapter?
2. Go to www.stern.nyu.edu/~adamodar/New_Home_Page/datafile/wacc.htm. Review the debt–equity ratios for firms in different industries. Select five service industries and five manufacturing industries. Compute the average debt–equity ratio for the service firms and that for the manufacturing firms. Compare these two figures. Are your results consistent with the theories discussed in this chapter?

MINI CASE

Your family owns a popular bar and grill just off campus. The firm is a corporation with stock that has been publicly distributed. You are talking to your parents one night and learn that the business is totally debt free. When you mention that you had learned in your finance class that borrowing money can often increase firm value, your family looks skeptical. They argue that if they borrowed money, they would have to pay interest to a bank. This would reduce their income and should lower firm value.
   a. Without using any numbers, discuss the concept of leverage and how it affects return on investment.
   b. Distinguish between operating leverage and financial leverage.
   c. Discuss how increased debt can increase firm value.
   You family is mildly interested, but still thinks the firm would be better off debt free. When they realize you are starting to get annoyed, they offer to let you "run the numbers."
   You begin by contacting the bank and find that it is eager to lend the firm money. The firm is currently capitalized with 200,000 shares outstanding at $20 per share. Using data provided by the bank for the cost of debt and the Internet for the cost of equity for firms similar to your

family's with varying levels of debt, you prepare the following chart:

Debt/ Equity Ratio	Cost of Debt	Cost of Equity
0%	—	16%
25	8%	17.5
50	10	19
75	14	25
100	20	28

Earnings before interest and taxes are expected to be $500,000. The tax rate is 40%.
   d. Compute the net income for each level of debt listed above. (Hints: Total assets = Share price × Number of shares. Equity = Total assets − Debt. Debt = Total assets × Debt − equity ratio.)
   e. Compute the return on equity (Net income/ Total equity).
   f. Compute the WACC.
   g. Discuss which level of financing results in the highest ROE. Should debt be used to finance the firm?

Financial Statement and Ratio Analysis

Chapter Objectives

By the end of this chapter you should be able to:

1. Explain why managers, investors, and potential creditors need ratios to help them interpret financial statements

2. Distinguish between time series analysis and cross-sectional analysis

3. Compute the most frequently used financial ratios

4. Perform an analysis of a firm using financial ratios

5. Use the Du Pont method to see the tradeoff between margin and turnover

In Chapter 1 we learned that the goal of the financial manager is to maximize shareholder wealth, which occurs when the firm's stock price is maximized. In this chapter we want to get more pragmatic. How does the financial manager know that he or she is moving the company in the right direction and how do investors in the firm's stock evaluate the performance of the managers? Both look at the firm's financial statements for answers to these and other questions. Firm managers use accounting information to help them manage the firm. Outsiders use accounting information to evaluate the firm.

Financial analysis is the process of using financial information to assist in investment and financial decision making. Financial analysis can help managers with employee performance evaluations, efficiency analysis, and identification of problem areas within the firm. It can also help managers identify strengths on which the firm should build. Externally, financial analysis is useful for credit managers evaluating loan requests and investors considering stock and bond purchases.

Financial analysis uses a variety of information. Financial statements are available in the firm's annual reports. Additional information is required by the Securities and Exchange Commission (SEC) on all publicly held corporations. Additionally, economic, industry, and market data are available for analysts. Table 14.1 reports some of these sources of information.

This chapter will initially focus on the interpretation and analysis of financial statements. This includes the use of common-sized financial statements, ratio analysis, and the Du Pont ratio. We will also review some of the market-based ratios that provide insight about what the market for stocks and bonds believes about the future prospects of the firm.

There are many companies that evaluate firms and provide summaries. Value Line is among the best known and is available for research at most libraries. Figure 14.1 is a sample page from the Value Line book.

Another valuable resource is *Standard & Poor's Stock Report.* This is also widely available. A sample page is shown in Figure 14.2.

REVIEW OF FINANCIAL STATEMENTS

All students enrolled in this course will have completed one or more courses in basic accounting methods. This chapter will not attempt to repeat this material or provide a review of basic accounting. We present the basic financial statements (Tables 14.2 through 14.4) as a reference only and urge students to review their accounting class notes if they need a refresher.

Balance Sheet

The **balance sheet** provides the details of the accounting identity

$$\text{Assets} = \text{Liabilities} + \text{Owners' equity}$$

or

$$\text{Investments} = \text{Investments paid for with debt} + \text{Investments paid for with equity}$$

TABLE 14.1 Sources of Financial Information

SEC Registration Statement: Contains financial statement information as well as information that describes the business and management of the firm.

10-K: An annual report required of all publicly held firms that contains virtually all of the information included in the firm's annual report as well as other financial information required by the SEC.

10-Q: A required quarterly report that is not as comprehensive as the 10-K, but is more current.

8-K: A statement that describes significant events that affect the firm, such as mergers or lawsuits.

Disclosure: A CD-ROM database that is widely available in libraries and contains company financial information.

Internet sites: The Internet may be the first place you search for financial data. Many firms now publish their annual reports and most recent financial data on their home pages. Additionally, many brokerage firms and news services post financial data that is either free or very inexpensive.

FIGURE 14.1
Value Line Report on J. C. Penney

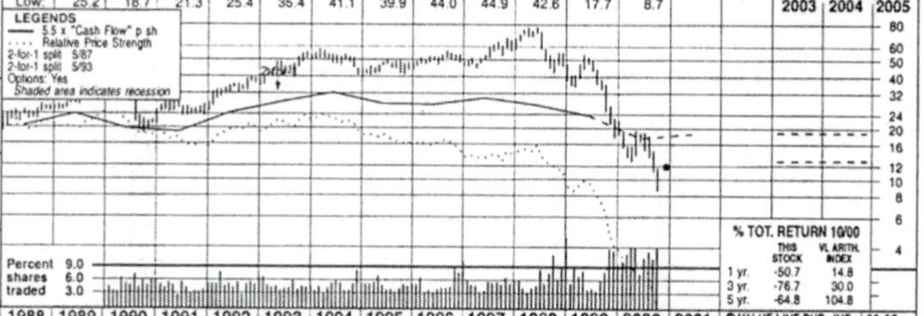

The right-hand side of the balance sheet lists the firm's sources of capital. The left-hand side shows how this capital has been put to work by the firm. A sample balance sheet is shown in Table 14.2. The balance sheet is a snapshot of the firm. That is, it provides information about the condition of the firm at one particular point in time.

FIGURE 14.2 Standard & Poor's Report on J. C. Penney

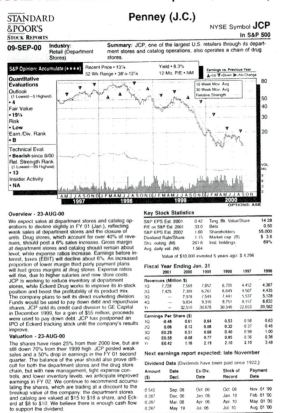

STANDARD &POOR'S STOCK REPORTS

Penney (J.C.)

NYSE Symbol **JCP**
In S&P 500

09-SEP-00 **Industry:** Retail (Department Stores)

Summary: JCP, one of the largest U.S. retailers through its department stores and catalog operations, also operates a chain of drug stores.

S&P Opinion: Accumulate (★★★★) Recent Price • 13⅞ 52 Wk Range • 38¼-12⅞ Yield • 8.3% 12-Mo. P/E • NM

Quantitative Evaluations
Outlook (1 Lowest—5 Highest) • 4
Fair Value • 19¼
Risk • Low
Earn./Div. Rank • B
Technical Eval. • **Bearish** since 8/00
Rel. Strength Rank (1 Lowest—99 Highest) • 13
Insider Activity • NA

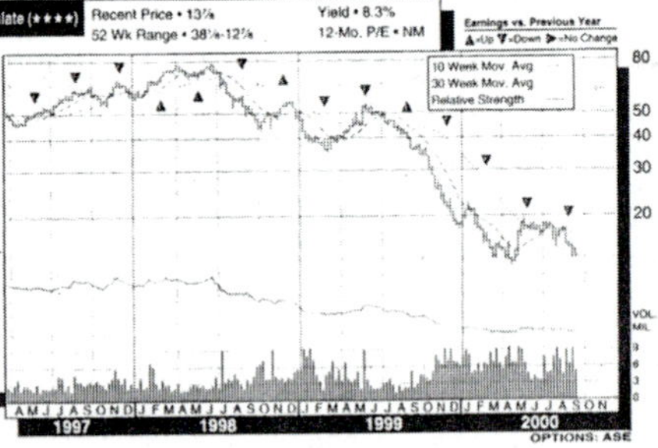

Overview - 23-AUG-00

We expect sales at department stores and catalog operations to decline slightly in FY 01 (Jan.), reflecting weak sales at department stores and the closure of units. Drug stores, which account for over 40% of revenues, should post a 6% sales increase. Gross margin at department stores and catalog should remain about level, while expense ratios increase. Earnings before interest, taxes (EBIT) will decline about 6%. An increased proportion of lower margin third party payment plans will hurt gross margins at drug stores. Expense ratios will rise, due to higher salaries and new store costs. JCP is working to reduce inventory at department stores, while Eckerd Drug works to improve its in-stock position and boost the profitability of its product mix. The company plans to sell its direct marketing division. Funds would be used to pay down debt and repurchase shares. JCP sold its credit card division to GE Capital in December 1999, for a gain of $55 million; proceeds were used to pay down debt. JCP has postponed an IPO of Eckerd tracking stock until the company's results improve.

Valuation - 23-AUG-00

The shares have risen 25% from their 2000 low, but are still down 70% from their 1999 high. JCP posted weak sales and a 50% drop in earnings in the FY 01 second quarter. The balance of the year should also prove difficult for both the department stores and the drug store chain, but with new management, tight expense controls, and lower inventory levels, we anticipate improved earnings in FY 02. We continue to recommend accumulating the shares, which are trading at a discount to the breakup value of the company: the department stores and catalog are valued at $15 to $18 a share, and Eckerd at $8 to $10. We believe there is enough cash flow to support the dividend.

Key Stock Statistics

S&P EPS Est. 2001	0.42	Tang. Bk. Value/Share	14.28
P/E on S&P Est. 2001	33.0	Beta	0.50
S&P EPS Est. 2002	1.60	Shareholders	55,000
Dividend Rate/Share	1.15	Market cap. (B)	$ 3.6
Shs. outstg. (M)	261.6	Inst. holdings	69%
Avg. daily vol. (M)	1.564		

Value of $10,000 invested 5 years ago: $ 4,296

Fiscal Year Ending Jan. 31

	2001	2000	1999	1998	1997	1996
Revenues (Million $)						
1Q	7,728	7,569	7,052	6,705	4,452	4,367
2Q	7,425	7,309	6,761	6,649	4,507	4,435
3Q	--	7,978	7,549	7,441	5,537	5,128
4Q	--	9,834	9,316	9,751	8,157	6,632
Yr.	--	32,510	30,678	30,546	22,653	20,562
Earnings Per Share ($)						
1Q	-0.48	0.61	0.64	0.53	0.58	0.63
2Q	0.06	0.12	0.08	0.32	0.37	0.46
3Q	E0.29	0.51	0.68	0.40	0.98	1.00
4Q	E0.55	-0.08	0.77	0.85	0.36	0.38
Yr.	E0.42	1.16	2.19	2.10	2.10	3.48

Next earnings report expected: late November

Dividend Data (Dividends have been paid since 1922.)

Amount ($)	Date Decl.	Ex-Div. Date	Stock of Record	Payment Date
0.545	Sep. 08	Oct. 06	Oct. 08	Nov. 01 '99
0.287	Dec. 06	Jan. 06	Jan. 10	Feb. 01 '00
0.287	Mar. 08	Apr. 06	Apr. 10	May. 01 '00
0.287	May 19	Jul. 06	Jul. 10	Aug. 01 '00

STANDARD &POOR'S STOCK REPORTS

J.C. Penney Company, Inc.

09-SEP-00

Business Summary - 23-AUG-00

Retail giant J.C. Penney Co. (JCP), with its 1,177 domestic and international stores, and its Eckerd drug store chain, has grown via acquisitions into a 2,600-store chain, one of the largest in the U.S.

JCP's main business is still the operation of its eponymous department store chain. The company's department stores and its complementary catalog operation, the largest in the U.S., accounted for 61% of total revenues in FY 00 (Jan.). Major merchandise areas include women's apparel and accessories, menswear, children's apparel, and home lines. The international division operates seven JCPenney stores, including five in Puerto Rico and two in Mexico. In 1998, the company expanded its international operations by acquiring Lojas Renner S.A. of Brazil, operating 21 stores in 15 cities. Another 14 stores were added in these countries in 1999, with 14 more planned for 2000.

Over the past few years, JCP has worked to shed its image as a mass merchandiser, aiming to be perceived instead as a department store chain. It remodeled stores into a department store ambiance, and developed private brands. The company currently offers 34 private brands, of which eight dominate: The Original Arizona Jean Company ($1 billion in annual sales); St. John's Bay ($800 million); Worthington; Stafford; Hunt Club; Jacqueline Ferrar; USA Olympic; and JCPenney Home Collection. JCP also offers popular national brands to complement its private brands.

The company's Internet store opened three years ago. In 1999, the entire fall and winter catalog was available on-line. Sales from Internet shopping, which are reported as a component of catalog sales, increased to $102 million in 1999, from $15 million. Catalog sales totaled $3.9 billion in 1999 and 1998.

In March 1999, the company acquired the New York-based Genovese drug store chain, with 141 stores and $800 million in annual revenues. In the first quarter of FY 01, JCP closed 289 underperforming Eckerd drug stores. The company planned to open 200 new and relocated drug stores in 2000, as well as 300 Express Photo centers. The Eckerd Health Services pharmacy benefit management service (PBM) includes more than 50,000 participating pharmacies, as well as one of the largest retail mail service pharmacies in the U.S.

JCPenney credit card sales totaled $7.4 billion in FY 00, or 37.9% of eligible sales. In December 1999, the company sold its proprietary credit card receivables to GE Capital.

Per Share Data ($) (Year Ended Jan. 31)	2000	1999	1998	1997	1996	1995	1994	1993	1992	1991
Tangible Bk. Val.	14.28	15.04	15.50	15.73	23.58	23.27	21.59	20.04	15.02	15.86
Cash Flow	3.87	4.40	4.46	4.13	5.15	5.65	5.10	4.46	2.33	3.56
Earnings	1.16	2.19	2.10	2.29	3.48	4.29	3.79	3.15	0.98	2.29
Dividends	2.19	2.18	2.14	2.08	1.92	1.68	1.80	1.32	1.32	1.32
Payout Ratio	188%	100%	102%	91%	55%	38%	47%	42%	134%	58%
Cal. Yrs.	1999	1998	1997	1996	1995	1994	1993	1992	1991	1990
Prices - High	54⅜	78¾	68¾	57	50	59	56⅜	40¼	29¾	37⅞
- Low	17⅞	42¾	44¼	44	39¼	41	35⅜	25⅜	21¼	18¾
P/E Ratio - High	47	36	32	25	14	14	15	13	30	16
- Low	15	19	21	19	11	10	9	8	22	8
Income Statement Analysis (Million $)										
Revs.	32,510	30,678	30,546	22,653	20,562	21,706	19,578	19,085	17,295	17,410
Oper. Inc.	1,681	2,253	1,687	1,075	1,200	2,292	1,943	1,825	1,485	1,432
Depr.	710	637	584	381	341	323	316	308	314	299
Int. Exp.	673	663	648	414	383	320	289	324	327	331
Pretax Inc.	531	955	925	909	1,341	1,699	1,554	1,250	468	832
Eff. Tax Rate	37%	38%	39%	38%	38%	38%	39%	38%	44%	31%
Net Inc.	336	594	566	565	838	1,057	944	777	264	577
Balance Sheet & Other Fin. Data (Million $)										
Cash	1,233	96.0	287	131	173	261	173	397	111	137
Curr. Assets	8,472	11,125	11,484	11,712	9,409	9,468	8,565	6,970	6,695	6,799
Total Assets	20,888	23,638	23,493	22,088	17,102	16,202	14,788	13,563	12,520	12,325
Curr. Liab.	4,465	5,970	6,137	7,966	4,020	4,481	3,883	3,077	2,409	2,662
LT Debt	5,844	7,143	6,986	4,565	4,080	3,335	2,929	3,171	3,354	3,135
Common Eqty.	6,782	6,694	6,831	5,526	5,509	5,292	5,096	4,486	3,504	3,697
Total Cap.	14,087	15,829	15,668	11,879	11,152	9,989	9,307	8,707	8,335	8,550
Cap. Exp.	631	744	824	704	717	550	480	453	515	637
Cash Flow	1,010	1,193	1,110	946	1,179	1,340	1,220	1,052	544	842
Curr. Ratio	1.9	1.9	1.9	1.5	2.3	2.1	2.2	2.3	2.8	2.6
% LT Debt of Cap.	41.5	45.1	44.6	38.4	36.6	33.4	31.5	36.4	40.2	36.7
% Net Inc. of Revs.	1.0	1.9	1.9	2.5	4.1	4.9	4.8	4.1	1.5	3.3
% Ret. on Assets	1.5	2.5	2.5	2.9	4.8	6.9	6.8	5.9	2.1	4.7
% Ret. on Equity	4.5	8.2	8.6	9.5	14.8	19.9	18.8	17.5	6.4	15.0

Data as orig. reptd.; bef. results of disc. opers/spec. items. Per share data adj. for stk. divs. Bold denotes diluted EPS (FASB 128) prior periods restated. E-Estimated. NA-Not Available. NM-Not Meaningful. NR-Not Ranked.

Office—6501 Legacy Dr., Plano, TX 75024-3698. **Registrar & Transfer Agent**—ChaseMellon Shareholder Services, S. Hackensack, NJ. **Tel**—(972) 431-1000. **Website**—http://www.jcpenney.com **Chrmn & CEO**—J. E. Oesterreicher. **EVP & CFO**—D. A. McKay. **EVP & Secy**—C. R. Lotter. **Investor Contact**—Wynn C. Watkins (972-431-1972). **Dirs**—M. A. Burns, T. J. Engibous, K. B. Foster, E. Jordan Jr., J. E. Oesterreicher, J. C. Pfeiffer, A. W. Richards, F. Sanchez-Loaeza, C. S. Sanford Jr., R. G. Turner. **Transfer Agent & Registrar**—ChaseMellon Shareholder Services, S. Hackensack, NJ. **Incorporated**—in Delaware in 1924. **Empl**— 291,000. **S&P Analyst:** Karen J. Sack, CFA

However, by reviewing a series of balance sheets, the analyst can identify changes in the firm over time.

In addition to the balance sheet, we can discuss the financial balance sheet. The financial balance sheet is not really a new statement; it is a way of looking at a firm's assets, liabilities, and equity that emphasizes why they exist. Assets are owned only for the income they can produce. Liabilities and owners' equity fund the purchase of these assets.

Assets Generate Income (Left-Hand Side)

The left-hand side of the balance sheet lists the firm's assets. *The only reason for a firm to hold an asset is if it can produce income.* The assets of the firm produce the firm's income. There is no reason for a firm to hold an asset if it is not currently or expected in the future to produce income for the firm. In Chapter 1 we noted that assets that satisfy only the needs of managers represent agency costs to the firm. Exotic wood desks do not increase firm sales or revenues and so should not be purchased by the firm. Alaska National Bank

TABLE 14.2   Sample Balance Sheet

Current assets	Current liabilities
Cash	Accounts payable
Marketable securities	Accrued expenses
Accounts receivable	Short-term notes
Inventories	
Total current assets	Total current liabilities
Fixed assets	Long-term liabilities
Machinery and equipment	Long-term notes
Buildings	Mortgages
Land	
Total fixed assets	Total long-term liabilities
Other assets	Equity
Investments	Preferred stock
Patents	Common stock
	Par value
	Paid in capital
Total other assets	Retained earnings
Total assets	**Total liabilities and equity**

of the North went bankrupt in 1987. Among its assets was an extensive collection of valuable Alaskan art. The art had appreciated little while owned by the bank, but the capital invested in the art was diverted from the core business of the bank. Certainly this was not the sole cause of the bank's failure, but it may be symptomatic of a more pervasive problem: not investing the firm's assets to generate income.

Think of the left-hand side entries as investments. Even cash balances should be considered an investment because no more should be held than is necessary to support expected sales. If a store holds too little cash at the beginning of a day to make change, it will lose sales. If too much is held, it loses whatever the cash could have earned had it been invested elsewhere. Similarly, over- or underinvesting in inventory will reduce the firm's net income from its theoretical maximum. We spend a substantial amount of our time in this course investigating how companies select assets that will produce optimal earnings for the firm.

Financing the Assets (Right-Hand Side)

For every dollar in assets the firm has, there will be either a dollar of liability or a dollar of equity on the right-hand side of the balance sheet. The right-hand side of the balance sheet shows how the firm is financing its assets. An all-equity firm has chosen to finance all of its investments with stock. Most firms choose to use a mixture of equity and debt. We discovered in Chapter 13 that at low levels, debt is often less costly than equity because interest payments are tax deductible whereas dividend payments are not. By adjusting the mix of debt and equity, the firm can achieve the lowest cost of financing.

It is tempting to think of equity financing as costless. However, if shareholders do not receive a fair return on their investment in the firm, they will sell their stock. This will depress the stock price, which leads to managers getting fired. Any manager who fails to recognize the importance of keeping shareholders satisfied is unlikely to have a long tenure.

In summary, the left-hand side of the balance sheet reports the assets that earn the income and the right-hand side finances these assets.

Income Statement

The **income statement** tells us how the firm has performed over a period of time (as opposed to the balance sheet, which tells us the state of the firm at one point in time). Income can be broken down as follows:

Income = Revenues + Gains − Expenses − Losses

Income statements usually have two sections. The first reports the results of operating activities. This includes sales minus operating expenses. Financing activities are reported in the second section. Interest expense, taxes, and preferred dividends are subtracted to arrive at net income. A sample income statement appears in Table 14.3.

Statement of Cash Flows

Many students are not as comfortable with the statement of cash flows as they are with the income statement and balance sheet. However, it provides insight not readily available from the other statements. In finance we are particularly concerned with cash flows rather than accounting earnings. This statement shows how cash flows have changed. The first section provides the cash flows from operating activities. This refers to the usual business activity of the firm. The second shows cash flows from investments. This includes interest income, increases in asset values, and other investment activity. The third section shows the cash flows from financing. For example, if the firm borrows

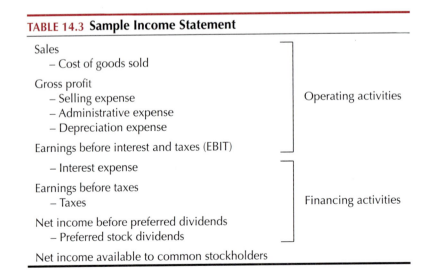

TABLE 14.3 Sample Income Statement

Sales	
− Cost of goods sold	
Gross profit	
− Selling expense	Operating activities
− Administrative expense	
− Depreciation expense	
Earnings before interest and taxes (EBIT)	
− Interest expense	
Earnings before taxes	
− Taxes	Financing activities
Net income before preferred dividends	
− Preferred stock dividends	
Net income available to common stockholders	

money, cash flows are increased. Alternatively, if the firm pays off debt, cash flows are reduced. A sample statement of cash flows is shown in Table 14.4.

Tables 14.29 and 14.30 (on pp. 389 and 390) report the balance sheet and income statements for J. C. Penney for 1997–1999. Review these statements carefully to ensure that you know where each statement reports each item.

GOALS OF FINANCIAL ANALYSIS

Exactly what can we hope to accomplish by analyzing the financial aspects of a firm? We will *not* find many absolute answers. For example, if a firm has been suffering declining sales and profits over the last several years, we may want to know why. Realistically, we are unlikely to find one specific cause for its problems. What we may find are a number of red flags that cause us to focus on specific portions of its operations.

Outsiders conduct financial analysis differently than do managers, also called *insiders*. Clearly, insiders have access to information and background unavailable to others in the market. This gives them an advantage when ratios raise questions. For example, suppose a firm discovers that it has a falling profit margin. It also has found that its inventory is not selling as quickly as in the past. Insiders can order an analysis to determine which specific items are not moving well. Outsiders may only speculate about the quality of the inventory mix. However, both insiders and outsiders have a common goal of attempting to identify the strengths and weaknesses of the firm.

Study Tip

Ratio analysis requires that you look for interactions. One ratio may give a clue that there is a problem and that clue must be followed by reviewing other ratios. Ratio analysis is a skill that can be honed only with practice.

TABLE 14.4 Sample Statement of Cash Flows

Cash Flow from Operations
  Net profit after taxes
  +Depreciation
  +Decrease in accounts receivable
  +Decrease in inventories
  +Increase in accounts payable
  +Decrease in accruals
    Cash provided by operations

Cash Flow from Investments
  Increase in fixed assets
  Change in business ownership
    Cash provided by investment activities

Cash Flow from Financing
  +Decrease in notes payable
  +Increase in long-term debt
  +Changes in stockholder equity
  −Dividends paid
    Cash provided by financing activities

**Net increase/decrease in cash
  and marketable securities**

Identify Company Problems

One goal of financial analysis is to identify problems that affect the firm. By identifying problems early, managers can make corrections to improve firm performance. Some problems may be hard to identify. A firm that seems to be earning profits but is constantly short of cash may turn to financial analysis to determine why this is occurring.

Investors also are interested in identifying companies with problems as early as possible. No one wants to stay on a sinking ship any longer than necessary. Analysts hope that they can identify firms with problems before other investors so that they can sell their stock before the price drops.

Identify Company Strengths

Another equally important purpose of financial analysis is to identify company strengths so that they can be enhanced and used to their greatest potential. In the early 1970s, J. C. Penney found that it was not able to compete with high-volume discount stores such as K-Mart. However, it was able to sell good-quality clothing. This discovery led to a major refocusing of the firm that involved discontinuing its automotive, appliance, and furniture departments and upscaling its clothing lines. Because of these changes, it succeeded where many of its competitors failed.

Investors are equally eager to identify firms with special strengths. By buying stock in these firms early, investors hope to realize greater gains.

Both investors and managers look at available financial data in two ways when conducting their analysis: cross-sectionally and in time series.

Cross-Sectional Analysis

Most **financial ratios** mean little when viewed in isolation. For example, an inventory turnover ratio tells us how many times per year the company's inventory is sold (we will discuss this ratio further later in the chapter). A value of 20 is not interesting until we learn that other firms in the industry have an inventory turnover ratio of 3. Similarly, gross profit margins, liquidity ratios, and activity ratios all vary substantially depending on the industry. Clearly, a grocery store will turn over its inventory more often than will an auto dealer.

Cross-sectional analysis is the comparison of one firm to other similar firms. A cross section of an industry is used as a comparison for the firm's numbers. There are a variety of sources of cross-sectional information. Value Line, Robert Morris & Associates, and Dun & Bradstreet all publish industry average ratio statistics.

Notice in Figure 14.3 that several figures are reported for each ratio. LQ is the average for the lower quartile, MED is the mean, and UQ is the average for the upper quartile. By providing the analysts with upper and lower quartile figures, the books give a feel for how large a deviation is significant.

The most common way to identify a firm's industry is by its Standard Industry Classification (SIC) code. These are four-digit codes given to firms by the government for statistical reporting purposes. All industry ratio resource books are organized around SIC codes. The first digit of the four-digit code puts the firm in a broad business type. Each

FIGURE 14.3 Sample of Industry Ratios

Page 17

	SIC 5311 DEPARTMENT STORES INDUSTRY ASSETS $5,000,000-$25,000,000 1998 (21 Establishments)		SIC 5311 DEPARTMENT STORES INDUSTRY ASSETS OVER $50,000,000 1998 (50 Establishments)		SIC 5331 VARIETY STORES (NO BREAKDOWN) 1998 (422 Establishments)		SIC 5331 VARIETY STORES INDUSTRY ASSETS UNDER $100,000 1998 (36 Establishments)	
	$	%	$	%	$	%	$	%
Cash	1,330,108	16.1	16,945,001	3.7	63,561	15.8	12,411	18.5
Accounts Receivable	743,539	9.0	48,087,165	10.5	18,103	4.5	134	0.2
Notes Receivable	—	—	—	—	2,816	0.7	67	0.1
Inventory	3,453,323	41.8	219,369,067	47.9	218,038	54.2	41,930	62.5
Other Current	660,923	8.0	14,655,136	3.2	12,471	3.1	1,476	2.2
Total Current	**6,187,893**	**74.9**	**299,056,369**	**65.3**	**314,989**	**78.3**	**56,018**	**83.5**
Fixed Assets	1,569,692	19.0	127,316,494	27.8	60,745	15.1	8,654	12.9
Other Non-current	503,954	6.1	31,600,137	6.9	26,551	6.6	2,415	3.6
Total Assets	**8,261,539**	**100.0**	**457,973,000**	**100.0**	**402,285**	**100.0**	**67,088**	**100.0**
Accounts Payable	941,815	11.4	69,153,923	15.1	51,895	12.9	5,501	8.2
Bank Loans	—	—	457,973	0.1	402	0.1	—	—
Notes Payable	57,831	0.7	17,860,947	3.9	8,448	2.1	3,019	4.5
Other Current	784,846	9.5	51,750,949	11.3	48,676	12.1	14,491	21.6
Total Current	**1,784,492**	**21.6**	**139,223,792**	**30.4**	**109,422**	**27.2**	**23,011**	**34.3**
Other Long Term	950,077	11.5	149,299,198	32.6	34,999	8.7	4,897	7.3
Deferred Credits	8,262	0.1	1,373,919	0.3	402	0.1	—	—
Net Worth	5,518,708	66.8	168,076,091	36.7	257,462	64.0	39,179	58.4
Total Liab & Net Worth	**8,261,539**	**100.0**	**457,973,000**	**100.0**	**402,285**	**100.0**	**67,088**	**100.0**
Net Sales	31,279,023	100.0	201,852,937	100.0	1,069,674	100.0	220,342	100.0
Gross Profit	10,009,287	32.0	53,692,881	26.6	365,829	34.2	84,611	38.4
Net Profit After Tax	218,953	0.7	—	—	43,857	4.1	15,424	7.0
Working Capital	4,403,401	—	159,832,577	—	205,567	—	33,007	—

RATIOS	UQ	MED	LQ	UQ	MED	LQ	UQ	MED	LQ	UQ	MED	LQ
SOLVENCY												
Quick Ratio (times)	3.0	1.3	0.7	0.9	0.5	0.2	2.6	0.8	0.2	2.4	0.8	0.3
Current Ratio (times)	6.5	4.7	2.3	2.7	2.1	1.6	10.4	3.8	1.8	16.6	6.6	1.3
Curr Liab To Nw (%)	11.1	20.6	89.1	48.6	64.4	82.4	7.6	27.6	72.3	5.9	14.2	94.8
Curr Liab To Inv (%)	28.8	39.2	80.0	55.1	67.1	94.6	14.8	37.4	83.4	7.5	18.5	82.9
Total Liab To Nw (%)	16.2	52.1	89.1	102.6	161.1	211.1	9.5	39.4	101.2	6.0	40.9	151.8
Fixed Assets To Nw (%)	9.8	23.6	59.6	53.4	74.9	114.5	5.8	15.6	39.5	6.0	13.2	59.9
EFFICIENCY												
Coll Period (days)	2.5	14.4	42.6	4.8	16.1	56.2	2.2	5.5	15.0	1.6	2.2	2.6
Sales To Inv (times)	8.2	5.1	4.2	5.2	4.5	3.8	8.2	4.7	3.3	9.8	5.9	3.3
Assets To Sales (%)	30.3	51.7	98.1	45.1	54.1	75.1	25.0	39.0	58.1	16.9	25.2	46.7
Sales To Nwc (times)	8.1	4.4	2.8	7.3	5.3	4.1	10.3	5.3	2.8	11.2	4.3	2.9
Acct Pay To Sales (%)	3.6	4.8	7.9	5.9	7.7	10.0	2.0	4.2	7.3	0.9	2.4	4.3
PROFITABILITY												
Return On Sales (%)	3.2	1.0	(0.7)	2.8	1.5	(0.4)	7.0	2.7	0.8	13.6	5.0	1.3
Return On Assets (%)	4.4	3.3	1.0	5.5	3.5	1.7	16.0	6.3	2.0	25.3	12.3	2.0
Return On Nw (%)	7.2	4.5	1.0	16.3	9.3	4.9	25.8	11.2	3.7	45.4	22.1	2.1

succeeding digit breaks the industry type down into finer units. For example, all financial firms have an SIC code that begins with 6. This includes insurance, banks, and real estate firms. SIC codes starting with 60 are reserved for banks, 63 for insurance firms, and so on. Many firms are assigned multiple SIC codes. For example, Disclosure Inc., a CD-ROM database available at most libraries, lists eight SIC codes for Xerox Corp. The first one listed is usually deemed the dominant industry for the firm. Table 14.5 lists the SIC codes Disclosure reports for Xerox.

Many times firms may be included in an SIC category used for preparing industry ratios that are not appropriate comparisons. For example, SIC 2080 includes Coca-Cola and Pepsi. However, it also includes Coors, Seagrams, and Clearly Canadian.

Many firms do not have any clear industry to use for comparison, such as conglomerates that do business in dozens of different industries. There are no good guidelines to use for picking comparison numbers for these types of firms. In other cases, the firm under study so dominates the industry that the industry ratios are simply

TABLE 14.5 **Primary and Secondary SIC Codes for Xerox Corp.**
Xerox Corp
Primary SIC Code:
3861 Photographic Equipment and Supplies
SIC Codes:
3861 Photographic Equipment and Supplies
3579 Office Machines
6331 Fire, Marine, and Casualty Insurance
6159 Miscellaneous Business Credit Institutions
5111 Printing and Writing Paper
6211 Security Brokers and Dealers
6311 Life Insurance

mirroring that firm. Consider General Motors. With so few firms in the auto manufacturing business, what happens to GM happens to the industry.

One solution to the problem of finding good comparison numbers is to create your own list of competitors. Compare the firm under analysis to the averages found from this list. Often this approach yields far better comparison numbers than can be found in the published reference materials.

When comparing one firm with another, it is important to recognize that a firm should not be satisfied being just average. To succeed, a firm must be better than its competition. For this reason, the best firm to use for comparison may be the top performing firm in the industry.

Time Series Analysis

Another equally important method of financial analysis is **time series analysis**, which involves comparing the firm's current performance with that of prior periods. This method allows the analyst to identify a trend, a change over time that moves fairly consistently in one direction. Unless the firm has undergone some type of major restructuring, prior period numbers are a near perfect comparison to use against today's figures.

Analysts must be careful to correct for changes and extraordinary items that may invalidate the comparison numbers. For example, if a firm sells a major division, a one-time gain will be recognized, but future revenues will be lower. Comparing this downsized firm without adjustment would lead to incorrect conclusions.

Both cross-sectional and time series analysis are important. For this reason, analysts should use both.

COMMON-SIZED FINANCIAL STATEMENTS

Financial statements themselves cannot be compared across an industry or across time because of scale differences. One way of standardizing financial statements is to divide each line item by a constant. In effect, this converts every entry into a ratio. This allows useful comparisons.

To prepare a common-sized balance sheet, all balance sheet line items are divided by total assets. Similarly, a **common-sized income statement** is prepared by dividing each line item by sales. *Thus, common-sized statements are just a specialized type of ratio analysis in which the denominator of every ratio is either total assets or total sales*.

Common-Sized Balance Sheet

As noted earlier, in the common-sized balance sheet we express each item as a percentage of total assets. Balance sheets restated in this way are easy to read and interpret. Changes in the structure of the firm are readily apparent when common-sized statements list entries for several years together.

Common-sized statements are easily prepared using spreadsheet software. Simply input the data from the firm's balance sheet, then use a formula to divide each entry by total assets. In our comprehensive example at the end of this chapter, Table 14.31 reports the common-sized balance sheet for J. C. Penney (p. 391).

Note that every entry is now a percentage of total assets.

Common-Sized Income Statement

The common-sized income statement is prepared by dividing each entry by sales. This expresses each item as a percentage of total sales. This statement tells us what happens to each dollar of sales as it works its way to the bottom line. It is easy to pick out the firm's gross and net margins from this statement. One purpose for this statement is to review a firm's cost controls. In the end-of-chapter comprehensive example, Table 14.32 reports the common-sized income statement for J. C. Penney (p. 392).

As useful as the common-sized statements are, analysts often seek information not provided by this simple technique. Instead, other ratios must be computed. These are discussed in the next section.

FINANCIAL RATIO ANALYSIS

In this section we introduce and briefly discuss a number of the more common financial ratios. This is not an exhaustive list. Many ratios can be used. In fact, it is not uncommon for analysts to create specialized ratios to look at a factor peculiar to a firm or industry. For example, revenues and costs per mile flown are often computed for airlines.

The formulas presented here for each ratio may differ from those reported elsewhere. An effort has been made in the writing of this section to locate the most common definition for each formula, but for some there is simply no consensus among reporting agencies. This means that when you are comparing ratios computed by different sources, you must be sure that they are all computed in the same way.

Ratios

The ratios are presented in groups to facilitate understanding. We have grouped the ratios into five categories:

- Profitability ratios
- Liquidity ratios
- Activity ratios
- Financing ratios
- Market ratios

Different firms put different levels of emphasis on the categories. For example, service firms are very concerned with how rapidly they collect on accounts receivable but are not too concerned with inventory usage because inventory is usually a minor cost factor. Manufacturing firms, however, must pay close attention to their inventories, whereas collections are often not a problem.

After presenting the formula for each ratio, we will demonstrate how the formula is calculated using a simple balance sheet and income statement for a fictional company, Risky Ventures, Inc., presented in Tables 14.6 and 14.7. We also provide a number of examples from familiar firms to show how the ratio varies with different companies. At the end of this section we will use the J. C. Penney financial statements in a comprehensive example to compute all of the ratios.

As you review this section pay attention to what the ratio is intended to measure and whether it is generally better if the ratio is higher or lower. Also note the unit of measure and what change might improve the ratio.

Profitability Ratios

We begin our discussion of ratio analysis with the profitability ratios because they are ultimately the most important. If a firm is generating acceptable profits, analysts tend to

TABLE 14.6 Risky Ventures, Inc.

Income Statement, Year Ending December 31, 2001

Net sales revenue		$30,000,000
Less: Cost of goods sold		−21,000,000
Gross profits		9,000,000
Less: Operating expenses:		
Selling expense	$2,500,000	
General and administration expense	1,500,000	
Depreciation expense	1,000,000	
Total operating expense		−$5,000,000
Operating profits		$4,000,000
Less: Interest expense		−2,000,000
Net profits before tax		$2,000,000
Less: Taxes (40%)		−800,000
Net profits after tax		**$1,200,000**

be more forgiving of deviations in other ratios. For example, low inventory turnover may be due to high prices. If this is a corporate strategy that produces high profits, investors are unlikely to complain. On the other hand, if the profits are not there, low inventory turnover will be viewed as a serious shortcoming.

Profitability ratios measure how effectively the firm uses its resources to generate income. The first three of the ratios reported here are probably the best known and most widely used of all financial ratios. Investors are happier the greater the profitability ratios are.

Return on Equity (ROE)　Many analysts consider **return on equity (ROE)** to be the most important of all ratios, which is why we present it first. The area of most

---

TABLE 14.7　Risky Ventures, Inc.

Balance Sheet, December 31, 2001

Assets	
Current assets	
Cash	$1,000,000
Marketable securities	3,000,000
Accounts receivable	12,000,000
Inventories	7,500,000
Total current assets	$23,500,000
Gross fixed assets	
Land and buildings	$11,000,000
Machinery and equipment	20,000,000
Furniture and fixtures	8,500,000
Total gross fixed assets	$39,500,000
Less: Accumulated depreciation	−13,000,000
Net fixed assets	$26,500,000
Total assets	$50,000,000
Liabilities and Stockholders' Equity	
Current liabilities	
Accounts payable	$8,000,000
Notes payable	8,000,000
Accruals	500,000
Total current liabilities	$16,500,000
Long-term debt (annual required of $800,000)	$20,000,000
Total liabilities	$36,500,000
Stockholders' equity	
Preferred stock (100,000 shares, Div = $2.00/share)	$2,500,000
Common stock (1 million shares at $5.00 par)	5,000,000
Paid in capital in excess of par on common stock	4,000,000
Retained earnings	2,000,000
Total stockholders' equity	$13,500,000
Total liabilities and stockholders' equity	$50,000,000

concern to shareholders is the return they receive on their invested dollar. This is what is reported by return on equity:[1]

$$\text{Return on equity} = \frac{\text{Net income after tax}}{\text{Common equity}} \quad (14.1)$$

$$\text{Return on equity} = \frac{\$1.2}{\$11.0} = 0.1091$$

Note that all examples are in millions.

The ROE tells us what the firm earns on every dollar of equity. Note that this return is based on the book value of equity. Because the market value of the stock may have changed substantially since it was booked, this is called an *accounting* rate of return rather than a *market* rate of return. If the market price of stock has risen since the stock was sold, the ROE will overstate the return to recent buyers of the stock. Some examples of ROE from familiar firms are presented in Table 14.8.

Return on Assets (ROA)   The **return on assets (ROA)** is a measure of profit per dollar of assets:

$$\text{Return on assets} = \frac{\text{Net income after tax}}{\text{Total assets}} \quad (14.2)$$

$$\text{Return on assets} = \frac{\$1.2}{\$50} = 0.02$$

This is sometimes also called the firm's *return on investment*. It measures the overall effectiveness of management in producing profits with available assets. For firms financed solely with equity, Total assets = Total equity, so ROA would equal ROE. However, because total assets for most firms exceed total equity, the ROA will be lower than ROE. This is clearly evident when you compare Table 14.8 and Table 14.9.

TABLE 14.8 Return on Equity

Company	2000	1999	1998	1997
Barnes & Noble	15.24%	13.61%	12.16%	11.23%
Dell Computer	31.39	62.90	73.01	65.88
Home Depot	18.80	18.47	16.34	15.75
Wal-Mart	21.58	20.98	19.06	17.83

TABLE 14.9 Return on Assets

Company	2000	1999	1998	1997
Barnes & Noble	5.34%	5.11%	4.06%	3.54%
Dell Computer	14.52	21.23	22.12	17.74
Home Depot	13.58	11.99	10.33	10.04
Wal-Mart	7.92	8.86	7.77	7.72

[1]The example calculations are based on the figures in Tables 14.6 and 14.7.

Gross Profit Margin   The **gross profit margin** is the gross profit (before operating expenses, interest, taxes, and preferred dividends) earned on each dollar of sales:

$$\text{Gross profit margin} = \frac{\text{Sales} - \text{Cost of goods sold}}{\text{Sales}} = \frac{\text{Gross profit}}{\text{Sales}} \quad (14.3)$$

$$\text{Gross profit margin} = \frac{\$9}{\$30} = 0.3$$

All expenses of the firm must be paid out of the gross profit margin. Gross profit margin reflects the gross profit a firm earns on each sale. Table 14.10 shows sample values for gross profit margin.

TABLE 14.10 Gross Profit Margin

Company	2000	1999	1998	1997
Barnes & Noble	28.75%	28.71%	27.80%	35.89%
Dell Computer	21.27	23.07	22.63	22.08
Home Depot	30.89	29.71	29.24	29.00
Wal-Mart	22.86	22.36	22.17	21.61

Operating Profit Margin   The **operating profit margin** goes one step further than the gross profit margin by subtracting operating expenses as well as the cost of goods sold from sales:

$$\text{Operating profit margin} = \frac{\text{Operating profits}}{\text{Sales}} \quad (14.4)$$

$$\text{Operating profit margin} = \frac{\$4}{\$30} = 0.13$$

The operating profit margin ignores any financial or tax charges and measures only the profits earned on operations. Table 14.11 demonstrates that operating profit margins vary widely by industry.

TABLE 14.11 Operating Profit Margin

Company	2000	1999	1998	1997
Barnes & Noble	9.47%	9.21%	8.02%	7.33%
Dell Computer	10.34	11.78	11.22	9.81
Home Depot	11.08	10.04	9.52	9.04
Wal-Mart	6.47	6.12	5.80	5.60

Net Profit Margin   The **net profit margin** is the percentage of each sales dollar that remains after all costs have been deducted, including taxes and preferred dividends:

$$\text{Net profit margin} = \frac{\text{Net income after tax}}{\text{Sales}} \quad (14.5)$$

$$\text{Net profit margin} = \frac{\$1.2}{\$30} = 0.04$$

Table 14.12 reports the net profit margin for a sample of firms.

TABLE 14.12 Net Profit Margin

Company	2000	1999	1998	1997
Barnes & Noble	3.70%	3.07%	2.31%	2.09%
Dell Computer	6.59	8.00	7.66	6.84
Home Depot	6.04	5.34	4.80	4.80
Wal-Mart	3.38	3.22	2.99	2.91

Note that there are several different profit margins. Some reporting services are careless about disclosing which profit margin they are reporting. *Generally, if a ratio is called the profit margin, the reference is usually to the net profit margin.*

Taken together, these profitability ratios give the analyst insight into the performance of the firm. If the return on equity is not acceptable, the various profit margin accounts can be reviewed to determine whether the problem lies with cost of goods sold, operating expenses, or financing cost.

Self-Test Review Question*

You have reviewed the ratios for Bongo Corp. and find the ROE is lower than that of the industry. After further investigation you determine that the net profit margin is low despite normal gross and operating profit margins. What else might you look at to confirm the source of Bongo Corp's problems?

Liquidity Ratios

A liquid firm is one that can meet its various short-term debt and credit obligations. Those who extend credit to a firm are particularly concerned with the firm's liquidity. It is not unusual for a firm to be making profits but not to have sufficient cash on hand to pay its creditors. The following **liquidity ratios** point out problems of this nature.

Current Ratio   The **current ratio** is a widely reported ratio of particular interest to creditors. It is one measure of the firm's ability to meet its short-term obligations:

$$\text{Current ratio} = \frac{\text{Current assets}}{\text{Current liabilities}} \qquad (14.6)$$

$$\text{Current ratio} = \frac{\$23.5}{\$16.5} = 1.42$$

In theory, current assets will be converted into cash within 1 year, so they should be available to pay current liabilities. Generally, this is true and the current ratio is an effective measure of a firm's liquidity. Of course, the exact timing of when assets are converted and when liabilities are due is not reflected by this ratio. A current ratio of 1 would mean that a firm has sufficient current assets to meet its current liabilities. Note in Table 14.13

that most firms maintain a current ratio well over 1. This is to provide a safety cushion in case there are cash flow timing problems or unforeseen problems or opportunities arise.

TABLE 14.13 Current Ratios

Company	2000	1999	1998	1997
Barnes & Noble	1.35	1.41	1.37	1.33
Dell Computer	1.48	1.72	1.45	1.66
Home Depot	1.75	1.73	1.82	2.01
Wal-Mart	0.94	1.26	1.34	1.64

Quick Ratio (Acid Test)   The **quick ratio** (or acid test) is very similar to the current ratio except that inventory is subtracted from current assets:

$$\text{Quick ratio} = \frac{\text{Current assets} - \text{Inventory}}{\text{Current liabilities}} \qquad (14.7)$$

$$\text{Quick ratio} = \frac{\$23.5 - \$7.5}{\$16.5} = 0.97$$

Because inventory may not always be easily converted into cash, the quick ratio is a more conservative measure of liquidity than is the current ratio. Note in Table 14.14 that for some industries the quick ratio falls well below 1.

TABLE 14.14 Quick Ratios

Company	2000	1999	1998	1997
Barnes & Noble	0.09	0.11	0.08	0.09
Dell Computer	1.31	1.53	1.23	1.36
Home Depot	0.21	0.19	0.30	0.51
Wal-Mart	0.12	0.18	0.17	0.16

Net Working Capital   The **net working capital** is not really a ratio, so it cannot be used in cross-sectional analysis. However, it is a useful measure of a firm's overall liquidity and can be reviewed using time series. Table 14.15 reports sample values for net working capital.

TABLE 14.15 Net Working Capital (millions)

Company	2000	1999	1998	1997
Barnes & Noble	$ 318.668	$ 325.989	$ 264.719	$ 212.692
Dell Computer	2,489.000	2,644.000	1,215.000	1,089.000
Home Depot	2,734.000	2,076.000	2,004.000	1,867.247
Wal-Mart	(1,447.000)	4,370.000	4,892.000	7,036.000

$$\text{Net working capital} = \text{Current assets} - \text{Current liabilities} \qquad (14.8)$$

$$\text{Net working capital} = \$23,500,000 - 16,500,000 = \$7,000,000$$

It is not clear whether greater net working capital is always good for shareholders. Recent research shows that reducing net working capital to the lowest possible level puts more assets to work earning revenues for the firm.

There is a great deal of disagreement among analysts as to how liquid a firm should be. It is not necessarily bad for a firm to have low current and quick ratios as well as low net working capital if the firm can meet its obligations. Consider which firm you would rather own: one that could make $100 of sales with only $5 of inventory and $1 of cash or one that required $50 of inventory and $10 of cash to make that same $100 of sales. Many efficiently run companies get by with fewer current assets than poorly run firms. For example, K-Mart's current ratio in 2000 was 2.00, compared with Wal-Mart's 0.94, yet K-Mart earned 2.7% on equity while Wal-Mart earned 21.6%.

Self-Test Review Question*

You are analyzing a firm and note that its current ratio has increased from 2.1 to 2.5 over the last 2 years. Is this good news?

Study Tip

Review the previous paragraph. It points out how ratio analysis is often a detective job in which there are no absolute rules to follow. The analyst must use the clues provided by the ratios to track down the source of the firm's problems.

Activity Ratios

Activity ratios measure the efficiency with which assets are converted to sales or cash. Generally, greater activity is good. Activity ratios go hand in hand with the liquidity ratios. If inventory is not turning over, current assets are not being converted to cash and the firm will have trouble paying its bills. If problems are suggested by the liquidity ratios, the analyst can review the activity ratios to see whether they provide clues to the problem. We begin our review of activity ratios with several that look at turnover.

Inventory Turnover The **inventory turnover ratio** measures how many times per year the inventory is completely sold and replaced:

$$\text{Inventory turnover} = \frac{\text{Cost of goods sold}}{\text{Inventory}} \tag{14.9}$$

$$\text{Inventory turnover} = \frac{\$21}{\$7.5} = 2.8$$

Some forms of this equation call for using average inventory in the denominator instead of end-of-period inventory. This is appropriate if beginning- and end-of-period inventory levels are very different. Average inventory is computed by summing the beginning and ending inventory levels and dividing by 2.

A falling inventory turnover ratio can be an indication of unsellable or obsolete inventory. On the other hand, net profit may be increased by selling fewer more expensive items. As always, a change in one ratio, say falling inventory turnover, must be viewed in context with other ratios, say increased profit margins. Notice in Table 14.16 that inventory turnover varies widely by industry.

TABLE 14.16 Inventory Turnover Ratios

Company	2000	1999	1998	1997
Barnes & Noble	2.43	2.38	2.55	2.13
Dell Computer	59.91	55.47	39.41	17.78
Home Depot	5.43	5.38	5.42	5.67
Wal-Mart	6.90	6.37	5.67	5.16

Fixed Asset Turnover   The inventory turnover ratio focuses on a particular asset inventory. A broader understanding of firm activity can be gleaned from the **fixed asset turnover ratio**, which measures how effectively fixed assets are being used (Table 14.17). The larger the fixed asset turnover, the more sales the firm is generating with a dollar of fixed assets:

TABLE 14.17 Fixed Asset Turnover

Company	2000	1999	1998	1997
Barnes & Noble	6.47	6.06	6.10	6.49
Dell Computer	39.23	42.18	42.73	37.48
Home Depot	4.18	4.12	4.04	3.95
Wal-Mart	5.33	5.55	5.37	5.35

$$\text{Fixed asset turnover} = \frac{\text{Sales}}{\text{Fixed assets}} \tag{14.10}$$

$$\text{Fixed asset turnover} = \frac{\$30}{\$26.5} = 1.13$$

Fixed asset turnover varies widely among industries. For example, Dell Computer generates $39.23 per $1.00 of fixed assets, whereas Home Depot generates about $4.18 in sales per $1.00 of fixed assets.

Total Asset Turnover   An even broader measure of activity is the **total asset turnover ratio**. It is determined mostly by accounts receivable turnover (discussed next), inventory turnover, and fixed asset turnover:

$$\text{Total asset turnover} = \frac{\text{Sales}}{\text{Total assets}} \tag{14.11}$$

$$\text{Total asset turnover} = \frac{\$30}{\$50} = 0.6$$

Total assets include both fixed assets and current assets. If fixed asset turnover is acceptable but total asset turnover is low, then we have a clue that there may be a problem with current assets. If the inventory turnover ratio is good, then the firm may have an excess of some other current asset, say cash or accounts receivable. Further investigation would be needed to determine which one is causing problems. Table 14.18 reports several sample values for total asset turnover.

TABLE 14.18 **Total Asset Turnover**

Company	2000	1999	1998	1997
Barnes & Noble	1.65	1.77	1.84	1.77
Dell Computer	2.75	3.27	3.40	3.02
Home Depot	2.52	2.45	2.35	2.34
Wal-Mart	2.74	2.89	2.78	2.72

The next several ratios can also be called *management ratios* because they reflect management policies toward receivables, collections, and payments. Problems indicated by these ratios may be caused by management inattention or fundamental problems with the underlying assets or liabilities.

Accounts Receivable Turnover   The **accounts receivable turnover ratio** is the number of times per year accounts receivable are paid and replaced:

$$\text{Accounts receivable turnover} = \frac{\text{Sales}}{\text{Accounts receivable}} \qquad (14.12)$$

$$\text{Accounts receivable turnover} = \frac{\$30}{\$12} = 2.5$$

As with all ratios, the analyst must be careful not to draw incorrect assumptions from changes in ratios. Slower accounts receivable turnover could be caused by collection problems, but it could also be caused by a new credit policy that gives customers more time to pay. If this new credit policy increases sales and net profits, it should not be criticized. Accounts receivable turnover ranges from 9.20 to 134.21 in Table 14.19.

TABLE 14.19 **Accounts Receivable Turnover**

Company	2000	1999	1998	1997
Barnes & Noble	60.23	59.29	62.56	51.77
Dell Computer	9.79	9.20	10.32	9.53
Home Depot	72.79	58.96	51.16	54.74
Wal-Mart	134.21	131.46	129.55	123.51

Average Collection Period   The **average collection period ratio** may be difficult for outsiders to compute because it requires the analyst to input daily credit sales. Often, total sales are substituted for credit sales if most sales are known to be on credit.

$$\text{Average collection period} = \frac{\text{Accounts receivable}}{\text{Daily credit sales}} \qquad (14.13)$$

$$\text{Average collection period} = \frac{\$12}{\left(\$30/365 \text{ days}\right)} = 146 \text{ days}$$

Analysts often have trouble determining what proportion of sales were made on credit and which were for cash. Most firms do not separate these on their published financial reports. In the above example, we substituted total sales for daily credit sales. If all sales are *not* made on credit, this will underestimate the true average collection period.

An alternative method of computing the average collection period is to divide the receivables turnover into 365:

$$\text{Average collection period} = \frac{365 \text{ days}}{\text{Receivables turnover}} \qquad (14.14)$$

This is also called the *days sales in receivables* ratio. Again, this gives a meaningful result only if all or most sales are on credit. Table 14.20 reports sample values for the average collection period.

TABLE 14.20 Average Collection Period (days)

Company	2000	1999	1998	1997
Barnes & Noble	6	6	6	7
Dell Computer	37	39	35	38
Home Depot	5	6	7	7
Wal-Mart	3	3	3	3

Average Payment Period   The **average payment period** is used to determine whether a firm is having trouble paying its bills. It must be used cautiously because many firms stretch their payables to conserve cash and to take advantage of interest-free loans from suppliers. Table 14.21 demonstrates that the average payment period is usually between 1 and 2 months.

TABLE 14.21 Average Payment Period (days)

Company	2000	1999	1998	1997
Barnes & Noble	81	80	77	85
Dell Computer	63	61	62	64
Home Depot	26	26	27	27
Wal-Mart	36	35	35	33

$$\text{Average payment period} = \frac{\text{Accounts payable}}{\text{Average purchases per day}}$$

$$\text{Average payment period} = \frac{\text{Accounts payable}}{\text{Annual purchases}/365} \qquad (14.15)$$

$$\text{Average payment period} = \frac{\$8}{\left(\$21/365 \text{ days}\right)} = 139$$

Note that we used the cost of goods sold to represent the average annual purchases.

Financing Ratios

Financing ratios measure how leveraged the firm is. For this reason they are also called *financial leverage ratios* or simply *leverage ratios*. As we discussed in Chapter 13, firm risk is closely tied to the firm's leverage.

Study Tip

Many students confuse the debt ratio with the debt–equity ratio. Note that the debt ratio seldom exceeds 100%, whereas the debt–equity ratio often does.

Debt Ratio   The **debt ratio** measures the proportion of assets financed by debt:

$$\text{Debt ratio} = \frac{\text{Total liabilities}}{\text{Total assets}} \qquad (14.16)$$

$$\text{Debt ratio} = \frac{\$36.5}{\$50} = 0.73$$

The greater the debt ratio, the more leveraged, and hence more risky, is the firm. Table 14.22 shows sample debt ratios.

TABLE 14.22 Debt Ratio

Company	2000	1999	1998	1997
Barnes & Noble	17.88%	13.78%	17.90%	22.81%
Dell Computer	4.43	7.45	3.82	1.50
Home Depot	4.56	11.73	11.68	13.37
Wal-Mart	31.39	21.23	23.83	26.85

Debt–Equity Ratio   The **debt–equity ratio** shows the relationship between the suppliers of long-term debt and equity:

$$\text{Debt-equity ratio} = \frac{\text{Long-term debt}}{\text{Stockholders' equity}} \qquad (14.17)$$

$$\text{Debt-equity ratio} = \frac{\$20}{\$13.5} = 1.48$$

It is another measure of leverage that is used in conjunction with the debt ratio. Table 14.23 presents sample debt–equity ratios.

TABLE 14.23 Debt–Equity Ratio

Company	2000	1999	1998	1997
Barnes & Noble	50.99%	36.70%	53.56%	63.60%
Dell Computer	9.57	22.06	1.31	1.66
Home Depot	6.08	17.92	18.36	20.93
Wal-Mart	64.54	45.50	52.28	58.43

Times Interest Earned   The **times interest earned ratio**, often called the TIE ratio, measures the firm's ability to meet its interest payments:

$$\text{Times interest earned} = \frac{\text{EBIT}}{\text{Interest expense}} \qquad (14.18)$$

$$\text{Times interest earned} = \frac{\$4}{\$2} = 2$$

This ratio does not actually measure leverage; rather, it indicates the firm's ability to service the debt it already has incurred. The TIE ratio is primarily of interest to the firm's creditors, who want to be sure the firm can make its interest payments. Table 14.24 provides sample TIE ratios.

TABLE 14.24 **Times Interest Earned**

Company	2000	1999	1998	1997
Barnes & Noble	9.67	7.17	3.88	3.01
Dell Computer	73.09	81.15	457.00	107.71
Home Depot	53.11	40.03	32.38	40.17
Wal-Mart	9.42	9.56	7.90	6.46

Market Ratios

The **market ratios** are distinct from the other ratios in that they are based, at least in part, on information not contained in the firm's financial statements. The term *market* is used as a reference to the financial markets where security prices are established. Market ratios are closely watched by those considering security purchases.

Earnings per Share (EPS)   **Earnings per share ratios** report the net income per share of stock:

$$EPS = \frac{\text{Net income available to stockholders}}{\text{Number of shares outstanding}} \qquad (14.19)$$

$$EPS = \frac{\$1.2 - \$0.2}{1} = 1$$

This ratio helps investors adjust for additional stock issues when reviewing company performance over time. Because a firm can choose to issue any number of shares of stock, it is impossible to compare EPS across companies. For example, if a firm has 100 shares outstanding and earns $1,000, EPS is $10. If the firm has 1,000 shares outstanding and earns $1,000, EPS is $1. Table 14.25 demonstrates the difficulty of comparing EPS across firms.

TABLE 14.25 **Earnings per Share Ratios**

Company	2000	1999	1998	1997
Barnes & Noble	1.87	1.35	0.96	0.74
Dell Computer	0.66	0.58	0.36	0.17
Home Depot	1.03	0.73	0.53	0.43
Wal-Mart	1.25	0.99	0.78	0.67

Notice that net income is adjusted to reflect only what is available to shareholders by subtracting dividend payments that are due preferred shareholders (100,000 shares with a $2 per share dividend = $200,000).

Price/Earnings Ratio (PE)   The **price/earnings (PE) ratio** is one of the more interesting ratios because it provides clues as to what other investors in the market are projecting about the firm's future. Table 14.26 reports a number of firms' PE ratios. Interpreting these ratios can be difficult. A high PE ratio may mean that the market is projecting that future earnings will increase. When earnings increase, if the price remains constant, the PE will fall back to a normal level.

TABLE 14.26 Price/Earnings Ratios

Company	2000	1999	1998	1997
Barnes & Noble	10.54	45.11	38.72	−19.82
Dell Computer	58.24	95.92	39.70	31.19
Home Depot	58.58	59.31	40.16	27.35
Wal-Mart	46.80	46.49	27.08	18.70

$$PE = \frac{\text{Market price of common stock}}{\text{Earnings per share}} \tag{14.20}$$

$$PE = \frac{\$20}{\$1} = 20$$

The PE ratio calculation requires that the analyst know the current market price of the firm's stock. For this example we assumed it was $20.

Of course, as earnings fall, the PE may rise and become very large. Most reporting services do not report the PE when earnings are very small or negative. The press uses various terminology when referring to a firm's PE ratio. It may say the stock is selling for 20 times earnings or that the stock has a multiple of 20.

Another interpretation of the PE is that it shows how much investors are willing to pay for each dollar of earnings. A firm with a PE of 20 means that investors are paying $20 for each dollar of earnings. This raises the question of why investors would pay more per dollar of earnings for one stock than for another. Consider that when Planet Hollywood went public, its stock sold at 112 times earnings (PE = 112). Microsoft regularly sells at about 30 times earnings. By comparison, Compaq computer has a PE of 19.6 and General Electric has a PE of 38.9. One reason investors may pay a premium for a stock is that they may think future earnings will be higher. Another reason is that investors may think the firm is less risky than another, so each dollar of earnings is more valuable. We will return to this discussion in Chapter 18.

Market-to-Book Ratio   The **market-to-book ratio** is another way of measuring how the market values the firm. If the ratio is greater than 1, it means that the market is valuing the firm at a premium over the acquisition price of its assets.

$$\text{Market-to-book ratio} = \frac{\text{Market value per share}}{\text{Book value per share}} \tag{14.21}$$

$$\text{Market-to-book ratio} = \frac{\$20}{\$13.5/1} = 1.48$$

Note that book value per share is computed by dividing total equity (not just common equity) by the number of shares outstanding. The market value per share is simply the firm's stock price. Sample market-to-book ratios are reported in Table 14.27.

TABLE 14.27 Market-to-Book Ratio

Company	2000	1999	1998	1997
Barnes & Noble	1.56	3.79	4.06	2.27
Dell Computer	18.65	54.78	24.76	14.20
Home Depot	10.57	10.21	6.24	3.99
Wal-Mart	9.45	9.06	4.82	3.17

Before moving on to the comprehensive example that follows, take a moment to review the formulas for these ratios, which are summarized in Table 14.28.

TABLE 14.28 Summary of Common Ratios

Profitability Ratios

$$\text{Return on equity} = \frac{\text{Net income after tax}}{\text{Common equity}}$$

$$\text{Return on assets} = \frac{\text{Net income after tax}}{\text{Total assets}}$$

$$\text{Gross profit margin} = \frac{\text{Sales} - \text{Cost of goods sold}}{\text{Sales}} = \frac{\text{Gross profits}}{\text{Sales}}$$

$$\text{Operating profit margin} = \frac{\text{Operating profits}}{\text{Sales}}$$

$$\text{Net profit margin} = \frac{\text{Net income after tax}}{\text{Sales}}$$

Activity Ratios

$$\text{Inventory turnover} = \frac{\text{Cost of goods sold}}{\text{Inventory}}$$

$$\text{Fixed asset turnover} = \frac{\text{Sales}}{\text{Fixed assets}}$$

$$\text{Total asset turnover} = \frac{\text{Sales}}{\text{Total assets}}$$

$$\text{Receivables turnover} = \frac{\text{Sales}}{\text{Accounts receivable}}$$

$$\text{Average collection period} = \frac{\text{Accounts receivable}}{\text{Daily credit sales}}$$

$$\text{Average collection period} = \frac{365 \text{ days}}{\text{Receivables turnover}}$$

$$\text{Average payment period} = \frac{\text{Accounts payable}}{\text{Average purchases per day}}$$

$$\text{Average payment period} = \frac{\text{Accounts payable}}{\text{Average purchases/365}}$$

Liquidity Ratios

$$\text{Current ratio} = \frac{\text{Current assets}}{\text{Current liabilities}}$$

$$\text{Quick ratio} = \frac{\text{Current assets} - \text{Inventory}}{\text{Current liabilities}}$$

$$\text{Net working capital} = \text{Current assets} - \text{Current liabilities}$$

Financing Ratios

$$\text{Debt ratio} = \frac{\text{Total liabilities}}{\text{Total assets}}$$

$$\text{Debt–equity ratio} = \frac{\text{Long-term debt}}{\text{Stockholders' equity}}$$

$$\text{Times interest earned} = \frac{\text{EBIT}}{\text{Interest}}$$

Market Ratios

$$\text{EPS} = \frac{\text{Net income}}{\text{Number of shares outstanding}}$$

$$\text{Market-to-book ratio} = \frac{\text{Market value per share}}{\text{Book value per share}}$$

$$\text{P/E} = \frac{\text{Market price of common stock}}{\text{Earnings per share}}$$

Comprehensive Example: J. C. Penney

In this section we use J. C. Penney's actual balance sheet and income statement to compute each of the ratios previously introduced. The following tables provide J. C. Penney's financial statements: Table 14.29 (balance sheet), Table 14.30 (income statement), Table 14.31 (common-sized balance sheet), and Table 14.32 (common-sized income statement). By tracking the numbers from the financial statements to the ratios, you can follow how each ratio is constructed. The ratios are presented in Table 14.33, which will provide a useful reference for your own future ratio analysis projects.

Computing J. C. Penney's Ratios

Table 14.33 uses J. C. Penney's income statement and balance sheet to compute the ratios discussed in the previous sections. Notice that when real data for real companies are used, some ratios are not meaningful or cannot be computed. For example, we do not know average credit sales for J. C. Penney, so we cannot compute its average collection period.

The common-sized balance sheet reports each line entry divided by total assets. The common-sized income statement reports each line item divided by total sales.

Study Tip

Notice how we proceed in our analysis. We begin by computing all of the ratios and putting them into groups. We next analyze each group to spot problems. Finally, we attempt to confirm our initial conclusions by reviewing the ratios across different categories.

Analysis

Now that the ratios have been computed (see Table 14.33), we can begin our analysis of J. C. Penney by reviewing the ratios in each category as a group. For example, we look at all of the profitability ratios to determine whether J. C. Penney's earnings have been acceptable. Similarly, we can look at the liquidity, activity, financing, and market ratios as groups of ratios to determine whether the firm is performing well or poorly in each area. Once we have a general understanding of the firm's performance strengths and weaknesses, we can look at the ratios in aggregate to see if the theories reached during the analysis-by-type phase of the study are sustained.

To conduct ratio analysis, we need a ratio history. This will allow us to establish a trend. Industry ratios will allow us to conduct a cross-sectional study. The most recent industry ratio is included in Table 14.33 along with the 10-year trend in J. C. Penney's ratios.

Our initial review shows that J. C. Penney has a profitability problem. Its gross profit margin, operating profit margin, and net profit margin are lower than the industry, and more importantly, the 10-year trend in all of its profitability ratios has been deteriorating.

Liquidity appears to be a strong point for J. C. Penney. The relatively low current ratio indicates the firm is operating with fewer current assets than normal. This is a sign of efficiency. However, the low quick ratio when compared to the current ratio suggests that J. C. Penney may be holding excessive or slow-moving inventory. If this is true, we would expect to see low inventory turnover. A look ahead at this ratio shows that inventory turnover is indeed somewhat below the industry average.

The activity ratios are generally unexciting, with the exception of inventory turnover, since J. C. Penney does not have sufficient receivables to be meaningful.

J. C. Penney has been reducing its debt load. The times interest earned is still above norms.

When all of these ratios are taken together, we see that the firm has lower profitability than others in its industry and that there may be a deteriorating trend. While

TABLE 14.29 Consolidated Balance Sheets for J. C. Penny Company, Inc. and Subsidiaries ($ in millions)

	2000	1999
Assets		
Current assets		
Cash (including short-term investments of $1,233 and $95)	$ 1,233	$ 96
Retained interest in JCP Master Credit Card Trust	—	415
Receivables, net (bad debt reserve of $20 and $149)	1,138	4,268
Merchandise inventory (including LIFO reserves of $270 and $227)	5,947	6,060
Prepaid expenses	154	168
Total current assets	8,472	11,007
Property and equipment		
Land and buildings	3,089	3,109
Furniture and Fixtures	3,955	4,045
Leasehold improvements	1,151	1,179
Accumulated depreciation	(2,883)	(2,875)
Property and equipment, net	5,312	5,458
Investments, principally held by Direct Marketing	1,827	1,961
Deferred policy acquisition costs	929	847
Goodwill and other intangible assets, net (accumulated amortization of $340 and $227)	3,056	2,941
Other assets	1,292	1,294
Total assets	**$20, 888**	**$23,508**
Liabilities and Stockholders' Equity		
Current liabilities		
Accounts payable and accrued expenses	$ 3,351	$ 3,443
Short-term debt	330	1,924
Current maturities of long-term debt	625	438
Deferred taxes	159	107
Total current liabilities	4,465	5,912
Long-term debt	5,844	7,143
Deferred taxes	1,461	1,512
Insurance policy and claims reserve	1,017	946
Other liabilities	873	893
Total liabilities	**$13,660**	**$16,406**
Stockholders' equity		
Preferred stock authorized, 25 million shares; issued and outstanding, 0.7 million and 0.8 million shares Series B ESOP convertible preferred	$ 446	$ 475
Common stock, par value 50 cents: authorized, 1,250 million shares; issued and outstanding 261 million and 250 million shares	3,266	2,850
Reinvested earnings	3,590	3,791
Accumulated other comprehensive income/(loss)	(74)	(14)
Total stockholder equity	**$ 7,228**	**$ 7,102**
Total liabilities and stockholder equity	**$20,888**	**$23,508**

TABLE 14.30 **Consolidated Statement of Income for J. C. Penny Company, Inc. and Subsidiaries ($ in millions)**

	2000	1999
Revenue		
Retail sales, net	$31,391	$29,439
Direct marketing revenue	1,119	1,022
Total revenue	**$32,510**	**$30,461**
Costs and Expenses		
Cost of goods sold	$23,374	21,642
Selling, general, and administrative expenses	7,164	6,623
Cost and expenses of direct marketing	872	785
Real estate and other	(28)	(26)
Net interest expense and credit operations	299	391
Acquisition amortization	129	113
Other charges and credits, net	169	(22)
Total costs and expenses	**$31,979**	**$29,506**
Income before income taxes	531	955
Income taxes	195	361
Net income	**$ 336**	**$ 594**

sales have grown, they have not grown as rapidly as have costs. One area of concern to J. C. Penney should be that their inventory turnover ratios are slowing and are substantially lower than the industry. This indicates that their products are not selling as well as they should. The firm appears to be reducing margins by lowering prices to move its inventory, but this is resulting in reduced ROE and ROA. Figure 14.4 shows that, due to the problems the firm has encountered, the market price of J. C. Penney's stock has fallen even while the S&P 500 has gone up.

FIGURE 14.4 **Relative Prices of S&P 500 and J. C. Penney, 1996–2001**

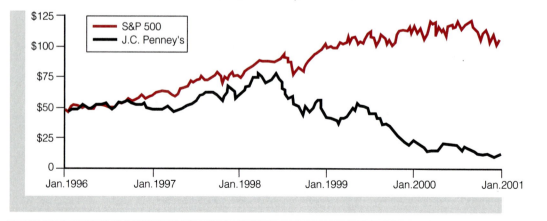

TABLE 14.31 Common-sized Balance Sheet for J. C. Penny Company, Inc. and Subsidiaries ($ in millions)

	2000	1999
Assets		
Current assets		
Cash (including short-term investments of $1,233 and $95)	5.90%	0.41%
Retained interest in JCP Master Credit Card Trust	0.00	1.77
Receivables, net (bad debt reserve of $20 and $149)	5.45	18.16
Merchandise inventory (including LIFO reserves of $270 and $227)	28.47	25.78
Prepaid expenses	0.74	0.71
Total current assets	**40.56%**	**46.82%**
Property and equipment		
Land and buildings	14.79%	13.23%
Furniture and Fixtures	18.93	17.21
Leasehold improvements	5.51	5.02
Accumulated depreciation	−13.80	−12.23
Property and equipment, net	**25.43%**	**23.22%**
Investments, principally held by Direct Marketing	8.75%	8.34%
Deferred policy acquisition costs	4.45	3.60
Goodwill and other intangible assets, net (accumulated amortization of $340 and $227)	14.63	12.51
Other assets	6.19	5.50%
Total assets	**100.00%**	**100.00%**
Liabilities and Stockholders' Equity		
Current liabilities		
Accounts payable and accrued expenses	16.04%	14.65%
Short-term debt	1.58	8.18
Current maturities of long-term debt	2.99	1.86
Deferred taxes	0.76	0.46
Total current liabilities	**21.38%**	**25.12%**
Long-term debt	27.98%	30.39%
Deferred taxes	6.99	6.43
Insurance policy and claims reserve	4.87	4.02
Other liabilities	4.18	3.80
Total liabilities	**65.40%**	**69.79%**
Stockholders' equity		
Preferred stock authorized, 25 million shares; issued and outstanding, 0.7 million and 0.8 million shares Series B ESOP convertible preferred	2.14%	2.02%
Common stock, par value 50 cents: authorized, 1,250 million shares; issued and outstanding 261 million and 250 million shares	15.64	12.12
Reinvested earnings	17.19	16.13
Accumulated other comprehensive income/(loss)	−0.35	−0.06
Total stockholder equity	**34.60%**	**30.21%**
Total liabilities and stockholder equity	**100.00%**	**100.00%**

TABLE 14.32 Common-sized Income statement for J. C. Penny Company, Inc. and Subsidiaries ($ in millions)

	2000	1999
Revenue		
Retail sales, net	96.56%	96.64%
Direct marketing revenue	3.44	3.36
Total revenue	**100.00%**	**100.00%**
Costs and Expenses		
Cost of goods sold	71.90%	71.05%
Selling, general, and administrative expenses	22.04	21.74
Cost and expenses of Direct Marketing	2.68	2.58
Real estate and other	−0.09	−0.09
Net interest expense and credit operations	0.92	1.28
Acquisition amortization	0.40	0.37
Other charges and credits, net	0.52	−0.07
Total costs and expenses	**98.37%**	**96.86%**
Income before income taxes	**1.63%**	**3.14%**
Income taxes	0.60	1.19
Net income	**1.03%**	**1.95%**

Let us summarize how we proceeded with our analysis of J. C. Penney. First we computed a large number of ratios and organized them by type. We then collected historical and industry data for comparison. We next reviewed the ratios by type, looking for clues about where there may be problems. When a ratio suggested a problem, we looked for confirmation in other ratios. Finally, we looked at the ratios in aggregate to summarize our analysis of the company.

EXTENSION 14.1

Du Pont Ratio Analysis

In the last section, we introduced and demonstrated one approach to financial analysis. Although this method is effective, it is time-consuming. An alternative method for identifying firm problems and using ratios is provided by **Du Pont ratio analysis**. This method of analysis was developed at the Du Pont Corporation and is now often used by analysts. Its primary contribution is to help organize and give direction to our analysis.

There Is a Tradeoff Among Margin, Volume, and Leverage

As we noted at the beginning of the last section, the most important ratio is the return on equity. The firm can change its ROE by adjusting any one of three components.

- It can have high turnover of its product.
- It can have large margins on each sale.
- It can be highly leveraged.

TABLE 14.33 Summary of Ratios for J. C. Penney

Formula	2000	1999	Industry	10-Year Trend
Profitability Ratios				
Return on equity = $\dfrac{\text{Net income after tax}}{\text{Common equity}}$	336 ÷ 6,782 = 4.95%	594 ÷ 6,627 = 8.96%	5.20%	⇓
Return on assets = $\dfrac{\text{Net income after tax}}{\text{Total assets}}$	336 ÷ 20,888 = 1.61%	594 ÷ 23,508 = 2.53%	0.84%	⇓
Gross profit margin = $\dfrac{\text{Sales − Cost of goods sold}}{\text{Sales}} = \dfrac{\text{Gross profits}}{\text{Sales}}$	9,136 ÷ 32,510 = 28.10%	8,819 ÷ 30,461 = 28.95%	33.98%	⇓
Operating profit margin = $\dfrac{\text{Operating profits}}{\text{Sales}}$	830 ÷ 32,510 = 2.55%	1,346 ÷ 30,461 = 4.42%	4.95%	⇓
Net profit margin = $\dfrac{\text{Net income after tax}}{\text{Sales}}$	336 ÷ 32,510 = 1.03%	594 ÷ 30,461 = 1.95%	2.2%	⇓
Liquidity Ratios				
Current ratio = $\dfrac{\text{Current assets}}{\text{Current liabilities}}$	8,472 ÷ 4,465 = 1.90	11,007 ÷ 5,912 = 1.86	2.33	⇓
Quick ratio = $\dfrac{\text{Current assets − Inventory}}{\text{Current liabilities}}$	(8,472 − 5,947) ÷ 4,465 = 0.57	(11,007 − 6,060) ÷ 5,912 = 0.84	0.78	⇓
Net working capital = Current assets − Current liabilities	8,472 − 4,465 = 4,007	11,007 − 5,912 = 5,095	NA	≈
Activity Ratios				
Inventory turnover = $\dfrac{\text{Cost of goods sold}}{\text{Inventory}}$	23,374 ÷ 5,947 = 3.93 ×	21,642 ÷ 6,060 = 3.57 ×	4.5 ×	≈
Fixed asset turnover = $\dfrac{\text{Sales}}{\text{Fixed assets}}$	32,510 ÷ 5,312 = 6.12 ×	30,461 ÷ 5,458 = 5.58 ×	13.3 ×	⇑
Total asset turnover = $\dfrac{\text{Sales}}{\text{Total assets}}$	32,510 ÷ 20,888 = 1.56 ×	30,461 ÷ 23,508 = 1.30 ×	2.6 ×	≈
Receivables turnover = $\dfrac{\text{Sales}}{\text{Accounts receivable}}$	32,510 ÷ 1,138 = 28.57 ×	30,461 ÷ 4,268 = 7.14 ×	29.8 ×	⇑
Average collection period = $\dfrac{\text{Accounts receivable}}{\text{Daily credit sales}}$ Average collection period = $\dfrac{365 \text{ days}}{\text{Receivables turnover}}$	365 ÷ 28.57 = 12.76 days	365 ÷ 7.14 = 51.12 days	40.38 days	⇓
Average payment period = $\dfrac{\text{Accounts payable}}{\text{Average purchases per day}}$ Average payment period = $\dfrac{\text{Accounts payable}}{\text{Average purchases/365}}$	3,351 ÷ (23,374 ÷ 365) = 52.33 days	3,443 ÷ (21,642 ÷ 365) = 58.07 days	42.61 days	≈

(Continued)

TABLE 14.33 Summary of Ratios for J. C. Penney *(continued)*

Formula	2000	1999	Industry	10-Year Trend
Financing Ratios				
Debt ratio = $\dfrac{\text{Total liabilities}}{\text{Total assets}}$	13,660 ÷ 20,888 = 65.40%	16,406 ÷ 23,508 = 69.79%	30.67%	≈
Debt–equity ratio = $\dfrac{\text{Long-term debt}}{\text{Stockholders' equity}}$	5,844 ÷ 7,228 = 80.85%	7,143 ÷ 7,102 = 100.6%	72.14%	≈
Times interest earned = $\dfrac{\text{Earnings before interest and taxes (EBIT)}}{\text{Interest}}$	(531 + 299) ÷ 299 = 2.78 ×	(955 + 391) ÷ 391 = 3.44 ×	2.23 ×	⇓
Market Ratios				
EPS = $\dfrac{\text{Net income}}{\text{Number of shares outstanding}}$	336 ÷ 250 = 1.34	594 ÷ 250 = 2.38	NA	⇓
P/E = $\dfrac{\text{Market price of common stock}}{\text{Earnings per share}}$	19.625 ÷ 1.34 = 14.65	39.000 ÷ 2.38 = 16.39	31.47	⇓
Market-to-book ratio = $\dfrac{\text{Market value per share}}{\text{Book value per share}}$	19.625 ÷ (7,228 ÷ 250) = 0.679	39.000 ÷ (7,102 ÷ 250) = 1.37	1.40	≈

For example, in 1996 Carmike Cinemas has a turnover of 172.3 whereas Freidman's Jewelers has a turnover of only 3.34. Clearly Freidman's must earn more per sale than does Carmike. Similarly, a modest return on assets can result in a high ROE if the firm is highly leveraged. If a firm's ROE is declining or is below that of its competitors, we can review its turnover, margins, and leverage to see which appears to be the source of the problem. Once we have narrowed the scope of our analysis, we can investigate why this problem exists.

Calculation

The Du Pont analysis computes ROE as the product of margin, turnover, and leverage:

$$\text{ROE} = \text{Net profit margin} \times \text{Total asset turnover} \times \text{Equity multiplier} \quad (14.22)$$

The equity multiplier is a measure of the firm's leverage. The Du Pont relationship can be rewritten using the ratio formulas that follow:[2]

$$\text{ROE} = \frac{\text{Net income}}{\text{Sales}} \times \frac{\text{Sales}}{\text{Total assets}} \times \frac{1}{1 - \dfrac{\text{Total debt}}{\text{Total assets}}} \quad (14.23)$$

---

[2]Equation 14.23 requires that preferred stock be included with debt since our calculation of ROE is based only on common stock.

FIGURE 14.5 Du Pont Ratio

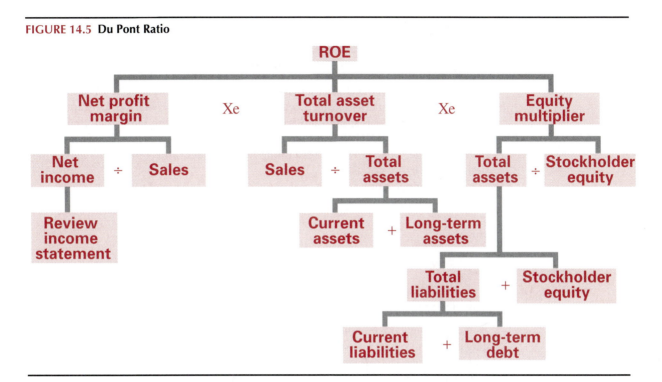

There is nothing mystical about this equation. With a little algebra it collapses to net income divided by equity. However, it is extremely useful as a tool to establish a beginning point for analysis. If ROE is declining or not as high as that of the firm's competitors, determine whether the problems seem to be with the margin, turnover, or leverage of the firm. Note that high leverage may mask problems with margin and turnover.

Once you have located the problem, examine the inputs to the troublesome ratio for additional clues. For example, if total asset turnover is declining, is it because sales have dropped or because the firm has acquired additional assets? Figure 14.5 can be used to track through the ratios to the source of the problem.

In Table 14.34 we have computed the Du Pont ratio for the last 10 years for J. C. Penney. We can easily see that the problem lies with the decline in profit margin since 1995.

TABLE 14.34 DuPont Analysis for J. C. Penney

	2000	1999	1998	1997	1996	1995	1994	1993	1992	1991
Profit margin	1.03%	1.95%	1.81%	2.33%	3.80%	4.87%	4.70%	4.07%	1.53%	3.31%
Total asset turnover	1.56	1.30	1.37	1.24	1.32	1.40	1.42	1.46	1.39	1.39
Equity multiplier	3.08	3.53	3.41	4.00	3.10	3.06	2.90	3.02	3.12	2.89
ROE	4.95%	8.95%	8.48%	11.53%	15.62%	20.89%	19.32%	18.01%	6.63%	13.34%

EXTENSION 14.2

Economic Value Added

This chapter has introduced many ways to evaluate the performance of a firm. Another method gaining popularity is called **economic value added (EVA)**. The concept behind its calculation and use is simple and appealing. Shareholders are most interested in how much a firm earns above what is needed to meet its minimum costs. This extra is what shareholders get to keep. While accounting numbers and ratios hint at this figure, they often obscure it.

The economic value added is computed using the following formula:

$$EVA = EBIT(1 - T) - (WACC \times Invested\ capital) \qquad (14.24)$$

where

$$
\begin{aligned}
EBIT &= \text{earnings before interest and taxes (operating income)} \\
T &= \text{marginal tax rate} \\
WACC &= \text{the weighted average cost of capital as in Chapter 12} \\
\text{Invested capital} &= \text{the sum of long-term capital and equity}
\end{aligned}
$$

Let us review this equation. The first term to the right of the equals sign adjusts operating income to reflect taxes. This gives us a value for income before subtracting out any interest expense. We can look at this term as the income available to pay for the capital used by the firm.

The second term computes the cost of capital for the firm. The firm's capital is the sum of the long-term debt and equity. The cost of this capital is found by multiplying by the weighted average cost of capital as we learned to compute in Chapter 12.

A positive EVA is interpreted as meaning that the firm is earning more than its capital cost. The extra represents an addition to shareholder wealth. Example 14.1 demonstrates the calculation of EVA.

E X A M P L E 14.1   Calculation of EVA

Compute EVA given the following information obtained from the balance sheet and income statement of Datamarine Corp.:

$$
\begin{aligned}
EBIT &= \$12,350,500 \\
\text{Tax rate} &= 44\% \\
WACC &= 14\%, \text{ based on the CAPM and average bond yields} \\
\text{Invested capital} &= \$35,550,000 \text{ found by adding together long-term debt, stockholder} \\
&\quad\ \text{equity, and reatined earnings.}
\end{aligned}
$$

Solution
Using the given figures in Equation 14.24:

$$
\begin{aligned}
EVA &= EBIT(1 - T) - \left(WACC \times Invested\ capital\right) \\
EVA &= \$12,350,500(1 - 0.44) - \left(0.14 \times \$35,550,000\right) \\
EVA &= \$6,916,280 - \$4,977,000 \\
EVA &= \$1,939,280
\end{aligned}
$$

Datamarine's shareholders are nearly $2 million better off due to the activity of the firm this year.

One of the reasons for the growing popularity of EVA is its strong link to owner wealth maximization. Overall, the stockholders of Datamarine in our example are $2 million wealthier. EVA can be used to determine how much can be paid in dividends without reducing shareholder wealth. Simply divide EVA by the number of shares outstanding to determine the maximum dividend per share.

Let us review what factors will increase EVA. If managers run the firm in such a way as to increase EBIT through increased efficiency or sales, EVA will go up. Similarly, anything that reduces WACC, such as lower risk, will increase EVA. This is consistent with our views of how stockholder wealth is maximized.

EVA is widely used as a method of determining employee compensation and bonuses. We have already discussed the idea of using stock price to motivate managers and to align their interest with those of stockholders so as to reduce agency costs. This works well for senior managers who clearly have enough influence on the overall activities of the firm to affect its stock price. The stock price is not as useful for motivating lower-level managers, who may not feel that what they do has a meaningful effect on the stock price. EVA can be applied to divisions, departments, or any other units that have separately prepared financial statements. Since the actions that increase EVA are often in the best interest of stockholders, EVA makes an attractive motivational tool. For example, managers who are compensated according to their unit's EVA will become aware of the cost of capital and want to get rid of underutilized assets. They will also want to reduce their working capital.

The concept of EVA is closely related to that of NPV. The idea behind NPV is that we accept a project if it returns more than its investment costs, after adjusting for the time value of money. Since EVA uses current period figures, no time value adjustment is needed. One way of looking at the EVA is that it is the NPV of the whole firm for one period.

EVA is not a panacea. While it has some attractive features, it also has some faults. Primary among them is that EVA only considers the current year's earnings. Thus it rewards projects with quick paybacks and penalizes long-term investments. This, of course, was the problem with compensating managers for maximizing profits.

Another problem with EVA is that it may not be as simple to compute as shown here. The original developer of EVA, Stern Stewart Management Services, indicates that more than 160 adjustments to financial statements are required to better estimate the true economic value of a firm's performance. Compustat, a well-known source of accounting data, charges an additional $6,000 per year to firms for this one statistic, in addition to the $10,000 yearly subscription cost.

Introduced in the early 1980s, EVA is currently achieving almost fadlike acceptance among corporations. We will have to watch its use over the next decade to determine whether EVA is indeed a fad or represents a meaningful and effective tool for corporate management.

Careers in Finance

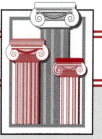

Trust Officer

Most banks have trust departments that employ trust officers. The purpose of a trust department is to handle financial affairs for someone. The types of services offered and the types of clients vary.

Many people assign trust departments as executors for wills and have the trust department manage the assets of underage heirs. Trust departments also handle investments for small pension funds and credit unions.

Trust officers are responsible for following the directions of their clients. They will determine exactly what level of risk the client wants to take and invest their assets strictly according to these instructions.

A trust may provide financial protection should a client ever become ill or incapacitated for a prolonged period. Trusts can continue beyond the client's lifetime, and they can be a source of income and support for their family or one or more designated beneficiaries.

Trust officers provide professional, unbiased, confidential investment management. As trustee, their goal is to meet their clients' requirements and protect their assets. Trust departments can serve as a sole trustee or work cooperatively with others, such as investment advisors and co-trustees.

Trust officers blend investment skills with banking skills to provide a full-service environment. This is a very challenging and competitive field of financial service and one that should be considered.

Putting the Ratios to Work

Now that we have a number of tools to use for analyzing firms, we need to decide how to proceed. The task can seem overwhelming until we decide on an organized approach.

The financial analysis of a firm should include the following steps:

1. Analysis of the economy in which the firm operates
2. Analysis of the industry in which the firm operates
3. Analysis of the competitors that currently challenge the firm
4. Analysis of the strengths and weaknesses of the firm, using common-sized statements and ratios

There are two primary methods you can follow to accomplish step 4. The first is to begin with the Du Pont ratio and let it lead you through the ratios. The second method is to summarize the ratios by type. For example, summarize the profitability ratios, then the liquidity ratios, and so on.

The weakness of this second method is that it can ignore ratio interactions.

Ratio Interaction

Ratio interaction is the effect one ratio has on another. For example, if sales fall, inventory turnover will also fall if inventory is held constant. The goal of ratio analysis is to locate the most fundamental cause of a firm's problem. We do not want to recommend that a firm adjust its inventory if the real problem is that its cost of goods sold is higher than that of its competitors. Because no two firms are likely to have the exact same problem, no two approaches to financial analysis are the same. The analyst must take on the role of a detective where ratios provide clues that must be tracked down and explained.

Reading Between the Lines

Often ratios simply do not tell the whole story. The analyst can only hope that they will provide flags that will prompt investigation and lead to the truth about the firm. For example, a banker reviews the statements of a credit applicant, looking for items that stand out as unusual. These unusual items generate questions that can be posed to the borrower. The customer's responses to these questions may put the issue to rest or may generate new, more probing questions.

It is important to recognize that ratio analysis is not useful for all firms. Conglomerates are especially difficult to analyze because widely different divisions may be combined on the financial statements. Insiders to the firm usually have departmental or divisional statements to use for management purposes, but outsiders may not have sufficient details to draw meaningful conclusions.

CHAPTER SUMMARY

The primary financial statements are the balance sheet, the income statement, and the statement of cash flows. The balance sheet provides a snapshot of the condition of the firm at one point in time. The right-hand side of the balance sheet lists the sources of capital the firm has used. The left-hand side of the balance sheet tells us how the firm has put the capital to work earning income.

The income statement provides information about income earned by the firm over a period of time. Finally, the statement of cash flows tells us how funds were raised and spent.

Financial ratios are helpful to both managers and analysts in that they allow the firm to be compared with other firms and with itself across time. This lets the analyst identify firm strengths and weaknesses.

The common-sized financial statement restates the balance sheet as a percentage of total assets and the income statement as a percentage of total sales. In essence, every line item becomes a ratio. These statements are useful for spotting trends over time that require management's attention.

The ratios are best analyzed in categories. The usual categories are profitability, liquidity, activity, financing, and market ratios. It is wise to compute all of the ratios in each category before drawing any strong conclusions.

The Du Pont ratio is useful for tracking down problems within a firm. Return on equity is computed as the product of net profit margin, total asset turnover, and leverage. If the return on equity is declining, the problem can usually be traced to one of these factors. This can help the analyst pinpoint the source of the firm's problems.

Economic values added (EVA) is a statistic that measures how much a firm earns above what is needed to meet its minimum costs. Its value lies in its application to motivating departmental managers. Its main weakness is that it only considers current year earnings.

KEY WORDS

accounts receivable
   turnover ratio 382
activity ratios 380
average collection period
   ratio 382

average payment
   period 383
balance sheet 364
common-sized income
   statement 373

cross-sectional
   analysis 370
current ratio 378
debt ratio 384
debt–equity ratio 384

Du Pont ratio analysis 392
earnings per share
   ratio 385
economic value added
   (EVA) 396

DISCUSSION QUESTIONS

1. Where can the financial analysts go to find information about companies and industry competitors?
2. The financial balance sheet is another way of looking at the relationship between the left-hand side of the balance sheet and the right-hand side. Explain this relationship.
3. What is meant by the statement that the balance sheet is a snapshot of the firm whereas the income statement shows the performance over time?
4. What is the difference between cross-sectional analysis and time series analysis?
5. Why is it necessary to conduct both cross-sectional analysis and time series analysis? Can ratios be used if not compared with another ratio?
6. What are the categories of ratios? What is the reason for segregating the ratios into categories?
7. What is the most important ratio? Why?

8. There are three profit margin ratios. What are they and what does each measure?
9. Is it always good when the current ratio increases? Suggest a possible scenario in which an increasing current ratio may indicate that the firm is having problems.
10. What does it mean if a firm's price/earnings ratio has increased over the last several years?
11. Describe the process the analyst should follow to conduct a ratio analysis of a firm.
12. What is the value of the Du Pont ratio analysis methodology? (Extension 14.1)
13. Describe how you would conduct a Du Pont analysis. (Extension 14.1)
14. What features of EVA have led to its increasing popularity as a motivational tool? What is its primary weakness?

PROBLEMS

1. Use the following balance sheet and income statement to compute the following ratios:

Balance Sheet

Assets	1996	1995
Current assets		
Cash	$ 1,013	$ 2,025
Accounts receivable	6,652	5,109
Inventories	6,700	10,611
Total current assets	$14,365	$17,745
Property, plant, and equipment	10,237	8,418
Accumulated depreciation	(5,741)	(4,165)
Net prop., plant, and equip.	4,496	4,253
Total assets	$18,861	$21,998

Balance Sheet

Liabilities and Equity	1996	1995
Current liabilities		
Accounts payable	$ 2,331	$ 1,184
Current long-term debt	2,000	1,995
Accrued expenses	3,158	2,808
Total current liabilities	$ 7,489	$ 5,987
Long-term debt	6,910	15,600
Total liabilities	$14,399	$21,587
Preferred stock	40	17
Common stock	129	138
Retained earnings	4,293	256
Total shareholders' equity	$ 4,462	$ 411
Total liabilities and equity	$18,861	$21,998

Income Statement

	1996	1995
Net sales	$69,169	$52,857
Cost of goods sold	(57,292)	(45,179)
Gross profit	$11,877	$ 7,678
Selling, general and admin.		
expenses	(5,353)	(5,547)
Income before deprec. and amort.	$ 6,524	$ 2,131
Depreciation and amortization	(697)	(531)
Nonoperating income	272	713
Earnings before interest and taxes	$ 6,099	$ 2,313
Interest expense	(875)	(1,245)
Income before tax	$ 5,224	$ 1,068
Taxes	(2,090)	(427)
Net income	$ 3,134	$ 641

    a. ROE
    b. ROA
    c. Gross profit margin
    d. Operating profit margin
    e. Net profit margin
    f. Current ratio
    g. Net working capital
    h. Inventory turnover
    i. Fixed asset turnover
    j. Total asset turnover
    k. Receivables turnover
    l. Average collection period
    m. Average payment period
    n. Debt ratio
    o. Debt–equity ratio
    p. TIE ratio

2. Using the balance sheet and income statement from problem 1, prepare a common-sized income statement and balance sheet.
3. Using the financial statements from problem 1, prepare a Du Pont analysis. What does it suggest that you look at more carefully?
4. Complete the balance sheet and sales information in the table that follows for Hyer Industries using the following financial data:

Debt ratio: 40%
Quick ratio: 1.25x

Total assets turnover: 3.5x
Average collection period: 39 days (based on total sales)
Gross profit margin on sales: 21%
Inventory turnover ratio: 11x

Balance Sheet

Cash	_____	Accounts payable	_____
Accounts receivable	_____	Long-term debt	95,000
Inventories	_____	Common stock	_____
Fixed assets	_____	Retained earnings	135,000
Total assets	450,000	Total liabilities and equity	_____
Sales	_____	Cost of goods sold	_____

5. You have been hired to examine the following data for Cyndee's Design Company as of December 31, 1997:

Sales	$800,000	Current ratio	2.31
Total assets	$600,000	Inventory turnover	6.45
Total liabilities	$362,000	Total asset turnover	1.33
Net income	$ 40,000		

    a. Compute the debt ratio, return on assets (ROA), return on equity (ROE), and net profit margin.
    b. Comment on the general position of the firm using the data you computed.
6. Doris Company has $1.4 million in current assets and $1.1 million in current liabilities. If it uses $0.7 million of cash to pay off some of its accounts payable, what will happen to the current ratio? What happens to net working capital?
7. Claire Cosmetics maintains a net profit margin of 6% and a total asset turnover ratio of 2.
    a. Calculate the ROA for the firm.
    b. If its debt–equity ratio is 40%, long-term debt is $10,000, its interest payments and taxes are each $6,000, and EBIT is $24,000, what is its ROE?
    c. Calculate and discuss ratios that show Claire's ability to meet the interest payments.
8. Skip's Repair Shop has an average accounts receivable of $9,651. Sales for the year were $13,836. What is the shop's accounts receivable turnover? What are its day's sales in receivables?
9. Assume a national corporation has a net income of $3.9 million and 150,000 shares of common stock. Currently, the stock is on the market for $27.50. Compute the earnings per share and the price/earnings ratio.

SELF-TEST PROBLEMS

1. Use the given income statement and balance sheet to compute the following ratios:

a. ROE
b. ROA
c. Gross profit margin
d. Operating profit margin
e. Net profit margin
f. Current ratio
g. Quick ratio
h. Net working capital
i. Inventory turnover

j. Fixed asset turnover
k. Total asset turnover
l. Receivables turnover
m. Average collection period
n. Average payment period
o. Debt ratio
p. Debt–equity ratio
q. TIE ratio

Income Statement

	2001	2000	1999
Sales	$77,425	$63,750	$59,625
Cost of sales	(62,800)	(53,750)	(51,050)
Gross profit	$14,625	$10,000	$ 8,575
Selling, general, and			
admin. expenses	(4,750)	(4,250)	(3,900)
Income before deprec. and amort.	$ 9,875	$ 5,750	$ 4,675
Depreciation and amortization	775	650	575
Nonoperating income	925	325	(125)
EBIT	$11,575	$ 6,725	$ 5,125
Interest expense	(575)	(750)	(1,025)
Income before tax	$11,000	$ 5,975	$ 4,100
Taxes	(5,250)	(2,825)	(2,075)
Net Income	$ 5,750	$ 3,150	$ 2,025

Balance Sheet

Assets	2001	2000	1999	Liabilities and equity	2001	2000	1999
Current assets				Current liabilities			
Cash	$ 875	$ 1,150	$ 1,175	Accounts payable	$ 5,275	$ 3,750	$ 2,850
Accounts receivable	4,850	4,225	3,950	Current long-term debt	1,500	1,975	2,225
Inventories	7,425	6,750	6,325	Accrued expenses	4,250	3,275	2,650
Prepaid expenses	825	475	275	Total current liabilities	$11,025	$ 9,000	$ 7,725
Total current assets	$13,975	$12,600	$11,725	Long-term debt	4,550	6,650	7,775
Property, plant, and equip.	17,950	15,475	14,425	Total liabilities	$15,575	$15,650	$15,500
Accumulated depreciation	(6,850)	(6,025)	(5,375)	Preferred stock	250	250	250
Net prop., plant, and equip.	$11,100	$ 9,450	$ 9,050	Common stock	5,275	4,125	4,125
Total assets	$25,075	$22,050	$20,775	Retained earnings	3,975	2,025	900
				Total shareholder's equity	$ 9,500	$ 6,400	$ 5,275
				Total liabilities and equity	$25,075	$22,050	$20,775

2. Using the financial statements from problem 1, prepare a common-sized balance sheet and income statement.
3. Using the financial statements from problem 1, prepare a Du Pont analysis. (Extension 14.1)
4. Compute the profitability ratios for Evergreen Inc. using the following information:

Sales	$6,125 million
Gross profit	$1,425 million
Operating profit	$975 million
Net income	$550 million
Total assets	$3,750 million
Common equity	$1,625 million

5. Compute the liquidity ratios for Evergreen Inc. using the following information:

Inventory	$625 million
Current assets	$1,325 million
Current liabilities	$1,125 million

6. Compute the activity ratios for Evergreen Inc. using the information from problems 4 and 5, in addition to the following:

Accounts receivable	$475 million
Accounts payable	$675 million
Cost of sales	$4,700 million
Fixed assets	$2,425 million

7. Compute the financing ratios for Evergreen Inc. using the information from problems 4, 5, and 6, in addition to the following:

Preferred stock	$0 million
Interest expense	$60 million

8. Evergreen Inc. currently has 475 million shares outstanding valued at $52.50 per share. Using the information from problems 4 through 7, compute the market ratios.

9. Assume an international conglomerate has a net income of $975 million, stockholder's equity of $3,525 million, and 850 million shares outstanding currently valued in the market at $57.50 per share. Compute the market ratios.

10. Use the Du Pont model to analyze the following data from East Coast Distributors: (Extension 14.1)

	2001	2000	1999
Sales	$1,500	$1,200	$975
Net income	$95	$70	$60
Total assets	$775	$600	$450
Stockholder's equity	$240	$230	$225

WEB EXPLORATION

1. Table 14.1 lists several sources of data about firms. Go to www.quote.com/quotecom/stocks/ and input a stock name in the Get Quote box. Click on the SEC button. You will see a long list of required filing documents. Click to sort by document type. Review each document to familiarize yourself with where to find different types of data.

2. Go to quicken.excite.com/investments/quotes and look up information on J. C. Penney (symbol = JCP). Review each of the menu items listed on the left of the screen. Write a summary of how J. C. Penney has responded to the problems raised by the comprehensive example in this chapter.

MINI CASE

You are applying for a position in the finance department at Buy Mart stores. Before going in for the second interview, you decide that you should become very familiar with current condition of the firm. Buy Mart is a major retail chain that competes with K-Mart, Wal-Mart, and Target in many markets. Use Buy Mart's income statement and balance sheet provided here to compute the ratios discussed in this chapter. In addition, compute the common-sized income and balance sheet. Use the ratios to discuss the strengths and weaknesses of the firm and to suggest areas where management should focus attention. Find industry numbers to help with your cross-sectional analysis.

Buy Mart's Balance Sheet
(figures in millions)

Fiscal Year Ending	2001	2000	Fiscal Year Ending	2001	2000
Assets			*Assets*		
Current assets:			Property, plant, and equipment		
Cash	406	458	Property, plant and equipment	10,768	10,116
Marketable securities	NA	NA	Less accumulated depreciation	5,028	4,815
Account receivable	NA	NA	Net property, plant, and equipment	5,740	5,301
Inventories	6,354	6,635			
Other current assets	973	1,092	Invest & adv to subs	200	94
Total current assets	7,733	8,882	Deposits and other assets	613	1,180
			Total Assets	14,286	16,397

Buy Mart's Balance Sheet
(figures in millions continued)

Fiscal Year Ending	2001	2000	Fiscal Year Ending	2001	2000
Liabilities & Stockholder's Equity			Liabilities & Stockholder's Equity		
Current liabilities:			Stockholders' equity:	1,478	1,629
Account payable	2,009	1993	Preferred stock	980	NA
Current long-term debt	156	7	Common stock	486	486
Accrued expenses	1,437	1,264	Capital surplus	1,608	1,624
Total current liabilities	3,602	3,264	Retained earnings	3,105	3,326
Long-term debt	2,121	3,935	Treasury stock	(37)	(92)
			Other equities	(70)	(64)
Non-current capital leases	1,478	1,629	Total shareholer's equity	6,072	5,280
Other long-term liabilities	1,478	1,629			
			Total Liabilities & Stockholders' Equity	14,286	15,397

Notes: The stock price on Dec 31, 2000, was $7.00, and on Dec 31, 2001, was $10.50. There were 486 million shares outstanding Dec 31, 2001, and 460 million outstanding on Dec. 31, 2000.

Buy Mart's Income Statement
($000,000's)

Fiscal Year Ending	2001	2000	Fiscal Year Ending	2001	2000
Net sales	31,437	34,654	Income before taxes	330	(750)
Cost of goods sold	24,390	26,996	Provision for income taxes	(68)	(222)
Gross profit	7,047	7,658	Other income	(31)	38
General and admin expenses	6,264	7,554	Net income before ex. items	231	(490)
Income before dep. and amort.	783	104	Ex. items and disc. ops	(451)	81
Non-operating income	NA	(408)	Net income	(220)	(571)
Interest expense	453	446			

Financial Planning, Forecasting, and Cash Budgets

Chapter Objectives

By the end of this chapter you should be able to:

1. Establish the need for financial forecasting
2. Make sales forecasts
3. Understand how to prepare cash budgets
4. Prepare pro forma statements
5. Determine external funds needed
6. Project the maximum sustainable growth rate

Good ideas, good products, and a good work ethic are not enough to succeed in business; it also takes money. Money may not be available unless your future financial plans ensure that it is. In this chapter we investigate how firms plan for success. Clearly, no firm plans for failure, but a failure to plan can lead to just that. Financial managers spend a substantial amount of their time in the planning process. This is because raising funds and investing funds take time. The more lead time the financial manager has to identify good projects for investment or to secure new sources of funds, the better the firm is likely to do.

A budget is a forecast of the future. In Chapters 10 and 11 we investigated how capital budgets are prepared. Projects are identified, analyzed, and either accepted or rejected. This chapter is a natural extension of that process. Once we have identified a capital budget, we need to determine how to implement it. The new projects eventually will generate revenues, but initially they will consume capital. The financial manager must determine the source of this capital. Cash budgets and pro formas, which are longer-term cash flow budgets, help in this process. This chapter also expands on the lessons learned in Chapter 14 because ratios provide a means for predicting the future.

Planning is a multistep process. It usually begins with the capital budget, which identifies what assets are to be acquired in the future and what new revenues are projected. This leads to the preparation of long-term financial plans. Long-term financial plans allow the manager to prepare short-term financial plans, called *cash budgets.* Together, these plans help managers direct the company's future rather than just react to it.

In the next section, we discuss the stages in the financial planning process. We then look at methods of gauging the key input to most financial plans: estimated sales. Using this estimate of sales, we develop the cash budget and long-term pro formas.

FINANCIAL PLANNING PROCESS

Financial forecasting is not an easy exercise. It involves making difficult projections about future events. It requires gathering input from a variety of sources, both inside and outside the firm. Is it really worth the effort?

Consider Intel, the world's leader in microchip manufacturing. During the late 1980s and 1990s, the firm enjoyed rapid growth in both sales and profits. By the beginning of the year 2001, however, personal computer sales had begun to slow substantially as consumers began to realize that their old computers were sufficient to satisfy their computing requirements. Intel must meet this problem by planning alternative business opportunities. Intel announced in early 2001 its forecast that the market for chips to be used in appliances and consumer devices would be the growth market this decade. By redirecting its resources toward the development of these products, Intel expects to continue its growth.

Weitek, in contrast, represents an example of ineffective planning. The firm, a maker of coprocessor chips, failed after Intel incorporated the math coprocessor into the 486 chip in the late 1980s. Clearly, effective planning can help firms survive such challenges.

The planning process can be broken down into two stages: long-term strategic goals and short-term operating plans.

Long-Term Strategic Goals

Every chapter thus far has repeated that the goal of the financial manager is to maximize shareholder wealth. However, this does not happen by accident. After reviewing its strengths, the firm identifies its opportunities and formulates strategies. For example, one of Disney's strengths is its brand name recognition and the public trust this name engenders about the quality of its entertainment. Faced with the question of how to continue its rapid growth when its theme parks appear to be stalled (Disneyland Paris has been a bust and Virginia has rejected Disney's America), Disney has now embarked on a plan to develop "places that were once wonderful that aren't wonderful anymore," according to a Disney corporate representative. It is currently revitalizing the once crime-ridden theater district on New York's 42nd Street. Similar plans include Chicago's State Street. The strategic plan is to create a series of Disney-branded, smaller-than-a-theme-park products that you can put on a 42nd Street anywhere in the world.

Once a firm has devised its strategic plan, and there may be many separate strategic plans for large conglomerates such as Disney, the **investment strategy** must be developed. This identifies specific investments using the capital budgeting process.

Managers need to identify the advantages the firm has over other firms and use those advantages to succeed. **Comparative advantage** is the edge a firm has over others because of production, distribution, or servicing. As an example, Apple Computer succeeded because it had a superior operating system. With the advantage of the Apple operating system eroded by the new Windows product, Apple must work hard to catch up. Apple has attempted to compete against Windows PCs by offering innovative designs and features. Unfortunately, with the loss of its comparative advantage from its operating system, Apple has had a difficult time showing consistent profits.

A **competitive advantage** exists when one firm has an edge because of the input and output markets in which it operates. For example, Intel has a tremendous competitive advantage over new entrants into the microchip business because of the huge cost of entry. With chip plants costing upward of $100 million, few firms have the resources to compete. Intel is benefiting from its competitive advantage by integrating more functions onto its chips.

Self-Test Review Questions*

1. Where should managers look for new ideas for company projects?
2. What is the purpose of the investment strategy?

Short-Term Operating Plans

Once strategic plans have been formulated, the firm converts those strategies into action plans. Plans for accomplishing strategies are called short-term operating plans. All capital budgeting decisions should be made with the strategic plan in mind. Although the senior management of the firm establishes the firm's strategies, others within the firm are usually responsible for their implementation.

Because the markets are very competitive, positive-NPV projects arise where the firm is taking advantage of a comparative or a competitive advantage. Let us expand on this concept further. Suppose that you have performed an analysis of a piece of equipment and have determined that it has a positive NPV. You might ask, "Why?" If the purchase of the machine will add value to the firm, every company will want to buy it. The demand for the machine will raise its cost until it no longer adds value to the firm. Therefore, the machine will have a positive NPV to a firm *only* when the firm has some comparative or competitive advantage in its use. For example, Disney can probably make its investment in New York's 42nd Street pay off because of the competitive advantage its brand name gives it. Most other firms would not find the investment to be profitable.

We leave further discussion of strategic planning to other courses and focus the balance of this chapter on financial planning. **Financial planning** is the allocation of a firm's resources to achieve its investment plans. This process usually begins with the sales forecast.

SALES FORECAST

The sales forecast is the beginning point for most financial forecasting. As we will show later, both cash budgets and pro formas require accurate sales forecasts to be reliable and useful. The sales figure is the driver that determines the balances in most other accounts. When we prepare spreadsheets, most formulas in them are tied to sales. Overly conservative or optimistic sales forecasts may leave the firm without the cash it needs to sustain business. You may be surprised to learn that it is as easy to run out of cash during periods of high sales growth as during periods of low sales. Each scenario can consume needed funds. Because sales forecasts are critical to everything that follows, we will investigate several forecasting methods.

The first step in forecasting sales is to gain an understanding of the state of the economy and its projected future. The economy tends to follow **business cycles**, which are periods in which the economy heats up and cools down. Sales, revenues, and profits tend to increase for a period, then level off or decline for a period. During the peaks of the business cycle, firms expand rapidly and growth tends to be high. As the economy enters a trough, businesses cut back and growth slows or disappears entirely. Business cycles are difficult to predict far ahead.

The second step in the forecasting process is to analyze the firm's industry. Is the industry in a declining market or a growth market? In the early 1970s, Post Versalog produced the finest slide rules available. Every engineer yearned for one of the enameled bamboo devices. When the electronic calculator was invented, Post found itself in a declining industry. It is not always that easy to identify the state of the industry. In the 1980s, the steel industry in the United States was declining. A massive reinvestment in plant modernization rejuvenated the entire industry and enabled it to compete around the world.

Finally, you must identify your competitors and determine what impact they are likely to have on your future. Consider the market for notebook computers. Industry analysts predict that notebook computer sales will increase 28% per year for the next several years, twice the growth rate of desktop computers. In 1996, Toshiba was the industry leader, with 26% of the market. Should it have predicted growth to be 28%? Probably not. Toshiba faced tough competition from IBM, Dell, and Gateway, all of which planned to capture a large share of this market. A thorough understanding of the firm's competitors and what they are doing is required to make forecasts that prove accurate.

Once you have an understanding of the economy, the industry, and the competition, you can make sales forecasts using historical average growth rates, regression analysis, and management opinions.

Estimating Sales Using the Historical Average Growth Rate

Perhaps the easiest and most widely used approach to estimating future sales growth is to compute the historical compounded average growth rate and apply it to future periods. Chapter 6 discussed how to compute compound average growth rates. To review, past sales are used to represent the present value. Most recent sales represent the future value. The number of periods is the number of *intervals* between the past sales and current sales. Finally, the figures are put into the future value formula and used to solve for the interest rate.

Self-Test Review Question*

What is the beginning point for most financial planning models?

Study Tip

You can find the *n*th root of a number on your calculator by raising the number to $1/n$. For example, the 4th root of 100 is equal to $100^{0.25}$.

E X A M P L E **15.1**   **Computing Average Compounded Growth Rate**

Average revenues (sales) for the 6,099 firms tracked by Morningstar's Equity Data are listed in the following table. What is the average compounded growth rate for the average company in the United States since 1997? What is the average sales forecast for 2002?

Year	Average Sales (Millions)
1997	$945.3
1998	985.9
1999	1,019.9
2000	1,053.6
2001	1,135.2

Solution
PV = $945.3, FV = $1,135.2, $n = 4$. Use the formula for future value of a lump sum:

$$FV = PV(1 + i)^n$$

$$\$1,135.2 = \$945.3(1 + i)^4$$

$$\frac{\$1,135.20}{\$945.30} = (1 + i)^4$$

$$\sqrt[4]{\frac{\$1,135.20}{\$945.30}} - 1 = i$$

$$0.0468 = i$$

This problem also can be solved using financial tables:

$$\$1,135.20 = \$945.30(FVIF_{4,i})$$

$$\$1,135.20/\$945.30 = FVIF_{4,i}$$

$$1.2009 = FVIF_{4,i}$$

The FVIF for four periods at 4% is 1.1699 and at 5% is 1.2155. We would estimate that the growth rate is about 4.5% using this method. You can also solve for growth rates using a financial calculator. Review Chapter 6 for a demonstration of how this is done.

The average firm in the United States experienced a 4.68% compounded growth rate between 1997 and 2001. Multiply 2001 sales by 1 plus this growth rate to forecast 2002 sales:

$$\text{Next year's sales} = \text{This year's sales} \times (1 + \text{Growth rate})$$

$$\text{1995 forecasted sales} = \$1,135.2 \times 1.0468 = \$1,188.33$$

FIGURE 15.1
Projecting Sales Growth

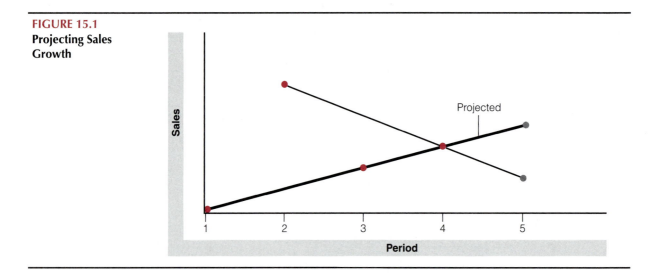

There are several problems with the above method. The first occurs if the periods used in the calculation of the growth rate are not normal years. Review Figure 15.1. Note the difference in projected growth if years 2 and 4 are used rather than years 1 and 4. This points out an important issue when making sales forecasts. The forecast is very dependent on the periods chosen for analysis. Generally, the longer the term used in making predictions, the more likely that annual variations will be smoothed out. However, is it appropriate to use sales from far in the past as an indication of what next year's sales may be? Not necessarily. The company or the economy may have changed substantially during the intervening years.

Self-Test Review Question*

Assume sales in 1996 were $1,000 and sales in 2000 were $1,800. What is the average compounded growth rate in sales?

Estimating Sales Using Regression Analysis

A more sophisticated approach to estimating sales is to apply ordinary least-squares regression analysis. *Regression analysis* finds the best-fitting line through a series of points. The line is found that minimizes the squared deviations between the points and the line. Once this line is determined, it can be extrapolated to predict future sales. Excel and Lotus have regression functions available that make finding the line easy.[1] Regression uses every year's sales, unlike the average growth rate approach, which only uses

---

[1]The regression analysis tool in Excel is an optional feature that is not automatically loaded. If it is not available on your computer system, it must be added.

*FV = PV(1 + i)^4, 1,800 = 1,000(1 + i)^4, (1.8)$^{0.25}$ − 1 = i = 0.1583 = 15.83%.

the first and last years. This makes regression analysis somewhat less sensitive to the years chosen for analysis.

E X A M P L E 15.2   Future Sales Using Regression

Use regression analysis to forecast 2002 sales for Quickfreeze Homemade Ice Cream. The 1997–2001 sales are as follows:

Year	Average Sales (millions)
1997	$ 77.0
1998	97.0
1999	132.0
2000	140.3
2001	148.8

Solution

In the following graph, Excel was used to plot a trend line using regression. The equation of the line that best fits the data is $y = 18.69x - 37{,}111$. Plugging 2002 into this equation for x, we predict 2002 sales to be $175.55 million. The r^2 is a measure of how well the line fits the data. An r^2 of 0.9293 means that 92.93% of the variation of sales is predicted by the equation and the year.

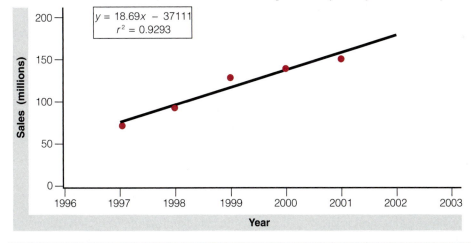

Regression analysis is helpful if the firm's sales have been growing at a constant rate and the trend is expected to continue. The method has the advantage of smoothing year-to-year variations while still allowing for every year to affect the trend. This does not guarantee its reliability. Review Figure 15.2. Do you think the regression line does a good job of forecasting sales for the Independent Insurance Group? Not really. Simple regression attempted to fit a straight line where a curved line would have fit better. Graphing the data will help you determine whether another method of forecasting sales should be tried. In this case a nonlinear regression line would have been a better choice.

Always review the data carefully before accepting the results of your statistical analysis. Common sense should rule. If your result does not appear reasonable, it probably is not and the forecast should be prepared using another method.

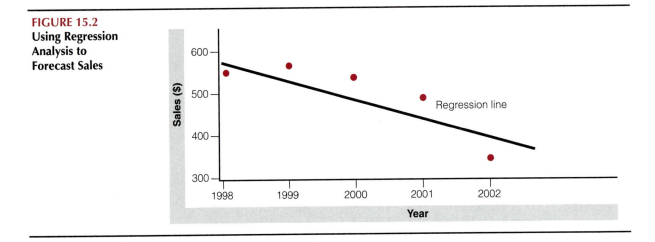

FIGURE 15.2
Using Regression Analysis to Forecast Sales

Estimating Sales Using Management Opinions

When trend analyses such as average compounded growth and regression fail to provide believable results, management opinions gain value. Historically, managers have been shown to be overly optimistic in their forecasts. However, they often can add the insight that is missing from simple trends. They may be better than outsiders at evaluating the effect of changing industry or competitive factors on the firm's revenues.

Ultimately, the financial manager must gather all of the forecasts available, adjust them based on economic, industry, and competitive information, and factor in management's insight to arrive at the best estimate of future sales. Note that new products, processes, and other such developments should be included in the forecast.

FORECASTING WITH THE PERCENTAGE OF SALES METHOD

The financial manager is keenly concerned with maintaining sufficient funds to meet the firm's immediate needs. *A firm can rapidly outgrow its cash supply and find itself in serious financial distress because of its success*. One important purpose of financial forecasting is to make sure that the firm does not run out of capital.

The most accurate method of forecasting cash requirements is with cash budgets and pro formas, which are discussed in the following sections. However, the percentage of sales method is an easy-to-use approach that offers a first approximation of the firm's financing needs, or the additional funds needed, for future periods. In this section we will discuss using the percentage of sales method to estimate additional funds needed. Two approaches to this method may be used: the tabular approach and the equation approach. Because the tabular approach better demonstrates the theory behind the percentage of sales method, we begin there.

TABLE 15.1 Tabular Approach to Percentage of Sales Method
(1998 sales = $20, predicted 1999 sales = $25)

	1998	% of Sales × Projected Sales =		1999
Assets				
Current assets	$ 5	5/20 = 25%	× 25	= $ 6.25
Fixed assets[1]	15	NA		15.00
Total assets	$20			$21.25
Liabilities and owners' equity				
Current liabilities	$ 3	3/20 = 0.15	× 25	= $ 3.75
Notes payable[2]	1	NA		1.00
Long-term debt	10	NA		10.00
Total liabilities	$14			$14.75
Common stock	$ 4	NA		$ 4.00
Retained earnings[3]	2	2 + [0.06 × 25 × (1 − 0.7)]		= 2.45
Total equity	$ 6			$6.45
Financing provided				$21.20
Additional funds needed				$0.05[4]
Total	$20			$21.25

[1]If fixed assets are expected to increase as a result of the sales increase, they should be adjusted along with current assets.

[2]Notes payable are not usually spontaneous in the sense that they increase automatically with sales. It usually requires a request from management to increase them. Notes payable may be a source of additional funds needed.

[3]The net profit margin is 6% and the dividend payout ratio is 70%. This means that 6% of every sales dollar is available for shareholders but only 30% is retained to use to finance growth. In this example net income will be $1.50, found as ($25 × 0.06), and $0.45 will be retained ($1.50 × 0.3).

[4]If the increase in liabilities and owners' equity was greater than the increase in sales, a surplus would result. A surplus is entered as a negative number.

Additional Funds Needed: Tabular Approach

The percentage of sales method involves estimating assets, liabilities, expenses, and income as a percentage of sales. The following steps are used to construct the balance sheet in Table 15.1.

1. Estimate future sales.

2. Compute the percentage of current sales for each item that varies with sales.

3. Multiply the percentage of sales by estimated future sales.

4. Compute the additions to equity due to current year income.

5. Use additional funds needed as a plug figure to balance.

The example shown in Table 15.1 assumes that sales will increase to $25 from $20. The net profit margin is 6% and the payout ratio is 70%. Once you have estimated future sales, you must next identify the accounts that increase in proportion to sales. When sales increase, certain assets also spontaneously increase. For example, accounts receivable rise with sales. Similarly, inventories and cash usually rise proportionately with sales. The better you know the firm, the better you will be able to determine which accounts will increase with sales and which will not. The ratio of each different account balance divided by sales for the accounts that change is computed in the second column of Table 15.1. Next, multiply this ratio by projected sales. Repeat this for every asset and liability account that fluctuates with sales. For example, this firm requires $5 of current assets to generate $20 of sales. In other words, the firm operates with a ratio of current assets to sales of 25% (5/20 = 25%). If sales increase to $25 and this ratio is to be maintained, current assets must increase by 1.25 times $25. This means that next period's current assets must be $6.25 (0.25 × $25 = 6.25). The same method is used to compute next period's current liabilities.

Retained earnings increase from the addition of current period income. The new retained earnings amount is computed in a three-step process. First, multiply the net profit margin by the forecasted sales to estimate net profit. For example, in Table 15.1 the net profit margin of 0.06 is multiplied by forecasted sales of $25 to compute estimated net income. Next, multiply the estimated net income by 1 minus the dividend payout ratio to determine how much of the net income will be retained to finance growth. In Table 15.1 net income (which is 0.06 × $25) is multiplied by (1 − 0.7). Finally, add the original retained earnings to get the new retained earnings. Again looking at Table 15.1, the original net income of $2 is added to [0.06 × $25 × (1 − 0.7)] to get the forecasted retained earnings of $2.45.

Let us review what we have done so far. First, we found how much assets will increase if sales increase as projected. This increase in assets must be financed somehow. Part of the financing comes from a spontaneous increase in liabilities. Specifically, current liabilities such as accounts payable often increase with sales. Finally, part of the needed financing comes from the portion of net income that is not distributed as dividends.

We are now ready to estimate additional funds needed (AFN). ***If the increase in assets is greater than the spontaneous increase in liabilities and equity, additional funds are required. This is the plug figure that balances total assets to liabilities and owners' equity.***

In the example provided, the firm requires $0.05 in additional funds. The firm may choose to raise this from an increase in notes payable, long-term debt, or equity. For example, a smaller dividend could be paid. Another option available to management is to curtail growth so that it does not need additional funds. Remember, the purpose of financial planning is to give management options. By projecting that a cash shortage will occur, management can choose the option that best fits the firm's strategic plan. Suppose that the analysis showed a cash surplus. This information also would increase management's options. The firm could choose to push growth more aggressively, pay off a portion of its debt, or invest the surplus in higher-yield long-term securities.

Self-Test Review Questions*

1. Why may a firm need additional funds even if it is growing rapidly?
2. What may a firm do if it finds it needs additional funds?

---

*1. Growth requires more assets because typically more inventory and equipment are needed to support a higher level of sales.

2. Slow its growth, raise additional funds, or operate more efficiently.

Additional Funds Needed: Using the Equation Approach

The tabular approach to computing AFN provides analysts the opportunity to pick which specific accounts will vary with sales. The equation approach is simpler and may be more appropriate if only a rough estimate of cash requirements is needed. The equation for estimating additional funds needed is given here:

$$\text{AFN} = \frac{A^*}{S}\Delta S - \frac{L^*}{S}\Delta S - \left[\text{PM} \times S^1 \times (1 - d)\right] \tag{15.1}$$

where

> AFN = additional funds needed
> A^* = assets that increase proportionately to sales, such as accounts receivables or inventory
> S = prior year sales, which should come from the same period as the asset balances used to form the ratio
> ΔS = the change in sales (Projected sales − Last period sales)
> L^* = liabilities that are expected to change proportionately with sales, such as accounts payable
> PM = net profit margin, equal to net income divided by sales
> S^1 = projected sales for next period
> d = the dividend payout ratio, which is equal to total common dividends paid divided by net income

Compare Equation 15.1 and Table 15.1. They both accomplish the same task. Equation 15.1 summarizes what is done in the table. The increase in assets due to an increase in sales is determined by the first term to the right of the equals sign. Spontaneous sources of financing, which include increases in liabilities and retained earnings, are then subtracted from this figure. AFN is computed here using the figures from Table 15.1:

$$\text{AFN} = \frac{\$5}{20}\$5 - \frac{\$3}{20}\$5 - \left[\$25 \times 0.06 \times (1 - 0.7)\right] = \$0.05$$

We get the same AFN using the equation as we found using the tabular method. This will not always be the case. As sales increase, the profit margin will gradually change and slightly different estimates of additional funds needed will be computed. One advantage of the equation is that it can easily be used in a spreadsheet to map the AFN at different projected sales or payout ratios. Because sales are only an estimate, a graph of AFN at various sales levels will help management determine the likelihood that additional funds will be required. Figure 15.3 is a graph of AFN for various sales projections.

In Figure 15.3, if sales are below about $24, no additional funds are required. As sales increase above $24, more funds must be raised. Figure 15.3 points out an important issue in finance. *Firms can grow too fast*. Success can lead to failure unless it is well managed. The good news is that growth firms are usually able to raise additional capital from a number of sources as long as they start the process before they find themselves in financial distress.

FIGURE 15.3
AFN with Different Sales Growth Projections

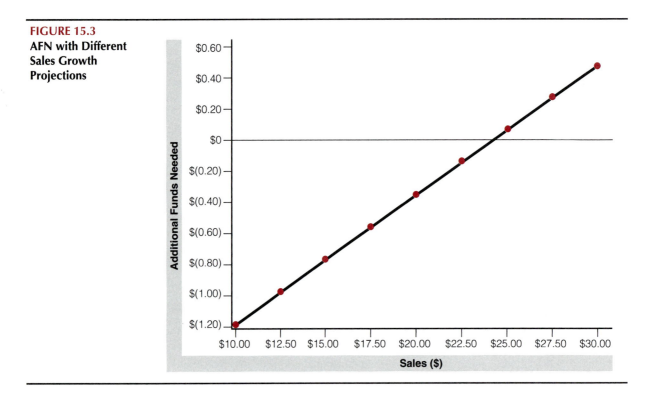

In this section we learned two approaches to determining when excess funds will be needed. However, there are several deficiencies in these approaches. The most serious is that they assume a fixed relationship between sales and the asset and liability accounts. Although the relationship often remains fairly stable over time, it can vary. Second, both methods fail to allow for lumpy growth. Lumpy growth refers to the fact that many assets increase in large discrete units. For example, a warehouse functions over a wide range of sales, but once it is at capacity, a new one must be built. Other economies of scale also may exist that are not adequately captured by the simple models discussed so far. These issues should be kept in mind when using these models.

PROJECTING THE MAXIMUM RATE OF GROWTH

Additional funds needed and growth are clearly closely related topics. In Figure 15.3, the line crosses the x-axis at about $24. This means that as long as the firm does not increase sales beyond $24, no external funds are required. We can express this in terms of sales growth by computing the percentage change between the previous period and $24:

$$\text{Sales growth} = \frac{\$24 - \$20}{\$20} \approx 20\%$$

Maximum Internal Growth Rate

An interesting question managers may raise is, What growth rate can the firm maintain without requiring external funds? This is called the **internal growth rate** because it is the rate of growth that can be achieved solely with internal financing. We can modify Equation 15.1 by setting AFN = 0 to provide the answer. With some algebra, we derive the following formula:[2]

$$\text{Internal growth rate} = \frac{\text{ROA} \times (1 - d)}{1 - \text{ROA} \times (1 - d)} \tag{15.2}$$

ROA is the return on assets (defined in Chapter 14) and d is the dividend payout ratio. This equation does not exactly match the results found using the above methods because it does not allow for any increase in current liabilities. Because this increase is often small compared with the increase in assets required, this simplification is usually acceptable.

> ### E X A M P L E   1 5 . 3   Maximum Internal Growth Rate
>
> ROA for The Gap, Inc., a clothing retailer, is 16.43%. The firm's dividend payout ratio is 20.91%. What maximum rate of growth can The Gap maintain using internally generated funds only?
>
> **Solution**
> Using Equation 15.2 and plugging in the values where appropriate, we get the following:
>
> $$g_i = \frac{\text{ROA}(1 - d)}{1 - [\text{ROA}(1 - d)]}$$
>
> $$g_i = \frac{0.1643(1 - 0.2091)}{1 - [0.1643(1 - 0.2091)]}$$
>
> $$g_i = \frac{0.1299}{0.8701}$$
>
> $$g_i = 0.1493 = 14.93\%$$
>
> The Gap can grow 14.93% per year indefinitely without resorting to outside capital.

Maximum Sustainable Growth Rate

The internal growth rate is the growth rate a firm can maintain without *any* outside financing. There is an alternative growth rate that may be of more interest. Recall from Chapter 13 that the optimal capital structure is the one that maximizes the firm's share

---

[2]Note that ΔS is equal to $(S \times g)$, S^1 is equal to $S(1 + g)$, and the increase in liabilities is usually small enough to be assumed equal to zero.

price. This optimal capital structure often requires the firm to obtain a given proportion of its capital from debt. The amount of debt in the optimal capital structure is the debt capacity of the firm. As a firm grows and accumulates retained earnings, the percentage of debt will fall unless additional funds are borrowed.

The **maximum sustainable growth rate** is the rate of growth a firm can maintain while keeping its financial leverage constant and not issuing additional equity. As we discussed in Chapter 13, firms tend to be reluctant to issue equity and more willing to issue debt. The equation for the maximum sustainable growth rate is given here:

$$\text{Maximum sustainable growth rate} = \frac{\text{ROE} \times (1 - d)}{1 - \left[\text{ROE} \times (1 - d)\right]} \tag{15.3}$$

E X A M P L E 15.4   Maximum Sustainable Growth Rate

The ROE for The Gap, Inc. is 24.32%. The dividend payout ratio is 20.91%. What is the firm's maximum sustainable growth rate?

Solution

Using Equation 15.3 and plugging in the figures where appropriate yields

$$\text{MSG} = \frac{\text{ROE} \times (1 - d)}{1 - \left[\text{ROE} \times (1 - d)\right]}$$

$$\text{MSG} = \frac{0.2432 \times (1 - 0.2091)}{1 - \left[0.2432 \times (1 - 0.2091)\right]}$$

$$\text{MSG} = \frac{0.1923}{0.8077} = 0.2381 = 23.81\%$$

The Gap can grow at 23.81% indefinitely without issuing additional equity. Earlier we found that The Gap's internal growth rate was 14.93%. Because debt is increasing, the maximum sustainable growth rate is greater than the internal growth rate.

Self-Test Review Question*

What is the difference between the maximum internal growth rate and the maximum sustainable growth rate?

How to Influence the Growth Rate

In Chapter 14 we developed the Du Pont method, which shows ROE to be affected by the profit margin, total asset turnover, and leverage. If we review Equation 15.3, we see that anything that increases ROE will increase the maximum sustainable growth rate. Putting Equation 15.3 together with the Du Pont ratio shows that the following factors affect a firm's ability to sustain its growth without issuing additional equity.

*The maximum internal growth rate is the maximum growth the firm can have without needing any outside funds. The maximum sustainable growth rate is the maximum growth rate the firm can maintain without requiring additional equity. However, *debt* will be increased.

- *Profit margin:* The greater the profit on sales, the more cash is available to finance growth.
- *Total asset turnover:* The more rapidly assets turn over, the more sales are generated by each dollar of assets. This decreases the amount of assets needed as sales increase.
- *Financial leverage:* The greater the percentage of debt in the firm's optimal capital structure, the less equity is required to support growth.
- *Dividend payout ratio:* The greater the net income kept by the firm to finance growth, the greater is the maximum sustainable growth rate.

Every firm should know its sustainable growth rate. If growth exceeds this rate, management can expect cash flow problems to develop. It also helps to illustrate the effect management can have on the growth of the firm. Increasing profitability, turnover, and leverage increases the rate at which a firm can grow.

Keep in mind that Equations 15.1–15.3 provide only approximations. They require that the asset and liability accounts change proportionately with sales. In the following sections we will discuss cash budgets and pro formas. These tools allow the analyst to be as precise as desired when making financial forecasts.

CASH BUDGET

The **cash budget** is a detailed statement of cash inflows and outflows that summarizes the cash position of the firm. Cash budgets are prepared for various intervals. A weekly cash budget would include the cash inflows and outflows during the next week. In one example, the financial manager of Sadler Development Company claims to have spent 80% of his time developing cash budgets for the firm during its peak construction periods. Weekly cash outflows were fairly constant due to payrolls and purchases. However, bank loan disbursements were made only when specific phases of the construction were completed. Often, Sadler found that disbursements exceeded revenues. By constructing detailed cash budgets, management was able to delay certain disbursements and to adjust construction schedules to ensure that paychecks did not bounce. Although the employees were not told, the firm occasionally worked them overtime to complete a phase of a project so that a loan disbursement could be requested and the employees paid on time.

Although many firms are not as cash strapped as Sadler, every firm can benefit from knowing its cash position. If the cash budget shows that a firm will be short of cash at some point in the future, it will have time to make arrangements for a loan, an equity infusion, or deferred disbursements. If the cash budget shows that the firm will have a cash surplus, those funds can be invested in income-producing securities or otherwise put to work.

Compilation of the Cash Budget

This section presents a simple approach to preparing a cash budget. It can be modified to work for most firms. Keep in mind that the cash budget is simply a tool that can be modified to fit the needs of the firm and management.

In its simplest form the cash budget contains the following elements:

> Cash receipts
>   − Cash disbursements
>   Net cash flow
>   + Beginning cash balance
>   − Required cash balance
>   Required external funds needed/excess cash balance

Cash receipts: Not all sales generate cash receipts. Usually a portion of sales are for cash and the rest are for credit. Some firms sell entirely on credit, such as Anheuser Busch, a liquor distributor, whereas others sell for cash, such as Kroger grocery stores. To determine cash receipts, multiply the portion of sales that are for cash by the sales amount. For example, if 75% of all sales are for cash, then you can estimate cash receipts by multiplying the total sales by 0.75.

Each month a portion of the outstanding credit sales will be collected. Determine this figure and add it to the current month cash receipts figure.

Cash disbursements: Cash disbursements include cash purchases, payment of accounts payable, rent, wages, and all other cash outlays including interest, tax, and dividend payments. Determining whether an item is a cash disbursement is simple. If it reduces the bank account, it is a cash disbursement. It is often helpful to prepare a separate schedule if the list of disbursements is very extensive. Cash receipts − Cash disbursements = Net cash flow.

Beginning cash balance: The beginning cash balance is the balance forwarded from the previous period. For example, if a monthly cash budget is being prepared, the ending cash balance from January becomes the beginning cash balance for February.

Required cash balance: Most firms establish a desired minimum cash balance that must be maintained. This is to cover unexpected cash requirements. The amount may be small if the firm has established a loan arrangement to quickly supply emergency funds. Funds must be added to the balance if the net balance falls below this minimum.

The beginning cash balance is added to the net cash flow and the required cash balance is subtracted. The result is either the required external funds needed if the figure is negative or the excess cash balance if the figure is positive.

The following demonstrates the compilation of a cash budget: Assume that sales increase at 10% per month beginning in January. November and December sales were $9,500 and $10,000, respectively. Cost of goods sold equals 60% of sales, but is not paid until the following month. All sales are for credit, with 80% collected the following month and 20% collected during the second month. Wages are $1,000, rent is $1,500, taxes are $500, and a $1,000 loan payment is due in February. Monthly interest expense is $200. The cash balance at the end of December is $3,000 and the firm does not want to hold any less cash than this.

To prepare a cash budget, first organize the data into cash receipts and cash disbursements. For a simple cash budget such as this, it is advisable to include these schedules in the budget (Table 15.2).

Sales are listed on the cash budget for reference only. Sales are not cash. Some sales are on credit, which increases the account receivable balance rather than the cash account

TABLE 15.2 Cash Budget

	November	December	January	February	March
Sales	$9,500	$10,000	$11,000	$12,100	$13,310
Cash receipts					
Last month			$ 8,000	$ 8,800	$ 9,680
Prior month			1,900	2,000	2,200
Total collections			$ 9,900	$10,800	$11,880
Disbursements					
COGS			$ 6,000	$ 6,600	$ 7,260
Wages			1,000	1,000	1,000
Rent			1,500	1,500	1,500
Taxes			500	500	500
Loan PMT and interest			200	1,200	200
Total disbursements			$ 9,200	$10,800	$10,460
Net cash flow			$ 700	$ 0	$ 1,420
Plus beginning cash flow			3,000	3,700	3,700
Total cash			$ 3,700	$ 3,700	$ 5,120
Less minimum balance			3,000	3,000	3,000
AFN/Surplus			$ 700	$ 700	$ 2,120

balance. However, the sales forecast provides the beginning point for estimating cash receipts. Formulas are used wherever possible in spreadsheets so that assumptions can be changed easily.

Once the net cash flow has been computed, the beginning balance is added and the minimum balance is subtracted. This shows what cash is surplus or whether any external funds are required. In this example, $700 was a surplus during January and February. There is a $2,120 surplus in March.

The first step is to put the sales figures on the budget as a reference because they will be used to compute cash receipts. Cash receipts are the total of payments made on sales from the last 2 months. For example, in January payments are received from sales made in November and December. Eighty percent of December's sales of $10,000 equals $8,000; 20% of November's sales of $9,500 is $1,900.

Cost of goods sold (COGS) is computed as 60% of the prior month's sales. For example, January's COGS is computed as 60% of December's sales of $10,000. The other cash disbursements are also included in the cash budget.

Total disbursements are then subtracted from total collections to compute the net cash flow. The net cash flow is added to the beginning cash balance, and the minimum balance is then subtracted. The result is either the additional funds needed or the surplus. The ending cash balance is carried forward to the next period.

Uncertainty and the Cash Budget

Few firms are able to predict month-to-month cash flows with certainty. If the firm has been established for a long time, a track record will be available. Similarly, a

FIGURE 15.4
Sensitivity of Cash Flow to Sales Growth

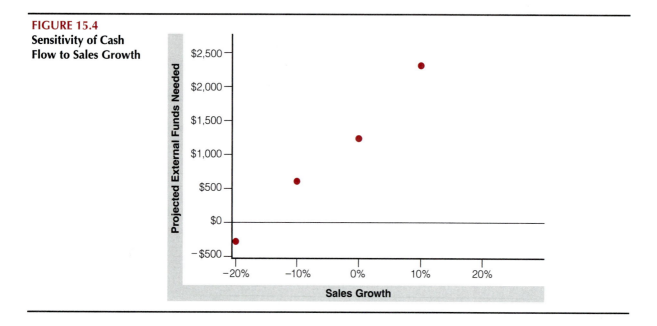

well-established firm may have more predictable sales because it may be past its stage of rapid growth. On the other hand, some firms' cash flows are very difficult to predict. For example, Sadco Development sold properties. It was impossible for the firm to accurately predict when a particular property would sell. Even when it did sell, it was difficult to determine precisely when the proceeds from the sale would be received.

The usual approach to dealing with uncertain cash flows is to prepare multiple cash budgets that reflect different scenarios. Again, by using formulas in electronic spreadsheets it is an easy matter to create as many cash budgets as are useful.

One problem you will find if you attempt to prepare many spreadsheets is assimilating all of the information. Therefore, you may find it helpful to graph the data. For example, if you prepare multiple cash budgets for various sales growth rates, you can graph the sales growth against external funds needed to create a picture of the firm's sensitivity to the growth rate. Figure 15.4 graphs this data for the earlier example.

In this section we have mainly discussed monthly cash budgets. In fact, many firms prepare daily and weekly cash budgets as well. These can follow the same format or can be simplified to fit the needs of the firm.

Self-Test Review Questions*

1. What is the appropriate interval to use for preparing cash budgets?
2. What line items should appear in the cash budget?
3. Should interest expense be included in the cash budget?

---

*1.   Any interval that is useful to management is acceptable, including daily, weekly, and monthly budgets.
2.   All cash disbursements and cash receipts should appear in the cash budget.
3.   Yes, because it is a cash disbursement.

EXTENSION 15.1

Pro Forma Financial Statements

Pro forma financial statements may project 1, 2, or more years into the future. Pro forma statements may be prepared using the percentage of sales method as a basis. The advantage to the pro forma approach to forecasting is that a much greater degree of flexibility is possible than by using the percentage of sales method discussed earlier. We begin our discussion of pro formas by demonstrating the preparation of very simple pro forma statements. We then demonstrate how more accurate forecasts can be achieved by improving on this model.

Preparing Simple Pro Forma Statements

Review the following balance sheet and income statement:

Income Statement

Sales	$100
Costs	70
Net income	$ 30

Balance Sheet

Assets	$200	Liabilities	$ 50
		Equity	150
Total assets	$200	Total	$200

If we assume that all assets and liabilities change in direct proportion to sales and that sales increase 10%, we can construct the following pro forma statements:

Pro Forma Income Statement

	2001	(1 + g)	2002
Sales	100	1.1	110
Costs	70	1.1	77
Net income	30		33

Pro Forma Balance Sheet

	2001	Adjustments	2002
Assets	$200	× 1.1	$220
Total assets	$200	× 1.1	$220
Liabilities	$ 50	× 1	$ 50
Equity	150	× 1	150
Addition to retained earnings		+ 33	33
Subtract from retained earnings		− 13	− 13
Total	$200		$220

Total assets increased by 10% because sales increased 10%. Liabilities and equity did not change because the purpose of the pro forma is to determine whether these sources of capital need to increase to finance the growth. We are assuming that there are no spontaneous increases in liabilities. Net income is projected to be $33 and is added to equity. Dividends are the plug figures that are adjusted to make the statement balance.

The assumptions required to construct these pro formas are unrealistic. It would be unusual for all assets to increase in direct proportion to sales. It would also be unusual for liabilities not to increase. Similarly, only variable costs should increase with sales. What these simple statements do demonstrate is the basic model that pro formas take. In the next section we will show how we can improve on this approach.

Study Tip

Many students fail to make the balance sheet balance. *Always* be sure that the assets equal the liabilities and owners' equity. This can be done by adding an adjustment line item or by adjusting the debt or equity accounts.

Improving on the Simple Pro Forma Method

Let us review a more complete set of financial statements and see how more accurate pro forma statements can be constructed.

Income Statement (2001)		
		Explanation
Sales	$100	
Cost of goods sold	47	47% of sales
EBIT	$ 53	
Interest	3	10% of debt
Earnings before taxes	$ 50	
Taxes	20	40% of EBIT
Net income	$ 30	
Dividends	$ 10	1/3 of net income
Addition to retained earnings	$ 20	

Balance Sheet		
Assets		
Current assets	$ 40	40% of sales
Fixed assets	160	Reflects excess capacity
Net assets	$200	
Liabilities and owners' equity		
Current liabilities	20	20% of sales
Long-term debt	30	Interest at 10%
Shareholders equity	150	Includes $20 retained earnings from current year
Total liabilities and equity	$200	

The revised statements show that only a portion of the costs vary directly with sales. Part of net income depends on interest expense and taxes. The balance sheet shows that a large portion of the assets are fixed. The comment notes that there is excess capacity. This implies that over the range of expected sales, fixed assets will not increase. We can also observe that current liabilities will fluctuate with sales. This will provide some spontaneous financing. We can now construct more accurate pro forma financial statements.

Pro Forma Income Statement Construction

	2001	Adjustment	2002
Sales	$100	× 1.10	$110.00
Cost of goods sold	47	× 1.10	51.70
EBIT	$ 53		$ 58.30
Interest	3		3.00
Earnings before taxes	$ 50		$ 55.30
Taxes (40% of EBT)	20		22.12
Net income	$ 30		$ 33.18
Dividends (NI × 0.33)	$ 10	$33.18 ÷ 3	$ 11.06
Addition to retained earnings	$ 20		$ 22.12

Pro Forma Balance Sheet Construction

	2001	Adjustment	2002
Assets			
Current assets	$ 40	× 1.1	$ 44.00
Fixed assets	160	none	160.00
Total assets	$200		$204.00
Liabilities and owners' equity			
Current liabilities	$ 20	× 1.1	$ 22.00
Long-term debt	30	none	30.00
Shareholders equity	150	22.12	172.12
AFN (surplus)			$ (20.12)
Total	$200		$204.00

The sales and cost of goods sold increase together. Other expenses are unchanged. Different assumptions could change this. More complicated income statements may include many separate line items, some of which vary with sales and some of which do not. The analyst must decide which vary and by how much. There is no rule that requires every expense and income item to vary proportionately with sales. This is just a convenient method of estimating changes that is often reasonably accurate.

In our example, only the current assets increase with sales because we are told that there is excess capacity. If there were not excess capacity, fixed assets also would increase. If the firm had decided on any capital expenditures, these would have been included as a change in assets. Additionally, if the firm had had new capital expenditures, the income the firm projected these new assets to generate would need to be included in the pro forma income statement. Our example did not include new expenditures.

A line has been added to the balance sheet for additional funds needed or surpluses. This line is used to balance the assets to the liabilities and owners' equity.

We have completed a first-stage pro forma statement. We can now decide what to do about the surplus or deficit that results. Remember to always make the balance sheet balance. The analyst must decide how the firm will handle surpluses or deficits and adjust accounts accordingly. In the following balance sheet, the $20.12 surplus from our example above is used to pay off long-term debt.

Second Stage Pro Forma Balance Sheet			
	2001	**Adjustments**	**2002**
Assets			
Net working capital	$ 40.00	× 1.1	$ 44.00
Fixed assets	160.00	none	160.00
Total assets	$200.00		$204.00
Liabilities and owners' equity			
Current liabilities	$ 20.00	× 1.1	$ 22.00
Long-term debt	30.00	− $20.12	9.88
Shareholders' equity	150.00	+ $22.12	172.12
Total liabilities and owners' equity	$200.00		$204.00

Now that long-term debt has been reduced, interest expense falls. This changes net income in the pro forma income statement, and more funds are available for retained earnings. These funds can in turn be used to pay off additional debt, which will continue the process. Depending on the magnitude of the adjustments, several iterations may be required to derive an accurate set of pro forma statements.

The important point to remember about pro forma statements is that they are a management tool that is useful only if the inputs reflect management's best estimate of the future. If the best estimate is not achieved using the percentage of sales method, another method should be explored. In practice, each line item should be individually forecasted using management's insight and experience. Once first-stage pro forma statements have been constructed, management can decide how it will address using the surplus or raising the additional funds needed. These decisions should be reflected in the second-stage pro formas.

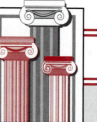

Careers in Finance

Property Manager

Students having an interest in real estate may choose to pursue a career in property management. Property managers assume a large number of tasks related to maintaining and managing commercial property on behalf of investors. These duties will include setting lease rates and arranging lease contracts, acquiring and selling property, and overseeing maintenance. Many property managers even-

tually move into developing property on their own after acquiring the knowledge needed to be successful.

Property managers will rely heavily on the lessons discussed in this chapter. They will prepare cash budgets and pro formas as a means of projecting the cash flows a given property is likely to generate. They will also need to have an extensive knowledge of real estate law and taxes.

CHAPTER SUMMARY

The financial planning process can be viewed in two parts: the development of long-term strategic goals and the formulation of short-term operating plans. A firm should review where it has an advantage over other firms and focus on those areas. Once the goals of the firm have been established and operating plans developed for meeting those goals, the firm can focus on financial planning, the process of allocating the firm's resources to achieve its investment plans.

The most important step in financial planning is developing the sales forecast because most other numbers tie back to it. The sales forecast can be estimated using average compounded growth rates, regression analysis, or management projections. Each method has its strengths and weaknesses, so it is often best to use all of them.

Once a sales forecast has been prepared, the firm can begin determining whether there will be sufficient capital to fund its projected growth. Many businesses are surprised to learn that it is possible to be too successful. By growing too rapidly, a firm can outstrip its ability to raise capital and find it difficult to pay bills and meet other financial obligations.

The percentage of sales method for estimating additional funds needed is based on the assumption that the ratio between most account balances and sales remains constant as the firm grows. For example, as sales increase, inventory is assumed to increase by the same percentage. The percentage of sales method can be performed using either a tabular approach or a simplifying equation. These methods also are effective at projecting how fast the firm can grow without requiring any outside financing (maximum internal growth rate) or without issuing additional equity (maximum sustainable growth rate).

Cash budgets are detailed plans that show cash inflows and outflows daily, weekly, or monthly. Every cash receipt is recorded at the time it is expected to be received, and every cash disbursement is recorded at the time it is expected to be made. The cash budget allows the firm to project cash shortages and surpluses in advance.

Pro forma financial statements project the firm's financial statements one or more years into the future. They are constructed using the projected growth rates. Several passes may be required to develop an accurate set of pro forma statements.

KEY WORDS

business cycle 408	competitive advantage 407	investment strategy 407	pro forma financial
cash budget 419	financial planning 407	maximum sustainable	statements 423
comparative advantage 407	internal growth rate 417	growth rate 418	

DISCUSSION QUESTIONS

1. Distinguish between long-term strategic goals and short-term operating plans. Which must be prepared first?
2. Is it theoretically likely that a firm will have a positive-NPV project in an area in which it has no comparative or competitive advantage? What does this suggest about how a firm should go about expanding and selecting projects?
3. What are the three methods for projecting sales? What are the weaknesses and strengths of each method?
4. What is the beginning point for preparing an estimate of external funds needed for a cash budget?
5. How is it possible for a firm to grow too fast? If a firm is growing too fast, what steps can it take to slow its growth?
6. Why is it important to review the precise periods used to estimate the compounded average growth rate carefully before using them?
7. What is the advantage of using regression analysis instead of the compounded growth method to compute future sales? What is the weakness of the regression method?
8. Why is the $5 of current assets multiplied by 1.25 in the first line of Table 15.1?
9. Will the tabular approach to estimating additional funds needed always provide the same result as the equation approach?
10. What is the difference between the maximum internal growth rate and the maximum sustainable growth rate?
11. How was the $10,800 figure for total collections in February computed in Table 15.2?
12. What is shown in the second-stage pro forma balance sheet? (Extension 15.1)

PROBLEMS

1. In 1997, sales were $2.2 million; in 1998, sales were $2.5 million; in 1999, sales fell to $1.8 million; in 2000, sales were $2.4 million; and in 2001, sales were $3 million.
   a. Compute the compounded average growth rate.
   b. Project 2002 sales.
   c. Plot the sales and your sales projection on a graph.
   d. Would your answer to part a have changed significantly if you had only used data for 1999 through 2001?
   e. Review the graph prepared in part c. Do you believe your sales projection to be the best one possible given the data?
   f. Draw a line on the graph prepared in part c that best fits the data. Is this superior to using the average compounded growth rate?

2. Use the following balance sheet for Feeble Corp. to estimate additional funds needed following the tabular approach. Assume that current sales are $100, and next year's sales are projected to be $150. The net profit margin is 5% and the payout ratio is 50%. The firm has excess capacity.

Feeble Corp. Balance Sheet

Assets	
Current assets	$ 35
Fixed assets	200
Total assets	$235
Liabilities and owners' equity	
Current liabilities	$ 10
Notes payable	2
Long-term debt	150
Total liabilities	$162
Common stock	$ 30
Retained earnings	43
Total	$235

3. Current assets are $200, sales are $1,000, current liabilities are $30, the profit margin is 8%, and the firm is not paying dividends. If sales increase 30%, what additional funds are needed? (Hint: Use the equation approach.)

4. Use the data from problem 2 to estimate AFN using the equation approach.

5. If the return on assets is 15% and the dividend payout ratio is 50%, what is the maximum internal growth rate? Recompute the maximum internal growth rate for a return on assets of 10%, then 20%. Recompute the maximum internal growth rate for a dividend payout ratio of 0%, then 25%.

6. Compute the maximum sustainable growth rate under the following conditions:
   a. ROE = 25%, dividend payout ratio is 0%.
   b. ROE = 25%, dividend payout ratio is 20%.
   c. ROE = 10%, dividend payout ratio is 0%.
   d. ROE = 10%, dividend payout ratio is 20%.

7. Predict the effect of the following on the maximum sustainable growth rate (i.e., will the maximum sustainable growth rate increase, decrease, or remain unchanged):
   a. Profit margin increases.
   b. Total asset turnover falls.
   c. The firm increases its target debt ratio.
   d. Dividend payout ratio falls.

8. A new firm opened for business in January. Prepare a cash budget from January to June using the following information. January and February sales were $150,000 and $175,000, respectively. Sales from March through June are expected to increase 5% per month from the February sales amount. Cost of goods sold is 50% of sales. Purchases are paid for the month following when they are sold. Forty percent of sales are for cash. Fifty percent of sales are paid during the following month and 10% are paid 2 months later. Rent is $20,000. Wages are $14,000. Loan payments of $10,000 are due monthly. Taxes of $25,000 are due in March and June. Other miscellaneous expenses total $30,000. The cash balance at the beginning of January is $15,000. A minimum cash balance of $10,000 must be maintained.

9. Prepare a pro forma balance sheet and income statement using the following data. Assume sales growth is estimated to be 15%. The firm has excess capacity in its fixed assets.

   Now assume that fixed assets are being used at full capacity. What are AFN and the projected ratios? (Extension 15.1)

Income Statement

Net sales	$15,000
Cost of goods sold	7,500
EBIT	$ 7,500
Interest	2,000
Earnings before taxes	5,500
Taxes	2,200
Net income	$ 3,300
Dividends paid	1,500
Addition to retained earnings	$ 1,800

Balance Sheet

Assets	
Cash	$ 2,000
Inventory	3,500
Accounts receivable	1,500
Fixed assets	10,000
Total assets	$17,000
Liabilities and owner's equity	
Accounts payable	$ 1,200
Notes payable	3,000
Long-term notes	5,000
Total liabilities	$ 9,200
Common stock	$ 4,000
Retained earnings	3,800
Total liabilities and owner's equity	$17,000

10. You have been given the following information on the Crum Company. Crum expects sales to grow by 50% in the next year, and operating costs should increase at the same rate. Fixed assets were being operated at 40% of capacity, but all other assets were used to full capacity. Underused fixed assets cannot be sold. Current assets and spontaneous liabilities should increase at the same rate as sales. The company plans to finance any external funds needed as 35% notes payable and 65% common stock.

Income Statement

Sales	$1,000.00
Operating cost	800.00
EBIT	$ 200.00
Interest	16.00
EBT	$ 184.00
Taxes	73.60
Net income	$ 110.40
Dividends (60%)	$ 66.24
Addition to RE	$ 44.16

Balance Sheet

Current assets	$ 700.00
Net fixed assets	300.00
Total assets	$1,000.00
A/P and accruals	150.00
N/P (8%)	200.00
Common stock	150.00
Retained earnings	500.00
Total liabilities and equity	$1,000.00
Profit margin	11.04%
ROE	16.98%
Debt/asset ratio	35%
Current ratio	2 times
Payout ratio	60%

a. Compute AFN using the equation approach.
b. What are Crum's projected ratios and AFN using the balance sheet method (compute only the ratios listed above after the balance sheet)? (Extension 15.1)

11. You have been given the following information on the Acme Company. Acme expects sales to grow by 25%. Operating costs should increase at the same rate. Fixed assets were being operated at 60% of capacity, but all other assets were used to full capacity. Underused fixed assets cannot be sold. Current assets and spontaneous liabilities should increase at half the rate of sales because of economies of scale. The company plans to finance any external funds needed as 25% notes payable (8%), 30% long-term debt (9%), and 45% common stock. If there is a surplus, notes payable and long-term debt will be retired in equal amounts. (Hint: When using a spreadsheet program, you will need to use an *if* statement.)

Income Statement

Sales	$5,000.00
Operating cost	2,000.00
EBIT	$3,000.00
Interest	611.00
EBT	2,389.00
Taxes	955.60
Net income	$1,433.40
Dividends (50%)	$1,075.05
Addition to RE	$ 358.35

Balance Sheet

Cash	$ 500.00
Inventory	2,500.00
Accounts receivable	700.00
Net fixed assets	13,500.00
Total assets	$17,200.00
A/P and accruals	$ 2,000.00
Notes/Payable (8%)	3,700.00
Long-term debt (9%)	3,500.00
Common stock	5,500.00
Retained earnings	2,500.00
Total liabilities and equity	$17,200.00
Profit margin	29%
ROE	18%
Debt/asset ratio	33%
Current ratio	.65
Payout ratio	75%

a. Compute AFN using the equation approach.
b. What are Acme's projected ratios and AFN using the balance sheet method (compute only the ratios listed below the balance sheet)?
c. Now assume that fixed assets are being used at full capacity. They will increase at half the rate of growth in sales. What are AFN and the projected ratios? (Extension 15.1)

SELF-TEST PROBLEMS

You have been given the attached information on Risky Ventures, Inc. Risky Ventures expects sales to grow by 35% in 2002. Operating costs should increase at one-half this rate. Fixed assets were being operated at 60% of capacity in 2001, but all other assets were used to full capacity. Underutilized fixed assets cannot be sold. Current assets and spontaneous liabilities should increase at three-quarters the rate of sales during 2002 due to economies of scale. The company plans to finance any external funds needed as 25% notes payable (8%), 30% long-term debt (9%), and 45% common stock. If there is a surplus, notes payable and long-term debt will be retired in equal proportions (this will require you to use an *if* statement in your spreadsheet).

	2001
Sales	$15,000.00
Operating cost	6,000.00
EBIT	$ 9,000.00
Interest	2,360.00
EBT	$ 6,640.00
Taxes	2,656.00
Net income	**$ 3,984.00**

	2001
Dividends (payout = 50%)	$ 1,992.00
Addition to RE	$ 1,992.00
Cash	$ 1,500.00
Inventory	7,500.00
Accounts receivable	2,000.00
Net fixed assets	52,500.00
Total assets	$63,500.00
A/P and accruals	$ 6,000.00
Notes/Payable (8%)	9,250.00
Long-term debt (9%)	18,000.00
Common stock	25,500.00
Retained earnings	4,750.00
Total liabilties and equity	**$63,500.00**

1. Compute AFN using the equation approach (Equation 15.1).
2. Compute AFN using the balance sheet method.

WEB EXPLORATION

1. We have looked at a number of sites offering information on stocks in other Web Exploration assignments. We continue this exercise by looking at a site that offers data different from what we have seen before. Go to www.411stocks.com. This site provides the usual basic fundamental data and current trading information, and it also has financial ratios, balance sheet and income statement data, and analysts' recommendations. Look up the data for General Electric (symbol = GE). Do analysts currently recommend this firm? Why does it appear that the analysts are making this recommendation?

2. Another site that reports analysts' projections can be found at www.bulldogresearch.com. Go to this site and look up General Electric (symbol = GE). Go to the Snapshot view offered on the left-hand margin. What is the consensus recommendation? Go to the Home page. Read about the awards given to analysts by Bulldog Research. Discuss the goal of this site.

MINI CASE

You have been given the attached information on the Microweb Company. Operating costs should increase at the same rate as sales, while overhead costs should increase at 25% of the increase in sales (e.g., if sales increase at 50%, overhead increases at 12.5%). Fixed assets were being operated at 40% of capacity in 2001, but all other assets were used to full capacity. (If fixed assets were being used at full capacity, they would increase at half the rate of the increase in sales.) Underutilized fixed assets cannot be sold. Current assets and spontaneous liabilities should increase at 80% of the increase in sales. The company plans to finance any external funds needed as 35% notes payable and 65% common stock. If there is any cash surplus during any year, notes will be paid off first and then the cash balance will accumulate.

	2001
Sales	$1,000.00
Operating cost	700.00
Overhead cost	100.00
EBIT	$ 200.00
Interest (8% of NP)	16.00
EBT	184.00
Taxes	73.60
Net income	**$ 110.40**
Current assets	$ 700.00
Net fixed assets	300.00
Total assets	**$1,000.00**

	2001
A/P and accruals	$ 150.00
N/P	200.00
Common stock	150.00
Retained earnings	500.00
Total liabilities and equity	**$1,000.00**
Dividends (60%) 2001	$66.24
Addition to RE (2001)	$44.16

Ratios

Profit margin	11.04%
ROE	16.98%
Debt/asset ratio	35%
Current ratio	4.67 ×

a. Compute AFN for 2002 using the equation approach and assuming sales increase 50%. (Recognize that the equation approach will not allow you to satisfy some of the assumptions provided in the problem.)

b. What are Microweb's projected ratios and AFN using the spreadsheet method assuming sales increase 50% (compute only the listed ratios for 2002)? Do a first and second pass.

The Management of Working Capital

Chapter Objectives

By the end of this chapter you should be able to:

1. Use the economic order quantity method to compute the optimal inventory level

2. Understand the nature of float and how it affects a firm's cash requirements

3. Use the Baumol model to estimate optimal cash levels

4. Use the Miller–Orr model to estimate optimal cash levels

5. Understand the tradeoff between different credit policies

In the last several chapters we focused much of our attention on evaluating and managing long-term assets. We now shift our focus to short-term assets and liabilities. The major short-term assets include cash, accounts receivable, and inventory. Current assets make up 15 to 50% of most firms' assets. Effectively managing these assets can produce major savings. For example, if Ford Motor Company were to speed up its collection of accounts receivable by just 1 day, earnings would increase by about $250 million per year. Although not all companies have this potential savings, all firms must carefully manage their current assets. Consider Wal-Mart's inventory control system. In the highly competitive discount retailing industry, any cost savings are extremely important. Wal-Mart has made a science of inventory control, and many industry analysts point to this as the single most important reason for the firm's success.

In this chapter, we will study each of the major types of current assets. Our goal is to determine what managers can do to optimize the return on each type of asset. In addition we will review the primary short-term sources of funds. The major short-term liability is accounts payable. Most firms both give credit and take advantage of credit offered by the firms with which they do business. We will extend our discussion of credit policy to how it affects a firm's liability management.

HOW TO MANAGE INVENTORY

Inventory represents a major asset for many firms. Typical manufacturing firms have at least 15% of their assets tied up in inventory, and retailers can have 25% or more of their total assets in inventory. With so much of the firm's net worth at stake, managers must make every effort to manage it wisely. We should recognize that the financial manager may not have primary control over the level of inventory. Marketing, purchasing, and production also have input into the inventory decision. Marketing and production typically argue for greater inventory, whereas finance attempts to point out its cost.

Reasons to Hold Inventories

For a manufacturing firm, there are three types of inventory: raw materials, work in process, and finished goods. Retailers typically hold only goods ready for resale. The type of inventory influences why it is held and how much is required. Retailers can seldom sell a product they do not have in inventory, although mail-order houses, Web retailers, and some distributors are successful in this area. The growth of the "category killers"[1] makes this point. Category killers are stores the size of aircraft hangars stocked with every conceivable variety of a particular line of merchandise. The first was Toys R Us. Recently, many new category killers have emerged. For example, Garden Ridge Corp. of Houston, Texas, stocks more than 4,000 kinds of candles and 3,000 styles of baskets, silk flowers, and housewares. Clearly, shoppers love a selection and stores that fail to offer it may not be able to compete. On the other hand, inventory is expensive to hold. In manufacturing, where inventory does not necessarily influence sales, tight inventory control can be especially valuable.

Costs of Holding Inventory

The combined costs of holding inventory are called **carrying costs**, which represent all of the direct and opportunity costs of keeping inventory on hand. As inventory levels increase, so do each of the following costs:

- The opportunity cost of funds tied up in inventory
- Storage cost
- Insurance cost
- The cost of obsolescence, damage, and theft

At the other end of the spectrum are costs that fall as inventory increases. Shortage costs are associated with the consequences of running out of inventory. An entire assembly line can be shut down for lack of a certain type of bolt. Shortage costs can be enormous, and many firms maintain large inventories to ensure that a stockout never occurs.

Firms also must be aware of reorder costs. These are costs related to the processing, restocking, and paying for each new order. We generally assume that each new order has

[1]*Forbes,* vol. 157 (11), June 3, 1996, p. 114.

a fixed cost, although certainly some variation exists because of differences in order size. Clearly, reorder costs fall when larger inventory levels are maintained. To see this, review Figure 16.1.

If a firm sells 10,000 units a month and reorders new inventory once each month, then each order will be for 10,000 units. Because the inventory begins at 10,000 and falls to 0, the average inventory during the month is 5,000. The second panel in Figure 16.1 shows what happens when the firm reorders twice per month. The firm still sells 10,000 units, but now 5,000 units are ordered at a time and the average inventory falls to 2,500. With four orders per month, the average inventory level falls to

FIGURE 16.1
Relationship of Average Inventory and Order Size and Frequency

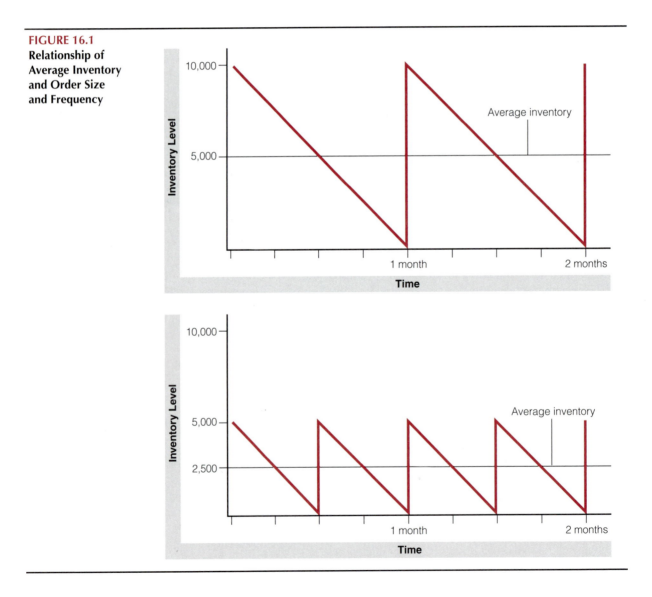

1,250. With more orders, the average order size and inventory level continue to fall. The costs of holding inventory fall, but reorder costs increase. The question then becomes, how many orders per month is optimal?

Optimal Inventory Level

Office Depot is a discount office supply store that stocks and sells, among many other items, copy paper. One store estimates that it sells about $250,000 of a particular type of paper per year with a cost of $3.29 per ream. If the store ordered only once per year, it would order $250,000/$3.29 = 75,988 reams. Because the paper sells continuously throughout the year, the average number of reams on hand would be 75,988/2 = 37,994. All of the carrying costs listed earlier apply to holding this inventory of paper. If the local Office Depot orders the paper twice per year, the order amount drops to 37,994 and the average inventory drops to 37,994/2 = 18,997. If the number of orders per year increases, carrying costs decline, but the reorder costs increase.

Figure 16.2 graphs the costs of holding inventory. As the size of the average inventory order increases, reorder costs fall, but carrying costs increase. The goal of inventory management is to find the order size that minimizes the total costs of holding inventory, or the optimal inventory level. This occurs on the graph at Q^*. Note that Q^* is independent of the total annual inventory purchases during the year, because that

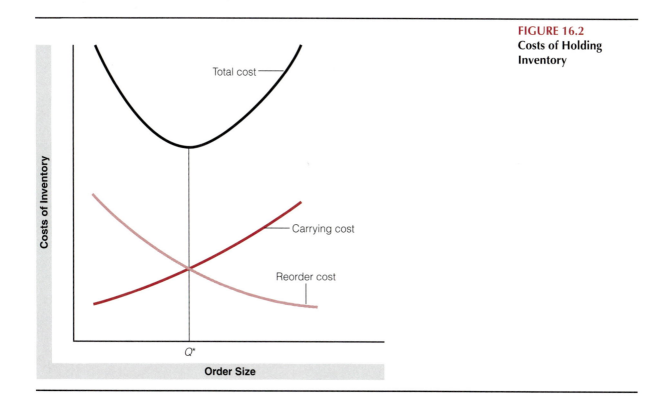

FIGURE 16.2
Costs of Holding Inventory

is dictated by sales. What we are concerned with here is determining the amount of inventory that should be kept on hand at any particular moment.

Self-Test Review Question*

What is the average inventory if a company orders 10,000 units per year and makes 6 orders per year?

Computing the Economic Order Quantity

The **economic order quantity model** is the best-known and simplest approach for computing the optimal inventory level, Q^*. Notice in Figure 16.2 that the minimum total cost occurs where carrying costs are equal to order costs. You can derive the economic order quantity (EOQ) model by setting carrying costs equal to order costs and solving for Q^*.

We first need to derive an equation to compute the carrying cost. This cost includes the opportunity cost of the funds tied up in inventory, the costs of shelf space and storage, insurance, and so forth. Suppose that these costs are estimated to be $0.50 per ream of paper. The annual total carrying cost is

$$\text{Total carrying cost} = \text{Carrying cost per ream} \times \text{Average inventory}$$

$$= CC \times \frac{Q}{2} \tag{16.1}$$

where Q is the number of reams of paper in each order.

Next we need an equation to compute the total order cost. This cost involves the clerical and handling expense required to place and pay for an order. Each order costs the same, and the number of orders per year is the annual number of units sold divided by the number of reams purchased each time an order is placed:

$$\text{Total order cost} = \text{Order cost} \times \text{Orders per year}$$

$$= OC \times \frac{\text{Sales}}{Q} \tag{16.2}$$

Study Tip

Note that "Sales" is the number of units sold, not the number of dollars received.

Notice that as Q increases in Equation 16.1, the total carrying cost also increases because Q is in the numerator. However, in Equation 16.2, Q is in the denominator, so as it increases total order cost falls. Next, let us set Equation 16.1 equal to Equation 16.2 and solve for Q^*:

$$CC \times \frac{Q^*}{2} = OC \times \frac{S}{Q^*}$$

$$CC \times \frac{\left(Q^*\right)^2}{2} = OC \times S$$

$$\left(Q^*\right)^2 = \frac{2 \times OC \times S}{CC}$$

$$Q^* = \sqrt{\frac{2 \times OC \times S}{CC}} \tag{16.3}$$

where

$Q*$ = the optimal number of units purchased by each order
CC = the carrying cost per unit
OC = the order cost per order
S = the number of units sold per year

Continuing our example, if the carrying cost per ream of paper is $0.50, the order cost per order is $20.00, and the number of reams sold per year is 75,988, then $Q*$, the optimal number of reams of paper to purchase with each order, is found using Equation 16.3:

$$Q^* = \sqrt{\frac{2 \times OC \times S}{CC}}$$

$$Q^* = \sqrt{\frac{2 \times \$20 \times 75{,}988}{0.50}}$$

$$Q^* = 2{,}465.57 = 2{,}466$$

Office Depot should order 2,466 reams of paper each time it orders. Notice that we rounded our result up to the nearest whole number because only whole reams of paper can be ordered. If we order 2,466 reams with each order, then we will make 75,988/2,466 = 30.81 orders per year or about one every couple of weeks. We can determine from Equation 16.3 that as order cost increases, the number of units purchased with each order increases and the number of orders per year falls. Conversely, when carrying costs increase, the number of units purchased with each order falls so the number of orders per year increases.

E X A M P L E   16.1   Economic Order Quantity

Lady Footlocker expects to sell about 500 pairs of a particular style of running shoe this year from one store. Suppose the ordering and restocking costs are $20 per order and that the carrying cost is $2.75 per pair. What is the EOQ for this one style of shoe?

Solution
The CC is $2.75, the sales are 500, and the OC is $20. Use Equation 16.3 to compute EOQ:

$$Q^* = \sqrt{\frac{2 \times OC \times S}{CC}}$$

$$Q^* = \sqrt{\frac{2 \times \$20 \times 500}{2.75}}$$

$$Q^* = 85.28 = 86$$

Lady Footlocker should order 86 pairs of shoes each time it places an order. The store will place 500/86 = 5.81 = 6 orders per year, or one order every 2 months.

Study Tip

$Q*$ is the economic order quantity, EOQ. Do not confuse $Q*$ with Q, the number of units in each historic order.

Self-Test Review Question*

Your firm will sell 12,000 pencils this year. Order costs are $15 and carrying costs are $0.02 per pencil. What is the EOQ?

Problems with the EOQ

The EOQ assumes that the firm lets the inventory run down to zero before new inventory is purchased. In reality, firms prefer to order before this point to avoid stockouts and the resulting production delays or loss of customers.

A safety stock is a minimum level of inventory that a firm keeps on hand. Ideally, the inventory level never falls below this level except in emergencies, such as when the supplier has problems or demand unexpectedly surges. Holding a safety stock does not change the fundamentals of the EOQ. The first order is simply increased to include the extra number of units to be held as safety stock. Subsequent orders represent the EOQ.

Firms also must consider the delay between when the order is placed and when delivery occurs. The timing of the order should be such that delivery is made as inventory hits zero or reaches the safety stock.

Figure 16.3 illustrates when an order will be placed, allowing for delivery delay and a safety stock. When the inventory falls to point A, an order is placed. This allows time for delivery. The inventory arrives when the inventory level has fallen to point B. The new inventory returns the stock to point C. Management experience is required to determine the time difference between points A and B and how large a safety stock is required.

FIGURE 16.3
Reorder Point with Safety Stock

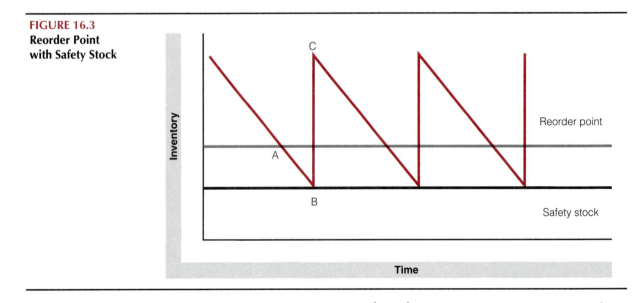

*EOQ = [(2 × $15 × 12,000) ÷ 0.02]^{0.5} = 4,243 pencils per order.

Other Inventory Methods

Some firms choose a much simpler approach to inventory control. The method is sometimes called the basket method. In essence, inventory is separated into three bins (baskets) when it arrives. The first is the normal operating inventory. When this bin is empty, new inventory is ordered and the firm operates out of the second bin. The third bin is the safety stock. You may have seen a related inventory approach taken by your bank to encourage you to order replacement checks on time. A reorder slip is inserted into the check supply box when about three-quarters of the order has been used. If you order when you find this slip, you should not run out of checks. This approach may be appropriate for low-valued inventory items or when inventory represents a very small part of the firm's assets. For example, a law firm may use the basket approach to control office supplies.

An alternative to holding inventory is the just-in-time inventory method. Popularized by Japanese manufacturing firms, this method requires a very close relationship between the supplier and the buyer to function safely. The idea behind just-in-time inventory is that parts and supplies are delivered just as the firm needs them, often mere hours ahead of time. This removes the need for the firm to store or control inventory.

The downside of just-in-time inventory is that it increases the likelihood of a stockout. If the supplier is not reliable, any savings the method provides will be lost when the plant is shut down by a parts shortage. However, technology has made the just-in-time inventory method and its derivatives easier to manage. By tying the buyer's computer system to its own system, the supplier is able to track parts usage and production requirements so that the parts can be delivered as needed.

Many major retailers have adopted the just-in-time inventory concept. Wal-Mart, for example, requires many of its suppliers to restock shelves from the supplier's inventory so that the store is not required to inventory the item itself.

HOW TO MANAGE CASH

In one sense, holding cash is a waste of resources. Cash balances in themselves do not generate any income and there is typically little or no interest paid on corporate checking account balances. Still, virtually all firms keep significant amounts of cash on hand. In this section we will investigate ways to minimize cash and to compute the optimal level of cash that a firm should hold.

Two Types of Float

Float occurs because of delays in the banking system; it is the difference in time between when a check is written and when it actually clears. Most students have learned the basics of float management with their own funds. In 1980 Congress mandated as part of the Depository Institutions Deregulation and Monetary Control Act that the Federal Reserve take steps to reduce the amount of time required for checks to be collected and paid. Despite the increased use of electronic fund transfers and other techniques, float remains a part of our financial system. The result of float is that there is a difference between your actual bank balance and what your books reflect. Whether the bank shows a greater or smaller balance than your books depends on whether disbursement or collection float dominates.

Disbursement Float

Disbursement float occurs when there is a delay between when the firm issues a check and when the funds are removed from the checking account balance at the bank. For example, if your parents mail a check to the university to pay your tuition, the check may be in the mail 2 or 3 days and it may be several more days before the university's bank presents the check to your parents' bank for payment. It is only then that the funds are removed from the checking account.

Disbursement float works to increase the balance in your account relative to your book balance. A corporation can issue checks and not put the funds into the bank for several days if the financial managers can predict float accurately.

Collection Float

Collection float occurs when there is a delay between when you receive payment and when the bank gives you credit. Suppose that you deposit a check into your account at the bank. The bank must process that check but will not receive the funds for several days. Therefore, it may put a hold on your account while the check clears. Clearing a check is the process of sending it through the banking system and having funds transferred back. A hold is an annotation that is put on a checking account that prevents funds that have not been cleared from being spent. The available balance is the amount of funds on deposit that can be spent. Large corporate checks may have holds put on them because the bank does not want to disburse large sums that it has not yet received. Smaller personal checks may have holds placed by the bank if the bank is uncertain that the check is good.

Net Float

Disbursement float increases the available balance and collection float decreases the available balance. A firm should be more concerned with the available balance than with the book balance because this is what can be used to pay bills. We calculate the net float as the difference between the firm's available balance and the firm's book balance:

$$\text{Net float} = \text{Available balance} - \text{Firm's book balance}$$

E X A M P L E 16.2   Computing Net Float

Suppose that on January 1 you write a $300 check to order a new hard drive for your computer. Your favorite uncle sends you a check for $200 on January 3 to help with the cost. It takes 5 days for your check to clear and 3 days for your uncle's check to clear. If you started with $150 in your account, what is the net float on January 4 and will your check bounce? Assume the bank places a 3-day hold on your uncle's check because you have a history of bouncing checks.

Solution
The net float is the difference between the available balance and the book balance. The $300 will not have been presented for payment on January 4 and the $200 will still have a hold. The

result is that the available balance will be $150, the original starting balance. The book balance will be $150 + $200 − $300 = $50. The net float on January 4 is

$$\text{Net float} = \$150 - \$50 = \$100$$

The critical date is January 5 because that is when your check will be presented for payment. We need to determine whether the available balance is greater than $300 on that date. Your uncle's check will not be available until January 6, so the available balance on January 5 is $150 − $300 = −$150. So the bank would return the check for the hard drive unpaid.

Self-Test Review Question*

Is the goal of float management to increase or decrease disbursement float? Collection float?

How to Manage Float

The objective of float management is to speed up collections while slowing down disbursements. This will result in the greatest available balance for a given commitment of funds. Several kinds of delay affect float:

- The time the check is in the mail
- The time the firm spends processing the check
- The time the bank requires to clear the check

Many firms aggressively seek ways to reduce these sources of float in their receivables while increasing the time for their disbursements. In 1985, E. F. Hutton pleaded guilty to 2,000 counts of mail and wire fraud. Cash managers at the firm had created nearly $1 billion of float by moving funds between branches and various bank accounts. Check kiting is when checks are written with the sole purpose of creating float. Unfortunately for E. F. Hutton, this is against the law. Clearly, there are both legal and ethical limits to how aggressively float management policies can be pursued.

Speeding Up Collections

There are several frequently used methods to speed the processing of accounts receivable. The faster these accounts are collected, the faster the funds become available for use by the firm. As mentioned earlier, the amount of savings is considerable for firms with large accounts receivable.

Using Lockboxes   One popular method for speeding collections is to use lockboxes. A **lockbox** is an arrangement with a bank in which customers mail their payments to a post office box controlled by the bank. Several times per day the bank checks the box and all payments are taken back to the bank, where they are recorded and deposited into the firm's accounts. The bank then transmits the payment data to the firm, which in turn updates its customer's records. A firm may have any number of lockboxes scattered

*The goal is to increase disbursement float and to decrease collection float.

FIGURE 16.4 **Lockbox Arrangement**

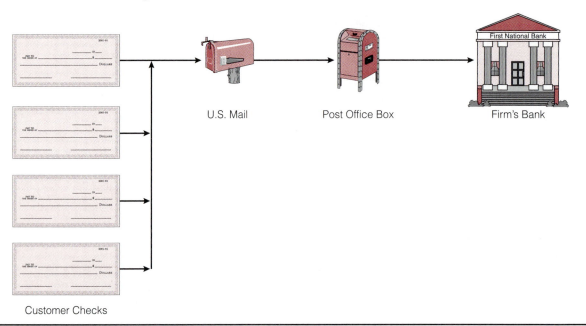

throughout the country. These reduce both the time payments are in the mail and the time it takes the company to process the payments. A typical lockbox arrangement is illustrated in Figure 16.4.

Using Concentration Banking   **Concentration banking** refers to having a number of bank accounts that serve as collection points that are then concentrated into one central account. Concentration banks are often used along with lockboxes. Payments are received and processed by many banks. The funds are then transferred into a central account. This greatly simplifies the bookkeeping required by the firm and the larger balance may allow the firm to negotiate favorable terms from the con-centration bank.

Much of the responsibility for the day-to-day operation of lockboxes and concen-tration banks can be shifted to the banks that are involved. Bank services are nego-tiable and the industry is very competitive. A large firm may find that a bank is willing to handle all the details of a lockbox system and concentrating the cash in return for the firm's cash deposits. Sometimes the bank may require a **compensating balance**, an agreed-upon balance that the firm must maintain in its accounts to compensate the bank for the services it provides. A concentration banking arrangement is illustrated in Figure 16.5.

Using Electronic Funds Transfer   The use of electronic funds transfer systems has dramatically increased in the last two decades. **Electronic funds transfer (EFT)** is

FIGURE 16.5 Concentration Banking

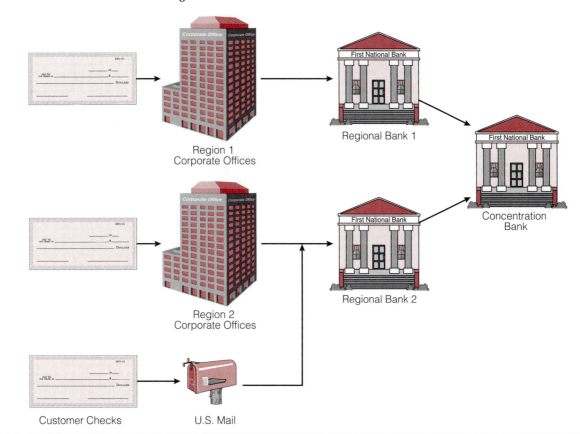

Region 1
Corporate Offices

Regional Bank 1

First National Bank

Concentration
Bank

Region 2
Corporate Offices

Regional Bank 2

Customer Checks

U.S. Mail

the process of transferring funds from bank to bank electronically. The system is also called the Fed wire or simply the wire, because funds usually are wired through accounts that banks hold at the Federal Reserve Bank. EFTs are often used for deducting regular payments from customer accounts. For example, most insurance companies and many mortgage companies encourage customers to sign up for automatic payment services because this reduces late payments and speeds processing. The primary bank in a concentration banking arrangement also uses EFT to transfer funds from subaccounts to the primary account. One advantage of EFT is that it is precisely predictable, meaning that the firm knows exactly what the float will be. This is a significant aid to cash management.

Selecting the Right Banks   Which bank is used for deposits also can affect float. If you and your customer both bank at the same bank, the deposit does not have to be transferred elsewhere. Your firm receives credit for the deposit the day it is made, and your customer's account is reduced that same day. Firms that have many customers in one community may find it beneficial to conduct a study to determine which bank or banks are used by most of their customers. This may be a significant criterion to consider when choosing a bank.

Slowing Down Disbursements

From the firm's point of view, it is desirable to increase disbursement float because this increases the available balance. Therefore, some firms have developed strategies to increase mail and processing float.

Remote Disbursements   The most common approach to increasing disbursement float is to pay bills with checks drawn on a distant bank. For example, a firm could maintain two accounts, one at a bank on the West Coast and one at a bank on the East Coast. All bills received from East Coast firms could be paid with checks drawn on the West Coast account and vice versa. The firms might even arrange for the checks to be mailed from remote sites to increase mail float.

Few suppliers are likely to be fooled by these remote disbursement strategies, and they may impose costly terms on the firm. Some firms have such large buying power that suppliers must tolerate slow payment and remote payment because the business received is critical to their survival. For example, if Wal-Mart chose to delay payment to a small supplier of brushes, it is unlikely that the brush maker would have much recourse. It becomes an ethical question whether firms in positions of control should take advantage of smaller companies in this way.

Zero Balance Accounts   A less controversial method of maintaining the lowest necessary cash balance is by using a **zero balance account**. This is an arrangement in which the bank moves only enough funds into a transaction account to cover checks presented for payment that day. The rest of the firm's cash can be left in interest-bearing accounts until needed. There may be many subaccounts that all have zero balances and are fed from a master account. Instead of maintaining balances in each account for unexpected disbursements, the firm holds a single cash buffer in the master account. The zero balance account can effectively free up cash to be used elsewhere.

What Is the Value of Reducing Float?

Some of the methods for reducing float and increasing the available balance may seem to consume a significant amount of time and energy. A reasonable question to ask is whether such activities are worth the effort. Consider Farah Inc., a manufacturer of casual clothing. Its average daily sales are about $700,000, mostly on credit. If Farah could speed up collections by 1 day and the interest rate is 0.02% per day (or $0.0002 \times 365 = 7.3\%$ per year), earnings would increase by $0.0002 \times \$700,000 = \$140.00$ per day, or $\$140 \times 365 = \$51,100$ per year. In other words, even a small firm such as Farah could afford to hire an employee to do nothing but manage cash and still come out ahead. Clearly the benefits of cash management increase dramatically for larger firms.

Computing the Optimal Cash Balance

Our discussion so far has centered on methods for reducing float by speeding up collections and slowing down disbursements. Another related question is, How much cash should a firm hold? In 1995 Kirk Kerkorian made an attempt to buy Chrysler Motor Company because it had over $7 billion in cash. He argued that with that kind of cash surplus "someone is going to come after them. Why not me?"[2] Kerkorian felt that the excess cash should be returned to shareholders rather than being held as idle funds by the firm. His takeover attempt failed, but Chrysler was shocked into increasing its dividends.

Reasons to Hold Cash   Traditionally, there are three reasons why firms should hold cash. The most obvious is to satisfy transactional needs. Beyond this reason we can identify two others: the precautionary motive and the speculative motive.

The **transactional motive** for holding cash is the need to pay debts that arise as a regular consequence of doing business. These include disbursements to pay wages, trade debts, taxes, and so forth. Cash inflows occur as goods and services are sold and these inflows should be sufficient to cover the outflows. In a perfect world, cash deposits made each day would cover that day's cash disbursements and any extra could be invested or returned to shareholders. The problem is that cash inflows and cash outflows are not perfectly synchronized. As a result, some level of cash is needed as a buffer.

The **precautionary motive** for holding cash is the need for a safety supply to act as a financial reserve against unexpected events. For example, suppose a major customer is unable to pay its bill as expected and projected on the cash budget. This means that you will have less cash than forecasted and will be unable to pay your bills unless a safety stock is available. The size of the precautionary balance depends on the reliability of the firm's cash flows and the speed with which its other assets can be converted into cash. Money market instruments and T-bills can be converted to cash very quickly and thus reduce the need for large cash balances.

The **speculative motive** for holding cash is to take advantage of bargain purchases or opportunities that might arise. Again, the frequency with which such opportunities arise varies by firm and industry. A used car dealer may require large speculative balances so that it can buy cars that are offered at irregular intervals.

Cost of Cash   The primary cost of holding cash is the opportunity cost of lost interest income. Because there is a cost of holding excess cash, why would any firm hold more than is required to meet its minimum expected needs? The reason is that there is a cost of converting other assets into cash or borrowing funds. To determine the optimal cash balance we must weigh the benefits of holding cash against the opportunity and conversion costs of holding more than is needed at any particular moment.

How much cash should a firm hold? The more cash it has, the lower are its conversion and borrowing costs, but the higher are the opportunity costs of not investing in income-producing assets. We want to hold the amount of cash that results in the

---

[2]*Fortune,* June 24, 1996, pp. 50–61. In fact, Kerkorian was accurate in his prediction that Chrysler would be acquired. It merged with Daimler-Benz AG in 1998.

minimum total costs. The Baumol and the Miller–Orr models can help us compute this optimal amount.

Using the Baumol and Miller–Orr Models to Compute the Optimal Cash Conversion Amount

Baumol Model

Earlier in this chapter we investigated the economic order quantity (EOQ) model used to determine the optimal inventory level. Baumol applied this model to estimating the optimal cash levels to hold. The resulting **Baumol model** determines the amount of cash that minimizes the sum of the holding costs and the transaction costs. The holding costs include the administration of the cash accounts as well as the opportunity cost of holding cash. The transaction costs are the costs of converting assets into cash or borrowing.

If you keep a reservoir of cash that is steadily drawn down to pay expenses, it will need replenishing at regular intervals. The pattern of cash balances assumes the sawtooth pattern we saw for inventory levels earlier. The management of cash is very similar to the inventory problem. To compute the optimal order quantity using the EOQ model, you needed to know the inventory carrying cost, order cost, and total annual sales. We can simply redefine these variables to solve the cash problem. Instead of units per order, Q^* becomes the value of short-term securities sold or loans obtained each time cash is replenished. Cost per order is the cost per sale of securities. The carrying cost of cash is the interest rate. Finally, total cash disbursements for the year replace annual sales. With these substitutions, we define the Baumol model for the optimal cash conversion amount to be

$$Q^* = \sqrt{\frac{2 \times \text{Annual cash disbursements} \times \text{Cost per sale of securities}}{\text{Interest rate}}} \tag{16.4}$$

As interest rates increase, fewer securities are converted to cash so more conversion cycles are required. If the cost per sale of securities is high (i.e., if you must borrow the funds), more cash is converted and there are fewer cycles. These results are reasonable because you will want to hold as much cash in interest-bearing securities as possible if the reward for doing so is high. Similarly, if the cost of obtaining cash is high (i.e., if you must go through the loan process), you will want to do this as infrequently as possible.

Study Tip

The variance of the cash flows can be computed with Excel. Determine the cash balance at a fixed interval over a large number of periods and use the built-in Excel function to determine the variance of the cash balance.

EXAMPLE 16.3   Optimal Cash Conversion Amount

Lillian Vernon Corporation has annual cash expenditures of about $175 million. If the firm's cash conversion cost is $100 and it can earn 5% on funds invested in short-term securities, what is the optimal amount of securities that should be sold at one time?

Solution
Using Equation 16.4 we find

$$Q^* = \sqrt{\frac{2 \times \text{Annual cash disbursements} \times \text{Cost per sale of securities}}{\text{Interest rate}}}$$

$$Q^* = \sqrt{\frac{2 \times \$175,000,000 \times \$100}{0.05}}$$

$$Q^* = \$836,660$$

According to the Baumol model, Lillian Vernon should convert $836,660 in securities into cash each time it needs to replenish its cash balances.

Self-Test Review Question*

Your firm has annual expenditures of $100,000. The cash conversion cost is $50 and it earns 7% on invested money. How much should be converted to cash at one time?

Miller–Orr Model

The Baumol model assumes that cash is used at a steady rate over time, but this does not always happen. In fact, the number of exceptions probably exceeds the cases when the assumption holds. For example, cash inflows may occur when receivables are paid. Cash outflows may occur at the same time or after a delay. We need a model that allows for more flexibility in the cash flow patterns. The **Miller–Orr model** depends on the variation in the cash flows, as well as the transaction cost of converting funds.[3] High and low limits are set which trigger conversion.

To understand the Miller–Orr model, begin by reviewing Figure 16.6. The cash balance meanders up and down over time. The firm sets a lower and upper limit. As long as the cash balance is within these bounds, no action is taken. This allows for the usual variations in cash flows to occur without the firm incurring transaction costs. At some point, however, the cash balance falls to the lower limit. This triggers the firm to sell securities to raise the cash balance up to the return point. Similarly, when the cash balance builds to the upper limit, securities are purchased so that the cash balance again drops to the return point. This process continues with the firm buying and selling short-term securities whenever the cash balance reaches the upper or lower limit. The amount of securities bought and sold is always whatever is required to bring the cash balance back to the return point.

To put the Miller–Orr model to use, the firm must compute the spread between the upper and lower limits and the return point. The spread is a function of the variability of the cash flows over time, the transaction costs, and the interest rate. When the cash flow variance is high, we will want a larger spread to accommodate the normal range of cash balances. We also will want a wider spread when the cost of converting cash is high. Conversely, if the opportunity cost of holding cash is high, as measured by the interest

---

[3]M. H. Miller and D. Orr, "A Model of the Demand for Money by Firms," *Quarterly Journal of Economics*, vol. 80, August 1966, pp. 414–434.

* $Q^* = [(2 \times \$100,000 \times \$50) \div 0.07]^{0.5} = \$11,952.$

FIGURE 16.6

Using the Miller–Orr Model to Compute the Economic Order Quantity

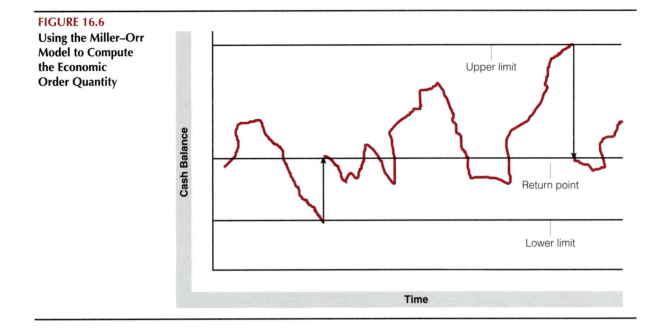

rate, we will want a narrower spread. Miller and Orr provide the formula for computing the spread between the upper and lower limit as

$$\text{Spread} = 3\left(\sqrt[3]{\frac{3}{4} \times \frac{\text{Transaction cost} \times \text{Variance of cash flow}}{\text{Interest rate}}}\right) \qquad (16.5)$$

The firm sets the lower limit as the safety stock it desires. The spread is added to this safety stock to compute the upper limit. The firm then computes the variance of the cash flows. This is easily done with any spreadsheet software and on most financial calculators. Actual daily cash balances for the last several months can be collected and used for this purpose.

The next step is to compute the return point. Note that the return point is not halfway between the upper and lower limit. Instead it is one-third of the way between the upper and lower limit. This means that the firm will hit the lower limit more often than the upper limit. Although this does not minimize the number of transactions (as would be the case if a return point was chosen halfway between the upper and lower limits), it does minimize the sum of the transaction costs and interest cost. The return point is found by Equation 16.6:

$$\text{Return point} = \text{Lower limit} + \frac{\text{Spread}}{3} \qquad (16.6)$$

Let us summarize the steps in implementing the Miller–Orr model.

1. Determine the variance of the cash flows.

2. Estimate the transaction costs for converting securities into cash.

3. Decide on a safety stock to be the lower limit for the cash balance.

4. Compute the spread between the upper and lower limit using Equation 16.5 and the current short-term interest rate.

5. Compute the upper limit by adding the spread to the lower limit.

6. Compute the return point using Equation 16.6.

E X A M P L E 16.4   Miller–Orr Cash Management Model

Suppose that Lillian Vernon's variance of cash flows was $10 million, its conversion cost was $100, and its short-term interest rate was 5%. If the firm wanted to maintain a $100,000 safety stock, what would be the spread, the upper limit, and the return point?

Solution

Use Equation 16.5 to compute the spread:

$$\text{Spread} = 3\left(\sqrt[3]{\frac{3}{4} \times \frac{\text{Transaction cost} \times \text{Variance of cash flow}}{\text{Interest rate}}}\right)$$

$$\text{Spread} = 3\left(\sqrt[3]{\frac{3}{4} \times \frac{\$100 \times \$10,000,000}{0.000137}}\right) = \$52,873$$

Note that the 5% annual interest rate must be converted to a *daily* rate because a daily variance is used.

To find the upper limit, the spread is added to the lower limit:

$$\text{Upper limit} = \text{Lower limit} + \text{Spread}$$

$$\text{Upper limit} = \$100,000 + \$52,873 = \$152,873$$

The return point is computed using Equation 16.6:

$$\text{Return point} = \text{Lower limit} + \frac{\text{Spread}}{3}$$

$$\text{Return point} = \$100,000 + \frac{\$52,873}{3} = \$117,624$$

Lillian Vernon would sell $17,624 in securities whenever the cash balance fell to $100,000 (this would return the balance to $117,624). The firm would buy $152,873 − $117,624 = $35,249 in short-term securities whenever the cash balance rose to $152,873 (this would return the balance to $117,624). If the cash balance remained between $100,000 and $152,873, the firm would not adjust the cash balance. The solution is presented graphically in Figure 16.7. The firm would buy securities at points A and B and sell at point C.

Like the Baumol model, the Miller–Orr model is based on assumptions that are probably not very realistic. It assumes that cash flows are entirely random and unpredictable. In fact, company managers are often able to predict cash flows quite accurately. Many firms have seasonal cash flow patterns, such as around Christmas or during the summer season. Other firms, such as grocery stores, have very predictable daily and weekly patterns. We discussed in Chapter 15 how cash budgets are prepared to take advantage of

FIGURE 16.7
Solution to
Example 16.4

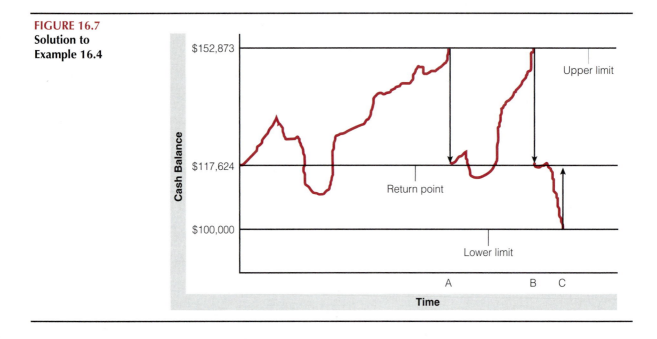

this managerial insight to predict cash flows. Which approach is better, the cash budget or the cash flow models presented here? Undoubtedly, the cash budget, which includes all known seasonalities and management's judgment, will outperform these rigid models. They simply help us understand the problem of cash management and possibly provide clues on how the unpredictable portion of cash variability may be handled.

Investing Idle Cash   We have said little about what should be done with surplus cash balances. Several options are available to firms. Recall from Chapter 2 that the money markets are for the investment of short-term funds. Many of the securities discussed in the money market section of Chapter 2 would be good ones to use for warehousing funds. Recall that money market securities have very low risk and usually pay low interest rates. Typical money market securities include commercial paper, certificates of deposit, repurchase agreements, and Treasury bills. All of these securities are very liquid and low risk.

Another alternative to purchasing securities is to invest in money market mutual funds. These are managed funds that invest only in short-term securities. The advantage of the money market mutual fund is that there may be very low transaction costs. The cash management models we have studied in this chapter point out the significance of minimizing these costs.

A final investment option may be to let the bank invest the idle funds on behalf of the firm. Bank interest rates are usually not as high as what a firm could obtain independently, but the bank may be able to invest *all* idle funds so that the net return may be greater than through some other method. The financial manager will want to investigate all of these options before selecting the one that provides the highest income for the firm.

HOW TO MANAGE ACCOUNTS RECEIVABLE

In this section we will investigate the management of accounts receivable. In Chapter 14 we learned a number of ratios that managers can use to track accounts receivable, such as the accounts receivable turnover ratio and average collection period. Although these ratios deserve management attention, there is much more to managing accounts receivable than simply attempting to collect what is due as fast as possible. For example, firm managers must decide how aggressively collection efforts should be pursued, who should receive credit, and what discounts the firm will give to customers who pay promptly. All of these problems could be avoided if the firm simply refused to offer credit. Therefore, let us begin our discussion by reviewing why credit is offered.

Why Credit Is Offered

The primary reason for offering credit is to stimulate sales. For example, the furniture industry in many parts of the country has learned to use credit as a major marketing tool. Furniture Fair in the East advertises with "buy now with no payments for a year" and other attractive financing opportunities. The only reason the store offers these terms is because they induce customers to buy furniture.

Alternatively, in many industries trade credit is so frequently offered that any firm failing to give credit would probably not survive. For example, lumber stores usually allow contractors to buy on credit. The real decision in cases such as this is not whether to offer credit, but rather what terms to offer.

Developing a Credit Policy

Once a firm has decided to offer credit, either because the competitive nature of the industry demands it or because the firm expects increased sales, it must then decide on the credit terms. A firm's **credit policy** stipulates how it will handle each phase of the credit decision. This includes what goods will be sold on credit, who will receive credit, what the credit terms will be, and how the firm will collect on delinquent accounts.

There are three elements to the typical credit sale: the credit period, the discount amount, and the discount period.

Credit Period

The credit period is the length of time the customer has before payment is due. Although the credit period varies among industries, it is usually between 30 and 120 days. Longer credit periods often are offered as a means of inducing customers to buy the firm's products. For example, some small grocery stores have negotiated with Coca-Cola distributors to stock only Coke brand products in exchange for 90- or 120-day credit periods.

Not all customers are given the same terms. Higher-value customers, those with an established credit history, and those whose business is most desired, either for its prestige or constancy, may be given longer periods to pay.

Another factor to consider when establishing the credit period is the buyer's inventory period and receivables cycle. The inventory period is the length of time it takes the buyer to acquire, process, and sell the inventory. The receivables cycle is the length of time it takes to collect on the sale. The longer the buyer's inventory receivables cycle, the longer the credit period the buyer will require. The credit period serves to finance a portion of the buyer's operating cycle (the inventory period plus the receivables cycle). Trade credit, as this is often called, is often an important part of a firm's capital structure.

If the credit period is longer than the buyer's operating cycle, then the supplier is financing a portion of the buyer's operations beyond what is related to inventory. For this reason, we typically avoid credit periods that exceed the customer's operating cycle.

Other issues that the firm should consider before establishing the credit period include whether the product is perishable or has continuing collateral value, consumer demand for the product, the credit risk of the buyer, and the competition in the market.

Cash Discounts

Cash discounts are widely used as a method to speed up the collection of accounts receivable. The usual terms offer a 1 or 2% discount if the customer pays the outstanding balance within some short period, such as 10 days. Credit terms are quoted using a shorthand notation in which the discount and discount period are listed first and the credit period is listed last. For example, 2/10, net 30 means that a 2% discount is available if the customer pays the bill within 10 days; otherwise the bill is due in full in 30 days. In this case, by forgoing the 2% discount the customer obtains a $30 - 10 = 20$-day loan for 2% of the amount due. Although this may initially seem like a low interest rate, remember that the 2% is for only 20 days. An important question that both the supplier and the customer may ask is, What is the annualized cost of this credit?

To compute the effective annual rate for a cash discount, we first need to determine how many discount periods there are in a year. There are $365/20 = 18.25$ discount periods in one year. If the amount of the discount is 2%, then the customer is paying $2 to borrow $98 for 20 days. The holding period cost of the loan is $$2/$98 = 0.02041$. We annualize this by compounding this rate for one year:

$$\text{Effective annual rate (EAR)} = (1.02041)^{18.25} - 1 = 0.4459 = 44.59\%$$

Alternatively, the annual percentage rate is the interest rate per period multiplied by the number of periods:

$$\text{Annual percentage rate (APR)} = 0.02041 \times 18.25 = 0.3725 = 37.25\%$$

Whether compounding is considered or not (EAR versus APR), from both the buyer's and seller's viewpoints, this is very high cost financing. The seller is paying a high rate of interest to speed collections and the buyer is paying a very high rate of interest to borrow short-term money. It is important that buyers keep the correct perspective when dealing with trade credit. The price after the discount is taken is not really a discounted price. This is the price the typical customer will pay who visits the seller's place of business and purchases the goods across the counter. The undiscounted price reflects a markup over the real price that includes the cost of financing the purchase for the credit period. It is *not* free credit, as some business managers are inclined to think. In fact, it is very expensive credit that usually should be financed with some other source of short-term money. Trade credit is free only for the length of the discount period, for example, the 10 days in the 2/10, net 30 terms.

Despite the high cost to buyers, trade credit remains a very popular means of financing. With this in mind, suppliers must establish an optimal credit policy. Theoretically, the optimal credit policy is one in which the increased profit from sales is exactly equal to the increase in the cost of carrying and administering accounts receivable. Let us identify these costs more precisely.

Cost of Credit

The cost of credit includes three separate factors. First, there is the cost of holding increased current assets in the form of accounts receivable. If most customers pay within the discount period, there are no offsetting revenues. If most customers fail to take advantage of the discount, or if no discount is offered, the increased prices paid by credit customers can turn out to be a revenue source. For example, General Motors offers credit to car buyers. Part of its motivation is to sell cars, but it has realized that the firm's credit division makes money for the firm. This division has been spun off as a wholly owned subsidiary called General Motors Acceptance Corporation (GMAC). GMAC is an example of a captive finance company, a company with the mandate to provide financing for its parent company's customers.

A second cost of credit is bad debt losses. In a later section we will discuss the factors that determine who is to receive credit. For now, we should realize that if credit is extended, there is a chance that it will not be repaid. Default rates of 1 or 2% are not unusual, even for firms with careful screening procedures.

The third cost of offering credit is the cost of administering the accounts receivable. Staff must be employed to analyze credit, send out bills, and collect on past due accounts. This entire department can be eliminated if no credit is offered.

Total Cost of Credit Curve and the Optimal Amount of Credit

We now can combine the cost of receivables with their revenues to generate a total cost curve, as shown in Figure 16.8. The downward-sloping line represents revenues earned by extending credit and increasing sales. The more credit is offered, the more sales will be generated and the more income the firm will receive.

The upward-sloping line represents the combined cost of offering credit. Increased trade credit requires more administration and more bad debt losses. For example, as credit is offered to less creditworthy customers, bad debt losses increase. There may be offsetting revenues from increased prices charged to credit customers.

FIGURE 16.8
Net Cost of
Exteding Credit

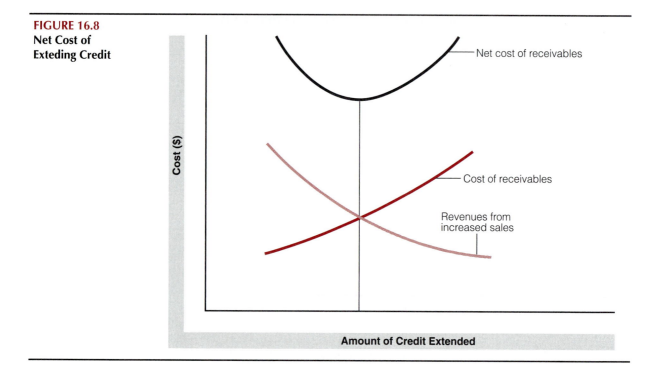

The net cost of receivables curve combines the income from advancing credit with the cost of offering credit. The optimal credit policy is one in which the net cost of receivables curve is lowest. The general shape of this curve should look very familiar to you by now, but it is difficult to quantify the costs and revenues. Most firms must experiment with their credit policy to find the terms that minimize costs. A typical approach is to begin with a credit policy that is standard for the industry. The firm can then make small adjustments and carefully observe the resulting effects.

Five Cs of Credit Analysis

Once the firm has made the decision to extend credit it must decide to whom credit will be extended and how much credit will be allowed. Some firms use complex computer programs to analyze credit applications. Many others rely on less sophisticated methods. Because firm managers often do not know nearly as much about the finances of customers as they might like, they must find alternative methods for judging creditworthiness. The classic approach is to use the five Cs of credit:

- *Character:* The willingness of the borrower to pay obligations owed.
- *Capacity:* The ability of the borrower to pay. If the capacity to pay is not present, the best intentions of the borrower are of little use.

- *Capital:* The financial reserves of the firm. The more capital the firm has at its disposal, the more likely is repayment.
- *Conditions:* The general economic and business climate. Favorable conditions increase the probability of repayment.
- *Collateral:* The value of the assets that could be seized if the customer does not pay on the debt. If all else fails, the customer may be forced to liquidate to pay debts. The lender's priority of payment in the event of liquidation and the value of the assets affect the likelihood of repayment.

A variety of sources of information are available to the firm considering offering a customer credit. The best information may be from the firm's own prior experience with the customer. When this is unavailable, the manager may obtain information from credit rating companies such as Dun & Bradstreet and TRW. Dun & Bradstreet provides financial statement information and TRW provides payment history. Most firms require their customers to complete a credit application before large sums are extended. This credit application can authorize the firm to contact the customer's bank or other creditors. Typically, the lower the credit level being considered, the less expense a firm will incur analyzing a customer's credit history.

Collection of Accounts Receivable (Monitoring)

An important part of the overall credit policy is the firm's collection policy. The collection policy begins with careful monitoring of accounts receivable.

Monitoring Accounts Receivable

In Chapter 14 we introduced several activity ratios that the firm's management can use to track accounts receivable. The most important of these is the average collection period, which tells managers how long the average credit remains outstanding. With experience, managers learn to factor out seasonal variation in the average collection period and use it to help evaluate how well the credit policy is functioning. If the average collection period begins to stretch out, it may be that many customers are taking a little longer to pay or a few are taking much longer. Either alternative requires additional investigation.

Another tool managers use to evaluate the firm's accounts receivable is an **aging schedule**. An aging schedule is simply a list of the amounts due, organized by due dates. Most modern accounting packages used by even the smallest firms have built-in accounts receivable aging schedules. An example of an aging schedule is presented in Table 16.1.

Any interval may be used for reporting purposes. The first one usually extends from zero to the end of the discount period and the second period goes from the end of the discount period to the end of the credit period. In the example cited earlier, with credit terms of 2/10, net 30, an aging schedule similar to the one in Table 16.1 would be useful to track how many customers are taking advantage of the discount and how many are truly delinquent. Based on the aging schedule in Table 16.1, there are eight customers who should be watched, three of whom require careful monitoring.

TABLE 16.1 Aging Schedule

Age of Account	Amount	Number of Accounts
0–10 days	$100,000	60
11–30 days	75,000	40
31–45 days	10,000	5
46–60 days	3,000	2
Over 60 days	1,500	1

Collection Effort

Most computerized accounting packages also print specialized reports that list the details of delinquent accounts so that the firm can follow up with additional collection efforts. An important part of the overall credit policy is collection procedures. Firms usually are concerned with treading a middle ground between losing customers by being too aggressive with collections versus having bad debt losses because they are too lax. The firm should follow a sequence of steps that are progressively more insistent:

1. The accounts receivable department sends a past due letter or notice as soon as the account is past due.

2. The firm makes a telephone call to the customer. Depending on the nature of the relationship with the customer, the telephone call may be made by someone who has dealt with the customer or by someone from the collection department.

3. If the above fails to elicit payment, the firm may turn the account over to a credit company that specializes in collection.

4. Finally, if all else has failed, the customer may be sued for payment.

Management must closely monitor the activities of both the sales force and the collection department. Clearly, they operate with different primary motives. The sales personnel are most concerned with moving the product. If their compensation is based on their sales volume, they will tend to sell to customers who may be known credit risks. On the other hand, the collection department may antagonize normally good customers by being overly threatening. It is the responsibility of management to balance these two opposing approaches to maximize profits and, as always, to maximize shareholder wealth.

SHORT-TERM FINANCING ALTERNATIVES

So far, this chapter has focused on short-term asset management. When a firm requires more short-term assets than it can accumulate through careful management, it may use alternative sources. The two alternatives that will be discussed in this chapter are short-term bank loans and trade credit. There are many sources of short-term funds. One that is not recommended is discussed in Box 16.1.

Box 16.1 Desperate Situations Require Desperate Measures

One source of short-term funds seldom mentioned in the textbooks is credit cards. Clearly, they are not a usual source of funds and are a high-cost method of borrowing, but they are used more often than many suspect.

A group of partners at an architectural firm in Alaska bought out the majority partner's ownership interest. The terms of the buyout required that the partners pay a substantial amount of the funds 1 year after the buyout or lose their ownership interest. When revenues did not materialize as the partners had projected, they found themselves without the required payment. Their bank was not interested in extending additional funds to the new partners because they did not have a track record. After many sleepless nights the partners agreed to each obtain the maximum cash advance they could on all of their credit cards. This was done and the money was used to make the payment.

Fortunately, the firm soon after obtained a large contract with an advance payment that permitted them to pay off the credit card debt. How often credit cards are used to fund company expenses is unknown. Desperate managers take desperate measures.

Bank Loans

Many businesses use banks to supply short-term funds needed for the firm's operations. Banks tend to specialize in customizing short-term loans. In fact, these short-term business loans are the bread and butter for most banks. The advantage to the bank is that it can charge fees every time a new loan is made. The advantage to the firm is that the bank can be much more flexible in its terms and conditions than is possible with publicly issued debt.

Recall from Chapter 4 that short-term interest rates tend to be lower than long-term rates (with a normal-shaped yield curve). This means that firms may prefer to obtain short-term loans instead of long-term because they may be less costly. Of course, there is additional risk from using short-term money in that the cost of borrowing can rise if interest rates increase.

Self-Liquidating Loans

Short-term bank loans are often self-liquidating, meaning that the loan is made to finance an asset that will pay off the loans. For example, a bank may make a loan to finance accounts receivable. When the receivables are paid, the proceeds are given to the bank to retire the debt.

Receivable financing usually requires that the firm pledge its accounts receivable to the bank as collateral for the loan. The bank will lend the firm no more than 80% of the book value of receivables. Additionally, accounts that are past due are often excluded from financing. If the firm defaults on its loan, the bank can notify those who owe the firm money that all payments are to be made to the bank.

Inventory financing is also a very common type of short-term financing. The firm borrows a portion of the value of its inventory and pays off the loan from the proceeds generated by selling the inventory. For example, an auto dealer may borrow money to pay for its inventory of cars. Each time a car is sold, the car dealer must pay an agreed-upon amount to the bank.

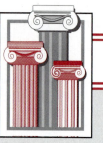

Careers in Finance

Current Asset Management

This chapter demonstrates that firms must watch their float and current accounts carefully to avoid the lost opportunity of investing surplus current assets. Managing bank accounts, payment schedules, bank float, and inventory levels can be a full-time job even in relatively small firms. Current asset management at larger firms may involve whole departments. These departments usually report to the Chief Financial Officer.

A great deal of current asset management is now computerized, relieving much of the tedium that existed at one time. Now current asset managers can focus on implementing, reviewing, and monitoring the effectiveness of various innovative cash and inventory strategies.

Current asset managers usually have degrees in either finance or accounting. They need a solid background in computer accounting applications. Salaries begin in the mid $30,000s and can reach the mid $70,000s at larger firms.

Banks often require that the firm completely pay off its short-term loans every year. This is to keep the short-term money from becoming used to finance long-term assets.

Lines of Credit

Firms often reach an agreement with banks regarding how much credit the bank will extend. The total amount that can be borrowed is the firm's line of credit. Usually, once the line of credit has been established, little effort is required by the firm to obtain a disbursement of funds. For example, a firm may have a line of credit of $100,000. If the current total of loans outstanding is $50,000, a request for a $25,000 loan secured by accounts receivable can often be obtained almost immediately and without even a bank visit.

Banks monitor firms by requiring that periodic financial statements be submitted to the bank. The bank's loan officers occasionally visit the firm. At least once per year the bank and the firm review the line of credit to see whether it is adequately serving the company.

Trade Credit

Earlier in this chapter we discussed the use of accounts receivables from the standpoint of a firm offering credit to its customers to increase sales. Most firms both offer credit and receive credit. Credit offered by suppliers and used by firms that sell products or services is known as **trade credit**. Trade credit can be a significant source of capital for many firms. In some cases it is very simple to obtain. By placing an order for goods that will be delivered before payment is expected, a firm obtains a short-term loan. In the business world, most goods are sold in this manner.

As a firm establishes a relationship with a supplier, the amount of trade credit usually increases. Additionally, trade credit is often included in the negotiations for goods and services.

It is important that the cost of trade credit be fully understood. Discounts given for paying within a limited time period actually represent price increases charged for paying after the discount period. The cost of this is very high compared with virtually any other source of short-term financing. Typically, it should be used only if no other option is available to the firm.

CHAPTER SUMMARY

The management of short-term assets typically occupies a substantial portion of the financial manager's time and energy. Short-term assets include inventory, cash, and accounts receivable.

Firms want to hold a level of inventory that balances the cost of holding inventory against the cost of ordering and restocking. Additionally, firms may want a safety stock to prevent losses due to running out of inventory. The economic order quantity model sets the cost of ordering against the cost of holding inventory. The first order is increased to include the safety stock. The reorder must be placed so that the order arrives as the level of inventory falls to the safety stock.

Cash management involves increasing the speed with which payments are received and slowing down disbursements. Often firms can take advantage of float by making disbursements from remote locations, and they can reduce collection times by using lockboxes or remote collection points. As with inventory, there is often a cost of converting securities into cash. At times, securities must be sold to increase cash. The optimal conversion amount balances the cost of converting against the interest income that is lost by holding large cash balances.

Accounts receivable are held as a method of increasing sales. Competitive pressure often forces firms into offering trade credit. A firm must develop a credit policy to direct the management of accounts receivable. The credit policy dictates who is to receive trade credit, the terms of the credit agreement, and how past due accounts are to be collected. Often firms offer discounts to companies that pay within a short period of time. The correct way to look at discounts is that the discount price is the normal price of the merchandise because this is what anyone buying across the counter would pay. The undiscounted price is a markup that can reflect a very high cost of borrowing. For example, a 2% discount that is not taken can be the equivalent of borrowing funds at an effective interest rate of 45% per year.

Part of the credit policy involves who will receive credit and how much. The five Cs of credit (character, capacity, capital, conditions, and collateral) should all be considered in this process. Once credit has been extended, outstanding balances must be monitored to reduce the amount of losses from nonpayment.

Part of working capital management includes short-term liability management. Firms obtain short-term credit principally from banks or as trade credit. Banks lend money secured by accounts receivable or inventory. Trade credit is often easily obtained, but firms should be aware of the high cost of exceeding the discount period when paying the credit.

KEY WORDS

aging schedule 455
Baumol model 446
carrying costs 433
collection float 440
compensating balance 442

concentration banking 442
credit policy 451
disbursement float 440
economic order quantity
    model 436

electronic funds transfer
    (EFT) 442
lockbox 441
Miller–Orr model 447
precautionary motive 445

speculative motives 445
trade credit 458
transactional motives 445
zero balance account 444

DISCUSSION QUESTIONS

1. What are the costs of holding inventory?
2. How is the average inventory amount computed from the average reorder amount?

3. What costs are compared with carrying costs when the optimal reorder amount is computed?
4. Explain the concept behind the economic order quantity.

5. What is the purpose of a safety stock in the context of inventory management?

6. What is the primary risk the firm takes when using a just-in-time inventory method?

7. Distinguish between disbursement float, collection float, and net float.

8. Discuss how collections can be speeded up.

9. What ethical issues arise when a firm considers methods of slowing down disbursements?

10. Will it ever make sense to hire an employee strictly to manage the firm's float?

11. Discuss the similarities between computing the optimal cash conversion amount and the optimal reorder amount. (Extension 16.1)

12. What elements make up the credit policy?

13. What are the five Cs of credit analysis?

14. How are most short-term business loans secured?

PROBLEMS

1. If beginning inventory is $100 and ending inventory is $50, what is the average inventory?

2. Assume beginning inventory is $150,000 and ending inventory is $25,000, what are total carrying costs if the carrying cost per unit is $0.15?

3. If the firm sells 50,000 units per year and makes 10 orders per year, what is the total order cost if each order costs $20?

4. Assume a car dealer has carrying costs per car of $250. The order costs are $150. The dealer sells 3,000 cars per year.
   a. What is the optimal number of cars that should be ordered at one time?
   b. Assume that sales increase to 4,000 cars per year. What is the new optimal order quantity?
   c. A new office manager is hired who increases the order cost to $175. If sales stay at 4,000 cars per year, what is the optimal order quantity?

5. A grocery store sells 10,000 heads of lettuce per year. Order costs are $1.50 and holding costs are $0.25 per head. Compute the optimal order quantity.

6. A manufacturing plant requires ten-penny nails to produce its product. If it runs out of the nails, the whole plant shuts down. The company uses 15,000 nails per year. Order costs are $25 per order and carrying costs are $0.02.
   a. What is the optimal order quantity?
   b. Assume that the firm wants a safety stock of 3,000 nails. What will the first order be and what will each subsequent order be?

7. If you write $5,000 in checks that are either in the mail or still clearing the banking system and had an original bank balance of $10,000, what are your available balance, your book balance, and your net float?

8. You write three checks. The first one is for $200 and will clear in 1 day. The second one is for $300 and will clear in 2 days. The third one is for $400 and will clear in 3 days. If your bank balance was $1,000 at the time the checks were written, what is the available balance and net float after 1, 2, and 3 days?

9. Your firm holds $1,500,000 in short-term securities. These securities earn 5%. It costs $500 in commissions to convert the securities to cash. If the firm has annual cash disbursements of $20,000,000, what is the optimal conversion amount? (Extension 16.1)

10. Your firm has computed that its cash flow variance is $25,000. Conversion costs are $150 and the firm earns 5.75% on short-term funds. If the firm wants to hold a $5,000 safety stock, what are the spread, the upper limit, the lower limit, and the return point according to the Miller–Orr model? (Extension 16.1)

11. You start work at a new firm and learn that it is the company policy to never take a trade discount. When you ask your boss about this, she says that the firm needs the trade credit to avoid borrowing more money. You tell her it would be cheaper to borrow than to miss taking the discounts. She tells you to prove it. You learn that most of your suppliers offer terms of 1/20, net 30. Compute the effective annual rate and the annual percentage rate. If the firm's cost of borrowed funds is 15%, should it take the discounts?

SELF-TEST PROBLEMS

1. What is the average inventory if a company orders 8,000 units per month and places 4 orders per month?
2. If the average inventory is 2,000 units and the number of units ordered per month is 12,000, compute the number of orders per month.
3. If the average inventory of a company is 5,000 units and it places 4 orders a month, how many units does it order per month?
4. If beginning inventory is $200 and ending inventory is $150, what is the average inventory?
5. If beginning inventory is 16,000 units, closing inventory is 10,000 units, and the total carrying cost is $26,000, what is the carrying cost per unit?
6. If total carrying cost is $40,000, carrying cost per unit is $4, and opening inventory is 15,000 units, compute closing inventory.
7. If sales are 400,000 units, total order cost is $60,000, and ordering cost is $6, what is the number of units ordered per order?
8. If total order cost is $40,000, sales are 400,000 units, and number of units ordered per order is 20, compute order cost.
9. If carrying cost is $3, sales are 6,000 units, and ordering cost is $100, compute EOQ.
10. If EOQ is 100, sales are 1,000 units, and ordering cost is $10, compute carrying cost.
11. If EOQ is 200, sales are 5,000 units, and carrying cost is $2, compute ordering cost.
12. The available balance of Company A is $200. On January 3, if Company A has deposited a check for $100 and written a check for $150, what will be its net float on that day?
13. On January 10, Company B deposited a check for $500 and wrote a check for $600. What would be its net float on that day if its available balance on that day were $100?
14. John writes three checks. The first one is for $300 and will clear in 1 day. The second one is for $400 and will clear in 2 days, and the third one is for $500 and will clear in 3 days. If John's bank balance was $2,000 at the time the checks were written, what are the available balance and the net float after 2 days?
15. If Company A has average daily credit sales of $800,000, by how much will its earnings per year increase if it speeds up collection by 1 day, assuming an interest rate of 8.5% per year?
16. If Company C speeds up its collection by 1 day, its earnings will increase by $60,000. Assuming the interest rate to be 7.3% per year, what are the average daily sales of Company C?
17. Company X has annual expenditures of $100,000. The cash conversion cost is $100, and it earns 10% on invested money. How much should be converted to cash at one time? What is the firm's optimal cash conversion amount according to the Baumol model? (Extension 16.1)?
18. The cash conversion cost for Company Y is $200, and it earns 8% on invested money. What is its annual cash expenditure if it needs to convert $15,000 to cash at one time? What is the firm's annual cash expenditure if $15,000 is its optimal cash conversion amount according to the Baumol model? (Extension 16.1)?
19. Company Z's variance of cash flows is $1 million, its conversion cost is $100, and its short-term interest rate is 6%. If the company wanted to maintain a $120,000 safety stock, what would be the spread, the upper limit, and the return point according to the Miller-Orr model? (Extension 16.1)?
20. The terms of a sale are 2/10, net 30. If the cost of an item is $1,000 and the payment is made on the 9th day after the item is acquired, compute the amount that is required to be paid.

WEB EXPLORATION

1. As we near the end of your course in finance, it is a good time to look at the job opportunities available to finance graduates. Go to finance.pro2net.com/. This site is a free source of job information and career advice.
2. One important factor in choosing a career is the compensation that you can expect to receive. Go to www.jobs-careers.com/accounting/. Click on Salary Wizard on the left side of the screen. Find a job that appeals to you in the financial arena and obtain a salary report for the part of the country in which you plan to live after graduation. Compare several different options and report on your favorite.

MINI CASE

Your company is experiencing rapid growth. While this has generated increasing profits and bodes well for the future, the firm finds itself short of cash to pay current bills. The company president is tackling the problem from a number of sides. She has applied for a line of credit from the firm's primary bank, hopes to sell additional equity early next year, and is talking to suppliers about extended trade credit. She has asked you to look into reducing inventory and to suggest ways of increasing cash balances.

a. The firm currently orders inventory once every month. The carrying cost per unit is $0.25, the order cost is $25.00, and the firm sells about 50,000 units per year. Does this order frequency appear about right?

b. What other issues should be reviewed when determining the optimal inventory level?

c. What other inventory monitoring methods should the firm consider?

d. You have determined that little can be done to reduce inventory, and so you now look at the management of cash as an opportunity to relieve your liquidity problem. What types of float are there? What is the firm's goal with regard to each?

e. Discuss what the firm could do to reduce collection float.

f. As you continue looking for sources of cash, you notice that the firm has a large amount of accounts receivable. The president thinks that the company's customers may pay faster if a discount is offered for early payment. Is this a good idea?

g. A careful review of the accounts payable aging schedule reveals several customers are very late. What actions should the firm take to remedy this problem?

PART **IV**

Bringing It All Together

CHAPTER **17**
International Finance

CHAPTER **18**
Applying Financial Concepts: A Case Study

International Finance

As of December 1997, foreign countries have invested $1.23 trillion in the United States. To put that figure in perspective, about one-quarter of the entire national debt of the United States can be said to be financed by investments coming from foreign nations. Similarly, U.S. banks report investments in foreign countries of $500 billion. Additionally, about one-fifth of the U.S. gross national product (the total output of goods and services in the economy) is now accounted for by exports and imports, *double* the percentage of just 20 years ago. Clearly, tremendous quantities of goods and sums of money are flowing back and forth between countries, and the number of foreign transactions is increasing.

There are many reasons for this increase in international activity. First, most foreign nations are now open to foreign trade, partly because of the collapse of socialism in Eastern Europe and partly because of improved communications that link one side of the world with the other instantly and cheaply. Second, many countries have recognized the benefits of specialization. Recall our discussion in Chapter 15 of the importance of comparative advantages to firms looking for growth opportunities. A comparative advantage is an edge a firm has because of production, distribution, or servicing. For example, in the United States, firms in states with climates conducive to growing oranges specialize in orange production while choosing to import manufactured goods from the northern states. Likewise, the firms in midwestern states produce beef while importing lumber from the northwestern states. Around the world, countries specialize in products for which they have a climate, resource, or skill that places them at a comparative advantage over other countries. In turn, they import goods for which they are at a comparative disadvantage. Globally, the result is that the lowest-cost producer supplies a particular product and everyone benefits.

A third and particularly important reason for increased long-term international trade is the high rate of return possible from foreign investments. For example, McDonald's invested heavily to open the first foreign fast-food outlet in Moscow's Red Square in 1992. The motivation for this investment was not the revenues McDonald's expected from this one outlet; rather, McDonald's wanted the opportunity to introduce the Big Mac to the entire Russian nation.

International trade has many advantages for Americans, despite many complaints about jobs being lost when goods are produced in foreign nations. One primary benefit is that international competition has forced American firms to perform better. For instance, in the 1950s and 1960s, few foreign cars were sold in the United States. The "Big Three"—Ford, General Motors, and Chrysler—completely dominated the auto market. In the 1970s Japan began exporting high-quality cars that were better built, longer lasting, and less expensive than those produced by American manufacturers. Year after year, reliability studies convinced many consumers to buy these foreign cars and the Big Three watched their market share and profits decline. In the 1980s, American quality began improving, and by the 1990s the quality advantage enjoyed by Japan had been dramatically reduced. Today, largely as a result of the competitive pressure, the quality issue is no longer of paramount concern to buyers. This quality improvement has been extended to many products, and we all enjoy better quality and lower prices because of international competition.

Although international commerce involves issues that cross many business disciplines, in this chapter we investigate the more important financial aspects of international business. This includes reviewing:

- How currency exchange rates are established and what they accomplish
- How exchange rate risk affects international trade
- Other areas of international risk that firms incur
- How the international markets can be used to raise capital

BASICS OF EXCHANGE RATES

Few will argue the value of international trade to both firms and consumers. The question is, How can firms do business in countries where goods and services are priced in foreign currencies? The answer lies in exchange rates that allow the firm to convert its domestic currency into foreign currency and back. The **exchange rate** is the price of one country's money quoted in terms of another country's money. For example, if you are planning a trip to England and have located a hotel in London that will cost 50 pounds, you may well wonder what this will cost in U.S. dollars. The exchange rate is used to make this conversion.

Exchange rates make international commerce possible, but they also add both risk and complexity to international trade. We will investigate exchange rates by examining their role in international trade. We will then learn how to read exchange rate quotes. Finally, we will learn how exchange rates are established and what factors cause them to change over time.

Role of Exchange Rates

Exchange rates tell us how to convert one currency into another. The need to do this is easy to understand. If you are quoted the price of a product in terms of a foreign currency, you must determine what that product will cost in your own currency in order to know whether the price is acceptable. Exchange rates are important because they affect the relative price of domestic and foreign products. For example, suppose you are an importer of Porsche 911s. You learn that the new model will sell for 143,718 marks in Germany. How much will this car cost in U.S. dollars? If the exchange rate is $0.59144 to the mark (U.S. dollar equivalent = 0.59144), the car will cost $85,000 (143,718 marks × 0.59144 = $85,000). If the exchange rate changes to $0.6206 to the mark, then the domestic price of the Porsche becomes $89,191.39 (143,718 marks × 0.6206 = $89,191.39). Conversely, if the exchange rate falls, the car becomes cheaper in U.S. dollars. These changes could significantly affect your ability to sell the cars.

From this simple example we can make two deductions. First, exchange rates have a powerful effect on exports and imports because they affect the price of imports for buyers. If the domestic price increases because of a change in the exchange rate, demand is likely to fall. Alternatively, if the exchange rate makes foreign goods less expensive, demand will increase and imports are likely to rise. For example, in the early 1970s the exchange rate between Japan and the United States made Japanese cars cheap and demand increased dramatically, nearly bankrupting Chrysler Corporation. In the early 1990s, exchange rates made Japanese cars more expensive and demand fell, resulting in record profits for domestic auto manufacturers.

The second conclusion we can draw from our Porsche example is that exchange rates introduce a new kind of risk to international trade: **exchange rate risk,** or the risk of loss due to exchange rates moving over time. For example, suppose a U.S. exporter agrees to sell goods abroad in exchange for a sum to be paid in a foreign currency when the goods are delivered in about 2 months. If the value of the foreign currency falls relative to the dollar, the exporter may take a loss on the sale. We will discuss methods to reduce exchange rate risk later in this chapter.

Reading Exchange Rate Quotes

Exchange rate quotes are published in the financial press. Figure 17.1 is a clip from the *Wall Street Journal*'s Currency Trading column. Until you get used to the format of this

FIGURE 17.1

Wall Street Journal **Currency Trading Column**

CURRENCY TRADING

Thursday, January 18, 2001
EXCHANGE RATES

The New York foreign exchange mid-range rates below apply to trading among banks in amounts of $1 million and more, as quoted at 4 p.m. Eastern time by Reuters and other sources. Retail transactions provide fewer units of foreign currency per dollar. Rates for the 12 Euro currency countries are derived from the latest dollar-euro rate using the exchange ratios set 1/1/99.

COUNTRY	U.S. $ EQUIV. Thu	Wed	CURRENCY PER U.S. $ Thu	Wed
Argentina (Peso)	1.0002	1.0002	.9998	.9998
Australia (Dollar)	.5588	.5537	1.7894	1.8059
Austria (Schilling)	.06870	.06793	14.556	14.722
Bahrain (Dinar)	2.6525	2.6525	.3770	.3770
Belgium (Franc)	.0234	.0232	42.6719	43.1581
Brazil (Real)	.5116	.5112	1.9545	1.9560
Britain (Pound)	1.4735	1.4745	.6787	.6782
1-month forward	1.4734	1.4745	.6787	.6782
3-months forward	1.4730	1.4743	.6789	.6783
6-months forward	1.4721	1.4736	.6793	.6786
Canada (Dollar)	.6612	.6619	1.5123	1.5108
1-month forward	.6614	.6620	1.5120	1.5105
3-months forward	.6615	.6622	1.5118	1.5102
6-months forward	.6618	.6626	1.5111	1.5092
Chile (Peso)	.001748	.001748	571.95	572.05
China (Renminbi)	.1208	.1208	8.2764	8.2764
Colombia (Peso)	.0004440	.0004459	2252.50	2242.50
Czech. Rep. (Koruna)				
Commercial rate	.02677	.02630	37.352	38.018
Denmark (Krone)	.1266	.1252	7.8978	7.9878
Ecuador (US Dollar)-e	1.0000	1.0000	1.0000	1.0000
Finland (Markka)	.1590	.1572	6.2894	6.3611
France (Franc)	.1441	.1425	6.9388	7.0178
1-month forward	.1442	.1426	6.9332	7.0114
3-months forward	.1444	.1428	6.9246	7.0024
6-months forward	.1446	.1431	6.9135	6.9893
Germany (Mark)	.4833	.4779	2.0689	2.0925
1-month forward	.4837	.4783	2.0672	2.0906
3-months forward	.4844	.4790	2.0646	2.0879
6-months forward	.4851	.4798	2.0614	2.0840
Greece (Drachma)	.002774	.002743	360.45	364.56
Hong Kong (Dollar)	.1282	.1282	7.7995	7.7998
Hungary (Forint)	.003564	.003527	280.56	283.52
India (Rupee)	.02155	.02154	46.395	46.435
Indonesia (Rupiah)	.0001058	.0001058	9450.00	9450.00
Ireland (Punt)	1.2003	1.1868	.8331	.8426
Israel (Shekel)	.2420	.2433	4.1325	4.1100

COUNTRY	U.S. $ EQUIV. Thu	Wed	CURRENCY PER U.S. $ Thu	Wed
Italy (Lira)	.0004882	.0004827	2048.20	2071.54
Japan (Yen)	.008473	.008413	118.02	118.87
1-month forward	.008512	.008453	117.49	118.30
3-months forward	.008583	.008523	116.51	117.33
6-months forward	.008687	.008629	115.12	115.90
Jordan (Dinar)	1.4065	1.4065	.7110	.7110
Kuwait (Dinar)	3.2690	3.2669	.3059	.3061
Lebanon (Pound)	.0006634	.0006634	1507.50	1507.50
Malaysia (Ringgit)-b	.2632	.2632	3.8000	3.8000
Malta (Lira)	2.3031	2.2894	.4342	.4368
Mexico (Peso)				
Floating rate	.1018	.1014	9.8250	9.8650
Netherland (Guilder)	.4290	.4241	2.3311	2.3577
New Zealand (Dollar)	.4495	.4461	2.2247	2.2416
Norway (Krone)	.1150	.1141	8.6945	8.7657
Pakistan (Rupee)	.01696	.01693	58.950	59.050
Peru (new Sol)	.2841	.2842	3.5200	3.5188
Philippines (Peso)	.01826	.01840	54.750	54.350
Poland (Zloty)-d	.2442	.2429	4.0955	4.1175
Portugal (Escudo)	.004715	.004662	212.07	214.49
Russia (Ruble)-a	.03526	.03519	28.360	28.419
Saudi Arabia (Riyal)	.2666	.2666	3.7508	3.7509
Singapore (Dollar)	.5754	.5767	1.7380	1.7340
Slovak Rep. (Koruna)	.02162	.02131	46.264	46.931
South Africa (Rand)	.1271	.1276	7.8675	7.8350
South Korea (Won)	.0007782	.0007825	1285.00	1278.00
Spain (Peseta)	.005682	.005618	176.00	178.01
Sweden (Krona)	.1061	.1049	9.4210	9.5330
Switzerland (Franc)	.6183	.6079	1.6174	1.6451
1-month forward	.6195	.6092	1.6143	1.6415
3-months forward	.6216	.6113	1.6087	1.6358
6-months forward	.6246	.6144	1.6010	1.6275
Taiwan (Dollar)	.03066	.03066	32.620	32.620
Thailand (Baht)	.02312	.02309	43.250	43.300
Turkey (Lira)	.00000149	.00000149	669870.00	673280.00
United Arab (Dirham)	.2723	.2723	3.6729	3.6728
Uruguay (New Peso)				
Financial	.07941	.07929	12.593	12.613
Venezuela (Bolivar)	.001430	.001430	699.25	699.40
SDR	1.2997	1.2997	.7694	.7694
Euro	.9454	.9347	1.0578	1.0699

Special Drawing Rights (SDR) are based on exchange rates for the U.S., German, British, French, and Japanese currencies. Source: International Monetary Fund.
a-Russian Central Bank rate. b-Government rate. d-Floating rate; trading band suspended on 4/11/00. e-Adopted U.S. dollar as of 9/11/00. Foreign Exchange rates are available from Readers' Reference Service (413) 592-3600.

Source: Wall Street Journal (1/19/2001).

list, it can be quite confusing. The first two columns list the U.S. dollar equivalent of one unit of a foreign currency. The third and fourth columns list the amount of foreign currency one U.S. dollar will buy. An example may help clarify this.

Suppose you are going to England and are interested in the number of British pounds you can buy with $1. This information is provided by the "Currency per U.S. Dollar" columns. In our example, we see that you can buy 0.6787 pounds for each dollar you exchange. When you come home from your trip and want to exchange the pounds you have left over back into dollars, you will use the U.S. dollar equivalent exchange rate. For every pound you exchange, you will receive 1.4735 dollars.

The entry in the "U.S. $ Equivalent" column is the reciprocal of the "Currency per U.S. $" column. To verify this, divide 0.6787 into 1 to get 1.4735 (1/0.6787 = 1.4735). Table 17.1 summarizes how to use the Currency Trading column.

TABLE 17.1 Using the Currency Trading Column to Convert Currency

To convert U.S. dollars into a foreign currency	Multiply by "Currency per U.S. $" column
To convert a foreign currency into U.S. dollars	Multiply by "U.S. $ Equivalent" column

Study Tip

It is not unusual to be confused by exchange rate conversions. The terminology used to explain whether a given exchange rate is converting from dollars to a foreign currency or from a foreign currency into dollars is sometimes difficult to interpret. Do not let this very common problem discourage you. Foreign traders often acknowledge having struggled with this initially, but after a short time of actually trading, it becomes quite easy.

E X A M P L E 17.1   Using Exchange Rate Quotes

Suppose that you are planning a trip to England and have located a hotel on the Internet that lists the price of the rooms as 50 pounds per night. How much will these rooms cost you in U.S. dollars?

Solution

$$\text{U.S. \$ equivalent} = \text{Number of pounds} \times \text{Price of pounds in terms of U.S. dollars}$$

$$\text{U.S. equivalent of 50 pounds} = 50 \text{ pounds} \times \$1.4735 = \$73.67$$

Your hotel room will cost $73.67 per night based on the exchange rates now in effect. If those rates change by the time you are required to pay for the room, the cost in dollars may be more or less than $73.67, depending on how the rates change.

Self-Test Review Questions*

Use Figure 17.1 to make the following conversions.
1. Convert 200 pounds sterling into U.S. dollars.
2. Convert 10,000 Japanese yen into U.S. dollars.
3. Convert $200 U.S. into German marks.

We cannot overemphasize the importance of understanding exchange rates when dealing with international trade. Because goods are bought or sold in different currencies, the firm must determine the effect on profits after converting all cash flows into dollar equivalents. Additionally, the financial manager must appreciate the effect on cash flows and profits of changes in exchange rates. We will investigate these issues in the following sections.

Foreign Exchange Markets

There is no central place that you can go to watch foreign exchange rates being determined; they are not traded on organized exchanges such as the New York Stock Exchange. Instead the foreign exchange market is organized much like the over-the-counter stock market, where hundreds of dealers conduct business over telephones and

*1. 200 pounds × 1.4735 = $294.70.
2. 10,000 yen × 0.008473 = $84.73.
3. $200 × 2.0689 = 413.78 marks.

computers. The volume of these transactions worldwide exceeds $1 trillion per day. Because of the rapid flow of information among these traders, the market is very competitive and functions much like a centralized market. Trades in the foreign exchange market are denominated in units of $1 million or more.

The exchange rates listed in the *Wall Street Journal* reflect what traders in these wholesale markets receive. If you are planning to exchange dollars for an upcoming trip to England, you will buy foreign currency from dealers such as American Express or a bank. Because retail exchange rates allow for a profit to the dealer, you will receive less foreign currency than indicated by the exchange rates quoted in the *Wall Street Journal* column. It is often worth shopping for the best exchange rates if substantial amounts are to be converted. Large money center banks often offer the best exchange rate; airport- and hotel-based dealers may be much worse. When a credit card is used to buy foreign goods, the credit card issuer automatically makes the exchange. Most issuers provide fair exchange rates.

There are two ways to exchange funds in the currency markets. The most common is called a **spot transaction**, which involves the exchange of bank deposits immediately (actually, it usually takes 2 days for the transaction to clear the bank). The **spot exchange rate** is the exchange rate applied to the spot transaction. Spot transactions and spot exchange rates apply to exchanges of funds that occur at the present rather that at some point in the future.

Forward transactions involve the exchange of funds at some prespecified point in the future and **forward exchange rates** are the exchange rates put into forward exchange contracts. Forward transactions are used by businesses that want to reduce exchange rate risk. By entering into a forward contract, they protect themselves from undesirable shifts in exchange rates by locking into a specified rate. Of course, by using a forward transaction, the firm loses the possibility of benefiting from favorable exchange rate movements. In effect, the exchange rate risk has been transferred from the firm to a speculator in the exchange rate market who buys the forward contract. Exchange rate speculators are often employed by large money center banks that trade extensively in the foreign markets. They project future exchange rates for contracts to be settled 30, 90, and 180 days in the future. Refer again to Figure 17.1. Under the listing for the British pound are quotes for 1 month forward, 3 months forward, and 6 months forward. These rates show the direction of change in the exchange rate that is expected by speculators. We will discuss how forward exchange rates can be used by businesses to reduce risk in a later section.

The financial press often reports on the strength of the dollar. On a daily basis, analysts watch how the rate of exchange between the dollar and other foreign currencies changes. *If the value of the dollar increases on average, meaning $1 will buy more foreign currency, then the dollar has strengthened. Alternatively, if the dollar buys less foreign currency, then it has weakened.*

Another term used to describe an increase in the strength of a currency is **appreciation**. When the dollar appreciates against the pound, a dollar can buy more pounds than before. Similarly, **depreciation** means that the dollar has weakened relative to another currency and that the dollar will buy fewer units of the foreign currency.

Now that we know how exchange rates are quoted and who uses them, the next step is to investigate what factors cause exchange rates to be set at a particular level and what factors cause them to change.

Explaining the Level of Exchange Rates

In order for a firm to properly assess the risk of doing business in the international marketplace, we must understand how exchange rates are established and what factors could cause them to change over time. Unfortunately, there is no single factor at work, nor a simple explanation. Instead, many issues affect exchange rates, including the supply and demand for each country's currency, the relative prices of goods, and the returns that can be earned on international investments in securities.

Supply and Demand for Currency Affect Exchange Rates

Suppose that a U.S. firm sells goods in Japan through one of its subsidiaries. The subsidiary receives yen that must be converted back into U.S. dollars. This increases the demand for dollars and the supply of yen in the exchange markets. Similarly, when Toyota sells cars in the United States, it must convert U.S. dollars back into yen in order to transfer the profits back to the parent company. This increases the demand for yen and the supply of dollars on the international exchange markets.

As long as the flow of currencies between countries is equal, the exchange rate can remain constant. However, when the demand for one currency increases and the supply of another increases, the exchange rate adjusts so that the market for the currencies reaches equilibrium. For example, if Japan consistently sells more goods in the United States than the United States sells in Japan, Japanese firms may have trouble converting their U.S. dollars into yen. The excess dollars offered for sale in the currency markets cause the value of the dollar to fall compared with the value of the yen. This is reflected in a devaluation of the dollar–yen exchange rate.

What happens when the dollar becomes weak compared with another currency? If the dollar weakens against the yen, Japanese goods become more expensive to U.S. consumers and U.S. goods become less expensive to Japanese consumers. This causes reduced sales of Japanese products in the United States and increased sales of U.S. products in Japan. Thus, we see that the exchange markets are self-correcting in the long run. We witnessed this in the early 1990s, when the dollar prices of Japanese cars increased significantly, largely because of a weakening of the U.S. dollar. This reduced their demand and concurrently reduced the supply of dollars being offered in the currency markets.

Governments become very concerned with their exchange rates because they directly affect the domestic economy. When exports decrease because of an appreciating currency, domestic firms will have slower growth and reduced profits, and they will employ fewer workers. The country's central bank may attempt to affect the exchange rate by buying or selling currencies. However, because of the size of the markets, a central bank cannot control the level of exchange rates in the long run.

In addition to the supply and demand for currencies, other factors also affect the level of exchange rates. Foremost among these is the relative price of goods in different countries. We discuss this in the next section.

Relative Prices Affect Exchange Rates: The Law of One Price

To understand how the relative prices of goods and services between countries affect exchange rates, we must first introduce a concept called the law of one price. The **law of one price** says that two identical products produced in two different countries should cost the same to traders in any other country. For example, oil produced in Kuwait and oil produced in Saudi Arabia should cost the same to traders in the United States. *The reasoning behind this idea is that if the law of one price did not hold, buyers would shun the product that is more expensive and buy only the cheaper one. This increased demand for the cheaper product would increase its price while the lack of demand for the more expensive product would lower its price. These price changes would continue until the prices of the two goods became equal.*

For example, the law of one price says that if oil sells for 75.01 riyals in Saudi Arabia and 6.118 dinars in Kuwait, then the price of oil from both countries should be the same to a buyer in the United States. In this example, $20 U.S. converts to 75.01 riyals ($20 × 3.7508 = 75.01 riyals) and to 6.118 dinars in Kuwait ($20 × 0.3059 = 6.118 dinars), so that the cost in dollars is the same from both countries. If it was not, the demand for the expensive oil would drop and the demand for the cheap oil would rise, which, as noted above, would eventually drive prices back in line with each other.

Before we continue to investigate the role of exchange rates in the law of one price, we must first acknowledge its limitations. Oil is a homogeneous good (one barrel of oil is much like another barrel)[1] and cheaply transported so traders can take advantage of price differences that may emerge. Some products are not so easily substituted or transported. For example, if you learn that haircuts cost less in France than in England, there is little you can do to earn a profit with this opportunity. Because haircuts are not transportable, the forces of supply and demand will not cause prices to adjust. In addition, it is often difficult to determine whether goods from different countries are truly the same. For example, many connoisseurs believe California and Washington wines are now equivalent to the best French wines. Others disagree. It gets even more difficult. For example, how does a particular bottle of 1978 Chateau St. Michelle merlot compare to a bottle of 1978 Chateau Lafite Rothschild? Such comparisons are matters of opinion and are not addressed by the law of one price.

Purchasing Power Parity   Remember that our reason for discussing the law of one price was to explain exchange rates and how they change over time. The idea behind **purchasing power parity (PPP)** is that exchange rates must adjust over time to keep purchasing power constant among currencies and to maintain the law of one price despite different currencies. In the examples presented above, we assumed that exchange rates did just that. If a slice of pizza cost $2.00 in Atlanta, Georgia, and the exchange rate between dollars and English pounds is 0.6787 pounds to the dollar, then the pizza should cost 1.36 pounds in England ($2.00 × 0.6787 = 1.36 pounds). *The purchasing power parity theory says that the exchange rate between dollars and pounds will adjust to*

---

[1]Actually, oil has grades, which affect its price. In the search for a truly homogeneous good, a number of products were suggested and rejected. Even grains of rice, to those who know, differ in quality.

Study Tip

Purchasing power parity can be thought of as the law of one price applied to national price levels through the exchange rate rather than to the individual prices of goods.

ensure that the price of the pizza is indeed the same in both countries, after adjustment using the exchange rate.

We can state the formula for purchasing power parity more formally as an equation. If S_0 is the spot exchange rate between English pounds and U.S. dollars (read as the dollar price of pounds) and $P_\$$ is the price of pizza in dollars and $P_£$ is the price in pounds, then purchasing power parity says that

$$P_\$ = S_0 \times P_£ \tag{17.1}$$

Purchasing power parity says that the price of a good in the United States is equal to the price of that same good in another country when multiplied by the exchange rate. If this condition did not hold, two things would occur. First, the price of the goods would change because merchants would buy the cheap good and avoid the expensive one. Thus, the forces of supply and demand would cause the prices to adjust.

A second thing that would happen is that the exchange rate itself would adjust. Suppose the price of oil in Saudi Arabia was below that of oil coming from Alaska, even after adjusting for exchange rates. Oil companies would be converting U.S. dollars into riyals to buy Saudi oil. This would increase the international supply of dollars and increase the demand for riyals. As a result, the value of the riyal would increase compared with the value of the dollar, and this would be reflected in a change in the dollar/riyal exchange rate. Because it would take more dollars to buy a riyal, the dollar cost of Saudi oil will increase. The combined effect of the price changes and the exchange rate adjustments would bring purchasing power parity into line.

To review:

- Purchasing power parity (PPP) says that the price of a good in one country will equal its price in another country after adjustment for exchange rates.
- The PPP theory depends on traders taking advantage of deviations from PPP by buying the cheap good and selling the expensive one. This trading causes the prices of the goods and the exchange rate to adjust.
- PPP will not hold if the goods are not transportable or identical.
- Strict PPP requires that transportation costs be zero and that the good be perfectly substitutable. Some goods that are technically transportable are legally restricted from moving across borders due to tariffs, taxes, and other political restraints.

Few goods meet all of these conditions. Transportation costs are seldom zero, and few goods are identical to their counterparts around the world. As a result, PPP is seldom found to hold exactly. In fact, large deviations often occur. For example, in 1996 a Ford Probe, which sold for around $20,000 in the United States, was selling (poorly) for a little over the equivalent of $30,000 in Japan. Transportation costs, taxes, and various tariffs caused a significant deviation from PPP.

Changes in Purchasing Power Parity (Relative PPP)   We have been discussing absolute purchasing power parity, which posits that exchange rates are determined by the differences in the prices of goods at a *particular point in time*. Although absolute PPP may not hold very often, it does provide a basis for understanding how long-term changes in price levels between countries can affect exchange rates. Consider what happens to the *relative* prices of goods if one country experiences a higher level of inflation than another. For example, suppose that PPP holds between the United States and Mexico today and that the exchange rate is 8 pesos to $1 (currency per U.S. dollar = 8). Now suppose that Mexico's inflation rate is 20% per year and the U.S. inflation rate is 0% per year. If the exchange rate does not adjust to reflect the changing prices in each country, PPP will soon be violated. In this example, because the prices of goods in Mexico are appreciating 20% per year faster than in the United States, the exchange rate must adjust 20% per year as well. If the currency per U.S. dollar = 8 pesos initially, it must appreciate 20% to 9.6 due to inflation differences (8 × 1.2 = 9.6). Now it takes 9.6 pesos (rather than 8 pesos) to buy $1. This is an example of **relative purchasing power parity**: Changes in inflation rates cause exchange rates to adjust. The following example demonstrates how this adjustment to the exchange rate maintains PPP.

E X A M P L E 17.2   Maintaining PPP

A merchant in the United States has been importing wool shirts from England for the last several years. The price of the shirts to the importer is 10 pounds per shirt. The exchange rate is $2 per pound (the U.S. dollar equivalent = 2). If inflation is 10% in England and 0% in the United States, how must the exchange rate adjust for the price to the importer to remain unchanged?

Solution

We must first compute the original price of the wool shirts in dollars. This is found by multiplying the U.S. dollar equivalent by the price of the shirts in pounds:

Dollar price of shirts = Pound price of shirt × U.S. dollar equivalent

Dollar price of shirts = 10 pounds × $2 = $20

Now if inflation in England causes the price of the shirts to increase 10% to 11 pounds, the exchange rate must adjust so that the dollar price remains constant at $20:

Dollar price of shirts = Pound price of shirt × U.S. dollar equivalent

$20 = 11 pounds × U.S. dollar equivalent

$20/11 = $1.8182

The U.S. dollar equivalent falls to 1.8182 from 2. Notice that the currency per U.S. dollar, which is the reciprocal of the U.S. dollar equivalent, is 0.55 (1/1.8182 = 0.55).

In Example 17.2, the exchange rate adjusts so that the price in U.S. dollars is constant, but what would happen if the United States were also experiencing inflation? If the U.S. inflation rate were equal to that in England, then the exchange rate would not need to adjust. However, if there were a difference, the exchange rate would have to compensate. For example, if the inflation rate is 10% in England and 6% in the United States, the U.S. dollar equivalent must adjust up 4% (10% − 6% = 4%). In Example 17.2, the new exchange rate would be 0.52.[2]

We can formalize this relationship with Equation 17.2:

$$E(S_t) = S_0 \times [1 + (Inf_f - Inf_{US})]^t \tag{17.2}$$

where

$$
\begin{aligned}
E(S_t) &= \text{expected currency per U.S. dollar exchange rate at time } t \\
S_0 &= \text{current spot exchange rate (currency per U.S. dollar)} \\
Inf_f &= \text{foreign rate of inflation} \\
Inf_{US} &= \text{U.S. rate of inflation} \\
t &= \text{number of years}
\end{aligned}
$$

E X A M P L E 17.3   Relative PPP

If the inflation rate in the United States is expected to average 3% in the future and the inflation rate in England is expected to average 5%, what spot rate is expected to be in effect in 3 years? Assume the currency per U.S. dollar exchange rate is now 0.62.

Solution
Using Equation 17.2 we obtain

$$
\begin{aligned}
E(S_3) &= S_0 \times [1 + (Inf_f - Inf_{US})]^t \\
E(S_3) &= 0.6200 \times [1 + (0.05 - 0.03)]^3 \\
E(S_3) &= 0.6200 \times 1.0612 = 0.6579
\end{aligned}
$$

Because of the greater inflation in England than in the United States, the number of pounds you can buy with $1 is expected to increase to 0.6579 from 0.62 after 3 years.

Study Tip

Absolute purchasing power parity describes the relationship between the prices of goods at a particular point in time. Relative purchasing power parity focuses on the changes over time in the relative prices of goods between countries. Absolute PPP does not hold well when examined; relative PPP does a good job of explaining exchange rate movements over the long run.

The exchange rate expected to be in effect in 3 years is 0.6579 in Example 17.3. This demonstrates how forward exchange rates are established. Traders must anticipate the relative inflation rates between two countries and set a forward rate that compensates for the difference. The forward rate represents a best guess as to what the spot rate will be in the future.

We have already noted that absolute purchasing power parity does not hold very well for most goods because of transportation costs and other restrictions to trade. We might now ask how *changes* in relative PPP (*relative* purchasing power parity) reflect differences in inflation rates. Studies show that in the short run, relative purchasing power parity does not explain changes in exchange rates well. However, over the long run, relative PPP does do a good job of explaining exchange rate changes. The reason for this is that in the short run other factors affect the prices of goods, such as changes in demand, droughts, and production problems. These influences tend to cancel in the long run, where the relationship between inflation and exchange rates dominates the short-run effects.

---

[2]The price of the shirt in the United States would be $20 × 1.06 = $21.20 and the price in England would be 10 pounds × $1.10 = 11 pounds. $21.20/11 = 1.9273. 1/1.9273 = 0.52.

Self-Test Review Questions*

1. What does the law of one price say about prices around the world?
2. What does purchasing power parity say establishes exchange rates?
3. What factor causes exchange rates to change over time?
4. Does relative purchasing power parity hold better than absolute purchasing power parity? Why?
5. Does relative PPP hold better in the short run or the long run? Why?

EXTENTION 17.1

Interest Rate Parity

Another factor that influences exchange rates is the return earned on investments in different countries. Exchange rates must adjust so that there is no reason for funds to flow from one country just to take advantage of better returns.

In the last section we explained the purchasing power parity theory by arguing that if it did not hold, traders could buy the goods in the cheaper country and sell them where they are more expensive. However, we also noted that various restrictions on trade prevented purchasing power parity from being true much of the time. What if there were a good that was essentially costless to transport, was exactly equivalent around the world, and had an easily obtainable price quote? We might expect this particular good to adhere to PPP very accurately. In fact, there is such a good: money. Money can be transferred from one country to another electronically, has a universal value, and has an easy-to-determine price: the interest rate. Interest rates behave so much better than the prices of goods that a special term has been applied to international interest rate relationships: **interest rate parity (IRP)**. Understanding interest rate parity requires that we first understand interest rate arbitrage.

Interest Rate Arbitrage

To **arbitrage**, you buy and sell something so that you have zero net investment and then earn a return on the transaction. For example, if you can invest $1 in a risk-free dollar-denominated investment while simultaneously borrowing $1 at the rate paid on British pounds, you have zero net investment. If you can earn a return for doing this transaction, you have an arbitrage opportunity. Interest rate arbitrage maintains the interest rate parity relationship.

Table 17.2 lists the interest rates available on risk-free deposits in different countries in December 1992. This date was chosen because of the wide variation in interest rates at that time. Upon initial examination, you might think it is wise to borrow Eurodollars

dominate.

5. Long run, because in the long run relative price changes tend to cancel each other and inflation effects

4. Relative PPP holds best because changes are more detectable than absolute levels.

3. Inflation.

cost the same.

2. The law of one price causes exchange rates to adjust so that after adjusting for exchange rates all goods

*1. All goods should cost the same.

TABLE 17.2 Interest Rates, December, 1992

	Percent per Year
Eurodollars	3.70%
United Kingdom	9.56
Canada	6.76
Germany	9.42
Switzerland	7.67
Netherlands	9.25
France	10.14
Italy	13.91
Belgium	9.31
Japan	4.39

(dollar-denominated deposits available in foreign countries) at 3.70% and invest in Italian lira at 13.91%. Let us examine this transaction in greater detail.

To invest in Italian lira you must:

- Convert your dollars to lira using the spot exchange rate.
- Buy the Italian risk-free investment.
- Convert the lira back to dollars when the investment matures. To make this a risk-free transaction, you would lock in a future exchange rate by buying a forward exchange contract.

Let us find out how much we could earn if we borrowed $10,000 in Eurodollars at 3.70%, converted the $10,000 into lira, invested at 13.91%, and finally converted the lira back into dollars. Assume that lira per U.S. dollar (S_0) is 1,700. In the first step, you must convert the $10,000 into lira by multiplying by the S_0:

$$\text{Liras} = \$10,000 \times 1,700 = 17,000,000 \text{ lira}$$

You now invest these liras at 13.91% so you will have 19,364,700 liras at the end of 1 year:

$$\text{Liras at end of year} = \text{Liras invested} \times (1 + \text{Interest rate})$$
$$\text{Liras at end of year} = 17,000,000 \times 1.1391 = 19,364,700 \text{ lira}$$

Now, you must convert your lira back into dollars. To be sure that you do not suffer if exchange rates move, you lock in an exchange rate at the time of the initial investment by buying a contract that lets you convert liras back into dollars when your investment matures. Suppose that this forward contract sets the U.S. dollar equivalent to be 0.000537 (multiplying by the U.S. dollar equivalent will convert your lira into dollars). Then,

$$\text{Dollars from investment} = \text{Liras at end of year} \times \text{U.S. dollar equivalent forward rate}$$
$$\text{Dollars from investment} = 19,364,700 \times \$.000537 = \$10,398.84$$

To determine your net income from the investment you must compute how much the loan of the $10,000 cost you. You borrowed $10,000 at 3.70% for 1 year so you will have to pay back $10,000 times $(1 + 0.0370)$:

Amount due on loan of $10,000 = Loan amount $\times$ (1 + Interest rate)

Amount due on loan of $10,000 = $10,000 $\times$ 1.0370 = $10,370

The net income is $10,398.84 − $10,370 = $28.84. You are investing none of your own equity in this transaction, and it is completely riskless because you are investing in risk-free securities and have locked in a contract to convert the liras to dollars when the investment matures; thus you have a positive arbitrage opportunity. As long as the opportunity continues to exist, you, as well as other arbiters, will continue to borrow more dollars and invest in more lira-denominated investments. Predictably, as the demand for dollars increases, the cost of dollars will rise. This means that the interest cost on borrowed dollars will rise. Similarly, as investments flow into Italy, the return on the investments will fall. Finally, as the demand for forward contracts rises, the rate will increase. Eventually, all of these forces will cause the arbitrage opportunity to disappear.

We can summarize the interest rate parity relationship by noting that when no arbitrage opportunity exists, the return earned on an investment in dollars must equal the return earned when dollars are converted to a foreign currency, invested, and then converted back to dollars. This is shown by the following equation:

$$1 + R_\$ = [S_0 \times (1 + R_{for})]/F_1 \tag{17.3}$$

where

$R_\$$ = the risk-free rate of return on an investment denominated in dollars
S_0 = the spot exchange rate quoted as the currency per U.S. dollar
R_{for} = the risk-free rate of return on an investment denominated in foreign currency
F_1 = the forward exchange rate available at the time of the investment, quoted as currency per U.S. dollar

The term on the left side of the equal sign is what will result from investing $1 domestically. The term on the right is what will result from a foreign investment after converting to and from the foreign currency. By rearranging Equation 17.3 we arrive at the equation that represents the interest rate parity relationship:

$$F_1 \div S_0 = (1 + R_{for}) \div (1 + R_\$) \tag{17.4}$$

Let us use Equation 17.4 to estimate what forward exchange rate was likely to be quoted to investors in 1992:

$$F_1 \div S_0 = (1 + R_{for}) \div (1 + R_\$)$$

$$F_1 \div 1,700 = 1.1391 \div 1.037$$

$$F_1 = 1,867.38 \text{ currency per U.S. dollar or}$$

$$1 \div 1,867.38 = 0.0005355$$

If the forward rate had been 0.0005355 in our example rather than 0.000537, we would not have earned any arbitrage profits from our foreign investment. Because speculators can take advantage of arbitrage opportunities so quickly and costlessly, few arbitrage opportunities last long. The result is that tests of interest rate parity show that it holds very well around the world. *In other words, it is rare that similar risk investments in one country earn more than in another country, after converting money to and from the foreign currency using spot and forward exchange rates*. This does not mean that speculators cannot earn high returns with foreign investments. If they believe that the forward exchange rate over- or underestimates what the true rate of inflation will be in a country, speculators can invest without the benefit of a forward contract and instead convert the foreign income back to dollars at the future spot rate. However, this is no longer a risk-free investment, so it does not affect interest rate parity.

The point of this section is that arbitrageurs, working to make profits for themselves with riskless transactions, also help exchange rates adjust to their correct levels rapidly and accurately.

Self-Test Review Questions*

1. Why does interest rate parity seem to work well, whereas purchasing power parity does not?
2. If you find a foreign interest rate quoted that is higher than the domestic interest rate, should you invest in the foreign country? Why not?
3. Which two investments does interest rate parity say should equal each other?

INTERNATIONAL FINANCE RISK

Engaging in international business involves risk not normally faced when doing business domestically. For example, we discussed exchange rate risk earlier and demonstrated that a business may suffer losses due to unexpected changes in exchange rates. Firms investing in foreign countries are also subject to political risk: the risk that changing politics may adversely affect the business's interests. We examine these sources of risk in this section.

*1. Because money can be moved around the world easily to take advantage of disparities that arise.
2. No, because interest rate parity says that by the time you convert to the foreign currency and back, your earnings would be the same as with a domestic investment.
3. The return on a domestic investment should equal the return on a foreign investment after dollars are converted to and from the foreign currency.

EXTENSION 17.2

Controlling Exchange Rate Risk

In the last section we used futures contracts (contracts that lock in forward rates) to lock in an exchange rate when setting up a risk-free arbitrage for interest rates. These futures contracts can also be used to reduce the exchange rate risk associated with normal international business transactions by allowing the firm to hedge against exchange rate fluctuations. The concept behind a hedge is straightforward. If a drop in the exchange rate will cost a firm money, a futures contract is sold so that the same drop will cause the value of the hedge to increase by exactly the amount of the loss. The gain on the futures contract cancels the loss suffered from the change in exchange rates on the business transaction being hedged. If exchange rates move so that the original business transaction would have enjoyed a gain due to exchange rates, a loss will occur on the futures contract. Either way, the firm ends up earning the same as if exchange rates had not moved. The exchange rate risk is transferred to a speculator, who essentially insures the firm against exchange rate losses.

For example, suppose a firm decides to buy land for a manufacturing facility in Mexico, but the transaction will not be completed for 6 months. If the price of the land is 8,000,000 pesos and the exchange rate is $1 equals 8 pesos, the price of the land is $1,000,000 (8,000,000 × 1/8 = $1,000,000). If the value of the peso were to increase to $1 equals 7 pesos, the cost of the land would increase to $1,142,857 (8,000,000 × 1/7 = $1,142,857), a loss of $142,857 to the purchasing firm.

To prevent a loss due to exchange rate changes, the financial manager of the firm will enter into a contract to purchase pesos in 6 months for a prespecified price, say $1 equals 7.95 pesos. If the exchange rate falls to $1 equals 7 pesos, the futures contract will appreciate in value by an amount sufficient to offset most of the loss. Although this

Box 17.1 The Euro Nails U.S. Firms in 2000

Despite the availability of hedges, many firms choose not to hedge their foreign exchange risk. This turned out to be a mistake for many firms doing business in Europe since the introduction of the euro. The euro is a new currency created by the Economic and Monetary Union on January 1, 1999. By the end of its first year the currency had plunged over 20% against the U.S. dollar. This cost Goodyear about $68 million, Caterpillar about $294 million, and McDonalds's about $910 million.

The euro's 20% fall was unprecedented and most companies did not foresee any reason to hedge against it. U.S. companies must convert their foreign revenues and earnings into dollars. So if a firm earns 1 million euros, but the euro's

value drops from $1 per euro to 90 cents per euro, they would be worth only $900,000, not $1 million. An option to sell euros at $1 each would prevent the loss; however, hedging is not cheap. According to Goldman, Sachs & Co., hedging $500 million worth of earnings costs about $26 million.

Peter Gerhard, managing director and global head of foreign exchange at Goldman Sachs, figures only about 30% of U.S. companies buy options to hedge earnings. "There isn't a company on earth that has a 100% hedging program," says Allan Kessler, J.P. Morgan & Co.'s vice president of foreign exchange.

Source: *Businessweek*, December 4, 2000, p. 157.

TABLE 17.3 Interest Rate Hedge

Land

Land cost in pesos	Initial exchange rate	$ Cost of land
8,000,000 pesos	$1 to 8 pesos	$1,000,000
	New exchange rate	
8,000,000 pesos	$1 to 7 pesos	$1,142,857
	Loss due to exchange rate change	$ 142,857

Forward Contract

Amount of forward contract	Contract exchange rate	$ Value of contract
8,000,000 pesos	$1 to 7.95 pesos	$1,006,289
	New exchange rate	
	$1 to 7 pesos	$1,142,857
	Gains from sale of contract	$ 136,568
	Net gain (loss) due to exchange rate change	($ 6,289)

arrangement effectively prevents the firm from taking a loss on the land, it also prevents the firm from gaining from exchange rate increases, which would make the dollar cost of the land cheaper. This is because if exchange rates increase, say to $1 equals 9 pesos, the dollar cost of the land would be less, but the value of the futures contract would have fallen by enough to offset most of the gain. Table 17.3 shows the gain and loss from forming hedges with futures contracts.

The value of the forward contract increases to $1,142,857 because it lets the holder buy pesos at a more favorable exchange rate. The increase in the value of the contract offsets most of the loss on the purchase price of the land. This is not a perfect hedge because the forward rate is below the current spot rate.

An alternative method of avoiding exchange rate risk is to insist that contracts be denominated in U.S. dollars. The U.S. dollar has become as close to a worldwide currency as there is. Its stability and the size of the U.S. economy allow it to be used in trade around the world. This means that businesses in many countries are willing to accept dollars in exchange for goods because these dollars can be used to satisfy other obligations of the foreign firm. Although establishing contracts in dollars is not always possible, it is clearly one avenue that international firms should investigate.

Political Risk

Although it is possible to create hedges to reduce exchange rate risk, it is much more difficult to deal with political risk. Suppose that your firm has built a facility in a small South American country to process coffee before shipping it to plants in the United States for final packaging. If the government of that country is overthrown, the new government may not choose to recognize any ownership claims established under the old regime. In fact, the new government may see taking your firm's plant (a process called nationalization or expropriation) as an opportunity to enrich itself. For example, China nationalized all business assets owned by foreign firms in 1949, as did Cuba in 1959. More recently, events in Yugoslavia in 1995 and 1996 caused losses to foreign firms.

Other less drastic circumstances can arise from political problems. The local government in a foreign country may impose import or export duties or tariffs that may make the operation of a firm from another country unprofitable. Labor laws may change, causing the cost of labor to rise, erasing the advantage initially provided by the foreign location. One of the more common risks is that the local government will impose additional unexpected taxes on businesses from other countries. The foreign government may choose to tax the income, the property, or the value added by the manufacturer. Firms doing business in foreign countries must recognize that the government has little interest in the outside firm's health and often makes every effort to extract as much benefit as possible from businesses headquartered in other countries. In addition to high taxes, governments may require foreign firms to hire local labor, which may prevent the firm from using its own specialized personnel. Finally, the foreign government may pass laws limiting the ability of the outside firm to convert currency; such a rule prevents outside firms from taking profits or income out of the country.

Offsetting the increased risk of doing business in a foreign nation are the benefits realized from increased diversification. In Chapter 7 we discussed the benefits of investing in a variety of different firms and projects to reduce firm-specific risk. We concluded that diversification could almost eliminate firm-specific risk but could not reduce market risk, the risk due to interest rate changes, raw material shortages, and changing economic conditions. However, by investing in foreign countries, firms may reduce the risk usually equated with the market as a whole because different economies do not necessarily move together. For example, in 1993–1995, Japan was experiencing a recession while the United States' economy was very strong. Alternatively, in 1989–1991, the United States suffered a mild recession while Japan's economy was strong. Firms doing business in both countries would have had smaller fluctuations in income than firms with operations limited to one country. The economies of many developing countries are less closely related to that of the United States. This makes them attractive to domestic companies seeking to stabilize their cash flows. In Chapter 7 we learned that it was possible to reduce the risk of a portfolio by adding a high-risk investment if it was negatively correlated with other investments. Similarly, the risk of a firm can be reduced by adding investments in high-risk countries if their economies have a low correlation with business cycles of the firm's other investments. In fact, the desire to insulate the firm's income from fluctuations is often one of the driving motivations behind foreign investment and expansion.

Certainly, firms that do business in foreign countries are alert to all forms of political change that might affect their profitability. In addition to this attentiveness, large companies may form allegiances with foreign governments to reduce political risk. For example, joint ventures that include the foreign government as a partner may result in more favorable taxes and a reduced chance of nationalization.

FOREIGN INVESTMENTS

Foreign investments may offer returns and opportunities for growth far greater than can be achieved domestically. Evaluating these opportunities involves the same principle used to evaluate any investment: maximizing the value of the firm by accepting positive net present value projects.

Evaluating Foreign Investments

The process of evaluating foreign investments, though conceptually the same as evaluating any investment, includes additional issues of which analysts should be particularly aware. First, estimating the cash flows is more difficult than on similar domestic projects. This is because the international firm may not be as aware of indirect expenses and operating conditions as it is when operating in more familiar territory. Given the problems that firms have in accurately estimating cash flows domestically, estimating them in foreign countries can add a whole new level of error.

The usual method for adjusting a project's cash flows for increased risk is to increase the discount rate used when computing the net present value of the cash flows. The analyst usually determines the amount of the increase from experience with similar projects or from examining the risk of other firms performing similar activities. However, the financial analyst may have little experience to draw on for evaluating a foreign investment and there may be no other firms to use for comparison. As a result, the evaluation may not have a great deal of value. As firms grow more familiar with a particular part of the world, it becomes easier to properly evaluate and quantify risk.

How Foreign Investments Are Financed

Although both domestic and international firms have access to foreign markets, more international firms take advantage of the opportunities foreign markets offer for raising capital. Of course, international firms may finance their international investments with the usual sources of capital, such as retained earnings, bank loans, or domestically marketed bonds and stock. The international financial markets offer attractive alternatives to these sources. One such source is the Eurodollar market. **Eurodollars** are dollar-denominated deposits held in foreign banks. Firms may often borrow short-term funds in the Eurodollar market at attractive interest rates. Eurodollar loans are usually unsecured and have maturities from 30 days to a year. The interest rate on the loans tends to be based on the London interbank offer rate **LIBOR**. LIBOR is similar to the prime rate quoted by large banks in the United States but is set by large international banks for loans among themselves. The lowest-risk borrower pays 0.75 to 1% above the LIBOR rate.

Firms may also issue **Eurobonds** to attract long-term funds. Eurobonds may be in dollars or in the currency of another country with a strong economy, such as Germany. It is even possible to split a Eurobond issue so that part of it is denominated in one currency and the balance is in another. The primary advantage of Eurobonds is that they are not subject to Securities and Exchange (SEC) registration and disclosure rules, which can substantially delay the issue and increase costs.

Box 17.2 Egypt's Markets Are Discovered

In 1961 almost every Egyptian company of any size was seized by the government. For the next three decades the Cairo Stock Exchange's trading floor served as a quiet café. In 1997 it had 107 traders glued to computers following the action on its 600 publicly traded companies. By 2001 more than 1,000 firms traded on the Cairo Stock Exchange. There is even a Web page you can visit (www.egyptse.com). The government has begun to privatize much of what had been socialized earlier. The economy is healthy and the action is attracting international attention. The result is that a trickle of foreign investment into Egypt has begun. As privatization efforts continue and investors gain confidence in the government, the new Cairo Stock Exchange could become a major international institution and source of funding for Egypt's companies.

Source: www.egyptse.com.

Foreign countries also have stock exchanges in which equity capital can be raised and shares of foreign firms can be traded. Box 17.2 discusses the reemergence of the Cairo Stock Exchange.

INTERNATIONAL TRADE AGREEMENTS

Historically, many countries have passed laws restricting international trade. These laws were motivated by the desire to protect the domestic economy from unfair or unbeatable competition from foreign firms. Some of the laws subtly restrict trade, such as limits on how much profit a foreign firm could take out of the country. Other laws are much more blatant in their effort to restrict trade, such as quotas that limit the number of units of a particular product that can be imported.

Trade wars often result when one country imposes some type of trade restriction on another. This often leads to retaliatory trade restrictions being placed on the first country. These trade wars can escalate to the point where trade between countries is effectively eliminated. As business becomes increasingly global, there has been a movement to break down some of these restrictions to encourage free trade. A recent example is the passage of the **North American Free Trade Agreement (NAFTA)**.

NAFTA was signed in 1994 to reduce trade barriers among Canada, Mexico, and the United States. Proponents of NAFTA argue that reducing tariffs and quotas will increase exports by Mexico and Canada. This will improve their economies so that they will import more U.S. goods. The net result is hoped to improve the economies of all three countries and to make them more able to compete globally. Opponents of the treaty are concerned that it will cause jobs to shift from the United States to Mexico, where labor is less expensive. It is still too early to determine which side of the argument was correct.

The **Economic and Monetary Union (EMU)** is an alliance formed in 1993 to minimize trade barriers among most Western European countries. The countries that signed the Maastricht Treaty creating the EMU were Austria, Belgium, Finland, France, Germany, Ireland, Italy, Luxembourg, the Netherlands, Portugal, and Spain. The goal of the

Careers in Finance

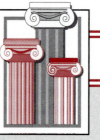

Budget Manager

A budget manager directs and coordinates the activities of the personnel who formulate, monitor, and present budgets for controlling funds at public and private organizations. The budget manager directs the compilation of data based on statistical projections and analysis of past and current years to prepare budgets and to justify funds requested. The budget manager correlates appropriations for specific programs with appropriations for divisional programs and includes items for emergency funds. Most firms will require a bachelor's degree and 5–7 years of experience in the field or in a related area. A wide degree of creativity and latitude is usually expected. Salaries should range between $39,000 and $53,000.

EMU is to encourage joint business ventures, improve business relationships, and coordinate economic policies. Each member of the union recognizes the professional degrees of the other EMU members. A common passport has been adopted.

The best-known goal of the EMU is to establish a common currency for use by all the countries signing the treaty. This has been much more difficult to achieve than first anticipated. As we discussed earlier in this chapter, in order for the currencies of two countries to remain synchronized they must have similar rates of inflation. This requires a high degree of coordination among the countries attempting to use the common currency. However, no country is eager to give up its right to conduct its own economic policy and to do what is best for its own population. Yet at times this is what is required to match inflation rates.

A major milestone for the EMU was the introduction of the **euro**, the new single currency for Europe, on January 1, 1999. On that date, the 11 member countries gave up the sovereignty of their national currency and handed over control of monetary policy to the European Central Bank (ECB) based in Frankfurt, Germany. A fixed euro conversion rate was set for each participating currency. Foreign exchange operations in the euro began. National banknotes and coins were not replaced, but banking became possible both in the euro and in the national currency.

Production of euro coins and banknotes began. On January 1, 2002, euro notes and coins will replace notes and coins in national currencies, which will be withdrawn within 2 months. From then on the national currencies will no longer be valid for everyday use. The reason for the delay between the introduction of the euro and its use in everyday transactions is that it will take several years to print and mint the new money. The EMU will need about 12 billion banknotes and around 80 billion coins.

The EMU has established a Web site to help address the concerns and questions of the people who will be affected by the changeover. You can visit this site at europa.eu.int/euro/html/home5.html?lang=5.

The recent treaties are another indication of the globalization of the world's economies. There is little doubt that this trend will continue in the future.

CHAPTER SUMMARY

A major part of the study of international finance is developing an understanding of the role of exchange rates. Spot rates are quoted for the immediate exchange of funds. Forward rates are quoted for the exchange of funds at some point in the future.

One factor that influences the exchange rate is the supply of a currency being offered for sale in the foreign currency markets. The concept of purchasing power parity also helps explain how exchange rates aid international trade. They adjust so that the price of a good in one country equals the price of the same good in another country after converting from one currency to another. For PPP to hold well, the goods must be easily transportable and equivalent, a condition that seldom exists. As a result, purchasing power parity does not hold very well in the short run. Over the long run, however, exchange rates adjust to compensate for inflation and PPP is found to function much better.

Interest rate parity says that a domestic investment will earn the same return as one made in a foreign country after converting funds from the domestic currency into the foreign currency and back again. Because of low transaction costs, we find that interest rate parity holds very well when tested in both the short run and the long run. When deviations from interest rate parity occur, arbitrage opportunities exist. An arbitrage opportunity occurs when a profit can be made with zero net investment. Speculators taking advantage of arbitrage opportunities keep exchange rates and interest rate parity in line.

Investing internationally adds several types of risk to the firm. One type is exchange rate risk, the risk that exchange rates will move unfavorably before a payment is due. Firms can reduce exchange rate risk by hedging with futures contracts or denominating contracts in dollars.

International firms are also subject to political risk, the risk that changing politics will be costly to the firm's operations. Foreign governments may choose to take ownership of the firm's assets, impose additional taxes, change labor laws, or impose tariffs that reduce the international investment's profitability.

The international markets provide alternative sources of capital in the form of Eurodollars and Eurobonds. Firms can borrow Eurodollars at a markup over LIBOR, the rate large international banks charge on loans among themselves.

International trade agreements are changing the international landscape in both North America and Europe. NAFTA, signed in 1994, reduced trade barriers between Canada, Mexico, and the United States. The European Union has provided a single trade currency and dropped most barriers to trade among its 11 member countries.

KEY WORDS

appreciation 469
arbitrage 475
depreciation 469
Economic and Monetary Union (EMU) 483
euro 484
Eurobonds 482

Eurodollars 482
exchange rate 466
exchange rate risk 466
forward exchange rate 469
forward transactions 469
interest rate parity (IRP) 475

law of one price 471
LIBOR 482
North American Free Trade Agreement (NAFTA) 483
purchasing power parity (PPP) 471

relative purchasing power parity 473
spot exchange rate 469
spot transaction 469

DISCUSSION QUESTIONS

1. What happens to the supply of dollars in the foreign exchange markets if the United States imports more than it exports?
2. If the supply of dollars in the foreign exchange markets grows, what will happen to the value of the dollar compared with other currencies?
3. If the dollar falls in value relative to other currencies, are imports to the United States likely to increase or decrease? Why?
4. Distinguish between a spot exchange rate and a forward exchange rate. What is the purpose of a forward rate?
5. Can you tell anything about the market's expectations regarding the relative inflation rate between two countries by looking at the forward rate?
6. What does the law of one price say about the relative prices of goods in different countries?
7. What factors tend to make the law of one price not work well?

8. What factor is primarily responsible for changes in exchange rates? Explain how this factor is taken into consideration by the purchasing power parity relationship.

9. Explain how interest rate arbitrage keeps international interest rates at levels such that investments in foreign countries provide the same yield.

10. Explain how a hedge can be used to reduce exchange rate risk incurred in international trade.

11. What are the sources of risk a firm faces doing business in a global setting?

PROBLEMS

1. Use the Currency Trading data in Figure 17.1 to make the following conversions.
   a. Convert $100 U.S. to British pounds.
   b. Convert $250 U.S. to Japanese yen.
   c. Convert $500 U.S. to Swiss francs.
   d. Convert 10,000 South Korean wons to U.S. dollars.
   e. Convert 300 Jordanian dinars to U.S. dollars.
   f. Convert 50 British pounds to Japanese yen. (Hint: Try converting the pounds to dollars, then to yen.)

2. As the import manager for a department store, you want to buy 10,000 shirts made in Mexico. If the supplier in Mexico demands to be paid in pesos and the price of the order is 400,000 pesos, what is the cost of each shirt in U.S. dollars?

3. Assume that oil costs $20 per barrel in the United States and that the exchange rate between the U.S. and Mexico is $1 U.S. = 8 pesos. Assuming purchasing power parity holds, what should the price of oil be in Mexico, expressed in pesos?

4. If inflation in the United States is expected to average 3% in the future and the inflation rate in Germany is expected to be 6%, what spot rate will be in effect after 5 years if the current spot exchange rate is $1 U.S. equals 1.75 marks? Is the U.S. dollar appreciating or depreciating against the mark? (Extension 17.1)

5. What would the 1-year forward rate be if inflation in the United States is 3%, inflation in France is 8%, and the current spot exchange rate is $1 equals 6 francs? Is the U.S. dollar appreciating or depreciating against the franc? (Extension 17.1)

6. Assume that the interest rate in Mexico is 7% and in the United States it is 5%. If the spot exchange rate is $1 U.S. equals 8 pesos, what is the 1-year forward rate predicted by interest rate parity? (Extension 17.1)

7. You just contracted to purchase 1 million pounds of sugar from Brazil to be delivered in 3 months. You must pay for the sugar in Brazilian reals when the shipment arrives. You are concerned that the cost of reals may increase against the dollar and this increase could be costly for your firm. Set up a hedge that will protect your firm if you are paying $0.25 per pound for the sugar at the current spot rate of $1 U.S. equals 1.10 reals, and you can buy a futures contract that locks in an exchange rate of $1 U.S. equals 1.105 reals. (Extension 17.2)

SELF-TEST PROBLEMS

For the following problems use the Currency Trading data in Figure 17.1. In some cases you will have to first convert a foreign currency into U.S. dollars and then convert these dollars into another foreign currency.
   1. Convert $150 U.S. to British pounds.
   2. Convert 600 Japanese yen to U.S. dollars.
   3. Convert $400 U.S. to Saudi Arabian riyals.
   4. Convert 18,000 Indian rupees to U.S. dollars.
   5. Convert 200 New Zealand dollars to Colombian pesos.
   6. Convert 200 Spanish peseta to Indian rupees.
   7. Convert 500 Hong Kong dollars to U.S. dollars.
   8. Convert 200 Bahraini dinars to British pounds.
   9. Convert 500 United Arab Emirates dirhams to Pakistani rupees.
   10. Convert 200 Australian dollars to U.S. dollars.
   11. The inflation rate in the United States is 3%, and the inflation rate in India is 6%. What would be the 1-year forward rate in Indian rupees?
   12. The inflation rate in the United States is 3%, and the inflation rate in Britain is 4%. What would be the 2-year forward rate in British pounds?
   13. The inflation rate in the United States is 3%, and in Turkey it is 15%. What would be the 3-year forward rate in Turkish lira?

14. The inflation rate in the United States is 4%, and in Denmark it is 3%. What would be the 3-year forward rate in Danish krone?
15. The interest rate in the United States is 5%, and the interest rate in India is 8%. What would be the 1-year forward rate in Indian rupees?
16. The interest rate in the United States is 5%, and the interest rate in Britain is 7%. What would be the 1-year forward rate in British pounds?
17. The interest rate in the United States is 5%, and in Turkey it is 12%. What would be the 1-year forward rate in Turkish lira?
18. The interest rate in the United States is 5%, and in Denmark it is 4%. What would be the 1-year forward rate in Danish krone?

WEB EXPLORATION

1. The Federal Reserve maintains a Web site that lists the exchange rate between the United States and many other currencies. Go to www.federalreserve.gov/releases/ H10/hist/thru89.htm. Go to the historical data from 1990 on and find the euro. What has been the percentage change in the euro–dollar exchange rate between the euro's introduction and now? What has been the annual percentage change in the euro–dollar exchange rate for each year since then?

2. International travelers and businesspeople frequently need to accurately convert from one currency to another. It is often easy to find the rate needed to convert the U.S. dollar to another currency. It can be more difficult to find cross-conversion rates. Go to www.oanda.com/convert/classic. This site lets you convert from any currency to any other currency. How many Lithuanian litas can you currently buy with one Chilean peso?

MINI CASE

You have just been hired as a financial consultant for a firm that supplies components used in cell phone antennas. The firm is doing well and has even begun penetrating the global market with sales to Germany, France, and Spain. The management of the company is considering expanding their global presence and wants to use your international experience to help them avoid making mistakes.

The firm's initial concern is with transferring profits earned overseas back to the United States. Since all of the countries they do business with are members of the EMU, all foreign earnings are denominated in euros.

a. The firm's managers want to know if they should consider hedging their foreign profits. They ask you to evaluate the dollar–euro exchange rate to determine the size of the risk they are taking by not setting up a hedge. (Review Extension 17.1.)

   i. Go to www.federalreserve.gov/releases/ H10/hist/ and find the dollar–euro exchange rate. Put the exchange rates for the last 12 months into an Excel spreadsheet. (The method for moving data into spreadsheets in described in the Chapter 2 Mini Case.)

Examine the trend by graphing the data and plotting a trendline. (The method for plotting trendlines is discussed in the Chapter 2 Mini Case.) You may need to delete any cells with NR or other nonnumeric data to get the graphics to work properly. Compute the mean exchange rate and the standard deviation of the exchange rate over the last year using the Excel functions.

   ii. You recognize that many issues should be considered when deciding whether the firm should set up a hedge. These include such factors as the cost of the hedge, the probability that the firm could make a profit on the exchange rate, the amount of profits at stake relative to the total profits of the firm, and management's willingness to gamble on exchange rates. Address each of these issues in light of the current economic climate in Europe and your results from part i.

b. Firm management has expressed the idea that the best opportunities for international growth may be in less developed nations where cell phone use is just becoming commonplace. Since many of these countries never developed the wired phone systems used by the industrialized nations, cell phones could be the answer to their communications needs.

   i. Identify the different types of risk faced by the firm if it attempts to do business in developing nations.

   ii. You have learned that the firm's Chief Financial Officer has prepared a capital budget that includes intensive international investment. The basis for this is a series of projects that have positive NPVs. After further investigation, you learn that the CFO used the firm's current cost of capital as the discount rate in these calculations. The company's president has asked you to comment on these project calculations. What do you say?

c. Cash flows from the last several years have been so good for the firm that it finds a need to invest its excess for about a year. After this time the cash will be needed to fund its expansion plans. The CFO has noticed that the interest rates offered on government bonds issued in some of the developing nations where the firm plans to expand have much higher interest rates than do U.S. government bonds. He is recommending to the president that the excess funds be invested in these foreign bonds. The president asks for your recommendation. What is your answer?

Applying Financial Concepts: A Case Study

Chapter Objectives

By the end of this chapter you should be able to:

1. Choose between leasing or purchasing assets
2. Compute the value of a private company
3. Evaluate an acquisition
4. Develop a personal financial savings plan

You have been introduced to many different financial concepts, theories, and methods in this course. For example, you can now evaluate whether a business should invest in a particular asset, determine what its stock and bond prices should be, and understand the issues involved in its capital structure decision. Additionally, you now have a basic understanding of how investments by both individuals and businesses are selected and what you can do to minimize risk without jeopardizing returns. You also have learned how the markets interact with various financial intermediaries to facilitate the transfer of funds from those with a surplus to those with investment opportunities.

More important than the list of specific financial problems you have learned to solve are the tools you have acquired. Just as a carpenter can build many things with his or her tools, you can solve many different problems with the financial tools you have acquired. You may never be called upon to actually compute the price of a share of stock or to recommend a capital structure to a firm (although someday you might). However, the theories and lessons learned in this text have prepared you to solve the problems that you will actually encounter.

In this chapter we will follow the career of a fictitious businessperson named Alena Green. We address a number of seemingly unrelated problems that surface with regard to her business and financial life and will help her make decisions regarding how to finance her initial expansion into a chain of coffee shops. Next, we look at the difficult problem of how to value a privately owned company so that it can be sold to the public. We then evaluate whether she should acquire a competitor. Finally, as Alena's wealth increases, she decides that she would like to develop a financial plan for her personal life that will allow her to retire young and to enjoy the fruits of her success. We help her to put together such a strategy.

After each problem is introduced, we evaluate how you might apply the methods you already know in order to solve the problem. If you continue to take more advanced courses in finance, you will find that this chapter is an excellent primer on how to approach case studies. If this is your last finance course, you will gain the confidence you need to tackle the financial problems you will face in business and in your personal life.

AMERICA'S COFFEE HOUSE

Alena Green opened her first small coffee shop in 1980, shortly after she graduated from college with a degree in finance. She had enjoyed the atmosphere at the coffee shop that was near her campus and tried to mimic its relaxed style and cozy setting. She thought she had improved on the original concept by adding fresh pastries. Additionally, she featured live folk and blues guitar music during the evenings.

It took her 2 years to get the combination of coffee products, food, price, and decor right. However, once all the parts were in place, customers came. On Fridays and Saturdays it was standing room only from 4:00 P.M. until midnight. Alena's America's Coffee House (ACH) was the most popular meeting place in town, and her coffee was the standard against which all other coffee was judged. Musicians vied with each other for the exposure they received performing on the small stage at ACH.

By the mid-1980s Alena was earning around $60,000 per year from her coffee shop. With a flash of insight she realized that her shop was operating at near full capacity and that if she wanted to increase her income she was going to have to expand. The decision to expand was hard to make. She fully realized the increased risk of having a manager run stores instead of attending to every detail personally, as she had in the past. Additionally, she did not have the cash on hand to buy all of the fixtures needed to open additional coffee shops. Despite these concerns, Alena also realized that she was getting bored running her one store and she thought she would enjoy the challenge that expansion would provide. She prepared pro formas that she thought were both realistic and conservative. She found that the expansion had a positive net present value. Over a cup of her own premium gold coffee one night with her best friend, she decided to go for it.

The next day she began the search for her second location. She wanted to be far enough away from her original location to avoid stealing her own customers, but close enough that she could easily monitor both stores without spending all of her time commuting. Her first coffee shop had targeted the student population at the large state university. She thought it would make sense to locate near another university, but a different thought occurred to her. Alena had noticed that many of the university's professors seemed to enjoy meeting at ACH. She wondered if other older people might as well. Being something of a risk taker, Alena decided that she would open her second store in an area surrounded by high-tech research and production facilities. Success here would mean that she could open in a wide variety of different locations.

After several months of searching, Alena found what she considered the perfect site. It had excellent exposure, it was exactly the size she deemed appropriate, and the lease price was reasonable. Her first major problem was how to finance all of the required furniture, fixtures, and equipment.

LEASE VERSUS PURCHASE DECISIONS

Alena's first stop was to see her banker, Joe Snail. Her borrowing requirements had been modest over the years. She had financed an occasional upgrade to her coffee machines and had once borrowed to do some remodeling. Nevertheless, Joe considered her account valuable. She maintained her payroll account and personal accounts with the bank and had always handled them professionally. He respected her business sense and agreed that an expansion had a very good chance of succeeding. Furthermore, she owned most of the equipment in her original store debt free. Joe informed Alena that he would need to see the details of her loan request, but he fully expected that the bank would be happy to provide financing.

Alena was pleased with her reception at the bank, but she realized she had another option. A leasing company had contacted her several months earlier expressing an interest in her business. Acme Leasing specialized in leasing restaurant equipment. Her next step was to contact Acme to see whether it was still interested. Acme was as enthusiastic as her bank. It would be Alena's decision whether she would lease or buy the equipment. She was sure that her finance background would help her make the right choice.

Although she had never actually been taught to evaluate leases, she felt confident that she could do it. She began by listing what she did know about leases. Acme Leasing had explained the two types of leases she could obtain. An **operating lease** is short-term (usually less than 5 years) and may be canceled at any time. At the end of an operating lease, Alena could renew it, return the assets, or buy the assets for their market value. Additionally, Acme would pay for any maintenance, insurance, or taxes during the lease term.

The alternative to the operating lease is the **financial** (or **capital**) **lease**. Acme carefully explained that if Alena chose a capital lease, she would be obligated for the term of the lease. She also would pay her own maintenance, insurance, and tax expenses. One benefit of the capital lease would be that when it matured she would be able to purchase the assets at a bargain price.

Alena decided that she would prefer the operating lease. She liked the idea of being able to get out of it easily if things went poorly. However, she still thought it might be best to buy what she needed to open the new coffee shop outright using funds obtained with a loan. To make this decision she decided to take the following steps:

- Identify the cash flows under the purchase (loan) option.
- Identify the cash flows under the lease option.

- Compute the present value of the cash flows from each option.
- Choose the alternative with the lowest present value (of outflows).

The cash flows under the purchase option include the loan payment, the maintenance expense, and the tax shield provided by depreciation and the deductibility of interest payments. Alena remembered that loan payments are computed using the present value of an annuity formula, where the PV is the loan amount. The purchase price of the equipment and fixtures needed to open her second coffee shop came to $200,000. She contacted Joe at the bank and found that he would offer her a loan with a 10% interest rate repayable in equal annual payments over 5 years. She computed the annual payments as follows:

$$PV = PMT(PVIFA_{5 \text{ years, } 10\%})$$
$$\$200,000 = PMT(3.7908)$$
$$Pmt = \$52,760$$

(Using a financial calculator, $I = 10\%$, $N = 5$, $PV = \$200,000$, compute PMT = $52,759.50)

Alena found the interest amount each year that can be deducted from taxable income by multiplying the remaining balance by 10%. The interest for the first year is $200,000 × 0.10 = $20,000. The rest of the $52,760 payment reduces the balance so that less interest is paid the following year. For example, $32,760 ($52,760 − $20,000 = $32,760) is left of the first year's payment after paying interest to reduce principal. The principal balance due at the end of the first year is $200,000 − $32,760 = $167,240. The interest owed on this at the end of the second year is 0.10 × $167,240 = $16,724. Each year the balance falls so that the interest due goes down. This lets more of the payment be applied to reducing the principal.

Alena used the 5-year MACRS depreciation table to compute the depreciation deduction. Because of the half-year convention, there is a small depreciation balance in the sixth year.[1] The equipment suppliers quoted her a maintenance contract price of $4,700 per year.

Alena put all of the data into a spreadsheet and computed the present value of the cash flows from purchasing. She discounted the cash flows at 6% since they were known with certainty. Her worksheet appears in Table 18.1.

Alena reviewed Table 18.1 and recognized that her goal was to find the financing option that resulted in the lowest present value of cash flows possible. This is because she is computing the present value of cash outflows. She wanted the cash outflows as small as possible.

Her next step was to compute the estimated cash flows from leasing the asset. After thinking about the problem for awhile, Alena decided this would be even simpler than computing those for the purchase. First, the maintenance and depreciation expenses are taken by Acme Leasing. Second, she would be able to deduct the entire lease payment from her taxes. To make the two scenarios comparable, she wanted to

---

[1]See Chapter 11 for a more complete discussion of MACRS and the half-year convention.

TABLE 18.1 Cash Flows from Purchasing Equipment

	Year					
	1	2	3	4	5	6
1. Loan payment	$ 52,760	$52,760	$52,760	$52,760	$52,760	
2. Maintenance	4,700	4,700	4,700	4,700	4,700	
3. Interest portion	20,000	16,724	13,120	9,157	4,796	
4. Depreciation	40,000	64,000	38,000	24,000	22,000	12,000
5. Total tax deductions	64,700	85,424	55,820	37,857	31,496	12,000
6. Tax shield	25,880	34,170	22,328	15,143	12,598	4,800
7. After-tax cash flow	31,580	23,290	35,132	42,317	44,862	(4,800)
8. PVIF	0.9434	0.8900	0.8396	0.7921	0.7473	0.7050
9. Present value of CF	$ 29,793	$20,728	$29,497	$33,519	$33,525	$(3,384)
10. Sum of PV of cash flows	**$143,678**					

Row 1: The total loan payment as calculated above.
Row 2: The amount of the maintenance contract.
Row 3: The portion of each loan payment that goes to pay accrued interest.
Row 4: The depreciation of the assets based on the MACRS 5-year asset table.
Row 5: The sum of rows 2, 3, and 4.
Row 6: The amount of the tax deduction found by multiplying row 5 times 0.40.
Row 7: The after-tax cash flow found by summing row 1 and 2 and subtracting row 6.
Row 8: The present value interest factors used to compute the present values (6%).
Row 9: The present value of the cash flows from each year.
Row 10: The sum of the present cash values of the cash flows from purchasing the asset.

include the cost of purchasing the equipment at the end of the lease term. After a lengthy conversation with Acme Leasing, Alena prepared the worksheet that appears in Table 18.2.

Alena noted that the present value cost of purchasing is less than the present value cost of leasing the equipment. She also noted that the present value costs were quite close. With this in mind she considered the qualitative issues as well. She began by making a list of the advantages and disadvantages of leases.

Advantages to Leases

- Because the entire lease payment is deductible, in effect, land becomes tax deductible. However, this did not apply to Alena's situation.

- Leasing provides 100% financing because no down payment is required. In her case, Alena would not have to pledge her other assets as security, leaving them available as security should she need a loan in the future.

- If the equipment becomes obsolete by the time the lease matures, rather than purchasing the assets, Alena can let them revert to the lessor.

- The terms of most lease agreements are less restrictive than those of many long-term loans.

- Many operating leases have cancellation clauses that allow the lessee to get out of the contract if the equipment is no longer needed.

TABLE 18.2 Cost of Leasing the Equipment

	Year					
	1	2	3	4	5	6
1. Lease payment	$ 27,741	$27,741	$27,741	$27,741	$ 27,741	
2. Tax shield	11,096	11,096	11,096	11,096	11,096	
3. Buyout option					100,000	
4. After tax cash flow	16,645	16,645	16,645	16,645	116,645	
5. PVIF	0.9434	0.8900	0.8396	0.7921	0.7473	
6. Present value of CF	$ 15,703	$14,814	$13,975	$13,184	$ 87,169	
7. Sum of PV of cash flows	**$144,845**					

Row 1: The lease payment quoted by Acme Leasing.
Row 2: The tax shield provided by the lease payment, computed as 0.4 times the lease amount.
Row 3: The cost of buying the assets at the end of the lease, as agreed in the lease contract with Acme.
Row 4: The after-tax cash flow found by subtracting row 2 from row 1 and adding row 3.
Row 5: The present value interest factors used to compute the present values (6%).
Row 6: The present value of the cash flows from each year.
Row 7: The sum of the present values of the cash flows from leasing the asset.

Disadvantages to Leases

- Leases do not usually state the interest cost and many provide for a high rate of return to the lessor.

- The assets revert to the lessor unless they are purchased when the lease matures. This purchase requires that either cash or alternative financing be arranged at that time.

- Because the property is not owned by the lessee, material changes or alterations cannot be made without the approval of the lessor.

- If a capital lease is selected and the coffee house fails before the lease expires, Alena would still be responsible for the payments, but she would not be able to sell the assets. If they had been purchased, she would be able to liquidate the assets to pay off the loan.

After considerable deliberation, Alena decided to obtain the loan and to buy the assets outright. Her decision was based primarily on the issue of not wanting to deal with finding alternative financing to purchase the assets when the lease expires and wanting the flexibility to modify the assets if her design of the coffee house changes.

ACH #2 was also a raging success. Business executives, engineers, designers, and local artists all found the atmosphere perfect for quiet discussion and relaxation. Alena knew she had a winning formula when she drove by a nearly empty Starbuck's Coffee before arriving at her store and finding customers standing against the walls waiting for tables to open.

Her confidence thus enhanced, she began opening new stores rapidly. She continued to follow the original formula that had worked so well. Occasionally a store would not perform as well as expected, and she was ruthless about closing it quickly. This policy kept her managers working diligently and maintained the reputation of the chain. As her firm grew, Alena began considering whether she should take her firm public. Before we find out her decision, let us first review the financial tools she used to analyze her financing option.

Lease Review

Lease analysis is conducted using the same tools and concepts as are used to evaluate any capital expenditure. Instead of computing the present value of the income, however, you compute the present value of the costs. The present value of the costs of purchasing is compared with the present value of the costs of leasing. The option with the lowest present value cost is accepted.

Let us review the concepts that were needed to conduct lease analysis:

- Present value calculations
- Loan payment calculations
- Loan amortization to compute interest deductions
- Cash flow estimations
- Depreciation computations

All of these methods were introduced earlier in the text. However, they are all applied to a simple lease versus purchase computation.

VALUING AN EXISTING PRIVATE COMPANY AND GOING PUBLIC

When Alena Green opened her first coffee house, she formed a corporation. She owned all of the stock of this corporation and was the chief executive officer, chief financial officer, and chair of the board. Of course, she was also the janitor. As her firm grew, Alena added staff to help her manage her business. However, she continued to hold all of the stock in the firm. When stock is held by only a few individuals, it is said to be **privately** or **closely held**. Because the stock of privately held firms rarely, if ever, sells, no market price is established.

Alena was aware that there were many issues to consider about whether she should **go public**, which would mean selling a substantial portion of her stock to outside investors. After reviewing the question with her managers, she compiled a list of the advantages and disadvantages of going public.

Advantages of Going Public

- *Access to capital:* One of the biggest reasons for taking a firm public is to increase its ability to raise money. Privately held firms are limited in their ability to obtain capital. They may go to their existing owners to raise money, use retained earnings from the company's ongoing operations, or go to banks for loans. Alena had been borrowing heavily during her expansion and realized that the firm needed equity. She also realized that it is very difficult for a closely held firm to raise external capital. Minority shareholders have virtually no control over the firm and little recourse if the majority stockholder takes actions that harm minority stockholders. For example, anyone considering investing in ACH would know that Alena could avoid paying dividends by simply increasing her wages as president to the point that no residual cash was available. Additionally, minority shareholders of a closely held firm may find it difficult to obtain information about the firm's profits and its real net worth. Going public, on the other hand, brings with it both public disclosure of information and regulation by the Securities and Exchange Commission (SEC). These factors greatly increase people's willingness to invest in the company and hence make it easier for the firm to increase its equity.

- *Increases founder's liquidity:* Alena knew that her company was worth a great deal, but all of her wealth was tied up in the firm. She wanted to take a cruise to Alaska, but despite her ownership of the business, its expansion had consumed every dollar it had generated, leaving her feeling poor. After years of working 7 days a week with long hours, she felt a deep need to enjoy some benefit from her success. Selling part of her ownership interest in the firm would give her the funds to do this.

- *Allows diversification:* One concern Alena had was that all of her wealth was tied up in the business. She often found herself lying awake at night wondering what would happen if coffee went out of vogue. Suppose research showed that coffee drinking caused baldness or premature wrinkling. Her largely yuppie crowd could disappear overnight. Alena remembered from her finance class that it was important to diversify. She would not be compensated for the risk of holding nondiversified assets. Unfortunately, her ownership of ACH precluded investing in any other assets or securities.

- *Values the firm:* Although Alena had a vague idea of what her coffee house chain was worth, the lack of a public market for shares of its stock made accurately assessing its value impossible. She had considered giving incentive stock options to the managers of each store, but wanted to know the value of the stock she was giving away. She also knew that privately held firms can cause problems for heirs when the founder dies because they must be valued for estate taxes. State and federal tax appraisers often put too high a value on private companies, causing increased taxes. When a firm is publicly held, the competition for assets among traders establishes the firm's market value, so these questions disappear.

Disadvantages of Going Public

- *Reporting costs:* Publicly held firms must report to the SEC quarterly and annually. The SEC specifies what must be included in these reports. This information is often available for large firms, but its collection may require extra time and effort on the part of small companies.

- *Public disclosure:* The SEC requires public disclosure of facts many owners might prefer to keep confidential. For example, the SEC requires that the number of shares held by insiders be made public. This essentially notifies the world of the managers' net worth. Many managers also worry that operating data may be valuable to competitors.

- *Managerial freedom:* The owners of closely held companies have a great deal of freedom with regard to how the firm is run. For example, owner/managers can pay themselves whatever salaries they see fit. Similarly, they can often charge expenses to the company and engage in other self-dealing activities that are aimed at reducing taxes. Such arrangements are often much more difficult if the company is publicly held. For instance, outside shareholders often elect some of the members of the board of directors. These directors are responsible for setting senior management salaries and approving benefit packages. They are unlikely to approve excessive compensation.

- *Maintaining control:* Once a majority of a firm's shares are in the public's hands, there is always a chance that another firm could buy enough shares to gain control of the board of directors. An outside firm might use a process called a **tender offer** to encourage shareholders to sell. In a tender offer, a firm makes an offer to buy shares at a prespecified price. This price is often above the current market price of the shares and reflects the additional value the acquiring firm places on gaining control. Once the outside firm has gained control of the board of directors, existing management can be terminated or the target firm can be merged with the acquiring firm and cease to exist as an independent company.

Alena was very disturbed with the idea of giving up total control of her company and somewhat concerned that another firm might attempt a takeover. However, she decided that her need for outside equity for continued expansion left her no real choice but to approach an investment banking firm about taking ACH public.

Establishing Its Value

The investment bankers were eager to help with an **initial public offering (IPO)**, a first offer of stock to the public, for ACH. They thought ACH had excellent growth potential and were impressed with the management provided by Alena Green and her team. They explained to Alena that they would prepare the **prospectus**, a document required by the SEC to gain approval for a public security sale, and that they would see to the marketing of the stock. The major hurdle was establishing the market price of the company. Alena remembered from her finance course that stock prices are set by finding the present value of the future dividends. However, ACH had never paid a dividend, so this approach did not seem useful.

The investment bankers suggested an alternative method that Alena thought had merit. This was to multiply the PE ratio of similar types of businesses by ACH's projected earnings per share. The result would be the market price per share:

$$\frac{\text{Price}}{\text{Earnings per share}} \times \text{Earnings per share} = \text{Price}$$

Alena put together the following table to help estimate the next year's earnings:

Annual Net Income for America's Coffee House				
1998	1999	2000	2001	2002
$557,000	$570,000	$620,000	$670,000	$730,000

Alena computed the average annual compounded growth rate using the present value formula she learned in her finance class:

$$PV = FV\left(PVIF_{4,i}\right)$$

$$\$557,000 = \$730,000\left(PVIF_{4,i}\right)$$

$$\frac{\$557,000}{\$730,000} = 0.7630 = PVIF_{4,7\%}$$

She solved for the ($PVIF_{4,i}$) and then looked up the interest rate on the PVIF table that corresponded to 0.763. This occurred when the interest rate was 7%. Alena thought this growth rate underestimated the growth potential of the firm. She decided to also compute the most recent growth rate. The firm grew at about 9% between 2001 and 2002:

$$\frac{\$730,000 - \$670,000}{\$670,000} = 0.0895 \approx 9\%$$

With estimated growth ranging between 7% and 9%, Alena and the investment bankers agreed that a future growth rate of 8.5% seemed reasonable considering that the stock offering would provide additional funds to open new coffee houses. The next year's projected earnings were then found by multiplying the 2002 earnings times 1.085:

$$2003 \text{ projected earnings} = 2002 \text{ earnings} \times (1.085)$$

$$2003 \text{ projected earnings} = \$730,000 (1.085)$$

$$2003 \text{ projected earnings} = \$792,050$$

Alena currently held all of the 200,000 shares of stock that the firm had issued when the corporation was founded. If 300,000 additional shares were issued a total of 500,000 would be outstanding. With 500,000 shares of stock issued, earnings per share would be

$$\frac{\text{Projected annual earnings}}{\text{Number of shares outstanding}} = \text{Earnings per share}$$

$$\frac{\$792,050}{500,000} = \$1.58$$

With a projected earnings per share of $1.58, the last problem was to find PE ratios for firms similar to ACH. The investment bankers also assisted with this effort, and a number of firms were reviewed. After discarding some for being more or less risky than ACH and averaging the others, Alena and her investment bankers agreed that a PE ratio of 17 would fairly value the firm. The market price of the shares was found by multiplying the 2003 projected earnings per share of $1.58 by the PE ratio of 17:

$$\$1.58 \times 17 = \$26.86$$

Alena was now able to compute the market value of her company: 500,000 shares valued at $26.86:

$$\text{Value of firm} = \text{Number of shares outstanding} \times \text{Market price per share}$$
$$\text{Value of firm} = 500{,}000 \times \$26.86 = \$13{,}430{,}000$$

ACH will be worth nearly $13.5 million after the new shares are issued. If 300,000 shares were issued, a total of $8,058,000 would be raised from the public to support continued expansion. Alena's 200,000 shares gave her an ownership interest in the company of $5,372,000 (200,000 × $26.86 = $5,372,000). Because no other single investor would be likely to gather more than this percentage ownership, Alena would remain in control. She can sell some of her shares to raise funds for diversification and personal cash flow.[2]

Alena agreed to the price, and the investment bankers moved ahead with the sale of the stock. Their nationwide network of brokers was advised of the pending IPO. The brokers contacted their customers and advised them that ACH was likely to be a wise investment. They solicited advance sales so that by the time the actual stock was available, all of it had been presold.

The ACH chain continued to grow and expand over the next year. However, there was one large market in Florida that was causing ACH trouble. The Aromatic Bean coffee house chain had already opened stores in the most desirable locations. Although ACH management thought it could outperform the competition, it would be difficult with inferior locations. Management was somewhat surprised, however, when the owner of the Aromatic Bean called and suggested that ACH buy them out. Before we evaluate this offer, however, let us first point out the financial skills we used to take ACH public.

Review of Valuing a Privately Held Firm

To take a firm public, the owner must determine whether the advantages of increased access to capital are more valuable than the disadvantages of complying with the SEC regulations imposed on public firms. Once the mostly qualitative decision has been reached, the investment bankers and the owner must agree on the firm's value. This requires the use of several financial tools. Private firm valuation requires:

- Knowledge of financial markets and the role played by investment bankers
- An understanding of the PE ratio and its use in valuation
- An understanding of discounted cash flow methods and their use in valuation
- The use of compound value to compute compounded growth rates
- The use of growth rates to project a future income level
- An understanding of how to determine the market value of a firm (i.e., the product of the market price of the stock times the number of shares outstanding)

---

[2]Had new shares not been issued, the value of the firm would have been about $5.3 million. Without the influx of new capital, the projected growth rate would have been much lower and a smaller PE ratio would have been used to value the shares.

EVALUATING A POSSIBLE CORPORATE ACQUISITION

When Alena learned of Aromatic Bean's interest in a merger, she once again called on her financial training. She knew that, at least in theory, the analysis was simple. The decision to acquire another firm was just like any other capital budgeting decision. If the present value of the cash flows resulting from the merger were greater than the present value of the price paid for the company, she should acquire Aromatic Bean. Otherwise, she should let the opportunity pass.

The difficulty, as Alena saw it, was to accurately estimate the incremental cash flows that would be generated by the acquisition. Certainly, the cash flows that Aromatic Bean had earned in the past would be a good guide as to what could be expected in the future. However, Alena thought that there would be **synergy** achieved by combining the two firms. For example, the Florida chain would benefit from ACH's national advertising and buying power. Additionally, ACH's existing management team could absorb the new stores without adding overhead or staff.

Estimating the Target Firm's Cash Flows

Alena told her staff to visit the Aromatic Bean's offices and collect information. She told them to prepare pro forma income statements of the Aromatic Bean company for the next 5 years. Her chief financial officer reported back shortly with the information shown in Table 18.3.

TABLE 18.3 Pro Forma Income Statement for Aromatic Bean Post Merger (000s)

	Last Year	Plus 1	Plus 2	Plus 3	Plus 4	Plus 5
Net sales	$2,500	$2,875	$3,220	$3,542	$3,825	$4,093
− Cost of goods sold	1,650	1,725	1,868	2,054	2,219	2,374
− Selling and admin. expense	300	200	175	150	125	125
− Depreciation	225	450	450	450	450	450
EBIT	$ 325	$ 500	$ 727	$ 888	$1,031	$1,144
− Interest expense	25	25	25	25	25	25
EBT	$ 300	$ 475	$ 702	$ 863	$1,006	$1,119
− Taxes	120	190	281	345	402	448
Net income	$ 180	$ 285	$ 421	$ 518	$ 604	$ 671
+ Depreciation	225	450	450	450	450	450
Net cash flow	$ 405	$ 735	$ 871	$ 968	$1,054	$1,121

Assumptions:
1. The net sales grow at 15% the first year after acquisition, 12% the second, 10% the third, 8% the fourth, and then at 7% thereafter.
2. Cost of goods sold drops from 66% of sales to 60% after one year and then stabilizes at 58% thereafter.
3. Selling and administration expense drops due to consolidation with ACH.
4. Depreciation increases due to remodeling expenses.
5. Interest expense is included in the cash flows. Because the net income all goes to equity holders, the return on equity will be used to calculate the present value of the cash flows.

Determining the Target's Value

The next step is to determine the present value of the cash flows. Alena's CFO pointed out that an acceptable method for computing the cash flows from a merger is to include interest expense in the cash flows so that all residual cash flows go to equity holders. Done this way, the cash flows are discounted at the cost of equity.

Alena thought that the acquisition would slightly increase ACH's risk because she would have to increase debt to finance the purchase. She estimated that ACH's beta would increase from 1.20 to 1.35 as a result. She then used the CAPM equation to compute her cost of equity. She found the risk-free rate of return by looking up the rate offered on Treasury bills. She used the long-term return on the stock market, which is 12%, as the return on the market.

$$\text{Required return} = Rf + \beta\,(R_m - R_f)$$
$$\text{Required return} = 0.05 + 1.35\,(0.12 - 0.05)$$
$$\text{Required return} = 0.14$$

The present value of the cash flows was calculated as follows:

$$PV = \frac{\$735}{(1.14)^1} + \frac{\$871}{(1.14)^2} + \frac{\$968}{(1.14)^3} + \frac{\$1,054}{(1.14)^4} + \frac{\$1,121}{(1.14)^5} + \frac{\left[\frac{\$1,121(1.07)}{0.14 - 0.07}\right]}{(1.14)^5}$$

$$PV = \$645 + \$670 + \$653 + \$624 + \$582 + \$8,900$$

$$PV = \$12,074$$

Because she expected the firm to continue growing indefinitely, Alena used the Gordon growth model to project the present value of an infinitely growing earnings stream. The present value of the cash flow stream the acquisition would produce is $12,074,000 ($12,074 × 1,000 = $12,074,000). This is the maximum she could pay for the Aromatic Bean, including her remodeling expenses. Her managers had inspected all of the properties and had given her a remodeling estimate of $2,000,000. Thus, her maximum purchase price could not exceed $10.1 million.

Alena directed her attorneys to open negotiations with a $7-million offer. This was met with howls of protest from the Aromatic Bean representatives, who counteroffered $15 million. The negotiations lasted for 2 months. The two parties considered cash, combinations of cash and stock in ACH, all ACH stock, and different prices for each combination. Additionally, the negotiations included the issues such as which employees were to be retained and whether the old management of Aromatic Bean could open any new coffee shops. Ultimately, Aromatic Bean managers agreed to sell for an exchange of stock in ACH worth $9 million. They opted for stock instead of cash to avoid the taxes they would otherwise owe. Additionally, ACH received an agreement from the managers of Aromatic Bean not to compete for a period of 5 years.

Review of Analyzing an Acquisition

Once again we are able to tackle a rather complex and significant issue using the tools learned earlier in the text under a variety of different headings. To evaluate an opportunity to acquire another firm, you need to:

- Project future net income based on historical income statements
- Adjust net income figures to reflect synergies achieved from the acquisition
- Estimate the required return on the combined firm using the CAPM
- Compute the present value of an infinite series using the Gordon growth model
- Compute the present value of net income before the infinite growth period
- Understand how the present value of the net income translates into a bid price for the target firm

Mergers continue to be a common occurrence in business.

PERSONAL FINANCIAL PLANNING

Over the years Alena had taken little out of the company. She had kept dividends low so that the company could fund its growth without incurring excessive debt. She also had kept her own salary low. She continued to live in a modest home and to drive mid-priced cars. With the success of ACH, Alena found she could delegate more work to subordinates and begin enjoying her wealth. She liked to go to Utah twice per year to ski at the luxurious Park City. She also planned to begin enjoying her other passions, boating and scuba diving. Now at the age of 45, she realized that she needed to tend to her future. She had married a musician, Marvin, who had performed at her coffee houses. She loved Marvin dearly, but she knew his talents would never earn him much. Providing for their retirement was up to her. She needed to determine how much to put aside in retirement investments to reach their goals.

Alena turned once again to her finance background to help her work through the problem. She identified the following steps that would be needed to develop a personal financial plan:

- Identify assets and resources
- Identify specific goals
- Compute financial requirements to meet these goals

Alena wanted to leave the bulk of her wealth to her two children. For this reason, she did not want to build a plan that would require her to liquidate her stock holdings during her retirement. Instead, she wanted to put a fixed amount every year into a retirement plan so that when she retired, she could live off the earnings and principal in the account for the rest of her life. Her ownership interest in ACH would be passed on within the family.

Alena and Marvin spent a great deal of time discussing their retirement goals. When they thought they knew what they wanted, they prepared the following list:

- North Carolina beachfront house
- Park City Ski Resort condo
- 50-foot Hatteras yacht
- Annual income with the spending power provided today by $250,000

The second step in preparing their financial plan called for them to compute how much money they would need to meet these goals. This required that they determine the cost of each asset in today's dollars and then estimate the cost when they retired. After consulting with various financial advisors and reviewing the rate of inflation over the last 20 years, they decided that they would be comfortable assuming inflation would increase at an average annual compounded rate of 4%. Although they hoped this was a little high, they thought they would rather overestimate inflation than underestimate it and not have the spending power they desired.

Providing for Asset Accumulation

They also decided that the cost of the real estate they planned to acquire should increase at a rate above the average inflation rate. They decided to use a 10% rate of increase. They realized that there was some risk to this assumption because real estate price changes often deviate substantially from the average inflation rate. However, they knew that if property prices began increasing rapidly, they could sell stock and make their real estate purchases. They could then replace the stock before they retired. Their research into yacht price increases led them to assume prices would keep pace with the inflation rate. With these thoughts in mind, they did some research and prepared Table 18.4.

To adjust for inflation, Alena multiplied the current value of the assets by the future value interest factor for 20 years at the appropriate inflation rate. For example, a beach house that costs $325,000 today will cost $2,186,437 in 20 years if it appreciates at 10% per year ($325,000 \times 1.10^{20} = $2,186,437$). In all, by the time the Greens reached their retirement, they would require $7,295,379 to buy the assets they wanted.

TABLE 18.4 Projected Future Cost of Assets

Retirement Asset	Current Value	Inflation Rate	Cost in 20 Years
North Carolina beach house	$325,000	0.10	$2,186,437
Ski condo	$450,000	0.10	$3,027,375
Yacht	$950,000	0.04	$2,081,567
Purchase price of assets			$7,295,379

Providing for Retirement Income

The next problem was to compute the amount of money Alena must have in her retirement nest egg to provide a constant income equal to $250,000 in today's dollars after adjusting for inflation. Alena decided that she needed to provide income for 25 years. The problem was complicated by the fact that she could not assume that inflation would stop once she retired. In other words, once she computed how much she would need her first year of retirement, another calculation would be required to compute what would be needed the second, and so on. She first identified the steps needed in the calculations, and then prepared a spreadsheet.

- Compute the future value of $250,000 after 20 years at 4% inflation.
- Compute the annual income required during each of the following 25 years assuming inflation continues at 4%.
- Compute the present value of the 25 yearly payments to determine the size of the retirement nest egg.
- Use the future value of an annuity formula to compute how much must be saved every year until retirement to build the nest egg.

Future value of $250,000: The amount of the first annual retirement payment is computed in the same way as the inflation-adjusted asset values were computed:

$$\text{Future income required} = \$250,000 \times 1.04^{20}$$

$$\text{Future income required} = \$547,781$$

During her first year of retirement, Alena will need $547,781 to have the spending power provided by $250,000 today.

Annual income required during each year: The income required during the first year of retirement is multiplied by 1.04 to find the income required during the second year. The process continues for each of the subsequent 23 years. To make the calculations easier, Alena prepared the spreadsheet shown in Table 18.5.

The second column lists the amount required each year after adjusting for inflation. The third column is the PVIF at 10%. The 10% factors were used to compute the present value because Alena thought that she could earn at least this much on average by investing in the stock market. The last column lists the present value of the amount required each year. The sum of this column is the amount that must be in the nest egg to provide the cash flows listed in the second column. Alena remembered that the present value of a cash flow stream will let you reproduce that cash flow stream exactly.

When Alena showed her worksheet to her husband, Marvin, he told her that she must have made a mistake. How could $7,571,696 provide for 25 years of retirement when they would need over $1 million just to get through the first 2 years? Alena reminded him that the nest egg would continue earning interest each year at 10%. For example, during the first year the income on the nest egg would be 10% of $7,571,696, which is $757,170. Only $547,781 is needed that year so the balance actually increases.

TABLE 18.5 Calculation of Nest Egg Required for Retirement

Year	Retirement Dollars Required	PVIF	PV
1	$ 547,781	1	$ 547,781
2	569,692	0.9091	517,902
3	592,480	0.8264	489,653
4	616,179	0.7513	462,944
5	640,826	0.6830	437,693
6	666,459	0.6209	413,819
7	693,118	0.5645	391,247
8	720,842	0.5132	369,906
9	749,676	0.4665	349,729
10	779,663	0.4241	330,653
11	810,850	0.3855	312,618
12	843,284	0.3505	295,566
13	877,015	0.3186	279,444
14	912,096	0.2897	264,202
15	948,579	0.2633	249,791
16	986,523	0.2394	236,166
17	1,025,984	0.2176	223,284
18	1,067,023	0.1978	211,105
19	1,109,704	0.1799	199,590
20	1,154,092	0.1635	188,703
21	1,200,256	0.1486	178,410
22	1,248,266	0.1351	168,679
23	1,298,196	0.1228	159,478
24	1,350,124	0.1117	150,779
25	1,404,129	0.1015	142,555
Nest egg required			**$7,571,696**

In later years, after inflation increases the amount required, the interest income will not be sufficient so a portion of the principal will be used. After 25 years the balance in the retirement account should be zero.

Summing the amount of money required to purchase the assets they want at retirement ($7,295,379 from Table 18.4) and the amount of cash they need in their retirement account ($7,571,696 from Table 18.5), Alena and Marvin need to accumulate $14,867,075 over the next 20 years.

Accumulating a Nest Egg

Once Alena knew how much she wanted to accumulate over the next 20 years, she was able to begin working on a plan to make it happen. The first step was to determine how much must be saved each year. The second step was to negotiate her compensation package with the directors of ACH.

Careers in Finance

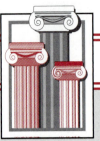

Obtaining an MBA

Now that your course in introductory finance is almost over, it may be time for many of you to seriously consider what you will do upon graduation. We have investigated a number of career opportunities that are available to finance and business majors. Another option that should be considered is continuing your education by obtaining an MBA.

The number of business students obtaining MBAs has increased over the last decade to the point where it is almost a requirement for those who want to be competitive in the marketplace. The decision that must be made before you graduate is whether you would prefer to continue with your education now or go to work for a few years first. Most of the more prestigious MBA programs require a minimum of two years of business experience before you can be admitted to their programs. Less competitive programs have less stringent requirements.

Studies show that businesspeople with MBAs earn around 15% more than those with only undergraduate degrees. They also report greater job satisfaction and better long-term promotion potential.

Every business student should consider obtaining an MBA. Consider when doing so is right for you.

Computing the amount that must be saved each year was a simple exercise using the future value of an annuity formula. She knew the future amount, the interest rate, and the term. She just needed to solve for the payment:

$$FV_{annuity} = PMT\left(FVIFA_{n,i}\right)$$

$$\$14{,}867{,}075 = PMT\left(FVIFA_{20\,years,10\%}\right)$$

$$\$14{,}867{,}075 = PMT\left(57.275\right)$$

$$\frac{\$14{,}867{,}075}{57.275} = PMT$$

$$PMT = \$259{,}574$$

When Alena reviewed her numbers with the chief financial officer of ACH, he pointed out that she had made a serious error. She had not accounted for taxes. If the money was put into a tax-exempt retirement account, she would have to pay a large portion of it to the IRS if she withdrew enough in her first year of retirement to purchase the assets she desired. The annual amount would have to be increased sufficiently so that $259,574 could be invested after deductions for taxes. Assuming that state and federal taxes total about 35%, Alena determined that the actual annual compensation she needed was

$$\frac{After\text{-}tax\ requirement}{1 - Tax\ rate} = Pretax\ requirement$$

$$\frac{\$259{,}574}{1 - 0.35} = \$399{,}345$$

To pay taxes and still be able to put aside $259,574, Alena would need retirement compensation to total $399,345.[3]

For the senior executive officer of one of the largest and most profitable coffee house chains in the country, this compensation request was not deemed inappropriate by her board and was readily approved.

Review of Financial Planning

In this last section we found another application of time value of money principles. The following skills were required to provide a simple retirement plan:

- Inflation adjustment of prices using future value techniques
- Appreciation adjustment of prices using future value techniques
- Inflation adjustment of cash flows using future value techniques and spreadsheet skills
- Calculation of the retirement balance needed using present value equations
- Calculation of annual payments required using future value of annuity equations

All of the techniques applied were learned in Chapter 6, "The Time Value of Money," and they are brought together here to solve a problem that most of us face. Of course, not all of us will be attempting to finance a ski resort condo and yacht. Yet we will each have a list of goals that we want to accomplish during our lives. Some of these goals may require that we set aside money now in order to finance them later. The simple techniques applied in this chapter can be used in a wide variety of situations.

---

[3]The IRS allows limited amounts of money to be saved pretax. In effect this delays paying taxes and lets the worker invest these tax dollars. While Alena's plan would provide what she wanted, she could do so at a lower cost to ACH by taking advantage of tax saving strategies. These strategies are beyond the scope of this text, however. Even well-versed financial executives consult tax planning experts when establishing their retirement plans. This example greatly simplifies tax planning issues. For example, we have ignored the taxes that will be paid on withdrawals.

CHAPTER SUMMARY

The purpose of this chapter was twofold. Most important was to point out the wide variety of financial and business problems you are now equipped to analyze using the skills learned in this course. Second, we wanted to briefly introduce a number of common business problems and demonstrate an acceptable method of analysis for each. We used the case of America's Coffee House, established by Alena Green, to illustrate the application of several financial techniques and principles.

The first problem addressed in this chapter was how to analyze lease versus purchase financing options. The analysis closely followed the method learned earlier for capital budgeting. The cash flows for each financing option were identified and the present value was computed. Because financing represents a cost, the option with the lowest present value was favored. However, qualitative issues also were considered.

As ACH continued to expand, its need for additional capital increased. The company realized that going public would give it access to the additional capital it required. The problem with going public is the firm must be valued so that the stock price can be set fairly. The investment bankers hired to help with ACH's public offering suggested using the price/earnings ratio for similar firms and ACH's projected earnings to compute a fair market value. This done, the firm was taken public.

A second method for valuing a firm was explored when a competitor suggested a merger. In this case a discounted cash flow approach was applied to the net income of the target. The projected net income of the target firm was discounted back to the present to determine the maximum amount ACH could pay for the company. The managers of the target firm agreed to an exchange of stock, and the deal was consummated.

The last problem explored in this chapter was how Alena could provide for her retirement. She first listed her financial goals. This included what real estate she wanted to own by the time she retired and how much annual income she thought she would need. She then adjusted all of these amounts to compensate for inflation and appreciation in costs. Finally, she computed how much she must save to have

a retirement nest egg sufficient to buy the assets and provide the required annual cash flows. After adjusting for taxes, she negotiated a contract with the ACH board to fund her needs.

The important point to understand about this chapter is that you now have a complete box of tools to use to analyze a wide variety of financial problems and issues. Some of these problems may be unique to you or to the company you will work for, so solutions will not be clearly outlined in textbooks. However, if you accurately estimate cash flows, always adjust for the time value of money, and apply the financial concepts learned in this course, there will be few problems that you are not prepared to tackle. At times you may require the assistance of experts to help with the analysis. For example, a tax expert should be consulted when a retirement plan is prepared and investment bankers can help with taking a firm public. However, your financial background will allow you to talk intelligently to these consultants and get the most from their advice.

KEY WORDS

financial (capital) lease 491	initial public offering	privately (closely) held 495	tender offer 497
go public 495	(IPO) 497	prospectus 497	
	operating lease 491	synergy 500	

DISCUSSION QUESTIONS

1. When conducting a lease versus purchase analysis, why do we choose the option with the lowest present value?
2. What are the arguments for and against using an operating lease as opposed to a financial lease?
3. Identify the qualitative issues that must be considered when making a lease versus purchase decision.
4. What are the advantages of going public? What are the disadvantages?

5. Identify the basic financial concepts used to conduct a lease versus purchase analysis.
6. Identify the basic financial concepts used to value a firm in the process of going public.
7. What basic financial concepts are used to evaluate a potential takeover target?
8. What basic financial concepts are used in personal financial planning?

PROBLEMS

1. You are attempting to decide between accepting a lease or obtaining a loan to purchase some equipment. The lease payment is $3,000 per year. After 3 years you may buy the equipment for $500. You are not responsible for maintenance if you lease. The alternative is to purchase the equipment with an $8,000 loan. Maintenance is expected to be $200 per month. Assuming the loan has a 10% interest rate, taxes are 40%, and the cost of capital is 12%, which option should you choose?

2. You are evaluating a lease that offers annual payments of $25,000 for 5 years. Under this lease you are responsible for maintenance at $2,500 per year. At the end of the lease you can purchase the asset for $5,000. Alternatively, you can obtain a $60,000 five-year loan to purchase the asset. If you must pay 12% for this loan, taxes are 40%, and the discount rate is 10%, which option should you choose?

3. Assume a firm's earnings have been growing at 5% for the last several years and this growth is expected to continue. Last year's earnings were $1.2 million. There are 1 million shares of stock outstanding.
   a. What should the price per share of stock be if the PE for comparable firms is 23?
   b. Based on your answer to part a, what would be the total value of the firm?
   c. If 500,000 new shares of stock are issued and projected earnings rise to $1.9 million, what will be the new price per share?
4. You are evaluating an acquisition that will cost $20,000. The firm will add $4,000 to net cash flows for the next 10 years because of the acquisition. If the discount rate is 12%, should you make the acquisition?
5. If you want to buy a condo when you retire and the condo currently costs $120,000, what will it cost in 35 years if inflation causes prices to increase at 4% per year?
6. You have decided that you will need 70% of your current income to be happy during your retirement. You cur-rently earn $50,000. You do not plan to retire for 35 years and inflation should equal 3% per year. How much will you need for your first year of retirement?
7. You have determined that you will need $100,000 during your first year of retirement. You expect to earn 10% on your investments and you assume inflation will average 3%. How much must you have at the beginning of your retirement to last 35 years? (Hint: Find the present value of the annuity using the net interest rate [i.e., 10% − 3%]).
8. If you will need $2,000,000 in a nest egg to retire, how much must you save every year if you can earn 12% for the next 35 years?
9. Prepare your own financial plan using the methods outlined in the chapter. You will need to decide what assets you will need during retirement and how much money you will need annually. Determine the following:
   a. Total nest egg needed to retire
   b. Annual payments needed to accumulate nest egg

SELF-TEST PROBLEMS

1. Net annual income for Company X was $603,000 in 1999 and $705,000 in 2000. Compute the growth rate.
2. Using the growth rate from problem 1, estimate earnings for 2001.
3. Using the earnings estimation from problem 2, calculate earnings per share (EPS) if the number of shares outstanding is 600,000.
4. Calculate the market price of the shares using the EPS as obtained in problem 3 if the PE ratio is 18.
5. Using the data from problems 1–4, calculate the value of Company X.
6. If the after-tax requirement is $317,000 and the pretax requirement is $470,000, compute the tax rate.
7. If the tax rate is 35% and the after-tax requirement is $270,000, compute the pretax requirement.
8. Compute the required return if the long-term return on the stock market is 15% and the risk-free rate of return is 6%. Beta is 1.40.
9. Compute beta if the required return is 15%, the long-term return on the stock market is 13%, and the risk-free rate of return is 5%.
10. Compute the future value of $4,166 invested to earn interest at 8% compounded semiannually for 20 years.
11. Find the present value of $9,500 due in 4 years at 12% compounded quarterly.
12. Compute the future value of $5,920 invested to earn interest at 12% compounded quarterly for 4 years.
13. Find the present value of $20,000 due in 20 years at 8% compounded semiannually.
14. What is the PV of an annuity of $8,000 per year for 5 years if the interest rate is 10% compounded annually?
15. What is the FV of an annuity of $10,000 per month for 1 year if the interest rate is 12% compounded annually?

WEB EXPLORATION

1. It has become very popular to lease autos, since the down payment is usually lower and the monthly payments are often less. The calculator at the following site takes an MSRP, bargained discount (%), down payment, lease length, and lending rate to calculate estimated lease payments.

   a. Go to www.interest.com/hugh/calc/lease.cgi. First, find the lease rate on a $25,000 car (the amount you are paying is $25,000) for which you put down 10% assuming an 8% new car lending rate. The lease is for 36 months, and the value of the car at the end of the lease is estimated to be $15,000. Assume a 6% sales tax.

   b. Now adjust the down payment until the monthly payment is $300.

2. In this chapter we looked at how Alena prepared for her future. Go to www.interest.com/hugh/calc/wealth.cgi. This site allows you to input your income and net worth to determine whether you are on track for retirement.

While it is very simplistic and leaves off all the planning issues discussed in this chapter, it can be fun to see if you or your parents meet the rule of thumb for retirement investing.

3. Go to www.interest.com/hugh/calc/retire.cgi. This site provides a simple retirement calculator. Assume that you would like to have $70,000 in today's dollars when you retire in 40 years. Assume that you will need this income stream for 25 years, that it will earn 10%, and that inflation will average 3%. Now try adjusting these assumptions to see what impact they have on your retirement needs.

4. One point made in this chapter was that retirement funds are eroded by the effects of inflation. It is interesting to compute what goods would have cost at some point in the past after adjusting for inflation. Go to www.interest.com/hugh/calc/cpi.cgi. What would a milkshake that cost $2.50 today have cost the year that you were born?

Appendix A

TABLE A1 Future Value of $1 (FVIF)

Period	1%	2%	3%	4%	5%	6%	7%	8%	9%	10%	12%	14%	15%	16%	18%	20%	25%	30%
1	1.010	1.020	1.030	1.040	1.050	1.060	1.070	1.080	1.090	1.100	1.120	1.140	1.150	1.160	1.180	1.200	1.250	1.300
2	1.020	1.040	1.061	1.082	1.102	1.124	1.145	1.166	1.188	1.210	1.254	1.300	1.323	1.346	1.392	1.440	1.563	1.690
3	1.030	1.061	1.093	1.125	1.158	1.191	1.225	1.260	1.295	1.331	1.405	1.482	1.521	1.561	1.643	1.728	1.953	2.197
4	1.041	1.082	1.126	1.170	1.216	1.262	1.311	1.360	1.412	1.464	1.574	1.689	1.749	1.811	1.939	2.074	2.441	2.856
5	1.051	1.104	1.159	1.217	1.276	1.338	1.403	1.469	1.539	1.611	1.762	1.925	2.011	2.100	2.288	2.488	3.052	3.713
6	1.062	1.126	1.194	1.265	1.340	1.419	1.501	1.587	1.677	1.772	1.974	2.195	2.313	2.436	2.700	2.986	3.815	4.827
7	1.072	1.149	1.230	1.316	1.407	1.504	1.606	1.714	1.828	1.949	2.211	2.502	2.660	2.826	3.185	3.583	4.768	6.275
8	1.083	1.172	1.267	1.369	1.477	1.594	1.718	1.851	1.993	2.144	2.476	2.853	3.059	3.278	3.759	4.300	5.960	8.157
9	1.094	1.195	1.305	1.423	1.551	1.689	1.838	1.999	2.172	2.358	2.773	3.252	3.518	3.803	4.435	5.160	7.451	10.604
10	1.105	1.219	1.344	1.480	1.629	1.791	1.967	2.159	2.367	2.594	3.106	3.707	4.046	4.411	5.234	6.192	9.313	13.786
11	1.116	1.243	1.384	1.539	1.710	1.898	2.105	2.332	2.580	2.853	3.479	4.226	4.652	5.117	6.176	7.430	11.642	17.922
12	1.127	1.268	1.426	1.601	1.796	2.012	2.252	2.518	2.813	3.138	3.896	4.818	5.350	5.936	7.288	8.916	14.552	23.298
13	1.138	1.294	1.469	1.665	1.886	2.133	2.410	2.720	3.066	3.452	4.363	5.492	6.153	6.886	8.599	10.699	18.190	30.288
14	1.149	1.319	1.513	1.732	1.980	2.261	2.579	2.937	3.342	3.797	4.887	6.261	7.076	7.988	10.147	12.839	22.737	39.374
15	1.161	1.346	1.558	1.801	2.079	2.397	2.759	3.172	3.642	4.177	5.474	7.138	8.137	9.266	11.974	15.407	28.422	51.186
16	1.173	1.373	1.605	1.873	2.183	2.540	2.952	3.426	3.970	4.595	6.130	8.137	9.358	10.748	14.129	18.488	35.527	66.542
17	1.184	1.400	1.653	1.948	2.292	2.693	3.159	3.700	4.328	5.054	6.866	9.276	10.761	12.468	16.672	22.186	44.409	86.504
18	1.196	1.428	1.702	2.026	2.407	2.854	3.380	3.996	4.717	5.560	7.690	10.575	12.375	14.463	19.673	26.623	55.511	112.46
19	1.208	1.457	1.754	2.107	2.527	3.026	3.617	4.316	5.142	6.116	8.613	12.056	14.232	16.777	23.214	31.948	69.389	146.19
20	1.220	1.486	1.806	2.191	2.653	3.207	3.870	4.661	5.604	6.727	9.646	13.743	16.367	19.461	27.393	38.338	86.736	190.05
25	1.282	1.641	2.094	2.666	3.386	4.292	5.427	6.848	8.623	10.835	17.000	26.462	32.919	40.874	62.669	95.396	264.70	705.64
30	1.348	1.811	2.427	3.243	4.322	5.743	7.612	10.063	13.268	17.449	29.960	50.950	66.212	85.850	143.371	237.376	807.79	2620.00
35	1.417	2.000	2.814	3.946	5.516	7.686	10.677	14.785	20.414	28.102	52.800	98.100	133.176	180.314	327.997	590.668	2465.190	9727.860
60	1.817	3.281	5.892	10.520	18.679	32.988	57.946	101.257	176.031	304.482	897.597	2595.919	4383.999	7370.201	20555.140	56347.514	652530.447	*

Note: The basic equation for finding the future value interest factor (FVIF) is: $FVIF_{i,n} = (1 + i)^n$ where i is the interest rate and n is the number of periods in years.
*Value exceeds 1 million.

TABLE A2 Future Value of a $1 Ordinary Annuity (FVIFA)

Period	1%	2%	3%	4%	5%	6%	7%	8%	9%	10%	12%	14%	16%	18%	20%	25%	30%
1	1.000	1.000	1.000	1.000	1.000	1.000	1.000	1.000	1.000	1.000	1.000	1.000	1.000	1.000	1.000	1.000	1.000
2	2.010	2.020	2.030	2.040	2.050	2.060	2.070	2.080	2.090	2.100	2.120	2.140	2.160	2.180	2.200	2.250	2.300
3	3.030	3.060	3.091	3.122	3.153	3.184	3.215	3.246	3.278	3.310	3.374	3.440	3.506	3.572	3.640	3.813	3.990
4	4.060	4.122	4.184	4.246	4.310	4.375	4.440	4.506	4.573	4.641	4.779	4.921	5.066	5.215	5.368	5.766	6.187
5	5.101	5.204	5.309	5.416	5.526	5.637	5.751	5.867	5.985	6.105	6.353	6.610	6.877	7.154	7.442	8.207	9.043
6	6.152	6.308	6.468	6.633	6.802	6.975	7.153	7.336	7.523	7.716	8.115	8.536	8.977	9.442	9.930	11.259	12.756
7	7.214	7.434	7.662	7.898	8.142	8.394	8.654	8.923	9.200	9.487	10.089	10.730	11.414	12.142	12.916	15.073	17.583
8	8.286	8.583	8.892	9.214	9.549	9.897	10.260	10.637	11.028	11.436	12.300	13.233	14.240	15.327	16.499	19.842	23.858
9	9.369	9.755	10.159	10.583	11.027	11.491	11.978	12.488	13.021	13.579	14.776	16.085	17.519	19.086	20.799	25.802	32.015
10	10.462	10.950	11.464	12.006	12.578	13.181	13.816	14.487	15.193	15.937	17.549	19.337	21.321	23.521	25.959	33.253	42.619
11	11.567	12.169	12.808	13.486	14.207	14.972	15.784	16.645	17.560	18.531	20.655	23.044	25.733	28.755	32.150	42.566	56.405
12	12.683	13.412	14.192	15.026	15.917	16.870	17.888	18.977	20.141	21.384	24.133	27.271	30.850	34.931	38.580	54.208	74.327
13	13.809	14.680	15.618	16.627	17.713	18.882	20.141	21.495	22.953	24.523	28.029	32.089	36.786	42.219	48.497	68.760	97.625
14	14.947	15.974	17.086	18.292	19.599	21.015	22.550	24.215	26.019	27.975	32.393	37.581	43.672	50.818	59.196	86.949	127.91
15	16.097	17.293	18.599	20.024	21.579	23.276	25.129	27.152	29.361	31.772	37.280	43.842	51.660	60.965	72.035	109.69	167.29
16	17.258	18.639	20.157	21.825	23.657	25.673	27.888	30.324	33.003	35.950	42.753	50.980	60.925	72.939	87.442	138.11	218.47
17	18.430	20.012	21.762	23.698	25.840	28.213	30.840	33.750	36.974	40.545	48.884	59.118	71.673	87.068	105.931	173.64	285.01
18	19.615	21.412	23.414	25.645	28.132	30.906	33.999	37.450	41.301	45.599	55.750	68.394	84.141	103.740	128.117	218.04	371.52
19	20.811	22.841	25.117	27.671	30.539	33.760	37.379	41.466	46.018	51.159	63.440	78.969	98.603	123.414	154.740	273.56	483.97
20	22.019	24.297	26.870	29.778	33.066	36.786	40.995	45.762	51.160	57.275	72.052	91.025	115.380	146.628	186.688	342.94	630.17
25	28.243	32.030	36.459	41.646	47.727	54.865	63.249	73.106	84.701	98.347	133.334	181.871	249.214	342.603	471.981	1054.79	2348.80
30	34.785	40.568	47.575	56.085	66.439	79.058	94.461	113.283	136.308	164.494	241.333	356.787	530.312	790.948	1181.882	3227.17	8730.00
35	41.660	49.994	60.462	73.652	90.320	111.435	138.237	172.317	215.711	271.024	431.663	693.573	1120.713	1816.652	2948.341	9856.761	32422.868
60	81.670	114.052	163.053	237.991	353.584	533.128	813.520	1253.213	1944.792	3034.816	7471.641	18353.133	46057.509	114189.666	281732.572	*	*

Note: The basic equation for finding the future value interest factor of an ordinary annuity (FVIFA) is: $\mathrm{FVIFA}_{i,n} = \sum_{}^{n}(1 + i)^{t-1} = \frac{(1 + i)^n - 1}{i}$ where i is the interest rate and n is the number of periods in years.

Future Value of a $1 Annuity Due (FVIFAD)   The future value interest factor of an annuity due (FVIFAD) may be found by using the following formula to convert FVIFA values found in Table A2:

FVIFADt,n = $\mathrm{FVIFA}_{t,n}$(1 + i) where i is the interest rate and n is the number of periods in years.

*Value exceeds 1 million.

TABLE A3 Present Value of $1 (PVIF)

Period	1%	2%	3%	4%	5%	6%	7%	8%	9%	10%	12%	14%	15%	16%	18%	20%	25%	30%
1	.990	.980	.971	.962	.952	.943	.935	.926	.917	.909	.893	.877	.870	.862	.847	.833	.800	.769
2	.980	.961	.943	.925	.907	.890	.873	.857	.842	.826	.797	.769	.756	.743	.718	.694	.640	.592
3	.971	.942	.915	.889	.864	.840	.816	.794	.772	.751	.712	.675	.658	.641	.609	.579	.512	.455
4	.961	.924	.888	.855	.823	.792	.763	.735	.708	.683	.636	.592	.572	.552	.516	.482	.410	.350
5	.951	.906	.863	.822	.784	.747	.713	.681	.650	.621	.567	.519	.497	.476	.437	.402	.328	.269
6	.942	.888	.837	.790	.746	.705	.666	.630	.596	.564	.507	.456	.432	.410	.370	.335	.262	.207
7	.933	.871	.813	.760	.711	.665	.623	.583	.547	.513	.452	.400	.376	.354	.314	.279	.210	.159
8	.923	.853	.789	.731	.677	.627	.582	.540	.502	.467	.404	.351	.327	.305	.266	.233	.168	.123
9	.914	.837	.766	.703	.645	.592	.544	.500	.460	.424	.361	.308	.284	.263	.225	.194	.134	.094
10	.905	.820	.744	.676	.614	.558	.508	.463	.422	.386	.322	.270	.247	.227	.191	.162	.107	.073
11	.896	.804	.722	.650	.585	.527	.475	.429	.388	.350	.287	.237	.215	.195	.162	.135	.086	.056
12	.887	.788	.701	.625	.557	.497	.444	.397	.356	.319	.257	.208	.187	.168	.137	.112	.069	.043
13	.879	.773	.681	.601	.530	.469	.415	.368	.326	.290	.229	.182	.163	.145	.116	.093	.055	.033
14	.870	.758	.661	.577	.505	.442	.388	.340	.299	.263	.205	.160	.141	.125	.099	.078	.044	.025
15	.861	.743	.642	.555	.481	.417	.362	.315	.275	.239	.183	.140	.123	.108	.084	.065	.035	.020
16	.853	.728	.623	.534	.458	.394	.339	.292	.252	.218	.163	.123	.107	.093	.071	.054	.028	.015
17	.844	.714	.605	.513	.436	.371	.317	.270	.231	.198	.146	.108	.093	.080	.060	.045	.023	.012
18	.836	.700	.587	.494	.416	.350	.296	.250	.212	.180	.130	.095	.081	.069	.051	.038	.018	.009
19	.828	.686	.570	.475	.396	.331	.277	.232	.194	.164	.116	.083	.070	.060	.043	.031	.014	.007
20	.820	.673	.554	.456	.377	.312	.258	.215	.178	.149	.104	.073	.061	.051	.037	.026	.012	.005
25	.780	.610	.478	.375	.295	.233	.184	.146	.116	.092	.059	.038	.030	.024	.016	.010	.004	.001
30	.742	.552	.412	.308	.231	.174	.131	.099	.075	.057	.033	.020	.015	.012	.007	.004	.001	.000
35	.706	.500	.355	.253	.181	.130	.094	.068	.049	.036	.019	.010	.008	.006	.003	.002	*	*
60	.550	.305	.170	.095	.054	.030	.017	.010	.006	.003	.001	*	.000	.000	*	*	*	*

Note: The basic equation for finding the present value interest factor (PVIF) is: $PVIF_{i,n} = \dfrac{1}{(1+i)^n}$ where i is the interest or discount rate and n is the number of periods in years.

TABLE A4 Present Value of $1 Ordinary Annuity (PVIFA)

Period	1%	2%	3%	4%	5%	6%	7%	8%	9%	10%	12%	14%	16%	18%	20%	25%	30%
1	0.990	0.980	0.971	0.962	0.952	0.943	0.935	0.926	0.917	0.909	0.893	0.877	0.862	0.847	0.833	.800	.769
2	1.970	1.942	1.913	1.886	1.859	1.833	1.808	1.783	1.759	1.736	1.690	1.647	1.605	1.566	1.528	1.440	1.361
3	2.941	2.884	2.829	2.775	2.723	2.673	2.624	2.577	2.531	2.487	2.402	2.322	2.246	2.174	2.106	1.952	1.816
4	3.902	3.808	3.717	3.630	3.546	3.465	3.387	3.312	3.240	3.170	3.037	2.914	2.798	2.690	2.589	2.362	2.166
5	4.853	4.713	4.580	4.452	4.329	4.212	4.100	3.993	3.890	3.791	3.605	3.433	3.274	3.127	2.991	2.689	2.436
6	5.795	5.601	5.417	5.242	5.076	4.917	4.767	4.623	4.486	4.355	4.111	3.889	3.685	3.498	3.326	2.951	2.643
7	6.728	6.472	6.230	6.002	5.786	5.582	5.389	5.206	5.033	4.868	4.564	4.288	4.039	3.812	3.605	3.161	2.802
8	7.652	7.325	7.020	6.733	6.463	6.210	5.971	5.747	5.535	5.335	4.968	4.639	4.344	4.078	3.837	3.329	2.925
9	8.566	8.162	7.786	7.435	7.108	6.802	6.515	6.247	5.995	5.759	5.328	4.946	4.607	4.303	4.031	3.463	3.019
10	9.471	8.983	8.530	8.111	7.722	7.360	7.024	6.710	6.418	6.145	5.650	5.216	4.833	4.494	4.193	3.571	3.092
11	10.368	9.787	9.253	8.760	8.306	7.887	7.499	7.139	6.805	6.495	5.938	5.453	5.029	4.656	4.327	3.656	3.147
12	11.255	10.575	9.954	9.385	8.863	8.384	7.943	7.536	7.161	6.814	6.194	5.660	5.197	4.793	4.439	3.725	3.190
13	12.134	11.348	10.635	9.986	9.394	8.853	8.358	7.904	7.487	7.103	6.424	5.842	5.342	4.910	4.533	3.780	3.223
14	13.004	12.106	11.296	10.563	9.899	9.295	8.745	8.244	7.786	7.367	6.628	6.002	5.468	5.008	4.611	3.824	3.249
15	13.865	12.849	11.938	11.118	10.380	9.712	9.108	8.559	8.061	7.606	6.811	6.142	5.575	5.092	4.675	3.859	3.268
16	14.718	13.578	12.561	11.652	10.838	10.106	9.447	8.851	8.313	7.824	6.974	6.265	5.668	5.162	4.730	3.887	3.283
17	15.562	14.292	13.166	12.166	11.274	10.477	9.763	9.122	8.544	8.022	7.120	5.373	5.749	4.222	4.775	3.910	3.295
18	16.398	14.992	13.754	12.659	11.690	10.828	10.059	9.372	8.756	8.201	7.250	6.467	5.818	5.273	4.812	3.928	3.304
19	17.226	15.678	14.324	13.134	12.085	11.158	10.336	9.604	8.950	8.365	7.366	6.550	5.877	5.316	4.843	3.942	3.311
20	18.046	16.351	14.877	13.590	12.462	11.470	10.594	9.818	9.129	8.514	7.469	6.623	5.929	5.353	4.870	3.954	3.316
25	22.023	19.523	17.413	15.622	14.094	12.783	11.654	10.675	9.823	9.077	7.843	6.873	6.097	5.467	4.948	3.985	3.329
30	25.808	22.396	19.600	17.292	15.372	13.765	12.409	11.258	10.274	9.427	8.055	7.003	6.177	5.517	4.979	3.995	3.332
35	29.409	24.999	21.487	18.665	16.374	14.498	12.948	11.655	10.567	9.644	8.176	7.070	6.215	5.539	4.992	3.998	3.333
60	44.955	34.761	27.676	22.623	18.929	16.161	14.039	12.377	11.048	9.967	8.324	7.140	6.249	5.555	5.000	4.000	3.333

Note: The basic equation for finding the present value interest factor of an ordinary annuity (PVIFA) is: $\text{PVIFA}_{i,n} = \sum_{t=1}^{n} \frac{1}{(1+i)^t} = \frac{1 - \frac{1}{(1+i)^n}}{i}$ where i is the interest or discount rate and n is the number of periods in years.

Present Value of a $1 Annuity Due (PVIFAD) The present value interest factor of an annuity due (PVIFAD) may be found by suing the following formula to convert PVIFA values found in Table A4:

$\text{PVIFAS}_{i,n} = \text{PVIFA}_{i,n}(1+i)$ where i is the interest or discount rate and n is the number of periods in years.

Appendix B

CHAPTER 1
1. a. 10%
    b. 8.333%
    c. 11.11%
    d. Good deals disappear fast in efficient markets

CHAPTER 2
1. $1,103.125
3. 130-5

CHAPTER 3
1. $575
3. $2,250

CHAPTER 4
1. 3
3. Yr 1 6%
    Yr 2 7%
    Yr 3 8%
5. 1 Year = 3% + 3% + 1% + 4% + .1% = 11.1%
    5 Year = 3% + 2.3% + 1% + 4% + .1%(5) = 10.8%
    10 Year = 3% + 2.1% + 1% + 4% + .1%(10) = 11.1%
    20 Year = 3% + 2.075% + 1% + 4% + .1%(20) = 12.075%

CHAPTER 5
1. $2,300
3. Not all of the money loaned out by banks will be redeposited. Some will be used as transactional balances held by the individuals receiving the loans. Also, not all the banks will lend the maximum amount permitted by law. It may be because there is not enough loan requests for the bank or it may be that bank management is conservative and wants to maintain excess reserves.

CHAPTER 6
Problems
1.

3. a. $100 * (1.06)^{30} = \$574.35$
    a. $5,000 * (1.10)^{25} = \$54,173.52$
    b. $12,500 * (1.12)^{7} = \$27,633.52$
    c. $23,200 * (1.14)^{10} = \$86,007.53$
5. a. $500(2.7183)^{.08*2} = \$584.92$
    b. $300(2.7183)^{.06*5} = \$403.17$
    c. $300(2.7183)^{.10*7} = \$593.98$
7. FV = $4,136
9. PV = $816.30
11. a. $37,908
    b. $113,004
13. a. $100,000
    b. $400,000
    c. $625,000
15. a. $1,917.14
    b. $3,956.95
17. a. $924,487.40
    b. $609,695.44
    c. In part a, a total of $16,000 was invested. In part b, $64,000 was invested into the retirement fund. Plan A seems to be the better retirement investment.
19.

Year	Beginning Balance	Payment	Accrued Interest	Principal Payment	Ending Balance
1	$100,000.00	$11,682.95	$8,000.00	$3,682.95	$96,317.05
2	$96,317.05	$11,682.95	$7,705.36	$3,977.58	$92,339.46

21. 85.15 months

Self-Test Problems
1. $889.73
2. $1,348.48
3. $876.72
4. $670.43
5. $1,493.89
6. $4,495.50
7. $481.59
8. $263.80
9. $6,666.67
10. $161.05
11. $148.59

12. $402.11
13. $1,000
14. $144,104
15. $11,713.54
16. $57.62
17. $122.02
18. 8%
19. $125,870
20. $1,464.29

The following answers are computed using a financial calculator. Rounding errors are to be expected if you are using the financial tables.

21. $239,061.37
22. $13,486.73 (use equation or calculator method)
23. $1,762.34
24. $5,407.16
25. $6,056.02
26. $186.28
27. $641.00
28. $481.59
29. $131.90
30. $1,485.95
31. .08243 = 8.24%
32. $162,169.87
33. $706.10 (use equation or calculator method)
34. 13% (use equation or calculator method)
35. $66.67

CHAPTER 7

Problems

1. 70%
3. 11.1%
5. a. Project 1: 5%
      Project 2: 5%
   b. Project 1: 4%
      Project 2: 10%
   c. Project 2
   d. Project 1
7. a. A 0.5
      B 0.8
      C - 5
   b. A
   c. C
   d. Coefficient of Variation
9. 8.31%

11.

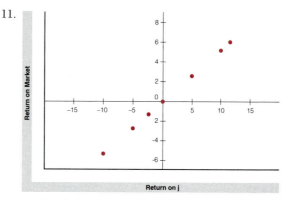

13. 7%; If inflation increases both the return on the market and the return on the risk free security will increase, so the risk premium is unchanged. The risk premium would rise if investors become more risk averse.
15. No: required return = 15%
17.

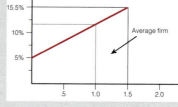

Self-Test Problems

1. 20%
2. 11%
3. .1374
4. 1.27
5. 14%
6. 11%
7. Fairchild and SWA
8. 4
9. .5

10. 1.25
11. .45
12. 15%
13. 10%
14. 20%
15. No
16. Fall
17. 3%
18. 1.5%
19. 1%
20. 2.8%

CHAPTER 8

Problems

1. $33,521.55
3. $924.18
5. PV = $148.64
7. 3.68%
9. a. $927.90
   b. 10.78%
   c. 1.22%
   d. $939.25
   e. $1.22%; Yes
11. $1,053.88

Self-Test Problems

1. $702,441.45
2. $522,860.82
3. $886.28
4. $1,086.59
5. $717.19
6. $972.73
7. problem 5
8. $884.17
9. $1,087.52
10. $904.90
11. 2.10%
12. 7.90%
13. Yes
14. 4.43%
15. 8.69%
16. 4.44%
17. 8.65%

CHAPTER 9

Problems

1. $50.00
3. 5.97%

5. $30.44
7. a. $34.67
   b. 9.18%
   c. $71.33
   d. $42.80
9. a. $1.80; $2.16; $2.592
   b. $2.80
   c. $34.99
   d. $1.55; $1.61; $1.66; $22.42
   e. $27.24
11. $13.88
13. $22.38

Self-Test Problems

1. $20
2. 10%
3. $20.00
4. $19.13
5. $14.97
6. $20.00
7. $31.50
8. $46.29
9. $15.75
10. $9.50
11. $45.45
12. $50.00
13. 10%
14. 12%
15. 12%
16. 15.5%
17. 17.65
18. $30.00
19. $3,200,000
20. $32

CHAPTER 10

Problems

1. a. 3.08; 2.80
   b. NPV: $55.16, $72.30; PI: 1.37, 1.48
   c. Investment 2

3.

Discount Rate	NPV
0	100
10	16.98
12.59	0

5. a. 4.44 years
   b. NPV: $4,708.75; PI: 1.12
   c. IRR: 15.29

7. $1,198.35; Accept
9. a. NPV: $78,819.75; PI: 1.0788
   b. IRR: 14.48
   c.

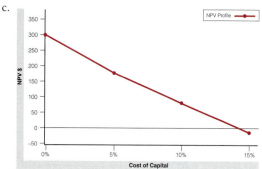

11. Payback: 4.64 years; NPV: $8,025.62; PI: 1.12; IRR: 17.09
13. a. 4.58 years
    b. $4,611.68
    c. 14.36%
    d. 13.13%
15.

	Treadmill	Step Machine
NPV	$50.87	$347.81
IRR	15.24%	20.88%
TV	$3,371.15	$4,957.58
MIRR	14.67%	17.64%
	Accept	Accept

Self-Test Problems

1. 5 years
2. 9.6 years
3. $769; accept
4. −$66,775; reject
5. $132,831; accept
6. −$419,655; reject
7. $114,621; accept
8. 0.96; reject
9. C, A, E, B, D
10. 36.31%
11. 21.48%
12. −8.36%
13. Project A; The reinvestment rate assumption is a problem when you are attempting to rank mutually exclusive projects with IRR. Thus, NPV is more useful when attempting to select among mutually exclusive projects.
14. 9.43%
15. IRR = 7.71%; MIRR = 9.83%
16. 16.5%
17. 19.3%

18. 19.19%
19. 31.38%
20. −$41,093; reject

CHAPTER 11

Problems

1. −$24,000
3. $2,070.00; $2,625; $1,507.50; $1,278.25
5. a. −$240,000.00
   b. $102,360; $113,400
   c. $162,240
   d. $57,273.87
7. a. −$155,000.00
   b. $18,900
   c. $23,900
9. a. Accept
   b. Accept

Self-Test Problems

1. −$215,000
2. −$215,000
3. $40,000
4. −$15,600 (loss); −$6,240; added
5. −$151,760
6. $64,103
7. $41,603; $49,103; $58,103; $68,903
8. $49,320, $67,880, $42,000, $33,680
9. $69,680
10. $334,410,223
11. −$166,873,735
12. $26,150,000
13. F, B, & D; total cost = $6 million; total NPV = $1.72 million
14. K_1 = 0.18; yes, NPV of $5,327
15. 3-year = $13,022,069; 6-year = $6,334,222; accept 3-year
16. 3-year = $26,394,184; 6-year = $12,838,714; accept 3-year
17. A = $331,144; B = $709,957; accept B
18. A = $773,256; B = $1,657,822; accept B

CHAPTER 12

Problems

1. a. 9%
   b. 6.4%
   c. 10.8%
3. 5.09%
5. 13.33%
7. 12%

9. a. 17%
   b. 18.4%
   c. 13.70%
   d. 14.71%
   e. $11,142.86
   f.

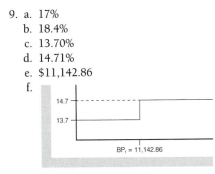

11. a. $71,428.57
    b. Retained earnings: $50,000; Debt financing: $21,428.57
13. a. 20%
    b. 18.1%
    c. $25,000,000; Below: 11.6%; Above: 12.3%

Self-Test Problems

1. 8.89%
2. 6.41%
3. 5.33%
4. 3.85%
5. 8.57%
6. 8.57%
7. 13.70%
8. 14.67%
9. 13.42%
10. 10.41%
11. 12.93%
12. 13.12%
13. 9.95%
14. No
15. $197,910.07
16. $316,656.11
17. $950,570.07
18. $197,910.07
19. 9.95%
20. 11.14%

CHAPTER 13

Problems

1. a. $36; $24
   b. $3; $9
   c. Leveraged at $4,000; unleveraged at $1,500
3. 5
5. DOL: 2; DFL 2; DTL: 4.0
7. 2,000 units

9. a. $297,500.00
   b.

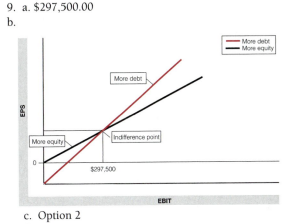

   c. Option 2
   d. Option 1

CHAPTER 14

Problems

1.

	1996	1995
a. ROE	70.2%	162.9%
b. ROA	16.6%	2.9%
c. Gross Profit Margin	17.2%	14.5%
d. Operating Profit Margin	8.8%	4.4
e. Net Profit margin	4.5%	1.2%
f. Current ratio	1.92	2.96
g. Net working Capital	6,876	11,758
h. Inventory Turnover	8.55	4.26
I. Fixed Asset Turnover	15.38	12.43
j. Total Assets Turnover	3.67	2.40
k. Receivable Turnover	10.40	10.35
l. Average Collection Period	35.10	35.28
m. Average Payment Period	14.85	9.57
n. Debt Ratio	0.76	0.98
o. Debt-Equity Ratio	1.55	37.96
p. Times Interest Earned	6.97	1.86

3. 1996: 70.86%; 1995: 162.33%; From the Du Pont analysis, we can observe that sales are increasing causing net income to increase also. The equity multiplier is decreasing which in turn made ROE decrease. With both the profit margin and the turnover ratio improved, the firm is actually healthier. The decline in ROE is due to the reduced leverage so the firm is now lower risk.
5. a. Debt Ratio: 60.33%; Return on Assets (ROA): 6.67%; Return on Equity (ROE): 16.80%; Net Profit Margin: 5.0%

520   Appendix B

b. The company has good liquidity to pay off its creditors. By looking at the inventory turnover, there seems not to have been excess inventory. The net profit margin indicates that there is not a heavy debt that is held by the firm.

7. a. 12%
   b. 48%
   c. 4
9. EPS: $26.00; P/E: 1.06

Self-Test Problems

1.

Ratios	2001	2000	1999
ROE	62.16%	51.22%	40.30%
ROA	22.93%	14.29%	9.75%
Gross profit margin	18.89%	15.69%	14.38%
Operating profit margin	12.75%	9.02%	7.84%
Net profit margin	7.43%	4.94%	3.40%
Current ratio	1.27	1.40	1.52
Quick ratio	0.59	0.65	0.70
Net working capital	$2,950	$3,600	$4,000
Inventory turnover	8.46	7.96	8.07
Fixed asset turnover	6.98	6.75	6.59
Total asset turnover	3.09	2.89	2.87
Receivables turnover	15.96	15.09	15.09
Average collection period	22.86	24.19	24.18
Average payment period	30.66	25.47	20.38
Debt ratio	62.11%	70.98%	74.61%
Debt-equity ratio	47.89%	103.91%	147.39%
TIE ratio	20.13	8.97	5.00

2.

Common-Sized Balance Sheet

	2001	2000	1999
Assets			
Current assets			
Cash	3.49%	5.22%	5.66%
Accounts receivable	19.34%	19.16%	19.01%
Inventories	29.61%	30.61%	30.45%
Prepaid expenses	3.29%	2.15%	1.32%
Total current assets	55.73%	57.14%	56.44%
Property, plant, and equip.	71.59%	70.18%	69.43%
Accumulated depreciation	−27.32%	−27.32%	−25.87%
Net prop., plant, and equip.	44.27%	42.86%	43.56%
Total assets	100.00%	100.00%	100.00%

Common-Sized Balance Sheet (cont.)

	2001	2000	1999
Liabilities and equity			
Current liabilities			
Accounts payable	21.04%	17.01%	13.72%
Current long-term debt	5.98%	8.96%	10.71%
Accrued expenses	16.95%	14.85%	12.76%
Total current liabilities	43.97%	40.82%	37.18%
Long-term debt	18.15%	30.16%	37.42%
Total Liabilities	62.11%	70.98%	74.61%
Preferred stock	1.00%	1.13%	1.20%
Common stock	21.04%	18.71%	19.86%
Retained earnings	15.85%	9.18%	4.33%
Total shareholder's equity	37.89%	29.02%	25.39%
Total liability and equity	100.00%	100.00%	100.00%

Common-Sized Income Statement

	2001	2000	1999
Sales	100.00%	100.00%	100.00%
Cost of sales	− 81.11%	− 84.31%	− 85.62%
Gross profit	18.89%	15.69%	14.38%
Selling, general and admin. expenses	− 6.13%	− 6.67%	− 6.54%
Income before deprec. and amort.	12.75%	9.02%	7.84%
Depreciation and amortization	1.00%	1.02%	0.96%
Nonoperating income	1.19%	0.51%	− 0.21%
EBIT	14.95%	10.55%	8.60%
Interest expense	− 0.74%	− 1.18%	− 1.72%
Income before tax	14.21%	9.37%	6.88%
Taxes	− 6.78%	− 4.43%	− 3.48%
Net Income	7.43%	4.94%	3.40%

3.

Dupont Analysis	2001	2000	1999
Profit margin	7.43%	4.94%	3.40%
Total asset turnover	3.09	2.89	2.87
Equity multiplier	2.64	3.45	3.94
ROE	62.16%	51.22%	40.30%

Note: Since ROE is based on common stock only, include preferred stock with debt when computing total debt. This way the ROE found with Dupont will match the ROE computed using the equation.

4. Sales $6,125 million
   Gross profit $1,425 million
   Operating profit $ 975 million
   Net income $ 550 million
   Total assets $3,750 million
   Common equity $1,625 million

   ROE   33.85%
   ROA   14.67%
   Gross profit margin   23.27%
   Operating profit margin   15.92%
   Net profit margin   8.98%

5. Inventory $ 625 million
   Current assets $1,325 million
   Current liabilities $1,125 million

   Current ratio   1.18
   Quick ratio   0.62
   NWC $ 200 million

6. Accounts receivable $ 475 million
   Accounts payable $ 675 million
   Cost of Sales $4,700 million
   Fixed assets $2,425 million

   Inventory turnover   7.52 X
   Fixed asset turnover   2.53 X
   Total asset turnover   1.63 X
   Receivables turnover   12.89 X
   Avg. collection period   28.31 days
   Avg. payment period   52.42 days

7. Preferred stock $ 0 million
   Interest expense $60 million

   Debt ratio   56.67%
   Debt-equity ratio   61.54%
   TIE ratio   16.25X

8. # of shares outstanding   475 million
   Market price $52.50 per share

   EPS $1.16
   P/E ratio   45.34
   Book value $3.42
   Market-to-book ratio   15.35

9. Net income $ 975 million
   # of shares outstanding $ 850 million
   Market price per share $57.50
   Stockholder's equity $3,525 million

   Book value per share $4.15
   EPS $1.15
   P/E ratio   50.13
   Market-to-book ratio   13.85

10.

	2001	2000	1999
Sales	$1,500	$1,200	$975
Net income	$ 95	$ 70	$ 60
Total Assets	$ 775	$ 600	$450
Stockholder's equity	$ 240	$ 230	$225
Net profit margin	6.33%	5.83%	6.15%
Total asset turnover	1.94	2.00	2.17
Equity multiplier	3.23	2.61	2.00
ROE	39.58%	30.43%	26.67%

CHAPTER 15

Problems

1. a. 8.0624%
   b. $3,241,872.26
   c.

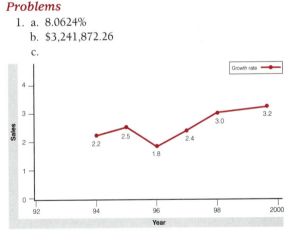

   d. Yes

e. No

f.

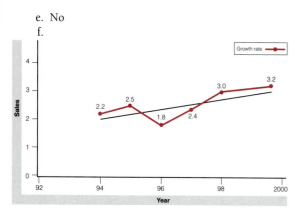

3. -$53

5. payout 8.11%, 5.26%, 11.11%;
   payout 17.65%, 11.11%, 25%;
   payout 12.68%, 8.11%, 17.65%

7. a. The growth rate would increase because the ROE would increase.

   b. The decrease in the ROE would cause the growth rate to also decrease.

   c. There is no change to the growth rate if the target debt ratio increases.

   d. If the dividend payout ratio falls, the growth rate will increase

9. Forcasted AFN $1,298 surplus $201.82 /AFN

11. a. -$28.125

    b. $258.35

	1996 factor	1997 1st Pass
Profit Margin	29%	30%
ROE	18%	22%
Debt/Asset Ratio	53%	52%
Current Ratio	.6491	.6996
Payout Ratio	75%	75%

	1996 factor	1997 1st Pass
	Forcasted AFN	$1,554.15
	Cum AFN	$1,554.15
Profit Margin	29%	30%
ROE	18%	22%
Debt/Asset Ratio	53%	48.84
Current Ratio	.6491	.6996
Payout Ratio	75%	75%

Self-Test Problems

1. a. Equation approach:
   Use Equation 15.1

$$\left(\frac{\$11{,}000}{\$15{,}000} \times \$5{,}250\right) - \left(\frac{\$6{,}000}{\$15{,}000} \times \$5{,}250\right) - [.2656 \times \$20{,}250 \times (1 - .5)] = \text{AFN}$$

$$\$3{,}850 - \$2100 - \$2{,}689.2 = -\$939.20$$

The equation method projects a surplus of $939.2. Note that the equation method and the balance sheet method will not give the same answer since the equation method does not allow for differing rates of growth in operating cost and spontaneous liabilities and assets.

b.

	2001 Adjustment		2002 Adjustment		2nd Pass 2002
Sales	$15,000.00	1.35	$20,250.00	1	$20,250.00
Operating cost	6,000.00	1.175	$ 7,050.00	1	$ 7,050.00
EBIT	9,000.00		13,200.00		13,200.00
Interest	2,360.00	1	2,360.00	(57.76)	2,302.24
EBT	6,640.00		10,840.00		10,897.76
Taxes	2,656.60		4,336.00		4,359.10
Net income	**$ 3,984.00**		**$ 6,504.00**		**$ 6,538.65**
Dividends (50%)	$ 1,992.00		$ 3,252.00		$ 3,269.33
Addition to R. E.	$ 1,992.00		$ 3,252.00		$17.33
Cash	$ 1,500.00	1.2625	$ 1,893.75	1	$ 1,893.75
Inventory	7,500.00	1.2625	$ 9,468.75	1	$ 9,468.75
Accounts Rec	2,000.00	1.2625	$ 2,525.00	1	$ 2,525.00
Net fixed assets	52,500.00	1	$52,500.00	1	$52,500.00
Total assets	**$63,500.00**		**$66,387.50**		**$66,387.50**
A/P and Accruals	6,000.00	1.2625	7,575.00	1	7,575.00
Notes/Payable (8%)	9,250.00	1	9,250.00	($339.75)	8,910.25
Long-term Debt (9%)	18,000.00	1	18,000.00	($339.75)	17,660.25
Common Stock	25,500.00	1	25,500.00	1	25,500.00
Retained earnings	4,750.00	$1,992.00	$ 6,742.00	$ 17.33	$ 6,759.33
Total Liab and Equity	**$63,500.00**		**$67,067.00**		**$66,404.83**
AFN (surplus)			**($679.50)**		**($17.33)**
Cum AFN					**($696.83)**

CHAPTER 16

Problems

1. $75
3. $200
5. 346.41
7. The available: $10,000; Book balance: $5,000; Net float: $5,000
9. $632,455.53
11. Effective Annual Rate (EAR): 44.32%; Annual percentage rate (APR): 36.87%; Take the discount

Self-Test Problems

1. 1,000 units
2. 3
3. 40,000 units
4. $175
5. $2
6. $5,000
7. 40 units

8. $2
9. 633 units
10. $1
11. $8
12. $50
13. $100
14. $1,300, $500
15. 68,000
16. $821,918
17. $14,142
18. $45,000
19. $23,095, $143,095, $127,698
20. $980

CHAPTER 17

Problems

1. a. 61.37 pounds
   b. 31,513.929 yen
   c. 741.75 francs
   d. $11.19
   e. $422.82
   f. 10,269.78 yen
3. 160 pesos
5. Depreciating
7. Contract for delivery of $275,000 reals which will cost $248,868.78

Self-Test Problems

1. 101.81 British Pounds
2. $5.08
3. 1500.32 Saudi Arabian Riyals
4. $387.90
5. 202,499.75 Columbian Pesos
6. 52.72 Indian Rupees
7. $64.10
8. 360.05 British Pounds
9. 8,026.04 Pakistan Rupees
10. $111.76
11. 47.79 Indian Rupees
12. 69.23 British Pounds
13. 941,119.12 Turkey Lira
14. 7.6632 Denmark Krone
15. 47.72 Indian Rupees
16. .6916 British Pounds
17. 714,527.99 Turkey Lira
18. 7.822 Denmark Krone

CHAPTER 18

Problems

1. Lease Option
3. a. $28.98
   b. 28,980,000
   c. $29.13
5. $473,530.68
7. $1,294,767.23

Self-Test Problems

1. 16.92%
2. $824,286
3. $1.37
4. $24.66
5. $14,796,000
6. 32.55%
7. $415,384.62
8. 18.6%
9. 1.25
10. $20,001
11. $5,920.40
12. $9499.82
13. $4,166
14. $30,326.40
15. $126,825

Glossary

accumulated depreciation: A periodic expense which reflects the decrease in value of an asset as it is used over time.

activity ratios: Used to measure the speed with which various accounts are converted into sales or cash.

agency costs: Costs borne by stockholders to prevent or minimize agency problems and to contribute to the maximization of the owners' wealth. They include monitoring and bonding expenditures, opportunity costs, and structuring expenditures.

Aging schedule: A schedule used to evaluate credit and/or collection policies that shows the proportion of the accounts receivable balance that has been outstanding for a specified period of time.

annual compounding: A method of computing future value where interest is earned on interest that is paid each year.

annuity due: An annuity for which the payments occur at the beginning of each period.

annuity: A stream of equal annual cash flows. These cash flows can be inflows of returns earned on investments or outflows of funds invested to earn future returns.

appreciation: An increase in value as when a currency increases in value relative to another currency.

asymmetric information: The situation in which managers of a firm have more information about operations and future prospects than do investors.

auction market: Markets for securities where prices are publicly announced and posted. Organized markets such as the NYSE are auction markets.

balance sheet: Summary statement of the firm's financial position at a given point in time.

balloon payment: At the maturity of a loan, a large lump-sum payment representing the entire loan principal if the periodic payments represent only interest.

banker's acceptances: Short-term, low-risk marketable securities arising from bank guarantees of business transactions; are sold by banks at a discount from their maturity value and provide yields slightly below those on negotiable CDs and commercial paper, but higher than those on U.S. Treasury issues.

bank holding company: A company that owns stock in one or more banks. The bank holding company may own other conpanies in addition to banks.

bank note: Banks issued notes before the Federal government that were used as currency. These bank notes were backed only by deposits held at the bank.

Baumol model: A model that provides for cost-efficient transactional cash balances; assumes that the demand for cash can be predicted with certainty and determines the economic conversion quantity (ECQ).

beta coefficient: A measure of nondiversifiable risk. An index of the degree of movement of an asset's return in response to a change in the market return.

bid price: Dealers will buy securities from investors at the bid price and will sell to investors at the ask price. The bid price is below the ask.

book value per share: The amount per share of common stock to be received if all of the firm's assets are sold for their book value and if the proceeds remaining after payment of all liabilities (including preferred stock) are divided among the common stockholders.

break point: The level of total new financing at which the cost of one of the financing components rises, thereby causing an upward shift in the weighted marginal cost of capital (WMCC).

business risk: The risk to the firm of being unable to cover operating costs.

business cycle: The economy has historically ebbed and flowed over time. The average time between peaks and slowdowns has been about 7 years.

capital asset pricing model (CAPM): Describes the relationship between the required return, or cost of common stock equity capital, and the nondiversifiable risk of the firm as measured by the beta coefficient.

capital budgeting process: Consists of five distinct but interrelated steps: proposal generation, review and analysis, decision making, implementation, and follow-up.

capital budgeting: A method for evaluating long-term investment opportunities where all cash flows are discounted to the present.

capital rationing: The financial situation in which a firm has only a fixed number of dollars for allocation among competing capital expenditures.

capital structure: The mix of long-term debt and equity maintained by the firm.

capital yield: The portion of the return an investor receives from an increase in the value of a security.

capitalized lease: A financial (capital) lease that has the present value of all its payments included as an asset and corresponding liability on the firm's balance sheet, as required by Financial Accounting Standards Board (FASB) Standard No. 13.

carrying costs: The variable costs per unit of holding an item in inventory for a specified time period.

cash budget (cash forecast): A statement of the firm's planned inflows and outflows of cash that is used to estimate its short-term cash requirements.

certainty equivalents (CEs): Risk-adjustment factors that represent the percent of estimated cash inflows that investors would be satisfied to receive for certain rather than the cash inflows that are possible for each year.

characteristic line: Beta is the slope of the characteristic line. The line is drawn to relate the return on a market portfolio to the return on a specific asset.

coefficient of variation (CV): A measure of relative dispersion used in comparing the risk of assets with differing expected returns.

collection float: The delay between the time when a payer or customer deducts a payment from its checking account ledger and the time when the payee or vendor actually receives the funds in a spendable form.

commercial paper: A short-term, unsecured promissory note issued by a corporation that has a very high credit standing, having a yield above that paid on U.S. Treasury issues and comparable to that available on negotiable CDs with similar maturities.

common-size income statement: An income statement in which each item is expressed as a percentage of sales.

compensating balance: A required checking account balance equal to a certain percentage of the borrower's short-term unsecured bank loan.

compounding: The process of computing future values where interest is earned on paid interest.

compounded return: A return that recognizes that interest has been earned on paid interest.

compounded interest: Interest earned on a given deposit that has become part of the principal at the end of a specified period.

concentration banking: A collection procedure in which payments are made to regionally dispersed collection centers, then deposited in local banks for quick clearing. Reduces collection float by shortening mail and clearing float.

corporate bond: A certificate indicating that a corporation has borrowed a certain amount of money from an institution or an individual and promises to repay it in the future under clearly defined terms.

corporate finance: An area of study in the field of finance that focuses on issues of importance to businesses, such as project evaluation, ratio analysis, and capital structure.

credit policy: The determination of credit selection, credit standards, and credit terms.

cross-sectional analysis: The comparison of different firms' financial ratios at the same point in time; involves comparing the firm's ratios to those of an industry leader or to industry averages.

current yield: A yield computed as the interest paid on a bond divided by the current price of the bond.

dealer markets: Markets where dealers take ownership of securities and make a market by buying or selling securities to and from investors.

Depository Institutions Deregulation and Monetary Control Act of 1980 (DIDMCA): Signaled the beginning of the "financial services revolution" by eliminating interest-rate ceilings on all accounts and permitting certain institutions to offer new types of accounts and services.

deeper markets: Markets that are active so that many securities can be quickly and easily sold.

deferred annuity: A series of equal payments which does not begin immediately, rather begins at some future date.

depository institutions: Financial institutions which accept deposits from customers and allow checks to be written against the deposits.

depreciation: The systematic charging of a portion of the costs of fixed assets against annual revenues over time.

disbursement float: The lapse between the time when a firm deducts a payment from its checking account ledger (disburses it) and the time when funds are actually withdrawn from its account.

discount loans: Loans on which interest is paid in advance by deducting it from the amount borrowed.

discount: The amount by which a bond sells at a value that is less than its par, or face, value.

discount rate: The rate of interest used to compute the present value of a cash flow.

discounting cash flows: The process of finding present values; the inverse of compounding interest.

diversification: The process of investing in a variety of different stocks or securities.

diversifiable risk: The portion of an asset's risk that is attributable to firm-specific, random causes; can be eliminated through diversification.

dividend yield: That portion of the return that comes from the payment of dividends. The balance of the yield comes from capital gains.

dual banking system: The chartering of banks by both Federal authorities and state authorities.

DuPont formula: Relates the firm's net profit margin and total asset turnover to its return on total assets (ROA). The ROA is the product of the net profit margin and the total asset turnover.

DuPont system of analysis: Used by management as a framework for dissecting the firm's financial statements and assessing its financial condition.

EBIT-EPS approach: An approach for selecting the capital structure that maximizes earnings per share (EPS) over the expected range of earnings before interest and taxes (EBIT).

economic order quantity (EOQ) model: An inventory management technique for determining an item's optimal order quantity, which is the one that minimizes the total of its order and carrying costs.

effective (true) interest rate: The rate of interest actually paid or earned; in personal finance, commonly called the annual percentage rate (APR).

efficient market hypothesis: Theory describing the behavior of an assumed "perfect" market in which securities are typically in equilibrium, security prices fully reflect all public information available and react swiftly to new information, and, since stocks are fairly priced, investors need not waste time looking for mispriced securities. A market that allocates funds to their most productive uses as a result of competition among wealth-maximizing investors that determines and publicizes prices that are believed to be close to their true value. An assumed "perfect" market in which there are many small investors, each having the same information and expectations with respect to securities; there are no restrictions on investment, no taxes, and no transaction costs; and all investors are rational, they view securities similarly, and they are risk-averse, preferring higher returns and lower risk.

efficient portfolio: A portfolio that maximizes return for a given level of risk or minimizes risk for a given level of return.

electronic funds transfer: A method of moving funds from one bank to another by wire.

Eurobond: A bond issued by an international borrower and sold to investors in countries with currencies other than the currency in which the bond is denominated. An international bond that is sold primarily in countries other than the country of the currency in which the issue is denominated.

Eurodollar deposits: Deposits of currency not native to the country in which the bank is located; negotiable, usually pay interest at maturity, and are typically denominated in units of $1 million. Provide yields above nearly all other marketable securities with similar maturities.

equal annual annuity: A method to adjusted capital budgeting analysis for different lives by converting each option into a perpetuity.

exchange rate: The factor that is used to convert the value of one currency into another currency.

expected return: The return that is expected to be earned each period on a given asset over an infinite time horizon.

Federal deposit insurance corporation: The agency that administers the insurance program that protects depositors at banks from losses due to bank failure.

federal funds: Loan transactions between commercial banks in which the Federal Reserve banks become involved.

finance: The art and science of managing money.

finance company: A firm that lends money to consumers, usually for the purchase of a product offered by a related company (example—General Motors Acceptance Company)

financial (or capital) lease: A longer-term lease than an operating lease that is noncancelable and obligates the lessee to make payments for the use of an asset over a predefined period of time; the total payments over the term of the lease are greater than the lessor's initial cost of the leased asset.

financial analysis: A general term referring to a variety of methods for analyzing investment opportunities and company strength.

financial institution: An intermediary that channels the savings of individuals, businesses, and governments into loans or investments.

financial leverage: The magnification of risk and return introduced through the use of fixed-cost financing such as debt and preferred stock. The potential use of fixed financial costs to magnify the effects of changes in earning before interest and taxes (EBIT) on the firm's earnings per share (EPS).

financial markets: Provide a forum in which suppliers of funds and demanders of loans and investments can transact business directly.

financial planning: Planning that begins with long-term (strategic) financial plans that in turn guide the formulation of short-term (operating) plans and budgets.

financial risk: The risk to the firm of being unable to cover required financial obligations (interest, lease payments, preferred stock dividends.)

financial ratios: Ratios that convert balance sheet and income statement data into standardized values that can be compared across time and to other firms.

financial system: Banks, investors, borrowers, firms and exchanges that are all involved in the process of moving funds from those with an excess to those who can put it to work make up the financial system.

firm specific risk: The risk peculiar to a particular firm, such as management quality and strikes, that can be eliminated by diversifying across many firms.

flotation costs: The total costs of issuing and selling a security.

forward exchange rate: The rate of exchange between two currencies at some specified future date.

forward transaction: A financial arrangement where prices or exchange rates are agreed upon in the present for an exchange that will occur in the future.

future value: The value of a present amount at a future date found by applying compound interest over a specified period of time.

Gordon growth model: A common name for the constant growth model that is widely cited in dividend valuation.

generalized dividend theory: The theory that the value of stock is computed as the present value of all future dividends the firm will pay.

going public: The process where a corporation owned by a limited number of investors offers shares of stock to the general public.

holding period return: The return earned on an investment since its inception, not annualized.

income statement: Provides a financial summary of the firm's operating results during a specified period.

indenture: A contract that accompanies a bond that spells out the details of the terms, conditions, and limitations surrounding the bond.

initial cash flow: The relevant cash outflow for a proposed project at time zero.

interstate banking: A relatively recent trend where a bank expands across state lines.

interest rate premium: An additional return earned by an investor for accepting an investment with unwanted conditions, such as a call previous or a long time until maturity.

interest rate parity: A theory that interest rates around the world will adjust so that investors will earn the same return, regardless where they invest.

initial public offering: The first time that a security is offered to the public for sale.

interest rate risk: The chance of a loss due to changing interest rates affecting the value of a security.

internal growth rate: The maximum rate of growth a firm can maintain without the use of outside financing.

internal rate of return (IRR): The discount rate that equates the present value of cash inflows with the initial investment associated with a project, thereby causing NPV = \$0.

inverted yield curve: A downward-sloping yield curve that indicates generally cheaper long-term borrowing costs than short-term borrowing costs.

investment banker: A financial intermediary that purchases securities from corporate and government issuers and resells them to the general public in the primary market.

investments: An area of study in finance that focuses on how dollars invested today can be used to earn dollars in the future.

investment company: A firm that receives money from many people and invests it on their behalf.

investment opportunities schedule (IOS): A ranking of investment possibilities from best (highest returns) to worst (lowest returns). The graph that plots project IRRs in descending order against total dollar investment.

investment strategy: The method an investor may choose to follow when investing that considers risk, return, and timing.

law of one price: A theory that says the forces of supply and demand should cause the prices of goods to adjust around the world so that a product costs the same.

life insurance: An insurance product that pays beneficiaries when the insured dies.

liquidity preference theory: Theory suggesting that for any given issuer, long-term interest rates tend to be higher than short-term rates due to the lower liquidity and higher responsiveness to general interest rate movements of longer-term securities; causes the yield curve to be upward-sloping.

liquidity: A firm's ability to satisfy its short-term obligations as they come due.

liquidity ratios: ratios that examine how able a firm is to pay its current liabilities.

load fund: A fund that charges a fee when funds are either deposited or withdrawn.

lockbox system: A collection procedure in which payers send their payments to a nearby post office box that is emptied by the firm's bank several times daily; the bank deposits the payment checks in the firm's account. Reduces collection float by shortening processing float as well as mail and clearing float.

London Interbank Offered Rate (LIBOR): The base rate that is used to price all Eurocurrency loans.

market maker: A dealer who either buys or sells securities so that there is always a market for them, thus increasing the liquidity of the markets.

market order: An order placed with a broker to purchase securities where the buyer will pay whatever the price of the securities currently is.

market ratios: Ratios that are based on the firm's security prices, such as stock price.

market risk: The risk of a security that cannot be diversified away and reflects how the securities price fluctuates with the market. Market risk is also called systematic risk and nondiversifiable risk.

maximum sustainable growth rate: That rate of growth that a firm can maintain without adding equity capital nor changing its capital structure.

marginal cost of capital schedule: A graph or table that shows the cost of obtaining an additional dollar of financing.

Miller-Orr model: A model that provides for cost-efficient transactional cash balances; assumes uncertain cash flows and determines an upper limit and return point for cash balances.

money market mutual funds: Professionally managed portfolios of various popular marketable securities, having instant liquidity, competitive yields, and low transaction costs.

municipal bonds: Bonds issued by municipalities, many of which are exempt from state and federal taxation on their earnings.

negotiable certificates of deposit (CDs): Negotiable instruments representing specific cash deposits in commercial banks, having varying maturities and yields based on size, maturity, and prevailing money market conditions. Yields are generally above those on U.S. Treasury issues and comparable to those on commercial paper with similar maturities.

net present value (NPV): A sophisticated capital budgeting technique; found by subtracting a project's initial investment from the present value of its cash inflows discounted at a rate equal to the firm's cost of capital.

net present value profiles: Graphs that depict the net present value of a project for various discount rates.

no-load fund: A mutual fund that does not charge a fee for either making deposits or withdrawals.

nominal rate of interest: The actual rate of interest charged by the supplier of funds and paid by the demander. In the international context, the stated interest rate charged on financing when only the MNC parent's currency is involved.

nondiversifiable risk: The relevant portion of an asset's risk attributable to market factors that affect all firms; cannot be eliminated through diversification.

nonnotification basis: The basis on which a borrower, having pledged an account receivable, continues to collect the account payments without notifying the account customer.

open end fund: A fund that accepts deposits constantly. This is contrasted with a closed end fund that sells a fixed number of shares like a conventional stock corporation.

operating lease: A cancelable contractual arrangement whereby the lessee agrees to make periodic payments to the lessor, often for five or fewer years, for an asset's services; generally, the total payments over the term of the lease are less than the lessor's initial cost of the leased asset.

operating leverage: The potential use of fixed operating costs to magnify the effects of changes in sales on the firm's earnings before interest and taxes (EBIT).

opportunity cost: The returns that are given up by choosing one option over another.

ordinary annuity: An annuity for which the payments occur at the end of each period.

organized securities market: Tangible organizations that act as secondary markets in which outstanding securities are resold.

over-the-counter (OTC) exchange: Not an organization but an intangible market for the purchase and sale of securities not listed by the organized exchanges.

payback period: The exact amount of time required for a firm to recover its initial investment in a project as calculated from cash inflows.

pension fund: A fund established to hold investments until an individual retires.

portfolio: A collection, or group, of assets.

precautionary motives: Cash balances and inventories that are held which are greater than are usually required to protect against unforseen needs.

present value: The current dollar value of a future amount. The amount of money that would have to be invested today at a given interest rate over a specified period to equal the future amount.

price/earnings (P/E) ratio: Reflects the amount investors are willing to pay for each dollar of the firm's earnings; the higher the P/E ratio, the greater the investor confidence in the firm.

premium: Bonds selling at a premium are selling for a price above their par value.

primary market: Financial market in which securities are initially issued; the only market in which the issuer is directly involved in the transaction.

privately owned stock: All common stock of a firm owned by a single individual.

profitability analysis: An analysis of those ratios that relate to profit margins and the earnings of the firm.

profitability index: A ratio formed by dividing the present value of the cash inflows from a project by the present value of the cash outflows.

property and casualty insurance: Insurance that protects against losses to property and against damage.

prospectus: A portion of a security registration statement filed with the SEC that details the firm's operating and financial position; it must be made available to all potential buyers.

proxy battle: The attempt by a nonmanagement group to gain control of the management of a firm through the solicitation of a sufficient number of proxy votes.

proxy statement: A statement giving the votes of a stockholder or stockholders to another party.

public offering: The nonexclusive sale of either bonds or stock to the general public.

publicly held corporations: Corporations whose stock is traded on either an organized securities exchange or the over-the-counter exchange and/or those with more than $5 million in assets and 500 or more stockholders.

publicly owned stock: Common stock of a firm owned by a broad group of unrelated individual and (or) institutional investors.

purchase options: Provisions frequently included in both operating and financial leases that allow the lessee to purchase the leased asset at maturity, typically for a prespecified price.

put option: An option to sell a given number of shares of a stock (typically 100) on or before a specified future date at a stated striking price.

putable bonds: See Table 12.4.

pyramiding: An arrangement among holding companies wherein one holding company controls other holding companies, thereby causing an even greater magnification of earnings and losses.

quarterly compounding: Compounding of interest over four periods within the year.

quick (acid-test) ratio: A measure of liquidity calculated by dividing the firm's current assets minus inventory by current liabilities.

range: A measure of an asset's risk, which is found by subtracting the pessimistic (worst) outcome from the optimistic (best) outcome.

ranking approach: The ranking of capital expenditure projects on the basis of some predetermined measure such as the rate of return.

ratio analysis: Involves the methods of calculating and interpreting financial ratios to assess the firm's performance and status.

ratio of exchange in market price: The ratio of the market price per share of the acquiring firm paid to each dollar of market price per share of the target firm.

ratio of exchange: The ratio of the amount paid per share of the target company to the per-share market price of the acquiring firm.

raw materials inventory: Items purchased by the firm for use in the manufacture of a finished product.

real rate of interest: The rate that creates an equilibrium between the supply of savings and the demand for investment funds in a perfect world, without inflation, where funds suppliers and demanders have no liquidity preference and all outcomes are certain.

recapitalization: The reorganization procedure under which a failed firm's debts are generally exchanged for equity or the maturities of existing debts are extended.

recaptured depreciation: The portion of the sale price that is above book value and below the initial purchase price.

recovery period: The appropriate depreciable life of a particular asset as determined by MACRS.

red herring: On a prospectus, a statement, printed in red ink, indicating the tentative nature of a security offer while it is being reviewed by the SEC.

red-line method: Unsophisticated inventory management technique in which a reorder is placed when sufficient use of inventory items from a bin exposes a red line drawn inside the bin.

regular dividend policy: A dividend policy based on the payment of a fixed-dollar dividend in each period.

relevant cash flows: The incremental after-tax cash outflow (investment) and resulting subsequent inflows associated with a proposed capital expenditure.

renewal options: Provisions especially common in operating leases that grant the lessee the option to release assets at their expiration.

reorder point: The point at which to reorder inventory, expressed equationally as: lead time in days × daily usage.

repurchase agreement: An agreement whereby a bank of securities dealers sells a firm specific securities and agrees to repurchase them at a specific price and time.

required return: A specified return required each period by investors for a given level of risk. The cost of funds obtained by selling an ownership (or equity) interest; it reflects the funds supplier's level of expected return.

required total financing: Amount of funds needed by the firm if the ending cash for the period is less than the desired minimum cash balance; typically represented by notes payable.

residual theory of dividends: A theory that the dividend paid by a firm should be the amount left over after all acceptable investment opportunities have been undertaken.

restrictive covenants: Contractual clauses in long-term debt agreement that place certain operating and financial constraints on the borrower.

retained earnings: The cumulative total of all earnings, net of dividends, that have been retained and reinvested in the firm since its inception.

return on equity (ROE): Measures the return earned on the owners' (both preferred and common stockholders') investment in the firm.

return on total assets (ROA): Measures the overall effectiveness of management in generating profits with its available assets; also called return on investment.

return: The total gain or loss experienced on behalf of the owner of an investment over a given period of time; calculated by dividing the asset's change in value plus any cash distributions during the period by its beginning-of-period investment value.

reverse stock split: A method that is used to raise the market price of a firm's stock by exchanging a certain number of outstanding shares for one new share of stock.

revolving credit agreement: A line of credit guaranteed to the borrower by the bank for a stated time period and regardless of the scarcity of money.

risk premium: The amount by which the required discount rate for a project exceeds the risk-free rate.

risk-adjusted discount rate (RADR): The rate of return that must be earned on a given project to compensate the firm's owners adequately, thereby resulting in the maintenance or improvement of share price.

risk-averse: The attitude toward risk in which an increased return would be required for an increase in risk.

risk-free rate of interest, RF: The required return on a risk-free asset, typically a three-month U.S. Treasury bill.

risk-free rate: The rate of return that one would earn on a virtually riskless investment such as a U.S. Treasury Bill.

risk-indifferent: The attitude toward risk in which no change in return would be required for an increase in risk.

risk-return tradeoff: The expectation that for accepting greater risk, investors must be compensated with greater returns.

risk-seeking: The attitude toward risk in which a decreased return would be accepted for an increase in risk.

risk: The chance of financial loss, or more formally, the variability of returns associated with a given asset: The chance that actual outcomes may differ from those expected. The probability that a firm will be unable to pay its bills as they come due.

S corporation: A tax-reporting entity whose earnings are taxed not as a corporation but as the incomes of its stockholders, thus avoiding the usual double taxation on corporate earnings.

safety motive: A motive for holding cash or near-cash—to protect the firm against being unable to satisfy unexpected demands for cash.

safety of principal: The ease of salability of a security for close to its initial value.

safety stocks: Extra inventories that can be drawn down when actual lead times and/or usage rates are greater than expected.

sale-leaseback arrangement: A lease under which the lessee sells an asset for cash to a prospective lessor and then leases back the same asset, making fixed periodic payments for its use.

sales forecast: The prediction of the firm's sales over a given period, based on external and/or internal data, and used as the key input to the short-term financial planning process.

scenario analysis: A behavioral approach that evaluates the impact on return of simultaneous changes in a number of variables.

seasonal need: Financing requirements for temporary current assets, which vary over the year.

secondary market: Financial market in which pre-owned securities (those that are not new issues) are traded.

secured creditors: Creditors who have specific assets pledged as collateral and in liquidation of the failed firm receive proceeds from the sale of those assets.

secured loan: A loan that has specific assets pledged as collateral.

secured short-term financing: Short-term financing (loans) obtained by pledging specific assets as collateral.

Securities and Exchange Commission (SEC): The federal regulatory body that governs the sale and listing of securities.

securities exchanges: Organizations that provide the marketplace in which firms can raise funds through the sale of new securities and purchasers can resell securities.

security agreement: The agreement between the borrower and the lender that specifies the collateral held against a secured loan.

security market line (SML): The depiction of the capital asset pricing model (CAPM) as a graph that reflects the required return for each level of nondiversifiable risk (beta).

selling group: A group of brokerage firms, each of which agrees to sell a portion of a security issue and expects to make a profit on the spread between the price at which they buy and sell the securities.

semiannual compounding: Compounding of interest over two periods within the year.

sensitivity analysis: A behavioral approach for assessing risk that uses a number of possible return estimates to obtain a sense of the variability among outcomes.

serial bonds: An issue of bonds for which a certain proportion matures each year.

shark repellents: Antitakeover amendments to a corporate charter that constrain the firm's ability to transfer managerial control of the firm as a result of a merger.

shelf registration: An SEC procedure that allows firms with more than $150 million in outstanding common stock to file a "master registration statement" covering a two-year period and then, during that period, to sell securities that have already been approved under the master statement.

short-term (operating) financial plans: Planned short-term financial actions and the anticipated financial impact of those actions.

short-term financial management: Management of current assets and current liabilities.

short-term self-liquidating loan: An unsecured short-term loan in which the use to which the borrowed money is put provides the mechanism through which the loan is repaid.

signal: A financing action by management that is believed to reflect its view with respect to the firm's stock value; generally, debt financing is viewed as a positive signal that management believes that the stock is "undervalued," and a stock issue is viewed as a negative signal that management believes that the stock is "overvalued."

simulation: A statistically based behavioral approach used in capital budgeting to get a feel for risk by applying predetermined probability distributions and random numbers to estimate risky outcomes.

single-payment note: A short-term, one-time loan payable as a single amount at its maturity.

sinking-fund requirement: A restrictive provision that is often included in a bond indenture providing for the systematic retirement of bonds prior to their maturity.

small (ordinary) stock dividend: A stock dividend that represents less than 20 to 25 percent of the common stock outstanding at the time the dividend is declared.

sole proprietorship: A business owned by one person and operated for his or her own profit.

speculative motive: A motive for holding cash or near-cash—to put unneeded funds to work or to be able to quickly take advantage of unexpected opportunities that may arise.

spin-off: A form of divestiture in which an operating unit becomes an independent company by issuing shares in it on a pro rata basis to the parent company's shareholders.

sponsored ADR: An ADR for which the issuing (foreign) company absorbs the legal and financial costs of creating and trading a security.

spontaneous financing: Financing that arises from the normal operations of the firm, the two major short-term sources of which are accounts payable and accruals.

spot exchange rate: The rate of exchange between two currencies on any given day.

spread: The difference between the price paid for a security by the investment banker and the sale price.

staggered funding: A way to play the float by depositing a certain proportion of a payroll or payment into the firm's checking account on several successive days following the actual issuance of checks.

stakeholder: Groups such as employees, customers, suppliers, creditors, and others who have a direct economic link to the firm.

standard debt provisions: Provisions in long-term debt agreements specifying certain criteria of satisfactory record keeping and reporting, tax payment, and general business maintenance on the part of the borrowing firm; normally, they do not place a burden on the financially sound business.

standard deviation: The most common statistical indicator of an asset's risk; it measures the dispersion around the expected value.

standby arrangement: A formal guarantee that any shares that are not subscribed or sold publicly will be purchased by the investment banker.

statement of cash flows: Provides a summary of the firm's operating, investment, and financing cash flows and reconciles them with changes in its cash and marketable securities during the period of concern.

statement of retained earnings: Reconciles the net income earned during a given year and any cash dividends paid with the change in retained earnings between the start and end of that year.

stock dividend: The payment to existing owners of a dividend in the form of stock.

stock options: An incentive allowing management to purchase stock at the market price set at the time of the grant. Options, generally extended to management, that permit purchase of the firm's common stock at a specified price over a stated period of time.

stock repurchase: The repurchasing by the firm of outstanding shares of its common stock in the marketplace; desired effects of stock repurchases are that they enhance shareholder value and/or help to discourage unfriendly takeovers.

stock rights: Provide stockholders with the privilege to purchase additional shares of stock in direct proportion to their number of owned shares.

stock split: A method that is commonly used to lower the market price of a firm's stock by increasing the number of shares belonging to each shareholder.

stock swap transaction: An acquisition method in which the acquiring firm exchanges its shares for shares of the target company according to a predetermined ratio.

stock-purchase plans: An employee fringe benefit that allows the purchase of a firm's stock at a discount or on a matching basis with a part of the cost absorbed by the firm.

stock-purchase warrant: An instrument that gives its holder the right to purchase a certain number of shares of common stock at a specified price over a certain period of time.

stockholders' report: Annual report required of publicly held corporations that summarizes and documents for stockholders the firm's financial activities during the past year.

stockholders: The true owners of the firm by virtue of their equity in the form of preferred and common stock.

straight bond value: The price at which a convertible bond would sell in the market without the conversion feature.

straight bond: A bond that is nonconvertible, having no conversion feature.

straight preferred stock: Preferred stock that is nonconvertible, having no conversion feature.

strategic merger: A merger transaction undertaken to achieve economies of scale.

stretching accounts payable: Paying bills as late as possible without damaging one's credit rating.

striking price: The price at which the holder of a call option can buy (or the holder of a put option can sell) a specified amount of stock at any time before the option's expiration date.

subordinated debentures: See Table 12.3.

subordination: In a long-term debt agreement, the stipulation that all subsequent or less important creditors agree to wait until all claims of the senior debt are satisfied before having their claims satisfied.

subscription price: The price at which stock rights are exercisable for a specified period of time; is set below the prevailing market price.

subsidiaries: The companies controlled by a holding company.

supervoting shares: Stock that carries with it more votes per share than a share of regular common stock.

takeover defenses: Strategies for fighting hostile takeovers.

target capital structure: The desired optimal mix of debt and equity financing that most firms attempt to achieve and maintain.

target company: The firm in a merger transaction that the acquiring company is pursuing.

target dividend-payout ratio: A policy under which the firm attempts to pay out a certain percentage of earnings as a stated dollar dividend, which it adjusts toward a target payout as proven earnings increases occur.

target weights: Either book or market value weights based on desired capital structure proportions; used in calculating the weighted average cost of capital.

tax loss carryback/carryforward: A tax benefit that allows corporations experiencing operating losses to carry tax losses back up to 3 years and forward for as many as 15 years. In a merger, the tax loss of one of the firms that can be applied against a limited amount of future income of the merged firm either over 15 years or until the total tax loss has been fully recovered, whichever is shorter.

tax on sale of old asset: Tax that depends upon the relationship between the old asset's sale price, initial purchase price, and book value.

technical insolvency: Business failure that occurs when a firm is unable to pay its liabilities as they come due.

tender offer: A formal offer to purchase a given number of shares of a firm's stock at a specified price.

term (long-term) loan: A loan made by a financial institution to a business and having an initial maturity of more than one year.

term loan agreement: A formal contract, ranging from a few to a few hundred pages, specifying the conditions under which a financial institution has made a long-term loan.

term structure of interest rates: The relationship between the interest rate and the time to maturity.

terminal cash flow: The after-tax nonoperating cash flow occurring in the final year of a project, usually attributable to liquidation of the project.

time line: A horizontal line on which time zero is at the leftmost end and future periods are shown as you move from left to right; can be used to depict investment cash flows.

time-series analysis: Evaluation of the firm's financial performance over time utilizing financial ratio analysis.

times interest earned ratio: Measures the firm's ability to make contractual interest payments.

total asset turnover: Indicates the efficiency with which the firm uses all its assets to gene rate sales.

total cost: The sum of the order costs and carrying costs of inventory.

total leverage: The potential use of fixed costs, both operating and financial, to magnify the effect of changes in sales on the firm's earnings per share (EPS).

total quality management (TQM): The application of quality principles to all aspects of a company's operations.

total risk: The combination of a security's nondiversifiable and diversifiable risk.

transactions motive: A motive for holding cash or near-cash—to make planned payments for items such as materials and wages.

transfer prices: Prices that subsidiaries charge each other for the goods and services traded between them.

treasurer: The officer responsible for the firm's financial activities, such as financial planning and fund raising, making capital expenditure decisions, managing cash, managing credit activities, and managing the pension fund.

Treasury bills: U.S. Treasury obligations issued weekly on an auction basis, having varying maturities, generally under a year, and virtually no risk.

Treasury notes: U.S. Treasury obligations with initial maturities of between one and ten years, paying interest at a stated rate semiannually, and having virtually no risk.

treasury stock: The number of shares of outstanding stock that have been repurchased and held by the firm; shown on the firm's balance sheet as a deduction from stockholders' equity.

trust receipt inventory loan: An agreement under which the lender advances 80 to 100 percent of the cost of the borrower's relatively expensive inventory items in exchange for the borrower's promise to immediately repay the loan, with accrued interest, upon the sale of each item.

trustee: A paid individual, corporation, or commercial bank trust department that acts as the third party to a bond indenture to ensure that the issuer does not default on its contractual responsibilities to the bondholders.

two-tier offer: A tender offer in which the terms offered are more attractive to those who tender shares early.

U.S. Treasury bills (T-bills): Short-term IOUs issued by the U.S. Treasury; considered the risk-free asset.

uncorrelated: Describes two series that lack any relationship or interaction and therefore have a correlation coefficient close to zero.

underpriced: Stock sold at a price below its current market price.

undersubscribed issue: A security issue whose shares are not immediately sold.

underwriting syndicate: A group of investment banking firms, each of which will underwrite a portion of a large security issue, thus lessening the risk of loss to any single firm.

underwriting: The process in which an investment banker buys a security issue from the issuing firm at a lower price than that for which he or she plans to sell it, thereby guaranteeing the issuer a specified amount from the issue and assuming the risk of price changes between the time of purchase and the time of sale.

unitary tax laws: Laws in some U.S. states that tax multinationals (both American and foreign) on a percentage of their total worldwide income rather than the usual taxation of the MNCs' earnings arising within their jurisdiction.

unlimited funds: The financial situation in which a firm is able to accept all independent projects that provide an acceptable return.

unlimited liability: The condition imposed by a sole proprietorship (or general partnership) allowing the owner's total wealth to be taken to satisfy creditors.

unsecured loan: A loan that has no assets pledged as collateral.

unsecured short-term financing: Short-term financing obtained without pledging specific assets as collateral.

unsecured, or general, creditors: Creditors who have a general claim against all the firm's assets other than those specifically pledged as collateral.

valuation: The process that links risk and return to determine the worth of an asset.

value dating: A procedure used by non-U.S. banks to delay, often for days or even weeks, the availability of funds deposited with them.

variable growth model: A dividend valuation approach that allows for a change in the dividend growth rate.

vertical merger: A merger in which a firm acquires a supplier or a customer.

voluntary reorganization: A petition filed by a failed firm on its own behalf for reorganizing its structure and paying its creditors.

voluntary settlement: An arrangement between a technically insolvent or bankrupt firm and its creditors enabling it to bypass many of the costs involved in legal bankruptcy proceedings.

warehouse receipt loan: An arrangement in which the lender receives control of the pledged inventory collateral, which is warehoused by a designated agent on the lender's behalf.

warrant premium: The difference between the actual market value and theoretical value of a warrant.

weighted average cost of capital (WACC): Reflects the expected average future cost of funds over the long run; determined by weighting the cost of each specific type of capital by its proportion in the firm's capital structure.

weighted marginal cost of capital (WMCC) schedule: Graph that relates the firm's weighted average cost of capital (WACC) to the level of total new financing.

weighted marginal cost of capital (WMCC): The firm's weighted average cost of capital (WACC) associated with its next dollar of total new financing.

white knight: A takeover defense in which the target firm finds an acquirer more to its liking than the initial hostile acquirer and prompts the two to compete to take over the firm.

wire transfers: Telegraphic communications that, via bookkeeping entries, remove funds from the payer's bank and deposit them into the payee's bank, thereby reducing collection float.

work-in-process inventory: All items that are currently in production.

working capital: Current assets, which represent the portion of investment that circulates from one form to another in the ordinary conduct of business.

yield curve: A graph of the term structure of interest rates that depicts the relationship between the yield to maturity of a security (y-axis) and the time to maturity (x-axis); it shows the pattern of interest rates on securities of equal quality and different maturity.

yield to maturity (YTM): The rate of return investors earn if they buy a bond at a specific price and hold it until maturity. Assumes that issuer makes all scheduled interest and principal payments as promised. Annual rate of interest earned on a security purchased on a given day and held to maturity.

zero-balance account: A checking account in which a zero balance is maintained and the firm is required to deposit funds to cover checks drawn on the account only as they are presented for payment.

zero-growth model: An approach to dividend valuation that assumes a constant, nongrowing dividend stream.

Index

TABLE A3 Present Value of $1 (PVIF)

Period	1%	2%	3%	4%	5%	6%	7%	8%	9%	10%	12%	14%	15%	16%	18%	20%	25%	30%
1	.990	.980	.971	.962	.952	.943	.935	.926	.917	.909	.893	.877	.870	.862	.847	.833	.800	.769
2	.980	.961	.943	.925	.907	.890	.873	.857	.842	.826	.797	.769	.756	.743	.718	.694	.640	.592
3	.971	.942	.915	.889	.864	.840	.816	.794	.772	.751	.712	.675	.658	.641	.609	.579	.512	.455
4	.961	.924	.888	.855	.823	.792	.763	.735	.708	.683	.636	.592	.572	.552	.516	.482	.410	.350
5	.951	.906	.863	.822	.784	.747	.713	.681	.650	.621	.567	.519	.497	.476	.437	.402	.328	.269
6	.942	.888	.837	.790	.746	.705	.666	.630	.596	.564	.507	.456	.432	.410	.370	.335	.262	.207
7	.933	.871	.813	.760	.711	.665	.623	.583	.547	.513	.452	.400	.376	.354	.314	.279	.210	.159
8	.923	.853	.789	.731	.677	.627	.582	.540	.502	.467	.404	.351	.327	.305	.266	.233	.168	.123
9	.914	.837	.766	.703	.645	.592	.544	.500	.460	.424	.361	.308	.284	.263	.225	.194	.134	.094
10	.905	.820	.744	.676	.614	.558	.508	.463	.422	.386	.322	.270	.247	.227	.191	.162	.107	.073
11	.896	.804	.722	.650	.585	.527	.475	.429	.388	.350	.287	.237	.215	.195	.162	.135	.086	.056
12	.887	.788	.701	.625	.557	.497	.444	.397	.356	.319	.257	.208	.187	.168	.137	.112	.069	.043
13	.879	.773	.681	.601	.530	.469	.415	.368	.326	.290	.229	.182	.163	.145	.116	.093	.055	.033
14	.870	.758	.661	.577	.505	.442	.388	.340	.299	.263	.205	.160	.141	.125	.099	.078	.044	.025
15	.861	.743	.642	.555	.481	.417	.362	.315	.275	.239	.183	.140	.123	.108	.084	.065	.035	.020
16	.853	.728	.623	.534	.458	.394	.339	.292	.252	.218	.163	.123	.107	.093	.071	.054	.028	.015
17	.844	.714	.605	.513	.436	.371	.317	.270	.231	.198	.146	.108	.093	.080	.060	.045	.023	.012
18	.836	.700	.587	.494	.416	.350	.296	.250	.212	.180	.130	.095	.081	.069	.051	.038	.018	.009
19	.828	.686	.570	.475	.396	.331	.277	.232	.194	.164	.116	.083	.070	.060	.043	.031	.014	.007
20	.820	.673	.554	.456	.377	.312	.258	.215	.178	.149	.104	.073	.061	.051	.037	.026	.012	.005
25	.780	.610	.478	.375	.295	.233	.184	.146	.116	.092	.059	.038	.030	.024	.016	.010	.004	.001
30	.742	.552	.412	.308	.231	.174	.131	.099	.075	.057	.033	.020	.015	.012	.007	.004	.001	.000

Note: The basic equation for finding the present value interest factor (PVIF) is: $\text{PVIF}_{i,n} = \dfrac{1}{(1+i)^n}$ where i is the interest or discount rate and n is the number of periods in years.

TABLE A4 Present Value of $1 Ordinary Annuity (PVIFA)

Period	1%	2%	3%	4%	5%	6%	7%	8%	9%	10%	12%	14%	16%	18%	20%	25%	30%
1	0.990	0.980	0.971	0.962	0.952	0.943	0.935	0.926	0.917	0.909	0.893	0.877	0.862	0.847	0.833	.800	.769
2	1.970	1.942	1.913	1.886	1.859	1.833	1.808	1.783	1.759	1.736	1.690	1.647	1.605	1.566	1.528	1.440	1.361
3	2.941	2.884	2.829	2.775	2.723	2.673	2.624	2.577	2.531	2.487	2.402	2.322	2.246	2.174	2.106	1.952	1.816
4	3.902	3.808	3.717	3.630	3.546	3.465	3.387	3.312	3.240	3.170	3.037	2.914	2.798	2.690	2.589	2.362	2.166
5	4.853	4.713	4.580	4.452	4.329	4.212	4.100	3.993	3.890	3.791	3.605	3.433	3.274	3.127	2.991	2.689	2.436
6	5.795	5.601	5.417	5.242	5.076	4.917	4.767	4.623	4.486	4.355	4.111	3.889	3.685	3.498	3.326	2.951	2.643
7	6.728	6.472	6.230	6.002	5.786	5.582	5.389	5.206	5.033	4.868	4.564	4.288	4.039	3.812	3.605	3.161	2.802
8	7.652	7.325	7.020	6.733	6.463	6.210	5.971	5.747	5.535	5.335	4.968	4.639	4.344	4.078	3.837	3.329	2.925
9	8.566	8.162	7.786	7.435	7.108	6.802	6.515	6.247	5.995	5.759	5.328	4.946	4.607	4.303	4.031	3.463	3.019
10	9.471	8.983	8.530	8.111	7.722	7.360	7.024	6.710	6.418	6.145	5.650	5.216	4.833	4.494	4.193	3.571	3.092
11	10.368	9.787	9.253	8.760	8.306	7.887	7.499	7.139	6.805	6.495	5.938	5.453	5.029	4.656	4.327	3.656	3.147
12	11.255	10.575	9.954	9.385	8.863	8.384	7.943	7.536	7.161	6.814	6.194	5.660	5.197	4.793	4.439	3.725	3.190
13	12.134	11.348	10.635	9.986	9.394	8.853	8.358	7.904	7.487	7.103	6.424	5.842	5.342	4.910	4.533	3.780	3.223
14	13.004	12.106	11.296	10.563	9.899	9.295	8.745	8.244	7.786	7.367	6.628	6.002	5.468	5.008	4.611	3.824	3.249
15	13.865	12.849	11.938	11.118	10.380	9.712	9.108	8.559	8.061	7.606	6.811	6.142	5.575	5.092	4.675	3.859	3.268
16	14.718	13.578	12.561	11.652	10.838	10.106	9.447	8.851	8.313	7.824	6.974	6.265	5.668	5.162	4.730	3.887	3.283
17	15.562	14.292	13.166	12.166	11.274	10.477	9.763	9.122	8.544	8.022	7.120	5.373	5.749	4.222	4.775	3.910	3.295
18	16.398	14.992	13.754	12.659	11.690	10.828	10.059	9.372	8.756	8.201	7.250	6.467	5.818	5.273	4.812	3.928	3.304
19	17.226	15.678	14.324	13.134	12.085	11.158	10.336	9.604	8.950	8.365	7.366	6.550	5.877	5.316	4.843	3.942	3.311
20	18.046	16.351	14.877	13.590	12.462	11.470	10.594	9.818	9.129	8.514	7.469	6.623	5.929	5.353	4.870	3.954	3.316
25	22.023	19.523	17.413	15.622	14.094	12.783	11.654	10.675	9.823	9.077	7.843	6.873	6.097	5.467	4.948	3.985	3.329
30	25.808	22.396	19.600	17.292	15.372	13.765	12.409	11.258	10.274	9.427	8.055	7.003	6.177	5.517	4.979	3.995	3.332

Note: The basic equation for finding the present value interest factor of an ordinary annuity (PVIFA) is: $\text{PVIFA}_{i,n} = \sum_{t=1}^{n} \dfrac{1}{(1+i)^t} = \dfrac{1 - \dfrac{1}{(1+i)^n}}{i}$ where i is the interest or discount rate and n is the number of periods in years.

Present Value of a $1 Annuity Due (PVIFAD) The present value interest factor of an annuity due (PVIFAD) may be found by suing the following formula to convert PVIFA values found in Table A4:

$\text{PVIFAS}_{i,n} = \text{PVIFA}_{i,n}(1 + i)$ where i is the interest or discount rate and n is the number of periods in years.